WHAT IS THE PLAY?

WHAT IS THE PLAY?

RICHARD A. CASSELL, *Butler University*

HENRY KNEPLER, *Illinois Institute of Technology*

SCOTT, FORESMAN AND COMPANY

L. C. Catalog Card No. 67-13095

Regional offices of Scott, Foresman and Company are located in Atlanta, Dallas, Glenview, Palo Alto, and Oakland, N. J.

Contents

LIST OF ILLUSTRATIONS

Pictures of the playwrights are credited to the following sources: Eugene O'Neill—Culver Pictures; Bernard Shaw—Culver Pictures; William Shakespeare—Historical Pictures Service; Henrik Ibsen—Brown Brothers; Thornton Wilder—Brown Brothers; Molière—The Bettmann Archive Inc; Ben Jonson—Historical Pictures Service; Robert Lowell—*Newsweek,* Phil Macmullan; Sophocles—The Bettmann Archive Inc; Jean Anouilh—Historical Pictures Service; Friedrich Dürrenmatt—Wide World Photos; Michel de Ghelderode—Charles Leirens, Paris, courtesy Hill & Wang, Inc.

THE PLAYS IN CHRONOLOGICAL ORDER

Sophocles	*Antigone* (441 B.C.)
William Shakespeare	*King Henry IV, Part 1* (1597)
Ben Jonson	*The Alchemist* (1610)
Molière	*Scapin* (1671)
Henrik Ibsen	*An Enemy of the People* (1882)
Bernard Shaw	*Arms and the Man* (1894)
Michel de Ghelderode	*Christopher Columbus* (1927)
Eugene O'Neill	*Hughie* (1941-1942)
Jean Anouilh	*Antigone* (1942)
Thornton Wilder	*The Matchmaker* (1954)
Friedrich Dürrenmatt	*The Visit* (1956)
Robert Lowell	*My Kinsman, Major Molineux* (1964)

Introduction

On any evening of the week, those who want to watch can find a situation comedy on television. These programs, which carry the same main characters from week to week—and usually the same jokes—are almost invariably filmed without an audience. Yet, when you watch them, you find they are plentifully laced with laughter. Why do the producers go to the trouble of dubbing in a fictitious audience? Obviously because they believe that this action will increase the appeal of the show. The comedy itself unrolls in the living room before an audience of one or two people. But the laughter envelops these solitary watchers and gives them the illusion that they are part of a large audience, all watching together, all laughing together.... Here is illustrated a basic point regarding theater, for television is theater, too: the performance of a play involves large numbers of people—it is a communal experience. A community on stage and behind it performs for a community in front of it or surrounding it.

The idea of a communal experience is one of the chief distinctions between the play and other forms of literature. The novel, for example, has a solitary reader, even if it is a best seller. The sole intermediary between reader and writer is the printed page, and the reader, therefore, receives the work, essentially as the novelist wrote it. The play, on the other hand, presents a different situation, because it is meant to be produced on stage, and to be seen and heard by large numbers of people sitting together. Reading a play is a substitute experience. True, reading and rereading Shakespeare, for example, will reveal elements of beauty and thought which a performance may leave hidden, but merely reading Shakespeare—without being at some point exposed to competent performances of at least a few of his plays—will leave hidden many elements that only the experience in the theater can bring to light.

That experience actually begins when the audience gathers in the theater. The low rumble of voices lends an atmosphere of expectancy as the patrons wait for the lights to dim and the curtain to rise—to reveal the lobby of a cheap hotel, or a chamber in a medieval castle, or whatever the world of the play is. The illusion of that world must engross the audience immediately, and involve it in the fortunes and conflicts of the characters on stage. In our time the playwright can use lights, curtains, and elaborate stage sets to enhance the illusion. But the need to involve the audience is the same now as it was for the ancient Greek or Elizabethan playwrights who wrote their plays for performances given in daylight, in open-air theaters, and on stages almost devoid of sets or props as we understand them today, and who had, therefore, to rely on the spoken word for many explanations or situations which can today be rendered by visual means.

The visual element of theater, the immediacy of human actions in front of us, opens up opportunities for the playwright which the novelist, for example, does not have. But performance and theater audience also pose problems the novelist can ignore. To engross the audience, and to keep it engrossed, the playwright must use his time well; he must simplify, compress, and keep his play moving forward, making every moment count, because he cannot exceed the time an audience is willing to sit. (The reader of a novel can skim or skip a paragraph or a speech; he can put the novel down when he wishes, begin reading again when he will. A member of the audience has no such opportunity, though a play reader, of course, has.)

However, the playwright must not rush too much, because if the plot of the play develops too rapidly, or the characters are too loosely sketched in, the audience will become disinvolved. (A reader can backtrack if he has missed a point, but a playgoer cannot check back to find out what happened in a previous scene.) Even the intermission, the period for conversation and exercise which the modern audience demands, presents a challenge for the playwright. He cannot afford to let these ten or fifteen minutes loosen the hold of the play. Some modern plays provide instructive points as to how the playwright copes with this problem: the ending of the first act of The Visit, *or of the second act of* An Enemy of the People *are examples.*

A good and effective play, therefore, has to cast and keep its spell from beginning to end—and even beyond the end, when it unites the audience for the last time to applaud the cast of characters, who are now turned back to being individual actors, stepping forward to receive a tribute for their ability and at the same time to release some of the tension they provided through their performance. Then the lights come up, and the audience—individuals once more—disperses; but, if play and performance were of a high order, almost everyone will retain a residue of emotion and thought which is never quite lost in time.

Closely linked to the audience and its demands are the physical and economic conditions of the theater. These are also among the complex considerations which influence the playwright's craft. In Shakespeare's day, for example, the needs were relatively simple, because performances were given in the open, stage sets and props were few, and only costumes were elaborate. Scenes could shift rapidly from palace to tavern, or from Italy to Greece, by means of a few descriptive lines of dialogue.

In addition to the actors, the company needed only a prompter and a few stagehands to complete the performance. Today, a large and complex community behind the stage is generally necessary to bring the performance about. This increases expenses and makes play production a risky undertaking. If the Lord Chamberlain's Men, the company of actors to which Shakespeare belonged, put on a play that did not find audience approval, they could drop it with little loss after a few performances. If a play on Broadway is unable to attract a large audience, it may be a financial disaster for many people. Modern conditions of performance, therefore, favor the tried and true and mitigate against experiment, innovation, and unknown actors and playwrights.

The play reader's enjoyment is, of course, enhanced to the degree that he can imagine an actual performance and reconstruct in his mind the setting, the movements of characters, and the intonations of their speeches. As an aid in this direction, this book attempts to acquaint the reader with the different conditions of performance and the effects they have produced on the audience. In his essay "Some Thoughts on Playwriting," Thornton Wilder, himself a major playwright, discusses the problems of the theater today and some of the effects of its physical conditions on both writer and audience. Raymond Williams in his essay attempts to recreate, as far as possible, the conditions of a performance of Antigone *in ancient Athens. Oscar G. Brockett sets forth the conditions of the stage and audience in Shakespeare's day. From Shaw's review of a late nineteenth-century revival of* Henry IV, *the student can gather information about a Shakespearean performance seventy years ago, which used the kind of theater auditorium which is still current, but in ways in which we no longer perform Shakespeare today.*

What is true of works of art in general is true of plays: only a small part of what is produced survives the age in which it is created. Most plays of our time disappear like most movies and television shows —without a trace, and without being remembered. A few remain because they retain their meanings in later ages, or rather, because later ages see new, timely meanings in them. The composition and character of audiences change from age to age, just as the physical conditions of performances change. The Greek drama, the earliest drama of Western Man of which we have accurate records, was still related to its source: religious observance. Attending a Greek play was, as Arthur Miller points out in his essay "Of Social Plays," a true communal experience because the audience which saw it was unified in its main beliefs about the world. If Sophocles' Antigone *retains its power to move a vastly different audience 2500 years after it was written, an audience no longer unified in its world view, it must be because the* play deals with basic concerns of man which are timeless; Anouilh, in recreating *Antigone* in our time, takes up some of the concerns which are particularly significant to us.

The drama of Shakespeare's time, in contrast to the ancient Greek, is purely secular in character. Dramatic production had disappeared with the Roman Empire, and the Dark Ages were concerned with sheer human survival too immediately to permit the luxury of contemplation on which drama ultimately rests. Drama arose again in the Middle Ages, and again in connection with religious observance. The medieval Roman Catholic church at first fostered the new, simple drama based on the Bible, and on the propagation of moral precepts. But as the drama became more elaborate and diversified, the Church divorced itself from it, and by the time of Shakespeare it had become transformed by Renaissance sentiments into a sophisticated amalgam of individual characterization, philosophic thought, national sentiment, and poetry. Jonson's didactic statements about vice, as exemplified in *The Alchemist*, differ greatly from the simple black-and-white precepts of medieval morality plays. In the play of *Everyman*, for example, the character named Death promises God in the opening scene:

"Lord, I will in the world go run over all,
And cruelly out search both great and small.
Every man will I beset that liveth beastly
Out of God's laws, and dreadeth not folly.
He that loveth riches I will strike with my dart. . ."

In the theater, though, change is often paired with tradition. Molière's misers and con men, lovers and servants, are not only seventeenth-century French; they retain meaning for our time, and are at the same time direct descendants of characters created by Aristophanes, Plautus, and Terence—the great writers of comedy in ancient Greece and Rome. Scapin, the trickster, has also much in common with Dolly Levi, a contemporary trickster in *The Matchmaker*.

The modern realistic drama—realistic in its stage setting and in the dialogue of its characters—begins with Ibsen who brought the moral and social issues of his time to the stage, often demonstrating, once the furor about them had died down, that these problems did not really differ from those of other ages. Shaw, who learned much from Ibsen, shows a view of soldiering, for example, which differs little from that of Shakespeare's Falstaff, or from some views of our own time.

Since Ibsen and Shaw, the drama has gone many different ways, and has often turned away from realism to the symbolic or the surreal.

At its simplest it may be a full-dimensional character portrayal and little else, as in Hughie, *the portrait of human isolation in the modern metropolis. Or it may go back into the past to seek a meaning for the human condition, as Lowell does in* My Kinsman, Major Molineux *or, quite differently, Ghelderode in* Christopher Columbus. *Or it may starkly raise an age-old moral problem in a modern setting as Dürrenmatt does in* The Visit, *or modernize an age-old problem in an ancient setting, as Anouilh does in his* Antigone.

Television has, since the Second World War, made heavy inroads into the movie public. The former casual movie goer now looks at television, and movies have therefore become fewer. The effect of television on movies repeats the effect of movies on the live stage. The number of theaters declined in the early twentieth century, because the casual theater goer began to go to the movies instead. But the theater has not died out, and shows no sign of disappearing, just as the film, transformed in many ways, will survive in the age of television. An evening at a play may not answer more than very imperfectly what a play is. But the live performance will, if it is good, have meaning and create an excitement of a kind that has entranced audiences from antiquity to the present.

Eugene O'Neill

(1886-1953)

HUGHIE

Eugene O'Neill began his career as a dramatist with a series of one-act plays. In 1941-1942, toward the end of his life, after many experiments with different kinds of plays, he returned to the short form and projected a series of one-act plays called By Way of Obit of which, as far as we know, only one, Hughie, was completed. Hughie had its first production in Swedish at the Royal Dramatic Theater in Stockholm on March 29, 1957, and was first given in New York on December 22, 1964.

In Hughie, the dramatic action is pared to a minimum; the play is close to being a dramatic monologue or a first-person short story. It represents drama in its most elementary form: voice and gesture. "Drama" in its original Greek means "a doing"; this is to say that talking (or singing, or chanting) and body movements must convey most of the meaning, aided usually by the setting, though stage scenery is not a necessary requirement in drama. What is necessary are men acting—or living.

Seeing or reading a play is in a certain way like observing people in everyday life, in that we try to understand and evaluate them on the basis of what they say and do. The real difference between a story (in novel, play, or poem) and life is that a story, so often unlike life, completes an action. This is true of every play in this text, from the realistic An Enemy of the People to the surrealistic Christopher Columbus. Something happens which moves our emotions and leads us to infer the meaning or the value of what has happened. More clearly and purposefully than people in real life, the playwright under the pressure of his own vision directs our thoughts and feelings about the completed experience he sets before us. His aim is conviction or, better, enthrallment.

Though scenery as such may not be necessary, there must be a setting —a time and a place for the action, a world, whether "real" or fanciful. The lobby of a third-rate hotel defines the world of Hughie, a world remote from the bright lights of Broadway and its superficial life, a dead world of silence punctuated only by the rumblings of the periodic el train or by the garbage men bouncing cans. The night clerk with his expressionless eyes is beyond boredom, creating imaginary gun fights and spectacular fires; Erie Smith is the stereotype of "a Broadway sport and a Wise Guy," loud shirt and tie, dead-pan expression and all, who is down on his luck since Hughie, the previous night clerk, has taken sick and died.

The dialogue between them, actually more a rambling monologue by Erie Smith, gradually reveals two very lonely men. Their search for *a defense against that loneliness gradually develops O'Neill's statement of the human condition. We need to observe, however, that a play, like any valid work of art, does more than simply make a statement about life or any other thing. Any statement one might devise is inadequate to express the full emotional, intellectual, and moral impact of the work. To make his point O'Neill need not convince us that his cheap Broadway hotel is like our world, and that we are all in a way like Erie Smith and Hughie. But, if he is successful, he will show us convincingly what it is like to be a Hughie or an Erie. To come to understand what others experience is a major share of the pleasure derived from a play.*

HUGHIE

Characters

"ERIE" SMITH, *a teller of tales*
A NIGHT CLERK

Scene

The desk and a section of lobby of a small hotel on a West Side street in midtown New York. It is between 3 and 4 A.M. *of a day in the summer of 1928.*

It is one of those hotels, built in the decade 1900-1910 on the side streets of the Great White Way sector, which began as respectable second class but soon were forced to deteriorate in order to survive. Following the First World War and Prohibition, it had given up all pretense of respectability, and now is anything a paying guest wants it to be, a third-class dump, catering to the catch-as-catch-can trade. But still it does not prosper. It has not shared in the Great Hollow Boom of the 10 *twenties. The Everlasting Opulence of the New Economic Law has overlooked it. It manages to keep running by cutting the overhead for service, repairs, and cleanliness to a minimum.*

The desk faces left along a section of seedy lobby with shabby chairs. The street entrance is off-stage, left. Behind the desk are a telephone switchboard and the operator's stool. At right, the usual numbered tiers of mailboxes, and above them a clock.

The Night Clerk sits on the stool, facing front, his back to the switchboard. There is nothing to do. He is not thinking. He is not sleepy. He simply droops and stares acquiescently at nothing. It would be dis- 20 *couraging to glance at the clock. He knows there are several hours to go before his shift is over. Anyway, he does not need to look at clocks. He has been a night clerk in New York hotels so long he can tell time by sounds in the street.*

He is in his early forties. Tall, thin, with a scrawny neck and jutting Adam's apple. His face is long and narrow, greasy with perspiration, sallow, studded with pimples from ingrowing hairs. His nose is large and without character. So is his mouth. So are his ears. So is his thinning brown hair, powdered with dandruff. Behind horn-rimmed spectacles, his blank brown eyes contain no discernible expression. One would 30 *say they had even forgotten how it feels to be bored. He wears an ill-fitting blue serge suit, white shirt and collar, a blue tie. The suit is old and shines at the elbows as if it had been waxed and polished.*

Footsteps echo in the deserted lobby as someone comes in from the street. The Night Clerk rises wearily. His eyes remain empty but his gummy lips part automatically in a welcoming The-Patron-Is-Always-Right grimace, intended as a smile. His big uneven teeth are in bad condition.

Erie Smith enters and approaches the desk. He is about the same age as the Clerk and has the same pasty, perspiry, night-life complexion. There the resemblance ends. Erie is around medium height but appears shorter because he is stout and his fat legs are too short for his body. So are his fat arms. His big head squats on a neck which seems part of his beefy shoulders. His face is round, his snub nose flattened at the tip. His blue eyes have drooping lids and puffy pouches under them. His sandy hair is falling out and the top of his head is bald. He walks to the desk with a breezy, familiar air, his gait a bit waddling because of his short legs. He carries a Panama hat and mops his face with a red-and-blue silk handkerchief. He wears a light grey suit cut in the extreme, tight-waisted, Broadway mode, the coat open to reveal an old and faded but expensive silk shirt in a shade of blue that sets teeth on edge, and a gay red-and-blue foulard tie, its knot stained by perspiration. His trousers are held up by a braided brown leather belt with a brass buckle. His shoes are tan and white, his socks white silk.

In manner, he is consciously a Broadway sport and a Wise Guy—the type of small-fry gambler and horse player, living hand to mouth on the fringe of the rackets. Infesting corners, doorways, cheap restaurants, the bars of minor speakeasies, he and his kind imagine they are in the Real Know, cynical oracles of the One True Grapevine.

Erie usually speaks in a low, guarded tone, his droop-lidded eyes suspiciously wary of nonexistent eavesdroppers. His face is set in the prescribed pattern of gambler's dead pan. His small, pursy mouth is always crooked in the cynical leer of one who possesses superior, inside information, and his shifty once-over glances never miss the price tags he detects on everything and everybody. Yet there is something phoney about his characterization of himself, some sentimental softness behind it which doesn't belong in the hard-boiled picture.

Erie avoids looking at the Night Clerk, as if he resented him.

Erie. (Peremptorily) Key. *(Then as the Night Clerk gropes with his memory—grudgingly)* Forgot you ain't seen me before. Erie Smith's the name. I'm an old timer in this fleabag. 492.

Night Clerk. (In a tone of one who is wearily relieved when he does not have to remember anything—he plucks out the key.) 492. Yes, sir.

Erie. (Taking the key, gives the Clerk the once-over. He appears not unfavorably impressed but his tone still holds resentment.) How long you been on the job? Four, five days, huh? I been off on a drunk. Come to now, though. Tapering off. Well, I'm glad they fired that young squirt they took on when Hughie got sick. One of them fresh wise punks. Couldn't tell him nothing. Pleased to meet you, Pal. Hope you stick around. *(He shoves out his hand. The Night Clerk takes* 80 *it obediently.)*

Night Clerk. (With a compliant, uninterested smile) Glad to know you, Mr. Smith.

Erie. What's your name?

Night Clerk. (As if he had half forgotten because what did it matter, anyway?) Hughes. Charlie Hughes.

Erie. (Starts) Huh? Hughes? Say, is that on the level?

Night Clerk. Charlie Hughes.

Erie. Well, I be damned! What the hell d'you know about that! *(Warming toward the Clerk)* Say, now I notice, you don't look like 90 Hughie, but you remind me of him somehow. You ain't by any chance related?

Night Clerk. You mean to the Hughes who had this job so long and died recently? No, sir. No relation.

Erie. (Gloomily) No, that's right. Hughie told me he didn't have no relations left—except his wife and kids, of course. *(He pauses—more gloomily.)* Yeah. The poor guy croaked last week. His funeral was what started me off on a bat. *(Then boastfully, as if defending himself against gloom)* Some drunk! I don't go on one often. It's bum dope in my book. A guy gets careless and gabs about things he 100 knows and when he comes to he's liable to find there's guys who'd feel easier if he wasn't around no more. That's the trouble with knowing things. Take my tip, Pal. Don't never know nothin'. Be a sap and stay healthy.

(His manner has become secretive, with sinister undertones. But the Night Clerk doesn't notice this. Long experience with guests who stop at his desk in the small hours to talk about themselves has given him a foolproof technique of self-defense. He appears to listen with agreeable submissiveness and be impressed, but his mind is blank and he doesn't hear unless a direct question is put to him, and sometimes not even 110 *then. Erie thinks he is impressed.)*

But hell, I always keep my noggin working, booze or no booze. I'm no sucker. What was I sayin'? Oh, some drunk. I sure hit the high spots. You shoulda seen the doll I made night before last. And did she take me to the cleaners! I'm a sucker for blondes. *(He pauses—giving the Night Clerk a cynical, contemptuous glance.)* You're married, ain't you?

Night Clerk. (Long ago he gave up caring whether questions were personal or not.) Yes, sir.

Erie. Yeah, I'd'a laid ten to one on it. You got that old look. Like 120 Hughie had. Maybe that's the resemblance. *(He chuckles contemptuously.)* Kids, too, I bet?

Night Clerk. Yes, sir. Three.

Erie. You're worse off than Hughie was. He only had two. Three, huh? Well, that's what comes of being careless! *(He laughs. The Night Clerk smiles at a guest. He had been a little offended when a guest first made that crack—must have been ten years ago—yes, Eddie, the oldest, is eleven now—or is it twelve? Erie goes on with good-natured tolerance.)* Well, I suppose marriage ain't such a bum racket, if you're 130 made for it. Hughie didn't seem to mind it much, although if you want my low-down, his wife is a bum—in spades! Oh, I don't mean cheatin'. With her puss and figure, she'd never make no one except she raided a blind asylum. *(The Night Clerk feels that he has been standing a long time and his feet are beginning to ache and he wishes 492 would stop talking and go to bed so he can sit down again and listen to the noises in the street and think about nothing. Erie gives him an amused, condescending glance.)* How old are you? Wait! Let me guess. You look fifty or over but I'll lay ten to one you're forty-three or maybe forty-four.

140 *Night Clerk.* I'm forty-three. *(He adds vaguely.)* Or maybe it is forty-four.

Erie. (Elated) I win, huh? I sure can call the turn on ages, Buddy. You ought to see the dolls get sored up when I work it on them! You're like Hughie. He looked like he'd never see fifty again and he was only forty-three. Me, I'm forty-five. Never think it, would you? Most of the dames don't think I've hit forty yet. *(The Night Clerk shifts his position so he can lean more on the desk. Maybe those shoes he sees advertised for fallen arches—But they cost eight dollars, so that's out—Get a pair when he goes to heaven. Erie is sizing him up with another cynical,* 150 *friendly glance.)* I make another bet about you. Born and raised in the sticks, wasn't you?

Night Clerk. (Faintly aroused and defensive) I come originally from Saginaw, Michigan, but I've lived here in the Big Town so long I I consider myself a New Yorker now. *(This is a long speech for him and he wonders sadly why he took the trouble to make it.)*

Erie. I don't deserve no medal for picking that one. Nearly every guy I know on the Big Stem—and I know most of 'em—hails from the sticks. Take me. You'd never guess it but I was dragged up in Erie, P-a. Ain't that a knockout! Erie, P-a! That's how I got my moniker. 160 No one calls me nothing but Erie. You better call me Erie, too, Pal, or I won't know when you're talkin' to me.

Night Clerk. All right, Erie.

Erie. Atta Boy. *(He chuckles.)* Here's another knockout. Smith is my real name. A Broadway guy like me named Smith and it's my real name! Ain't that a knockout! *(He explains carefully so there will be no misunderstanding.)* I don't remember nothing much about Erie,

P-a, you understand—or want to. Some punk burg! After grammar school, my Old Man put me to work in his store, dealing out groceries. Some punk job! I stuck it till I was eighteen before I took a run-out powder. *(The Night Clerk seems turned into a drooping waxwork,* 170 *draped along the desk. This is what he used to dread before he perfected his technique of not listening: The Guest's Story of His Life. He fixes his mind on his aching feet. Erie chuckles.)* Speaking of marriage, that was the big reason I ducked. A doll nearly had me hooked for the old shotgun ceremony. Closest I ever come to being played for a sucker. This doll in Erie—Daisy's her name—was one of them dumb wide-open dolls. All the guys give her a play. Then one day she wakes up and finds she's going to have a kid. I never figured she meant to frame me in particular. Way I always figured, she didn't have no idea who, so she holds a lottery all by herself. Put about a thousand guys' 180 names in a hat—all she could remember—and drew one out and I was it. Then she told her Ma, and her Ma told her Pa, and her Pa come round looking for me. But I was no fall guy even in them days. I took it on the lam. For Saratoga, to look the bangtails over. I'd started to be a horse player in Erie, though I'd never seen a track. I been one ever since. *(With a touch of bravado)* And I ain't done so bad, Pal. I've made some killings in my time the gang still gab about. I've been in the big bucks. More'n once, and I will be again. I've had tough breaks too, but what the hell, I always get by. When the horses won't run for me, there's draw or stud. When they're bad, there's a 190 crap game. And when they're all bad, there's always bucks to pick up for little errands I ain't talkin' about, which they give a guy who can keep his clam shut. Oh, I get along, Buddy. I get along fine. *(He waits for approving assent from the Night Clerk, but the latter is not hearing so intently he misses his cue until the expectant silence crashes his ears.)*

Night Clerk. (Hastily, gambling on "yes") Yes, Sir.

Erie. (Bitingly) Sorry if I'm keeping you up, Sport. *(With an aggrieved air)* Hughie was a wide-awake guy. He was always waiting for me to roll in. He'd say, "Hello, Erie, how'd the bangtails treat you?" Or, "How's luck?" Or, "Did you make the old bones behave?" Then 200 I'd tell him how I'd done. He'd ask, "What's new along the Big Stem?" and I'd tell him the latest off the grapevine. *(He grins with affectionate condescension.)* It used to hand me a laugh to hear old Hughie crackin' like a sport. In all the years I knew him, he never bet a buck on nothin'. *(Excusingly)* But it ain't his fault. He'd have took a chance, but how could he with his wife keepin' cases on every nickel of his salary? I showed him lots of ways he could cross her up, but he was too scared. *(He chuckles.)* The biggest knockout was when he'd kid me about dames. He'd crack, "What? No blonde to-night, Erie? You must be slippin'." Jeez, you never see a guy more bashful with a doll around 210 than Hughie was. I used to introduce him to the tramps I'd drag home with me. I'd wise them up to kid him along and pretend they'd fell for him. In two minutes, they'd have him hanging on the ropes. His face'd be red and he'd look like he wanted to crawl under the desk and hide. Some of them dolls was raw babies. They'd make him pretty raw propositions. He'd stutter like he was paralyzed. But he ate it up, just the same. He was tickled pink. I used to hope maybe I could nerve him up to do a little cheatin'. I'd offer to fix it for him with one of my dolls. Hell, I got plenty, I wouldn't have minded. I'd tell him, 220 "Just let that wife of yours know you're cheatin', and she'll have some respect for you." But he was too scared. *(He pauses—boastfully.)* Some queens I've brought here in my time, Brother—frails from the Follies, or the Scandals, or the Frolics,° that'd knock your eye out! And I still can make 'em. You watch. I ain't slippin'. *(He looks at the Night Clerk expecting reassurance, but the Clerk's mind has slipped away to the clanging bounce of garbage cans in the outer night. He is thinking: "A job I'd like. I'd bang those cans louder than they do! I'd wake up the whole damned city!" Erie mutters disgustedly to himself.)* Jesus, what a dummy! *(He makes a move in the direction of* 230 *the elevator, off right front—gloomily.)* Might as well hit the hay, I guess.

Night Clerk. (Comes to—with the nearest approach to feeling he has shown in many a long night—approvingly) Good night, Mr. Smith. I hope you have a good rest. *(But Erie stops, glancing around the deserted lobby with forlorn distaste, jiggling the room key in his hand.)*

Erie. What a crummy dump! What did I come back for? I shoulda stayed on a drunk. You'd never guess it, Buddy, but when I first come here this was a classy hotel—and clean, can you believe it? *(He scowls.)* 240 I've been campin' here, off and on, fifteen years, but I've got a good notion to move out. It ain't the same place since Hughie was took to the hospital. *(Gloomily)* Hell with going to bed! I'll just lie there worrying—*(He turns back to the desk. The Clerk's face would express despair, but the last time he was able to feel despair was back around World War days when the cost of living got so high and he was out of a job for three months. Erie leans on the desk—in a dejected, confidential tone.)* Believe me, Brother, I never been a guy to worry, but this time I'm on a spot where I got to, if I ain't a sap.

Night Clerk. (In the vague tone of a corpse which admits it once 250 *overheard a favorable rumor about life)* That's too bad, Mr. Smith. But they say most of the things we worry about never happen. *(His*

223. Follies . . . Scandals . . . Frolics, colorful New York stage productions in the early decades of the twentieth century, famous for their chorus girls and elaborate staging.

mind escapes to the street again to play bouncing cans with the garbage men.)

Erie. (Grimly) This thing happens, Pal. I ain't won a bet at nothin' since Hughie was took to the hospital. I'm jinxed. And that ain't all—But to hell with it! You're right, at that. Something always turns up for me. I was born lucky. I ain't worried. Just moaning low. Hell, who don't when they're getting over a drunk? You know how it is. The Brooklyn Boys march over the bridge with bloodhounds to hunt you down. And I'm still carrying the torch for Hughie. His checking 260 out was a real K.O. for me. Damn if I know why. Lots of guys I've been pals with, in a way, croaked from booze or something, or got rubbed out, but I always took it as part of the game. Hell, we all gotta croak. Here today, gone tomorrow, so what's the good of beefin'? When a guy's dead, he's dead. He don't give a damn, so why should anybody else? *(But this fatalistic philosophy is no comfort and Erie sighs.)* I miss Hughie, I guess. I guess I'd got to like him a lot. *(Again he explains carefully so there will be no misunderstanding.)* Not that I was ever real pals with him, you understand. He didn't run in my class. He didn't know none of the answers. He was just a sucker. *(He sighs* 270 *again.)* But I sure am sorry he's gone. You missed a lot not knowing Hughie, Pal. He sure was one grand little guy.

He stares at the lobby floor. The Night Clerk regards him with vacant, bulging eyes full of a vague envy for the blind. The garbage men have gone their predestined way. Time is that much older. The Clerk's mind remains in the street to greet the noise of a far-off el train. Its approach is pleasantly like a memory of hope; then it roars and rocks and rattles past the nearby corner, and the noise pleasantly deafens memory; then it recedes and dies, and there is something melancholy about that. But there is hope. Only so many el trains pass in one night, and each one 280 *passing leaves one less to pass, so the night recedes, too, until at last it must die and join all the other long nights in Nirvana, the Big Night of Nights. And that's life. "What I always tell Jess when she nags me to worry about something: 'That's life, isn't it? What can you do about it?'" Erie sighs again—then turns to the Clerk, his foolishly wary, wise-guy eyes defenseless, his poker face as self-betraying as a hurt dog's—appealingly.)*

Say, you do remind me of Hughie somehow, Pal. You got the same look on your map. *(But the Clerk's mind is far away attending the obsequies of night, and it takes it some time to get back. Erie is hurt—contemp-* 290 *tuously.)* But I guess it's only that old night clerk look! There's one of 'em born every minute!

Night Clerk. (His mind arrives just in time to catch this last—with a bright grimace.) Yes, Mr. Smith. That's what Barnum said, and it's certainly true, isn't it?

Erie. *(Grateful even for this sign of companionship, growls)* Nix on the Mr. Smith stuff, Charlie, There's ten of *them* born every minute. Call me Erie, like I told you.

Night Clerk. *(Automatically, as his mind tiptoes into the night*
300 *again)* All right, Erie.

Erie. *(Encouraged, leans on the desk, clacking his room key like a castanet)* Yeah. Hughie was one grand little guy. All the same, like I said, he wasn't the kind of guy you'd ever figger a guy like me would take to. Because he was a sucker, see—the kind of sap you'd take to the cleaners a million times and he'd never wise up he was took. Why, night after night, just for a gag, I'd get him to shoot crap with me here on the desk. With *my* dice. And he'd never ask to give 'em the once-over. Can you beat that! *(He chuckles—then earnestly.)* Not that I'd ever ring in no phoneys on a pal. I'm no heel. *(He chuckles again.)* And
310 anyway, I didn't need none to take Hughie because he never even made me knock 'em against nothing. Just a roll on the desk here. Boy, if they'd ever let me throw 'em that way in a real game, I'd be worth ten million dollars. *(He laughs.)* You'da thought Hughie woulda got wise something was out of order when, no matter how much he'd win on a run of luck like suckers have sometimes, I'd always take him to the cleaners in the end. But he never suspicioned nothing. All he'd say was "Gosh, Erie, no wonder you took up gambling. You sure were born lucky." *(He chuckles.)* Can you beat that? *(He hastens to explain earnestly.)* Of course, like I said, it was only a gag. We'd play with real
320 jack, just to make it look real, but it was all my jack. He never had no jack. His wife dealt him four bits a day for spending money. So I'd stake him at the start to half of what I got—in chicken feed, I mean. We'd pretend a cent was a buck, and a nickel was a fin and so on. Some big game! He got a big kick out of it. He'd get all het up. It give me a kick, too—especially when he'd say, "Gosh, Erie, I don't wonder you never worry about money, with your luck." *(He laughs.)* That guy would believe anything! Of course, I'd stall him off when he'd want to shoot nights when I didn't have a goddamned nickel. *(He chuckles.)* What laughs he used to hand me! He'd always call horses "the bangtails,"
330 like he'd known 'em all his life—and he'd never seen a race horse, not till I kidnaped him one day and took him down to Belmont. What a kick he got out of that! I got scared he'd pass out with excitement. And he wasn't doing no betting either. All he had was four bits. It was just the track, and the crowd, and the horses got him. Mostly the horses. *(With a surprised, reflective air)* Y'know, it's funny how a dumb, simple guy like Hughie will all of a sudden get something right. He says, "They're the most beautiful things in the world, I think." And he wins! I tell you, Pal, I'd rather sleep in the same stall with old Man o' War than make the whole damn Follies. What do you think?

Night Clerk. *(His mind darts back from a cruising taxi and blinks bewilderedly in the light: "Say yes.")* Yes, I agree with you, Mr.—I mean, Erie. 340

Erie. *(With good-natured contempt.)* Yeah? I bet you never seen one, except back at the old Fair Grounds in the sticks. I don't mean them kind of turtles. I mean a real horse. *(The Clerk wonders what horses have to do with anything—or for that matter, what anything has to do with anything—then gives it up. Erie takes up his tale.)* And what d'you think happened the next night? Damned if Hughie didn't dig two bucks out of his pants and try to slip 'em to me. "Let this ride on the nose of whatever horse you're betting on tomorrow," 350 he told me. I got sore. "Nix," I told him, "if you're going to start playin' sucker and bettin' on horse races, you don't get no assist from me." *(He grins wryly.)* Was that a laugh! Me advising a sucker not to bet when I've spent a lot of my life tellin' saps a story to make 'em bet! I said, "Where'd you grab this dough? Outa the Little Woman's purse, huh? What tale you going to give her when you lose it? She'll start breaking up the furniture with you!" "No," he says, "she'll just cry."

Jason Robards, Jr., as Erie Smith and Jack Dodson as the night clerk in the original American production of Hughie *at the Royale Theater, New York, 1964.*

"That's worse," I said, "no guy can beat that racket. I had a doll cry
on me once in a restaurant full of people till I had to promise her a
360 diamond engagement ring to sober her up." Well, anyway, Hughie
sneaked the two bucks back in the Little Woman's purse when he
went home that morning, and that was the end of that. *(Cynically)*
Boy Scouts got nothin' on me, Pal, when it comes to good deeds. That
was one I done. It's too bad I can't remember no others. *(He is well
wound up now and goes on without noticing that the Night Clerk's
mind has left the premises in his sole custody.)* Y'know I had Hughie
sized up for a sap the first time I see him. I'd just rolled in from Tia
Juana. I'd made a big killing down there and I was lousy with jack.
Came all the way in a drawing room, and I wasn't lonely in it neither.
370 There was a blonde movie doll on the train—and I was lucky in them
days. Used to follow the horses South every winter. I don't no more.
Sick of traveling. And I ain't as lucky as I was—*(Hastily)* Anyway,
this time I'm talkin' about, soon as I hit this lobby I see there's a new
night clerk, and while I'm signing up for the bridal suite I make a bet
with myself he's never been nothin' but a night clerk. And I win. At
first, he wouldn't open up. Not that he was cagey about gabbin' too
much. But like he couldn't think of nothin' about himself worth saying.
But after he'd seen me roll in here the last one every night, and I'd
stop to kid him along and tell him the tale of what I'd win that day, he
380 got friendly and talked. He'd come from a hick burg upstate. Graduated
from high school, and had a shot at different jobs in the old home town
but couldn't make the grade until he was took on as night clerk in the
hotel there. Then he made good. But he wasn't satisfied. Didn't like
being only a night clerk where everybody knew him. He'd read somewhere—in the Suckers' Almanac, I guess—that all a guy had to do
was come to the Big Town and Old Man Success would be waitin' at
the Grand Central to give him the key to the city. What a gag that is!
Even I believed that once, and no one could ever call me a sap. Well,
anyway, he made the break and come here and the only job he could
390 get was night clerk. Then he fell in love—or kidded himself he was—
and got married. Met her on a subway train. It stopped sudden and she
was jerked into him, and he put his arms around her, and they started
talking, and the poor boob never stood a chance. She was a salesgirl
in some punk department store, and she was sick of standing on her
dogs all day, and all the way home to Brooklyn, too. So, the way I
figger it, knowing Hughie and dames, she proposed and said "yes"
for him, and married him, and after that, of course, he never dared stop
being a night clerk, even if he could. *(He pauses.)* Maybe you think
I ain't giving her a square shake. Well, maybe I ain't. She never give
400 me one. She put me down as a bad influence, and let her chips ride.
And maybe Hughie couldn't have done no better. Dolls didn't call him

no riot. Hughie and her seemed happy enough the time he had me out to dinner in their flat. Well, not happy. Maybe contented. No, that's boosting it, too. Resigned comes nearer, as if each was givin' the other a break by thinking, "Well, what more could I expect?" *(Abruptly he addresses the Night Clerk with contemptuous good nature.)* How d'you and your Little Woman hit it off, Brother?

Night Clerk. (His mind has been counting the footfalls of the cop on the beat as they recede, sauntering longingly toward the dawn's release. "If he'd only shoot it out with a gunman some night! Nothing exciting has happened in any night I've ever lived through!" He stammers gropingly among the echoes of Erie's last words.) Oh—you mean *my* wife? Why, we get along all right, I guess. 410

Erie. (Disgustedly) Better lay off them headache pills, Pal. First thing you know, some guy is going to call you a dope.

(But the Night Clerk cannot take this seriously. It is years since he cared what anyone called him. So many guests have called him so many things. The Little Woman has, too. And, of course, he has, himself. But that's all past. Is daybreak coming now? No, too early yet. He can tell by the sound of that surface car. It is still lost in the night. Flat wheeled and tired. Distant the carbarn, and far away the sleep. Erie, having soothed resentment with his wisecrack, goes on with a friendly grin.) 420

Well, keep hoping, Pal. Hughie was as big a dope as you until I give him some interest in life. *(Slipping back into narrative)* That time he took me home to dinner. Was that a knockout! It took him a hell of a while to get up nerve to ask me. "Sure, Hughie," I told him, "I'll be tickled to death." I was thinking, I'd rather be shot. For one thing, he lived in Brooklyn, and I'd sooner take a trip to China. Another thing, I'm a guy that likes to eat what I order and not what somebody deals me. And he had kids and a wife, and the family racket is out of my line. But Hughie looked so tickled I wouldn't welsh on him. And it didn't work out so bad. Of course, what he called home was only a dump of a cheap flat. Still, it wasn't so bad for a change. His wife had done a lot of stuff to doll it up. Nothin' with no class, you understand. Just cheap stuff to make it comfortable. And his kids wasn't the gorillas I'd expected, neither. No throwin' spitballs in my soup or them kind of gags. They was quiet like Hughie. I kinda liked 'em. After dinner I started tellin' 'em a story about a race horse a guy I know owned once. I thought it was up to me to put out something, and kids like animal stories, and this one was true, at that. This old turtle never wins a race, but he was as foxy as ten guys, a natural born crook, the goddamnedest thief, he'd steal anything in reach that wasn't nailed down—Well, I didn't get far. Hughie's wife butt in and stopped me cold. Told the kids it was bedtime and hustled 'em off like I was giving 'em measles. It got 430 440

my goat, kinda. I coulda liked her—a little—if she'd give me a chance. Not that she was nothin' Ziegfeld° would want to glorify. When you call her plain, you give her all the breaks. *(Resentfully)* Well, to hell with it. She had me tagged for a bum, and seein' me made her sure
450 she was right. You can bet she told Hughie never invite me again, and he never did. He tried to apologize, but I shut him up quick. He says, "Irma was brought up strict. She can't help being narrow-minded about gamblers." I said, "What's it to me? I don't want to hear your dame troubles. I got plenty of my own. Remember that doll I brung home night before last? She gives me an argument I promised her ten bucks. I told her, 'Listen, Baby, I got an impediment in my speech. Maybe it sounded like ten, but it was two, and that's all you get. Hell, I don't want to buy your soul! What would I do with it?' Now she's peddling the news along Broadway I'm a rat and a chiseler, and of course all the rats
460 and chiselers believe her. Before she's through, I won't have a friend left." *(He pauses—confidentially.)* I switched the subject on Hughie, see, on purpose. He never did beef to me about his wife again. *(He gives a forced chuckle.)* Believe me, Pal, I can stop guys that start telling me their family troubles!

Night Clerk.

(His mind has hopped an ambulance clanging down Sixth, and is asking without curiosity: "Will he die, Doctor, or isn't he lucky?" "I'm afraid not, but he'll have to be absolutely quiet for months and months." "With a pretty nurse taking care of him?" "Probably not
470 *pretty." "Well, anyway, I claim he's lucky. And now I must get back to the hotel. 492 won't go to bed and insists on telling me jokes. It must have been a joke because he's chuckling." He laughs with a heartiness which has forgotten that heart is more than a word used in "Have a heart," an old slang expression.)*

Ha—Ha! That's a good one, Erie. That's the best I've heard in a long time!

Erie. *(For a moment is so hurt and depressed he hasn't the spirit to make a sarcastic crack. He stares at the floor, twirling his room key—to himself.)* Jesus, this sure is a dead dump. About as homey as
480 the Morgue. *(He glances up at the clock.)* Gettin' late. Better beat it up to my cell and grab some shut eye. *(He makes a move to detach himself from the desk but fails and remains wearily glued to it. His eyes prowl the lobby and finally come to rest on the Clerk's glistening, sallow face. He summons up strength for a withering crack.)* Why didn't you tell me you was deef, Buddy? I know guys is sensitive about them little afflictions, but I'll keep it confidential.

447. *Ziegfeld,* Florenz Ziegfeld (1869-1932), a theatrical producer who in 1907 introduced the lavish musical revue and the chorus line to the United States in annual productions known as the *Ziegfeld Follies.*

(But the Clerk's mind has rushed out to follow the siren wail of a fire engine. "A fireman's life must be exciting." His mind rides the engine, and asks a fireman with disinterested eagerness: "Where's the fire? Is it a real good one this time? Has it a good start? Will it be big enough, 490 *do you think?" Erie examines his face—bitingly.)*
Take my tip, Pal, and don't never try to buy from a dope peddler. He'll tell you you had enough already.

(The Clerk's mind continues its dialogue with the fireman: "I mean, big enough to burn down the whole damn city?" "Sorry, Brother, but there's no chance. There's too much stone and steel. There'd always be something left." "Yes, I guess you're right. There's too much stone and steel. I wasn't really hoping, anyway. It really doesn't matter to me." Erie gives him up and again attempts to pry himself from the desk, twirling his key frantically as if it were a fetish which might set him free.) 500
Well, me for the hay. *(But he can't dislodge himself—dully.)* Christ, it's lonely. I wish Hughie was here. By God, if he was, I'd tell him a tale that'd make his eyes pop! The bigger the story the harder he'd fall. He was that kind of sap. He thought gambling was romantic. I guess he saw me like a sort of dream guy, the sort of guy he'd like to be if he could take a chance. I guess he lived a sort of double life listening to me gabbin' about hittin' the high spots. Come to figger it, I'll bet he even cheated on his wife that way, using me and my dolls. *(He chuckles.)* No wonder he liked me, huh? And the bigger I made myself the more he lapped it up. I went easy on him at first. I didn't lie— 510 not any more'n a guy naturally does when he gabs about the bets he wins and the dolls he's made. But I soon see he was cryin' for more, and when a sucker cries for more, you're a dope if you don't let him have it. Every tramp I made got to be a Follies' doll. Hughie liked 'em to be Follies' dolls. Or in the Scandals or Frolics. He wanted me to be the Sheik of Araby, or something that any blonde 'd go round-heeled about. Well, I give him plenty of that. And I give him plenty of gambling tales. I explained my campin' in this dump was because I don't want to waste jack on nothin' but gambling. It was like dope to me, I told him. I couldn't quit. He lapped that up. He liked to kid himself I'm mixed 520 up in the racket. He thought gangsters was romantic. So I fed him some baloney about highjacking I'd done once. I told him I knew all the Big Shots. Well, so I do, most of 'em, to say hello, and sometimes they hello back. Who wouldn't know 'em that hangs around Broadway and the joints? I run errands for 'em sometimes, because there's dough in it, but I'm cagey about gettin' in where it ain't healthy. Hughie wanted to think me and Legs Diamond° was old pals. So I gave him that

527. Legs Diamond, Jack "Legs" Diamond, a small-time New York gangster and bootlegger, murdered gangland style in December of 1931. In 1926 he acted as a bodyguard for Arnold Rothstein.

too. I give him anything he cried for. *(Earnestly)* Don't get the wrong idea, Pal. What I fed Hughie wasn't all lies. The tales about gambling
530 wasn't. They was stories of big games and killings that really happened since I've been hangin' round. Only I wasn't in on 'em like I made out—except one or two from way back when I had a run of big luck and was in the bucks for a while until I was took to the cleaners. *(He stops to pay tribute of a sigh to the memory of brave days that were and that never were—then meditatively.)* Yeah, Hughie lapped up my stories like they was duck soup, or a beakful of heroin. I sure took him around with me in tales and showed him one hell of a time. *(He chuckles —then seriously.)* And, d'you know, it done me good, too, in a way. Sure. I'd get to seein' myself like he seen me. Some nights I'd come
540 back here without a buck, feeling lower than a snake's belly, and first thing you know I'd be lousy with jack, bettin' a grand a race. Oh, I was wise I was kiddin' myself. I ain't a sap. But what the hell, Hughie loved it, and it didn't cost nobody nothin', and if every guy along Broadway who kids himself was to drop dead there wouldn't be nobody left. Ain't it the truth, Charlie?

(He again stares at the Night Clerk appealingly, forgetting past rebuffs. The Clerk's face is taut with vacancy. His mind has been trying to fasten itself to some noise in the night, but a rare and threatening pause of silence has fallen on the city, and here he is, chained behind
550 *a hotel desk forever, awake when everyone else in the world is asleep, except Room 492, and he won't go to bed, he's still talking, and there is no escape.)*

Night Clerk. *(His glassy eyes stare through Erie's face. He stammers deferentially.)* Truth? I'm afraid I didn't get— What's the truth?

Erie. *(Hopelessly)* Nothing, Pal. Not a thing.

(His eyes fall to the floor. For a while he is too defeated even to twirl his room key. The Clerk's mind still cannot make a getaway because the city remains silent, and the night vaguely reminds him of death, and he is vaguely frightened, and now that he remembers, his feet are
560 *giving him hell, but that's no excuse not to act as if the Guest is always right: "I should have paid 492 more attention. After all, he is company. He is awake and alive. I should use him to help me live through the night. What's he been talking about? I must have caught some of it without meaning to." The Night Clerk's forehead puckers perspiringly as he tries to remember. Erie begins talking again but this time it is obviously aloud to himself, without hope of a listener.)*

I could tell by Hughie's face before he went to the hospital, he was through. I've seen the same look on guys' faces when they knew they was on the spot, just before guys caught up with them. I went to see him
570 twice in the hospital. The first time, his wife was there and give me a dirty look, but he cooked up a smile and said, "Hello, Erie, how're the

bangtails treating you?" I see he wants a big story to cheer him, but his wife butts in and says he's weak and he mustn't get excited. I felt like crackin', "Well, the Docs in this dump got the right dope. Just leave you with him and he'll never get excited." The second time I went, they wouldn't let me see him. That was near the end. I went to his funeral, too. There wasn't nobody but a coupla his wife's relations. I had to feel sorry for her. She looked like she ought to be parked in a coffin, too. The kids was bawlin'. There wasn't no flowers but a coupla lousy wreaths. It woulda been a punk showing for poor old Hughie, if 580 it hadn't been for my flower piece. *(He swells with pride.)* That was some display, Pal. It'd knock your eye out! Set me back a hundred bucks, and no kiddin'! A big horseshoe of red roses! I knew Hughie'd want a horseshoe because that made it look like he'd been a horse player. And around the top printed in forget-me-nots was "Good-by, Old Pal." Hughie liked to kid himself he was my pal. *(He adds sadly.)* And so he was, at that—even if he was a sucker.

(He pauses, his false poker face as nakedly forlorn as an organ grinder's monkey's. Outside, the spell of abnormal quiet presses suffocatingly upon the street, enters the deserted, dirty lobby. The Night Clerk's mind 590 *cowers away from it. He cringes behind the desk, his feet aching like hell. There is only one possible escape. If his mind could only fasten onto something 492 has said. "What's he been talking about? A clerk should always be attentive. You even are duty bound to laugh at a guest's smutty jokes, no matter how often you've heard them. That's the policy of the hotel. 492 has been gassing for hours. What's he been telling me? I must be slipping. Always before this I've been able to hear without bothering to listen, but now when I need company— Ah! I've got it! Gambling! He said a lot about gambling. That's something I've always wanted to know more about, too. Maybe he's a professional gambler.* 600 *Like Arnold Rothstein."°)*

Night Clerk. (Blurts out with an uncanny, almost lifelike eagerness) I beg your pardon, Mr.—Erie—but did I understand you to say you are a gambler by profession? Do you, by any chance, know the Big Shot, Arnold Rothstein? *(But this time it is Erie who doesn't hear him. And the Clerk's mind is now suddenly impervious to the threat of Night and Silence as it pursues an ideal of fame and glory within itself called Arnold Rothstein.)*

Erie. (With mournful longing) Christ, I wish Hughie was alive and kickin'. I'd tell him I win ten grand from the bookies, and ten grand 610 at stud, and ten grand in a crap game! I'd tell him I bought one of those Mercedes sport roadsters with nickel pipes sticking out of the

601. Arnold Rothstein, a New York business man and professional gambler, reputedly connected with bootlegging and dope peddling, murdered gangland style in November, 1928.

hood! I'd tell him I lay three babes from the Follies—two blondes and one brunette!

(The Night Clerk dreams, a rapt hero worship transfiguring his pimply face: "Arnold Rothstein! He must be some guy! I read a story about him. He'll gamble for any limit on anything, and always wins. The story said he wouldn't bother playing in a poker game unless the smallest bet you could make—one white chip—was a hundred dollars.
620 *Christ, that's going some! I'd like to have the dough to get in a game with him once! The last pot everyone would drop out but him and me. I'd say, 'Okay, Arnold, the sky's the limit,' and I'd raise him five grand, and he'd call, and I'd have a royal flush to his four aces. Then I'd say, 'Okay, Arnold, I'm a good sport, I'll give you a break. I'll cut you double or nothing. Just one cut. I want quick action for my dough.' And I'd cut the ace of spades and win again." Beatific vision swoons on the empty pools of the Night Clerk's eyes. He resembles a holy saint, recently elected to Paradise. Erie breaks the silence—bitterly resigned.)*
630 But Hughie's better off, at that, being dead. He's got all the luck. He needn't do no worryin' now. He's out of the racket. I mean, the whole goddamned racket. I mean life.

Night Clerk. (Kicked out of his dream—with detached, pleasant acquiescence) Yes, it is a goddamned racket when you stop to think, isn't it, 492? But we might as well make the best of it, because—Well, you can't burn it all down, can you? There's too much steel and stone. There'd always be something left to start it going again.

Erie. (Scowls bewilderedly) Say, what is this? What the hell you talkin' about?

640 *Night Clerk. (At a loss—in much confusion)* Why, to be frank, I really don't—Just something that came into my head.

Erie. (Bitingly, but showing he is comforted at having made some sort of contact) Get it out of your head quick, Charlie, or some guys in uniform will walk in here with a butterfly net and catch you. *(He changes the subject—earnestly.)* Listen, Pal, maybe you guess I was kiddin' about that flower piece for Hughie costing a hundred bucks? Well, I ain't! I didn't give a damn what it cost. It was up to me to give Hughie a big-time send-off, because I knew nobody else would.

Night Clerk. Oh, I'm not doubting your word, Erie. You won the
650 money gambling, I suppose—I mean, I beg your pardon if I'm mistaken, but you are a gambler, aren't you?

Erie. (Preoccupied) Yeah, sure, when I got scratch to put up. What of it? But I don't win that hundred bucks. I don't win a bet since Hughie was took to the hospital. I had to get down on my knees and beg every guy I know for a sawbuck here and a sawbuck there until I raised it.

Night Clerk. (His mind concentrated on the Big Ideal—insistently) Do you by any chance know—Arnold Rothstein?

Erie. (His train of thought interrupted—irritably) Arnold? What's he got to do with it? He wouldn't loan a guy like me a nickel to save my grandmother from streetwalking. 660

Night Clerk. (With humble awe) Then you do know him!

Erie. Sure I know the bastard. Who don't on Broadway? And he knows me—when he wants to. He uses me to run errands when there ain't no one else handy. But he ain't my trouble, Pal. My trouble is, some of these guys I put the bite on is dead wrong G's, and they expect to be paid back next Tuesday, or else I'm outa luck and have to take it on the lam, or I'll get beat up and maybe sent to a hospital. *(He suddenly rouses himself and there is something pathetically but genuinely gallant about him.)* But what the hell. I was wise I was takin' a chance. I've always took a chance, and if I lose I pay, and no welshing! It sure was worth it to give Hughie the big send-off. *(He pauses. The Night Clerk hasn't paid any attention except to his own dream. A question is trembling on his parted lips, but before he can get it out Erie goes on gloomily.)* But even that ain't my big worry, Charlie. My big worry is the run of bad luck I've had since Hughie got took to the hospital. Not a win. That ain't natural. I've always been a lucky guy—lucky enough to get by and pay up, I mean. I wouldn't never worry about owing guys, like I owe them guys. I'd always know I'd make a win that'd fix it. But now I got a lousy hunch when I lost Hughie I lost my luck—I mean, I've lost the old confidence. He used to give me confidence. *(He turns away from the desk.)* No use gabbin' here all night. You can't do me no good. *(He starts toward the elevator.)* 670 680

Night Clerk. (Pleadingly) Just a minute, Erie, if you don't mind. *(With awe)* So you're an old friend of Arnold Rothstein! Would you mind telling me if it's really true when Arnold Rothstein plays poker, one white chip is—a hundred dollars?

Erie. (Dully exasperated) Say, for Christ's sake, what's it to you—? *(He stops abruptly, staring probingly at the Clerk. There is a pause. Suddenly his face lights up with a saving revelation. He grins warmly and saunters confidently back to the desk.)* Say, Charlie, why didn't you put me wise before, you was interested in gambling? Hell, I got you all wrong, Pal. I been tellin' myself, this guy ain't like old Hughie. He ain't got no sportin' blood. He's just a dope. *(Generously)* Now I see you're a right guy. Shake. *(He shoves out his hand which the Clerk clasps with a limp pleasure. Erie goes on with gathering warmth and self-assurance.)* That's the stuff. You and me'll get along. I'll give you all the breaks, like I give Hughie. 690

Night Clerk. (Gratefully) Thank you, Erie. *(Then insistently)* Is it true when Arnold Rothstein plays poker, one white chip— 700

Erie. *(With magnificent carelessness)* Sets you back a hundred bucks? Sure. Why not? Arnold's in the bucks, ain't he? And when you're in the bucks, a C note is chicken feed. I ought to know, Pal. I was in the bucks when Arnold was a piker. Why, one time down in New Orleans I lit a cigar with a C note, just for a gag, y'understand. I was with a bunch of high class dolls and I wanted to see their eyes pop out—and believe me, they sure popped! After that, I coulda made 'em one at a time or all together! Hell, I once win twenty grand on a single race. That's action! A good crap game is action, too. Hell, I've been in
710 games where there was a hundred grand in real folding money lying around the floor. That's travelin'! *(He darts a quick glance at the Clerk's face and begins to hedge warily. But he needn't. The Clerk sees him now as the Gambler in 492, the Friend of Arnold Rothstein —and nothing is incredible. Erie goes on.)* Of course, I wouldn't kid you. I'm not in the bucks now—not right this moment. You know how it is, Charlie. Down today and up tomorrow. I got some dough ridin' on the nose of a turtle in the 4th at Saratoga. I hear a story he'll be so full of hop, if the joc can keep him from jumpin' over the grandstand, he'll win by a mile. So if I roll in here with a blonde that'll
720 knock your eyes out, don't be surprised. *(He winks and chuckles.)*

Night Clerk. *(Ingratiatingly pally, smiling)* Oh, you can't surprise me that way. I've been a night clerk in New York all my life, almost. *(He tries out a wink himself.)* I'll forget the house rules, Erie.

Erie. *(Dryly)* Yeah. The manager wouldn't like you to remember something he ain't heard of yet. *(Then slyly feeling his way)* How about shootin' a little crap, Charlie? I mean just in fun, like I used to with Hughie. I know you can't afford takin' no chances. I'll stake you, see? I got a coupla bucks. We gotta use real jack or it don't look real. It's all my jack, get it? You can't lose. I just want to show you how
730 I'll take you to the cleaners. It'll give me confidence. *(He has taken two one-dollar bills and some change from his pocket. He pushes most of it across to the Clerk.)* Here y'are. *(He produces a pair of dice—carelessly.)* Want to give these dice the once-over before we start?

Night Clerk. *(Earnestly)* What do you think I am? I know I can trust you.

Erie. *(Smiles)* You remind me a lot of Hughie, Pal. He always trusted me. Well, don't blame me if I'm lucky. *(He clicks the dice in his hand —thoughtfully.)* Y'know, it's time I quit carryin' the torch for Hughie.
740 Hell, what's the use? It don't do him no good. He's gone. Like we all gotta go. Him yesterday, me or you tomorrow, and who cares, and what's the difference? It's all in the racket, huh? *(His soul is purged of grief, his confidence restored.)* I shoot two bits.

Night Clerk. (Manfully, with an excited dead-pan expression he hopes resembles Arnold Rothstein's) I fade you.

Erie. (Throws the dice) Four's my point. *(Gathers them up swiftly and throws them again)* Four it is. *(He takes the money.)* Easy when you got my luck—and know how. Huh, Charlie? *(He chuckles, giving the Night Clerk the slyly amused, contemptuous, affectionate wink with which a Wise Guy regales a Sucker.)* 750

(Curtain)

Comments and Questions

In the published version of Hughie *you have read, O'Neill transcends the stage limitations of conveying experience directly through voice and gesture by his detailing for us the inner thoughts of the clerk. He is using the traditional freedom of the writer of novels and short stories to go into the minds of his characters; the device is of obvious help to the reader and actor, especially in understanding the clerk's unconscious outburst, when he refers to the burning buildings of his earlier daydream. How might the clerk's secret thoughts be made clear to the audience? (Note sound effects, characteristic gestures to indicate sore feet, and the like.)*

In characterizing Erie, the problem is somewhat different. One long-standing technique of the dramatist to allow a character to think out loud is the soliloquy, but since soliloquies are inappropriate in a realistic setting, O'Neill does the next best thing. He simply allows Erie to talk and to talk in such a way that he reveals even more than he might normally admit to himself. Hence, everything he says should be taken into account and evaluated before you decide you fully understand him. Of what importance for our understanding Erie are his remarks about Hughie's wife, or his agreeing with Hughie that horses are "the most beautiful things in the world," or his borrowing, if he did, a hundred dollars to buy a horseshoe of red roses for Hughie's funeral? Is Erie a character with whom we can be fully sympathetic? Why or why not?

One critic has called Hughie *a "perfectly constructed work." The reader should follow each step as Erie slowly and unwittingly bares his soul until he confronts the dreadful truth about himself. What is that truth? On the other hand, what evidence is there to suggest that Erie's self-knowledge is incomplete, that his new insight into himself is still tarnished by illusions of which he is unaware? Which of his lies does he still cling to in his despair?*

By the end of the play, Erie's "soul is purged of grief, his confidence restored." What is the turning point in this change from his despair? What does the change signify? Has Erie, then, really gained no insight into himself? Or is it possible that at the end he believes illusions he knows to be illusions? Does the play encourage the audience to draw inferences about the nature of the world at large, or about men in general?

Related Reading

Thornton Wilder, "Some Thoughts on Playwrighting," page 644

Bernard Shaw

(1856-1950)

ARMS AND THE MAN

In the 1890's Bernard Shaw, one of the major music and theater critics of London, turned to writing plays, and eventually became the most prolific and probably most important British playwright of modern times. His start was difficult, however, His earliest plays, some of which he collectively characterized as "unpleasant," were performed only in obscure theater clubs. Arms and the Man, *his fourth play, was the first to reach London's West End, the equivalent of Broadway in New York. It was first performed in London on April 21, 1894, and in New York on September 17, of the same year, but its initial success was small in both places. Revivals in the early twentieth century attracted increasingly large audiences. In 1909 it was made into an operetta.*

Shaw was a great admirer of Ibsen and did what he could as a critic and writer to advance Ibsen's cause with the public. Shaw was as concerned with social abuses, hypocrisies, and malpractices as Ibsen, but he used a different route to attack them in his plays. Ibsen is almost invariably earnest, dogged, direct in his social criticism. Shaw uses a kind of shock treatment combined with laughter. His comedies of ideas attempt to force us to revise our accepted notions, not by telling us how wrong they are, but by showing us how illogical and ridiculous.

In Arms and the Man *Shaw ridicules romantic and idealized notions about three topics: war, soldier-heroes, and love. For his setting he chose a very appropriate event of then-recent European history, the Serbo-Bulgarian War of 1885. In the late nineteenth century the Balkan states were the Banana republics of Europe—except that they were not republics but rather kingdoms, mostly ruled over by western European princes imported for that purpose. They also were, to use a more recent term, satellites of the great European powers. In 1885 Serbia happened to be a satellite of its neighbor, the Austro-Hungarian Empire. Bulgaria was a satellite of Russia (as it has again become, since World War II), so much so that all officers in the Bulgarian army above the rank of captain were Russians. A few months before the events which form the background of* Arms and the Man, *the Russian Czar, annoyed about some independent action of Bulgaria's, had withdrawn all his officers. The Serbians thought that this opened up a marvelous opportunity for a cheap victory and a gain of land and money. So on November 14, 1885, they invaded their neighbor along the main road from Serbia toward the Bulgarian capital, Sofia, across the Dragoman Pass which formed the border. At Slivnitza, near Sofia, on November 17, they met the Bulgarian army. Two days later, to everyone's surprise, the Bulgarians won the battle, chased the Serbians back over the Dragoman Pass, and proceeded with their own invasion. The Serbian army could not stop them, but an Austrian ultimatum did, and the whole war ended where it had begun, without any territory or spoils changing hands. It had taken just two weeks from start to finish.*

In 1914, twenty years after Shaw wrote Arms and the Man, *and two hundred miles from the Dragoman Pass, on the other side of Serbia, at Sarajevo, the assassination of an Austrian archduke by a Serbian revolutionary set off the First World War. But in the 1890's the Balkan nations were comical rather than sinister to Westerners, and in* Arms and the Man *Shaw has much fun with their haphazard view of Western civilization which they were trying to introduce into their own picturesque culture. Among these borrowings, he places some of the more ridiculous romantic notions of heroism and love. His real hero, if any, is a professional soldier who does not go in for heroics at all, while the hero, romantic style, has to be rescued periodically from his own quixotic bumbling. Probably the most resourceful and competent of all the characters is a servant girl.*

The play also spoofs the usual nineteenth-century melodrama. It opens, romantically, in a lady's bedchamber, where the sweet dreams of the heroine are rudely interrupted by a sinister invader, stealthily entering through the window. The bedchamber, however, as Shaw sets the scene, is not romantic, but a ridiculous mixture "half rich Bulgarian, half cheap Viennese"; and the invader is not a fierce Serbian but a professional Swiss soldier, with chocolate in his ammunition belt.

ARMS AND THE MAN

Characters

MAJOR PETKOFF
CATHERINE PETKOFF
RAINA PETKOFF
LOUKA
NICOLA
CAPTAIN BLUNTSCHLI
MAJOR SERGIUS SARANOFF
RUSSIAN OFFICER

Act I

Night. A lady's bedchamber in Bulgaria, in a small town near the Dragoman Pass, late in November in the year 1885. Through an open window with a little balcony a peak of the Balkans, wonderfully white and beautiful in the starlit snow, seems quite close at hand, though it is really miles away. The interior of the room is not like anything to be seen in the west of Europe. It is half rich Bulgarian, half cheap Viennese. Above the head of the bed, which stands against a little wall cutting off the left hand corner of the room, is a painted wooden shrine, blue and gold, with an ivory image of Christ, and a light hanging before it in a pierced metal ball suspended by three chains. The principal seat, placed towards the other side of the room and opposite the window, is a Turkish ottoman. The counterpane and hangings of the bed, the window curtains, the little carpet, and all the ornamental textile fabrics in the room are oriental and gorgeous: the paper on the walls is occidental and paltry. The washstand, against the wall on the side nearest the ottoman and window, consists of an enamelled iron basin with a pail beneath it in a painted metal frame, and a single towel on the rail at the side. The dressing table, between the bed and the window, is a common pine table, covered with a cloth of many colors, with an expensive toilet mirror on it. The door is on the side nearest the bed; and there is a chest of drawers between. This chest of drawers is also covered by a variegated native cloth; and on it there is a pile of paper backed novels, a box of chocolate creams, and a miniature easel with a large photograph of an extremely handsome officer, whose lofty bearing and magnetic glance can be felt even from the portrait. The room is lighted by a candle on the chest of drawers, and another on the dressing table with a box of matches beside it.

The window is hinged doorwise and stands wide open. Outside, a pair of wooden shutters, opening outwards, also stand open. On the

30 *balcony a young lady, intensely conscious of the romantic beauty of the night, and of the fact that her own youth and beauty are part of it, is gazing at the snowy Balkans. She is in her nightgown, well covered by a long mantle of furs, worth, on a moderate estimate, about three times the furniture of her room.*

Her reverie is interrupted by her mother, Catherine Petkoff, a woman over forty, imperiously energetic, with magnificent black hair and eyes, who might be a very splendid specimen of the wife of a mountain farmer, but is determined to be a Viennese lady, and to that end wears a fashionable tea gown on all occasions.

40 *Catherine. (Entering hastily, full of good news)* Raina! *(She pronounces it Rah-eena, with the stress on the ee.)* Raina! *(She goes to the bed, expecting to find Raina there.)* Why, where—? *(Raina looks into the room.)* Heavens, child! are you out in the night air instead of in your bed? You'll catch your death. Louka told me you were asleep.

Raina. (Dreamily) I sent her away. I wanted to be alone. The stars are so beautiful! What is the matter?

Catherine. Such news! There has been a battle.

Raina. (Her eyes dilating) Ah! *(She comes eagerly to Catherine.)*

Catherine. A great battle at Slivnitza! A victory! And it was won 50 by Sergius.

Raina. (With a cry of delight) Ah! *(They embrace rapturously.)* Oh, mother! *(Then, with sudden anxiety)* Is father safe?

Catherine. Of course: he sends me the news. Sergius is the hero of the hour, the idol of the regiment.

Raina. Tell me, tell me. How was it? *(Ecstatically)* Oh, mother! mother! mother! *(She pulls her mother down on the ottoman; and they kiss one another frantically.)*

Catherine. (With surging enthusiasm) You cant guess how splendid it is. A cavalry charge! think of that! He defied our Russian com- 60 manders°—acted without orders—led a charge on his own responsibility—headed it himself—was the first man to sweep through their guns. Cant you see it, Raina: our gallant splendid Bulgarians with their swords and eyes flashing, thundering down like an avalanche and scattering the wretched Serbs and their dandified Austrian officers like chaff. And you! you kept Sergius waiting a year before you would be betrothed to him. Oh, if you have a drop of Bulgarian blood in your veins, you will worship him when he comes back.

Raina. What will he care for my poor little worship after the acclamations of a whole army of heroes? But no matter: I am so happy! so

59-60. defied our Russian commanders. Shaw pretends that the Russian officers still command all of the Bulgarian Army. (See headnote to play, page 31.)

proud! *(She rises and walks about excitedly.)* It proves that all our 70
ideas were real after all.

Catherine. (Indignantly) Our ideas real! What do you mean?

Raina. Our ideas of what Sergius would do. Our patriotism. Our heroic ideals. I sometimes used to doubt whether they were anything but dreams. Oh, what faithless little creatures girls are! When I buckled on Sergius's sword he looked so noble: it was treason to think of disillusion or humiliation or failure. And yet—and yet—*(She sits down again suddenly.)* Promise me youll never tell him.

Catherine. Dont ask me for promises until I know what I'm promising.

Raina. Well, it came into my head just as he was holding me in his 80
arms and looking into my eyes, that perhaps we only had our heroic ideas because we are so fond of reading Byron and Pushkin,° and because we were so delighted with the opera that season at Bucharest.° Real life is so seldom like that! indeed never, as far as I knew it then. *(Remorsefully)* Only think, mother: I doubted him: I wondered whether all his heroic qualities and his soldiership might not prove mere imagination when he went into a real battle. I had an uneasy fear that he might cut a poor figure there beside all those clever officers from the Tsar's court.

Catherine. A poor figure! Shame on you! The Serbs have Austrian 90
officers who are just as clever as the Russians; but we have beaten them in every battle for all that.

Raina. (Laughing and snuggling against her mother) Yes: I was only a prosaic little coward. Oh, to think that it was all true! that Sergius is just as splendid and noble as he looks! that the world is really a glorious world for women who can see its glory and men who can act its romance! What happiness! what unspeakable fulfilment! *(They are interrupted by the entry of Louka, a handsome proud girl in a pretty Bulgarian peasant's dress with double apron, so defiant that her servility to Raina is almost insolent. She is afraid of Catherine,* 100
but even with her goes as far as she dares.)

Louka. If you please, madam, all the windows are to be closed and the shutters made fast. They say there may be shooting in the streets. *(Raina and Catherine rise together, alarmed.)* The Serbs are being chased right back through the pass; and they say they may run into the town. Our cavalry will be after them; and our people will be ready for them, you may be sure, now theyre running away. *(She goes out on the balcony, and pulls the outside shutters to; then steps back into the room.)*

82. Byron and Pushkin. Lord Byron (1788-1824) an English poet; Alexander Pushkin (1799-1837) a Russian poet. ***83. Bucharest,*** "the Paris of the Balkans" is the capital of neighboring Rumania.

110 *Catherine. (Businesslike, her housekeeping instincts aroused)* I must see that everything is made safe downstairs.

Raina. I wish our people were not so cruel. What glory is there in killing wretched fugitives?

Catherine. Cruel! Do you suppose they would hesitate to kill you —or worse?

Raina. (To Louka) Leave the shutters so that I can just close them if I hear any noise.

Catherine. (Authoritatively, turning on her way to the door) Oh no, dear: you must keep them fastened. You would be sure to drop
120 off to sleep and leave them open. Make them fast, Louka.

Louka. Yes, madam. *(She fastens them.)*

Raina. Dont be anxious about me. The moment I hear a shot, I shall blow out the candles and roll myself up in bed with my ears well covered.

Catherine. Quite the wisest thing you can do, my love. Goodnight.

Raina. Goodnight. *(Her emotion comes back for a moment.)* Wish me joy. *(They kiss.)* This is the happiest night of my life—if only there are no fugitives.

Catherine. Go to bed, dear; and dont think of them. *(She goes out.)*

130 *Louka. (Secretly, to Raina)* If you would like the shutters open, just give them a push like this *(She pushes them: they open: she pulls them to again.)* One of them ought to be bolted at the bottom; but the bolt's gone.

Raina. (With dignity, reproving her) Thanks, Louka; but we must do what we are told. *(Louka makes a grimace.)* Goodnight.

Louka. (Carelessly) Goodnight. *(She goes out swaggering.)*

(Raina, left alone, takes off her fur cloak and throws it on the ottoman. Then she goes to the chest of drawers, and adores the portrait there with feelings that are beyond all expression. She does not kiss it
140 *or press it to her breast, or shew it any mark of bodily affection; but she takes it in her hands and elevates it, like a priestess.)*

Raina. (Looking up at the picture) Oh, I shall never be unworthy of you any more, my soul's hero: never, never, never.

(She replaces it reverently. Then she selects a novel from the little pile of books. She turns over the leaves dreamily; finds her page; turns the book inside out at it; and, with a happy sigh, gets into bed and prepares to read herself to sleep. But before abandoning herself to fiction, she raises her eyes once more, thinking of the blessed reality, and murmurs) My hero! my hero!

150 *(A distant shot breaks the quiet of the night. She starts, listening; and two more shots, much nearer, follow, startling her so that she scrambles out of bed, and hastily blows out the candle on the chest of drawers. Then, putting her fingers in her ears, she runs to the dressing*

table, blows out the light there, and hurries back to bed in the dark, nothing being visible but the glimmer of the light in the pierced ball before the image, and the starlight seen through the slits at the top of the shutters. The firing breaks out again: there is a startling fusillade quite close at hand. Whilst it is still echoing, the shutters disappear, pulled open from without; and for an instant the rectangle of snowy starlight flashes out with the figure of a man silhouetted in black upon 160 *it. The shutters close immediately; and the room is dark again. But the silence is now broken by the sound of panting. Then there is a scratch; and the flame of a match is seen in the middle of the room.)*

Raina. (Crouching on the bed) Who's there? *(The match is out instantly.)* Who's there? Who is that?

A Man's Voice. (In the darkness, subduedly, but threateningly) Sh—sh! Dont call out; or youll be shot. Be good; and no harm will happen to you. *(She is heard leaving her bed, and making for the door.)* Take care: it's no use trying to run away. 170

Raina. But who—

The Voice. (Warning) Remember: if you raise your voice my revolver will go off. *(Commandingly)* Strike a light and let me see you. Do you hear?

(Another moment of silence and darkness as she retreats to the chest of drawers. Then she lights a candle; and the mystery is at an end. He is a man of about 35, in a deplorable plight, bespattered with mud and blood and snow, his belt and the strap of his revolver-case keeping together the torn ruins of the blue tunic of a Serbian artillery officer. All that the candlelight and his unwashed unkempt condition make it 180 *possible to discern is that he is of middling stature and undistinguished appearance, with strong neck and shoulders, roundish obstinate looking head covered with short crisp bronze curls, clear quick eyes and good brows and mouth, hopelessly prosaic nose like that of a strong minded baby, trim soldierlike carriage and energetic manner, and with all his wits about him in spite of his desperate predicament: even with a sense of the humor of it, without, however, the least intention of trifling with it or throwing away a chance. Reckoning up what he can guess about Raina: her age, her social position, her character, and the extent to which she is frightened, he continues, more politely but still* 190 *most determined.)*

Excuse my disturbing you; but you recognize my uniform? Serb! If I'm caught I shall be killed. *(Menacingly)* Do you understand that?

Raina. Yes.

The Man. Well, I dont intend to get killed if I can help it. *(Still more formidably)* Do you understand that? *(He locks the door quickly but quietly.)*

Raina. *(Disdainfully)* I suppose not. *(She draws herself up superbly, and looks him straight in the face, adding, with cutting emphasis.)* 200 Some soldiers, I know, are afraid to die.

The Man. *(With grim goodhumor)* All of them, dear lady, all of them, believe me. It is our duty to live as long as we can. Now, if you raise an alarm—

Raina. *(Cutting him short)* You will shoot me. How do you know that I am afraid to die?

The Man. *(Cunningly)* Ah; but suppose I dont shoot you, what will happen then? A lot of your cavalry will burst into this pretty room of yours and slaughter me here like a pig; for I'll fight like a demon: they shant get me into the street to amuse themselves with: I know what 210 they are. Are you prepared to receive that sort of company in your present undress? *(Raina, suddenly conscious of her nightgown, instinctively shrinks, and gathers it more closely about her neck. He watches her, and adds, pitilessly.)* Hardly presentable, eh? *(She turns to the ottoman. He raises his pistol instantly, and cries.)* Stop! *(She stops.)* Where are you going?

Raina. *(With dignified patience)* Only to get my cloak.

The Man. *(Passing swiftly to the ottoman and snatching the cloak)* A good idea! I'll keep the cloak; and youll take care that nobody comes in and sees you without it. This is a better weapon than the revolver: 220 eh? *(He throws the pistol down on the ottoman.)*

Raina. *(Revolted)* It is not the weapon of a gentleman!

The Man. It's good enough for a man with only you to stand between him and death. *(As they look at one another for a moment, Raina hardly able to believe that even a Serbian officer can be so cynically and selfishly unchivalrous, they are startled by a sharp fusillade in the street. The chill of imminent death hushes the man's voice as he adds.)* Do you hear? If you are going to bring those blackguards in on me you shall receive them as you are.

(Clamor and disturbance. The pursuers in the street batter at the 230 *house door, shouting.)* Open the door! Open the door! Wake up, will you! *(A man servant's voice calls to them angrily from within.)* This is Major Petkoff's house: you cant come in here; *(But a renewal of the clamor, and a torrent of blows on the door, end with his letting a chain down with a clank, followed by a rush of heavy footsteps and a din of triumphant yells, dominated at last by the voice of Catherine, indignantly addressing an officer with)* What does this mean, sir? Do you know where you are? *(The noise subsides suddenly.)*

Louka. *(Outside, knocking at the bedroom door)* My lady! my lady! get up quick and open the door. If you dont they will break it down. 240 *(The fugitive throws up his head with the gesture of a man who sees that it is all over with him, and drops the manner he has been assuming to intimidate Raina.)*

The Man. *(Sincerely and kindly)* No use, dear: I'm done for. *(Flinging the cloak to her)* Quick! wrap yourself up: theyre coming.

Raina. Oh, thank you. *(She wraps herself up with intense relief.)*

The Man. *(Between his teeth)* Dont mention it.

Raina. *(Anxiously)* What will you do?

The Man. *(Grimly)* The first man in will find out. Keep out of the way; and dont look. It wont last long; but it will not be nice. *(He draws his sabre and faces the door, waiting.)* 250

Raina. *(Impulsively)* I'll help you. I'll save you.

The Man. You cant.

Raina. I can. I'll hide you. *(She drags him towards the window.)* Here! behind the curtains.

The Man. *(Yielding to her)* Theres just half a chance, if you keep your head.

Raina. *(Drawing the curtain before him)* S-sh! *(She makes for the ottoman.)*

The Man. *(Putting out his head)* Remember—

Raina. *(Running back to him)* Yes? 260

The Man. —nine soldiers out of ten are born fools.

Raina. Oh! *(She draws the curtain angrily before him.)*

The Man. *(Looking out at the other side)* If they find me, I promise you a fight: a devil of a fight. *(She stamps at him. He disappears hastily. She takes off her cloak, and throws it across the foot of the bed. Then, with a sleepy, disturbed air, she opens the door. Louka enters excitedly.)*

Louka. One of those beasts of Serbs has been seen climbing up the waterpipe to your balcony. Our men want to search for him; and they are so wild and drunk and furious. *(She makes for the other side* 270 *of the room to get as far from the door as possible.)* My lady says you are to dress at once, and to— *(She sees the revolver lying on the ottoman, and stops, petrified.)*

Raina. *(As if annoyed at being disturbed)* They shall not search here. Why have they been let in?

Catherine. *(Coming in hastily)* Raina, darling: are you safe? Have you seen anyone or heard anything?

Raina. I heard the shooting. Surely the soldiers will not dare come in here?

Catherine. I have found a Russian officer, thank Heaven: he knows 280 Sergius. *(Speaking through the door to someone outside)* Sir: will you come in now. My daughter will receive you.

(A young Russian officer, in Bulgarian uniform, enters, sword in hand.)

Officer. *(With soft feline politeness and stiff military carriage)* Good evening, gracious lady. I am sorry to intrude; but there is a Serb hiding on the balcony. Will you and the gracious lady your mother please to withdraw whilst we search?

Raina. *(Petulantly)* Nonsense, sir: you can see that there is no one on the balcony. *(She throws the shutters wide open and stands with her*
290 *back to the curtain where the man is hidden, pointing to the moonlit balcony. A couple of shots are fired right under the window; and a bullet shatters the glass opposite Raina, who winks and gasps, but stands her ground; whilst Catherine screams, and the officer, with a cry of* Take care! *rushes to the balcony.)*

The Officer. *(On the balcony, shouting savagely down to the street)* Cease firing there, you fools: do you hear? Cease firing, damn you! *(He glares down for a moment; then turns to Raina, trying to resume his polite manner.)* Could anyone have got in without your knowledge? Were you asleep?

300 *Raina.* No: I have not been to bed.

The Officer. *(Impatiently, coming back into the room)* Your neighbors have their heads so full of runaway Serbs that they see them everywhere. *(Politely)* Gracious lady: a thousand pardons. Goodnight. *(Military bow, which Raina returns coldly. Another to Catherine, who follows him out. Raina closes the shutters. She turns and sees Louka, who has been watching the scene curiously.)*

Raina. Dont leave my mother, Louka, until the soldiers go away.

(Louka glances at Raina, at the ottoman, at the curtain; then purses her lips secretively, laughs insolently, and goes out. Raina, highly
310 *offended by this demonstration, follows her to the door, and shuts it behind her with a slam, locking it violently. The man immediately steps out from behind the curtain, sheathing his sabre, and closes the shutters. Then, dismissing the danger from his mind in a businesslike way, he comes affably to Raina.)*

The Man. A narrow shave; but a miss is as good as a mile. Dear young lady: your servant to the death. I wish for your sake I had joined the Bulgarian army instead of the other one. I am not a native Serb.

Raina. *(Haughtily)* No: you are one of the Austrians who set the Serbs on to rob us of our national liberty, and who officer their army
320 for them. We hate them!

The Man. Austrian! not I. Dont hate me, dear young lady. I am a Swiss, fighting merely as a professional soldier. I joined the Serbs because they came first on the road from Switzerland. Be generous: youve beaten us hollow.

Raina. Have I not been generous?

The Man. Noble! Heroic! But I'm not saved yet. This particular rush will soon pass through; but the pursuit will go on all night by fits and starts. I must take my chance to get off in a quiet interval. *(Pleasantly)* You dont mind my waiting just a minute or two, do you?

Raina. *(Putting on her most genteel society manner)* Oh, not at all. 330
Wont you sit down?

The Man. Thanks. *(He sits on the foot of the bed. Raina walks with studied elegance to the ottoman and sits down. Unfortunately she sits on the pistol, and jumps up with a shriek. The man, all nerves, shies like a frightened horse to the other side of the room.)*

The Man. *(Irritably)* Dont frighten me like that. What is it?

Raina. Your revolver! It was staring that officer in the face all the time. What an escape!

The Man. *(Vexed at being unnecessarily terrified)* Oh, is that all?

Raina. *(Staring at him rather superciliously as she conceives a* 340 *poorer and poorer opinion of him, and feels proportionately more and more at her ease)* I am sorry I frightened you. *(She takes up the pistol and hands it to him.)* Pray take it to protect yourself against me.

The Man. *(Grinning wearily at the sarcasm as he takes the pistol)* No use, dear young lady: theres nothing in it. It's not loaded. *(He makes a grimace at it, and drops it disparagingly into his revolver case.)*

Raina. Load it by all means.

The Man. Ive no ammunition. What use are cartridges in battle? I always carry chocolate instead; and I finished the last cake of that hours ago. 350

Raina. *(Outraged in her most cherished ideals of manhood)* Chocolate! Do you stuff your pockets with sweets—like a schoolboy—even in the field?

The Man. *(Grinning)* Yes: isnt it contemptible? *(Hungrily)* I wish I had some now.

Raina. Allow me. *(She sails away scornfully to the chest of drawers, and returns with the box of confectionery in her hand.)* I am sorry I have eaten them all except these. *(She offers him the box.)*

The Man. *(Ravenously)* Youre an angel! *(He gobbles the contents.)* Creams! Delicious! *(He looks anxiously to see whether there are any* 360 *more. There are none: he can only scrape the box with his fingers and suck them. When that nourishment is exhausted he accepts the inevitable with pathetic goodhumor, and says, with grateful emotion)* Bless you, dear lady! You can always tell an old soldier by the inside of his holsters and cartridge boxes. The young ones carry pistols and cartridges: the old ones, grub. Thank you. *(He hands back the box. She snatches it contemptuously from him and throws it away. He shies again, as if she had meant to strike him.)* Ugh! Dont do things so suddenly, gracious lady. It's mean to revenge yourself because I frightened you just now.

Raina. *(Loftily)* Frighten me! Do you know, sir, that though I am 370 only a woman, I think I am at heart as brave as you.

The Man. I should think so. You havnt been under fire for three days as I have. I can stand two days without shewing it much; but no man can stand three days: I'm as nervous as a mouse. *(He sits down on the ottoman, and takes his head in his hands.)* Would you like to see me cry?

Raina. *(Alarmed)* No.

The Man. If you would, all you have to do is to scold me just as if I were a little boy and you my nurse. If I were in camp now, theyd play
380 all sorts of tricks on me.

Raina. *(A little moved)* I'm sorry. I wont scold you. *(Touched by the sympathy in her tone, he raises his head and looks gratefully at her: she immediately draws back and says stiffly.)* You must excuse me: our soldiers are not like that. *(She moves away from the ottoman.)*

The Man. Oh yes they are. There are only two sorts of soldiers: old ones and young ones. Ive served fourteen years: half of your fellows never smelt power before. Why, how is it that youve just beaten us? Sheer ignorance of the art of war, nothing else. *(Indignantly)* I never saw anything so unprofessional.

390 *Raina.* *(Ironically)* Oh! was it unprofessional to beat you?

The Man. Well, come! is it professional to throw a regiment of cavalry on a battery of machine guns, with the dead certainty that if the guns go off not a horse or man will ever get within fifty yards of the fire? I couldnt believe my eyes when I saw it.

Raina. *(Eagerly turning to him, as all her enthusiasm and her dreams of glory rush back on her)* Did you see the great cavalry charge? Oh, tell me about it. Describe it to me.

The Man. You never saw a cavalry charge, did you?

Raina. How could I?

400 *The Man.* Ah, perhaps not. No: of course not! Well, it's a funny sight. It's like slinging a handful of peas against a window pane: first one comes; then two or three close behind him; and then all the rest in a lump.

Raina. *(Her eyes dilating as she raises her clasped hands ecstatically)* Yes, first One! the bravest of the brave!

The Man. *(Prosaically)* Hm! you should see the poor devil pulling at his horse.

Raina. Why should he pull at his horse?

The Man. *(Impatient of so stupid a question)* It's running away
410 with him, of course: do you suppose the fellow wants to get there before the others and be killed? Then they all come. You can tell the young ones by their wildness and their slashing. The old ones come bunched up under the number one guard: they know that theyre mere projectiles, and that it's no use trying to fight. The wounds are mostly broken knees, from the horses cannoning together.

Raina. Ugh! But I dont believe the first man is a coward. I know he is a hero!

The Man. *(Goodhumoredly)* Thats what youd have said if youd seen the first man in the charge today.

Raina. *(Breathless, forgiving him everything)* Ah, I knew it! Tell me. Tell me about *him.* 420

The Man. He did it like an operatic tenor. A regular handsome fellow, with flashing eyes and lovely moustache, shouting his war-cry and charging like Don Quixote at the windmills. We did laugh.

Raina. You dared to laugh!

The Man. Yes; but when the sergeant ran up as white as a sheet, and told us theyd sent us the wrong ammunition, and that we couldnt fire a round for the next ten minutes, we laughed at the other side of our mouths. I never felt so sick in my life; though Ive been in one or two very tight places. And I hadnt even a revolver cartridge: only chocolate. We'd no bayonets: nothing. Of course, they just cut us to bits. And there was Don Quixote flourishing like a drum major, thinking he'd done the cleverest thing ever known, whereas he ought to be courtmartialled for it. Of all the fools ever let loose on a field of battle, that man must be the very maddest. He and his regiment simply committed suicide; only the pistol missed fire: thats all. 430

Raina. *(Deeply wounded, but steadfastly loyal to her ideals)* Indeed! Would you know him again if you saw him?

The Man. Shall I ever forget him! *(She again goes to the chest of drawers. He watches her with a vague hope that she may have something more for him to eat. She takes the portrait from its stand and brings it to him.)* 440

Raina. That is a photograph of the gentleman—the patriot and hero—to whom I am betrothed.

The Man. *(Recognizing it with a shock)* I'm really very sorry. *(Looking at her)* Was it fair to lead me on? *(He looks at the portrait again.)* Yes: thats Don Quixote: not a doubt of it. *(He stifles a laugh.)*

Raina. *(Quickly)* Why do you laugh?

The Man. *(Apologetic, but still greatly tickled)* I didnt laugh, I assure you. At least I didnt mean to. But when I think of him charging the windmills and imagining he was doing the finest thing—*(He chokes with suppressed laughter.)* 450

Raina. *(Sternly)* Give me back the portrait, sir.

The Man. *(With sincere remorse)* Of course. Certainly. I'm really very sorry. *(He hands her the picture. She deliberately kisses it and looks him straight in the face before returning to the chest of drawers to replace it. He follows her, apologizing.)* Perhaps I'm quite wrong, you know: no doubt I am. Most likely he had got wind of the cartridge business somehow, and knew it was a safe job.

460 *Raina.* That is to say, he was a pretender and a coward! You did not dare say that before.

The Man. *(With a comic gesture of despair)* It's no use, dear lady: I cant make you see it from the professional point of view. *(As he turns away to get back to the ottoman, a couple of distant shots threaten renewed trouble.)*

Raina. *(Sternly, as she sees him listening to the shots)* So much the better for you!

The Man. *(Turning)* How?

Raina. You are my enemy; and you are at my mercy. What would 470 I do if I were a professional soldier?

The Man. Ah, true, dear young lady: youre always right. I know how good youve been to me: to my last hour I shall remember those three chocolate creams. It was unsoldierly; but it was angelic.

Raina. *(Coldly)* Thank you. And now I will do a soldierly thing. You cannot stay here after what you have just said about my future husband; but I will go out on the balcony and see whether it is safe for you to climb down into the street. *(She turns to the window.)*

The Man. *(Changing countenance)* Down that waterpipe! Stop! Wait! I cant! I darent! The very thought of it makes me giddy. I came 480 up it fast enough with death behind me. But to face it now in cold blood—! *(He sinks on the ottoman.)* It's no use: I give up: I'm beaten. Give the alarm. *(He drops his head on his hands in the deepest dejection.)*

Raina. *(Disarmed by pity)* Come: dont be disheartened. *(She stoops over him almost maternally: he shakes his head.)* Oh, you are a very poor soldier: a chocolate cream soldier! Come, cheer up! it takes less courage to climb down than to face capture: remember that.

The Man. *(Dreamily, lulled by her voice)* No: capture only means death; and death is sleep: oh, sleep, sleep, sleep, undisturbed sleep! 490 Climbing down the pipe means doing something—exerting myself —thinking! Death ten times over first.

Raina. *(Softly and wonderingly, catching the rhythm of his weariness)* Are you as sleepy as that?

The Man. Ive not had two hours undisturbed sleep since I joined. I havnt closed my eyes for forty-eight hours.

Raina. *(At her wit's end)* But what am I to do with you?

The Man. *(Staggering up, roused by her desperation)* Of course. I must do something. *(He shakes himself; pulls himself together; and speaks with rallied vigor and courage.)* You see, sleep or no sleep, 500 hunger or no hunger, tired or not tired, you can always do a thing when you know it must be done. Well, that pipe must be got down: *(He hits himself on the chest.)* do you hear that, you chocolate cream soldier? *(He turns to the window.)*

Raina. *(Anxiously)* But if you fall?

The Man. I shall sleep as if the stones were a feather bed. Goodbye. *(He makes boldly for the window; and his hand is on the shutter when there is a terrible burst of firing in the street beneath.)*

Raina. *(Rushing to him)* Stop! *(She seizes him recklessly, and pulls him quite round.)* Theyll kill you.

The Man. *(Coolly, but attentively)* Never mind: this sort of thing is all in my day's work. I'm bound to take my chance. *(Decisively)* Now do what I tell you. Put out the candles; so that they shant see the light when I open the shutters. And keep away from the window, whatever you do. If they see me theyre sure to have a shot at me. 510

Raina. *(Clinging to him)* Theyre sure to see you: it's bright moonlight. I'll save you. Oh, how can you be so indifferent! You want me to save you, dont you?

The Man. I really dont want to be troublesome. *(She shakes him in her impatience.)* I am not indifferent, dear young lady, I assure you. But how is it to be done? 520

Raina. Come away from the window. *(She takes him firmly back to the middle of the room. The moment she releases him he turns mechanically towards the window again. She seizes him and turns him back, exclaiming)* Please! *(He becomes motionless, like a hypnotized rabbit, his fatigue gaining fast on him. She releases him, and addresses him patronizingly.)* Now listen. You must trust to our hospitality. You do not yet know in whose house you are. I am a Petkoff.

The Man. A pet what?

Raina. *(Rather indignantly)* I mean that I belong to the family of the Petkoffs, the richest and best known in our country. 530

The Man. Oh yes, of course. I beg your pardon. The Petkoffs, to be sure. How stupid of me!

Raina. You know you never heard of them until this moment. How can you stoop to pretend!

The Man. Forgive me: I'm too tired to think; and the change of subject was too much for me. Dont scold me.

Raina. I forgot. It might make you cry. *(He nods, quite seriously. She pouts and then resumes her patronizing tone.)* I must tell you that my father holds the highest command of any Bulgarian in our army. He is *(proudly)* a Major. 540

The Man. *(Pretending to be deeply impressed)* A Major! Bless me! Think of that!

Raina. You shewed great ignorance in thinking that it was necessary to climb up to the balcony because ours is the only private house that has two rows of windows. There is a flight of stairs inside to get up and down by.

The Man. Stairs! How grand! You live in great luxury indeed, dear young lady.

Raina. Do you know what a library is?

550 *The Man.* A library? A roomful of books?

Raina. Yes. We have one, the only one in Bulgaria.

The Man. Actually a real library! I should like to see that.

Raina. *(Affectedly)* I tell you these things to shew you that you are not in the house of ignorant country folk who would kill you the moment they saw your Serbian uniform, but among civilized people. We go to Bucharest every year for the opera season; and I have spent a whole month in Vienna.

The Man. I saw that, dear young lady. I saw at once that you knew the world.

560 *Raina.* Have you ever seen the opera of Ernani?°

The Man. Is that the one with the devil in it in red velvet, and a soldiers' chorus?

Raina. *(Contemptuously)* No!

The Man. *(Stifling a heavy sigh of weariness)* Then I dont know it.

Raina. I thought you might have remembered the great scene where Ernani, flying from his foes just as you are tonight, takes refuge in the castle of his bitterest enemy, an old Castilian noble. The noble refuses to give him up. His guest is sacred to him.

The Man. *(Quickly, waking up a little)* Have your people got that 570 notion?

Raina. *(With dignity)* My mother and I can understand that notion, as you call it. And if instead of threatening me with your pistol as you did you had simply thrown yourself as a fugitive on our hospitality, you would have been as safe as in your father's house.

The Man. Quite sure?

Raina. *(Turning her back on him in disgust)* Oh, it is useless to try to make you understand.

The Man. Dont be angry: you see how awkward it would be for me if there was any mistake. My father is a very hospitable man: he 580 keeps six hotels; but I couldnt trust him as far as that. What about your father?

Raina. He is away at Slivnitza fighting for his country. I answer for your safety. There is my hand in pledge of it. Will that reassure you? *(She offers him her hand.)*

The Man. *(Looking dubiously at his own hand)* Better not touch my hand, dear young lady. I must have a wash first.

Raina. *(Touched)* That is very nice of you. I see that you are a gentleman.

The Man. *(Puzzled)* Eh?

590 *Raina.* You must not think I am surprised. Bulgarians of really good standing—people in our position—wash their hands nearly every

560. opera of Ernani, by Guiseppe Verdi, composed in 1844.

day. So you see I can appreciate your delicacy. You may take my hand. *(She offers it again.)*

The Man. *(Kissing it with his hands behind his back)* Thanks, gracious young lady: I feel safe at last. And now would you mind breaking the news to your mother? I had better not stay here secretly longer than is necessary.

Raina. If you will be so good as to keep perfectly still whilst I am away.

The Man. Certainly. *(He sits down on the ottoman. Raina goes to the bed and wraps herself in the fur cloak. His eyes close. She goes to the door. Turning for a last look at him, she sees that he is dropping off to sleep.)* 600

Raina. *(At the door)* You are not going asleep, are you? *(He murmurs inarticulately: she runs to him and shakes him.)* Do you hear? Wake up: you are falling asleep.

The Man. Eh? Falling aslee—? Oh no: not the least in the world: I was only thinking. It's all right: I'm wide awake.

Raina. *(Severely)* Will you please stand up while I am away. *(He rises reluctantly.)* All the time, mind. 610

The Man. *(Standing unsteadily)* Certainly. Certainly: you may depend on me. *(Raina looks doubtfully at him. He smiles weakly. She goes reluctantly, turning again at the door, and almost catching him in the act of yawning. She goes out.)*

The Man. *(Drowsily)* Sleep, sleep, sleep, sleep, slee—*(The words trail off into a murmur. He wakes again with a shock on the point of falling.)* Where am I? Thats what I want to know: where am I? Must keep awake. Nothing keeps me awake except danger: remember that: *(Intently)* danger, danger, danger, dan—*(Trailing off again: another shock)* Wheres danger? Mus' find it. *(He starts off vaguely round the room in search of it.)* What am I looking for? Sleep—danger—dont know. *(He stumbles against the bed.)* Ah yes: now I know. All right now. I'm to go to bed, but not to sleep. Be sure not to sleep, because of danger. Not to lie down either, only sit down. *(He sits on the bed. A blissful expression comes into his face.)* Ah! *(With a happy sigh he sinks back at full length; lifts his boots into the bed with a final effort; and falls fast asleep instantly.)* 620

(Catherine comes in, followed by Raina.)

Raina. *(Looking at the ottoman)* He's gone! I left him here.

Catherine. Here! Then he must have climbed down from the— 630

Raina. *(Seeing him)* Oh! *(She points.)*

Catherine. *(Scandalized)* Well! *(She strides to the bed, Raina following until she is opposite her on the other side.)* He's fast asleep. The brute!

Raina. *(Anxiously)* Sh!

Catherine. *(Shaking him)* Sir! *(Shaking him again, harder)* Sir!! *(Vehemently, shaking very hard)* Sir!!!

Raina. *(Catching her arm)* Dont, mamma: the poor darling is worn out. Let him sleep.

640 *Catherine.* *(Letting him go, and turning amazed to Raina)* The poor darling! Raina!!! *(She looks sternly at her daughter. The man sleeps profoundly.)*

Act II

The sixth of March, 1886. In the garden of Major Petkoff's house. It is a fine spring morning: the garden looks fresh and pretty. Beyond the paling the tops of a couple of minarets can be seen, shewing that there is a valley there, with the little town in it. A few miles further the Balkan mountains rise and shut in the landscape. Looking towards them from within the garden, the side of the house is seen on the left, with a garden door reached by a little flight of steps. On the right the stable yard, with its gateway, encroaches on the garden. There are fruit bushes along the paling and house, covered with washing spread out to dry. A path runs
10 *by the house, and rises by two steps at the corner, where it turns out of sight. In the middle, a small table, with two bent wood chairs at it, is laid for breakfast with Turkish coffee pots, cups, rolls, etc.; but the cups have been used and the bread broken. There is a wooden garden seat against the wall on the right.*

Louka, smoking a cigaret, is standing between the table and the house, turning her back with angry disdain on a man servant who is lecturing her. He is a middle-aged man of cool temperament and low but clear and keen intelligence, with the complacency of the servant who values himself on his rank in servitude, and the imperturbability
20 *of the accurate calculator who has no illusions. He wears a white Bulgarian costume: jacket with embroidered border, sash, wide knickerbockers, and decorated gaiters. His head is shaved up to the crown, giving him a high Japanese forehead. His name is Nicola.*

Nicola. Be warned in time, Louka: mend your manners. I know the mistress. She is so grand that she never dreams that any servant could dare be disrespectful to her; but if she once suspects that you are defying her, out you go.

Louka. I do defy her. I will defy her. What do I care for her?

Nicola. If you quarrel with the family, I never can marry you. It's
30 the same as if you quarrelled with me!

Louka. You take her part against me, do you?

Nicola. *(Sedately)* I shall always be dependent on the good will of the family. When I leave their service and start a shop in Sofia, their custom will be half my capital: their bad word would ruin me.

Louka. You have no spirit. I should like to catch them saying a word against me!

Nicola. *(Pityingly)* I should have expected more sense from you, Louka. But youre young: youre young!

Louka. Yes; and you like me the better for it, dont you? But I know some family secrets they wouldnt care to have told, young as I am. Let 40 them quarrel with me if they dare!

Nicola. *(With compassionate superiority)* Do you know what they would do if they heard you talk like that?

Louka. What could they do?

Nicola. Discharge you for untruthfulness. Who would believe any stories you told after that? Who would give you another situation? Who in this house would dare be seen speaking to you ever again? How long would your father be left on his little farm? *(She impatiently throws away the end of her cigaret, and stamps on it.)* Child: you dont know the power such high people have over the like of you and me when we 50 try to rise out of our poverty against them. *(He goes to her and lowers his voice.)* Look at me, ten years in their service. Do you think I know no secrets? I know things about the mistress that she wouldnt have the master know for a thousand levas. I know things about him that she wouldnt let him hear the last of for six months if I blabbed them to her. I know things about Raina that would break off her match with Sergius if—

Louka. *(Turning on him quickly)* How do you know? I never told you!

Nicola. *(Opening his eyes cunningly)* So thats your little secret, 60 is it? I thought it might be something like that. Well, you take my advice and be respectful; and make the mistress feel that no matter what you know or dont know, she can depend on you to hold your tongue and serve the family faithfully. Thats what they like; and thats how youll make most out of them.

Louka. *(With searching scorn)* You have the soul of a servant, Nicola.

Nicola. *(Complacently)* Yes: thats the secret of success in service. *(A loud knocking with a whip handle on a wooden door is heard from the stable yard.)* 70

Male Voice Outside. Hollo! Hollo there! Nicola!

Louka. Master! back from the war!

Nicola. *(Quickly)* My word for it, Louka, the war's over. Off with you and get some fresh coffee. *(He runs out into the stable yard.)*

Louka. *(As she collects the coffee pot and cups on the tray, and carries it into the house)* Youll never put the soul of a servant into me. *(Major Petkoff comes from the stable yard, followed by Nicola. He is a cheerful, excitable, insignificant, unpolished man of about 50, naturally unambitious except as to his income and his importance in local*

80 *society, but just now greatly pleased with the military rank which the war has thrust on him as a man of consequence in his town. The fever of plucky patriotism which the Serbian attack roused in all the Bulgarians has pulled him through the war; but he is obviously glad to be home again.)*

Petkoff. *(Pointing to the table with his whip)* Breakfast out here, eh?

Nicola. Yes, sir. The mistress and Miss Raina have just gone in.

Petkoff. *(Sitting down and taking a roll)* Go in and say Ive come; and get me some fresh coffee.

90 *Nicola.* It's coming, sir. *(He goes to the house door. Louka, with fresh coffee, a clean cup, and a brandy bottle on her tray, meets him.)* Have you told the mistress?

Louka. Yes: she's coming. *(Nicola goes into the house. Louka brings the coffee to the table.)*

Petkoff. Well: the Serbs havnt run away with you, have they?

Louka. No, sir.

Petkoff. Thats right. Have you brought me some cognac?

Louka. *(Putting the bottle on the table)* Here, sir.

Petkoff. Thats right. *(He pours some into his coffee.)*

100 *(Catherine, who, having at this early hour made only a very perfunctory toilet, wears a Bulgarian apron over a once brilliant but now half worn-out dressing gown, and a colored handkerchief tied over her thick black hair, comes from the house with Turkish slippers on her bare feet, looking astonishingly handsome and stately under all the circumstances. Louka goes into the house.)*

Catherine. My dear Paul: what a surprise for us! *(She stoops over the back of his chair to kiss him.)* Have they brought you fresh coffee?

Petkoff. Yes: Louka's been looking after me. The war's over. The treaty was signed three days ago at Bucharest; and the decree for our

110 army to demobilize was issued yesterday.

Catherine. *(Springing erect, with flashing eyes)* Paul: have you let the Austrians force you to make peace?

Petkoff. *(Submissively)* My dear: they didnt consult me. What could *I* do? *(She sits down and turns away from him.)* But of course we saw to it that the treaty was an honorable one. It declares peace—

Catherine. *(Outraged)* Peace!

Petkoff. *(Appeasing her)*—but not friendly relations: remember that. They wanted to put that in; but I insisted on its being struck out. What more could I do?

120 *Catherine.* You could have annexed Serbia and made Prince Alexander° Emperor of the Balkans. Thats what I would have done.

120-121. Prince Alexander, Prince Alexander Batterbery, the ruler of Bulgaria, who was kidnapped by the Russians.

Petkoff. I dont doubt it in the least, my dear. But I should have had to subdue the whole Austrian Empire first; and that would have kept me too long away from you. I missed you greatly.

Catherine. (Relenting) Ah! *(She stretches her hand affectionately across the table to squeeze his.)*

Petkoff. And how have you been, my dear?

Catherine. Oh, my usual sore throats: thats all.

Petkoff. (With conviction) That comes from washing your neck every day. Ive often told you so. 130

Catherine. Nonsense, Paul!

Petkoff. (Over his coffee and cigaret) I dont believe in going too far with these modern customs. All this washing cant be good for the health: it's not natural. There was an Englishman at Philippopolis° who used to wet himself all over with cold water every morning when he got up. Disgusting! It all comes from the English: their climate makes them so dirty that they have to be perpetually washing themselves. Look at my father! he never had a bath in his life; and he lived to be ninety-eight, the healthiest man in Bulgaria. I dont mind a good wash once a week to keep up my position; but once a day is carrying the thing 140 to a ridiculous extreme.

Catherine. You are a barbarian at heart still, Paul. I hope you behaved yourself before all those Russian officers.

Petkoff. I did my best. I took care to let them know that we have a library.

Catherine. Ah; but you didnt tell them that we have an electric bell in it? I have had one put up.

Petkoff. Whats an electric bell?

Catherine. You touch a button; something tinkles in the kitchen; and then Nicola comes up. 150

Petkoff. Why not shout for him?

Catherine. Civilized people never shout for their servants. Ive learnt that while you were away.

Petkoff. Well, I'll tell you something Ive learnt too. Civilized people dont hang out their washing to dry where visitors can see it; so youd better have all that *(Indicating the clothes on the bushes)* put somewhere else.

Catherine. Oh, thats absurd, Paul: I dont believe really refined people notice such things.

Sergius. (Knocking at the stable gates) Gate, Nicola! 160

Petkoff. Theres Sergius. *(Shouting)* Hollo, Nicola!

Catherine. Oh, dont shout, Paul: it really isnt nice.

Petkoff. Bosh! *(He shouts louder than before.)* Nicola!

Nicola. (Appearing at the house door) Yes, sir.

134. Philippopolis, a town in Bulgaria.

Petkoff. Are you deaf? Dont you hear Major Saranoff knocking? Bring him round this way. *(He pronounces the name with the stress on the second syllable: Sarahnoff.)*

Nicola. Yes, major. *(He goes into the stable yard.)*

Petkoff. You must talk to him, my dear, until Raina takes him off
170 our hands. He bores my life out about our not promoting him. Over my head, if you please.

Catherine. He certainly ought to be promoted when he marries Raina. Besides, the country should insist on having at least one native general.

Petkoff. Yes; so that he could throw away whole brigades instead of regiments. It's no use, my dear: he hasnt the slightest chance of promotion until we're quite sure that the peace will be a lasting one.

Nicola. (At the gate, announcing) Major Sergius Saranoff! *(He goes into the house and returns presently with a third chair, which he*
180 *places at the table. He then withdraws.)*

(Major Sergius Saranoff, the original of the portrait in Raina's room, is a tall romantically handsome man, with the physical hardihood, the high spirit, and the susceptible imagination of an untamed mountaineer chieftain. But his remarkable personal distinction is of a characteristically civilized type. The ridges of his eyebrows, curving with an interrogative twist round the projections at the outer corners; his jealously observant eye; his nose, thin, keen, and apprehensive in spite of the pugnacious high bridge and large nostril; his assertive chin, would not be out of place in a Parisian salon, shewing that the clever imaginative
190 *barbarian has an acute critical faculty which has been thrown into intense activity by the arrival of western civilization in the Balkans. The result is precisely what the advent of nineteenth century thought first produced in England: to wit, Byronism. By his brooding on the perpetual failure, not only of others, but of himself, to live up to his ideals; by his consequent cynical scorn for humanity; by his jejune credulity as to the absolute validity of his concepts and the unworthiness of the world in disregarding them; by his wincings and mockeries under the sting of the petty disillusions which every hour spent among men brings to his sensitive observation, he has acquired the half tragic,*
200 *half ironic air, the mysterious moodiness, the suggestion of a strange and terrible history that has left nothing but undying remorse, by which Childe Harold° fascinated the grandmothers of his English contemporaries. It is clear that here or nowhere is Raina's ideal hero. Catherine is hardly less enthusiastic about him than her daughter, and much less reserved in shewing her enthusiasm. As he enters from the stable gate, she rises effusively to greet him. Petkoff is distinctly less disposed to make a fuss about him.)*

202. Childe Harold, *Childe Harold's Pilgrimage,* a long poem by Byron.

Petkoff. Here already, Sergius! Glad to see you.

Catherine. My dear Sergius! *(She holds out both her hands.)*

Sergius. *(Kissing them with scrupulous gallantry)* My dear mother, if I may call you so. 210

Petkoff. *(Drily)* Mother-in-law, Sergius: mother-in-law! Sit down; and have some coffee.

Sergius. Thank you: none for me. *(He gets away from the table with a certain distaste for Petkoff's enjoyment of it, and posts himself with conscious dignity against the rail of the steps leading to the house.)*

Catherine. You look superb. The campaign has improved you, Sergius. Everybody here is mad about you. We were all wild with enthusiasm about that magnificent cavalry charge.

Sergius. *(With grave irony)* Madam: it was the cradle and the grave of my military reputation. 220

Catherine. How so?

Sergius. I won the battle the wrong way when our worthy Russian generals were losing it the right way. In short, I upset their plans, and wounded their self-esteem. Two Cossack colonels had their regiments routed on the most correct principles of scientific warfare. Two major-generals got killed strictly according to military etiquette. The two colonels are now major-generals; and I am still a simple major.

Catherine. You shall not remain so, Sergius. The women are on your side; and they will see that justice is done you. 230

Sergius. It is too late. I have only waited for the peace to send in my resignation.

Petkoff. *(Dropping his cup in his amazement)* Your resignation!

Catherine. Oh, you must withdraw it!

Sergius. *(With resolute measured emphasis, folding his arms)* I never withdraw.

Petkoff. *(Vexed)* Now who could have supposed you were going to do such a thing?

Sergius. *(With fire)* Everyone that knew me. But enough of myself and my affairs. How is Raina; and where is Raina? 240

Raina. *(Suddenly coming round the corner of the house and standing at the top of the steps in the path)* Raina is here.

(She makes a charming picture as they turn to look at her. She wears an underdress of pale green silk, draped with an overdress of thin ecru canvas embroidered with gold. She is crowned with a dainty eastern cap of gold tinsel. Sergius goes impulsively to meet her. Posing regally, she presents her hand: he drops chivalrously on one knee and kisses it.)

Petkoff. *(Aside to Catherine, beaming with parental pride)* Pretty, isnt it? She always appears at the right moment. 250

Catherine. *(Impatiently)* Yes: she listens for it. It is an abominable habit.

(Sergius leads Raina forward with splendid gallantry. When they arrive at the table, she turns to him with a bend of the head: he bows; and thus they separate, he coming to his place, and she going behind her father's chair.)

Raina. (Stooping and kissing her father) Dear father! Welcome home!

Petkoff. (Patting her cheek) My little pet girl. *(He kisses her. She*
260 *goes to the chair left by Nicola for Sergius, and sits down.)*

Catherine. And so youre no longer a soldier, Sergius.

Sergius. I am no longer a soldier. Soldiering, my dear madam, is the coward's art of attacking mercilessly when you are strong, and keeping out of harm's way when you are weak. This is the whole secret of successful fighting. Get your enemy at a disadvantage; and never, on any account, fight him on equal terms.

Petkoff. They wouldnt let us make a fair stand-up fight of it. However, I suppose soldiering has to be a trade like any other trade.

Sergius. Precisely. But I have no ambition to shine as a tradesman;
270 so I have taken the advice of the bagman of a captain that settled the exchange of prisoners with us at Pirot,° and give it up.

Petkoff. What! that Swiss fellow? Sergius: Ive often thought of that exchange since. He over-reached us about those horses.

Sergius. Of course he over-reached us. His father was a hotel and livery stable keeper; and he owed his first step to his knowledge of horse-dealing. *(With mock enthusiasm)* Ah, he was a soldier: every inch a soldier! If only I had bought the horses for my regiment instead of foolishly leading it into danger, I should have been a field-marshal now!

280 *Catherine.* A Swiss? What was he doing in the Serbian army?

Petkoff. A volunteer, of course: keen on picking up his profession. *(Chuckling)* We shoudnt have been able to begin fighting if these foreigners hadnt shewn us how to do it: we knew nothing about it; and neither did the Serbs. Egad, there'd have been no war without them!

Raina. Are there many Swiss officers in the Serbian army?

Petkoff. No. All Austrians, just as our officers were all Russians. This was the only Swiss I came across. I'll never trust a Swiss again. He humbugged us into giving him fifty ablebodied men for two hundred
290 worn out chargers. They werent even eatable!

Sergius. We were two children in the hands of that consummate soldier, Major: simply two innocent little children.

Raina. What was he like?

Catherine. Oh, Raina, what a silly question!

271. Pirot, a town in Serbia.

Sergius. He was like a commercial traveller in uniform. Bourgeois to his boots!

Petkoff. (Grinning) Sergius: tell Catherine that queer story his friend told us about how he escaped after Slivnitza. You remember. About his being hid by two women.

Sergius. (With bitter irony) Oh yes: quite a romance! He was serving in the very battery I so unprofessionally charged. Being a thorough soldier, he ran away like the rest of them, with our cavalry at his heels. To escape their sabres he climbed a waterpipe and made his way into the bedroom of a young Bulgarian lady. The young lady was enchanted by his persuasive commercial traveller's manners. She very modestly entertained him for an hour or so, and then called in her mother lest her conduct should appear unmaidenly. The old lady was equally fascinated; and the fugitive was sent on his way in the morning, disguised in an old coat belonging to the master of the house, who was away at the war. 300 310

Raina. (Rising with marked stateliness) Your life in the camp has made you coarse, Sergius. I did not think you would have repeated such a story before me. *(She turns away coldly.)*

Catherine. (Also rising) She is right, Sergius. If such women exist, we should be spared the knowledge of them.

Petkoff. Pooh! nonsense! what does it matter?

Sergius. (Ashamed) No, Petkoff: I was wrong. *(To Raina, with earnest humility)* I beg your pardon. I have behaved abominably. Forgive me, Raina. *(She bows reservedly.)* And you too, madam. *(Catherine bows graciously and sits down. He proceeds solemnly, again addressing Raina.)* The glimpses I have had of the seamy side of life during the last few months have made me cynical; but I should not have brought my cynicism here: least of all into your presence, Raina. I—*(Here, turning to the others, he is evidently going to begin a long speech when the Major interrupts him.)* 320

Petkoff. Stuff and nonsense, Sergius! Thats quite enough fuss about nothing: a soldier's daughter should be able to stand up without flinching to a little strong conversation. *(He rises.)* Come: it's time for us to get to business. We have to make up our minds how those three regiments are to get back to Philippopolis: theres no forage for them on the Sofia route. *(He goes towards the house.)* Come along. *(Sergius is about to follow him when Catherine rises and intervenes.)* 330

Catherine. Oh, Paul, cant you spare Sergius for a few moments? Raina has hardly seen him yet. Perhaps I can help you to settle about the regiments.

Sergius. (Protesting) My dear madam, impossible: you—

Catherine. (Stopping him playfully) You stay here, my dear Sergius: theres no hurry. I have a word or two to say to Paul. *(Sergius instantly*

bows and steps back.) Now, dear *(Taking Petkoff's arm):* come and see
340 the electric bell.

Petkoff. Oh, very well, very well. *(They go into the house together affectionately. Sergius, left alone with Raina, looks anxiously at her, fearing that she is still offended. She smiles, and stretches out her arms to him.)*

Sergius. (Hastening to her) Am I forgiven?

Raina. (Placing her hands on his shoulders as she looks up at him with admiration and worship) My hero! My king!

Sergius. My queen! *(He kisses her on the forehead.)*

Raina. How I have envied you, Sergius! You have been out in the
350 world, on the field of battle, able to prove yourself there worthy of any woman in the world; whilst I have had to sit at home inactive —dreaming—useless—doing nothing that could give me the right to call myself worthy of any man.

Sergius. Dearest: all my deeds have been yours. You inspired me. I have gone through the war like a knight in a tournament with his lady looking down at him!

Raina. And you have never been absent from my thoughts for a moment. *(Very solemnly)* Sergius: I think we two have found the higher love. When I think of you, I feel that I could never do a base
360 deed or think an ignoble thought.

Sergius. My lady and my saint! *(He clasps her reverently.)*

Raina. (Returning his embrace) My lord and my—

Sergius. Sh—sh! Let me be the worshipper, dear. You little know how unworthy even the best man is of a girl's pure passion!

Raina. I trust you. I love you. You will never disappoint me, Sergius. *(Louka is heard singing within the house. They quickly release each other.)* I cant pretend to talk indifferently before her: my heart is too full. *(Louka comes from the house with her tray. She goes to the table, and begins to clear it, with her back turned to them.)* I will get my hat;
370 and then we can go out until lunch time. Wouldnt you like that?

Sergius. Be quick. If you are away five minutes, it will seem five hours.

(Raina runs to the top of the steps, and turns there to exchange looks with him and wave him a kiss with both hands. He looks after her with emotion for a moment; then turns slowly away, his face radiant with the loftiest exaltation. The movement shifts his field of vision, into the corner of which there now comes the tail of Louka's double apron. His attention is arrested at once. He takes a stealthy look at her, and begins to twirl his moustache mischievously, with his left
380 *hand akimbo on his hip. Finally, striking the ground with his heels in something of a cavalry swagger, he strolls over to the other side of the table, opposite her, and says)*

Louka: do you know what the higher love is?

Louka. (Astonished) No, sir.

Sergius. Very fatiguing thing to keep up for any length of time. Louka. One feels the need of some relief after it.

Louka. (Innocently) Perhaps you would like some coffee, sir? *(She stretches her hand across the table for the coffee pot.)*

Sergius. (Taking her hand) Thank you, Louka.

Louka. (Pretending to pull) Oh, sir, you know I didnt mean that. I'm surprised at you! 390

Sergius. (Coming clear of the table and drawing her with him) I am surprised at myself, Louka. What would Sergius, the hero of Slivnitza, say if he saw me now? What would Sergius, the apostle of the higher love, say if he saw me now? What would the half dozen Sergiuses who keep popping in and out of this handsome figure of mine say if they caught us here? *(Letting go her hand and slipping his arm dexterously round her waist)* Do you consider my figure handsome, Louka?

Louka. Let me go, sir. I shall be disgraced. *(She struggles: he holds her inexorably.)* Oh, will you let go? 400

Sergius. (Looking straight into her eyes) No.

Louka. Then stand back where we cant be seen. Have you no common sense?

Sergius. Ah! thats reasonable. *(He takes her into the stableyard gateway, where they are hidden from the house.)*

Louka. (Plaintively) I may have been seen from the windows: Miss Raina is sure to be spying about after you.

Sergius. (Stung: letting her go) Take care, Louka. I may be worthless enough to betray the higher love; but do not you insult it. 410

Louka. (Demurely) Not for the world, sir, I'm sure. May I go on with my work, please, now?

Sergius. (Again putting his arm round her) You are a provoking little witch, Louka. If you were in love with me, would you spy out of windows on me?

Louka. Well, you see, sir, since you say you are half a dozen different gentlemen all at once, I should have a great deal to look after.

Serguis. (Charmed) Witty as well as pretty. *(He tries to kiss her.)*

Louka. (Avoiding him) No: I dont want your kisses. Gentlefolk are all alike: you making love to me behind Miss Raina's back; and she doing the same behind yours. 420

Sergius. (Recoiling a step) Louka!

Louka. It shews how little you really care.

Sergius. (Dropping his familiarity, and speaking with freezing politeness) If our conversation is to continue, Louka, you will please

remember that a gentleman does not discuss the conduct of the lady he is engaged to with her maid.

Louka. It's so hard to know what a gentleman considers right. I
430 thought from your trying to kiss me that you had given up being so particular.

Sergius. *(Turning from her and striking his forehead as he comes back into the garden from the gateway)* Devil! devil!

Louka. Ha! ha! I expect one of the six of you is very like me, sir; though I am only Miss Raina's maid. *(She goes back to her work at the table, taking no further notice of him.)*

Sergius. *(Speaking to himself)* Which of the six is the real man? thats the question that torments me. One of them is a hero, another a buffoon, another a humbug, another perhaps a bit of a blackguard.
440 *(He pauses, and looks furtively at Louka as he adds, with deep bitterness)* And one, at least, is a coward: jealous, like all cowards. *(He goes to the table.)* Louka.

Louka. Yes?

Sergius. Who is my rival?

Louka. You shall never get that out of me, for love or money.

Sergius. Why?

Louka. Never mind why. Besides, you would tell that I told you; and I should lose my place.

Sergius. *(Holding out his right hand in affirmation)* No! on the
450 honor of a—*(He checks himself; and his hand drops, nerveless, as he concludes sardonically.)*—of a man capable of behaving as I have been behaving for the last five minutes. Who is he?

Louka. I dont know. I never saw him. I only heard his voice through the door of her room.

Sergius. Damnation! How dare you?

Louka. *(Retreating)* Oh, I mean no harm: youve no right to take up my words like that. The mistress knows all about it. And I tell you that if that gentleman ever comes here again, Miss Raina will marry him, whether he likes it or not. I know the difference between the sort
460 of manner you and she put on before one another and the real manner. *(Sergius shivers as if she had stabbed him. Then, setting his face like iron, he strides grimly to her, and grips her above the elbows with both hands.)*

Sergius. Now listen you to me.

Louka. *(Wincing)* Not so tight: youre hurting me.

Sergius. That doesnt matter. You have stained my honor by making me a party to your eavesdropping. And you have betrayed your mistress.

Louka. *(Writhing)* Please—

Sergius. That shews that you are an abominable little clod of common
470 clay, with the soul of a servant. *(He lets her go as if she were an unclean*

thing, and turns away, dusting his hands of her, to the bench by the wall, where he sits down with averted head, meditating gloomily.)

Louka. (Whimpering angrily with her hands up her sleeves, feeling her bruised arms) You know how to hurt with your tongue as well as with your hands. But I dont care, now Ive found out that whatever clay I'm made of, youre made of the same. As for her, she's a liar; and her fine airs are a cheat; and I'm worth six of her. *(She shakes the pain off hardily; tosses her head; and sets to work to put the things on the tray. He looks doubtfully at her. She finishes packing the tray, and laps the cloth over the edges, so as to carry all out together. As she stoops* 480 *to lift it, he rises.)*

Sergius. Louka! *(She stops and looks defiantly at him.)* A gentleman has no right to hurt a woman under any circumstances. *(With profound humility, uncovering his head)* I beg your pardon.

Louka. That sort of apology may satisfy a lady. Of what use is it to a servant?

Sergius. (Rudely crossed in his chivalry, throws it off with a bitter laugh, and says slightingly) Oh! you wish to be paid for the hurt? *(He puts on his shako, and takes some money from his pocket.)*

Louka. (Her eyes filling with tears in spite of herself) No: I want 490 my hurt made well.

Sergius. (Sobered by her tone) How?

(She rolls up her left sleeve; clasps her arm with the thumb and fingers of her right hand; and looks down at the bruise. Then she raises her head and looks straight at him. Finally, with a superb gesture, she presents her arm to be kissed. Amazed, he looks at her; at the arm; at her again; hesitates; and then, with shuddering intensity, exclaims Never! *and gets away as far as possible from her.)*

(Her arm drops. Without a word, and with unaffected dignity, she takes her tray, and is approaching the house when Raina returns, 500 *wearing a hat and jacket in the height of the Vienna fashion of the previous year, 1885. Louka makes way proudly for her, and then goes into the house.)*

Raina. I'm ready. Whats the matter? *(Gaily)* Have you been flirting with Louka?

Sergius. (Hastily) No, no. How can you think such a thing?

Raina. (Ashamed of herself) Forgive me, dear: it was only a jest. I am so happy to-day. *(He goes quickly to her, and kisses her hand remorsefully. Catherine comes out and calls to them from the top of the steps.)* 510

Catherine. (Coming down to them) I am sorry to disturb you, children; but Paul is distracted over those three regiments. He doesnt know how to send them to Philippopolis; and he objects to every suggestion of mine. You must go and help him, Sergius. He is in the library.

Raina. (Disappointed) But we are just going out for a walk.

Sergius. I shall not be long. Wait for me just five minutes. *(He runs up the steps to the door.)*

Raina. (Following him to the foot of the steps and looking up at him with timid coquetry) I shall go round and wait in full view of the library
520 windows. Be sure you draw father's attention to me. If you are a moment longer than five minutes, I shall go in and fetch you, regiments or no regiments.

Sergius. (Laughing) Very well. *(He goes in. Raina watches him until he is out of her sight. Then, with a perceptible relaxation of manner, she begins to pace up and down the garden in a brown study.)*

Catherine. Imagine their meeting that Swiss and hearing the whole story! The very first thing your father asked for was the old coat we sent him off in. A nice mess you have got us into!

Raina. (Gazing thoughtfully at the gravel as she walks) The little
530 beast!

Catherine. Little beast! What little beast?

Raina. To go and tell! Oh, if I had him here, I'd cram him with chocolate creams til he couldn't ever speak again!

Catherine. Dont talk such stuff. Tell me the truth, Raina. How long was he in your room before you came to me?

Raina. (Whisking round and recommencing her march in the opposite direction) Oh, I forget.

Catherine. You cannot forget! Did he really climb up after the soldiers were gone; or was he there when that officer searched the room?

540 *Raina.* No. Yes: I think he must have been there then.

Catherine. You think! Oh, Raina! Raina! Will anything ever make you straightforward? If Sergius finds out, it will be all over between you.

Raina. (With cool impertinence) Oh, I know Sergius is your pet. I sometimes wish you could marry him instead of me. You would just suit him. You would pet him, and spoil him, and mother him to perfection.

Catherine. (Opening her eyes very widely indeed) Well, upon my word!

Raina. (Capriciously: half to herself) I always feel a longing to do
550 or say something dreadful to him—to shock his propriety—to scandalize the five senses out of him. *(To Catherine, perversely)* I dont care whether he finds out about the chocolate cream soldier or not. I half hope he may. *(She again turns and strolls flippantly away up the path to the corner of the house.)*

Catherine. And what should I be able to say to your father, pray?

Raina. (Over her shoulder, from the top of the two steps) Oh, poor father! As if he could help himself! *(She turns the corner and passes out of sight.)*

Catherine. *(Looking after her, her fingers itching)* Oh, if you were only ten years younger! *(Louka comes from the house with a salver, which she carries hanging down by her side.)* Well? 560

Louka. Theres a gentleman just called, madam. A Serbian officer.

Catherine. *(Flaming)* A Serb! And how dare he—*(Checking herself bitterly)* Oh, I forgot. We are at peace now. I suppose we shall have them calling every day to pay their compliments. Well: if he is an officer why dont you tell your master? He is in the library with Major Saranoff. Why do you come to me?

Louka. But he asks for you, madam. And I dont think he knows who you are: he said the lady of the house. He gave me this little ticket for you. *(She takes a card out of her bosom; puts it on the salver; and offers it to Catherine.)* 570

Catherine. *(Reading)* "Captain Bluntschli"? Thats a German name.

Louka. Swiss, madam, I think.

Catherine. *(With a bound that makes Louka jump back)* Swiss! What is he like?

Louka. *(Timidly)* He has a big carpet bag, madam.

Catherine. Oh Heavens! he's come to return the coat. Send him away: say we're not at home: ask him to leave his address and I'll write to him. Oh stop: that will never do. Wait! *(She throws herself into a chair to think it out. Louka waits.)* The master and Major Saranoff are busy in the library, arnt they? 580

Louka. Yes, madam.

Catherine. *(Decisively)* Bring the gentleman out here at once. *(Peremptorily)* And be very polite to him. Dont delay. Here *(Impatiently snatching the salver from her)* leave that here; and go straight back to him.

Louka. Yes, madam *(Going).*

Catherine. Louka!

Louka. *(Stopping)* Yes, madam.

Catherine. Is the library door shut? 590

Louka. I think so, madam.

Catherine. If not, shut it as you pass through.

Louka. Yes, madam *(Going).*

Catherine. Stop! *(Louka stops.)* He will have to go that way. *(Indicating the gate of the stableyard)* Tell Nicola to bring his bag here after him. Dont forget.

Louka. *(Surprised)* His bag?

Catherine. Yes: here: as soon as possible. *(Vehemently)* Be quick! *(Louka runs into the house. Catherine snatches her apron off and throws it behind a bush. She then takes up the salver and uses it as a mirror, with the result that the handkerchief tied round her head follows the apron. A touch to her hair and a shake to her dressing gown* 600

make her presentable.) Oh, how? how? how can a man be such a fool! Such a moment to select! *(Louka appears at the door of the house, announcing* Captain Bluntschli. *She stands aside at the top of the steps to let him pass before she goes in again. He is the man of the midnight adventure in Raina's room, clean, well brushed, smartly uniformed, and out of trouble, but still unmistakably the same man. The moment Louka's back is turned, Catherine swoops on him with impet-
610 uous, urgent, coaxing appeal.)* Captain Bluntschli: I am very glad to see you; but you must leave this house at once. *(He raises his eyebrows.)* My husband has just returned with my future son-in-law; and they know nothing. If they did, the consequences would be terrible. You are a foreigner: you do not feel our national animosities as we do. We still hate the Serbs: the effect of the peace on my husband has been to make him feel like a lion baulked of his prey. If he discovers our secret, he will never forgive me; and my daughter's life will hardly be safe. Will you, like the chivalrous gentleman and soldier you are, leave at once before he finds you here?

620 *Bluntschli.* *(Disappointed, but philosophical)* At once, gracious lady. I only came to thank you and return the coat you lent me. If you will allow me to take it out of my bag and leave it with your servant as I pass out, I need detain you no further. *(He turns to go into the house.)*

Catherine. *(Catching him by the sleeve)* Oh, you must not think of going back that way. *(Coaxing him across to the stable gates)* This is the shortest way out. Many thanks. So glad to have been of service to you. Good-bye.

Bluntschli. But my bag?

630 *Catherine.* It shall be sent on. You will leave me your address.

Bluntschli. True. Allow me. *(He takes out his card-case, and stops to write his address, keeping Catherine in an agony of impatience. As he hands her the card, Petkoff, hatless, rushes from the house in a fluster of hospitality, followed by Sergius.)*

Petkoff. *(As he hurries down the steps)* My dear Captain Bluntschli—

Catherine. Oh Heavens! *(She sinks on the seat against the wall.)*

Petkoff. *(Too preoccupied to notice her as he shakes Bluntschli's hand heartily)* Those stupid people of mine thought I was out here, instead of in the—haw!—library. *(He cannot mention the library with-
640 out betraying how proud he is of it.)* I saw you through the window. I was wondering why you didnt come in. Saranoff is with me: you remember him, dont you?

Sergius. *(Saluting humorously, and then offering his hand with great charm of manner)* Welcome, our friend the enemy!

Petkoff. No longer the enemy, happily. *(Rather anxiously)* I hope youve called as a friend, and not about horses or prisoners.

Catherine. Oh, quite as a friend, Paul. I was just asking Captain Bluntschli to stay to lunch; but he declares he must go at once.

Sergius. *(Sardonically)* Impossible, Bluntschli. We want you here badly. We have to send on three cavalry regiments to Philippopolis; 650
and we dont in the least know how to do it.

Bluntschli. *(Suddenly attentive and businesslike)* Philippopolis? The forage is the trouble, I suppose.

Petkoff. *(Eagerly)* Yes: thats it. *(To Sergius)* He sees the whole thing at once.

Bluntschli. I think I can shew you how to manage that.

Sergius. Invaluable man! Come along! *(Towering over Bluntschli, he puts his hand on his shoulder and takes him to the steps, Petkoff following.)*

(Raina comes from the house as Bluntschli puts his foot on the first 660
step.)

Raina. Oh! The chocolate cream soldier! *(Bluntschli stands rigid. Sergius, amazed, looks at Raina, then at Petkoff, who looks back at him and then at his wife.)*

Catherine. *(With commanding presence of mind)* My dear Raina, don't you see that we have a guest here? Captain Bluntschli: one of our new Serbian friends. *(Raina bows: Bluntschli bows.)*

Raina. How silly of me! *(She comes down into the center of the group, between Bluntschli and Petkoff.)* I made a beautiful ornament this morning for the ice pudding; and that stupid Nicola has just put down 670
a pile of plates on it and spoilt it. *(To Bluntschli, winningly)* I hope you didnt think that you were the chocolate cream soldier, Captain Bluntschli.

Bluntschli. *(Laughing)* I assure you I did. *(Stealing a whimsical glance at her)* Your explanation was a relief.

Petkoff. *(Suspiciously, to Raina)* And since when, pray, have you taken to cooking?

Catherine. Oh, whilst you were away. It is her latest fancy.

Petkoff. *(Testily)* And has Nicola taken to drinking? He used to be careful enough. First he shews Captain Bluntschli out here when 680
he knew quite well I was in the library; and then he goes downstairs and breaks Raina's chocolate soldier. He must—*(Nicola appears at the top of the steps with the bag. He descends; places it respectfully before Bluntschli; and waits for further orders. General amazement. Nicola, unconscious of the effect he is producing, looks perfectly satisfied with himself. When Petkoff recovers his power of speech, he breaks out at him with)* Are you mad, Nicola?

Nicola. *(Taken aback)* Sir?

Petkoff. What have you brought that for?

Nicola. My lady's orders, major. Louka told me that— 690

Catherine. *(Interrupting him)* My orders! Why should I order you to bring Captain Bluntschli's luggage out here? What are you thinking of, Nicola?

Nicola. *(After a moment's bewilderment, picking up the bag as he addresses Bluntschli with the very perfection of servile discretion)* I beg your pardon, captain, I am sure. *(To Catherine)* My fault, madam: I hope youll overlook it. *(He bows, and is going to the steps with the bag, when Petkoff addresses him angrily.)*

Petkoff. Youd better go and slam that bag, too, down on Miss 700 Raina's ice pudding! *(This is too much for Nicola. The bag drops from his hand almost on his master's toes, eliciting a roar of)* Begone, you butter-fingered donkey.

Nicola. *(Snatching up the bag, and escaping into the house)* Yes, major.

Catherine. Oh, never mind, Paul: dont be angry.

Petkoff. *(Blustering)* Scoundrel! He's got out of hand while I was away. I'll teach him. Infernal blackguard! The sack next Saturday! I'll clear out the whole establishment—*(He is stifled by the caresses of his wife and daughter, who hang round his neck, petting him.)*

710 *Catherine.* Now, now, now, it mustnt be angry. He meant no harm. Be good to please me, dear. Sh-sh-sh-sh!

(Together)

Raina. Wow, wow, wow: not on your first day at home. I'll make another ice pudding. Tch-ch-ch!

Petkoff. *(Yielding)* Oh well, never mind. Come, Bluntschli: let's have no more nonsense about going away. You know very well youre not going back to Switzerland yet. Until you do go back youll stay with us.

Raina. Oh, do, Captain Bluntschli.

720 *Petkoff.* *(To Catherine)* Now, Catherine: it's of you he's afraid. Press him; and he'll stay.

Catherine. Of course I shall be only too delighted if *(Appealingly)* Captain Bluntschli really wishes to stay. He knows my wishes.

Bluntschli. *(In his driest military manner)* I am at madam's orders.

Sergius. *(Cordially)* That settles it!

Petkoff. *(Heartily)* Of course!

Raina. You see you must stay.

Bluntschli. *(Smiling)* Well, if I must, I must, *(Gesture of despair from Catherine)*

Act III

In the library after lunch. It is not much of a library. Its literary equipment consists of a single fixed shelf stocked with old paper covered novels, broken backed, coffee stained, torn and thumbed; and a couple of little hanging shelves with a few gift books on them: the rest of the wall space being occupied by trophies of war and the chase. But it is a most comfortable sitting room. A row of three large windows shews a mountain panorama, just now seen in one of its friendliest aspects in the mellowing afternoon light. In the corner next the right hand window a square earthenware stove, a perfect tower of glistening pottery, rises nearly to the ceiling and guarantees plenty of warmth. The otto- 10 *man is like that in Raina's room, and similarly placed; and the window seats are luxurious with decorated cushions. There is one object, however, hopelessly out of keeping with its surroundings. This is a small kitchen table, much the worse for wear, fitted as a writing table with an old canister full of pens, an eggcup filled with ink, and a deplorable scrap of heavily used pink blotting paper.*

At the side of this table, which stands to the left of anyone facing the window, Bluntschli is hard at work with a couple of maps before him, writing orders. At the head of it sits Sergius, who is supposed to be also at work, but is actually gnawing the feather of a pen, and 20 *contemplating Bluntschli's quick, sure, businesslike progress with a mixture of envious irritation at his own incapacity and awestruck wonder at an ability which seems to him almost miraculous, though its prosaic character forbids him to esteem it. The Major is comfortably established on the ottoman, with a newspaper in his hand and the tube of his hookah within easy reach. Catherine sits at the stove, with her back to them, embroidering. Raina, reclining on the divan, is gazing in a daydream out at the Balkan landscape, with a neglected novel in her lap.*

The door is on the same side as the stove, farther from the window. 30 *The button of the electric bell is at the opposite side, behind Bluntschli.*

Petkoff. (Looking up from his paper to watch how they are getting on at the table) Are you sure I cant help you in any way, Bluntschli?

Bluntschli. (Without interrupting his writing or looking up) Quite sure, thank you. Saranoff and I will manage it.

Sergius. (Grimly) Yes: we'll manage it. He finds out what to do; draws up the orders; and I sign em. Division of labor! *(Bluntschli passes him a paper.)* Another one? Thank you. *(He plants the paper squarely before him; sets his chair carefully parallel to it; and signs with his cheek on his elbow and his protruded tongue following the* 40 *movements of his pen.)* This hand is more accustomed to the sword than to the pen.

Petkoff. It's very good of you, Bluntschli: it is indeed, to let yourself be put upon in this way. Now are you quite sure I can do nothing?

Catherine. (In a low warning tone) You can stop interrupting, Paul.

Petkoff. (Starting and looking round at her) Eh? Oh! Quite right, my love: quite right. *(He takes his newspaper up again, but presently lets it drop.)* Ah, you havnt been campaigning, Catherine: you dont know how pleasant it is for us to sit here, after a good lunch, with nothing
50 to do but enjoy ourselves. Theres only one thing I want to make me thoroughly comfortable.

Catherine. What is that?

Petkoff. My old coat. I'm not at home in this one: I feel as if I were on parade.

Catherine. My dear Paul, how absurd you are about that old coat! It must be hanging in the blue closet where you left it.

Petkoff. My dear Catherine, I tell you Ive looked there. Am I to believe my own eyes or not? *(Catherine rises and crosses the room to press the button of the electric bell.)* What are you shewing off that
60 bell for? *(She looks at him majestically and silently resumes her chair and her needlework.)* My dear: if you think the obstinacy of your sex can make a coat out of two old dressing gowns of Raina's, your waterproof, and my mackintosh, youre mistaken. Thats exactly what the blue closet contains at present.

(Nicola presents himself.)

Catherine. Nicola: go to the blue closet and bring your master's old coat here: the braided one he wears in the house.

Nicola. Yes, madame. *(He goes out.)*

Petkoff. Catherine.

70 *Catherine.* Yes, Paul?

Petkoff. I bet you any piece of jewellery you like to order from Sofia against a week's housekeeping money that the coat isnt there.

Catherine. Done, Paul!

Petkoff. (Excited by the prospect of a gamble) Come: here's an opportunity for some sport. Wholl bet on it? Bluntschli: I'll give you six to one.

Bluntschli. (Imperturbably) It would be robbing you, major. Madame is sure to be right. *(Without looking up, he passes another batch of papers to Sergius.)*

80 *Sergius. (Also excited)* Bravo, Switzerland! Major: I bet my best charger against an Arab mare for Raina that Nicola finds the coat in the blue closet.

Petkoff. (Eagerly) Your best char—

Catherine. (Hastily interrupting him) Dont be foolish, Paul. An Arabian mare will cost you 50,000 levas.

Raina. (Suddenly coming out of her picturesque revery) Really, mother, if you are going to take the jewellery, I dont see why you should grudge me my Arab. *(Nicola comes back with the coat, and brings it to Petkoff, who can hardly believe his eyes.)*

Catherine. Where was it, Nicola? 90

Nicola. Hanging in the blue closet, madame.

Petkoff. Well, I am d—

Catherine. (Stopping him) Paul!

Petkoff. I could have sworn it wasnt there. Age is beginning to tell on me. I'm getting hallucinations. *(To Nicola)* Here: help me to change. Excuse me, Bluntschli. *(He begins changing coats, Nicola acting as valet.)* Remember: I didnt take that bet of yours, Sergius. Youd better give Raina that Arab steed yourself, since youve roused her expectations. Eh, Raina? *(He looks round at her; but she is again rapt in the landscape. With a little gush of parental affection and pride, he points* 100 *her out to them, and says)* She's dreaming, as usual.

Sergius. Assuredly she shall not be the loser.

Petkoff. So much the better for her. *I* shant come off so cheaply, I expect. *(The change is now complete. Nicola goes out with the discarded coat.)* Ah, now I feel at home at last. *(He sits down and takes his newspaper with a grunt of relief.)*

Bluntschli. (To Sergius, handing a paper) Thats the last order.

Petkoff. (Jumping up) What! Finished?

Bluntschli. Finished.

Petkoff. (With childlike envy) Havnt you anything for me to sign? 110

Bluntschli. Not necessary. His signature will do.

Petkoff. (Inflating his chest and thumping it) Ah well, I think weve done a thundering good day's work. Can I do anything more?

Bluntschli. You had better both see the fellows that are to take these. *(Sergius rises.)* Pack them off at once; and shew them that Ive marked on the orders the time they should hand them in by. Tell them that if they stop to drink or tell stories—if theyre five minutes late, theyll have the skin taken off their backs.

Sergius. (Stiffening indignantly) I'll say so. *(He strides to the door.)* And if one of them is man enough to spit in my face for insulting him, 120 I'll buy his discharge and give him a pension. *(He goes out.)*

Bluntschli. (Confidentially) Just see that he talks to them properly, major, will you?

Petkoff. (Officiously) Quite right, Bluntschli, quite right. I'll see to it. *(He goes to the door importantly, but hesitates on the threshold.)* By the bye, Catherine, you may as well come too. Theyll be far more frightened of you than of me.

Catherine. (Putting down her embroidery) I daresay I had better. You would only splutter at them. *(She goes out, Petkoff holding the door for her and following her.)* 130

Bluntschli. What an army! They make cannons out of cherry trees; and the officers send for their wives to keep discipline! *(He begins to fold and docket the papers. Raina, who has risen from the divan, marches slowly down the room with her hands clasped behind her, and looks mischievously at him.)*

Raina. You look ever so much nicer than when we last met. *(He looks up, surprised.)* What have you done to yourself?

Bluntschli. Washed; brushed; good night's sleep and breakfast. Thats all.

140 *Raina.* Did you get back safely that morning?

Bluntschli. Quite, thanks.

Raina. Were they angry with you for running away from Sergius's charge?

Bluntschli. (Grinning) No: they were glad; because theyd all just run away themselves.

Raina. (Going to the table, and leaning over it towards him) It must have made a lovely story for them: all that about me and my room.

Bluntschli. Capital story. But I only told it to one of them: a particular friend.

150 *Raina.* On whose discretion you could absolutely rely?

Bluntschli. Absolutely.

Raina. Hm! He told it all to my father and Sergius the day you exchanged the prisoners. *(She turns away and strolls carelessly across to the other side of the room.)*

Bluntschli. (Deeply concerned, and half incredulous) No! You dont mean that, do you?

Raina. (Turning, with sudden earnestness) I do indeed. But they dont know that it was in this house you took refuge. If Sergius knew, he would challenge you and kill you in a duel.

160 *Bluntschli.* Bless me! then dont tell him.

Raina. Please be serious, Captain Bluntschli. Can you not realize what it is to me to deceive him? I want to be quite perfect with Sergius: no meanness, no smallness, no deceit. My relation to him is the one really beautiful and noble part of my life. I hope you can understand that.

Bluntschli. (Sceptically) You mean that you wouldnt like him to find out that the story about the ice pudding was a—a—a—You know.

Raina. (Wincing) Ah, dont talk of it in that flippant way. I lied: I know it. But I did it to save your life. He would have killed you. That was the second time I ever uttered a falsehood. *(Bluntschli rises*
170 *quickly and looks doubtfully and somewhat severely at her.)* Do you remember the first time?

Bluntschli. I! No. Was I present?

Raina. Yes; and I told the officer who was searching for you that you were not present.

Bluntschli. True. I should have remembered it.

Raina. (Greatly encouraged) Ah, it is natural that you should forget it first. It cost you nothing: it cost me a lie! A lie!! *(She sits down on the ottoman, looking straight before her with her hands clasped round her knee. Bluntschli, quite touched, goes to the ottoman with a particularly reassuring and considerate air, and sits down beside her.)* 180

Bluntschli. My dear young lady, dont let this worry you. Remember: I'm a soldier. Now what are the two things that happen to a soldier so often that he comes to think nothing of them? One is hearing people tell lies *(Raina recoils.)* the other is getting his life saved in all sorts of ways by all sorts of people.

Raina. *(Rising in indignant protest)* And so he becomes a creature incapable of faith and of gratitude.

Bluntschli. *(Making a wry face)* Do you like gratitude? I dont. If pity is akin to love, gratitude is akin to the other thing.

Raina. Gratitude! *(Turning on him)* If you are incapable of gratitude 190 you are incapable of any noble sentiment. Even animals are grateful. Oh, I see now exactly what you think of me! You were not surprised to hear me lie. To you it was something I probably did every day! every hour!! That is how men think of women. *(She paces the room tragically.)*

Bluntschli. *(Dubiously)* Theres reason in everything. You said youd told only two lies in your whole life. Dear young lady: isnt that rather a short allowance? Im quite a straightforward man myself; but it wouldnt last me a whole morning.

Raina. *(Staring haughtily at him)* Do you know, sir, that you are 200 insulting me?

Bluntschli. I cant help it. When you strike that noble attitude and speak in that thrilling voice, I admire you; but I find it impossible to believe a single word you say.

Raina. *(Superbly)* Captain Bluntschli!

Bluntschli. *(Unmoved)* Yes?

Raina. *(Standing over him, as if she could not believe her senses)* Do you mean what you said just now? Do you know what you said just now?

Bluntschli. I do. 210

Raina. *(Gasping)* I! I!!! *(She points to herself incredulously, meaning "I, Raina Petkoff, tell lies!" He meets her gaze unflinchingly. She suddenly sits down beside him, and adds, with a complete change of manner from the heroic to a babyish familiarity.)* How did you find me out?

Bluntschli. *(Promptly)* Instinct, dear young lady. Instinct, and experience of the world.

Raina. *(Wonderingly)* Do you know, you are the first man I ever met who did not take me seriously?

Bluntschli. You mean, dont you, that I am the first man that has ever taken you quite seriously? 220

Raina. Yes: I suppose I do mean that. *(Cosily, quite at her ease with him)* How strange it is to be talked to in such a way! You know, I've always gone on like that.

Bluntschli. You mean the—?

Raina. I mean the noble attitude and the thrilling voice. *(They laugh together.)* I did it when I was a tiny child to my nurse. She believed in it. I do it before my parents. They believe in it. I do it before Sergius. He believes in it.

Bluntschli. Yes: he's a little in that line himself, isnt he?

230 *Raina.* *(Startled)* Oh! Do you think so?

Bluntschli. You know him better than I do.

Raina. I wonder—I wonder is he? If I thought that—! *(Discouraged)* Ah, well: what does it matter? I suppose, now youve found me out, you despise me.

Bluntschli. *(Warmly, rising)* No, my dear young lady, no, no, no a thousand times. It's part of your youth: part of your charm. I'm like all the rest of them: the nurse, your parents, Sergius: I'm your infatuated admirer.

Raina. *(Pleased)* Really?

240 *Bluntschli.* *(Slapping his breast smartly with his hand, German fashion)* Hand aufs Herz!° Really and truly.

Raina. *(Very happy)* But what did you think of me for giving you my portrait?

Bluntschli. *(Astonished)* Your portrait! You never gave me your portrait.

Raina. *(Quickly)* Do you mean to say you never got it?

Bluntschli. No. *(He sits down beside her, with renewed interest, and says, with some complacency.)* When did you send it to me?

Raina. *(Indignantly)* I did not send it to you. *(She turns her head*
250 *away, and adds, reluctantly)* It was in the pocket of that coat.

Bluntschli. *(Pursing his lips and rounding his eyes)* Oh-o-oh! I never found it. It must be there still.

Raina. *(Springing up)* There still! for my father to find the first time he puts his hand in his pocket! Oh, how could you be so stupid?

Bluntschli. *(Rising also)* It doesnt matter: I suppose it's only a photograph: how can he tell who it was intended for? Tell him he put it there himself.

Raina. *(Bitterly)* Yes: that is so clever! isnt it? *(Distractedly)* Oh! what shall I do?

260 *Bluntschli.* Ah, I see. You wrote something on it. That was rash.

Raina. *(Vexed almost to tears)* Oh, to have done such a thing for you, who care no more—except to laugh at me—oh! Are you sure nobody has touched it?

Bluntschli. Well, I cant be quite sure. You see, I couldnt carry it about with me all the time: one cant take much luggage on active service.

241. *Hand aufs Herz!* Cross my heart! (German).

Raina. What did you do with it?

Bluntschli. When I got through to Pirot I had to put it in safe keeping somehow. I thought of the railway cloak room; but thats the surest place to get looted in modern warfare. So I pawned it.

Raina. Pawned it!!! 270

Bluntschli. I know it doesnt sound nice; but it was much the safest plan. I redeemed it the day before yesterday. Heaven only knows whether the pawnbroker cleared out the pockets or not.

Raina. *(Furious: throwing the words right into his face)* You have a low shopkeeping mind. You think of things that would never come into a gentleman's head.

Bluntschli. *(Phlegmatically)* Thats the Swiss national character, dear lady. *(He returns to the table.)*

Raina. Oh, I wish I had never met you. *(She flounces away, and sits at the window fuming.)* 280

(Louka comes in with a heap of letters and telegrams on her salver, and crosses, with her bold free gait, to the table. Her left sleeve is looped up to the shoulder with a brooch, shewing her naked arm, with a broad gilt bracelet covering the bruise.)

Louka. *(To Bluntschli)* For you. *(She empties the salver with a fling on to the table.)* The messenger is waiting. *(She is determined not to be civil to an enemy, even if she must bring him his letters.)*

Bluntschli. *(To Raina)* Will you excuse me: the last postal delivery that reached me was three weeks ago. These are the subsequent accumulations. Four telegrams: a week old. *(He opens one.)* Oho! 290 Bad news!

Raina. *(Rising and advancing a little remorsefully)* Bad news?

Bluntschli. My father's dead. *(He looks at the telegram with his lips pursed, musing on the unexpected change in his arrangements. Louka crosses herself hastily.)*

Raina. Oh, how very sad!

Bluntschli. Yes: I shall have to start for home in an hour. He has left a lot of big hotels behind him to be looked after. *(He takes up a fat letter in a long blue envelope.)* Here's a whacking letter from the family solicitor.° *(He pulls out the enclosures and glances over them.)* Great 300 Heavens! Seventy! Two hundred! *(In a crescendo of dismay)* Four hundred! Four thousand!! Nine thousand six hundred!!! What on earth am I to do with them all?

Raina. *(Timidly)* Nine thousand hotels?

Bluntschli. Hotels! nonsense. If you only knew! Oh, it's too ridiculous! Excuse me: I must give my fellow orders about starting. *(He leaves the room hastily, with the documents in his hand.)*

300. solicitor, lawyer.

Louka. (Knowing instinctively that she can annoy Raina by disparaging Bluntschli) He has not much heart, that Swiss. He has not
310 a word of grief for his poor father.

Raina. (Bitterly) Grief! A man who has been doing nothing but killing people for years! What does he care? What does any soldier care? *(She goes to the door, restraining her tears with difficulty.)*

Louka. Major Saranoff has been fighting too; and he has plenty of heart left. *(Raina, at the door, draws herself up haughtily and goes out.)* Aha! I thought you wouldnt get much feeling out of your soldier. *(She is following Raina when Nicola enters with an armful of logs for the stove.)*

Nicola. (Grinning amorously at her) Ive been trying all the after-
320 noon to get a minute alone with you, my girl. *(His countenance changes as he notices her arm.)* Why, what fashion is that of wearing your sleeve, child?

Louka. (Proudly) My own fashion.

Nicola. Indeed! If the mistress catches you, she'll talk to you. *(He puts the logs down, and seats himself comfortable on the ottoman.)*

Louka. Is that any reason why you should take it on yourself to talk to me?

Nicola. Come! dont be so contrairy with me. Ive some good news
330 for you. *(She sits down beside him. He takes out some paper money. Louka, with an eager gleam in her eyes, tries to snatch it; but he shifts it quickly to his left hand, out of her reach.)* See! a twenty leva bill! Sergius gave me that, out of pure swagger. A fool and his money are soon parted. Theres ten levas more. The Swiss gave me that for backing up the mistress's and Raina's lies about him. He's no fool, he isnt. You should have heard old Catherine downstairs as polite as you please to me, telling me not to mind the Major being a little impatient; for they knew what a good servant I was—after making a fool and a liar of me before them all! The twenty will go to our savings; and you shall
340 have the ten to spend if youll only talk to me so as to remind me I'm a human being. I get tired of being a servant occasionally.

Louka. Yes: sell your manhood for 30 levas, and buy me for 10! *(Rising scornfully)* Keep your money. You were born to be a servant. I was not. When you set up your shop you will only be everybody's servant instead of somebody's servant. *(She goes moodily to the table and seats herself regally in Sergius's chair.)*

Nicola. (Picking up his logs, and going to the stove) Ah, wait til you see. We shall have our evenings to ourselves; and I shall be master in my own house, I promise you. *(He throws the logs down and kneels*
350 *at the stove.)*

Louka. You shall never be master in mine.

Nicola. (Turning, still on his knees, and squatting down rather forlornly on his calves, daunted by her implacable disdain) You have a great ambition in you, Louka. Remember: if any luck comes to you, it was I that made a woman of you.

Louka. You!

Nicola. (Scrambling up and going at her) Yes, me. Who was it made you give up wearing a couple of pounds of false black hair on your head and reddening your lips and cheeks like any other Bulgarian girl? I did. Who taught you to trim your nails, and keep your hands clean, and be dainty about yourself, like a fine Russian lady? Me: do you hear that? me! *(She tosses her head defiantly; and he turns away, adding, more coolly.)* Ive often thought that if Raina were out of the way, and you just a little less of a fool and Sergius just a little more of one, you might come to be one of my grandest customers, instead of only being my wife and costing me money. 360

Louka. I believe you would rather be my servant than my husband. You would make more out of me. Oh, I know that soul of yours.

Nicola. (Going closer to her for greater emphasis) Never you mind my soul; but just listen to my advice. If you want to be a lady, your present behavior to me wont do at all, unless when we're alone. It's too sharp and impudent; and impudence is a sort of familiarity; it shews affection for me. And dont you try being high and mighty with me, either. Youre like all country girls; you think it's genteel to treat a servant the way I treat a stableboy. Thats only your ignorance; and dont you forget it. And dont be so ready to defy everybody. Act as if you expected to have your own way, not as if you expected to be ordered about. The way to get on as a lady is the same as the way to get on as a servant: youve got to know your place: thats the secret of it. And you may depend on me to know my place if you get promoted. Think over it, my girl. I'll stand by you: one servant should always stand by another. 370 380

Louka. (Rising impatiently) Oh, I must behave in my own way. You take all the courage out of me with your coldblooded wisdom. Go and put those logs on the fire: thats the sort of thing you understand. *(Before Nicola can retort, Sergius comes in. He checks himself a moment on seeing Louka; then goes to the stove.)*

Sergius. (To Nicola) I am not in the way of your work, I hope.

Nicola. (In a smooth, elderly manner) Oh no, sir: thank you kindly. I was only speaking to this foolish girl about her habit of running up here to the library whenever she gets a chance, to look at the books. Thats the worst of her education, sir: it gives her habits above her station. *(To Louka)* Make that table tidy, Louka, for the Major. 390

(He goes out sedately.)

(Louka, without looking at Sergius, pretends to arrange the papers on the table. He crosses slowly to her, and studies the arrangement of her sleeve reflectively.)

Sergius. Let me see: is there a mark there? *(He turns up the bracelet and sees the bruise made by his grasp. She stands motionless, not looking*
400 *at him: fascinated, but on her guard.)* Ffff! Does it hurt?

Louka. Yes.

Sergius. Shall I cure it?

Louka. (Instantly withdrawing herself proudly, but still not looking at him) No. You cannot cure it now.

Sergius. (Masterfully) Quite sure? *(He makes a movement as if to take her in his arms.)*

Louka. Dont trifle with me, please. An officer should not trifle with a servant.

Sergius. (Indicating the bruise with a merciless stroke of his fore-
410 *finger)* That was no trifle, Louka.

Louka. (Flinching; then looking at him for the first time) Are you sorry?

Sergius. (With measured emphasis, folding his arms) I am never sorry.

Louka. (Wistfully) I wish I could believe a man could be as unlike a woman as that. I wonder are you really a brave man?

Sergius. (Unaffectedly, relaxing his attitude) Yes: I am a brave man. My heart jumped like a woman's at the first shot; but in the charge I found that I was brave. Yes: that at least is real about me.

420 *Louka.* Did you find in the charge that the men whose fathers are poor like mine were any less brave than the men who are rich like you.

Sergius. (With bitter levity) Not a bit. They all slashed and cursed and yelled like heroes. Psha! the courage to rage and kill is cheap. I have an English bull terrier who has as much of that sort of courage as the whole Bulgarian nation, and the whole Russian nation at its back. But he lets my groom thrash him, all the same. Thats your soldier all over! No, Louka: your poor men can cut throats; but they are afraid of their officers; they put up with insults and blows; they stand by and see one another punished like children: aye, and help to do it when they
430 are ordered. And the officers!!! Well *(With a short harsh laugh) I* am an officer. Oh, *(Fervently)* give me the man who will defy to the death any power on earth or in heaven that sets itself up against his own will and conscience: he alone is the brave man.

Louka. How easy it is to talk! Men never seem to me to grow up: they all have schoolboy's ideas. You dont know what true courage is.

Sergius. (Ironically) Indeed! I am willing to be instructed. *(He sits on the ottoman, sprawling magnificently.)*

Louka. Look at me! how much am I allowed to have my own will? I have to get your room ready for you: to sweep and dust, to fetch and carry. How could that degrade me if it did not degrade you to have it done for you? But *(With subdued passion)* if I were Empress of Russia, above everyone in the world, then!! Ah then, though according to you I could shew no courage at all, you should see, you should see. 440

Sergius. What would you do, most noble Empress?

Louka. I would marry the man I loved, which no other queen in Europe has the courage to do. If I loved you, though you would be as far beneath me as I am beneath you, I would dare to be the equal of my inferior. Would you dare as much if you loved me? No: if you felt the beginnings of love for me you would not let it grow. You would not dare: you would marry a rich man's daughter because you would be afraid of what other people would say of you. 450

Sergius. *(Bounding up)* You lie: it is not so, by all the stars! If I loved you, and I were the Czar himself, I would set you on the throne by my side. You know that I love another woman, a woman as high above you as heaven is above earth. And you are jealous of her.

Louka. I have no reason to be. She will never marry you now. The man I told you of has come back. She will marry the Swiss.

Sergius. *(Recoiling)* The Swiss!

Louka. A man worth ten of you. Then you can come to me; and I will refuse you. You are not good enough for me. *(She turns to the door.)* 460

Sergius. *(Springing after her and catching her fiercely in his arms)* I will kill the Swiss; and afterwards I will do as I please with you.

Louka. *(In his arms, passive and steadfast)* The Swiss will kill you, perhaps. He has beaten you in love. He may beat you in war.

Sergius. *(Tormentedly)* Do you think I believe that she—she! whose worst thoughts are higher than your best ones, is capable of trifling with another man behind my back?

Louka. Do you think she would believe the Swiss if he told her now that I am in your arms? 470

Sergius. *(Releasing her in despair)* Damnation! Oh, damnation! Mockery! mockery everywhere! everything I think is mocked by everything I do. *(He strikes himself frantically on the breast.)* Coward! liar! fool! Shall I kill myself like a man, or live and pretend to laugh at myself? *(She again turns to go.)* Louka! *(She stops near the door.)* Remember: you belong to me.

Louka. *(Turning)* What does that mean? An insult?

Sergius. *(Commandingly)* It means that you love me, and that I have had you here in my arms, and will perhaps have you there again. Whether that is an insult I neither know nor care: take it as you please. But *(Vehemently)* I will not be a coward and a trifler. If I choose to love 480 you, I dare marry you, in spite of all Bulgaria. If these hands ever touch you again, they shall touch my affianced bride.

Louka. We shall see whether you dare keep your word. And take care. I will not wait long.

Sergius. (Again folding his arms and standing motionless in the middle of the room) Yes: we shall see. And you shall wait my pleasure. *(Bluntschli, much preoccupied, with his papers still in his hand, enters, leaving the door open for Louka to go out. He goes across to the table,*
490 *glancing at her as he passes. Sergius, without altering his resolute attitude, watches him steadily. Louka goes out, leaving the door open.)*

Bluntschli. (Absently, sitting at the table as before, and putting down his papers) Thats a remarkable looking young woman.

Sergius. (Gravely, without moving) Captain Bluntschli.

Bluntschli. Eh?

Sergius. You have deceived me. You are my rival. I brook no rivals. At six o'clock I shall be in the drilling-ground on the Klissoura road, alone, on horseback, with my sabre. Do you understand?

Bluntschli. (Staring, but sitting quite at his ease) Oh, thank you:
500 thats a cavalry man's proposal. I'm in the artillery; and I have the choice of weapons. If I go, I shall take a machine gun. And there shall be no mistake about the cartridges this time.

Sergius. (Flushing, but with deadly coldness) Take care, sir. It is not our custom in Bulgaria to allow invitations of that kind to be trifled with.

Bluntschli. (Warmly) Pooh! dont talk to me about Bulgaria. You dont know what fighting is. But have it your own way. Bring your sabre along. I'll meet you.

Sergius. (Fiercely delighted to find his opponent a man of spirit)
510 Well said, Switzer. Shall I lend you my best horse?

Bluntschli. No: damn your horse! thank you all the same, my dear fellow. *(Raina comes in, and hears the next sentence.)* I shall fight you on foot. Horseback's too dangerous: I dont want to kill you if I can help it.

Raina. (Hurrying forward anxiously) I have heard what Captain Bluntschli said, Sergius. You are going to fight. Why? *(Sergius turns away in silence, and goes to the stove, where he stands watching her as she continues, to Bluntschli.)* What about?

Bluntschli. I dont know: he hasnt told me. Better not interfere,
520 dear young lady. No harm will be done: Ive often acted as sword instructor. He wont be able to touch me; and I'll not hurt him. It will save explanations. In the morning I shall be off home; and youll never see me or hear of me again. You and he will then make it up and live happily ever after.

Raina. *(Turning away deeply hurt, almost with a sob in her voice)* I never said I wanted to see you again.

Sergius. *(Striding forward)* Ha! That is a confession.

Raina. *(Haughtily)* What do you mean?

Sergius. You love that man!

Raina. *(Scandalized)* Sergius! 530

Sergius. You allow him to make love to you behind my back, just as you treat me as your affianced husband behind his. Bluntschli: you knew our relations; and you deceived me. It is for that that I call you to account, not for having received favors *I* never enjoyed.

Bluntschli. *(Jumping up indignantly)* Stuff! Rubbish! I have received no favors. Why, the young lady doesnt even know whether I'm married or not.

Raina. *(Forgetting herself)* Oh! *(Collapsing on the ottoman)* Are you?

Sergius. You see the young lady's concern, Captain Bluntschli. Denial is useless. You have enjoyed the privilege of being received 540 in her own room, late at night—

Bluntschli. *(Interrupting him pepperily)* Yes, you blockhead! she received me with a pistol at her head. Your cavalry were at my heels. I'd have blown out her brains if she'd uttered a cry.

Sergius. *(Taken aback)* Bluntschli! Raina: is this true?

Raina. *(Rising in wrathful majesty)* Oh, how dare you, how dare you?

Bluntschli. Apologize, man: apologize. *(He resumes his seat at the table.)*

Sergius. *(With the old measured emphasis, folding his arms)* I never apologize! 550

Raina. *(Passionately)* This is the doing of that friend of yours, Captain Bluntschli. It is he who is spreading this horrible story about me. *(She walks about excitedly.)*

Bluntschli. No: he's dead. Burnt alive.

Raina. *(Stopping, shocked)* Burnt alive!

Bluntschli. Shot in the hip in a woodyard. Couldnt drag himself out. Your fellows' shells set the timber on fire and burnt him, with half a dozen other poor devils in the same predicament.

Raina. How horrible!

Sergius. And how ridiculous! Oh, war! war! the dream of patriots 560 and heroes! A fraud, Bluntschli. A hollow sham, like love.

Raina. *(Outraged)* Like love! You say that before me!

Bluntschli. Come, Saranoff: that matter is explained.

Sergius. A hollow sham, I say. Would you have come back here if nothing had passed between you except at the muzzle of your pistol? Raina is mistaken about your friend who was burnt. He was not my informant.

Raina. Who then? *(Suddenly guessing the truth)* Ah, Louka! my maid! my servant! You were with her this morning all that time after
570 —after—Oh, what sort of god is this I have been worshipping! *(He meets her gaze with sardonic enjoyment of her disenchantment. Angered all the more, she goes closer to him, and says, in a lower, intenser tone.)* Do you know that I looked out of the window as I went upstairs, to have another sight of my hero; and I saw something I did not understand then. I know now that you were making love to her.

Sergius. (With grim humor) You saw that?

Raina. Only too well. *(She turns away, and throws herself on the divan under the centre window, quite overcome.)*

Sergius. (Cynically) Raina: our romance is shattered. Life's a farce.

580 *Bluntschli. (To Raina, whimsically)* You see: he's found himself out now.

Sergius. (Going to him) Bluntschli: I have allowed you to call me a blockhead. You may now call me a coward as well. I refuse to fight you. Do you know why?

Bluntschli. No; but it doesnt matter. I didnt ask the reason when you cried on; and I dont ask the reason now that you cry off. I'm a professional soldier: I fight when I have to, and am very glad to get out of it when I havnt to. Youre only an amateur: you think fighting's an amusement.

590 *Sergius. (Sitting down at the table, nose to nose with him)* You shall hear the reason all the same, my professional. The reason is that it takes two men—real men—men of heart, blood and honor—to make a genuine combat. I could no more fight with you than I could make love to an ugly woman. Youve no magnetism: youre not a man: youre a machine.

Bluntschli. (Apologetically) Quite true, quite true. I always was that sort of chap. I'm very sorry.

Sergius. Psha!

Bluntschli. But now that youve found that life isnt a farce, but some-
600 thing quite sensible and serious, what further obstacle is there to your happiness?

Raina. (Rising) You are very solicitous about my happiness and his. Do you forget his new love—Louka? It is not you that he must fight now, but his rival, Nicola.

Sergius. Rival!! *(Bounding half across the room)*

Raina. Dont you know that theyre engaged?

Sergius. Nicola! Are fresh abysses opening? Nicola!!

Raina. (Sarcastically) A shocking sacrifice, isnt it? Such beauty! such intellect! such modesty! wasted on a middle-aged servant man.
610 Really, Sergius, you cannot stand by and allow such a thing. It would be unworthy of your chivalry.

Sergius. (Losing all self-control) Viper! Viper! *(He rushes to and fro, raging.)*

Bluntschli. Look here, Saranoff: youre getting the worst of this.

Raina. (Getting angrier) Do you realize what he has done, Captain Bluntschli? He has set this girl as a spy on us; and her reward is that he makes love to her.

Sergius. False! Monstrous!

Raina. Monstrous! *(Confronting him)* Do you deny that she told you about Captain Bluntschli being in my room? 620

Sergius. No; but—

Raina. (Interrupting) Do you deny that you were making love to her when she told you?

Sergius. No; but I tell you—

Raina. (Cutting him short contemptuously) It is unnecessary to tell us anything more. That is quite enough for us. *(She turns away from him and sweeps majestically back to the window.)*

Bluntschli. (Quietly, as Sergius, in an agony of mortification, sinks on the ottoman, clutching his averted head between his fists) I told you you were getting the worst of it, Saranoff. 630

Sergius. Tiger cat!

Raina. (Running excitedly to Bluntschli) You hear this man calling me names, Captain Bluntschli?

Bluntschli. What else can he do, dear lady? He must defend himself somehow. Come *(Very persuasively)* dont quarrel. What good does it do? *(Raina, with a gasp, sits down on the ottoman, and after a vain effort to look vexedly at Bluntschli, falls a victim to her sense of humor, and actually leans back babyishly against the writhing shoulder of Sergius.)*

Sergius. Engaged to Nicola! Ha! ha! Ah well, Bluntschli, you are 640 right to take this huge imposture of a world coolly.

Raina. (Quaintly to Bluntschli, with an intuitive guess at his state of mind) I daresay you think us a couple of grown-up babies, dont you?

Sergius. (Grinning savagely) He does: he does. Swiss civilization nursetending Bulgarian barbarism, eh?

Bluntschli. (Blushing) Not at all, I assure you. I'm only very glad to get you two quieted. There! there! let's be pleasant and talk it over in a friendly way. Where is this other young lady?

Raina. Listening at the door, probably.

Sergius. (Shivering as if a bullet had struck him, and speaking with 650 *quiet but deep indignation)* I will prove that that, at least, is a calumny. *(He goes with dignity to the door and opens it. A yell of fury bursts from him as he looks out. He darts into the passage, and returns dragging in Louka, whom he flings violently against the table, exclaiming.)* Judge her, Bluntschli. You, the cool impartial man: judge the eaves dropper.

(Louka stands her ground, proud and silent.)

Bluntschli. (Shaking his head) I mustnt judge her. I once listened myself outside a tent when there was a mutiny brewing. It's all a question of the degree of provocation. My life was at stake.

660 *Louka.* My love was at stake. I am not ashamed.

Raina. (Contemptuously) Your love! Your curiosity, you mean.

Louka. (Facing her and retorting her contempt with interest) My love, stronger than anything you can feel, even for your chocolate cream soldier.

Sergius. (With quick suspicion, to Louka) What does that mean?

Louka. (Fiercely) It means—

Sergius. (Interrupting her slightingly) Oh, I remember: the ice pudding. A paltry taunt, girl!

(Major Petkoff enters, in his shirtsleeves.)

670 *Petkoff.* Excuse my shirtsleeves, gentlemen. Raina: somebody has been wearing that coat of mine: I'll swear it. Somebody with a differently shaped back. It's all burst open at the sleeve. Your mother is mending it. I wish she'd make haste: I shall catch cold. *(He looks more attentively at them.)* Is anything the matter?

Raina. No. *(She sits down at the stove, with a tranquil air.)*

Sergius. Oh no. *(He sits down at the end of the table, as at first.)*

Bluntschli. (Who is already seated) Nothing. Nothing.

Petkoff. (Sitting down on the ottoman in his old place) Thats all right. *(He notices Louka.)* Anything the matter, Louka?

680 *Louka.* No, sir.

Petkoff. (Genially) Thats all right. *(He sneezes.)* Go and ask your mistress for my coat, like a good girl, will you?

(Nicola enters with the coat. Louka makes a pretence of having business in the room by taking the little table with the hookah away to the wall near the windows.)

Raina. (Rising quickly as she sees the coat on Nicola's arm) Here it is, papa. Give it to me, Nicola; and do you put some more wood on the fire. *(She takes the coat, and brings it to the Major, who stands up to put it on. Nicola attends to the fire.)*

690 *Petkoff. (To Raina, teasing her affectionately)* Aha! Going to be very good to poor old papa just for one day after his return from the wars, eh?

Raina. (With solemn reproach) Ah, how can you say that to me, father?

Petkoff. Well, well, only a joke, little one. Come: give me a kiss: *(She kisses him.)* Now give me the coat.

Raina. No: I am going to put it on for you. Turn your back. *(He turns his back and feels behind him with his arms for the sleeves. She dexterously takes the photograph from the pocket and throws it on the table before Bluntschli, who covers it with a sheet of paper under the very nose of Sergius, who looks on amazed, with his suspicions roused in the highest degree. She then helps Petkoff on with his coat.)* There, dear! Now are you comfortable? 700

Petkoff. Quite, little love. Thanks. *(He sits down; and Raina returns to her seat near the stove.)* Oh, by the bye, Ive found something funny. Whats the meaning of this? *(He puts his hand into the picked pocket.)* Eh? Hallo! *(He tries the other pocket.)* Well, I could have sworn—! *(Much puzzled, he tries the breast pocket.)* I wonder—*(Trying the original pocket)* Where can it—? *(He rises, exclaiming)* Your mother's taken it!

Raina. (Very red) Taken what? 710

Petkoff. Your photograph, with the inscription: "Raina, to her Chocolate Cream Soldier: a Souvenir." Now you know theres something more in this than meets the eye; and I'm going to find it out. *(Shouting)* Nicola!

Nicola. (Coming to him) Sir!

Petkoff. Did you spoil any pastry of Miss Raina's this morning?

Nicola. You heard Miss Raina say that I did, sir.

Petkoff. I know that, you idiot. Was it true?

Nicola. I am sure Miss Raina is incapable of saying anything that is not true, sir. 720

Petkoff. Are you? Then I'm not. *(Turning to the others)* Come: do you think I dont see it all? *(He goes to Sergius, and slaps him on the shoulder.)* Sergius: youre the chocolate cream soldier, arnt you?

Sergius. (Starting up) I! A chocolate cream soldier! Certainly not.

Petkoff. Not! *(He looks at them. They are all very serious and very conscious.)* Do you mean to tell me that Raina sends things like that to other men?

Sergius. (Enigmatically) The world is not such an innocent place as we used to think, Petkoff.

Bluntschli. (Rising) It's all right, Major. I'm the chocolate cream soldier. *(Petkoff and Sergius are equally astonished.)* The gracious young lady saved my life by giving me chocolate creams when I was starving: shall I ever forget their flavour! My late friend Stolz told you the story at Pirot. I was the fugitive. 730

Petkoff. You! *(He gasps.)* Sergius: do you remember how those two women went on this morning when we mentioned it? *(Sergius smiles cynically. Petkoff confronts Raina severely.)* Youre a nice young woman, arnt you?

Raina. (Bitterly) Major Saranoff has changed his mind. And when I wrote that on the photograph, I did not know that Captain Bluntschli was married. 740

Bluntschli. (Startled into vehement protest) I'm not married.

Raina. (With deep reproach) You said you were.

Bluntschli. I did not. I positively did not. I never was married in my life.

Petkoff. (Exasperated) Raina: will you kindly inform me, if I am not asking too much, which of these gentlemen you are engaged to?

Raina. To neither of them. This young lady *(Introducing Louka, who faces them all proudly)* is the object of Major Saranoff's affections at present.

Petkoff. Louka! Are you mad, Sergius? Why, this girl's engaged to Nicola.

Nicola. I beg your pardon, sir. There is a mistake. Louka is not engaged to me.

Petkoff. Not engaged to you, you scoundrel! Why, you had twenty-five levas from me on the day of your betrothal; and she had that gilt bracelet from Miss Raina.

Nicola. (With cool unction) We gave it out so, sir. But it was only to give Louka protection. She had a soul above her station; and I have been no more than her confidential servant. I intend, as you know, sir, to set up a shop later on in Sofia; and I look forward to her custom and recommendation should she marry into the nobility.

(He goes out with impressive discretion, leaving them all staring after him.)

Petkoff. (Breaking the silence) Well, I am—hm!

Sergius. This is either the finest heroism or the most crawling baseness. Which is it, Bluntschli?

Bluntschli. Never mind whether it's heroism or baseness. Nicola's the ablest man Ive met in Bulgaria. I'll make him manager of a hotel if he can speak French and German.

Louka. (Suddenly breaking out at Sergius) I have been insulted by everyone here. You set them the example. You owe me an apology. *(Sergius, like a repeating clock of which the spring has been touched, immediately begins to fold his arms.)*

Bluntschli. (Before he can speak) It's no use. He never apologizes.

Louka. Not to you, his equal and his enemy. To me, his poor servant, he will not refuse to apologize.

Sergius. (Approvingly) You are right. *(He bends his knee in his grandest manner.)* Forgive me.

Louka. I forgive you. *(She timidly gives him her hand, which he kisses.)* That touch makes me your affianced wife.

Sergius. (Springing up) Ah! I forgot that.

Louka. (Coldly) You can withdraw if you like.

S[...]gius. Withdraw! Never! You belong to me. *(He puts his arm about*

[...]ine comes in and finds Louka in Sergius's arms, with all the [...]ing at them in bewildered astonishment.)

Catherine. What does this mean? *(Sergius releases Louka.)*

Petkoff. Well, my dear, it appears that Sergius is going to marry Louka instead of Raina. *(She is about to break out indignantly at him: he stops her by exclaiming testily.)* Dont blame me: Ive nothing to do with it. *(He retreats to the stove.)* 790

Catherine. Marry Louka! Sergius: you are bound by your word to us!

Sergius. (Folding his arms) Nothing binds me.

Bluntschli. (Much pleased by this piece of common sense) Saranoff: your hand. My congratulations. These heroics of yours have their practical side after all. *(To Louka)* Gracious young lady: the best wishes of a good Republican! *(He kisses her hand, to Raina's great disgust, and returns to his seat.)*

Catherine. Louka: you have been telling stories. 800

Louka. I have done Raina no harm.

Catherine. (Haughtily) Raina! *(Raina, equally indignant, almost snorts at the liberty.)*

Louka. I have a right to call her Raina: she calls me Louka. I told Major Saranoff she would never marry him if the Swiss gentleman came back.

Bluntschli. (Rising, much surprised) Hallo!

Louka. (Turning to Raina) I thought you were fonder of him than of Sergius. You know best whether I was right.

Bluntschli. What nonsense! I assure you, my dear Major, my dear Madame, the gracious young lady simply saved my life, nothing else. She never cared two straws for me. Why, bless my heart and soul, look at the young lady and look at me. She, rich, young, beautiful, with her imagination full of fairy princes and noble natures and cavalry charges and goodness knows what! And I, a commonplace Swiss soldier who hardly knows what a decent life is after fifteen years of barracks and battles: a vagabond, a man who has spoiled all his chances in life through an incurably romantic disposition, a man— 810

Sergius. (Starting as if a needle had pricked him and interrupting Bluntschli in incredulous amazement) Excuse me, Bluntschli: what did you say had spoiled your chances in life? 820

Bluntschli. (Promptly) An incurably romantic disposition. I ran away from home twice when I was a boy. I went into the army instead of into my father's business. I climbed the balcony of this house when a man of sense would have dived into the nearest cellar. I came sneaking back here to have another look at the young lady when any other man of my age would have sent the coat back—

Petkoff. My coat!

Bluntschli.—yes: thats the coat I mean—would have sent it back and gone quietly home. Do you suppose I am the sort of fellow a young girl falls in love with? Why, look at our ages! I'm thirty-four: I dont 830

suppose the young lady is much over seventeen. *(This estimate produces a marked sensation, all the rest turning and staring at one another. He proceeds innocently.)* All that adventure which was life or death to me, was only a schoolgirl's game to her—chocolate creams and hide and seek. Heres the proof! *(He takes the photograph from the table.)* Now, I ask you, would a woman who took the affair seriously have sent me this and written on it "Raina, to her Chocolate Cream Soldier: a Souvenir"? *(He exhibits the photograph triumphantly, as if it settled*
840 *the matter beyond all possibility of refutation.)*

Petkoff. Thats what I was looking for. How the deuce did it get there? *(He comes from the stove to look at it, and sits down on the ottoman.)*

Bluntschli. (To Raina, complacently) I have put everything right, I hope, gracious young lady.

Raina. (Going to the table to face him) I quite agree with your account of yourself. You are a romantic idiot. *(Bluntschli is unspeakably taken aback.)* Next time, I hope you will know the difference between a schoolgirl of seventeen and a woman of twenty-three.

Bluntschli. (Stupefied) Twenty-three! *(Raina snaps the photograph*
850 *contemptuously from his hand; tears it up; throws the pieces in his face; and sweeps back to her former place.)*

Sergius. (With grim enjoyment of his rival's discomfiture) Bluntschli: my one last belief is gone. Your sagacity is a fraud, like everything else. You have less sense than even I!

Bluntschli. (Overwhelmed) Twenty-three! Twenty-three!! *(He considers.)* Hm! *(Swiftly making up his mind and coming to his host)* In that case, Major Petkoff, I beg to propose formally to become a suitor for your daughter's hand, in place of Major Saranoff retired.

Raina. You dare!

860 *Bluntschli.* If you were twenty-three when you said those things to me this afternoon, I shall take them seriously.

Catherine. (Loftily polite) I doubt, sir, whether you quite realize either my daughter's position or that of Major Sergius Saranoff, whose place you propose to take. The Petkoffs and the Saranoffs are known as the richest and most important families in the country. Our position is almost historical: we can go back for twenty years.

Petkoff. Oh, never mind that, Catherine. *(To Bluntschli)* We should be most happy, Bluntschli, if it were only a question of your position; but hang it, you know, Raina is accustomed to a very comfortable es-
870 tablishment. Sergius keeps twenty horses.

Bluntschli. But who wants twenty horses? We're not going to keep [illegible]us.

[illegible]*erine. (Severely)* My daughter, sir, is accustomed to a first-rate

[illegible]*a.* Hush, mother: youre making me ridiculous.

Bluntschli. Oh well, if it comes to a question of an establishment, here goes! *(He darts impetuously to the table; seizes the papers in the blue envelope; and turns to Sergius.)* How many horses did you say?

Sergius. Twenty, noble Switzer.

Bluntschli. I have two hundred horses. *(They are amazed.)* How many carriages? 880

Sergius. Three.

Bluntschli. I have seventy. Twenty-four of them will hold twelve inside, besides two on the box, without counting the driver and conductor. How many tablecloths have you?

Sergius. How the deuce do I know?

Bluntschli. Have you four thousand?

Sergius. No.

Bluntschli. I have. I have nine thousand six hundred pairs of sheets and blankets, with two thousand four hundred eiderdown quilts. I have 890 ten thousand knives and forks, and the same quantity of dessert spoons. I have three hundred servants. I have six palatial establishments, besides two livery stables, a tea garden, and a private house. I have four medals for distinguished services; I have the rank of an officer and the standing of a gentleman; and I have three native languages. Shew me any man in Bulgaria that can offer as much!

Petkoff. (With childish awe) Are you Emperor of Switzerland?

Bluntschli. My rank is the highest known in Switzerland: I am a free citizen.

Catherine. Then, Captain Bluntschli, since you are my daughter's 900 choice—

Raina. (Mutinously) He's not.

Catherine. (Ignoring her)—I shall not stand in the way of her happiness. *(Petkoff is about to speak.)* That is Major Petkoff's feeling also.

Petkoff. Oh, I shall be only too glad. Two hundred horses! Whew!

Sergius. What says the lady?

Raina. (Pretending to sulk) The lady says that he can keep his tablecloths and his omnibuses. I am not here to be sold to the highest bidder. *(She turns her back on him.)*

Bluntschli. I wont take that answer. I appealed to you as a fugitive, 910 a beggar, and a starving man. You accepted me. You gave me your hand to kiss, your bed to sleep in, and your roof to shelter me.

Raina. I did not give them to the Emperor of Switzerland.

Bluntschli. Thats just what I say. *(He catches her by the shoulders and turns her face-to-face with him.)* Now tell us whom you did give them to.

Raina. (Succumbing with a shy smile) To my chocolate cream soldier.

Bluntschli. (With a boyish laugh of delight) Thatll do. Thank you. *(He looks at his watch and suddenly becomes businesslike.)* Time's up,

920 Major. Youve managed those regiments so well that youre sure to be asked to get rid of some of the infantry of the Timok division. Send them home by way of Lom Palanka. Saranoff: dont get married until I come back: I shall be here punctually at five in the evening on Tuesday fortnight. Gracious ladies *(His heels click.)* good evening. *(He makes them a military bow, and goes.)*

Sergius. What a man! Is he a man?

Comments and Questions

A look at Max Beerbohm's comments on seeing Arms and the Man *several years after its first production (p. 687) reminds us that, though a play does not change, attitudes toward it may. After two world wars and the atomic and hydrogen bombs, we obviously view a comedy like this one quite differently from the audiences of the eighteen-nineties. Is there any shock value left? Does Shaw puncture any ideals of war and soldiering still current? Does the level-headed, efficient, anti-heroic Bluntschli prefigure the most effective kind of contemporary soldier?*

In whatever way our attitudes today may differ from those of some seventy years ago, Arms and the Man *is still an amusing, effective comedy. Beerbohm finds the humorous tricks in the play inappropriate, but Shaw slyly uses the comic business about Petkoff's coat and Bluntschli's carpet bag to further the revelations of the plot. They should not distract you from the more subtle devices in characterization and theme that are designed to bring the audience around to a realistic and rational view of the subject. Toward the main characters—Bluntschli, Raina, Sergius and Louka—Shaw does not intend that we have a single reaction (as we do, for example, to the more stereotyped figures of Major and Mrs. Petkoff), but a series of responses, alternately favorable and unfavorable. By the end, not only is the action neatly and conventionally resolved in the manner of light comedy, but also the characters, in a much less conventional way, accept themselves and see others for what they really are. Precisely on what terms do Raina and Bluntschli accept each other? Sergius and Louka? Do you think Professor Elliott (p. 698) makes a reasonable comparison between Bluntschli and Falstaff in Shakespeare's* Henry IV?

The second act is particularly effective comedy. The quickly paced action offers a variety of humorous techniques: farcical situations which depend on hidden objects and mistaken identities; comic revelations and deceits in which the audience derives its amusement from knowing more than the characters on stage; verbal comedy—wisecracks, jokes, highflown language. Can you find some examples of these devices?

Related Reading

William Shakespeare, *Henry IV, Part I*, page 91
Max Beerbohm, "*Arms and the Man*," page 687
Robert C. Elliott, "Shaw's Captain Bluntschli: A Latter-Day Falstaff," page 698
Louis Kronenberger, "Some Prefatory Words on Comedy," page 680

William Shakespeare

(1564-1616)

KING HENRY IV, PART I

Shakespeare probably wrote the history play The First Part of King Henry the Fourth *in the fall of 1597. It is a sequel to his* Richard II, *written some two years before. In the earlier play Shakespeare described how Henry Bolingbroke, Earl of Hereford, forced his cousin King Richard II to abdicate his throne and then became king himself as Henry IV. Some months after this usurpation Richard was murdered at Pomfret Castle where he had been imprisoned, and Henry IV was strongly implicated in the murder. Richard had been king* dei gratia, *by divine right, as orderly succession was called, and Henry had disturbed that divine order. The moral implication of his actions made Henry uneasy for the rest of his life. At the end of the play* Richard II, *Henry IV promises to*

"make a voyage to the Holy Land
to wash this blood off from my guilty hand."

Henry IV, *Part I opens as the preceding play closed, with Henry's plans for his pilgrimage to the Holy Land.*

Henry IV is not only troubled by his conscience, but also by the forces he has unleashed. A revolution seldom ends at the point where the revolutionaries want it to end—with themselves in power and everything quiet once more—and Henry continued to reap the fruits of his action against the legitimate king in continued civil wars.

Henry's most valuable associates in gaining the throne had been members of the Percy family, the most powerful noblemen in the North of England near the Scottish border. In shifting their allegiance from Richard to Henry, the Percies had expected to gain even greater power by the side of the new king. When Henry IV wished to obtain the prisoners they had taken in the war with the Scots, because he wanted their ransom money to come to him, the Percies refused his authority, and a military conflict became inevitable. The Percies were doubly dangerous because one of them, Henry Hotspur, had married into the family of the Earls of March; and by descent the Earls of March had a better claim to the succession of Richard II than Henry IV himself. The childless Richard had reinforced this by proclaiming Edmund Earl of March as heir to the throne. The table on the following page explains these relationships.

Only in its outlines does the play follow the historical facts of the actual rebellion of the Percies and their defeat at Shrewsbury in 1403. Characteristically, Shakespeare freely adapted events and real characters to his own ends, and out of his own imagination created Sir John Falstaff, perhaps the most famous comic character in English literature. In fact, despite its title, the play is primarily about Henry IV's son, the Prince of Wales, and his supposed regeneration from habitué of the Boar's Head Tavern in Eastcheap to warrior and noble prince. However, it is neither the Prince nor the King who holds the center of the stage in Shakespeare's attention or in the audience's affection, but rather the characters who spring into life: Glendower, Hotspur, and most of all "this sanguine coward . . . this horseback breaker, this huge hill of flesh" Falstaff, who not only in bulk, but in sheer vivacity, overshadows the rest of the characters.

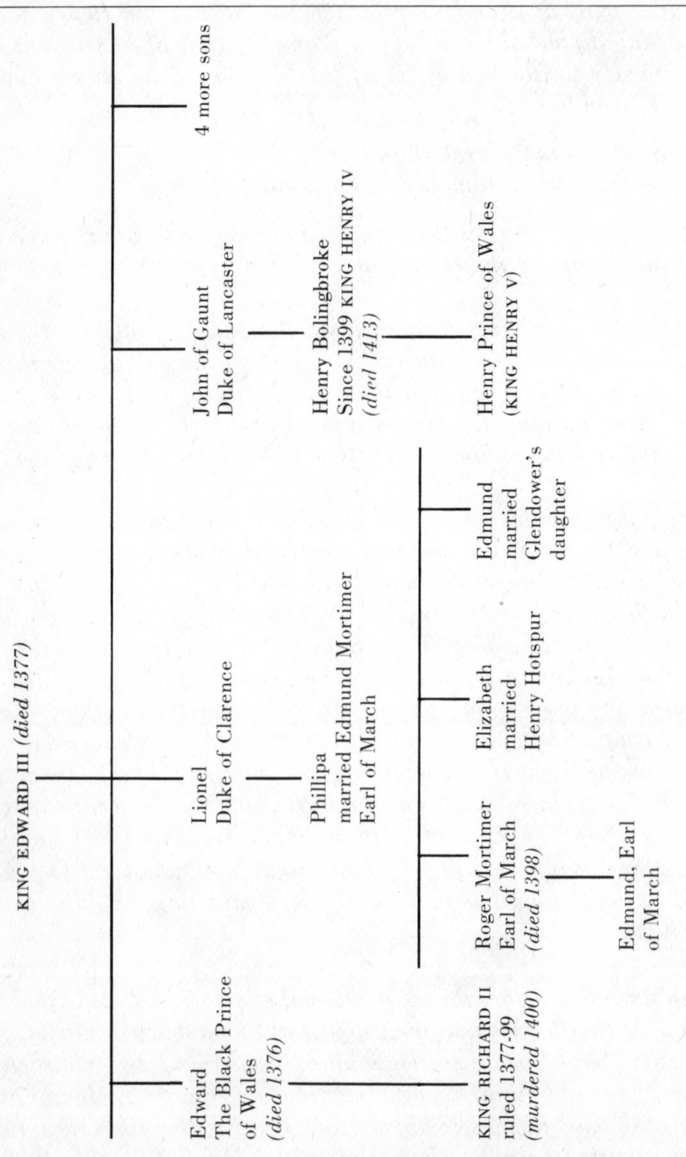

THE FIRST PART OF KING HENRY THE FOURTH

Characters

KING HENRY THE FOURTH
HENRY, PRINCE OF WALES } *sons to the King*
JOHN OF LANCASTER } *sons to the King*
EARL OF WESTMORELAND
SIR WALTER BLUNT
THOMAS PERCY, *Earl of Worcester*
HENRY PERCY, *Earl of Northumberland*
HENRY PERCY, *surnamed* HOTSPUR, *his son*
EDMUND MORTIMER, *Earl of March*
RICHARD SCROOP, *Archbishop of York*
ARCHIBALD, *Earl of Douglas*
OWEN GLENDOWER
SIR RICHARD VERNON
SIR JOHN FALSTAFF
SIR MICHAEL, *a friend to the Archbishop of York*
POINS
GADSHILL
PETO
BARDOLPH
LADY PERCY, *wife to Hotspur, and sister to Mortimer*
LADY MORTIMER, *daughter to Glendower, and wife to Mortimer*
MISTRESS QUICKLY, *hostess of a tavern in Eastcheap*
Lords Officers, Sheriff, Vintner, Chamberlain, Drawers, two Carriers, Travellers, and Attendants.

Scene: England.

Act I

Scene I. *London. The palace*

(Enter King Henry, Lord John of Lancaster, the Earl of Westmoreland, Sir Walter Blunt, and others)

King. So shaken as we are, so wan with care,
Find we a time for frighted peace to pant,
And breathe short-winded accents of new broils
To be commenced in strands afar remote.

Note: The footnotes for the play are from Hardin Craig's edition in his *The Complete Works of Shakespeare*, except for those in parentheses, which are the editors'.

No more the thirsty entrance of this soil
Shall daub her lips with her own children's blood;
No more shall trenching war° channel her fields,
Nor bruise her flowerets with the armed hoofs
Of hostile paces: those opposed eyes,
10 Which, like the meteors of a troubled heaven,
All of one nature, of one substance bred,
Did lately meet in the intestine shock°
And furious close° of civil butchery
Shall now, in mutual well-beseeming ranks,
March all one way and be no more opposed
Against acquaintance, kindred and allies:
The edge of war, like an ill-sheathed knife,
No more shall cut his master. Therefore, friends,
As far as to° the sepulchre of Christ,
20 Whose soldier now, under whose blessed cross
We are impressed and engaged to fight,
Forthwith a power of English shall we levy;
Whose arms were moulded in their mothers' womb
To chase these pagans in those holy fields
Over whose acres walk'd those blessed feet
Which fourteen hundred years ago were nail'd
For our advantage on the bitter cross.
But this our purpose now is twelve month old,
And bootless° 'tis to tell you we will go:
30 Therefore we meet not now.° Then let me hear
Of you, my gentle cousin° Westmoreland,
What yesternight our council did decree
In forwarding this dear expedience.°
Westmoreland. My liege, this haste was hot in question,°
And many limits of the charge° set down
But yesternight: when all athwart° there came
A post from Wales loaden with heavy news;
Whose worst° was, that the noble Mortimer,
Leading the men of Herefordshire to fight
40 Against the irregular° and wild Glendower,
Was by the rude hands of that Welshman taken,
A thousand of his people butchered;

7. (***trenching war,*** trench warfare.) **12.** (***intestine shock,*** civil war.) **13.** ***close,*** encounter. **19.** ***As far as to.*** There is an idea of motion in the word *levy,* line 22. **29.** (***bootless,*** needless.) **30.** (***Therefore we meet not now,*** this is not the reason for our meeting.) **31.** (***cousin,*** kinsman, generally used for relatives.) **33.** ***dear expedience,*** urgent expedition. **34.** ***hot in question,*** being hotly debated. **35.** ***limits of charge,*** military arrangements; possibly, estimates of expense. **36.** ***athwart,*** frustrating, interrupting. **38.** ***worst,*** i. e., worst news. **40.** ***irregular,*** lawless.

Upon whose dead corpse there was such misuse,
Such beastly shameless transformation,
By those Welshwomen done as may not be
Without much shame retold or spoken of.
King. It seems then that the tidings of this broil
Brake off our business for the Holy Land.
Westmoreland. This match'd with other° did, my gracious lord;
For more uneven° and unwelcome news 50
Came from the north and thus it did import:
On Holy-rood day,° the gallant Hotspur there,
Young Harry Percy and brave Archibald,
That ever-valiant and approved Scot,
At Holmedon met,
Where they did spend a sad and bloody hour;
As by° discharge of their artillery,
And shape of likelihood, the news was told;
For he that brought them, in the very heat
And pride of their contention did take horse, 60
Uncertain of the issue any way.
King. Here is a dear, a true industrious friend,
Sir Walter Blunt, new lighted from his horse,
Stain'd with the variation of each° soil
Betwixt that Holmedon and this seat of ours;
And he hath brought us smooth° and welcome news.
The Earl of Douglas is discomfited:
Ten thousand bold Scots, two and twenty knights,
Balk'd° in their own blood did Sir Walter see
On Holmedon's plains. Of prisoners, Hotspur took 70
Mordake the Earl of Fife, and eldest son
To beaten Douglas; and the Earl of Athol,
Of Murray, Angus, and Menteith:
And is not this an honourable spoil?
A gallant prize? ha, cousin, is it not?
Westmoreland. In faith,
It is a conquest for a prince to boast of.
King. Yea, there thou makest me sad and makest me sin
In envy that my Lord Northumberland
Should be the father to so blest a son, 80
A son who is the theme of honour's tongue;
Amongst a grove, the very straightest plant;

49. This . . . other, this piece of news matched with another. ***50. uneven,*** embarrassing. ***52.*** (***Holy-rood day,*** September 14.) ***57. by,*** i. e., judging from. ***64. the variation of each,*** every kind of. ***66. smooth,*** flattering, pleasant. ***69. Balk'd,*** heaped up in balks or ridges.

Who is sweet Fortune's minion and her pride:
Whilst I, by looking on the praise of him,
See riot and dishonour stain the brow
Of my young Harry. O that it could be proved
That some night-tripping fairy had exchanged
In cradle-clothes our children where they lay,
And call'd mine Percy, his Plantagenet!
90 Then would I have his Harry, and he mine.
But let him from my thoughts. What think you, coz,°
Of this young Percy's pride? the prisoners,
Which he in this adventure hath surprised,
To his own use he keeps; and sends me word,
I shall have none but Mordake Earl of Fife.

Westmoreland. This is his uncle's teaching: this is Worcester,
Malevolent° to you in all aspects;
Which makes him prune° himself, and bristle up
The crest of youth against your dignity.

100 *King.* But I have sent for him to answer this;
And for this cause awhile we must neglect
Our holy purpose to Jerusalem.
Cousin, on Wednesday next our council we
Will hold at Windsor; so inform the lords:
But come yourself with speed to us again;
For more is to be said and to be done
Than out of anger can be uttered.

Westmoreland. I will, my liege. *(Exeunt)*

Scene II. *London. An apartment of the Prince's*

(Enter the Prince of Wales and Falstaff)

Falstaff. Now, Hal, what time of day is it, lad?

Prince. Thou art so fat-witted, with drinking of old sack° and unbuttoning thee after supper and sleeping upon benches after noon, that thou has forgotten to demand that truly which thou wouldst truly know. What a devil hast thou to do with the time of the day? Unless hours were cups of sack and minutes capons and clocks the tongues of bawds° and dials the signs of leaping-houses° and the blessed sun himself a fair hot wench in flame-coloured taffeta, I see no reason why thou shouldst be so superfluous to demand the time of the day.

91. (***coz,*** cousin.) ***97. Malevolent, aspects,*** astrological terms. ***98. prune,*** preen (as a bird its feathers). ***2.*** (***sack,*** a dry white wine from Spain.) ***6.*** (***bawds,*** prostitutes.) ***7.*** (***leaping houses,*** brothels.)

Falstaff. Indeed, you come near me now,° Hal; for we that take purses go by the moon and the seven stars,° and not by Phœbus, he, 'that wandering knight so fair.'° And, I prithee, sweet wag, when thou art king, as, God save thy grace,—majesty I should say, for grace thou wilt have none,—

Prince. What, none?

Falstaff. No, by my troth, not so much as will serve to be prologue° to an egg and butter.

Prince. Well, how then? come, roundly, roundly.°

Falstaff. Marry, then, sweet wag, when thou art king, let not us that are squires of the night's body be called thieves of the day's beauty: let us be Diana's foresters, gentlemen of the shade, minions of the moon; and let men say we be men of good government, being governed, as the sea is, by our noble and chaste mistress the moon, under whose countenance we steal.°

Prince. Thou sayest well, and it holds well too; for the fortune of us that are the moon's men doth ebb and flow like the sea, being governed, as the sea is, by the moon. As, for proof, now: a purse of gold most resolutely snatched on Monday night and most dissolutely spent on Tuesday morning; got with swearing 'Lay by'° and spent with crying 'Bring in;'° now in as low an ebb as the foot of the ladder and by and by in as high a flow as the ridge of the gallows.

Falstaff. By the Lord, thou sayest true, lad. And is not my hostess of the tavern a most sweet wench?

Prince. As the honey of Hybla,° my old lad of the castle.° And is not a buff jerkin° a most sweet robe of durance?

Falstaff. How now, how now, mad wag! what, in thy quips and thy quiddities?° what a plague have I to do with a buff jerkin?

Prince. Why, what a pox have I to do with my hostess of the tavern?

Falstaff. Well, thou hast called her to a reckoning many a time and oft.

Prince. Did I ever call for thee to pay thy part?

Falstaff. No; I'll give thee thy due, thou has paid all there.

Prince. Yea, and elsewhere, so far as my coin would stretch; and where it would not, I have used my credit.

10. come near me now. Prince Hal's speech has been full of extravagant abuse; Falstaff parries by taking it in a sense of his own. ***11. the seven stars,*** the Pleiades. ***12. 'that . . . fair,'*** a line from some ballad. ***16. prologue,*** punning allusion to grace before meat. ***18. roundly,*** out with it. It is a wit combat. ***19-24.*** (Falstaff talks, in a style fashionable among the intelligentia, of the nightly activities of the highwayman.) ***29. 'Lay by,'*** a cry of highwaymen, like "Hands up!" ***30. 'Bring in,'*** i.e. the orders in the tavern. ***34. Hybla,*** a mountain region in Sicily near Syracuse, famed for honey. ***old lad of the castle,*** a pun on the name, Sir John Oldcastle, borne by Falstaff in the earlier versions of the Henry IV plays. ***35. buff jerkin,*** a leather jacket worn by officers of the law; a *robe of durance* in two senses, since *durance* means "imprisonment" and "durability." ***37. quiddities,*** subtleties of speech.

Falstaff. Yea, and so used it that, were it not here apparent that thou art heir apparent—But, I prithee, sweet wag, shall there be gallows standing in England when thou art king? and resolution thus fobbed° as it is with the rusty curb of old father antic° the law? Do not thou, when thou art king, hang a thief.

Prince. No; thou shalt.

Falstaff. Shall I? O rare! By the Lord, I'll be a brave judge.

Prince. Thou judgest false already: I mean, thou shalt have the hanging of the thieves and so become a rare hangman.

Falstaff. Well, Hal, well; and in some sort it jumps with my humour as well as waiting in the court,° I can tell you.

Prince. For obtaining of suits?°

Falstaff. Yea, for obtaining of suits, whereof the hangman hath no lean wardrobe. 'Sblood,° I am as melancholy as a gib cat° or a lugged bear.°

Prince. Or an old lion, or a lover's lute.

Falstaff. Yea, or the drone of a Lincolnshire bagpipe.

Prince. What sayest thou to a hare, or the melancholy of Moor-ditch?°

Falstaff. Thou has the most unsavoury similes and art indeed the most comparative, rascalliest, sweet young prince. But, Hal, I prithee, trouble me no more with vanity. I would to God thou and I knew where a commodity of good names were to be bought. An old lord of the council rated° me the other day in the street about you, sir, but I marked him not; and yet he talked very wisely, but I regarded him not; and yet he talked wisely, and in the street too.

Prince. Thou didst well; for wisdom° cries out in the streets, and no man regards it.

Falstaff. O, thou hast damnable iteration and art indeed able to corrupt a saint. Thou hast done much harm upon me,° Hal; God forgive thee for it! Before I knew thee, Hal, I knew nothing; and now am I, if a man should speak truly, little better than one of the wicked. I must give over this life, and I will give it over: by the Lord, an° I do not, I am a villain: I'll be damned for never a king's son in Christendom.

Prince. Where shall we take a purse to-morrow, Jack?

Falstaff. "Zounds,° where thou wilt, lad; I'll make one; an I do not, call me villain and baffle° me.

48. fobbed, cheated. ***antic,*** the buffoon of the old plays. ***55. waiting in the court,*** in a double sense, as a courtier and a judge. ***56. suits,*** suits at court and suits of clothes. ***58. 'S-blood,*** an oath. ***gib cat,*** tomcat. ***58-59. lugged bear,*** bear dragged by a rope. ***62-63. Moor-ditch,*** a foul ditch draining Moorfields. ***68.*** (***rated,*** berated.) ***71. wisdom cries out, etc.,*** an allusion to Proverbs 1:20-24. ***74. much harm upon me.*** Oldcastle was traditionally a religious hypocrite and a Lollard, or follower of John Wycliffe; Falstaff retains his faculty for insincere repentance. ***77.*** (***an,*** if.) ***80. 'Zounds,*** an oath, "God's wounds." ***81. baffle,*** hand up by the heels as a recreant knight.

Prince. I see a good amendment of life in thee; from praying to purse-taking.

Falstaff. Why, Hal, 'tis my vocation,° Hal; 'tis no sin for a man to labour in his vocation.

(Enter Poins)

Poins! Now shall we know if Gadshill have set a match.° O, if men were to be saved by merit, what hole in hell were hot enough for him? This is the most omnipotent villain that ever cried 'Stand' to a true man.

Prince. Good morrow, Ned.

Poins. Good morrow, sweet Hal. What says Monsieur Remorse? 90 what says Sir John Sack and Sugar? Jack! how agrees the devil and thee about thy soul, that thou soldest him on Good-Friday last for a cup of Madeira and a cold capon's leg?

Prince. Sir John stands to his word, the devil shall have his bargain; for he was never yet a breaker of proverbs: he will give the devil his due.

Poins. Then art thou damned for keeping thy word with the devil.

Prince. Else he had been damned for cozening° the devil.

Poins. But, my lads, my lads, to-morrow morning, by four o'clock, early at Gadshill! there are pilgrims going to Canterbury with rich offer- 100 ings, and traders riding to London with fat purses: I have vizards° for you all; you have horses for yourselves: Gadshill lies to-night in Rochester: I have bespoke supper to-morrow night in Eastcheap: we may do it as secure as sleep. If you will go, I will stuff your purses full of crowns; if you will not, tarry at home and be hanged.

Falstaff. Hear ye, Yedward;° if I tarry at home and go not, I'll hang you for going.

Poins. You will, chops?°

Falstaff. Hal, wilt thou make one?

Prince. Who, I rob? I a thief? not I, by my faith. 110

Falstaff. There's neither honesty, manhood, nor good fellowship in thee, nor thou camest not of the blood royal, if thou darest not stand for ten shillings.

Prince. Well, then, once in my days I'll be a madcap.

Falstaff. Why, that's well said.

Prince. Well, come what will, I'll tarry at home.

Falstaff. By the Lord, I'll be a traitor then, when thou art king.

Prince. I care not.

Poins. Sir John, I prithee, leave the prince and me alone: I will lay him down such reasons for this adventure that he shall go. 120

84. vocation, a cant term for religious conversion. ***86. set a match,*** arranged a robbery. ***98.*** (***cozening,*** cheating.) ***101. vizards,*** masks. ***106. Yedward,*** Edward; a colloquialism. ***108. chops,*** apparently alluding to Falstaff's fat jaws.

Falstaff. Well, God give thee the spirit of persuasion° and him the ears of profiting,° that what thou speakest may move and what he hears may be believed, that the true prince may, for recreation sake, prove a false thief; for the poor abuses of the time want countenance. Farewell: you shall find me in Eastcheap.

Prince. Farewell, thou latter spring! farewell, Allhallown summer!°

(Exit Falstaff)

Poins. Now, my good sweet honey lord, ride with us to-morrow: I have a jest to execute that I cannot manage alone. Falstaff, Bardolph, Peto and Gadshill shall rob those men that we have already waylaid;
130 yourself and I will not be there; and when they have the booty, if you and I do not rob them, cut this head off from my shoulders.

Prince. How shall we part with them in setting forth?

Poins. Why, we will set forth before or after them, and appoint them a place of meeting, wherein it is at our pleasure to fail, and then will they adventure upon the exploit themselves; which they shall have no sooner achieved, but we'll set upon them.

Prince. Yea, but 'tis like that they will know us by our horses, by our habits° and by every other appointment, to be ourselves.

Poins. Tut! our horses they shall not see; I'll tie them in the wood;
140 our vizards we will change after we leave them: and, sirrah, I have cases° of buckram for the nonce, to immask our noted° outward garments.

Prince. Yea, but I doubt they will be too hard for us.

Poins. Well, for two of them, I know them to be as true-bred cowards as ever turned back; and for the third, if he fight longer than he sees reason, I'll forswear arms. The virtue of this jest will be, the incomprehensible lies that this same fat rogue will tell us when we meet at supper: how thirty, at least, he fought with; what wards, what blows, what extremities he endured; and in the reproof of this lies the jest.

150 *Prince.* Well, I'll go with thee: provide us all things necessary and meet me to-morrow night in Eastcheap; there I'll sup. Farewell.

Poins. Farewell, my lord. *(Exit)*

Prince. I know you all, and will awhile uphold
The unyoked humour° of your idleness:
Yet herein will I imitate the sun,
Who doth permit the base contagious clouds
To smother up his beauty from the world,
That, when he please again to be himself,
Being wanted, he may be more wonder'd at,

121-122. spirit of persuasion, ears of profiting, cant phrases of religious connotation. ***126. Allhallown summer.*** Falstaff's summer (his youth) has lasted to All Saints' Day, November 1st. ***138.*** (***habits,*** clothes.) ***141. cases,*** suits. ***noted,*** known. ***154.*** (***unyoked humour,*** unrestrained follies.)

By breaking through the foul and ugly mists 160
Of vapours that did seem to strangle him.
If all the year were playing holidays,
To sport would be as tedious as to work;
But when they seldom come, they wish'd for come,
And nothing pleaseth but rare accidents.
So, when this loose behaviour I throw off
And pay the debt I never promised,
By how much better than my word I am,
By so much shall I falsify men's hopes;
And like bright metal on a sullen ground, 170
My reformation, glittering o'er my fault,
Shall show more goodly and attract more eyes
Than that which hath no foil to set it off.
I'll so offend, to make offence a skill;
Redeeming time when men think least I will. *(Exit)*

Scene III. *London. The palace.*

(Enter the King, Northumberland, Worcester, Hotspur, Sir Walter Blunt, with others)

King. My blood hath been too cold and temperate,
Unapt to stir at these indignities,
And you have found me;° for accordingly
You tread upon my patience: but be sure
I will from henceforth rather be myself,
Mighty and to be fear'd, than my condition;°
Which hath been smooth as oil, soft as young down,
And therefore lost that title of respect
Which the proud soul ne'er pays but to the proud.

Worcester. Our house, my sovereign liege, little deserves 10
The scourge of greatness to be used on it;
And that same greatness too which our own hands
Have holp to make so portly.°

Northumberland. My lord,—

King. Worcester, get thee gone; for I do see
Danger and disobedience in thine eye:
O, sir, your presence is too bold and peremptory,
And majesty might never yet endure
The moody° frontier° of a servant brow.
You have good leave to leave us: when we need 20

3. found me, i. e., found me so. ***6.*** (***condition,*** disposition.) ***13. portly,*** prosperous, with a suggestion of overprosperity. ***19. moody,*** passionate, angry. ***19. frontier,*** outwork or fortification; here with play on the word *front* or *brow.*

Your use and counsel, we shall send for you. *(Exit Worcester)*
You were about to speak. *(To Northumberland)*
Northumberland. Yea, my good lord.
Those prisoners in your highness' name demanded,
Which Harry Percy here at Holmedon took,
Were, as he says, not with such strength denied
As is deliver'd to your majesty:
Either envy, therefore, or misprision°
Is guilty of this fault and not my son.
Hotspur. My liege, I did deny no prisoners.
30 But I remember, when the fight was done,
When I was dry with rage and extreme toil,
Breathless and faint, leaning upon my sword,
Came there a certain lord, neat, and trimly dress'd,
Fresh as a bridegroom; and his chin new reap'd
Show'd like a stubble-land at harvest-home;°
He was perfumed like a milliner;°
And 'twixt his finger and his thumb he held
A pouncet-box,° which ever and anon
He gave his nose and took 't away again;
40 Who therewith angry, when it next came there,
Took it in snuff; and still he smiled and talk'd,
And as the soldiers bore dead bodies by,
He call'd them untaught knaves, unmannerly,
To bring a slovenly unhandsome corse
Betwixt the wind and his nobility.
With many holiday° and lady° terms
He question'd me; amongst the rest, demanded
My prisoners in your majesty's behalf.
I then, all smarting with my wounds being cold,
50 To be so pester'd with a popinjay,°
Out of my grief and my impatience,
Answer'd neglectingly I know not what,
He should, or he should not; for he made me mad
To see him shine so brisk and smell so sweet
And talk so like a waiting-gentlewoman
Of guns and drums and wounds,—God save the mark!°—
And telling me the sovereign'st thing on earth
Was parmaceti° for an inward bruise;

27. misprision, misunderstanding. ***35. harvest-home,*** end of harvest, fields being neat and bare. ***36. milliner,*** man dealing in fancy articles. ***38. pouncet-box,*** perfume box with perforated lid. ***46.*** (***holiday,*** as opposed to working day, or plain English, phrases.) ***lady,*** ladylike. ***50. popinjay,*** parrot. ***56. God save the mark.*** Probably originally a formula to avert evil omen; here an expression of impatience. ***58. parmaceti,*** spermaceti, sperm from the whale.

And that it was great pity, so it was,
This villanous salt-petre should be digg'd 60
Out of the bowels of the harmless earth,
Which many a good tall fellow had destroy'd
So cowardly; and but for these vile guns,
He would himself have been a soldier.
This bald unjointed chat of his, my lord,
I answer'd indirectly, as I said;
And I beseech you, let not his report
Come current for an accusation
Betwixt my love and your high majesty.
Blunt. The circumstance consider'd, good my lord, 70
Whate'er Lord Harry Percy then had said
To such a person and in such a place,
At such a time, with all the rest retold,
May reasonably die and never rise
To do him wrong or any way impeach
What then he said, so he unsay it now.
King. Why, yet he doth deny his prisoners,
But with proviso and exception,
That we at our own charge shall ransom straight
His brother-in-law, the foolish Mortimer; 80
Who, on my soul, hath wilfully betray'd
The lives of those that he did lead to fight
Against that great magician, damn'd Glendower,
Whose daughter, as we hear, the Earl of March°
Hath lately married. Shall our coffers, then,
Be emptied to redeem a traitor home?
Shall we buy treason? and indent° with fears,
When they have lost and forfeited themselves?
No, on the barren mountains let him starve;
For I shall never hold that man my friend 90
Whose tongue shall ask me for one penny cost
To ransom home revolted Mortimer.
Hotspur. Revolted Mortimer!
He never did fall off, my sovereign liege,
But by the chance of war: to prove that true
Needs no more but one tongue for all those wounds,
Those mouthed wounds, which valiantly he took,
When on the gentle Severn's sedgy bank,

80-84. Mortimer, Earl of March. There were two Edmund Mortimers, Shakespeare confuses them and combines the stories. It was the uncle (1378-1409?) who was captured by Glendower and married Glendower's daughter; it was the nephew (1391-1425), fourth earl of March, who had been proclaimed heir to King Richard II. ***87.*** (***indent,*** make an agreement.)

In single opposition, hand to hand,
100 He did confound the best part of an hour
In changing hardiment° with great Glendower:
Three times they breathed and three times did they drink,
Upon agreement, of swift Severn's flood;
Who then, affrighted with their bloody looks,
Ran fearfully among the trembling reeds,
And hid his crisp head in the hollow bank
Bloodstained with these valiant combatants.
Never did base and rotten policy
Colour her working with such deadly wounds;
110 Nor never could the noble Mortimer
Receive so many, and all willingly:
Then let not him be slander'd with revolt.
King. Thou dost belie° him, Percy, thou dost belie him;
He never did encounter with Glendower:
I tell thee,
He durst as well have met the devil alone
As Owen Glendower for an enemy.
Art thou not ashamed? But, sirrah,° henceforth
Let me not hear you speak of Mortimer:
120 Send me your prisoners with the speediest means
Or you shall hear in such a kind from me
As will displease you. My Lord Northumberland,
We license your departure with your son.
Send us your prisoners, or you will hear of it.
(Exeunt King Henry, Blunt, and train)
Hotspur. An if the devil come and roar for them,
I will not send them: I will after straight
And tell him so; for I will ease my heart,
Albeit I make a hazard of my head.
Northumberland. What, drunk with choler?° stay and pause awhile:
Here comes your uncle.
(Re-enter Worcester)
130 *Hotspur.* Speak of Mortimer!
'Zounds, I will speak of him; and let my soul
Want mercy, if I do not join with him:
Yea, on his part I'll empty all these veins,
And shed my dear blood drop by drop in the dust,
But I will lift the down-trod Mortimer

101. hardiment, bravery, daring. ***113.*** (***belie,*** lie about.) ***118.*** (***sirrah,*** a form of address used towards the lower classes. Here, a deliberate insult by the King.) ***129.*** (***choler,*** anger.)

As high in the air as this unthankful king,
As this ingrate and canker'd° Bolingbroke.
Northumberland. Brother, the king hath made your nephew mad.
Worcester. Who struck this heat up after I was gone?
Hotspur. He will, forsooth, have all my prisoners; 140
And when I urged the ransom once again
Of my wife's brother, then his cheek look'd pale,
And on my face he turn'd an eye of death,
Trembling even at the name of Mortimer.
Worcester. I cannot blame him: was not he proclaim'd
By Richard that dead is the next of blood?
Northumberland. He was; I heard the proclamation:
And then it was when the unhappy king,—
Whose wrongs in us God pardon!—did set forth
Upon his Irish expedition; 150
From whence he intercepted did return
To be deposed and shortly murdered.°
Worcester. And for whose death we in the world's wide mouth
Live scandalized and foully spoken of.
Hotspur. But, soft, I pray you; did King Richard then
Proclaim my brother° Edmund Mortimer
Heir to the crown?
Northumberland. He did; myself did hear it.
Hotspur. Nay, then I cannot blame his cousin king,
That wish'd him on the barren mountains starve.
But shall it be, that you, that set the crown 160
Upon the head of this forgetful man
And for his sake wear the detested blot
Of murderous subornation,° shall it be,
That you a world of curses° undergo,
Being the agents, or base second means,
The cords, the ladder, or the hangman rather?
O, pardon me that I descend so low,
To show the line and the predicament°
Wherein you range under this subtle king;
Shall it for shame be spoken in these days, 170
Or fill up chronicles in time to come,
That men of your nobility and power
Did gage them both in an unjust behalf,

137. canker'd, spoiled, malignant. ***145-152. I . . . murdered.*** These lines and the dialogue as a whole serve to connect this play with *Richard III* and to make clear the political situation back of the revolt. ***156.*** (***brother,*** brother-in-law.) ***163. subornation,*** oath-breaking, treason. ***164. a world of curses.*** Treason against the king was treason against God. ***168. predicament,*** category.

As both of you—God pardon it!—have done,
To put down Richard, that sweet lovely rose,
And plant this thorn, this canker,° Bolingbroke?
And shall it in more shame be further spoken,
That you are fool'd, discarded and shook off
By him for whom these shames ye underwent?
180 No; yet time serves wherein you may redeem
Your banish'd honours and restore yourselves
Into the good thoughts of the world again,
Revenge the jeering and disdain'd° contempt
Of this proud king, who studies day and night
To answer all the debt he owes to you
Even with the bloody payment of your deaths:
Therefore, I say,—

Worcester. Peace, cousin, say no more:
And now I will unclasp a secret book,
And to your quick-conceiving discontents
190 I'll read you matter deep and dangerous,
As full of peril and adventurous spirit
As to o'er-walk a current roaring loud
On the unsteadfast footing of a spear.

Hotspur. If he fall in, good night! or sink or swim:
Send danger from the east unto the west,
So honour cross it from the north to south,
And let them grapple: O, the blood more stirs
To rouse a lion than to start a hare!

Northumberland. Imagination of some great exploit
200 Drives him beyond the bounds of patience.

Hotspur. By heaven, methinks it were an easy leap,
To pluck bright honour from the pale-faced moon,
Or dive into the bottom of the deep,
Where fathom-line could never touch the ground,
And pluck up drowned honour by the locks;
So he that doth redeem her thence might wear
Without corrival° all her dignities:
But out upon this half-faced° fellowship!

Worcester. He apprehends a world of figures here,
210 But not the form of what he should attend.
Good cousin, give me audience for a while.

Hotspur. I cry you mercy.

Worcester. Those same noble Scots

176. canker, canker rose, dog rose. ***183. disdain'd,*** disdainful. ***207. corrival,*** rival, competitor. ***208. half-faced,*** half-hearted.

That are your prisoners,—
Hotspur. I'll keep them all;
By God, he shall not have a Scot of them;
No, if a Scot would save his soul, he shall not:
I'll keep them, by this hand.
Worcester. You start away
And lend no ear unto my purposes.
Those prisoners you shall keep.
Hotspur. Nay, I will; that's flat:
He said he would not ransom Mortimer; 220
Forbad my tongue to speak of Mortimer;
But I will find him when he lies asleep,
And in his ear I'll holla 'Mortimer!'
Nay,
I'll have a starling shall be taught to speak
Nothing but 'Mortimer,' and give it him,
To keep his anger still in motion.°
Worcester. Hear you, cousin; a word.
Hotspur. All studies here I solemnly defy,
Save how to gall and pinch this Bolingbroke:
And that same sword-and-buckler° Prince of Wales, 230
But that I think his father loves him not
And would be glad he met with some mischance,
I would have him poison'd° with a pot of ale.
Worcester. Farewell, kinsman: I'll talk to you
When you are better temper'd to attend.
Northumberland. Why, what a wasp-stung and impatient fool
Art thou to break into this woman's mood,
Tying thine ear to no tongue but thine own!
Hotspur. Why, look you, I am whipp'd and scourged
with rods,
Nettled and stung with pismires,° when I hear 240
Of this vile politician,° Bolingbroke.
In Richard's time,—what do you call the place?—
A plague upon it, it is in Gloucestershire;
'Twas where the madcap duke his uncle kept,
His uncle York; where I first bow'd my knee
Unto this king of smiles, this Bolingbroke,—
'Sblood!—
When you and he came back from Ravenspurgh.

226. in motion, i.e., he will not allow the spirits of anger to settle or be diverted. ***230. sword-and-buckler,*** arms improper for a prince, who should carry rapier and dagger. ***233. poison'd.*** This has been called malicious; it is only part of Hotspur's madness. ***240. pismires,*** ants. ***241. politician,*** deceitful schemer.

Northumberland. At Berkley castle.
250 *Hotspur*. You say true:
Why, what a candy° deal of courtesy
This fawning greyhound then did proffer me!
Look, 'when his infant fortune came to age,'
And 'gentle Harry Percy,' and 'kind cousin;'
O, the devil take such cozeners!° God forgive me!
Good uncle, tell your tale; I have done.
Worcester. Nay, if you have not, to it again;
We will stay° your leisure.
Hotspur. I have done, i' faith.
Worcester. Then once more to your Scottish prisoners.
260 Deliver them up without their ransom straight,
And make the Douglas' son your only mean°
For powers in Scotland; which, for divers reasons
Which I shall send you written, be assured,
Will easily be granted. You, my lord, *(To Northumberland)*
Your son in Scotland being thus employ'd,
Shall secretly into the bosom creep
Of that same noble prelate, well beloved,
The archbishop.
Hotspur. Of York, is it not?
270 *Worcester*. True; who bears hard
His brother's death at Bristol, the Lord Scroop.
I speak not this in estimation,°
As what I think might be, but what I know
Is ruminated, plotted and set down,
And only stays but to behold the face
Of that occasion that shall bring it on.
Hotspur. I smell it: upon my life, it will do well.
Northumberland. Before the game is afoot, thou still let'st slip.
Hotspur. Why, it cannot choose but be a noble plot:
280 And then the power of Scotland and of York,
To join with Mortimer, ha?
Worcester. And so they shall.
Hotspur. In faith, it is exceedingly well aim'd.
Worcester. And 'tis no little reason bids us speed,
To save our heads by raising of a head;°
For, bear ourselves as even as we can,
The king will always think him in our debt,
And think we think ourselves unsatisfied,

251. candy, sugared flattering. ***255. cozeners,*** cheats, with pun on "cousins." ***258.*** (***stay,*** await.) ***261. mean, i.e.,*** means of procuring. ***272. estimation,*** guesswork. ***284.*** (***head,*** army.)

Till he hath found a time to pay us home:
And see already how he doth begin
To make us strangers to his looks of love. 290
Hotspur. He does, he does: we'll be revenged on him.
Worcester. Cousin, farewell: no further go in this
Than I by letters shall direct your course.
When time is ripe, which will be suddenly,
I'll steal to Glendower and Lord Mortimer;
Where you and Douglas and our powers at once,
As I will fashion it, shall happily meet,
To bear our fortunes in our own strong arms,
Which now we hold at much uncertainty.
Northumberland. Farewell, good brother: we shall thrive, I trust. 300
Hotspur. Uncle, adieu: O, let the hours be short
Till fields and blows and groans applaud our sport! *(Exeunt)*

Act II

Scene I. *Rochester. An inn yard*

(Enter a Carrier° with a lantern in his hand)

1st Carrier. Heigh-ho! an it be not four by the day,° I'll be hanged: Charles' wain° is over the new chimney, and yet our horse° not packed. What, ostler!°

Ostler. (Within) Anon, anon.

1st Carrier. I prithee, Tom, beat Cut's saddle,° put a few flocks° in the point;° poor jade, is wrung in the withers out of all cess.°

(Enter another Carrier)

2nd Carrier. Peas and beans are as dank here as a dog, and that is the next° way to give poor jades the bots:° this house is turned upside down since Robin Ostler died.

1st Carrier. Poor fellow, never joyed since the price of oats rose; 10 it was the death of him.

2nd Carrier. I think this be the most villanous house in all London road for fleas: I am stung like a tench.

1st Carrier. Like a tench!° by the mass, there is ne'er a king christen° could be better bit than I have been since the first cock.

Stage Directions: ***Carrier,*** one whose trade was conveying goods, usually by pack horse. ***1. by the day,*** by the sun. ***2. Charles' wain,*** the constellation of the Great Bear. ***horse,*** horses. ***3.*** (***ostler,*** man in charge of the inn's stables.) ***5. Cut's saddle,*** packsaddle of the horse named *Cut,* meaning "bob-tailed." ***flocks,*** locks of wool. ***6. point, i.e.,*** of the saddle. ***cess,*** measure, estimate. ***8. next,*** nearest, quickest. ***bots,*** a disease of horses. ***14. tench,*** a kind of fish; probably an allusion to an ancient belief that the spots on certain fishes were due to flea bites. ***christen,*** in Christendom.

2nd Carrier. Why, they will allow us ne'er a jordan,° and then we leak in your chimney; and your chamber-lie breeds fleas like a loach.

1st Carrier. What, ostler! come away and be hanged! come away.

2nd Carrier. I have a gammon° of bacon and two razes° of ginger,
20 to be delivered as far as Charing-cross.

1st Carrier. God's body! the turkeys in my pannier° are quite starved. What, ostler! A plague on thee! hast thou never an eye in thy head? canst not hear? An 'twere not as good deed as drink, to break the pate on thee, I am a very villain. Come, and be hanged! hast no faith in thee?
(Enter Gadshill)

Gadshill. Good morrow, carriers. What 's o'clock?

1st Carrier. I think it be two o'clock.

Gadshill. I prithee, lend me thy lantern, to see my gelding in the stable.

1st Carrier. Nay, by God, soft; I know a trick worth two of that, i'
30 faith.

Gadshill. I pray thee, lend me thine.

2nd Carrier. Ay, when? canst tell?° Lend me thy lantern, quoth he? marry, I'll see thee hanged first.

Gadshill. Sirrah carrier, what time do you mean to come to London?

2nd Carrier. Time enough to go to bed with a candle, I warrant thee. Come neighbour Mugs, we'll call up the gentlemen: they will along with company, for they have great charge.° *(Exeunt Carriers)*

Gadshill. What, ho! chamberlain!°

Chamberlain. (Within) At hand, quoth pick-purse.°

40 *Gadshill.* That's even as fair as—at hand, quoth the chamberlain; for thou variest no more from picking of purses than giving direction doth from labouring; thou layest the plot how.
(Enter Chamberlain)

Chamberlain. Good morrow, Master Gadshill. It holds current° that I told you yesternight: there 's a franklin° in the wild of Kent° hath brought three hundred marks with him in gold: I heard him tell it to one of his company last night at supper; a kind of auditor; one that hath abundance of charge too, God knows what. They are up already, and call for eggs and butter: they will away presently.

Gadshill. Sirrah, if they meet not with Saint Nicholas' clerks,° I'll
50 give thee this neck.

16. (***jordan,*** chamber pot.) ***19. gammon,*** side. ***razes,*** roots. ***21. pannier,*** basket. ***32. Ay, when? canst tell?*** Don't you wish I would? ***37.*** (***great charge,*** much money.) ***38.*** (***chamberlain,*** man in charge of the inn's bedrooms.) ***39. At hand, quoth pick-purse,*** slang expression for "Coming immediately." Gadshill's reply shows the chamberlain's alliance with the robbers. ***43. holds current,*** holds true. ***44. franklin,*** a farmer owning his own land. ***wild of Kent,*** weald (wooded region) of Kent. ***49. Saint Nicholas' clerks,*** highwaymen. St. Nicholas was vulgarly supposed the patron of thieves.

Chamberlain. No, I'll none of it: I pray thee, keep that for the hangman; for I know thou worshippest Saint Nicholas as truly as a man of falsehood may.

Gadshill. What talkest thou to me of the hangman? if I hang, I'll make a fat pair of gallows; for if I hang, old Sir John hangs with me, and thou knowest he is no starveling. Tut! there are other Trojans° that thou dreamest not of, the which for sport sake are content to do the profession some grace; that would, if matters should be looked into, for their own credit sake, make all whole. I am joined with no foot landrakers,° no long-staff sixpenny strikers,° none of these mad mustachio purple-hued malt-worms;° but with nobility and tranquillity, burgomasters and great oneyers,° such as can hold in, such as will strike sooner than speak, and speak sooner than drink, and drink sooner than pray: and yet, 'zounds, I lie; for they pray continually to their saint, the commonwealth; or rather, not pray to her, but prey on her, for they ride up and down on her and make her their boots.° 60

Chamberlain. What, the commonwealth their boots? will she hold out water in foul way?

Gadshill. She will, she will; justice hath liquored° her. We steal as in a castle, cocksure; we have the receipt of fern-seed,° we walk invisible. 70

Chamberlain. Nay, by my faith, I think you are more beholding to the night than to fern-seed for your walking invisible.

Gadshill. Give me thy hand: thou shalt have a share in our purchase, as I am a true man.

Chamberlain. Nay, rather let me have it, as you are a false thief.

Gadshill. Go to; 'homo' is a common name to all men. Bid the ostler bring my gelding out of the stable. Farewell, you muddy knave.

(Exeunt)

Scene II. *The highway, near Gadshill*°

(Enter Prince Henry and Poins.)

Poins. Come, shelter, shelter: I have removed Falstaff's horse, and he frets like a gummed velvet.°

Prince. Stand close.

(Enter Falstaff)

56. Trojans, slang for "thieves." ***59-60. foot land-rakers,*** footpads. ***60. long-staff sixpenny strikers,*** robbers with long staves who would knock down their victims for sixpence. ***60-61. mustachio purple-hued malt-worms,*** common drunkards with mustaches stained with drink. ***62. oneyers,*** many conjectures; possibly, a coinage from *ones* with pun on *owner*. ***66. boots,*** booty, with pun on "boots." ***69. liquored,*** made waterproof by oiling, and made drunk. ***70. of fern-seed,*** i.e., of becoming invisible, since fern seed was popularly supposed to render its possessor invisible. ***(Gadshill,*** here used not as the character, but as a location.) ***2. (gummed velvet,*** cheap velvet, treated with gum to stiffen it, frayed quickly, i.e., Falstaff is frazzled.)

Falstaff. Poins! Poins, and be hanged! Poins!

Prince. Peace, ye fat-kidneyed rascal! what a brawling dost thou keep!

Falstaff. Where 's Poins, Hal?

Prince. He is walked up to the top of the hill: I'll go seek him.

Falstaff. I am accursed to rob in that thief's company: the rascal hath removed my horse, and tied him I know not where. If I travel
10 but four foot by the squier° further afoot, I shall break my wind. Well, I doubt not but to die a fair death for all this, if I 'scape hanging for killing that rogue. I have forsworn his company hourly any time this two and twenty years, and yet I am bewitched with the rogue's company. If the rascal have not given me medicines° to make me love him, I'll be hanged; it could not be else; I have drunk medicines. Poins! Hal! a plague upon you both! Bardolph! Peto! I'll starve ere I'll rob a foot further. An 'twere not as good a deed as drink, to turn true man° and to leave these rogues, I am the veriest varlet° that ever chewed with a tooth. Eight yards of uneven ground is threescore and ten miles afoot
20 with me; and the stony-hearted villains know it well enough: a plague upon it when thieves cannot be true one to another! *(They whistle.)* Whew! A plague upon you all! Give me my horse, you rogues; give me my horse, and be hanged!

Prince. Peace, ye fat-guts! lie down; lay thine ear close to the ground and list if thou canst hear the tread of travellers.

Falstaff. Have you any levers to lift me up again, being down? 'Sblood, I'll not bear mine own flesh so far afoot again for all the coin in thy father's exchequer. What a plague mean ye to colt° me thus?

Prince. Thou liest; thou art not colted, thou art uncolted.

30 *Falstaff.* I prithee, good Prince Hal, help me to my horse, good king's son.

Prince. Out, ye rogue! shall I be your ostler?

Falstaff. Go hang thyself in thine own heir-apparent garters!° If I be ta'en, I'll peach for this. An I have not ballads made on you all and sung to filthy tunes, let a cup of sack be my poison: when a jest is so forward, and afoot too! I hate it.

(Enter Gadshill, Bardolph and Peto with him)

Gadshill. Stand.

Falstaff. So I do, against my will.

Poins. O, 'tis our setter:° I know his voice. Bardolph, what news?

40 *Bardolph.* Case ye, case ye;° on with your vizards: there's money of the king's coming down the hill; 'tis going to the king's exchequer.

10. squier, square, measure. ***14. medicines,*** love potions. ***17. turn true man,*** turn honest man; possibly, turn informer. ***18.*** (***varlet,*** knave.) ***28. colt,*** cheat. ***33. garters,*** an allusion to a proverbial expression about hanging oneself in one's garters, with a pun on the Order of the Garter. ***39. setter,*** arranger of the robbery. ***40. Case ye,*** put on your disguises.

Falstaff. You lie, ye rogue; 'tis going to the king's tavern.

Gadshill. There's enough to make us all.

Falstaff. To be hanged.

Prince. Sirs, you four shall front them in the narrow lane; Ned Poins and I will walk lower: if they 'scape from your encounter, then they light on us.

Peto. How many be there of them?

Gadshill. Some eight or ten.

Falstaff. 'Zounds, will they not rob us? 50

Prince. What, a coward, Sir John Paunch?

Falstaff. Indeed, I am not John of Gaunt, your grandfather; but yet no coward, Hal.

Prince. Well, we leave that to the proof.

Poins. Sirrah Jack, thy horse stands behind the hedge: when thou needest him, there thou shalt find him. Farewell, and stand fast.

Falstaff. Now cannot I strike him, if I should be hanged.

Prince. Ned, where are our disguises?

Poins. Here, hard by: stand close. *(Exeunt Prince and Poins)*

Falstaff. Now, my masters, happy man be his dole,° say I: every man to his business. 60

(Enter the Travellers)

1st Traveller. Come, neighbour: the boy shall lead our horses down the hill; we'll walk afoot awhile, and ease our legs.

Thieves. Stand!

Travellers. Jesus bless us!

Falstaff. Strike; down with them; cut the villains' throats: ah! whoreson caterpillars!° bacon-fed knaves! they hate us youth: down with them; fleece them.

Travellers. O, we are undone, both we and ours for ever!

Falstaff. Hang ye, gorbellied° knaves, are ye undone? No, ye fat chuffs;° I would your store were here! On, bacons,° on! What, ye knaves! young men must live. You are grandjurors,° are ye? we'll jure ye, 'faith. *(Here they rob them and bind them.)* *(Exeunt)* 70

(Re-enter Prince Henry and Poins)

Prince. The thieves have bound the true men. Now could thou and I rob the thieves and go merrily to London, it would be argument for a week, laughter for a month and a good jest for ever.

Poins. Stand close; I hear them coming.

(Enter the Thieves again)

Falstaff. Come, my masters, let us share, and then to horse before day. An the Prince and Poins be not two arrant cowards, there's no

60. *happy man be his dole,* may happiness be his portion. **67. *caterpillars,*** those who thrive off the commonwealth. **70. *gorbellied,*** big-bellied. **71. *chuffs,*** churls, rich but miserly. ***bacons,*** swine. **72.** (***grandjurors,*** i.e., very respectable.)

80 equity° stirring: there 's no more valour in that Poins than in a wild-duck.

Prince. Your money!

Poins. Villains! *(As they are sharing, the Prince and Poins set upon them; they all run away; and Falstaff, after a blow or two, runs away too, leaving the booty behind them.)*

Prince. Got with much ease. Now merrily to horse:
The thieves are all scatter'd and possess'd with fear
So strongly that they dare not meet each other;
Each takes his fellow for an officer.
90 Away, good Ned. Falstaff sweats to death,
And lards the lean earth° as he walks along:
Were 't not for laughing, I should pity him.

Poins. How the fat rogue roar'd! *(Exeunt)*

Scene III. *Warkworth castle*

(Enter Hotspur, solus, reading a letter)

Hotspur. 'But, for mine own part, my lord, I could be well contented to be there, in respect of the love I bear your house.'° He could be contented: why is he not, then? In respect of the love he bears our house: he shows in this, he loves his own barn better than he loves our house. Let me see some more. 'The purpose you undertake is dangerous;'—why, that's certain: 'tis dangerous to take a cold, to sleep, to drink; but I tell you, my lord fool, out of this nettle, danger, we pluck this flower, safety. 'The purpose you undertake is dangerous; the friends you have named uncertain; the time itself unsorted; and your whole
10 plot too light for the counterpoise of so great an opposition.' Say you so, say you so? I say unto you again, you are a shallow cowardly hind°, and you lie. What a lack-brain is this! By the Lord, our plot is a good plot as ever was laid; our friends true and constant: a good plot, good friends, and full of expectation; an excellent plot, very good friends. What a frosty-spirited rogue is this! Why, my lord of York commends the plot and the general course of the action. 'Zounds, an I were now by this rascal, I could brain him with his lady's fan. Is there not my father, my uncle and myself? lord Edmund Mortimer, my lord of York and Owen Glendower? is there not besides the Douglas? have I not all their letters
20 to meet me in arms by the ninth of the next month? and are they not some of them set forward already? What a pagan rascal is this! an infidel! Ha! you shall see now in very sincerity of fear and cold heart, will he to the king and lay open all our proceedings. O, I could divide

80. equity, justice. ***91. lards the lean earth,*** an allusion to the practice on the part of butchers of inserting fat into lean meat. "Sweat" was not distinguished from fat. **2.** (***house,*** here: family.) ***11.*** (***hind,*** female deer, i.e., timid.)

myself and go to buffets,° for moving such a dish of skim milk with so honourable an action! Hang him! let him tell the king: we are prepared. I will set forward to-night.
(Enter Lady Percy)
How now, Kate! I must leave you within these two hours.
Lady Percy. O, my good lord, why are you thus alone?
For what offence have I this fortnight been
A banish'd woman from my Harry's bed? 30
Tell me, sweet lord, what is 't that takes from thee
Thy stomach,° pleasure and thy golden sleep?
Why dost thou bend thine eyes upon the earth,
And start so often when thou sit'st alone?
Why hast thou lost the fresh blood in thy cheeks;
And given my treasures and my rights of thee
To thick-eyed musing and cursed melancholy?
In thy faint slumbers I by thee have watch'd,
And heard thee murmur tales of iron wars;
Speak terms of manage to thy bounding steed; 40
Cry 'Courage! to the field!' And thou hast talk'd
Of sallies and retires, of trenches, tents,
Of palisadoes, frontiers, parapets,
Of basilisks,° of cannon, culverin,°
Of prisoners' ransom and of soldiers slain,
And all the currents° of a heady fight.
Thy spirit within thee hath been so at war
And thus hath so bestirr'd thee in thy sleep,
That beads of sweat have stood upon thy brow,
Like bubbles in a late-disturbed stream; 50
And in thy face strange motions have appear'd,
Such as we see when men restrain their breath
On some great sudden hest. O, what portents are these?
Some heavy business hath my lord in hand,
And I must know it, else he loves me not.
Hotspur. What, ho!
(Enter Servant)
Is Gilliams with packet gone?
Servant. He is, my lord, an hour ago.
Hotspur. Hath Butler brought those horses from the sheriff?
Servant. One horse, my lord, he brought even now.
Hotspur. What horse? a roan, a crop-ear, is it not? 60
Servant. It is, my lord.

24. (***go to buffets,*** come to blows.) **32.** (***stomach,*** appetite.) **44.** ***basilisks,*** large cannon. ***culverin,*** long cannon. **46.** ***currents,*** occurrences.

Hotspur. That roan shall be my throne.
Well, I will back him straight: O esperance!°
Bid Butler lead him forth into the park. *(Exit Servant)*
Lady Percy. But hear you, my lord.
Hotspur. What say'st thou, my lady?
Lady Percy. What is it carries you away?
Hotspur. Why, my horse, my love, my horse.
Lady Percy. Out, you mad-headed ape!
A weasel hath not such a deal of spleen
70 As you are toss'd with. In faith,
I'll know your business, Harry, that I will.
I fear my brother Mortimer doth stir
About his title, and hath sent for you
To line his enterprize: but if you go,—
Hotspur. So far afoot, I shall be weary, love.
Lady Percy. Come, come, you paraquito,° answer me
Directly unto this question that I ask:
In faith, I'll break thy little finger,° Harry,
An if thou wilt not tell me all things true.
80 *Hotspur.* Away,
Away, you trifler! Love! I love thee not,
I care not for thee, Kate: this is no world
To play with mammets° and to tilt with lips:
We must have bloody noses and crack'd crowns,°
And pass them current too. God's me, my horse!
What say'st thou, Kate? what would'st thou have with me?
Lady Percy. Do you not love me? do you not, indeed?
Well, do not then; for since you love me not,
I will not love myself. Do you not love me?
90 Nay, tell me if you speak in jest or no.
Hotspur. Come, wilt thou see me ride?
And when I am o' horseback, I will swear
I love thee infinitely. But hark you, Kate:
I must not have you henceforth question me
Whither I go, nor reason whereabout:
Whither I must, I must; and, to conclude,
This evening must I leave you, gentle Kate.
I know you wise, but yet no farther wise
Than Harry Percy's wife: constant you are,
100 But yet a woman: and for secrecy,

62. esperance, hope; the motto of the Percy family. ***76. paraquito,*** little parrot; term of endearment. ***78. break thy little finger.*** She probably squeezes his folded little finger. ***83. mammets,*** dolls; or else breasts. ***84. crowns,*** obvious pun on the coin called a "crown."

No lady closer; for I well believe
Thou wilt not utter what thou dost not know;
And so far will I trust thee, gentle Kate.
Lady Percy. How! so far?
Hotspur. Not an inch further. But hark you, Kate:
Whither I go, thither shall you go too;
To-day will I set forth, to-morrow you.
Will this content you, Kate?
Lady Percy. It must of force.° *(Exeunt)*

Scene IV. *The Boar's-Head Tavern, Eastcheap*

(Enter the Prince, and Poins)

Prince. Ned, prithee, come out of that fat° room, and lend me thy hand to laugh a little.

Poins. Where hast been, Hal?

Prince. With three or four loggerheads° amongst three or four score hogsheads. I have sounded the very base-string of humility. Sirrah, I am sworn brother to a leash of drawers;° and can call them all by their christen names, as Tom, Dick, and Francis. They take it already upon their salvation, that though I be but Prince of Wales, yet I am the king of courtesy; and tell me flatly I am no proud Jack, like Falstaff, but a Corinthian,° a lad of mettle, a good boy, by the Lord, so they call me, and when I am king of England, I shall command all the good lads in Eastcheap. They call drinking deep, dyeing scarlet; and when you breathe in your watering,° they cry 'hem!' and bid you play it off.° To conclude, I am so good a proficient in one quarter of an hour, that I can drink with any tinker in his own language° during my life. I tell thee, Ned, thou hast lost much honour, that thou wert not with me in this action. But, sweet Ned,—to sweeten which name of Ned, I give thee this pennyworth of sugar, clapped even now into my hand by an under-skinker,° one that never spake other English in his life than 'Eight shillings and sixpence,' and 'You are welcome,' with this shrill addition, 'Anon, anon, sir! Score a pint of bastard° in the Half-moon,'° or so. But, Ned, to drive away the time till Falstaff come, I prithee, do thou stand in some by-room, while I question my puny° drawer to what

108. It must of force. Some critics have unnecessarily seen in this interview evidence of cruelty on Hotspur's part and lack of marital confidence. ***1. fat,*** vat. ***4. loggerheads,*** blockheads. ***6. leash of drawers,*** i.e., three waiters (like three greyhounds). ***10. Corinthian,*** gay fellow, with suggestion of profligacy. ***13.*** (***watering,*** drinking.) (***play it off,*** drink it down.) ***15. tinker. . .language.*** Tinkers' language was cant or jargon, and tinkers were proverbial drinkers. ***19. under-skinker,*** under-tapster. ***21. bastard,*** sweet Spanish wine. ***Half-moon,*** name of a room in the inn. ***23. puny,*** in the ordinary sense with a pun on the original *puisné*, younger son, applied to the second drawer.

end he gave me the sugar; and do thou never leave calling 'Francis,' that his tale to me may be nothing but 'Anon.' Step aside, and I'll show thee a precedent.°

Poins. Francis!

Prince. Thou art perfect.

Poins. Francis! *(Exit Poins)*

(Enter Francis)

30 *Francis.* Anon, anon, sir. Look down into the Pomgarnet, Ralph.

Prince. Come hither, Francis.

Francis. My lord?

Prince. How long hast thou to serve, Francis?

Francis. Forsooth, five years, and as much as to—

Poins. (Within) Francis!

Francis. Anon, anon, sir.

Prince. Five year! by 'r lady, a long lease for the clinking of pewter. But, Francis, darest thou be so valiant as to play the coward with thy indenture and show it a fair pair of heels and run from it?

40 *Francis.* O Lord, sir, I'll be sworn upon all the books in England, I could find in my heart.

Poins. (Within) Francis!

Francis. Anon, sir.

Prince. How old art thou, Francis?

Francis. Let me see—about Michaelmas next I shall be—

Poins. (Within) Francis!

Francis. Anon, sir. Pray stay a little, my lord.

Prince. Nay, but hark you, Francis: for the sugar thou gavest me, 'twas a pennyworth, was 't not?

50 *Francis.* O Lord, I would it had been two!

Prince. I will give thee for it a thousand pound: ask me when thou wilt, and thou shalt have it.

Poins. (Within) Francis!

Francis. Anon, anon.

Prince. Anon, Francis? No, Francis; but to-morrow, Francis; or Francis, o'Thursday; or indeed, Francis, when thou wilt. But, Francis!

Francis. My lord?

Prince. Wilt thou rob this leathern jerkin, crystal-button, not-
60 pated,° agate-ring, puke-stocking,° caddis-garter,° smooth-tongue, Spanish-pouch,—

Francis. O Lord, sir, who do you mean?

26. precedent, example. ***59-60. not-pated,*** crop-haired. ***60. puke-stocking,*** dark-colored stocking. ***caddis-garter,*** worsted garter. Since garters were worn in sight, they needed to be of better stuff than common worsted. The prince's epithets seem to apply to the vintner, the boy's master.

Prince. Why, then, your brown bastard is your only drink; for look you, Francis, your white canvas doublet will sully: in Barbary, sir, it cannot come to so much.°

Francis. What, sir?

Poins. (Within) Francis!

Prince. Away, you rogue! dost thou not hear them call? *(Here they both call him; the drawer stands amazed, not knowing which way to go.)*

(Enter Vintner)

Vintner. What, standest thou still, and hearest such a calling? Look to the guests within. *(Exit Francis)* My lord, old Sir John, with half-a-dozen more, are at the door: shall I let them in? 70

Prince. Let them alone awhile, and then open the door. *(Exit Vintner.)* Poins!

(Re-enter Poins)

Poins. Anon, anon, sir.

Prince. Sirrah, Falstaff and the rest of the thieves are at the door: shall we be merry?

Poins. As merry as crickets, my lad. But hark ye; what cunning match have you made with this jest of the drawer? come, what 's the issue?

Prince. I am now of all humours that have showed themselves humours since the old days of goodman° Adam to the pupil age° of this present twelve o' clock at midnight. 80

(Re-enter Francis)

What's o'clock, Francis?

Francis. Anon, anon, sir. *(Exit)*

Prince. That ever this fellow should have fewer words than a parrot, and yet the son of a woman! His industry is up-stairs and down-stairs; his eloquence the parcel° of a reckoning. I am not yet of Percy's mind, the Hotspur of the north; he that kills me some six or seven dozen of Scots at a breakfast, washes his hands, and says to his wife 'Fie upon this quiet life! I want work.' 'O my sweet Harry,' says she, 'how many hast thou killed to-day?' 'Give my roan horse a drench,' says he; and answers 'Some fourteen,' an hour after; 'a trifle, a trifle.' I prithee, call in Falstaff: I'll play Percy, and that damned brawn shall play Dame Mortimer his wife. 'Rivo!'° says the drunkard. Call in ribs, call in tallow. 90

(Enter Falstaff, Gadshill, Bardolph, and Peto; Francis following with wine)

Poins. Welcome, Jack: where hast thou been?

Falstaff. A plague of all cowards, I say, and a vengeance too! marry, and amen! Give me a cup of sack, boy. Ere I lead this life long, I'll

65. Why. . .much. The prince talks complete nonsense in order to bewilder Francis. ***81. goodman,*** a sort of familiar title. ***pupil age,*** i.e. the day is young. ***87. parcel,*** item. ***94.*** (***Rivo,*** a drinker's exclamation, a toast.)

sew nether stocks° and mend them and foot them too. A plague of all
100 cowards! Give me a cup of sack, rogue. Is there no virtue extant?
(He drinks.)

Prince. Didst thou never see Titan° kiss a dish of butter? pitiful-hearted Titan,° that melted at the sweet tale of the sun's! if thou didst, they behold that compound.

Falstaff. You rogue, here's lime in this sack° too: there is nothing but roguery to be found in villanous man: yet a coward is worse than a cup of sack with lime in it. A villanous coward! Go thy ways, old Jack; die when thou wilt, if manhood, good manhood, be not forgot upon the face of the earth, then am I a shotten herring.° There live not three good
110 men unhanged in England; and one of them is fat and grows old: God help the while! a bad world, I say. I would I were a weaver;° I could sing psalms or any thing. A plague of all cowards, I say still.

Prince. How now, wool-sack! what mutter you?

Falstaff. A king's son! If I do not beat thee out of thy kingdom with a dagger of lath,° and drive all thy subjects afore thee like a flock of wild-geese, I'll never wear hair on my face more. You Prince of Wales!

Prince. Why, you whoreson round man, what 's the matter?

Falstaff. Are not you a coward? answer me to that: and Poins there?

Poins. 'Zounds, ye fat paunch, and ye call me coward, by the Lord,
120 I'll stab thee.

Falstaff. I call thee coward! I'll see thee damned ere I call thee coward: but I would give a thousand pound I could run as fast as thou canst.° You are straight enough in the shoulders, you care not who sees your back: call you that backing of your friends? A plague upon such backing! give me them that will face me. Give me a cup of sack: I am a rogue, if I drunk to-day.

Prince. O villain! thy lips are scarce wiped since thou drunkest last.

Falstaff. All 's one for that. *(He drinks.)* A plague of all cowards, still say I.

130 *Prince.* What 's the matter?

Falstaff. What 's the matter! there be four of us here have ta'en a thousand pound this day morning.

Prince. Where is it, Jack? where is it?

Falstaff. Where is it! taken from us it is: a hundred upon poor four of us.

Prince. What, a hundred, man?

99. nether stocks, stockings. ***102.*** (***Titan,*** the sun.) ***102-103. pitiful-hearted Titan.*** Theobald suggested *butter* for *Titan,* which still seems the best way to explain this apparently contradictory passage. ***105. lime in the sack,*** i.e. used as a preservative. ***109. shotten herring,*** a herring that has cast its roe and is thin. ***111. weaver,*** allusion to psalm-singing Protestants from Flanders, mainly weavers. ***115.*** (***dagger of lath,*** a wooden imitation dagger.) ***121-123. I call. . .canst.*** This is a typical example of Falstaff's method of turning aside an issue and at the same time maintaining his point.

Falstaff. I am a rogue, if I were not at half-sword° with a dozen of them two hours together. I have 'scaped by miracle. I am eight times thrust through the doublet, four through the hose; my buckler cut through and through; my sword hacked like a hand-saw—ecce signum!° 140
I never dealt better since I was a man: all would not do. A plague of all cowards! Let them speak: if they speak more or less than truth, they are villains and the sons of darkness.

Prince. Speak, sirs; how was it?

Gadshill. We four set upon some dozen—

Falstaff. Sixteen at least, my lord.

Gadshill. And bound them.

Peto. No, no, they were not bound.

Falstaff. You rogue, they were bound, every man of them; or I am a Jew else, an Ebrew Jew. 150

Gadshill. As we were sharing, some six or seven fresh men set upon us—

Falstaff. And unbound the rest, and then come in the other.

Prince. What, fought you with them all?

Falstaff. All! I know not what you call all; but if I fought not with fifty of them, I am a bunch of radish: if there were not two or three and fifty upon poor old Jack, then am I no two-legged creature.

Prince. Pray God you have not murdered some of them.

Falstaff. Nay, that 's past praying for: I have peppered two of them; two I am sure I have paid, two rogues in buckram° suits. I tell thee 160
what, Hal, if I tell thee a lie, spit in my face, call me horse. Thou knowest my old ward;° here I lay, and thus I bore my point. Four rogues in buckram let drive at me

Prince. What, four? thou saidst but two even now.

Falstaff. Four, Hal; I told thee four.

Poins. Ay, ay, he said four.

Falstaff. These four came all a-front, and mainly° thrust at me. I made me no more ado but took all their seven points in my target,° thus.

Prince. Seven? why, there were but four even now. 170

Falstaff. In buckram?

Poins. Ay, four, in buckram suits.

Falstaff. Seven, by these hilts, or I am a villain else.

Prince. Prithee, let him alone; we shall have more anon.

Falstaff. Dost thou hear me, Hal?

Prince. Ay, and mark thee too, Jack.

137. *half-sword,* fighting at close quarters. **140. *ecce signum,*** behold the proof; familiar words from the Mass. **160. *buckram,*** coarse linen cloth stiffened. **162. *ward,*** guard in fencing. **167. *mainly,*** powerfully. **168. *target,*** shield.

Falstaff. Do so, for it is worth the listening to. These nine in buckram that I told thee of—

Prince. So, two more already.

180 *Falstaff.* Their points° being broken,—

Poins. Down fell their hose.

Falstaff. Began to give me ground: but I followed me° close, came in foot and hand; and with a thought seven of the eleven I paid.

Prince. O monstrous! eleven buckram men grown out of two!

Falstaff. But, as the devil would have it, three misbegotten knaves in Kendal green° came at my back and let drive at me; for it was so dark, Hal, that thou couldst not see thy hand.

Prince. These lies are like their father that begets them; gross as a mountain, open, palpable. Why, thou clay-brained guts, thou knotty-190 pated fool, thou whoreson, obscene, greasy tallow-catch,°—

Falstaff. What, art thou mad? art thou mad? is not the truth the truth?

Prince. Why, how couldst thou know these men in Kendal green, when it was so dark thou couldst not see thy hand? come, tell us your reason: what sayest thou to this?

Poins. Come, your reason, Jack, your reason.

Falstaff. What, upon compulsion? 'Zounds, an I were at the strappado, or all the racks° in the world, I would not tell you on compulsion. Give you a reason on compulsion! if reasons were as plentiful as black-200 berries,° I would give no man a reason upon compulsion, I.

Prince. I'll be no longer guilty of this sin; this sanguine coward, this bed-presser, this horseback-breaker, this huge hill of flesh,—

Falstaff. 'Sblood, you starveling, you elf-skin, you dried neat's tongue, you bull's pizzle, you stock-fish!° O for breath to utter what is like thee! you tailor's-yard, you sheath, you bow-case, you vile standing-tuck,°—

Prince. Well, breathe awhile, and then to it again: and when thou hast tired thyself in base comparisons, hear me speak but this.

Poins. Mark, Jack.

210 *Prince.* We two saw you four set on four and bound them, and were masters of their wealth. Mark now, how a plain tale shall put you down. Then did we two set on you four; and, with a word, out-faced° you from your prize, and have it; yea, and can show it you here in the house:

180. points. Falstaff uses *points* to mean "swords"; Poins' reply introduces a pun on the same word meaning the "laces" by which the hose were attached to the doublet and so supported. ***182. followed me,*** a sort of reflexive or middle voice. ***186. Kendal green,*** green cloth worn by foresters. ***190. tallow-catch,*** explained as "tallow-tub," and as "tallow-keech," a roll of fat delivered by the butcher to the tallow chandler. ***197-198.*** (***strappado, racks,*** forms of torture.) ***199-200. reason. . .blackberries.*** Falstaff not only avoids the issue, but also turns it into a jest by punning on the word "raisins," which was pronounced nearly like *reasons.* ***204. stock-fish,*** dried cod. ***205-206. standing-tuck,*** rapier standing on end. ***212. out-faced,*** frightened.

and, Falstaff, you carried your guts away as nimbly, with as quick dexterity, and roared for mercy and still run and roared, as ever I heard bull-calf. What a slave art thou, to hack thy sword as thou hast done, and then say it was in fight! What trick, what device, what starting-hole,° canst thou now find out to hide thee from this open and apparent shame?

Poins. Come, let's hear, Jack; what trick hast thou now? 220

Falstaff. By the Lord, I knew ye as well as he that made ye. Why, hear you, my masters: was it for me to kill the heir-apparent? should I turn upon the true prince? why, thou knowest I am as valiant as Hercules: but beware instinct; the lion will not touch the true prince. Instinct is a great matter; I was now a coward on instinct. I shall think the better of myself and thee during my life; I for a valiant lion, and thou for a true prince. But, by the Lord, lads, I am glad you have the money. Hostess, clap to the doors: watch to-night, pray to-morrow. Gallants, lads, boys, hearts of gold, all the titles of good fellowship come to you! What, shall we be merry? shall we have a play extempore? 230

Prince. Content; and the argument shall be thy running away.

Falstaff. Ah, no more of that, Hal, an thou lovest me!

(Enter Hostess)

Hostess. O Jesu, my lord the prince!

Prince. How now, my lady the hostess! what sayest thou to me?

Hostess. Marry, my lord, there is a nobleman of the court at door would speak with you: he says he comes from your father.

Prince. Give him as much as will make him a royal° man, and send him back again to my mother.

Falstaff. What manner of man is he?

Hostess. An old man. 240

Falstaff. What doth gravity out of his bed at midnight? Shall I give him his answer?

Prince. Prithee, do, Jack.

Falstaff. 'Faith, and I'll send him packing. *(Exit)*

Prince. Now, sirs: by 'r lady, you fought fair; so did you, Peto; so did you, Bardolph: you are lions too, you ran away upon instinct, you will not touch the true prince; no, fie!

Bardolph. 'Faith, I ran when I saw others run.

Prince. 'Faith, tell me now in earnest, how came Falstaff's sword so hacked? 250

Peto. Why, he hacked it with his dagger, and said he would swear truth out of England but he would make you believe it was done in fight, and persuaded us to do the like.

218. starting-hole, point of shelter (like a rabbit's hole). The most famous of all Falstaff's evasions follows. ***237. royal.*** The man is a noble (6s.8d); give him 3s. 4d. and he will be a *royal* (10s.) *man.*

Bardolph. Yea, and to tickle our noses with spear-grass to make them bleed, and then to beslubber our garments with it and swear it was the blood of true men. I did that I did not this seven year before, I blushed to hear his monstrous devices.

Prince. O villain, thou stolest a cup of sack eighteen years ago, and wert taken with the manner, and ever since thou hast blushed ex-
260 tempore. Thou hadst fire and sword on thy side,° and yet thou rannest away: what instinct hadst thou for it?

Bardolph. My lord, do you see these meteors? do you behold these exhalations?

Prince. I do.

Bardolph. What think you they portend?

Prince. Hot livers and cold purses.°

Bardolph. Choler, my lord, if rightly taken.

Prince. No, if rightly taken, halter.°

(Re-enter Falstaff)

Here comes lean Jack, here comes bare-bone. How now, my sweet
270 creature of bombast!° How long is't ago, Jack, since thou sawest thine own knee?

Falstaff. My own knee! when I was about thy years, Hal, I was not an eagle's talon in the waist; I could have crept into any alderman's thumb-ring: a plague of sighing and grief! it blows a man up like a bladder. There 's villanous news abroad: here was Sir John Bracy from your father; you must to the court in the morning. That same mad fellow of the north, Percy, and he of Wales, that gave Amamon° the bastinado° and made Lucifer cuckold and swore the devil his true liegeman° upon the cross of a Welsh hook°—what a plague call you him?

280 *Poins.* O°, Glendower.

Falstaff. Owen, Owen, the same; and his son-in-law Mortimer, and old Northumberland, and that sprightly Scot of Scots, Douglas, that runs o' horseback up a hill perpendicular,—

Prince. He that rides at high speed and with his pistol° kills a sparrow flying.

Falstaff. You have hit it.

Prince. So did he never the sparrow.

Falstaff. Well, that rascal hath good mettle in him; he will not run.

Prince. Why, what a rascal art thou then, to praise him so for running!

290 *Falstaff.* O' horseback, ye cuckoo; but afoot he will not budge a foot.

260. fire. . .side. Bardolph is a drunkard, and his flaming face is continually harped upon. ***266. Hot. . .purses,*** livers made hot by drink, and purses made empty by spending. ***268. halter.*** The pun is on "collar" pronounced like *choler*. ***270. bombast,*** cotton padding. ***277. Amamon,*** name of a demon. ***278. bastinado,*** cudgel, or a beating with a cudgel. ***279.*** (***liegeman,*** subject, follower.) ***cross of a Welsh hook,*** cross formed by the axhead and the shaft in the Welsh halberd. ***280. O,*** possibly an abbreviation of *Owen*. ***284. pistol.*** There were, of course, no pistols in the time of King Henry's reign.

Prince. Yes, Jack, upon instinct.

Falstaff. I grant ye, upon instinct. Well, he is there too, and one Mordake, and a thousand blue-caps° more: Worcester is stolen away to-night; thy father's beard is turned white with the news: you may buy land now as cheap as stinking mackerel.

Prince. Why, then, it is like, if there come a hot June and this civil buffeting hold, we shall buy maidenheads as they buy hob-nails, by the hundreds.

Falstaff. By the mass, lad, thou sayest true; it is like we shall have good trading that way. But tell me, Hal, art not thou horrible afeard? 300 thou being heir-apparent, could the world pick thee out three such enemies again as that fiend Douglas, that spirit Percy, and that devil Glendower? Art thou not horribly afraid? doth not thy blood thrill at it?

Prince. Not a whit, i' faith; I lack some of thy instinct.

Falstaff. Well, thou wilt be horribly chid to-morrow when thou comest to thy father: if thou love me, practise an answer.

Prince. Do thou stand for my father, and examine me upon the particulars° of my life.

Falstaff. Shall I? content: this chair shall be my state,° this dagger 310 my sceptre, and this cushion my crown.

Prince. Thy state is taken for a joined-stool,° thy golden sceptre for a leaden dagger, and thy precious rich crown for a pitiful bald crown!

Falstaff. Well, an the fire of grace be not quite out of thee, now shalt thou be moved. Give me a cup of sack to make my eyes look red, that it may be thought I have wept; for I must speak in passion, and I will do it in King Cambyses'° vein.

Prince. Well, here is my leg.°

Falstaff. And here is my speech. Stand aside, nobility.

Hostess. O Jesu, this is excellent sport, i' faith! 320

Falstaff. Weep not, sweet queen; for trickling tears are vain.

Hostess. O, the father,° how he holds his countenance!°

Falstaff. For God's sake, lords, convey my tristful° queen; For tears do stop the flood-gates of her eyes.

Hostess. O Jesu, he doth it as like one of these harlotry° players as ever I see!

Falstaff. Peace, good pint-pot; peace, good tickle-brain.° Harry, I do not only marvel where thou spendest thy time, but also how thou

293. blue-caps, Scottish soldiers. ***309. particulars,*** details of a private nature. ***310.*** (***state,*** throne.) ***312. joined-stool,*** a stool made by a joiner, hence, of rough workmanship. ***317. King Cambyses' vein,*** allusion to Thomas Preston's bombastic tragedy *Cambises,* still preserved. ***318. leg,*** bow. ***322.*** (***the father,*** God the Father, an exclamation.) (***holds his countenance,*** keeps a straight face.) ***323.*** (***tristful,*** sad. Falstaff's lines sound like an old-fashioned play.) ***325. harlotry,*** vagabond. ***327. tickle-brain,*** strong drink.

art accompanied: for though the camomile,° the more it is trodden
330 on the faster it grows, yet youth, the more it is wasted the sooner it wears. That thou art my son, I have partly thy mother's word, partly my own opinion, but chiefly a villanous trick of thine eye and a foolish hanging of thy nether lip, that doth warrant me. If then thou be son to me, here lies the point; why, being son to me, art thou so pointed at? Shall the blessed sun of heaven prove a micher° and eat blackberries? a question not to be asked. Shall the son of England prove a thief and take purses? a question to be asked. There is a thing, Harry, which thou hast often heard of and it is known to many in our land by the name of pitch: this pitch, as ancient writers do report, doth defile;° so doth
340 the company thou keepest: for, Harry, now I do not speak to thee in drink but in tears, not in pleasure but in passion, not in words only, but in woes also: and yet there is a virtuous man whom I have often noted in thy company, but I know not his name.

Prince. What manner of man, an it like your majesty?

Falstaff. A goodly portly man, i' faith, and a corpulent; of a cheerful look, a pleasing eye and a most noble carriage; and, as I think, his age some fifty, or, by 'r lady, inclining to three score; and now I remember me, his name is Falstaff: if that man should be lewdly given, he deceiveth me; for, Harry, I see virtue in his looks. If then the tree may
350 be known by the fruit, as the fruit by the tree, then, peremptorily I speak it, there is virtue in that Falstaff: him keep with, the rest banish. And tell me now, thou naughty varlet, tell me, where hast thou been this month?

Prince. Dost thou speak like a king? Do thou stand for me, and I'll play my father.

Falstaff. Depose me? if thou dost it half so gravely, so majestically, both in word and matter, hang me up by the heels for a rabbit-sucker° or a poulter's° hare.

Prince. Well, here I am set.

360 *Falstaff.* And here I stand: judge, my masters.

Prince. Now, Harry, whence come you?

Falstaff. My noble lord, from Eastcheap.

Prince. The complaints I hear of thee are grievous.

Falstaff. 'Sblood, my lord, they are false: nay, I'll tickle ye° for a young prince, i' faith.

Prince. Swearest thou, ungracious boy? henceforth ne'er look on me. Thou art violently carried away from grace: there is a devil haunts

329. camomile. This parodies an actual passage in Lyly's *Euphues* and exaggerates the balance and alliteration of its style. ***335. micher,*** truant. ***339. pitch . . . defile,*** an allusion to the familiar proverb from Ecclesiasticus 13:1, about the defilement of touching pitch. This proverb appears also in Lyly's *Euphues*. ***357. rabbit-sucker,*** sucking rabbit. ***358. poulter's,*** poulterer's. ***364.*** (***I'll tickle ye.*** I'll show you how to be.)

thee in the likeness of an old fat man; a tun of man is thy companion. Why dost thou converse with that trunk of humours, that bolting-hutch° of beastliness, that swollen parcel of dropsies, that huge bom- 370 bard° of sack, that stuffed cloak-bag of guts, that roasted Manningtree ox° with the pudding in his belly, that reverend vice, that grey iniquity,° that father ruffian, that vanity in years? Wherein is he good, but to taste sack and drink it? wherein neat and cleanly, but to carve a capon and eat it? wherein cunning, but in craft? wherein crafty, but in villany? wherein villanous, but in all things? wherein worthy, but in nothing?

Falstaff. I would your grace would take me with you: whom means your grace?

Prince. That villanous abominable misleader of youth, Falstaff, 380 that old white-bearded Satan.

Falstaff. My lord, the man I know.

Prince. I know thou dost.

Falstaff. But to say I know more harm in him than in myself, were to say more than I know. That he is old, the more the pity, his white hairs do witness it; but that he is, saving your reverence, a whoremaster, that I utterly deny. If sack and sugar be a fault, God helped the wicked! if to be old and merry be a sin, then many an old host that I know is damned: if to be fat be to be hated, then Pharaoh's lean kine° are to be loved. No, my good lord; banish Peto, banish Bardolph, 390 banish Poins: but for sweet Jack Falstaff, kind Jack Falstaff, true Jack Falstaff, valiant Jack Falstaff, and therefore more valiant, being, as he is, old Jack Falstaff, banish not him thy Harry's company, banish not him thy Harry's company: banish plump Jack, and banish all the world.

Prince. I do, I will. *(A knocking heard.)*

(Exeunt Hostess, Francis, and Bardolph)

(Re-enter Bardolph, running)

Bardolph. O, my lord, my lord! the sheriff with a most monstrous watch is at the door.

Falstaff. Out, ye rogue! Play out the play: I have much to say in the behalf of that Falstaff. 400

(Re-enter the Hostess)

Hostess. O Jesu, my lord, my lord!

Prince. Heigh, heigh! the devil rides upon a fiddlestick:° what's the matter?

369-370. (***bolting-hutch,*** large round bin.) ***370-371.*** (***bombard,*** leather vessel for sack.) ***371-372. Manningtree ox.*** Manningtree, a town in Essex, had noted fairs where no doubt, oxen were roasted whole. ***372. vice . . . iniquity.*** These terms suggest another feature of Manningtree, which was the acting of morality plays; the word *vanity* also suggests a character in such plays. ***390.*** (***kine,*** cattle.) ***402. the devil. . .fiddlestick,*** proverbial; here, an exclamation meaning, What's all the fuss about?

Hostess. The sheriff and all the watch are at the door: they are come to search the house. Shall I let them in?

Falstaff. Dost thou hear, Hal? never call a true piece of gold a counterfeit: thou art essentially mad, without seeming so.

Prince. And thou a natural coward, without instinct.

Falstaff. I deny your major:° if you will deny the sheriff, so; if not,
410 let him enter: if I become not a cart° as well as another man, a plague on my bringing up! I hope I shall as soon be strangled with a halter as another.

Prince. Go, hide thee behind the arras: the rest walk up above. Now, my masters, for a true face and good conscience.

Falstaff. Both which I have had: but their date is out, and therefore I'll hide me.

Prince. Call in the sheriff.

(Exeunt all except the Prince and Peto)

(Enter Sheriff and the Carrier)

Now, master sheriff, what is your will with me?

Sheriff. First, pardon me, my lord. A hue and cry°
420 Hath follow'd certain men unto this house.

Prince. What men?

Sheriff. One of them is well known, my gracious lord,
A gross fat man.

Carrier. As fat as butter.

Prince. The man, I do assure you, is not here;
For I myself at this time have employ'd him.
And, sheriff, I will engage my word to thee
That I will, by to-morrow dinner-time,
Send him to answer thee, or any man,
For any thing he shall be charged withal:
430 And so let me entreat you leave the house.

Sheriff. I will, my lord. There are two gentlemen
Have in this robbery lost three hundred marks.

Prince. It may be so: if he have robb'd these men,
He shall be answerable; and so farewell.

Sheriff. Good night, my noble lord.

Prince. I think it is good morrow, is it not?

Sheriff. Indeed, my lord, I think it be two o'clock.

(Exeunt Sheriff and Carrier)

Prince. This oily rascal is known as well as Paul's.° Go, call him forth.

409. major, major proposition. Falstaff denies that he is a natural coward; he does not deny that he is affected by instinct. ***410. cart,*** hangman's cart, tumbril. ***419. hue and cry,*** pursuit of criminals by horn and halloo; technical term. ***439. Paul's.*** St. Paul's Cathedral, a familiar landmark.

Peto. Falstaff!—Fast asleep behind the arras, and snorting like a horse. 440

Prince. Hark, how hard he fetches breath. Search his pockets. *(He searcheth his pockets, and findeth certain papers.)* What has thou found?

Peto. Nothing but papers, my lord.

Prince. Let's see what they be: read them.

Peto. *(Reads)*

Item, A capon, ... 2s. 2d.
Item, Sauce, ... 4d.
Item, Sack, two gallons, ... 5s. 8d.
Item, Anchovies and sack after 450
supper, ... 2s. 6d.
Item, Bread, ... ob.°

Prince. O monstrous! but one half-pennyworth of bread to this intolerable deal of sack! What there is else, keep close; we'll read it at more advantage: there let him sleep till day. I'll to the court in the morning. We must all to the wars, and thy place shall be honourable. I'll procure this fat rogue a charge of foot;° and I know his death will be a march of twelve-score.° The money shall be paid back again with advantage. Be with me betimes in the morning; and so, good morrow, Peto. 460

Peto. Good morrow, good my lord. *(Exeunt)*

Act III

Scene I. *Bangor. The Archdeacon's house*

(Enter Hotspur, Worcester, Mortimer, and Glendower)

Mortimer, These promises are fair, the parties sure,
And our induction° full of prosperous hope.

Hotspur. Lord Mortimer, and cousin Glendower,
Will you sit down?
And uncle Worcester: a plague upon it!
I have forgot the map.°

Glendower. No, here it is.
Sit, cousin Percy; sit, good cousin Hotspur,
For by that name as oft as Lancaster°

452. ob., abbreviation for *obolus* (Greek coin) meaning "halfpenny." ***457. charge of foot,*** command of infantry. ***458. twelve-score,*** i.e. yards; a distance familiar from its use in archery. ***2. induction,*** beginning. ***6. map.*** The spectacle of rebels sitting down with a map to divide England into parts would have been duly shocking to the patriotic audience. There was such a conference, but later and not among these leaders. ***8. Lancaster,*** King Henry IV, formerly duke of Lancaster.

Doth speak of you, his cheek looks pale and with
10 A rising sigh he wisheth you in heaven.
Hotspur. And you in hell, as oft as he hears Owen
Glendower spoke of.
Glendower. I cannot blame him: at my nativity
The front° of heaven was full of fiery shapes,
Of burning cressets;° and at my birth
The frame and huge foundation of the earth
Shaked like a coward.
Hotspur. Why, so it would have done at the same season, if your mother's cat had but kittened, though yourself had never been
20 born.
Glendower. I say the earth did shake when I was born.
Hotspur. And I say the earth was not of my mind,
If you suppose as fearing you it shook.
Glendower. The heavens were all on fire, the earth did tremble.
Hotspur. O, then the earth shook to see the heavens on fire,
And not in fear of your nativity.
Diseased nature oftentimes breaks forth
In strange eruptions; oft the teeming earth
Is with a kind of colic pinch'd and vex'd
30 By the imprisoning of unruly wind
Within her womb; which, for enlargement striving,
Shakes the old beldam earth and topples down
Steeples and moss-grown towers. At your birth
Our grandam earth, having this distemperature,
In passion shook.°
Glendower. Cousin, of many men
I do not bear these crossings.° Give me leave
To tell you once again that at my birth
The front of heaven was full of fiery shapes,
40 The goats ran from the mountains, and the herds
Were strangely clamorous to the frighted fields.
These signs have mark'd me extraordinary;
And all the courses of my life do show
I am not in the roll of common men.
Where is he living, clipp'd in° with the sea
That chides the banks of England, Scotland, Wales,
Which calls me pupil, or hath read to me?°

14. front, face. ***15.*** (***burning cressets,*** blazing stars.) ***27-35. Diseased. . .shook.*** These lines give the currently accepted scientific explanation of earthquakes. ***37.*** (***crossings,*** disagreements.) ***45.*** (***clipp'd in,*** encircled by.) ***47.*** (***Which calls me pupil, or has read to me,*** who is my master or has been my tutor.)

And bring him out that is but woman's son
Can trace° me in the tedious ways of art°
And hold me pace in deep experiments. 50
Hotspur. I think there's no man speaks better Welsh.
I'll to dinner.
Mortimer. Peace, cousin Percy; you will make him mad.
Glendower. I can call spirits from the vasty deep.
Hotspur. Why, so can I, or so can any man;
But will they come when you do call for them?
Glendower. Why, I can teach you, cousin, to command
The devil.
Hotspur. And I can teach thee, coz, to shame the devil
By telling truth: tell truth and shame the devil. 60
If thou have power to raise him, bring him hither,
And I'll be sworn I have power to shame him hence.
O, while you live, tell truth and shame the devil!
Mortimer. Come, come, no more of this unprofitable chat.
Glendower. Three times hath Henry Bolingbroke made head
Against my power; thrice from the banks of Wye
And sandy-bottom'd Severn have I sent him
Bootless° home and weather-beaten back.
Hotspur. Home without boots, and in foul weather too!
How 'scapes he agues, in the devil's name? 70
Glendower. Come, here's the map: shall we divide our right
According to our threefold order ta'en?
Mortimer. The archdeacon° hath divided it
Into three limits very equally:
England, from Trent and Severn hitherto,
By south and east is to my part assign'd:
All westward, Wales beyond the Severn shore,
And all the fertile land within that bound,
To Owen Glendower: and, dear coz, to you
The remnant northward, lying off from Trent. 80
And our indentures tripartite are drawn;
Which being sealed interchangeably,°
A business that this night may execute,
To-morrow, cousin Percy, you and I
And my good Lord of Worcester will set forth
To meet your father and the Scottish power,

49. trace, follow, keep pace. (***tedious ways of art,*** tortuous way of magic.) ***68.*** (***Bootless,*** profitless.) ***73. archdeacon,*** an official of an Episcopal diocese. The divisions of the Kingdom are really very ancient; they appear in Geoffrey of Monmouth's *Chronicle,* and are those into which King Lear divided his kingdom. ***82.*** (***sealed interchangeably,*** each of the three parties applied his seal to each of the indentures.)

As is appointed us, at Shrewsbury.
My father° Glendower is not ready yet,
Nor shall we need his help these fourteen days.
90 Within that space you may have drawn together
Your tenants, friends and neighbouring gentlemen.
Glendower. A shorter time shall send me to you, lords:
And in my conduct shall your ladies come;
From whom you now must steal and take no leave,
For there will be a world of water shed
Upon the parting of your wives and you.
Hotspur. Methinks my moiety, north from Burton here,
In quantity equals not one of yours:
See how this river comes me cranking in,°
100 And cuts me from the best of all my land
A huge half-moon, a monstrous cantle° out.
I'll have the current in this place damm'd up;
And here the smug and silver Trent shall run
In a new channel, fair and evenly;
It shall not wind with such a deep indent,
To rob me of so rich a bottom here.
Glendower. Not wind? it shall, it must; you see it doth.
Mortimer. Yea, but
Mark how he bears his course, and runs me up
110 With like advantage on the other side;
Gelding the opposed continent° as much
As on the other side it takes from you.
Worcester. Yea, but a little charge° will trench him here
And on this north side win this cape of land;
And then he runs straight and even.
Hotspur. I'll have it so: a little charge will do it.
Glendower. I'll not have it alter'd.
Hotspur. Will not you?
Glendower. No, nor you shall not.
Hotspur. Who shall say me nay?
Glendower. Why, that will I.
120 *Hotspur.* Let me not understand you, then; speak it in Welsh.
Glendower. I can speak English, lord, as well as you;
For I was train'd up in the English court;
Where, being but young, I framed to the harp
Many an English ditty lovely well

88. father, father-in-law. ***99. comes me cranking in,*** comes bending in on my share; *me* is an ethical dative. ***101. cantle,*** piece. ***111.*** (***opposed continent,*** opposite bank.) ***113.*** (***charge,*** expense.)

And gave the tongue a helpful ornament,
A virtue that was never seen in you.°
Hotspur. Marry,°
And I am glad of it with all my heart:
I had rather be a kitten and cry mew
Than one of these same metre ballad-mongers; 130
I had rather hear a brazen canstick° turn'd,
Or a dry wheel grate on the axle-tree;
And that would set my teeth nothing on edge,
Nothing so much as mincing poetry:
'Tis like the forced gait of a shuffling nag.
Glendower. Come, you shall have Trent turn'd.
Hotspur. I do not care: I'll give thrice so much land
To any well-deserving friend;
But in the way of bargain, mark ye me,
I'll cavil on the ninth part of a hair. 140
Are the indentures drawn? shall we be gone?
Glendower. The moon shines fair; you may away by night:
I'll haste the writer° and withal
Break with° your wives of your departure hence:
I am afraid my daughter will run mad,
So much she doteth on her Mortimer. *(Exit)*
Mortimer. Fie, cousin Percy! how you cross my father!
Hotspur. I cannot choose: sometime he angers me
With telling me of the moldwarp° and the ant,
Of the dreamer Merlin° and his prophecies, 150
And of a dragon and a finless fish,
A clip-wing'd griffin° and a moulten raven,
A couching lion and a ramping° cat,
And such a deal of skimble-skamble° stuff
As puts me from my faith. I tell you what;
He held me last night at least nine hours
In reckoning up the several devils' names
That were his lackeys: I cried 'hum,' and 'well, go to,'
But mark'd him not a word. O, he is as tedious
As a tired horse, a railing wife; 160
Worse than a smoky house: I had rather live

122-126. For . . . you. Glendower had indeed been bred in the English court; he shows a characteristic Welsh pride in being a poet, and Hotspur an equally characteristic scorn of the fine arts. ***127.*** (***Marry,*** by the Virgin Mary.) ***131. canstick,*** candlestick. ***143. writer,*** the scrivener who would be drawing the indentures. ***144.*** (***Break with,*** break the news.) ***149. moldwarp,*** mole. ***150. Merlin,*** the traditional bard and prophet of the Welsh. ***152. griffin,*** a fabulous beast. ***153. ramping,*** rampant, advancing on its hind legs. ***154. skimble-skamble,*** confused and foolish.

With cheese and garlic in a windmill, far,
Than feed on cates° and have him talk to me
In any summer-house in Christendom.
Mortimer. In faith, he is a worthy gentleman,
Exceedingly well read, and profited
In strange concealments, valiant as a lion
And wondrous affable and as bountiful
As mines of India. Shall I tell you, cousin?
170 He holds your temper in a high respect
And curbs himself even of his natural scope
When you come 'cross his humour; faith, he does:
I warrant you, that man is not alive
Might so have tempted him as you have done,
Without the taste of danger and reproof:
But do not use it oft, let me entreat you.
Worcester. In faith, my lord, you are too wilful-blame;°
And since your coming hither have done enough
To put him quite beside his patience.
180 You must needs learn, lord, to amend this fault:
Though sometimes it show greatness, courage, blood,—
And that 's the dearest grace it renders you,—
Yet oftentimes it doth present harsh rage,
Defect of manners, want of government,
Pride, haughtiness, opinion and disdain:
The least of which haunting a nobleman
Loseth men's hearts andleaves behind a stain
Upon the beauty of all parts besides,
Beguiling them of commendation.
190 *Hotspur.* Well, I am school'd: good manners be your speed!
Here come our wives, and let us take our leave.
(Re-enter Glendower with the ladies)
Mortimer. This is the deadly spite that angers me;
My wife can speak no English, I no Welsh.
Glendower. My daughter weeps: she will not part with you;
She'll be a soldier too, she'll to the wars.
Mortimer. Good father, tell her that she and my aunt Percy
Shall follow in your conduct speedily. *(Gendower speaks to her in Welsh, and she answers him in the same.)*
Glendower. She is desperate here; a peevish self-will'd
200 harlotry,° one that no persuasion can do good upon. *(The lady speaks in Welsh.)*

163. (***cates,*** delicacies.) ***177. wilful-blame,*** wilfully guilty. ***200. harlotry,*** silly wench.

Mortimer. I understand thy looks: that pretty Welsh
Which thou pour'st down from these swelling heavens
I am too perfect in; and, but for shame,
In such a parley should I answer thee. *(The lady speaks again in Welsh.)*
I understand thy kisses and thou mine,
And that's a feeling disputation:°
But I will never be a truant, love,
Till I have learn'd thy language; for thy tongue
Makes Welsh as sweet as ditties highly penn'd, 210
Sung by a fair queen in a summer's bower,
With ravishing division,° to her lute.

Glendower. Nay, if you melt, then will she run mad. *(The lady speaks again in Welsh.)*

Mortimer. O, I am ignorance itself in this!

Glendower. She bids you on the wanton° rushes lay you down
And rest your gentle head upon her lap,
And she will sing the song that pleaseth you
And on your eyelids crown the god of sleep,
Charming your blood with pleasing heaviness, 220
Making such difference 'twixt wake and sleep
As is the difference betwixt day and night
The hour before the heavenly-harness'd team°
Begins his golden progress in the east.

Mortimer. With all my heart I'll sit and hear her sing:
By that time will our book,° I think, be drawn.

Glendower. Do so;
And those musicians that shall play to you
Hang in the air a thousand leagues from hence,
And straight they shall be here: sit, and attend. 230

Hotspur. Come, Kate, thou art perfect in lying down:
come, quick, quick, that I may lay my head in thy lap.

Lady Percy. Go, ye giddy goose. *(Music plays.)*

Hotspur. Now I perceive the devil understands Welsh;
And 'tis no marvel he is so humorous.°
By 'r lady, he is a good musician.

Lady Percy. Then should you be nothing but musical, for you are altogether governed by humours. Lie still, ye thief, and hear the lady sing in Welsh.

Hotspur. I had rather hear Lady, my brach,° howl in Irish. 240

Lady Percy. Wouldst thou have thy head broken?

207. disputation, conversation. ***212. division,*** variation (in music). ***216. wanton,*** soft, luxurious. ***223. (heavenly. . .harnessed team,*** the team of horses drawing the sun across the firmament.) ***226. book,*** document, indentures. ***235. humorous,*** capricious. ***240. brach,*** bitch hound.

Hotspur. No.
Lady Percy. Then be still.
Hotspur. Neither; 'tis a woman's fault.
Lady Percy. Now God help thee!
Hotspur. To the Welsh lady's bed.
Lady Percy. What's that?
Hotspur. Peace! she sings. *(Here the lady sings a Welsh song.)*
Hotspur. Come, Kate, I'll have your song too.
250 *Lady Percy.* Not mine, in good sooth.
Hotspur. Not yours, in good sooth! Heart! you swear like a comfit-maker's wife.° 'Not you, in good sooth,' and 'as true as I live,' and 'as God shall mend me,' and 'as sure as day,'
And givest such sarcenet° surety for thy oaths,
As if thou never walk'st further than Finsbury.°
Swear me, Kate, like a lady as thou art,
A good mouth-filling oath, and leave 'in sooth,'
And such protest of pepper-gingerbread,
To velvet-guards° and Sunday-citizens.
260 Come, sing.
Lady Percy. I will not sing.
Hotspur. 'Tis the next way to turn tailor,° or be red-breast teacher.° An the indentures be drawn, I'll away within these two hours; and so, come in when ye will. *(Exit)*
Glendower. Come, come, Lord Mortimer; you are as slow
As hot Lord Percy is on fire to go.
By this our book is drawn; we'll but seal,
And then to horse immediately.
Mort. With all my heart. *(Exeunt)*

Scene II. *London. The palace*

(Enter the King, Prince of Wales, and others)
King. Lords, give us leave;° the Prince of Wales and I
Must have some private conference: but be near at hand,
For we shall presently have need of you. *(Exeunt Lords)*
I know not whether God will have it so,
For some displeasing service I have done,
That, in his secret doom,° out of my blood

251-252. you swear. . .wife. Hotspur prefers more violent oaths in accordance with the fashion of the time, when even the queen herself swore vigorously. ***252. comfit-maker's,*** confectioner's. ***254. sarcenet,*** soft, from the silken material known as "sarcenet." ***255. Finsbury,*** an archery ground outside Moorgate, resorted to by citizens. ***259. velvet-guards,*** wearers of velvet trimmings. ***262. turn tailor.*** Tailors were noted for singing. (***red-breast teacher,*** a teacher of caged birds, especially robins.) ***1. give us leave,*** leave us. ***6.*** (***doom,*** judgment.)

He'll breed revengement and a scourge for me;
But thou dost in thy passages of life
Make me believe that thou art only mark'd
For the hot vengeance and the rod of heaven 10
To punish my mistreadings. Tell me else,
Could such inordinate and low desires,
Such poor, such bare, such lewd, such mean attempts,
Such barren pleasures, rude society,
As thou art match'd withal and grafted to,
Accompany the greatness of thy blood
And hold their level with thy princely heart?
Prince. So please your majesty, I would I could
Quit all offences with as clear excuse
As well as I am doubtless I can purge 20
Myself of many I am charged withal:
Yet such extenuation let me beg,
As, in reproof of many tales devised,
Which oft the ear of greatness needs must hear,
By smiling pick-thanks° and base newsmongers,
I may, for some things true, wherein my youth
Hath faulty wander'd and irregular,
Find pardon on my true submission.
King. God pardon thee! yet let me wonder, Harry,
At thy affections, which do hold a wing 30
Quite from the flight of all thy ancestors.
Thy place in council thou hast rudely lost,
Which by thy younger brother is supplied,
And art almost an alien to the hearts
Of all the court and princes of my blood:
The hope and expectation of thy time
Is ruin'd, and the soul of every man
Prophetically doth forethink thy fall.
Had I so lavish of my presence been,
So common-hackney'd° in the eyes of men, 40
So stale and cheap to vulgar company,
Opinion, that did help me to the crown,
Had still kept loyal to possession°
And left me in reputeless banishment,
A fellow of no mark nor likelihood.
By being seldom seen, I could not stir
But like a comet I was wonder'd at;

25. pick-thanks, flatterers. ***40.*** (***common-hackneyed,*** at everyone's beck and call.) ***43. to possession,*** i.e. to Richard II's sovereignty.

That men would tell their children 'This is he;'
Others would say 'Where, which is Bolingbroke?'
50 And then I stole all courtesy from heaven,°
And dress'd myself in such humility
That I did pluck allegiance from men's hearts,
Loud shouts and salutations from their mouths,
Even in the presence of the crowned king.
Thus did I keep my person fresh and new;
My presence, like a robe pontifical,
Ne'er seen but wonder'd at: and so my state,
Seldom but sumptuous, showed like a feast
And won by rareness such solemnity.
60 The skipping° king, he ambled up and down
With shallow jesters and rash bavin° wits,
Soon kindled and soon burnt; carded° his state,
Mingled his royalty with capering fools,
Had his great name profaned with their scorns
And gave his countenance, against his name,°
To laugh at gibing boys and stand the push°
Of every beardless vain comparative,°
Grew a companion to the common streets,
Enfeoff'd° himself to popularity;
70 That, being daily swallow'd by men's eyes,
They surfeited with honey and began
To loathe the taste of sweetness, whereof a little
More than a little is by much too much.
So when he had occasion to be seen,
He was but as the cuckoo is in June,
Heard, not regarded; seen, but with such eyes
As, sick and blunted with community,°
Afford no extraordinary gaze,
Such as is bent on sun-like majesty
80 When it shines seldom in admiring eyes;
But rather drowsed and hung their eyelids down,
Slept in his face and render'd such aspect
As cloudy° men use to their adversaries,
Being with his presence glutted, gorged and full.
And in that very line, Harry, standest thou;
For thou hast lost thy princely privilege

50. stole. . .heaven. He assumed a bearing of the utmost graciousness. ***60. skipping,*** flighty. ***61. bavin,*** brushwood, soon burnt out. ***62. carded,*** debased; a term applied to the adulteration of wool. ***65. name,*** i.e., dignity. ***66. stand the push,*** undergo the attack. ***67. comparative,*** rival (in wit). ***69. Enfeoff'd,*** gave himself up to. The king is expressing the current view of royal dignity and policy with reference to the populace. ***77. community,*** commonness. ***83.*** (***cloudy,*** sullen.)

With vile participation:° not an eye
But is a-weary of thy common sight,
Save mine, which hath desired to see thee more;
Which now doth that I would not have it do, 90
Make blind itself with foolish tenderness.

Prince. I shall hereafter, my thrice gracious lord,
Be more myself.

King. For all the world
As thou art to this hour was Richard then
When I from France set foot at Ravenspurgh,
And even as I was then is Percy now.
Now, by my sceptre and my soul to boot,
He hath more worthy interest° to the state
Than thou the shadow of succession;°
For of no right, nor colour like to right, 100
He doth fill fields with harness° in the realm,
Turns head against the lion's armed jaws,
And, being no more in debt to years than thou,
Leads ancient lords and reverend bishops on
To bloody battles and to bruising arms.
What never-dying honour hath he got
Against renowned Douglas! whose high deeds,
Whose hot incursions and great name in arms
Holds from all soldiers chief majority
And military title capital° 110
Through all the kingdoms that acknowledge Christ:
Thrice hath this Hotspur, Mars in swathling° clothes,
This infant warrior, in his enterprizes
Discomfited great Douglas, ta'en him once,
Enlarged° him and made a friend of him,
To fill the mouth of deep defiance up
And shake the peace and safety of our throne.
And what say you to this? Percy, Northumberland,
The Archbishop's grace of York, Douglas, Mortimer,
Capitulate° against us and are up. 120
But wherefore do I tell these news to thee?
Why, Harry, do I tell thee of my foes,
Which art my near'st and dearest enemy?
Thou that art like enough, through vassal° fear,

87. vile participation, base association or companionship. ***98. interest,*** claim. ***99. shadow of succession.*** Hal's claim is a shadow compared to the real services toward gaining the crown which Hotspur has rendered. ***101. harness,*** armor. ***109-110. (Holds. . .capital,*** keeps all other soldiers from claiming to be the greatest.) ***112. swathling,*** swaddling. ***115. Enlarged,*** released.) ***120. Capitulate,*** form a league. ***124. vassal,*** slavish.

Base inclination and the start of spleen,
To fight against me under Percy's pay,
To dog his heels and curtsy at his frowns,
To show how much thou art degenerate.
Prince. Do not think so; you shall not find it so:
130 And God forgive them that so much have sway'd
Your majesty's good thoughts away from me!
I will redeem all this on Percy's head
And in the closing of some glorious day
Be bold to tell you that I am your son;
When I will wear a garment all of blood
And stain my favours° in a bloody mask,
Which, wash'd away, shall scour my shame with it:
And that shall be the day, whene'er it lights,
That this same child of honour and renown,
140 This gallant Hotspur, this all-praised knight,
And your unthought-of Harry chance to meet.
For every honour sitting on his helm,
Would they were multitudes, and on my head
My shames redoubled! for the time will come,
That I shall make this northern youth exchange
His glorious deeds for my indignities.
Percy is but my factor,° good my lord,
To engross° up glorious deeds on my behalf;
And I will call him to so strict account,
150 That he shall render every glory up,
Yea, even the slightest worship of his time,
Or I will tear the reckoning from his heart.
This, in the name of God, I promise here:
The which if He be pleased I shall perform,
I do beseech your majesty may salve
The long-grown wounds of my intemperance:
If not, the end of life cancels all bands;°
And I will die a hundred thousand deaths
Ere break the smallest parcel of this vow.
160 *King.* A hundred thousand rebels die in this:
Thou shalt have charge and sovereign trust herein.
(Enter Blunt)
How now, good Blunt? thy looks are full of speed.
Blunt. So hath the business that I come to speak of.
Lord Mortimer of Scotland hath sent word
That Douglas and the English rebels met

136. (***favours,*** face.) ***147.*** (***factor,*** agent.) ***148.*** (***engross,*** buy up.) ***157.*** (***bands,*** bonds.)

The eleventh of this month at Shrewsbury:
A mighty and a fearful head they are,
If promises be kept on every hand,
As ever offer'd foul play in a state.
King. The Earl of Westmoreland set forth to-day;
With him my son, Lord John of Lancaster; 170
For this advertisement° is five days old:
On Wednesday next, Harry, you shall set forward;
On Thursday we ourselves will march: our meeting
Is Bridgenorth: and, Harry, you shall march
Through Gloucestershire; by which account,
Our business valued,° some twelve days hence
Our general forces at Bridgenorth shall meet.
Our hands are full of business: let's away;
Advantage feeds him fat,° while men delay. *(Exeunt)* 180

Scene III. *Eastcheap. The Boar's-Head Tavern*

(Enter Falstaff and Bardolph)

Falstaff. Bardolph, am I not fallen away vilely since this last action? do I not bate?° do I not dwindle? Why, my skin hangs about me like an old lady's loose gown; I am withered like an old apple-john.° Well, I'll repent, and that suddenly, while I am in some liking;° I shall be out of heart shortly, and then I shall have no strength to repent. An I have not forgotten what the inside of a church is made of, I am a pepper-corn,° a brewer's horse:° the inside of a church! Company, villanous company, hath been the spoil of me.

Bardolph. Sir John, you are so fretful, you cannot live long.

Falstaff. Why, there is it: come sing me a bawdy song; make me 10 merry. I was as virtuously given as a gentleman need to be; virtuous enough; swore little; diced not above seven times a week; went to a bawdy-house not above once in a quarter—of an hour; paid money that I borrowed, three or four times; lived well and in good compass: and now I live out of all order, out of all compass.

Bardolph. Why, you are so fat, Sir John, that you must needs be out of all compass,° out of all reasonable compass, Sir John.

Falstaff. Do thou amend thy face, and I'll amend my life: thou art our admiral,° thou bearest the lantern in the poop, but 'tis in the nose of thee; thou art the Knight of the Burning Lamp. 20

172. advertisement, tidings, news. ***177.*** (***Our business valued,*** evaluating the tasks we have.) ***180. Advantage. . .fat,*** opportunity feeds itself fat. ***2.*** (***bate,*** grow thin.) ***3. apple-john,*** a kind of apple still in perfect condition even when shriveled and withered. ***4. liking,*** (good) bodily condition. ***6-7. peppercorn,*** grain of pepper. ***7.*** (***brewer's horse,*** decrepit.) ***14. good compass,*** reasonable limits. ***17. compass,*** girth, circumference. ***19. admiral,*** flagship.

Bardolph. Why, Sir John, my face does you no harm.

Falstaff. No, I'll be sworn; I make as good use of it as many a man doth of a Death's-head or a memento mori:° I never see thy face but I think upon hell-fire and Dives° that lived in purple; for there he is in his robes, burning, burning. If thou wert any way given to virtue, I would swear by thy face: my oath should be 'By this fire, that's God's angel:'° but thou art altogether given over; and wert indeed, but for the light in thy face, the son of utter darkness. When thou rannest up Gadshill in the night to catch my horse, if I did not think thou hadst
30 been an ignis fatuus° or a ball of wildfire, there's no purchase in money. O, thou art a perpetual triumph, an everlasting bonfire-light! Thou hast saved me a thousand marks in links° and torches, walking with thee in the night betwixt tavern and tavern: but the sack that thou hast drunk me would have bought me lights as good cheap° at the dearest chandler's in Europe. I have maintained that salamander° of yours with fire any time this two and thirty years; God reward me for it!

Bardolph. 'Sblood, I would my face were in your belly!

Falstaff. God-a-mercy! so should I be sure to be heart-burned.

(Enter Hostess)

40 How now, Dame Partlet° the hen! have you inquired yet who picked my pocket?

Hostess. Why, Sir John, what do you think, Sir John? do you think I keep thieves in my house? I have searched, I have inquired, so has my husband, man by man, boy by boy, servant by servant: the tithe of a hair was never lost in my house before.

Falstaff. Ye lie, hostess: Bardolph was shaved and lost many a hair; and I'll be sworn my pocket was picked. Go to, you are a woman, go.

Hostess. Who, I? no; I defy thee: God's light, I was never called so in mine own house before.

50 *Falstaff.* Go to, I know you well enough.

Hostess. No, Sir John; you do not know me, Sir John. I know you, Sir John: you owe me money, Sir John; and now you pick a quarrel to beguile me of it: I bought you a dozen of shirts to your back.

Falstaff. Dowlas,° filthy dowlas: I have given them away to bakers' wives, and they have made bolters° of them.

Hostess. Now, as I am a true woman, holland° of eight shillings an ell.° You owe money here besides, Sir John, for your diet and by-drinkings, and money lent you, four and twenty pound.

23. memento mori, reminder of death, such as skull and crossbones. ***24. Dives,*** the rich man referred to in Luke 16:19-31. ***26-27.*** (***By. . .angel,*** either a biblical allusion or a parody of a line from a contemporary play.) ***30. ignis fatuus,*** will-o-the-wisp. ***32. links,*** torches. ***34. good cheap,*** cheap. ***35. salamander,*** a fabled monster able to live in fire. ***40. Partlet,*** traditional name of a hen. ***54. Dowlas,*** a coarse kind of linen. ***55. bolters,*** cloths for sifting meal. ***56. holland,*** fine linen. ***57. ell,*** a measure of a yard and a quarter.

Falstaff. He had his part of it; let him pay.

Hostess. He? alas, he is poor; he hath nothing. 60

Falstaff. How! poor? look upon his face; what call you rich? let them coin his nose, let them coin his cheeks: I'll not pay a denier.° What, will you make a younker° of me? shall I not take mine ease in mine inn but I shall have my pocket picked? I have lost a seal-ring of my grandfather's worth forty mark.

Hostess. O Jesu, I have heard the prince tell him, I know not how oft, that that ring was copper!

Falstaff. How! the prince is a Jack, a sneak-cup:° 'sblood, an he were here, I would cudgel him like a dog, if he would say so.

(Enter the Prince and Peto, marching, and Falstaff meets them playing on his truncheon like a fife.)

How now, lad! is the wind in that door, i' faith? must we all march? 70

Bardolph. Yea, two and two, Newgate° fashion.

Hostess. My lord, I pray you, hear me.

Prince. What sayest thou, Mistress Quickly? How doth thy husband? I love him well; he is an honest man.

Hostess. Good my lord, hear me.

Falstaff. Prithee, let her alone, and list to me.

Prince. What sayest thou, Jack?

Falstaff. The other night I fell asleep here behind the arras° and had my pocket picked: this house is turned bawdy-house; they pick pockets. 80

Prince. What didst thou lose, Jack?

Falstaff. Wilt thou believe me, Hal? three or four bonds of forty pound a-piece, and a seal-ring of my grandfather's.

Prince. A trifle, some eight-penny matter.

Hostess. So I told him, my lord; and I said I heard your grace say so: and, my lord, he speaks most vilely of you, like a foul-mouthed man as he is; and said he would cudgel you.

Prince. What! he did not?

Hostess. There's neither faith, truth, nor womanhood in me else.

Falstaff. There's no more faith in thee than in a stewed prune; 90 nor no more truth in thee than in a drawn fox;° and for womanhood, Maid Marian may be the deputy's wife of the ward to thee.° Go, you thing, go.

Hostess. Say, what thing! what thing?

Falstaff. What thing? why, a thing to thank God on.

Hostess. I am no thing to thank God on, I would thou shouldst know

62. denier, one twelfth of a sou; type of very small coin. ***63. younker,*** youth, greenhorn. ***68. sneak-cup.*** Nares defines this as "one who shirks his liquor"; Johnson modifies to *sneak-up*, meaning "a sneak." ***71. Newgate,*** famous city prison in London. ***78.*** (***arras,*** curtain.) ***91. drawn fox,*** fox driven from cover and wily in getting back. ***92.*** (***Maid. . .thee,*** Maid Marian, a member of Robin Hood's gang, is a lady compared to you.)

it; I am an honest man's wife: and, setting thy knighthood aside, thou art a knave to call me so.

Falstaff. Setting thy womanhood aside, thou art a beast to say
100 otherwise.

Hostess. Say, what beast, thou knave, thou?

Falstaff. What beast! why, an otter.

Prince. An otter, Sir John! why an otter?

Falstaff. Why, she's neither fish nor flesh; a man knows not where to have her.

Hostess. Thou art an unjust man in saying so: thou or any man knows where to have me, thou knave, thou!

Prince. Thou sayest true, hostess; and he slanders thee most grossly.

Hostess. So he doth you, my lord; and said this other day you ought°
110 him a thousand pound.

Prince. Sirrah, do I owe you a thousand pound?

Falstaff. A thousand pound, Hal! a million: thy love is worth a million: thou owest me thy love.

Hostess. Nay, my lord, he called you Jack, and said he would cudgel you.

Falstaff. Did I, Bardolph?

Bardolph. Indeed, Sir John, you said so.

Falstaff. Yea, if he said my ring was copper.

Prince. I say 'tis copper: darest thou be as good as thy word now?

120 *Falstaff.* Why, Hal, thou knowest, as thou art but man, I dare: but as thou art prince, I fear thee as I fear the roaring of the lion's whelp.

Prince. And why not as the lion?

Falstaff. The king himself is to be feared as the lion: dost thou think I'll fear thee as I fear thy father? nay, an I do, I pray God my girdle break.

Prince. O, if it should, how would thy guts fall about thy knees! But, sirrah, there's no room for faith, truth, nor honesty in this bosom of thine; it is all filled up with guts and midriff. Charge an honest woman
130 with picking thy pocket! why, thou whoreson, impudent, embossed° rascal, if there were anything in thy pocket but tavern-reckonings, memorandums of bawdy-houses, and one poor penny-worth of sugar-candy to make thee long-winded, if thy pocket were enriched with any other injuries° but these, I am a villain: and yet you will stand to it; you will not pocket up wrong: art thou not ashamed?

Falstaff. Dost thou hear, Hal? thou knowest in the state of innocency Adam fell; and what should poor Jack Falstaff do in the days of villany?

109. ought, owed. ***130. embossed,*** swollen (with fat). ***134. injuries,*** used by the prince in allusion to the pocketing of injuries, i.e. failing to resent them.

Thou seest I have more flesh than another man, and therefore more frailty. You confess then, you picked my pocket?

Prince. It appears so by the story. 140

Falstaff. Hostess, I forgive thee:° go, make ready breakfast; love thy husband, look to thy servants, cherish thy guests: thou shalt find me tractable to any honest reason: thou seest I am pacified still. Nay, prithee, be gone.

(Exit Hostess)

Now, Hal, to the news at court: for the robbery, lad, how is that answered?

Prince. O, my sweet beef, I must still be good angel to thee: the money is paid back again.

Falstaff. O, I do not like that paying back; 'tis a double labour.

Prince. I am good friends with my father and may do any thing. 150

Falstaff. Rob me the exchequer the first thing thou doest, and do it with unwashed hands° too.

Bardolph. Do, my lord.

Prince. I have procured thee, Jack, a charge of foot.

Falstaff. I would it had been of horse. Where shall I find one that can steal well? O for a fine thief, of the age of two and twenty or thereabouts! I am heinously unprovided. Well, God be thanked for these rebels, they offend none but the virtuous: I laud them, I praise them.

Prince. Bardolph! 160

Bardolph. My lord?

Prince. Go bear this letter to Lord John of Lancaster, to my brother John; this to my Lord of Westmoreland.

(Exit Bardolph)

Go, Peto, to horse, to horse; for thou and I have thirty miles to ride yet ere dinner time.

(Exit Peto)

Jack, meet me to-morrow in the Temple hall at two o'clock in the afternoon.
There shalt thou know thy charge; and there receive
Money and order for their furniture.°
The land is burning; Percy stands on high; 170
And either we or they must lower lie. *(Exit)*

Falstaff. Rare words! brave world! Hostess, my breakfast, come!
O, I could wish this tavern were my drum!° *(Exit)*

141. Hostess, I forgive thee. This most comic line is an indication of Falstaff's mastery. ***152. with unwashed hands,*** at once. ***169. furniture,*** equipment, provision. ***173. drum.*** Possibly Falstaff means to say that he could wish that he might recruit his soldiers by means of this tavern.

Act IV

Scene I. *The rebel camp near Shrewsbury*

(Enter Hotspur, Worcester, and Douglas)

Hotspur. Well said, my noble Scot: if speaking truth
In this fine age were not thought flattery,
Such attribution° should the Douglas have,
As not a soldier of this season's stamp
Should go so general current° through the world.
By God, I cannot flatter; I do defy
The tongues of soothers;° but a braver place
In my heart's love hath no man than yourself:
Nay, task me to my word;° approve° me, lord.

10 *Douglas.* Thou art the king of honour:
No man so potent breathes upon the ground
But I will beard° him.

Hotspur. Do so, and 'tis well.

(Enter a Messenger with letters)

What letters hast thou there?—I can but thank you.

Messenger. These letters come from your father.

Hotspur. Letters from him! why comes he not himself?

Messenger. He cannot come, my lord; he is grievous sick.

Hotspur. 'Zounds! how has he the leisure to be sick
In such a justling° time? Who leads his power?
Under whose government come they along?

20 *Messenger.* His letters bear his mind, not I, my lord.

Worcester. I prithee, tell me, doth he keep his bed?

Messenger. He did, my lord, four days ere I set forth;
And at the time of my departure thence
He was much fear'd by his physicians.

Worcester. I would the state of time had first been whole
Ere he by sickness had been visited:
His health was never better worth than now.

Hotspur. Sick now! droop now! this sickness doth infect
The very life-blood of our enterprise;
30 'Tis catching hither, even to our camp.
He writes me here, that inward sickness—
And that his friends by deputation° could not
So soon be drawn, nor did he think it meet

3. attribution, praise. ***4-5. stamp. . .current,*** a figure of speech derived from coining. ***7. soothers,*** flatterers. ***9. task. . .word,*** challenge me to make good my word. ***approve,*** test. ***12.*** (***beard,*** dare.) ***18. justling,*** jostling, busy. ***32.*** (***deputation,*** by his representatives.)

To lay so dangerous and dear a trust
On any soul removed but on his own.
Yet doth he give us bold advertisement,°
That with our small conjunction° we should on,
To see how fortune is disposed to us;
For, as he writes, there is no quailing now,
Because the king is certainly possess'd° 40
Of all our purposes. What say you to it?
Worcester. Your father's sickness is a maim to us.
Hotspur. A perilous gash, a very limb lopp'd off:
And yet, in faith, it is not; his present want°
Seems more than we shall find it: were it good
To set the exact wealth of all our states
All at one cast?° to set so rich a main°
On the nice hazard of one doubtful hour?
It were not good; for therein should we read
The very bottom and the soul of hope, 50
The very list,° the very utmost bound
Of all our fortunes.
Douglas. 'Faith, and so we should;
Where now remains a sweet reversion:°
We may boldly spend upon the hope of what
Is to come in:
A comfort of retirement lives in this.
Hotspur. A rendezvous, a home to fly unto,
If that the devil and mischance look big
Upon the maidenhead of our affairs.
Worcester. But yet I would your father had been here. 60
The quality and hair° of our attempt
Brooks no division: it will be thought
By some, that know not why he is away,
That wisdom, loyalty and mere dislike
Of our proceedings kept the earl from hence:
And think how such an apprehension
May turn the tide of fearful faction
And breed a kind of question in our cause;
For well you know we of the offering side°
Must keep aloof from strict arbitrement,° 70
And stop all sight-holes, every loop from whence

36. advertisement, counsel, advice. ***37. conjunction,*** joint force, with allusion to the conjunction of planets. ***40.*** (***possessed,*** informed.) ***44. want,*** i.e., the lack of him. ***47. cast,*** throw of the dice. ***47. main,*** number called by the caster before the dice are thrown. ***51. list,*** limit. ***53. reversion,*** part of an estate yet to be inherited; hope of future profit. ***61. hair,*** kind, nature. ***69. offering side,*** side which attacks. ***70. arbitrement,*** just inquiry or investigation.

The eye of reason may pry in upon us:
This absence of your father's draws a curtain,
That shows the ignorant a kind of fear
Before not dreamt of.

Hotspur. You strain too far.
I rather of his absence make this use:
It lends a lustre and more great opinion,
A larger dare to our great enterprise,
Than if the earl were here; for men must think,
80 If we without his help can make a head
To push against a kingdom, with his help
We shall o'erturn it topsy-turvy down.
Yet all goes well, yet all our joints are whole.

Douglas. As heart can think: there is not such a word
Spoke of in Scotland as this term of fear.
(Enter Sir Richard Vernon)

Hotspur. My cousin Vernon! welcome, by my soul.

Vernon. Pray God my news be worth a welcome, lord.
The Earl of Westmoreland, seven thousand strong,
Is marching hitherwards; with him Prince John.

Hotspur. No harm: what more?

90 *Vernon.* And further, I have learn'd,
The king himself in person is set forth,
Or hitherwards intended speedily,
With strong and mighty preparation.

Hotspur. He shall be welcome too. Where is his son,
The nimble-footed madcap Prince of Wales,
And his comrades, that daff'd° the world aside,
And bid it pass?

Vernon. All furnish'd,° all in arms;
All plumed like estridges° that with the wind
Baited° like eagles having lately bathed;
100 Glittering in golden coats, like images;°
As full of spirit as the month of May,
And gorgeous as the sun at midsummer;
Wanton as youthful goats, wild as young bulls.
I saw young Harry, with his beaver° on,
His cuisses° on his thighs, gallantly arm'd,
Rise from the ground like feather'd° Mercury,
And vaulted with such ease into his seat,

96. daff'd, put aside with a gesture. ***97. furnish'd,*** equipped. ***98. like estridges,*** a reference to ostrich plumes on crests. ***99.*** (***Baited,*** beat [their wings]). ***100. images.*** Images (of saints, etc.) were dressed in splendid robes for holidays. ***104. beaver,*** visor (of helmet). ***105. cuisses,*** armor for the thighs. ***106.*** (***feather'd,*** winged.)

As if an angel dropp'd down from the clouds,
To turn and wind a fiery Pegasus°
And witch° the world with noble horsemanship. 110

Hotspur. No more, no more: worse than the sun in March,
This praise doth nourish agues.° Let them come;
They come like sacrifices in their trim,°
And to the fire-eyed maid of smoky war
All hot and bleeding will we offer them:
The mailed Mars° shall on his altar sit
Up to the ears in blood. I am on fire
To hear this rich reprisal° is so nigh
And yet not ours. Come, let me taste my horse,
Who is to bear me like a thunderbolt 120
Against the bosom of the Prince of Wales:
Harry to Harry shall, hot horse to horse,
Meet and ne'er part till one drop down a corse.
O that Glendower were come!

Vernon. There is more news:
I learn'd in Worcester, as I rode along,
He cannot draw his power this fourteen days.

Douglas. That's the worst tidings that I hear of yet.

Worcester. Ay, by my faith, that bears a frosty sound.

Hotspur. What may the king's whole battle reach unto?

Vernon. To thirty thousand.

Hotspur. Forty let it be: 130
My father and Glendower being both away,
The powers of us may serve so great a day.
Come, let us take a muster speedily:
Doomsday is near; die all, die merrily.

Douglas. Talk not of dying: I am out of fear
Of death or death's hand for this one-half year. *(Exeunt)*

Scene II. *A public road near Coventry*

(Enter Falstaff and Bardolph)

Falstaff. Bardolph, get thee before to Coventry; fill me a bottle of sack: our soldiers shall march through; we'll to Sutton Co'fil'° to-night.

Bardolph. Will you give me money, captain?

109. wind a fiery Pegasus, turn or wheel like the winged horse of Greek mythology. ***110. witch,*** bewitch. ***111-112. worse. . .agues.*** Your praise causes me worse pain than the agues of March. ***113. trim,*** fine apparel, trappings. ***116.*** (***mailed Mars,*** the God Mars is his armor.) ***118. reprisal,*** prize. ***2. Sutton Co'fil',*** Sutton Coldfield in Warwickshire near Coventry.

Falstaff. Lay out, lay out.

Bardolph. This bottle makes an angel.°

Falstaff. An if it do, take it for thy labour; and if it make twenty, take them all; I'll answer the coinage.° Bid my lieutenant Peto meet me at town's end.

10 *Bardolph.* I will, captain: farewell. *(Exit)*

Falstaff. If I be not ashamed of my soldiers, I am a soused gurnet.° I have misused the king's press° damnably. I have got, in exchange of a hundred and fifty soldiers, three hundred and odd pounds. I press me none but good householders, yeomen's° sons; inquire me out contracted° bachelors, such as had been asked twice on the banns; such a commodity of warm slaves, as had as lieve hear the devil as a drum; such as fear the report of a caliver° worse than a struck° fowl or a hurt wild-duck. I pressed me none but such toasts-and-butter, with hearts in their bellies no bigger than pins' heads, and they have bought 20 out their services; and now my whole charge consists of ancients,° corporals, lieutenants, gentlemen of companies,° slaves as ragged as Lazarus in the painted cloth,° where the glutton's dogs licked his sores; and such as indeed were never soldiers, but discarded unjust serving-men, younger sons to younger brothers,° revolted tapsters and ostlers trade-fallen, the cankers° of a calm world and a long peace, ten times more dishonourable ragged than an old faced ancient: and such have I, to fill up the rooms of them that have bought out their services, that you would think that I had a hundred and fifty tattered prodigals° lately come from swine-keeping, from eating draff° and 30 husks. A mad fellow met me on the way and told me I had unloaded all the gibbets° and pressed the dead bodies. No eye hath seen such scare-crows. I'll not march through Coventry with them, that's flat: nay, and the villains march wide betwixt the legs, as if they had gyves° on; for indeed I had the most of them out of prison. There's but a shirt and a half in all my company; and the half shirt is two napkins tacked together and thrown over the shoulders like a herald's coat without sleeves; and the shirt, to say the truth, stolen from my host at Saint Alban's, or the red-nose innkeeper of Daventry.° But that's all one; they'll find linen enough on every hedge.°

6. makes an angel, i.e., that I have spent. ***angel,*** coin worth ten shillings. ***7-8.*** (Falstaff deliberately misunderstands Bardolph's "make" and nonsensically professes to believe that the bottle makes coins.) ***11. soused gurnet,*** a kind of pickled fish; a nasty dish. ***12. king's press,*** royal warrant for the drafting of troops. ***14. yeomen's,*** small freeholders'. ***15. contracted,*** engaged to be married. ***17. caliver,*** musket or harquebus. ***struck,*** wounded. ***20. ancients,*** standardbearers. ***21.*** (***gentlemen of companies,*** men of good family serving in the ranks—no ordinary privates.) ***22. painted cloth,*** hangings for a room; in this case painted with the story of Lazarus, Luke 16:20. ***24.*** (***younger brothers,*** young gentlemen who could have no hope of inheritance or fortune.) ***25. cankers,*** worms which destroy leaves and buds; used figuratively. ***29. prodigals.*** See Luke 15:15-16. ***Draff,*** hogwash. ***31.*** (***gibbets,*** gallows.) ***33. gyves,*** fetters. ***37-38. Saint Alban's, Daventry,*** towns on the road from London to Coventry. ***39.*** (***linen. . .hedge,*** linen drying in the open; i.e., they will steal.)

(Enter the Prince and Westmoreland)

Prince. How now, blown° Jack! how now, quilt! 40

Falstaff. What, Hal! how now, mad wag! what a devil dost thou in Warwickshire? My good Lord of Westmoreland, I cry you mercy: I thought your honour had already been at Shrewsbury.

Westmoreland. Faith, Sir John, 'tis more than time that I were there, and you too; but my powers are there already. The king, I can tell you, looks for us all: we must away all night.

Falstaff. Tut, never fear me: I am as vigilant as a cat to steal cream.

Prince. I think, to steal cream indeed, for thy theft hath already made thee butter. But tell me, Jack, whose fellows are these that come after?

Falstaff. Mine, Hal, mine. 50

Prince. I did never see such pitiful rascals.

Falstaff. Tut, tut; good enough to toss;° food for powder, food for powder,° they'll fill a pit as well as better: tush, man, mortal men, mortal men.

Westmoreland. Ay, but, Sir John, methinks they are exceeding poor and bare, too beggarly.

Falstaff. 'Faith, for their poverty, I know not where they had that; and for their bareness, I am sure they never learned that of me.

Prince. No, I'll be sworn; unless you call three fingers on the ribs bare. But, sirrah, make haste: Percy is already in the field. 60

Falstaff. What, is the king encamped?

Westmoreland. He is, Sir John: I fear we shall stay too long.

Falstaff. Well,
To the latter end of a fray and the beginning of a feast
Fits a dull fighter and a keen guest. *(Exeunt)*

Scene III. *The rebel camp near Shrewsbury*

(Enter Hotspur, Worcester, Douglas, and Vernon)

Hotspur. We'll fight with him to-night.

Worcester. It may not be.

Douglas. You give him then advantage.

Vernon. Not a whit.

Hotspur. Why say you so? looks he not for supply?

Vernon. So do we.

Hotspur. His is certain, ours is doubtful.

Worcester. Good cousin, be advised; stir not to-night.

Vernon. Do not, my lord.

Douglas. You do not counsel well:
You speak it out of fear and cold heart.

40. blown, swollen, inflated. **52-53.** (**good. . .powder,** i.e., cannon fodder.) **52. toss,** i.e., on a pike.

Vernon. Do me no slander, Douglas: by my life,
And I dare well maintain it with my life,
10 If well-respected° honour bid me on,
I hold as little counsel with weak fear
As you, my lord, or any Scot that this day lives:
Let it be seen to-morrow in the battle
Which of us fears.
Douglas. Yea, or to-night.
Vernon. Content.
Hotspur. To-night, say I.
Vernon. Come, come, it may not be. I wonder much,
Being men of such great leading as you are,
That you foresee not what impediments
Drag back our expedition: certain horse
20 Of my cousin Vernon's are not yet come up:
Your uncle Worcester's horse came but to-day;
And now their pride and mettle is asleep,
Their courage with hard labour tame and dull,
That not a horse is half the half of himself.
Hotspur. So are the horses of the enemy
In general, journey-bated° and brought low:
The better part of ours are full of rest.
Worcester. The number of the king exceedeth ours:
For God's sake, cousin, stay till all come in. *(The trumpet sounds a*
30 *parley.)*
(Enter Sir Walter Blunt)
Blunt. I come with gracious offers from the king,
If you vouchsafe me hearing and respect.
Hotspur. Welcome, Sir Walter Blunt; and would to God
You were of our determination!
Some of us love you well; and even those some
Envy your great deservings and good name,
Because you are not of our quality,
But stand against us like an enemy.
Blunt. And God defend but still I should stand so,
40 So long as out of limit and true rule
You stand against anointed majesty.
But to my charge. The king hath sent to know
The nature of your griefs, and whereupon
You conjure from the breast of civil peace
Such bold hostility, teaching his duteous land

10. well-respected, well weighed or considered. ***26. journey-bated,*** tired from the journey.

Audacious cruelty. If that the king
Have any way your good deserts forgot,
Which he confesseth to be manifold,
He bids you name your griefs; and with all speed
You shall have your desires with interest 50
And pardon absolute for yourself and these
Herein misled by your suggestion.°

Hotspur. The king is kind; and well we know the king
Knows at what time to promise, when to pay.
My father and my uncle and myself
Did give him that same royalty he wears;
And when he was not six and twenty strong,
Sick in the world's regard, wretched and low,
A poor unminded outlaw sneaking home,
My father gave him welcome to the shore; 60
And when he heard him swear and vow to God
He came but to be Duke of Lancaster,
To sue his livery° and beg his peace,
With tears of innocency and terms of zeal,
My father, in kind heart and pity moved,
Swore him assistance and perform'd it too.
Now when the lords and barons of the realm
Perceived Northumberland did lean to him,
The more and less° came in with cap and knee;
Met him in boroughs, cities, villages, 70
Attended him on bridges, stood in lanes,
Laid gifts before him, proffer'd him their oaths,
Gave him their heirs, as pages follow'd him
Even at the heels in golden multitudes.
He presently, as greatness knows itself,
Steps me a little higher than his vow
Made to my father, while his blood was poor,
Upon the naked shore at Ravenspurgh;
And now, forsooth, takes on him to reform
Some certain edicts and some strait decrees 80
That lie too heavy on the commonwealth,
Cries out upon abuses, seems to weep
Over his country's wrongs; and by this face,
This seeming brow of justice, did he win
The hearts of all that he did angle for;
Proceeded further; cut me off the heads

52. suggestions, prompting to evil. ***63. sue his livery,*** sue as an heir come of age for the delivery of his lands held by the crown. ***69. more and less,*** persons of all ranks.

Of all the favourites that the absent king
In deputation left behind him here,
When he was personal° in the Irish war.
Blunt. Tut, I came not to hear this.
90 *Hotspur.* Then to the point.
In short time after, he deposed the king;
Soon after that, deprived him of his life;
And in the neck of that, task'd° the whole state;
To make that worse, suffer'd his kinsman March,
Who is, if every owner were well placed,
Indeed his king, to be engaged in Wales,
There without ransom to lie forfeited;
Disgraced me in my happy victories,
Sought to entrap me by intelligence;°
100 Rated mine uncle from the council-board;
In rage dismiss'd my father from the court;
Broke oath on oath, committed wrong on wrong,
And in conclusion drove us to seek out
This head of safety;° and withal to pry
Into his title, the which we find
Too indirect for long continuance.
Blunt. Shall I return this answer to the king?
Hotspur. Not so, Sir Walter: we'll withdraw awhile.
Go to the king; and let there be impawn'd
110 Some surety for a safe return again,
And in the morning early shall my uncle
Bring him our purposes: and so farewell.
Blunt. I would you would accept of grace and love.
Hotspur. And may be so we shall.
Blunt. Pray God you do. *(Exeunt)*

Scene IV. *York. The Archbishop's palace*

(Enter the Archbishop of York and Sir Michael)
Archbishop. Hie, good Sir Michael; bear this sealed brief°
With winged haste to the lord marshal;
This to my cousin Scroop, and all the rest
To whom they are directed. If you knew
How much they do import, you would make haste.
Sir Michael. My good lord,
I guess their tenour.
Archbishop. Like enough you do.
To-morrow, good Sir Michael, is a day

89. *personal,* in person. **93. *task'd,*** laid taxes upon. **99. *intelligence,*** secret information, i.e., from spies. **104. *head of safety,*** armed force for their protection. **1. *brief,*** letter, dispatch.

Wherein the fortune of ten thousand men
Must bide the touch;° for, sir, at Shrewsbury, 10
As I am truly given to understand,
The king with mighty and quick-raised power
Meets with Lord Harry: and, I fear, Sir Michael,
What with the sickness of Northumberland,
Whose power was in the first proportion,
And what with Owen Glendower's absence thence,
Who with them was a rated sinew° too
And comes not in, o'er-ruled by prophecies,
I fear the power of Percy is too weak
To wage an instant trial with the king. 20

Sir Michael. Why, my good lord, you need not fear;
There is Douglas and Lord Mortimer.

Archbishop. No, Mortimer is not there.

Sir Michael. But there is Mordake, Vernon, Lord Harry Percy,
And there is my Lord of Worcester and a head
Of gallant warriors, noble gentlemen.

Archbishop. And so there is: but yet the king hath drawn
The special head of all the land together:
The Prince of Wales, Lord John of Lancaster,
The noble Westmoreland and warlike Blunt; 30
And many moe corrivals° and dear men
Of estimation° and command in arms.

Sir Michael. Doubt not, my lord, they shall be well opposed.

Archbishop. I hope no less, yet needful 'tis to fear;
And, to prevent the worst, Sir Michael, speed:
For if Lord Percy thrive not, ere the king
Dismiss his power, he means to visit us,
For he hath heard of our confederacy,
And 'tis but wisdom to make strong against him:
Therefore make haste. I must go write again 40
To other friends; and so farewell, Sir Michael. *(Exeunt)*

Act V

Scene I. *The King's camp near Shrewsbury*

(Enter the King, Prince of Wales, Lord John of Lancaster, Earl of Westmoreland, Sir Walter Blunt, and Falstaff)

King. How bloodily the sun begins to peer
Above yon busky° hill! the day looks pale
At his distemperature.°

10. bide the touch, put to the test (like gold). ***17. rated sinew,*** main strength or support reckoned upon. ***31. moe corrivals,*** more partners in the enterprise. ***32. estimation,*** reputation, importance. ***2. busky,*** bosky, bushy. ***3. distemperature,*** ill-humor, or possibly inclemency.

Prince. The southern wind
Doth play the trumpet to his purposes,
And by his hollow whistling in the leaves
Foretells a tempest and a blustering day.
King. Then with the losers let it sympathise,
For nothing can seem foul to those that win. (*The trumpet sounds.*)
(Enter Worcester and Vernon)
How now, my Lord of Worcester! 'tis not well
10 That you and I should meet upon such terms
As now we meet. You have deceived our trust,
And made us doff our easy robes of peace,
To crush our old limbs in ungentle steel:
This is not well, my lord, this is not well.
What say you to it? will you again unknit
This churlish knot of all-abhorred war?
And move in that obedient orb° again
Where you did give a fair and natural light,
And be no more an exhaled° meteor,
20 A prodigy of fear and a portent
Of broached° mischief to the unborn times?
Worcester. Hear me, my liege:
For mine own part, I could be well content
To entertain the lag-end of my life
With quiet hours; for I do protest,
I have not sought the day of this dislike.
King. You have not sought it! how comes it, then?
Falstaff. Rebellion lay in his way, and he found it.
Prince. Peace, chewet,° peace!
30 *Worcester.* It pleased your majesty to turn your looks
Of favour from myself and all our house;
And yet I must remember you, my lord,
We were the first and dearest of your friends.
For you my staff of office did I break
In Richard's time; and posted day and night
To meet you on the way, and kiss your hand,
When yet you were in place and in account
Nothing so strong and fortunate as I.
It was myself, my brother and his son,
40 That brought you home and boldly did outdare
The dangers of the time. You swore to us,
And you did swear that oath at Doncaster,

17. (***obedient orb,*** sphere of obedience.) ***19. exhaled,*** drawn forth or engendered by the sun.
21. broached, already begun. ***29. chewet,*** jackdaw.

That you did nothing purpose 'gainst the state;
Nor claim no further than your new-fall'n right,°
The seat of Gaunt, dukedom of Lancaster:
To this we swore our aid. But in short space
It rain'd down fortune showering on your head;
And such a flood of greatness fell on you,
What with our help, what with the absent king,
What with the injuries of a wanton time, 50
The seeming sufferances° that you had borne,
And the contrarious winds that held the king
So long in his unlucky Irish wars
That all in England did repute him dead:
And from this swarm of fair advantages
You took occasion to be quickly woo'd
To gripe the general sway into your hand;
Forgot your oath to us at Doncaster;
And being fed by us you used us so
As that ungentle gull,° the cuckoo's bird,° 60
Useth the sparrow; did oppress our nest;
Grew by our feeding to so great a bulk
That even our love durst not come near your sight
For fear of swallowing; but with nimble wing
We were enforced, for safety sake, to fly
Out of your sight and raise this present head;
Whereby we stand opposed by such means
As you yourself have forged against yourself
By unkind usage, dangerous countenance,°
And violation of all faith and troth 70
Sworn to us in your younger enterprise.

King. These things indeed you have articulate,°
Proclaim'd at market-crosses, read in churches,
To face° the garment of rebellion
With some fine colour that may please the eye
Of fickle changelings° and poor discontents,
Which gape and rub the elbow at the news
Of hurlyburly innovation:°
And never yet did insurrection want
Such water-colours to impaint his cause; 80

44. (***new-fall'n right,*** recent inheritance.) **51.** ***sufferances,*** suffering, distress. **60.** ***gull,*** unfledged nestling. ***cuckoo's bird,*** allusion to the cuckoo's habit of laying its eggs in the sparrow's nest. **69.** (***dangerous countenance,*** threatening looks.) **72.** ***articulate,*** set forth, specified. **74.** ***face,*** trim, adorn **76.** (***changelings,*** turncoats.) **78.** ***innovation,*** disturbance, commotion.

Nor moody beggars, starving for a time
Of pellmell havoc and confusion.

Prince. In both your armies there is many a soul
Shall pay full dearly for this encounter,
If once they join in trial. Tell your nephew,
The Prince of Wales doth join with all the world
In praise of Henry Percy: by my hopes,
This present enterprise set off his head,°
I do not think a braver gentleman,
90 More active-valiant or more valiant-young,
More daring or more bold, is now alive
To grace this latter age with noble deeds.
For my part, I may speak it to my shame,
I have a truant been to chivalry;
And so I hear he doth account me too;
Yet this before my father's majesty—
I am content that he shall take the odds
Of his great name and estimation,
And will, to save the blood on either side,
100 Try fortune with him in a single fight.

King. And, Prince of Wales, so dare we venture thee,
Albeit considerations infinite
Do make against it. No, good Worcester, no,
We love our people well; even those we love
That are misled upon your cousin's part;
And, will they take the offer of our grace,
Both he and they and you, yea, every man
Shall be my friend again and I'll be his:
So tell your cousin, and bring me word
110 What he will do: but if he will not yield,
Rebuke and dread correction wait on us°
And they shall do their office. So, be gone;
We will not now be troubled with reply:
We offer fair; take it advisedly. *(Exeunt Worcester and Vernon)*

Prince. It will not be accepted, on my life:
The Douglas and the Hotspur both together
Are confident against the world in arms.

King. Hence, therefore, every leader to his charge;
For, on their answer, will we set on them:
120 And God befriend us, as our cause is just!

(Exeunt all but the Prince of Wales and Falstaff)

88. set off his head, taken from his account. ***111. wait on us,*** are in attendance upon us.

Falstaff. Hal, if thou see me down in the battle and bestride me, so; 'tis a point of friendship.

Prince. Nothing but a colossus can do thee that friendship. Say thy prayers, and farewell.

Falstaff. I would 'twere bed-time, Hal, and all well.

Prince. Why, thou owest God a death.° *(Exit)*

Falstaff. 'Tis not due yet; I would be loath to pay him before his day. What need I be so forward with him that calls not on me? Well, 'tis no matter; honour pricks me on. Yea, but how if honour prick me off° when I come on? how then? Can honour set to a leg? no: or an arm? 130 no: or take away the grief of a wound? no. Honour hath no skill in surgery, then? no. What is honour? a word. What is in that word honour? what is that honour? air. A trim reckoning! Who hath it? he that died o'Wednesday. Doth he feel it? no. Doth he hear it? no. 'Tis insensible, then? Yea, to the dead. But will it not live with the living? no. Why? detraction° will not suffer it. Therefore I'll none of it. Honour is a mere scutcheon:° and so ends my catechism. *(Exit)*

Scene II. *The rebel camp*

(Enter Worcester and Vernon)

Worcester. O, no, my nephew must not know, Sir Richard,
The liberal and kind offer of the king.
Vernon. 'Twere best he did.
Worcester. Then are we all undone.
It is not possible, it cannot be,
The king should keep his word in loving us;
He will suspect us still and find a time
To punish this offence in other faults:
Suspicion all our lives shall be stuck full of eyes;
For treason is but trusted like the fox,
Who, ne'er so tame, so cherish'd and lock'd up, 10
Will have a wild trick of his ancestors.
Look how we can, or sad or merrily,
Interpretation will misquote our looks,
And we shall feed like oxen at a stall,
The better cherish'd, still the nearer death.
My nephew's trespass may be well forgot;
It hath the excuse of youth and heat of blood,
And an adopted name of privilege,°

126. thou...death, proverbial, with a pun on "debt." ***129-130. prick me off,*** probably mark me off as one dead. ***136.*** (***detraction,*** slander.) ***137. scutcheon,*** emblem of hatchment carried in funerals. ***18. adopted name of privilege.*** The meaning is that Hotspur has taken a nickname, "hotspur," to justify his rashness.

A hare-brain'd Hotspur, govern'd by a spleen:
20 All his offences live upon my head
And on his father's; we did train him on,
And, his corruption being ta'en from us,
We, as the spring of all, shall pay for all.
Therefore, good cousin, let not Harry know,
In any case, the offer of the king.

Vernon. Deliver what you will; I'll say 'tis so.
Here comes your cousin.

(Enter Hotspur and Douglas)

Hotspur. My uncle is return'd:
Deliver up my Lord of Westmoreland.
30 Uncle, what news?

Worcester. The king will bid you battle presently.

Douglas. Defy him by the Lord of Westmoreland.

Hotspur. Lord Douglas, go you and tell him so.

Douglas. Marry, and shall, and very willingly. *(Exit)*

Worcester. There is no seeming mercy in the king.

Hotspur. Did you beg any? God forbid!

Worcester. I told him gently of our grievances,
Of his oath-breaking; which he mended thus,
By now forswearing that he is forsworn:
40 He calls us rebels, traitors; and will scourge
With haughty arms this hateful name in us.

(Re-enter Douglas)

Douglas. Arm, gentlemen; to arms! for I have thrown
A brave defiance in King Henry's teeth,
And Westmoreland, that was engaged,° did bear it;
Which cannot choose but bring him quickly on.

Worcester. The Prince of Wales stepp'd forth before the king,
And, nephew, challenged you to single fight.

Hotspur. O, would the quarrel lay upon our heads,
And that no man might draw short breath to-day
50 But I and Harry Monmouth! Tell me, tell me,
How show'd his tasking?° seem'd it in contempt?

Vernon. No, by my soul; I never in my life
Did hear a challenge urged more modestly,
Unless a brother should a brother dare
To gentle exercise and proof of arms.
He gave you all the duties of a man;
Trimm'd up your praises with a princely tongue,
Spoke your deservings like a chronicle,

44. (***engaged,*** held as a hostage.) **51.** ***tasking,*** challenge.

Making you ever better than his praise
By still dispraising praise valued with you;° 60
And, which became him like a prince indeed,
He made a blushing cital° of himself;
And chid his truant youth with such a grace
As if he master'd there a double spirit
Of teaching and of learning instantly.
There did he pause: but let me tell the world,
If he outlive the envy of this day,
England did never owe so sweet a hope,
So much misconstrued in his wantonness.

Hotspur. Cousin, I think thou art enamoured 70
On his follies: never did I hear
Of any prince so wild a libertine.
But be he as he will, yet once ere night
I will embrace him with a soldier's arm,
That he shall shrink under my courtesy.
Arm, arm with speed: and, fellows, soldiers, friends,
Better consider what you have to do
Than I, that have not well the gift of tongue,
Can lift your blood up with persuasion.

(Enter a Messenger)

Messenger. My lord, here are letters for you. 80

Hotspur. I cannot read them now.
O gentlemen, the time of life is short!
To spend that shortness basely were too long,
If life did ride upon a dial's point,°
Still ending at the arrival of an hour.
An if we live, we live to tread on kings;
If die, brave death, when princes die with us!
Now, for our consciences, the arms are fair,
When the intent of bearing them is just.

(Enter another Messenger)

Messenger. My lord, prepare; the king comes on apace. 90

Hotspur. I thank him, that he cuts me from my tale,
For I profess not talking; only this—
Let each man do his best: and here draw I
A sword, whose temper I intend to stain
With the best blood that I can meet withal
In the adventure of this perilous day.
Now, Esperance! Percy! and set on.

60. (***By...you,*** by insisting that all praise still undervalued you.) ***62.*** (***cital,*** recital.) ***84. dial's point,*** hand of watch or clock.

Sound all the lofty instruments of war,
And by that music let us all embrace;
100 For, heaven to earth, some of us never shall
A second time do such a courtesy.
(The trumpets sound. They embrace, and exeunt.)

Scene III. *Plain between the camps*

(The King enters with his power. Alarum to the battle. Then enter Douglas and Sir Walter Blunt)

Blunt. What is thy name, that in the battle thus
Thou crossest me? what honour dost thou seek
Upon my head?

Douglas. Know then, my name is Douglas;
And I do haunt thee in the battle thus
Because some tell me that thou art a king.

Blunt. They tell thee true.

Douglas. The Lord of Stafford dear to-day hath bought
Thy likeness, for instead of thee, King Harry,
This sword hath ended him: so shall it thee,
10 Unless thou yield thee as my prisoner.

Blunt. I was not born a yielder, thou proud Scot;
And thou shalt find a king that will revenge
Lord Stafford's death. *(They fight. Douglas kills Blunt.)*
(Enter Hotspur)

Hotspur. O Douglas, hadst thou fought at Holmedon thus,
I never had triumph'd upon a Scot.

Douglas. All 's done, all 's won; here breathless lies the king.

Hotspur. Where?

Douglas. Here.

Hotspur. This, Douglas? no: I know this face full well:
20 A gallant knight he was, his name was Blunt;
Semblably furnish'd° like the king himself.

Douglas. A fool go with thy soul, whither it goes!
A borrow'd title hast thou bought too dear:
Why didst thou tell me that thou wert a king?

Hotspur. The king hath many marching in his coats.°

Douglas. Now, by my sword, I will kill all his coats;
I'll murder all his wardrobe, piece by piece,
Until I meet the king.

Hotspur. Up, and away!
Our soldiers stand full fairly for the day. *(Exeunt)*

21. *Semblably furnish'd,* similarly dressed. **25.** (***coats,*** coats of arms.)

(Alarum. Enter Falstaff, solus)

Falstaff. Though I could 'scape shot-free° at London, I fear the shot here; here's no scoring° but upon the pate. Soft! who are you? Sir Walter Blunt: there's honour for you! here's no vanity! I am as hot as molten lead, and as heavy too: God keep lead out of me! I need no more weight than mine own bowels. I have led my ragamuffins where they are peppered: there's not three of my hundred and fifty left alive; and they are for the town's end, to beg during life. But who comes here? 30

(Enter the Prince)

Prince. What, stand'st thou idle here? lend me thy sword:
Many a nobleman lies stark and stiff
Under the hoofs of vaunting enemies,
Whose deaths are yet unrevenged: I prithee, lend me thy sword. 40

Falstaff. O Hal, I prithee, give me leave to breathe awhile. Turk Gregory° never did such deeds in arms as I have done this day. I have paid Percy, I have made him sure.

Prince. He is, indeed; and living to kill thee. I prithee, lend me thy sword.

Falstaff. Nay, before God, Hal, if Percy be alive, thou get'st not my sword; but take my pistol, if thou wilt.

Prince. Give it me: what, is it in the case?

Falstaff. Ay, Hal; 'tis hot, 'tis hot; there's that will sack a city. *(The Prince draws it out, and finds it to be a bottle of sack.)* 50

Prince. What, is it a time to jest and dally now?

(He throws the bottle at him. Exit)

Falstaff. Well, if Percy be alive, I'll pierce° him, If he do come in my way, so: if he do not, if I come in his willingly, let him make a carbonado° of me. I like not such grinning honour as Sir Walter hath: give me life: which if I can save, so; it not, honour comes unlooked for, and there's an end. *(Exit)*

Scene IV. *Another part of the field*

(Alarum. Excursions.° Enter the King, the Prince, Lord John of Lancaster, and Earl of Westmoreland)

King. I prithee,
Harry, withdraw thyself; thou bleed'st too much.
Lord John of Lancaster, go you with him.

Lancaster. Not I, my lord, unless I did bleed too.

30. shot-free, scot-free, without paying. ***31. scoring,*** marking up of charges (often on the inn door). ***41-42. Turk Gregory,*** a sort of combined allusion to that famous pope Gregory the Great, and to the Grand Turk. ***52. Percy. . .pierce.*** Current pronunciation probably rendered the pun more obvious than it is now. ***53-54. carbonado,*** meat scored across for broiling. ***(Alarum. Excursions,*** noises of battle—trumpet calls, noise of rapid movements.)

Prince. I beseech your majesty, make up,°
Lest your retirement do amaze° your friends.
King. I will do so.
My Lord of Westmoreland, lead him to his tent.
Westmoreland. Come, my lord, I'll lead you to your tent.
10 *Prince.* Lead me, my lord? I do not need your help:
And God forbid a shallow scratch should drive
The Prince of Wales from such a field as this,
Where stain'd nobility lies trodden on,
And rebels' arms triumph in massacres!
Lancaster. We breathe too long: come, cousin Westmoreland,
Our duty this way lies; for God's sake, come.
(Exeunt Prince John and Westmoreland)
Prince. By God, thou hast deceived me, Lancaster;
I did not think thee lord of such a spirit:
Before, I loved thee as a brother, John;
20 But now, I do respect thee as my soul.
King. I saw him hold Lord Percy at the point
With lustier maintenance° than I did look for
Of such an ungrown warrior.
Prince. O, this boy
Lends mettle to us all! *(Exit)*
(Enter Douglas)
Douglas. Another king! they grow like Hydra's heads:°
I am the Douglas, fatal to all those
That wear those colours on them: what art thou,
That counterfeit'st the person of a king?
King. The king himself; who, Douglas, grieves at heart
30 So many of his shadows thou hast met
And not the very king. I have two boys
Seek Percy and thyself about the field:
But, seeing thou fall'st on me so luckily,
I will assay thee: so, defend thyself.
Douglas. I fear thou art another counterfeit;
And yet, in faith, thou bear'st thee like a king:
But mine I am sure thou art, whoe'er thou be,
And thus I win thee.
(They fight; the King being in danger, re-enter Prince of Wales)
Prince. Hold up thy head, vile Scot, or thou art like
40 Never to hold it up again! the spirits
Of valiant Shirley, Stafford, Blunt, are in my arms:
It is the Prince of Wales that threatens thee;

5. *make up,* go forward. **6. *amaze,*** alarm. **22. *maintenance,*** bearing demeanor. **25. *Hydra's heads,*** allusion to the Lernean Hydra, whose heads grew again as fast as they were cut off.

Who never promiseth but he means to pay. *(They fight: Douglas flies.)*
Cheerly, my lord: how fares your grace?
Sir Nicholas Gawsey hath for succour sent,
And so hath Clifton: I'll to Clifton straight.

King. Stay, and breathe awhile:
Thou hast redeem'd thy lost opinion,
And show'd thou makest some tender° of my life,
In this fair rescue thou hast brought to me. 50

Prince. O God! they did me too much injury
That ever said I hearken'd° for your death.
If it were so, I might have let alone
The insulting hand of Douglas over you,
Which would have been as speedy in your end
As all the poisonous potions in the world
And saved the treacherous labour of your son.

King. Make up to Clifton: I'll to Sir Nicholas Gawsey. *(Exit)*

(Enter Hotspur)

Hotspur. If I mistake not, thou art Harry Monmouth.

Prince. Thou speak'st as if I would deny my name. 60

Hotspur. My name is Harry Percy.

Prince. Why, then I see
A very valiant rebel of the name.
I am the Prince of Wales; and think not, Percy,
To share with me in glory any more:
Two stars keep not their motion in one sphere;°
Nor can one England brook a double reign,
Of Harry Percy and the Prince of Wales.

Hotspur. Nor shall it, Harry; for the hour is come
To end the one of us; and would to God
Thy name in arms were now as great as mine! 70

Prince. I'll make it greater ere I part from thee;
And all the budding honours on thy crest
I'll crop, to make a garland for my head.

Hotspur. I can no longer brook thy vanities. *(They fight.)*

(Enter Falstaff)

Falstaff. Well said, Hal! to it, Hal! Nay, you shall find
no boy's play here, I can tell you.

(Re-enter Douglas; he fights with Falstaff, who falls down as if he were dead, and exit Douglas. Hotspur is wounded, and falls.)

Hotspur. O, Harry, thou hast robb'd me of my youth!
I better brook the loss of brittle life
Than those proud titles thou hast won of me;

49. makest some tender, hast some care for. ***52. hearken'd,*** listened (as for welcome intelligence). ***65. Two...sphere,*** proverbial allusion to the fact that each planet has its own orbit.

80 They wound my thoughts worse than thy sword my flesh:
But thought's the slave of life, and life time's fool;
And time, that takes survey of all the world,
Must have a stop.° O, I could prophesy,
But that the earthy and cold hand of death
Lies on my tongue: no, Percy, thou art dust,
And food for—*(Dies)*

Prince. For worms, brave Percy: fare thee well, great heart!
Ill-weaved ambition, how much art thou shrunk!
When that this body did contain a spirit,
90 A kingdom for it was too small a bound;
But now two paces of the vilest earth
Is room enough: this earth that bears thee dead
Bears not alive so stout a gentleman.
If thou wert sensible of courtesy,
I should not make so dear a show of zeal:°
But let my favours° hide thy mangled face;
And, even in thy behalf, I'll thank myself
For doing these fair rites of tenderness.
Adieu, and take thy praise with thee to heaven!
100 Thy ignominy sleep with thee in the grave,
But not remember'd in thy epitaph! *(He spies Falstaff on the ground.)*
What, old acquaintance! could not all this flesh
Keep in a little life? Poor Jack, farewell!
I could have better spared a better man:
O, I should have a heavy miss of thee,
If I were much in love with vanity!°
Death hath not struck so fat a deer to-day,
Though many dearer, in this bloody fray.
Embowell'd° will I see thee by and by:
110 Till then in blood by noble Percy lie. *(Exit)*

Falstaff. (Rising up) Embowelled! if thou embowel me to-day, I'll give you leave to powder° me and eat me too to-morrow. 'Sblood, 'twas time to counterfeit, or that hot termagant° Scot had paid me scot and lot° too. Counterfeit? I lie, I am no counterfeit: to die, is to be a counterfeit; for he is but the counterfeit of a man who hath not the life of a man: but to counterfeit dying, when a man thereby liveth, is to be no counterfeit, but the true and perfect image of life indeed. The better part of valour is discretion; in the which better part I have saved my life. 'Zounds, I am afraid of this gunpowder Percy, though he be dead:

81-83. But...stop. Thought ends with life, and life is ended by time; and time, though it serve as the measure for the world, must itself come to an end. ***95.*** (***zeal,*** respect.) ***96. favours,*** knots of ribbon. ***106.*** (***vanity,*** folly.) ***109. Embowell'd,*** disemboweled, i.e., for burial. ***112. powder,*** salt. ***113. termagant,*** violent; derived from the name of a heathen god of the Saracens in the miracle play of St. Nicholas. ***113-114. scot and lot,*** used figuratively to denote complete payment.

how, if he should counterfeit too and rise? by my faith, I am afraid he 120
would prove the better counterfeit. Therefore I'll make him sure; yea,
and I'll swear I killed him. Why may not he rise as well as I? Nothing
confutes me but eyes, and nobody sees me. Therefore, sirrah *(Stabbing him)*, with a new wound in your thigh, come you along with me. *(Takes up Hotspur on his back°)*

(Re-enter the Prince of Wales and Lord John of Lancaster)

Prince. Come, brother John; full bravely hast thou flesh'd
Thy maiden sword.

Lancaster. But, soft! whom have we here?
Did you not tell me this fat man was dead?

Prince. I did; I saw him dead,
Breathless and bleeding on the ground. Art thou alive? 130
Or is it fantasy° that plays upon our eyesight?
I prithee, speak; we will not trust our eyes
Without our ears: thou art not what thou seem'st.

Falstaff. No, that's certain; I am not a double man: but if I be not Jack Falstaff, then am I a Jack. There is Percy *(Throwing the body down)*: if your father will do me any honour, so; if not, let him kill the next Percy himself. I look to be either earl or duke, I can assure you.

Prince. Why, Percy I killed myself and saw thee dead.

Falstaff. Didst thou? Lord, Lord, how this world is given to lying!
I grant you I was down and out of breath; and so was he: but we rose 140
both at an instant and fought a long hour by Shrewsbury clock. If I may be believed, so; if not, let them that should reward valour bear the sin upon their own heads. I'll take it upon my death, I gave him this wound in the thigh: if the man were alive and would deny it, 'zounds, I would make him eat a piece of my sword.

Lancaster. This is the strangest tale that ever I heard.

Prince. This is the strangest fellow, brother John.
Come, bring your luggage nobly on your back:
For my part, if a lie may do thee grace,
I'll gild it with the happiest terms I have. *(A retreat is sounded.)* 150
The trumpet sounds retreat;° the day is ours.
Come, brother, let us to the highest of the field,
To see what friends are living, who are dead.

(Exeunt Prince of Wales and Lancaster)

Falstaff. I'll follow, as they say, for reward. He that rewards me, God reward him! If I do grow great, I'll grow less; for I'll purge, and leave sack, and live cleanly as a nobleman should do. *(Exit)*

124-125. *Stage Direction:* ***Takes up, etc.*** Bodies of slain persons had to be removed from the stage in the Elizabethan theater. This is a famous example of Shakespeare's skill in having the duty performed naturally. ***131. fantasy.*** Note that the prince seems to show real fear at what he thinks is Falstaff's ghost. ***151.*** (***retreat,*** to recall the troops from the pursuit of the enemy.)

Scene V. *Another part of the field*

(The trumpets sound. Enter the King, Prince of Wales, Lord John of Lancaster, Earl of Westmoreland, with Worcester and Vernon prisoners)

King. Thus ever did rebellion find rebuke.
Ill-spirited Worcester! did not we send grace,
Pardon and terms of love to all of you?
And wouldst thou turn our offers contrary?
Misuse the tenour of thy kinsman's trust?
Three knights upon our party slain to-day,
A noble earl and many a creature else
Had been alive this hour,
If like a Christian thou hadst truly borne
10 Betwixt our armies true intelligence.
Worcester. What I have done my safety urged me to;
And I embrace this fortune patiently,
Since not to be avoided it falls on me.
King. Bear Worcester to the death and Vernon too:
Other offenders we will pause upon.
(Exeunt Worcester and Vernon, guarded)
How goes the field?
Prince. The noble Scot, Lord Douglas, when he saw
The fortune of the day quite turn'd from him,
The noble Percy slain, and all his men
20 Upon the foot of fear,° fled with the rest;
And falling from a hill, he was so bruised
That the pursuers took him. At my tent
The Douglas is; and I beseech your grace
I may dispose of him.
King. With all my heart.
Prince. Then, brother John of Lancaster, to you
This honourable bounty shall belong:
Go to the Douglas, and deliver him
Up to his pleasure, ransomless and free:
His valour shown upon our crests to-day
30 Hath taught us how to cherish such high deeds
Even in the bosom of our adversaries.
Lancaster. I thank your grace for this high courtesy,
Which I shall give away immediately.
King. Then this remains, that we divide our power.
You, son John, and my cousin Westmoreland
Towards York shall bend you with your dearest speed,
To meet Northumberland and the prelate Scroop,

20. Upon the foot of fear, in flight.

Who, as we hear, are busily in arms:
Myself and you, son Harry, will towards Wales,
To fight with Glendower and the Earl of March.
Rebellion in this land shall lose his sway,
Meeting the check of such another day:
And since this business so fair is done,
Let us not leave till all our own be won. *(Exeunt)*

Comments and Questions

Shakespeare does more than merely tell a story; he constructs a cross-section of English feudal society, which he closely examines and evaluates. The plot dealing with Prince Hal's assumption of responsibility prompted by the rebellion of the Percies serves as little more than a framework. Instead, Shakespeare underdramatizes the suspense inherent in a young man's reformation or in the intrigues of a rebellion. How does he do that? Excitement is achieved by artfully placing scenes from the court, the rebel positions, and the tavern against each other so that the actions and characters actually serve to comment on each other. The planning for the robbery, for example, is an echo of that for the rebellion; the mock interview of the Prince with his father in Act II, scene iv, ll. 361-396, contrasts comically with the actual interview that follows; what are some of the others? What, finally, is the effect of these scenes that reflect each other?

The contrasting personalities and virtues of the Prince and Hotspur are fully examined. From the beginning, careful preparation is made for the confrontation of the Prince and Hotspur in battle. In Act I, scene i, ll. 78-91, King Henry refers to Hotspur as "the theme of honor's tongue" and contrasts him to his dissolute "young Harry." Throughout, the theme of regeneration, reflected also in the King and humorously counterpointed in Falstaff, is enforced by that of honor. You will want to observe speeches and actions which dramatize the differences between these two young men and which comment on honor. How does Shakespeare make it clear that Hal does not change his colors overnight, that, in fact, there is no essential transformation in his character? (See Hal's soliloquy at the end of Act I, scene i.) Who, finally, is the better man? Who is the more appealing character? Do you agree with John Masefield's and Bernard Shaw's evaluation of the characters?

Your examination will be incomplete until you consider practically all the actions and speeches (especially the soliloquies) of Falstaff, who serves as a kind of comic counterpart to Hotspur and the Prince.

Shakespeare is clearly examining military and political honor, courage, and integrity from several points of view; in this connection also consider the characters of King Henry, Glendower, Worcester, and Douglas. Taking into account these various points of view, try to formulate in writing a statement of the play's theme. Finally, are there any scenes in the play which might be omitted without hindering the development of plot or theme? If so, why are they included?

Related Reading

Bernard Shaw, *Arms and the Man*, page 33 and his review of *Henry IV*, Part I, page 689

Oscar G. Brockett, "The Elizabethan Theater," page 656

Robert C. Elliott, "Shaw's Captain Bluntschli: A Latter-Day Falstaff," page 698

John Masefield, "*King Henry IV*, Part I," page 696

Henrik Ibsen

(1828-1906)

AN ENEMY OF THE PEOPLE

translated by Michael Meyer

In 1881 Henrik Ibsen completed his play Ghosts. *The major theaters of his native Scandinavia flatly refused to perform it, and when it was published in December, the reaction of the press infuriated the famous playwright. He knew very well that the ideas presented in* Ghosts *were novel and daring for their time, but they were important to him, and, until confronted by that wave of hostility, he had believed that he would obtain at least a respectful hearing for them.*

Ibsen's fury led him to write another play much more speedily than he had written any of the rest of his major works. The play was An Enemy of the People, *written in Rome between March and June, 1882.*

Like its predecessor, An Enemy of the People *is a drama of ideas, a play in which one of the author's main intentions is to express himself on certain problems. Though the play was prompted in part by Ibsen's anger at what he called "the majority," including both the liberal and the conservative elements of society, and though the ideas expressed were obviously important to him, it should not be thought that* An Enemy of the People *is merely a sounding board for his pet peeves or pet theories arranged in dramatic form.*

Ibsen's letters to friends and associates over a period of years clearly show that Dr. Stockmann in the play expresses many ideas held by the playwright: ideas about the timidity of society, its refusal to act rationally (an idea Ibsen shares with Bernard Shaw), and, particularly, society's aversion against that small, militant minority of individualists to whom the new holds no threat. At the time of writing An Enemy of the People, *Ibsen expressed the link between himself and Dr. Stockmann in a letter to his friend, the Danish critic Georg Brandes:*

"You are, of course, right when you say that we must all work for the spread of our ideas. But I maintain that a fighter in the intellectual vanguard cannot possibly gather a majority around him. In ten years the majority will possibly occupy the standpoint which Dr. Stockmann held at the public meeting. But during those ten years the doctor will not have been standing still; he will still be at least ten years ahead of the majority. The majority, the mass, the mob, will never catch up with him; and he can never have the majority with him. As regards myself at least, I am quite aware of such unceasing progress. At the point where I stood when I wrote each of my books there now stands a tolerably compact crowd; but I myself am no longer there. I am elsewhere; farther ahead, I hope."

To his publisher, Ibsen also admitted that "Dr. Stockmann and I got on most excellently; we agree about so many things," but he then goes on to give the clue that the Doctor is not a replica of himself: ". . . the Doctor has a more muddled head on his shoulders than I have, and he has besides certain characteristics which will permit people to tolerate various things from his lips which they might not accept so readily if they had issued from mine."

The distinction here between preacher and preachment is significant, for it indicates that Ibsen felt it necessary to create for his hero a congenial, sympathetic, even comic character unlike his own well-known dour, caustic personality. Dr. Stockmann's character transforms what might have been a completely serious drama into a play that verges on comedy at times. Perhaps, by transferring some of his deepset convictions and anger to a serio-comic muddled visionary, Ibsen achieved enough detachment to create a work of permanent interest instead of a polemical tract.

It takes, however, more than detachment to create an effective work of art that will last beyond the situation or mood which gave rise to it. The play has often been acclaimed as a "well-made" play. This is true if we look at the play itself, but it is less true if we fit it too literally into the mold of the "well-made" play as it was popularized by the French playwright Eugène Scribe (1791-1861) and his followers, who devised a tightly knit structure for their plays, full of intrigues, withheld information, surprises, coincidences, long series of convenient revelations from the past, and the like, so that the dramatist was a magician of excitement and suspense who could neatly resolve everything with a professional flourish of his wand.

In some of his earlier plays, Ibsen quite effectively had used "well-made" plots for dramatizing his ideas, as in Ghosts, *which progresses by a number of artfully placed revelations of earlier events that build up to the climactic scene. But Ibsen's mastery of dramatic technique enables him to avoid the arts of the magician. In* An Enemy of the People *there is no need for surprise discoveries or withheld revelations; what discoveries and revelations there are come about naturally and plausibly within the context of the plot. Ibsen prepares his way meticulously, establishing all the main relationships between the characters in Act I, using Act II to gather the forces opposed to Dr. Stockmann, and so on to the end.*

The basis of the plot seems to lie in two incidents of which Ibsen had knowledge. One concerned a doctor, the medical officer of a German health resort, who discovered an outbreak of cholera which he felt it his duty to make public. As a result the season of the resort was ruined, and the citizens of the town stoned his house and forced him to flee. The second incident concerned the attempt by a Norwegian chemist to force the Christiania (Oslo) Steam Kitchens to fufill their duty toward the poor. In a climactic meeting, much like the one in Act IV of the play, the chemist was defeated by the majority, who evidently preferred their comfortable ignorance of the conditions in the Steam Kitchens.

An Enemy of the People *was first performed in Christiania, Norway, on January 13, 1883. It did not reach New York until 1892 (in German) and London (in English) until the following year.*

AN ENEMY OF THE PEOPLE

Characters

DR. THOMAS STOCKMANN, *medical officer at the Baths*
MRS. STOCKMANN, *his wife*
PETRA, *their daughter, a schoolteacher*
EILIF
MORTEN } *their sons, aged thirteen and ten*
PETER STOCKMANN, *the Doctor's elder brother, Mayor and Chief Constable, Chairman of the Baths Committee, etc.*
MORTEN KIIL, *master tanner, foster father to Mrs. Stockmann*
HOVSTAD, *editor of the* People's Tribune
BILLING, *an employee on the newspaper*
HORSTER, *a sea captain*
ASLAKSEN, *a printer*
People at a public meeting—men of all classes, a few women and a bunch of schoolboys.

The action takes place in a coastal town in Southern Norway.

Act I

(Evening in Dr. Stockmann's living-room. It is humbly but neatly furnished and decorated. In the wall to the right are two doors, of which the further leads out to the hall and the nearer to the Doctor's study. In the opposite wall, facing the hall door, is a door that leads to the other rooms occupied by the family. In the middle of this wall stands a tiled stove; further downstage is a sofa with a mirror above it. In front of the sofa is an oval table with a cloth on it. Upon this table stands a lighted lamp with a shade. Upstage, an open door to the dining-room, in which can be seen a table laid for the evening meal, with a lamp on it.)

(At this table Billing is seated, a napkin tucked beneath his chin. Mrs. Stockmann is standing by the table, offering him a plate with a large joint of beef on it. The other places around the table are empty, and the table is in the disorder of a meal that has been finished.)

Mrs. Stockmann. There, Mr. Billing! But if you will come an hour late, you'll have to put up with cold meat.

Billing. (Eating) Oh, but this is capital. Absolutely capital!

Mrs. Stockmann. Well, you know how punctually my husband always likes to eat.

Billing. It doesn't bother me. I enjoy eating alone, without having to talk to anyone.

Mrs. Stockmann. Oh. Well, as long as you're *enjoying* it, that's—*(Listens towards the hall)* Ah, this must be Mr. Hovstad.

Billing. Very likely. 10

(Peter Stockmann enters wearing an overcoat and his mayoral hat, and carrying a stick.)

Mayor. Good evening to you, my dear sister-in-law.

Mrs. Stockmann. (Goes into the living-room) Why, good evening! Fancy seeing you here! How nice of you to come and call on us!

Mayor. I just happened to be passing, so— *(Glances towards the dining-room)* But I hear you have company.

Mrs. Stockmann. (A little embarrassed) Oh, no, no, that's no one. *(Quickly)* Won't you have something too?

Mayor. I? No, thank you! A cooked meal at night! My digestion 20 would never stand that!

Mrs. Stockmann. Oh, but surely just for once—

Mayor. No, no! It's very kind of you, but I'll stick to my tea and sandwiches. It's healthier in the long run; and a little less expensive.

Mrs. Stockmann. (Smiles) You speak as though Thomas and I were spendthrifts!

Mayor. Not you, my dear sister-in-law. Such a thought was far from my mind. *(Points towards the Doctor's study)* Isn't he at home?

Mrs. Stockmann. No, he's gone for a little walk with the boys.

Mayor. I wonder if that's wise so soon after a meal? *(Listens)* Ah, 30 this must be he.

Mrs. Stockmann. No, I don't think it can be, yet. *(A knock on the door)* Come in!

(Hovstad, the editor of the local newspaper, enters from the hall.)

Mrs. Stockmann. Oh—Mr. Hovstad—?

Hovstad. Yes. Please excuse me, I was detained down at the printer's. Good evening, Your Worship.

Mayor. (Greets him somewhat stiffly) Good evening. I suppose you are here on business?

Hovstad. Partly. About an article for my newspaper— 40

Mayor. I guessed as much. I hear my brother is a regular contributor to the *People's Tribune.*

Hovstad. Yes, he usually drops us a line when he thinks the truth needs to be told about something.

Mrs. Stockmann. (To Hovstad, pointing towards the dining-room) Er—won't you—?

Mayor. Great heavens, you mustn't think I blame him for writing for the kind of public he's most likely to find sympathetic to his ideas. Besides, I have no reason to bear your newspaper any ill will, Mr. Hovstad— 50

Hovstad. I should hope not.

Mayor. On the whole I think I may say that an admirable spirit of tolerance reigns in our town. A fine communal spirit! And the reason for this is that we have this great common interest that binds us together—an interest which is the close concern of every right-minded citizen—

Hovstad. You mean the Baths?°

Mayor. Exactly! Our magnificent new Baths! Mark my words, sir! These Baths will prove the very heart and essence of our life! There can be no doubt about it.

60 *Mrs. Stockmann.* Yes, that's just what Thomas says.

Mayor. It's really astounding the strides this place has made during the past two or three years! The town is becoming prosperous. People are waking up and beginning to live. Buildings and ground rents° are increasing in value every day.

Hovstad. And unemployment is going down.

Mayor. Yes, there's that too. The burden upon the propertied classes of poor relief has been most gratifyingly reduced—and will be still more if only we have a really good summer this year, with plenty of visitors. What we want most is invalids. They'll give the Baths a good

70 name.

Hovstad. And I hear the indications are promising.

Mayor. They are indeed. Enquiries about accommodation are pouring in every day.

Hovstad. Well then, the Doctor's article will be most opportune.

Mayor. Oh, has he written something new?

Hovstad. No, it's something he wrote last winter; a eulogy of the Baths and the excellent health facilities of the town. But I decided to hold it over.

Mayor. Ah, there was a snag somewhere?

80 *Hovstad.* No, it wasn't that. I just thought it would be better to wait till the spring. Now people are thinking about where to spend their summer holidays—

Mayor. Quite right! Quite right, Mr. Hovstad!

Mrs. Stockmann. Thomas never stops thinking about those Baths.

Mayor. Well, he is employed there.

Hovstad. Yes, and he was the one who really created it all, wasn't he?

Mayor. Was he? Really? Yes, I have heard that certain people do hold that opinion. I must say I was labouring under the delusion that I had some modest share in promoting the enterprise.

90 *Mrs. Stockmann.* That's what Thomas is always telling people.

56. Baths. Health resorts play an important role in Europe. Almost all of them center on baths and drinking springs or wells whose waters are said to cure specific afflictions. Baths have never played as important a role in America, though there are some, such as Warm Springs, Georgia, or Hot Springs, Arkansas. ***63. ground rents,*** land values.

Hovstad. No one denies that, Your Worship. You got it going and saw to all the practical details—we all know that. I only meant that the idea originated with the Doctor.

Mayor. Yes, my brother's always been full of ideas—unfortunately. But when things have to be done, another kind of man is needed, Mr. Hovstad. And I should have thought that least of all in this house would—

Mrs. Stockmann. But my dear brother-in-law—!

Hovstad. Surely Your Worship doesn't—?

Mrs. Stockmann. Do go inside and get yourself something to eat, Mr. Hovstad. My husband will be here any moment. 100

Hovstad. Thank you—just a bite, perhaps.

(Goes into the dining-room)

Mayor. (Lowers his voice slightly) It's extraordinary about people of peasant stock. They never learn the meaning of tact.

Mrs. Stockmann. But is it really anything to bother about? Can't you and Thomas share the honour as brothers?

Mayor. Well, I should have thought so; but it seems not everyone is content to share.

Mrs. Stockmann. Oh, nonsense! You and Thomas always get on so well together. Ah, this sounds like him. *(Goes over and opens the door leading to the hall)* 110

Dr. Stockmann. (Laughing and boisterous) Hullo, Catherine! I've another guest for you here! The more the merrier, what? Come in, Captain Horster! Hang your overcoat up there on the hook. No, of course, you don't wear an overcoat, do you? Fancy, Catherine, I bumped into him in the street! Had the devil of a job persuading him to come back with me!

(Captain Horster enters and shakes hands with Mrs. Stockmann.)

Dr. Stockmann. (In the doorway) Run along in now, lads. *(To Mrs. Stockmann)* They're hungry again already! This way, Captain Horster, you're going to have the finest roast beef you ever—! 120

(Drives Horster into the dining-room. Eilif and Morten go in too.)

Mrs. Stockmann. Thomas! Don't you see who's—?

Dr. Stockmann. (Turns in the doorway) Oh, hullo, Peter! *(Goes over and shakes his hand)* Well, it's good to see you!

Mayor. I'm afraid I can only spare a few minutes—

Dr. Stockmann. Rubbish, we'll be having some hot toddy soon. You haven't forgotten the toddy, Catherine?

Mrs. Stockmann. No, of course not. I've got the kettle on— 130

(Goes into the dining-room)

Mayor. Hot toddy too—!

Dr. Stockmann. Yes. Now sit down, and we'll have a good time.

Mayor. Thank you. I never partake in drinking parties.

Dr. Stockmann. But this isn't a party.

Mayor. Well, but—! *(Glances towards the dining-room)* It's really extraordinary the amount they eat!

Dr. Stockmann. (Rubs his hands) Yes, there's nothing better than to see young people tuck in, is there? Always hungry! That's the way it 140 should be! They've got to have food! Gives them strength! They're the ones who've got to ginger up the future, Peter.

Mayor. May one ask what it is that needs to be "gingered up," as you put it?

Dr. Stockmann. You must ask the young ones that—when the time comes. We can't see it, of course. Obviously—a couple of old fogeys like you and me—

Mayor. Well, really! That's a most extraordinary way to describe us—

Dr. Stockmann. Oh, you mustn't take me too seriously, Peter. I feel 150 so happy and exhilarated, you see! It's so wonderful to be alive at a time like this, with everything germinating and bursting all around us! Oh, it's a glorious age we live in! It's as though a whole new world were coming to birth before our eyes!

Mayor. Do you really feel that?

Dr. Stockmann. Yes. Of course, you can't see it as clearly as I do. You've spent your life in this background, so it doesn't make the same impression on you as it does on me. But I've had to spend all these years sitting up there in that damned northern backwater, hardly ever seeing a new face that had a stimulating word to say to me. To me it's 160 as though I had moved into the heart of some pulsing metropolis—

Mayor. Hm; metropolis—!

Dr. Stockmann. Oh, I know it must seem small in comparison with lots of other cities. But there's life here—promise—so many things to work and fight for! And that's what matters. *(Shouts)* Catherine, hasn't the post come yet?

Mrs. Stockmann. (From the dining-room) No, not yet.

Dr. Stockmann. And to be making a decent living, Peter! That's something one learns to appreciate when one's been living on the edge of starvation, as we have—

170 *Mayor.* Oh, surely!

Dr. Stockmann. Oh yes, I can tell you we were often pretty hard pressed up there. But now, we can live like lords! Today, for instance, we had roast beef for dinner; *and* there was enough left over for supper! Won't you have a bit? Let me show it to you anyway. Come on, have a look—

Mayor. No, really—

Dr. Stockmann. Well, look at this, then! Do you see? We've got a tablecloth!

Mayor. Yes, I've noticed it.

Dr. Stockmann. And a lampshade too! See? All from what Catherine's managed to save! It makes the room so cosy, don't you think? Come and stand here—no, no, no, not there! There, now! Look! See how the light sort of concentrates downwards? I really think it looks very elegant, don't you? 180

Mayor. Well, if one can indulge in that kind of luxury—

Dr. Stockmann. Oh, I think I can permit myself that now. Catherine says I earn almost as much as we spend.

Mayor. Almost!

Dr. Stockmann. Well, a man of science ought to live in a little style. I'm sure any magistrate spends far more in a year than I do. 190

Mayor. Yes, I should think so! After all, a magistrate is an important public official—

Dr. Stockmann. Well, a wholesale merchant, then. A man like that spends much more—

Mayor. His circumstances are different.

Dr. Stockmann. Oh, it isn't that I'm wasteful, Peter. I just can't deny myself the pleasure of having people around me! I need that, you know. I've been living outside the world for so long, and for me it's a necessity to be with people who are young, bold, and cheerful, and have lively, liberal minds—and that's what they are, all the men who are sitting in there enjoying a good meal! I wish you knew Hovstad a little better— 200

Mayor. That reminds me, Hovstad told me he's going to print another article by you.

Dr. Stockmann. An article by me?

Mayor. Yes, about the Baths. Something you wrote last winter.

Dr. Stockmann. Oh, that. No, I don't want them to print that now.

Mayor. No? But I should have thought now would be the most suitable time.

Dr. Stockmann. I dare say it would under ordinary circumstances. *(Walks across the room)* 210

Mayor. (Watches him) And what is extraordinary about the circumstances now?

Dr. Stockmann. (Stops) I'm sorry, Peter, I can't tell you that yet. Not this evening, anyway. There may be a great deal that's extraordinary; or there may be nothing at all. It may be my imagination—

Mayor. I must say you're making it all sound very mysterious. Is there something the matter? Something I mustn't be told about? I should have thought that I, as Chairman of the Baths Committee—

Dr. Stockmann. And I should have thought that I, as—well, let's not start flying off the handle. 220

Mayor. Heaven forbid. I'm not in the habit of flying off the handle, as you phrase it. But I must absolutely insist that all arrangements be made and executed through the proper channels and through the authorities legally appointed for that purpose. I cannot permit any underhand or backdoor methods.

Dr. Stockmann. Have I ever used underhand or backdoor methods?

Mayor. You will always insist on going your own way. And that's almost equally inadmissible in a well-ordered community. The individual must learn to fall in line with the general will, or, to be more accu-
230 rate, with that of the authorities whose business it is to watch over the common good.

Dr. Stockmann. I dare say. But what the hell has that to do with me?

Mayor. Because that, my dear Thomas, is what you seem never to be willing to learn. But take care. You'll pay for it some time. Well, I've warned you. Goodbye.

Dr. Stockmann. Are you raving mad? You're barking completely up the wrong tree—

Mayor. I'm not in the habit of doing that. Well, if you'll excuse me—
240 *(Bows towards the dining-room)* Goodbye, sister-in-law. Good day, gentlemen. *(Goes)*

Mrs. Stockmann. (Comes back into the living-room) Has he gone?

Dr. Stockmann. Yes, Catherine, and in a damned bad temper.

Mrs. Stockmann. Oh, Thomas, what have you done to him now?

Dr. Stockmann. Absolutely nothing. He can't expect me to account to him until the time comes.

Mrs. Stockmann. Account to him? For what?

Dr. Stockmann. Hm; never mind, Catherine. Why the devil doesn't the post come?

250 *(Hovstad, Billing, and Horster have got up from the dining table and come into the living-room. Eilif and Morten follow a few moments later.)*

Billing. (Stretches his arms) Ah, a meal like that makes one feel like a new man! By jingo, yes!

Hovstad. His Worship wasn't in a very cheerful mood tonight.

Dr. Stockmann. Oh, that's his stomach. He's got a bad digestion.

Hovstad. I expect we radical journalists stuck in his gullet.

Mrs. Stockmann. I thought you were getting on rather well with him.

Hovstad. Oh, it's only an armistice.

Billing. That's it! The word epitomises the situation in a nutshell.

260 *Dr. Stockmann.* Peter's a lonely man, poor fellow; we must remember that. He has no home where he can relax; only business, business. And all that damned tea he pours into himself! Well, lads, pull up your chairs! Catherine, where's that toddy?

Mrs. Stockmann. (Goes into the dining-room) It's just coming.

Dr. Stockmann. You sit down here on the sofa with me, Captain Horster. You're too rare a guest in this house! Sit, sit, gentlemen! *(The*

Gentlemen sit at the table. Mrs. Stockmann brings a tray with a kettle, decanters, glasses, etc.)

Mrs. Stockmann. Here you are. This is arrack, and this is rum; and there's the brandy. Now everyone must help himself. 270

Dr. Stockmann. (Takes a glass) Don't you worry about that! *(As the toddy is mixed)* But where are the cigars? Eilif, you know where the box is. Morten, you can bring me my pipe. *(The Boys go into the room on the right.)* I've a suspicion Eilif pinches a cigar once in a while, but I pretend I don't know! *(Shouts)* And my smoking cap, Morten! Catherine, can't you tell him where I've put it? Oh, good, he's found it. *(The Boys return with the things he asked for.)* Help yourself, my friends! I stick to my pipe, you know; this old friend's been my companion on many a stormy round up there in the north. *(Clinks his glass with theirs.)* Skol! Ah, I must say it's better to be sitting here, warm and relaxed! 280

Mrs. Stockmann. (Who is sitting, knitting) Will you be sailing soon, Captain Horster?

Horster. I expect to be off next week.

Mrs. Stockmann. It's America this time, isn't it?

Horster. That's the idea.

Billing. But then you won't be able to vote in the next council elections!

Horster. Is there going to be a new election?

Billing. Didn't you know?

Horster. No, such things don't interest me. 290

Billing. But you must care about public affairs?

Horster. No, I don't understand these matters.

Billing. All the same, one ought at least to vote.

Horster. Even if one doesn't understand what it's about?

Billing. Understand? What's that got to do with it? Society's like a ship; everyone's got to lend a hand at the rudder.

Horster. Not in my ship!

Hovstad. It's curious how little sailors bother about what goes on in their own country.

Billing. Most abnormal. 300

Dr. Stockmann. Sailors are like birds of passage; wherever they happen to be, they regard that as home. Which means the rest of us must be all the more active, Mr. Hovstad. Have you anything salutary to offer us in the *People's Tribune* tomorrow?

Hovstad. Nothing of local interest. But the day after, I thought of printing your article—

Dr. Stockmann. Oh God, yes, that article! No, look, you'll have to sit on that.

Hovstad. Oh? We've plenty of space just now; and I thought this would be the most suitable time— 310

Dr. Stockmann. Yes, yes, I dare say you're right, but you'll have to wait all the same. I'll explain later—

(Petra, in hat and cloak, with a pile of exercise books under her arm, enters from the hall.)

Petra. Good evening.

Dr. Stockmann. Hullo, Petra, is that you? *(The others greet her, and she them. She puts down her cloak, hat and books on a chair by the door.)*

Petra. And you're all sitting here having a party while I've been out
320 working!

Dr. Stockmann. Well, come and have a party too.

Billing. May I mix you a tiny glass?

Petra. (Comes over to the table) Thanks, I'll do it myself; you always make it too strong. Oh, by the way, Father, I've a letter for you. *(Goes over to the chair on which her things are lying)*

Dr. Stockmann. A letter? Who from?

Petra. (Looks in her coat pocket) The postman gave it to me just as I was going out—

Dr. Stockmann. (Gets up and goes over to her) Why on earth didn't
330 you let me have it before?

Petra. I really didn't have time to run up again. Here it is.

Dr. Stockmann. (Seizes the letter) Let me see it, child, let me see it! *(Looks at the envelope)* Yes, this is it!

Mrs. Stockmann. Is this what you've been waiting for so anxiously, Thomas?

Dr. Stockmann. It is indeed. I must go and read it at once. Where can I find a light, Catherine? Is there no lamp in my room again?

Mrs. Stockmann. Yes, there's one burning on your desk.

Dr. Stockmann. Good, good. Excuse me a moment—
340 *(Goes into the room on the right)*

Petra. What on earth can that be, Mother?

Mrs. Stockmann. I don't know. These last few days he's done nothing but ask about the post.

Billing. Probably some patient out of town—

Petra. Poor Father! He'll soon find he's bitten off more than he can chew. *(Mixes herself a glass)* Ah, that tastes good!

Hovstad. Have you been at evening classes tonight, too?

Petra. (Sips her drink) Two hours.

Billing. And four hours this morning at the technical college—
350 *Petra. (Sits at the table)* Five hours.

Mrs. Stockmann. And you've got exercises to correct tonight, I see.

Petra. Yes, lots.

Horster. You seem to have bitten off more than you can chew too, by the sound of it.

Petra. Yes, but I like it. One feels so wonderfully tired afterwards.

Billing. Wonderfully?
Petra. Yes. One sleeps so soundly, afterwards.
Morten. You must be very wicked, Petra.
Petra. Wicked?
Morten. Yes, if you work so much. Dr. Roerlund says work is a punishment for our sins. 360
Eilif. (Sniffs) Silly! Fancy believing stuff like that!
Mrs. Stockmann. Now, now, Eilif!
Billing. (Laughs) Ha! Very good!
Hovstad. Don't you want to work hard too, Morten?
Morten. No! Not me!
Hovstad. But surely you want to become something?
Morten. I want to be a Viking!
Eilif. But then you'll have to be a heathen.
Morten. All right, I'll be a heathen! 370
Billing. I'm with you there, Morten! That's just the way I feel!
Mrs. Stockmann. (Makes a sign) I'm sure you don't really, Mr. Billing.
Billing. By jingo, I do! I *am* a heathen, and I'm proud of it! Before long we'll all be heathens. Just you wait and see.
Morten. Shall we be able to do anything we like then?
Billing. Yes, Morten! You see—!
Mrs. Stockmann. Hurry off now, boys. I'm sure you've some homework to do.
Eilif. I can stay a few minutes longer—
Mrs. Stockmann. No, you can't. Be off, the pair of you! 380
(The Boys say good night and go into the room on the left.)
Hovstad. Do you really think it can do the boys any harm to hear this kind of thing?
Mrs. Stockmann. Well, I don't know. I just don't like it.
Petra. Oh, really, Mother! I think you're being very stupid.
Mrs. Stockmann. Perhaps I am; but I don't like it. Not here in the home.
Petra. Oh, there's so much fear of the truth everywhere! At home and at school. Here we've got to keep our mouths shut, and at school we have to stand up and tell lies to the children. 390
Horster. Lie to them?
Petra. Yes, surely you realise we have to teach them all kinds of things we don't believe in ourselves.
Billing. I fear that is all too true!
Petra. If only I had the money, I'd start a school of my own. And there things would be different.
Billing. Ah! Money!
Horster. If you mean that seriously, Miss Stockmann, I could gladly let you have a room at my place. My father's old house is almost empty; there's a great big dining-room downstairs— 400

Petra. (Laughs) Thank you! But I don't suppose it'll ever come to anything.

Hovstad. No, I think Miss Petra will probably turn to journalism. By the way, have you found time to look at that English novel you promised to translate for us?

Petra. Not yet. But I'll see you get it in time.

(Dr. Stockmann enters from his room with the letter open in his hand.)

Dr. Stockmann. (Waves the letter) Here's news that's going to set this town by the ears, believe you me!

410 *Billing.* News?

Mrs. Stockmann. Why, what's happened?

Dr. Stockmann. A great discovery has been made, Catherine!

Hovstad. Really?

Mrs. Stockmann. By you?

Dr. Stockmann. Precisely! By me! *(Walks up and down)* Now let them come as usual and say it's all madman's talk and I'm imagining things! But they'll have to watch their step this time! *(Laughs)* Yes, I fancy they'll have to watch their step!

Petra. Father, for Heaven's sake tell us what it is!

420 *Dr. Stockmann.* Yes, yes, just give me time and you'll hear everything. Oh, if only I had Peter here now! Well, it only goes to show how blindly we mortals can form our judgments—

Hovstad. What do you mean by that, Doctor?

Dr. Stockmann. (Stops by the table) Is it not popularly supposed that our town is a healthy place?

Hovstad. Yes, of course.

Dr. Stockmann. A quite unusually healthy place? A place which deserves to be recommended in the warmest possible terms both for the sick and for their more fortunate brethren?

430 *Mrs. Stockmann.* Yes, but my dear Thomas—!

Dr. Stockmann. And we ourselves have praised and recommended it, have we not? I have written thousands of words of eulogy both in the *People's Tribune*, and in pamphlets—

Hovstad. Yes, well, what of it?

Dr. Stockmann. These Baths, which have been called the artery of the town, and its central nerve and—and God knows what else—

Billing. "The pulsing heart of our city" is a phrase I once, in a festive moment, ventured to—

Dr. Stockmann. No doubt. But do you know what they really are, 440 these beloved Baths of ours which have been so puffed up and which have cost so much money? Do you know what they are?

Hovstad. No, what are they?

Dr. Stockmann. Nothing but a damned cesspit!

Petra. The Baths, Father?

Mrs. Stockmann. (Simultaneously) Our Baths!

Hovstad. (Simultaneously) But, Doctor—!

Billing. Absolutely incredible!

Dr. Stockmann. These Baths are a whited sepulchre—and a poisoned one at that. Dangerous to health in the highest degree! All that filth up at Moelledal—you know, that stinking refuse from the tanneries— 450 has infected the water in the pipes that feed the Pump Room. And that's not all. This damnable muck has even seeped out onto the beach—

Horster. Where the sea baths are?

Dr. Stockmann. Exactly!

Hovstad. But how can you be so sure about all this, Doctor?

Dr. Stockmann. I've investigated the whole thing most thoroughly. Oh, I've long suspected something of the kind. Last year there were a lot of curious complaints among visitors who'd come for the bathing —typhoid, and gastric troubles— 460

Mrs. Stockmann. Yes, so there were.

Dr. Stockmann. At the time we thought these people had brought the disease with them. But later, during the winter, I began to have other thoughts. So I set to work to analyse the water as closely as I was able.

Mrs. Stockmann. So that's what you've been toiling so hard at!

Dr. Stockmann. Yes, you may well say I have toiled, Catherine. But of course I lacked the proper scientific facilities. So I sent specimens of both the drinking water and the sea water to the University to have them analysed by a chemist. 470

Hovstad. And now you have that analysis?

Dr. Stockmann. (Shows the letter) Here it is! It establishes conclusively that the water here contains putrid organic matter—millions of bacteria! It is definitely noxious to the health even for external use.

Mrs. Stockmann. What a miracle you found this out in time!

Dr. Stockmann. You may well say that, Catherine.

Hovstad. And what do you intend to do now, Doctor?

Dr. Stockmann. Put the matter right, of course.

Hovstad. Can that be done?

Dr. Stockmann. It must be done! Otherwise the Baths are unusable 480 —and all our work has been wasted. But don't worry. I'm pretty sure I know what needs to be done.

Mrs. Stockmann. But, my dear Thomas, why have you kept all this so secret?

Dr. Stockmann. Did you expect me to go round the town talking about it before I was certain? No, thank you, I'm not that mad.

Petra. You might have told us—

Dr. Stockmann. I wasn't going to tell anyone. But tomorrow you can run along to the Badger and—

Mrs. Stockmann. Thomas, really! 490

Dr. Stockmann. Sorry; I mean your grandfather. It'll shock the old boy out of his skin. He thinks I'm a bit gone in the head anyway—oh, and there are plenty of others who think the same! I know! But now these good people shall see! Now they shall see! *(Walks around and rubs his hands)* There's going to be such a to-do in this town, Catherine! You've no idea! The whole water system will have to be relaid.

Hovstad. (Gets up) The whole of the water system—?

Dr. Stockmann. Of course. The intake is too low. It'll have to be raised much higher up.

500 *Petra.* Then you were right after all!

Dr. Stockmann. Yes, Petra, do you remember? I wrote protesting against the plans when they were about to start laying it. But no one would listen to me then. Well, now I'll give them a real broadside. Of course, I've written a full report to the Baths Committee; it's been ready for a whole week, I've only been waiting to receive this. *(Shows the letter)* But now I shall send it to them at once! *(Goes into his room and returns with a sheaf of papers)* Look at this! Ten foolscap pages —closely written! I'm sending the analysis with it. A newspaper, Catherine! Get me something to wrap these up in. Good! There, now!
510 Give it to—to—! *(Stamps his foot)* What the devil's her name? You know, the maid! Tell her to take it straight down to the Mayor.

(Mrs. Stockmann goes out through the dining-room with the parcel.)

Petra. What do you think Uncle Peter will say, Father?

Dr. Stockmann. What can he say? He must be grateful that so important a fact has been brought to light.

Hovstad. May I have your permission to print a short piece about your discovery in the *People's Tribune?*

Dr. Stockmann. I'd be very grateful if you would.

Hovstad. I think it's desirable that the community should be in-
520 formed as quickly as possible.

Dr. Stockmann. Yes, yes, of course.

Mrs. Stockmann. (Comes back) She's gone with it now.

Billing. You'll be the first citizen in the town, Doctor, by jingo, you will!

Dr. Stockmann. (Walks round contentedly) Oh, nonsense. I've really done nothing except my duty. I dug for treasure and struck lucky, that's all. All the same—!

Billing. Hovstad, don't you think the town ought to organize a torch-light procession in honour of Dr. Stockmann?

530 *Hovstad.* I'll suggest it, certainly.

Billing. And I'll have a word with Aslaksen.

Dr. Stockmann. No, my dear friends, please don't bother with that nonsense. I don't want any fuss made. And if the Baths Committee should decide to raise my salary, I won't accept it! It's no good, Catherine, I won't accept it!

Mrs. Stockmann. Quite right, Thomas.
Petra. (Raises her glass) Skol, Father!
Hovstad.
Billing. } *(Together)* Skol, skol, Doctor!
Horster. (Clinks his glass with the Doctor's) Here's hoping your discovery will bring you nothing but joy! 540
Dr. Stockmann. Thank you, my dear friends, thank you! I'm so deeply happy! Oh, it's good to know that one has the respect of one's fellow-citizens! Hurrah, Catherine! *(Seizes her round the neck with both hands and whirls round with her. Mrs. Stockmann screams and struggles. Laughter, applause, and cheers for the Doctor. The Boys stick their heads in through the door.)*

Act II

(The Doctor's living-room. The door to the dining-room is shut. Morning.)

Mrs. Stockmann. (Enters from the dining-room with a sealed letter in her hand, goes over to the door downstage right and peeps in) Are you at home, Thomas?
Dr. Stockmann. (Offstage) Yes, I've just come in. *(Enters)* What is it?
Mrs. Stockmann. A letter from your brother. *(Hands it to him)*
Dr. Stockmann. Aha, let's see what he says. *(Opens the envelope and reads)* "I return herewith the manuscript you sent me—" *(Reads on, mumbling)* Hm—!
Mrs. Stockmann. Well, what does he say?
Dr. Stockmann. (Puts the papers in his pocket) No, he just writes that he'll be coming up here to see me towards noon. 10
Mrs. Stockmann. You must remember to stay at home, then.
Dr. Stockmann. Oh, that'll be all right. I've finished my round for today.
Mrs. Stockmann. I'm very curious to know how he's taken it.
Dr. Stockmann. You'll see. He won't like the fact that I made this discovery and not he.
Mrs. Stockmann. Doesn't it worry you? It does me.
Dr. Stockmann. Well, he'll be happy at heart, of course. The trouble is, Peter gets so damned angry at the idea of anyone but himself doing anything for the good of the town. 20
Mrs. Stockmann. You know, Thomas, I really think you ought to share the honour with him. Couldn't you say it was he who started you thinking along these lines—?
Dr. Stockmann. Gladly, as far as I'm concerned. As long as I get the matter put right, I—
Old Morten Kiil. (Puts his head in through the door leading from the hall, looks around enquiringly, chuckles to himself and asks slyly) Is it—is it true?

30 *Mrs. Stockmann.* Why, Father!
Dr. Stockmann. Hullo, Father-in-law! Good morning, good morning!
Mrs. Stockmann. Well, aren't you going to come in?
Morten Kiil. I will if it's true. If not, I'll be off—
Dr. Stockmann. If what's true?
Morten Kiil. This nonsense about the water system. Is it true, eh?
Dr. Stockmann. Of course it's true. But how did you hear about it?
Morten Kiil. (Comes in) Petra looked in on her way to school—
Dr. Stockmann. Oh, did she?
Morten Kiil. Mm. And she told me. I thought she was just pulling
40 my leg. But that's not like Petra.
Dr. Stockmann. How could you think she'd do a thing like that?
Morten Kiil. Never trust anyone. That's my motto. You get made a fool of before you know where you are. So it is true, then?
Dr. Stockmann. Absolutely true. Sit down now, Father. *(Coaxes him onto the sofa)* Isn't it a stroke of luck for the town?
Morten Kiil. (Stifles a laugh) Stroke of luck for the town?
Dr. Stockmann. That I made this discovery in time—
Morten Kiil. (As before) Oh, yes, yes, yes! But I never thought you'd start playing monkey tricks with your own flesh and blood!
50 *Dr. Stockmann.* Monkey tricks?
Mrs. Stockmann. Father dear—?
Morten Kiil. (Rests his hands and chin on the handle of his stick and winks slyly at the Doctor) What was it, now? Didn't you say some animals had got into the water pipes?
Dr. Stockmann. Yes, bacteria.
Morten Kiil. Quite a number of them, so Petra told me. Regular army!
Dr. Stockmann. Millions, probably.
Morten Kiil. But no one can see them. Isn't that right?
Dr. Stockmann. Of course one can't *see* them.
60 *Morten Kiil. (Chuckles silently)* Devil take me if this isn't the best I've heard from you yet!
Dr. Stockmann. What do you mean?
Morten Kiil. But you'll never get the Mayor to believe a tale like that.
Dr. Stockmann. We'll see.
Morten Kiil. Do you think he's that daft?
Dr. Stockmann. I hope the whole town will be that daft.
Morten Kiil. The whole town! That's perfectly possible! Serve them right, it'll teach them a lesson! They hounded me out of the Council —yes, that's what I call it, for they drove me out like a dog, they did!
70 But now they're going to pay for it! You make fools of them, Stockmann!
Dr. Stockmann. But, Father—
Morten Kiil. You make fools of them, my boy! *(Gets up)* If you can put the Mayor and his friends out of countenance, I'll give a hundred crowns to the poor—immediately!

Dr. Stockmann. That's very generous of you.

Morten Kiil. I'm not a rich man, mind! But if you do that, I'll remember the poor to the tune of fifty crowns; at Christmas.

(Hovstad enters from the hall.)

Hovstad. Good morning! *(Stops)* Oh, am I intruding?

Dr. Stockmann. No, come in, come in! 80

Morten Kiil. (Chuckles again) Him! Is he in with you on this?

Hovstad. What do you mean?

Dr. Stockmann. Indeed he is.

Morten Kiil. I might have guessed it! So it's to be in the papers! Yes, you're a card all right, Stockmann! Well, you two put your heads together. I'm off.

Dr. Stockmann. Oh, Father, stay a little longer.

Morten Kiil. No, I'm off. Pull out all the tricks you know! By God, I'll see you don't lose by it! *(Goes. Mrs. Stockmann accompanies him out.)*

Dr. Stockmann. (Laughs) Imagine, Hovstad, the old man doesn't 90 believe a word I say about the water system!

Hovstad. Oh, so *that* was—?

Dr. Stockmann. Yes, that's what we were talking about. I suppose that's why you've come too?

Hovstad. Yes. Can you spare me a moment or two, Doctor?

Dr. Stockmann. As long as you want, my dear fellow.

Hovstad. Have you heard anything from the Mayor?

Dr. Stockmann. Not yet. He'll be along shortly.

Hovstad. I've been thinking a lot about this since last night.

Dr. Stockmann. Yes? 100

Hovstad. You're a doctor and a man of science, and to you this business of the water is something to be considered in isolation. I think you don't perhaps realise how it's tied up with a lot of other things.

Dr. Stockmann. I don't quite understand you. Let's sit down, my dear chap. No, over there on the sofa. *(Hovstad sits on the sofa, Dr. Stockmann in an armchair on the other side of the table.)*

Dr. Stockmann. Well?

Hovstad. You said yesterday that the pollution of the water was the result of impurities in the soil.

Dr. Stockmann. Yes, we're pretty certain that filthy swamp up at 110 Moelledal is the cause of the evil.

Hovstad. Forgive me, Doctor, but I believe the real cause of all the evil is to found in quite a different swamp.

Dr. Stockmann. Which one?

Hovstad. The swamp in which our whole communal life is slowly rotting.

Dr. Stockmann. Damn it, Mr. Hovstad, what kind of talk is this?

Hovstad. Little by little all the affairs of this town have fallen into the hands of a small clique of bureaucrats.

120 *Dr. Stockmann.* Oh, come, you can't group them all under that description.

Hovstad. No, but the ones who don't belong to it are the friends and hangers-on of the ones who do. It's the rich men, the ones with names —they're the people who rule our life.

Dr. Stockmann. They're shrewd and intelligent men.

Hovstad. Did they show shrewdness or intelligence when they laid the water pipes where they are now?

Dr. Stockmann. No, that was very stupid, of course. But it's going to be put right now.

130 *Hovstad.* You think they'll enjoy doing that?

Dr. Stockmann. Enjoy it or not, they'll be forced to do it.

Hovstad. If the press is allowed to use its influence.

Dr. Stockmann. That won't be necessary, my dear fellow. I'm sure my brother will—

Hovstad. I'm sorry, Doctor, but I intend to take this matter up myself.

Dr. Stockmann. In the newspaper?

Hovstad. When I took over the *People's Tribune* I did so with the fixed purpose of breaking up this ring of obstinate bigots who hold all the power in their hands.

140 *Dr. Stockmann.* But you told me yourself what happened as a result. The paper almost had to close down.

Hovstad. We had to play it easy then, that's true. There was a risk that if these men fell, the Baths might not be built. But now we have them, and these fine gentlemen have become dispensable.

Dr. Stockmann. Dispensable, perhaps. But we owe them a debt all the same.

Hovstad. Oh, that'll be handsomely acknowledged. But a radical writer like me can't let an opportunity like this pass unused. We must destroy the myth of these men's infallibility. It must be rooted out like 150 any other kind of superstition.

Dr. Stockmann Ah, I'm with you there. If it is a superstition, then away with it!

Hovstad. I'd prefer not to attack the Mayor, since he's your brother. But I know you feel as strongly as I do that truth must precede all other considerations.

Dr. Stockmann. Of course. *(Bursts out)* But—! But—!

Hovstad. You mustn't think ill of me. I'm not more ambitious or self-seeking than most men.

Dr. Stockmann. But my dear fellow, who suggests you are?

160 *Hovstad.* I'm the son of poor people, as you know, and I've had the chance to see what's needed most in the lower strata of society. It's to have a share in the control of public affairs. That's what develops ability, and knowledge, and human dignity.

Dr. Stockmann. I appreciate that.

Hovstad. And then I think a journalist has a lot to answer for if he neglects an opportunity to achieve emancipation for the masses—the small and the oppressed. Oh, I know—the big boys will call me a demagogue and all that—but I don't care. As long as my conscience is clear, I—

Dr. Stockmann. That's the point, yes! That's exactly it, Mr. Hovstad! All the same—damn it— *(A knock at the door)* Come in! 170

(Aslaksen, the printer, appears in the doorway leading from the hall. He is humbly but decently dressed in black, with a white and somewhat crumpled cravat, gloves, and a silk hat in his hand.)

Aslaksen. (Bows) I trust you'll forgive me for being so bold, Doctor—

Dr. Stockmann. (Gets up) Why, hullo! Aren't you Aslaksen the printer?

Aslaksen. I am indeed, Doctor.

Hovstad. (Gets up) Are you looking for me, Aslaksen?

Aslaksen. No, I had no idea I'd see you here. It was the Doctor himself I— 180

Dr. Stockmann. Well, what can I do for you?

Aslaksen. Is it true what Mr. Billing tells me, that you're thinking of getting us a better water system?

Dr. Stockmann. Yes, for the Baths.

Aslaksen. Ah, yes; I see. Well, I just came to say that I'm right behind you!

Hovstad. (To Dr. Stockmann) You see!

Dr. Stockmann. I'm most grateful; but—

Aslaksen. You might find it useful to have us tradespeople behind you. We form a pretty solid majority in this town—when we choose to, mind! And it's always good to have the majority behind you, Doctor. 190

Dr. Stockmann. True enough. But I don't see that any special effort is necessary here. Surely it's a perfectly straightforward matter—

Aslaksen. Yes, but you might be glad of us all the same. I know these local authorities. The boys in power don't like accepting suggestions from outside. So I thought it might not be out of place if we organized a little demonstration.

Hovstad. That's just what I feel.

Dr. Stockmann. Demonstration? In what way will you demonstrate? 200

Aslaksen. Oh, with restraint, Doctor. I always insist on restraint. Restraint is the primary virtue of every citizen. That's my opinion, anyway.

Dr. Stockmann. Yes, yes, Mr. Aslaksen. Your views are well known—

Aslaksen. Yes, I fancy they are. Now this business of the water system is very important to us tradespeople. It looks as though the Baths are going to prove as you might say a little goldmine for the

town. We'll all be depending on the Baths for our livelihood, especially us property owners. That's why we want to give the project every sup-
210 port we can. And seeing as I'm Chairman of the Property Owners' Association—

Dr. Stockmann. Yes?

Aslaksen. And seeing as I'm also on the Council of the Temperance Society—You do know I'm a temperance worker?

Dr. Stockmann. Yes, yes.

Aslaksen. Well, so it stands to reason I come into contact with a lot of people. And seeing as I'm known to be a level-headed and law-abiding citizen, as you said yourself, it means I have a certain influence in the town—I wield a little power—though I say it myself.

220 *Dr. Stockmann.* I'm well aware of that, Mr. Aslaksen.

Aslaksen. Yes, well—so it'd be an easy matter for me to arrange an address, if the occasion should arise.

Dr. Stockmann. An address?

Aslaksen. Yes, a kind of vote of thanks from the citizens of this town to you for having carried this important matter to a successful conclusion. Of course, it stands to reason the wording's got to be restrained, so it won't offend the authorities and the other people as has the power. And so long as we're careful about that, I don't think anyone can take offence, can they?

230 *Hovstad.* Well, even if they don't particularly like it, they—

Aslaksen. No, no, no! We mustn't offend authority, Mr. Hovstad! We can't afford to defy the people on whom our lives depend. I've seen plenty of that in my time, and no good ever came out of it. But the sober expression of liberal sentiments can cause no affront.

Dr. Stockmann. (Shakes his hand) My dear Mr. Aslaksen, I can't tell you how deeply happy I am to find all this support among my fellow-citizens. I am most moved, most moved. Well, now; what about a small glass of sherry?

Aslaksen. No, thank you! I never touch spirits.

240 *Dr. Stockmann.* A glass of beer, then? What do you say to that?

Aslaksen. No, thank you, not that either, Doctor. I never touch anything so early in the day. And now I must be getting back to town to talk to some of the other property owners and prepare the atmosphere.

Dr. Stockmann. It's really most kind of you, Mr. Aslaksen. But I simply cannot get it into my head that all this fuss is really necessary. I should have thought the matter would solve itself.

Aslaksen. The authorities move somewhat ponderously, Doctor. Heaven knows I don't intend any reflection on them—!

Hovstad. We'll give them a drubbing in print tomorrow, Mr. Aslaksen.

250 *Aslaksen.* But no violence, Mr. Hovstad! Proceed with restraint! Otherwise you'll get nowhere with them. You can rely on my judgment, for I have culled my knowledge in the school of life. Yes, well, I must

say goodbye. You know now that we tradespeople stand behind you like a wall, Doctor. You have the solid majority on your side, whatever else may happen.

Dr. Stockmann. Thank you, my dear Mr. Aslaksen. *(Shakes his hand)* Goodbye, goodbye!

Aslaksen. Are you coming down to the press too, Mr. Hovstad?

Hovstad. I'll follow later. I've a few things to arrange first.

Aslaksen. Yes, yes. 260

(Bows and goes out. Dr. Stockmann accompanies him out into the hall.)

Hovstad. (As the Doctor returns) Well, what do you say to that, Doctor? Don't you think it's time this town was shaken out of its torpidity and its weak-kneed half-heartedness?

Dr. Stockmann. You mean Aslaksen?

Hovstad. Yes, I do. Oh, he's honest enough in some respects, but he's stuck in the swamp. And most of the others are the same. They swing this way and that, and spend so much time looking at every side of the question that they never make a move in any direction.

Dr. Stockmann. But Aslaksen seemed very well-meaning, I thought. 270

Hovstad. There's something I regard as more important than that. To know your own mind and have the courage of your convictions.

Dr. Stockmann. Yes, you're right there.

Hovstad. That's why I'm so keen to seize this opportunity if I can't get these well-meaning idiots to act like men for once. All this grovelling to authority has got to be stopped. This blunder they've made about the water system is quite indefensible, and that fact's got to be drummed into the ears of every citizen who's got the right to vote.

Dr. Stockmann. Very well. If you think it's for the communal good, go ahead. But not till I've talked with my brother. 280

Hovstad. I'll get my editorial written anyway. And if the Mayor refuses to take action, then—

Dr. Stockmann. Oh, but that's unthinkable.

Hovstad. It's a possibility. And if it should happen—?

Dr. Stockmann. If it does, I promise you that—yes, you can print my report. Print the whole damned thing.

Hovstad. Is that a promise?

Dr. Stockmann. (Hands him the manuscript) Here it is. Take it with you. It won't do any harm for you to read through it; and you can give it back to me afterwards. 290

Hovstad. Right, I'll do that. Well, goodbye, Doctor.

Dr. Stockmann. Goodbye, goodbye! Don't you worry, Mr. Hovstad—everything's going to go quite smoothly. Quite smoothly!

Hovstad. Hm. We shall see. *(Nods and goes out through the hall)*

Dr. Stockmann. (Goes over to the dining-room and looks in) Catherine—! Oh, hullo, Petra, are you here?

Petra. (Enters) Yes, I've just got back from school.

Mrs. Stockmann. (Enters) Hasn't he come yet?

Dr. Stockmann. Peter? No. But I've been having a long talk with 300 Hovstad. He's quite excited about this discovery of mine. It seems it has a much wider significance than I'd supposed. So he's placed his newspaper at my disposal, if I should need it.

Mrs. Stockmann. But do you think you will?

Dr. Stockmann. Oh no, I'm sure I won't. But it's good to know that one has the free press on one's side—the mouthpiece of liberal opinion. And what do you think? I've had a visit from the Chairman of the Property Owners' Association!

Mrs. Stockmann. Oh? And what did he want?

Dr. Stockmann. He's going to support me too. They're all going to 310 support me, if there's any trouble. Catherine, do you know what I have behind me?

Mrs. Stockmann. Behind you? No, what have you behind you?

Dr. Stockmann. The solid majority.

Mrs. Stockmann. I see. And that's a good thing, is it?

Dr. Stockmann. Of course, it's a good thing! *(Rubs his hands and walks up and down)* How splendid to feel that one stands shoulder to shoulder with one's fellow-citizens in brotherly concord!

Petra. And that one's doing so much that's good and useful, Father.

Dr. Stockmann. Yes, and for one's home town too!

320 *Mrs. Stockmann.* There's the doorbell.

Dr. Stockmann. Ah, this must be him! *(A knock on the inner door)* Come in!

Mayor. (Enters from the hall) Good morning.

Dr. Stockmann. (Warmly) Hullo, Peter!

Mrs. Stockmann. Good morning, Brother-in-law. How are you?

Mayor. Oh, thank you; so-so. *(To the Doctor)* Last night, after office hours, I received a thesis from you regarding the state of the water at the Baths.

Dr. Stockmann. Yes. Have you read it?

330 *Mayor.* I have.

Dr. Stockmann. Well! What do you think?

Mayor. (Glances at the others) Hm—

Mrs. Stockmann. Come, Petra.

(She and Petra go into the room on the left.)

Mayor. (After a pause) Was it necessary to conduct all these investigations behind my back?

Dr. Stockmann. Well, until I was absolutely certain, I—

Mayor. And now you are?

Dr. Stockmann. Yes. Surely you must be convinced—?

340 *Mayor.* Is it your intention to place this document before the Baths Committee as an official statement?

Dr. Stockmann. Of course! Something must be done. And quickly.

Mayor. I find your phraseology in this document, as usual, somewhat extravagant. Among other things, you say that all we have to offer our visitors at present is a permanent state of ill-health.

Dr. Stockmann. Peter, how else can you describe it? Just think! That water's poisonous even if you bathe in it, let alone drink it! And we're offering this to unfortunate people who are ill and who have turned to us in good faith, and are paying us good money, in order to get their health back! 350

Mayor. And your conclusion is that we must build a sewer to drain away these aforesaid impurities from the swamp at Moelledal, and that the whole water system must be relaid.

Dr. Stockmann. Can you think of any other solution? I can't.

Mayor. This morning I called upon the town engineer. In the course of our discussion I half jokingly mentioned these proposals as a thing we might possibly undertake some time in the future.

Dr. Stockmann. Some time in the future?

Mayor. He smiled at what he obviously regarded as my extravagance —as I knew he would. Have you ever troubled to consider what these 360 alterations you suggest would cost? According to the information I received, the expense would probably run into several hundred thousand crowns.

Dr. Stockmann. Would it be that much?

Mayor. Yes. But that's not the worst. The work would take at least two years.

Dr. Stockmann. Two years, did you say? Two whole years?

Mayor. At least. And what do we do with the Baths in the meanwhile? Close them? Yes, we'd be forced to. You don't imagine anyone would come here once the rumour got around that the water was 370 impure?

Dr. Stockmann. But, Peter, it is!

Mayor. And for this to happen just now, when the whole enterprise is coming to fruition! There are other towns around with qualifications to be regarded as health resorts. Do you think they won't start trying to attract the market? Of course they will! And there we shall be! We'll probably have to abandon the whole expensive scheme, and you will have ruined the town that gave you birth.

Dr. Stockmann. I—ruined—!

Mayor. It's only as a health resort—a spa—that this town has any 380 future worth speaking of. Surely you realise that as well as I do.

Dr. Stockmann. But what do you propose we do?

Mayor. Your report has not completely convinced me that the situation is as dangerous as you imply.

Dr. Stockmann. Oh, Peter, if anything it's worse! Or at least it will be in the summer, once the hot weather starts.

Mayor. As I said, I believe that you are exaggerating the danger.

A capable medical officer must be able to take measures—He must know how to forestall such unpleasantnesses, and how to remedy them
390 if they should become obvious.

Dr. Stockmann. Go on.

Mayor. The existing water system at the Baths is a fact, and must be accepted as such. However, in due course I dare say the Committee might not be inflexibly opposed to considering whether without unreasonable pecuniary sacrifice it might not be possible to introduce certain improvements.

Dr. Stockmann. And you think I'd lend my name to such chicanery?

Mayor. Chicanery?

Dr. Stockmann. That's what it would be! A fraud, a lie, a crime
400 against the community, against the whole of society!

Mayor. As I have already pointed out, I have not succeeded in convincing myself that any immediate or critical danger exists.

Dr. Stockmann. Oh, yes you have! You must have! My arguments are irrefutable—I know they are! And you know that as well as I do, Peter! But you won't admit it, because it was you who forced through the proposal that the Baths and the water pipes should be sited where they are, and you refuse to admit that you made a gross blunder. Don't be such a fool, do you think I don't see through you?

Mayor. And suppose you were right? If I do guard my reputation
410 with a certain anxiety, it is because I have the welfare of our town at heart. Without moral authority I cannot guide and direct affairs as I deem most fit for the general good. For this, and diverse other reasons, it is vital to me that your report should not be placed before the Baths Committee. It must be suppressed for the general good. At a later date I shall bring the matter up for discussion, and we shall discreetly do the best we can. But nothing, not a single word, about this unfortunate matter must come to the public ear.

Dr. Stockmann. Well, it can't be stopped now, my dear Peter.

Mayor. It must and shall be stopped.

420 *Dr. Stockmann.* It can't, I tell you. Too many people know.

Mayor. Know? Who knows? You don't mean those fellows from the *People's Tribune—?*

Dr. Stockmann. Oh, yes, they too. The free press of our country will see to it that you do your duty.

Mayor. (After a short pause) You're an exceedingly foolish man, Thomas. Haven't you considered what the consequence of this action may be for you?

Dr. Stockmann. Consequence? Consequence for me?

Mayor. Yes. For you and for your family.

430 *Dr. Stockmann.* What the devil do you mean by that?

Mayor. I think I have always shown myself a good brother to you, whenever you've needed help.

Dr. Stockmann. You have, and I thank you for it.

Mayor. I'm not asking for thanks. To a certain extent I've been forced to do it—for my own sake. I always hoped I might be able to curb you a little if I could help to improve your economic position.

Dr. Stockmann. What! So it was only for your own sake that you—

Mayor. Partly, I said. It's painful for a public servant to see his next of kin spend his entire time compromising himself.

Dr. Stockmann. And you think I do that? 440

Mayor. Unfortunately you do, without knowing it. You have a restless, combative, rebellious nature. And then you've this unfortunate passion for rushing into print upon every possible—and impossible—subject. The moment you get an idea you have to sit down and write a newspaper article or a whole pamphlet about it.

Dr. Stockmann. Surely if a man gets hold of a new idea it's his duty as a citizen to tell it to the public?

Mayor. People don't want new ideas. They're best served by the good old accepted ideas they have already.

Dr. Stockmann. And you can say that to my face! 450

Mayor. Yes, Thomas. I'm going to speak bluntly to you for once. Up to now I've tried to avoid it, because I know how hasty you are; but now I've got to tell you the truth. You've no idea how much harm you do yourself by this impulsiveness of yours. You abuse the authorities, and even the government—you throw mud at them, you claim you've been cold-shouldered and persecuted. But what else can you expect, when you're such a difficult person?

Dr. Stockmann. Oh, so I'm difficult too, am I?

Mayor. Oh, Thomas, you're impossible to work with. I've discovered that for myself. You never consider anyone else's feelings. You even 460 seem to forget it's me you have to thank for getting you your job at the Baths—

Dr. Stockmann. It was mine by right! I was the first person to see that this town could become a flourishing watering place! And I was the only person who did see it at that time! For years I fought alone for this idea! I wrote, and wrote—

Mayor. No one denies that. But the time wasn't ripe then. Of course you weren't to know that, tucked away in your northern backwater. But as soon as the right moment arrived, I—and others—took the matter up— 470

Dr. Stockmann. Yes, and made a mess of my wonderful plan! Oh yes, it's becoming very clear now what brilliant fellows you were!

Mayor. As far as I can see, all you're looking for now is just another excuse for a fight. You've always got to pick a quarrel with your superiors—it's your old failing. You can't bear to have anyone in authority over you. You look askance at anyone who occupies a position higher than yours; you regard him as a personal enemy—and then, as far as you're concerned, one weapon of attack is as good as another. But now I've shown you what's at stake, for the whole town, and for myself too. 480 And I'm not prepared to compromise.

Dr. Stockmann. What do you mean?

Mayor. Since you have been so indiscreet as to discuss this delicate matter, which you ought to have kept a professional secret, the affair obviously cannot be hushed up. All kinds of rumours will spread around, and the malicious elements among us will feed these rumours with details of their own invention. It is therefore necessary that you publicly deny these rumours.

Dr. Stockmann. I don't understand you.

Mayor. I feel sure that on further investigation you will convince 490 yourself that the situation is not nearly as critical as you had at first supposed.

Dr. Stockmann. Aha; you feel sure, do you?

Mayor. I also feel sure you will publicly express your confidence that the Committee will painstakingly and conscientiously take all necessary measures to remedy any possible defects which may exist.

Dr. Stockmann. But you can't remedy the defect by just patching things up! I'm telling you, Peter, unless you start again from scratch, it's my absolute conviction that—

Mayor. As an employee you have no right to any independent con- 500 viction.

Dr. Stockmann. (Starts) No right!

Mayor. As an employee. As a private person—well, Heaven knows that's another matter. But as a subordinate official at the Baths you have no right to express any opinion which conflicts with that of your superiors.

Dr. Stockmann. This is going too far! I, a doctor, a man of science, have no right—!

Mayor. The question is not merely one of science. The problem is complex. The issues involved are both technical and economical.

510 *Dr. Stockmann.* I don't care how you define the damned thing! I must be free to say what I think about anything!

Mayor. Go ahead. As long as it isn't anything connected with the Baths. That we forbid you.

Dr. Stockmann. (Shouts) You forbid—! You—! Why, you're just a—

Mayor. *I* forbid you—I, your chief. And when I forbid you to do something, you must obey.

Dr. Stockmann. (Controls himself) Peter—if you weren't my brother—!

Petra. (Throws open the door) Father, don't put up with this!

520 *Mrs. Stockmann. (Follows her)* Petra, Petra!

Mayor. Ha! Eavesdroppers!

Mrs. Stockmann. You were talking so loud—we couldn't help hearing—

Petra. I was listening.

Mayor. Well, I'm not altogether sorry—

Dr. Stockmann. (Goes closer to him) You spoke to me of forbidding and obeying?

Mayor. You forced me to use that tone.

Dr. Stockmann. And you expect me to publicly swallow my own words?

Mayor. We regard it as an unavoidable necessity that you issue a statement on the lines I have indicated. 530

Dr. Stockmann. And if I don't—obey?

Mayor. Then we shall be forced to issue an explanation, to calm the public.

Dr. Stockmann. All right; but I shall write and refute you. I stick to my view. I shall prove that I am right and you are wrong. And what will you do then?

Mayor. Then I shall be unable to prevent your dismissal.

Dr. Stockmann. What—!

Petra. Father! Dismissal!

Mrs. Stockmann. Dismissal! 540

Mayor. Dismissal from your post as public medical officer. I shall feel compelled to apply for immediate notice to be served on you, barring you from any further connection with the Baths.

Dr. Stockmann. You'd have the impudence to do that?

Mayor. You're the one who's being impudent.

Petra. Uncle, this is a disgraceful way to treat a man like Father!

Mrs. Stockmann. Be quiet, Petra.

Mayor. (Looks at Petra) So we've opinions of our own already, have we? But of course! *(To Mrs. Stockmann)* Sister-in-law, you seem to be the most sensible person in this house. Use what influence you have 550 over your husband. Make him realise the consequences this will have both for his family and—

Dr. Stockmann. My family concerns no one but myself.

Mayor.—both for his family, and for the town he lives in.

Dr. Stockmann. I'm the one who has the town's real interests at heart! I want to expose the evils that sooner or later must come to light. I'm going to prove to people that I love this town where I was born.

Mayor. Oh, you're blind! All you're trying to do is to stop up the source of the town's prosperity. 560

Dr. Stockmann. That source is poisoned, man! Are you mad? We live by hawking filth and disease! And all this communal life you boast so much about is based upon a lie!

Mayor. That's pure imagination—if nothing worse. The man who casts such foul aspersions against the town he lives in is an enemy of society.

Dr. Stockmann. (Goes towards him) You dare to—!

Mrs. Stockmann. (Throws herself between them) Thomas!

Petra. (Grasps her father by the arm) Keep calm, Father!

570 *Mayor.* I shall not expose myself to violence. You've been warned. Consider what is your duty to yourself and your family. Goodbye.

(Goes)

Dr. Stockmann. (Walks up and down) And in my own house, too, Catherine!

Mrs. Stockmann. Yes, Thomas. It's a shame and a scandal—

Petra. I'd like to get my hands on him—!

Dr. Stockmann. It's my own fault. I ought to have exposed them long ago; I should have bared my teeth; and used them! Calling me an enemy of society! By God, I'm not going to take that lying down!

580 *Mrs. Stockmann.* But, Thomas dear, might is right—

Dr. Stockmann. I'm the one who's right!

Mrs. Stockmann. What's the good of being right if you don't have the might?

Petra. Mother, how can you speak like that?

Dr. Stockmann. So it's no use in a free society to have right on one's side? Don't be absurd, Catherine. Besides—don't I have the free press in front of me—and the solid majority behind me? That's might enough, I should have thought!

Mrs. Stockmann. For Heaven's sake, Thomas, surely you're not 590 thinking of setting yourself up against your brother?

Dr. Stockmann. What the devil else do you expect me to do? Don't you want me to stand up for what I believe to be right?

Petra. Yes, Father, you must!

Mrs. Stockmann. It'll do you no good. If they won't, they won't.

Dr. Stockmann. (Laughs) Oh, Catherine, just give me time. You'll see! I'm going to fight this war to the end.

Mrs. Stockmann. Yes, and the end will be that you'll lose your job. You'll see.

Dr. Stockmann. At least I shall have done my duty to the community; 600 my duty to society. And they call me an enemy of society—!

Mrs. Stockmann. What about your family, Thomas? And your home? Do you think you'll be doing your duty to the ones who depend on you?

Petra. Oh, Mother, don't always think only of us.

Mrs. Stockmann. It's easy for you to talk. You can stand on your own feet, if need be. But think of the boys, Thomas! And think of yourself too—and me—

Dr. Stockmann. You must be mad, Catherine! If I give in like a coward to Peter and his wretched gang, do you think I'd ever have another moment of happiness in my life?

610 *Mrs. Stockmann.* I don't know about that. But God preserve us from the happiness we're likely to enjoy if you go on digging your heels in.

You'll have no means of livelihood, no regular income. Didn't we have enough of that in the old days? Remember that, Thomas. Think what it'll mean.

Dr. Stockmann. (Writhes, fighting with himself, and clenches his fists) And these office lackeys can do this to a free and honourable man! Isn't it monstrous, Catherine?

Mrs. Stockmann. Yes, they've behaved very wickedly to you, that's true. But Heaven knows, there's so much injustice one has to put up with in this world. There are the boys, Thomas. Look at them. What's to become of them? No, no, you can't have the heart. 620

(Eilif and Morten have meanwhile entered, carrying their schoolbooks.)

Dr. Stockmann. My sons! *(Suddenly stands erect, his mind made up)* Even if my whole world crashes about me, I shall never bow my head. *(Goes towards his room)*

Mrs. Stockmann. Thomas, what are you going to do?

Dr. Stockmann. (In the doorway) I want to have the right to look my sons in the eyes when they grow up into free men! *(Goes into his room)*

Mrs. Stockmann. Oh, God help us!

Petra. Father's right, Mother! He'll never give in. 630

Act III

(The editorial office of the People's Tribune. *On the left in the background is the entrance door; to the right in the same wall is another door with glass panes through which the composing-room is visible. Another door is in the wall on the right. In the middle of the room is a big table covered with papers, newspapers, and books. Downstage left is a window; by it is a writing desk and a high chair. Two armchairs stand by the table, and there are other chairs along the walls. The room is gloomy and uncomfortable; the furniture is old, the armchairs dirty and torn. In the composing-room one or two Compositors are at work. Beyond them, a hand-press is being operated.)*

(Hovstad sits writing at the desk. After a few moments Billing enters right, with the Doctor's manuscript in his hand.)

Billing. I say, I say, I say!

Hovstad. (Writing) Have you read it?

Billing. (Puts the manuscript on the desk) I should say I have!

Hovstad. Pretty forceful, isn't it?

Billing. Forceful? He'll butcher them, by jingo! Every paragraph's a knock-out!

Hovstad. Those fellows won't give in at the first blow, though.

Billing. That's true. But we'll go on bashing them, punch after punch, till their whole damned oligarchy falls to the grounds! As I sat 10 in there reading this, it was as though I saw the revolution dawning from afar!

Hovstad. (Turns) Hush, don't let Aslaksen hear.

Billing. (Lowers his voice) Aslaksen's a coward, a jellyfish! He hasn't the guts of a man! But you'll have your way? You will publish the Doctor's article?

Hovstad. Yes, unless the Mayor backs down—

Billing. That'd be a damned nuisance!

20 *Hovstad.* Whichever way it turns out we can exploit the situation. If the Mayor doesn't agree to the Doctor's proposal, he'll have all the tradespeople down on him—the Property Owners' Association, and the rest. And if he does agree to it he'll antagonise all the big shareholders in the Baths who up to now have been his chief supporters—

Billing. Of course! They'll have to fork out a pile of money—

Hovstad. You bet they will. And then the clique will be broken, and day after day we'll drum it into the public that the Mayor's incompetent in more respects than one, and that all the responsible offices in the town, the whole municipal authority, ought to be handed over to people 30 of liberal opinions.

Billing. By jingo, that's the truth! I see it! I see it! We stand on the threshold of a revolution! *(A knock on the door)*

Hovstad. Quiet! *(Shouts)* Come in.

(Dr. Stockmann enters through the door upstage left.)

Hovstad. (Goes to greet him) Ah, here is the Doctor! Well?

Dr. Stockmann. Print away, Mr. Hovstad!

Hovstad. So it's come to that?

Billing. Hurrah!

Dr. Stockmann. Print away, I say! Yes, it's come to that all right. 40 Well, now they shall have it the way they want it. It's war now, Mr. Billing!

Billing. War to the death, I hope! Give it to them, Doctor!

Dr. Stockmann. This report is only the beginning. My head's already teeming with ideas for four or five other articles. Where's Aslaksen?

Billing. (Calls into the composing-room) Aslaksen, come here a moment!

Hovstad. Four or five other articles, did you say? On the same theme?

Dr. Stockmann. No—oh, good heavens no, my dear fellow! No, they'll be about quite different things. But it all stems from this busi- 50 ness of the water system and the sewer. One thing leads to another, you know. It's like when you start to pull down an old building. Exactly like that.

Billing. By jingo, that's true! You suddenly realise you'll never be finished till you've pulled down the whole rotten structure!

Aslaksen. (From the composing-room) Pulled down! You're surely not thinking of pulling the Baths down, Doctor?

Hovstad. No, no, don't get frightened.

Dr. Stockmann. No, we were talking about something else. Well, Mr. Hovstad, what do you think of my report?

Hovstad. I think it's an absolute masterpiece— 60

Dr. Stockmann. Do you think so? That makes me very happy—very happy.

Hovstad. It's so clear and to the point; you don't have to be a specialist to follow the argument. I'm sure you'll have every enlightened person on your side.

Aslaksen. Every discriminating one too, I trust?

Billing. Discriminating or not—you'll have the whole town behind you.

Aslaksen. Well then, I don't think we need be afraid to print it.

Dr. Stockmann. I should damn well hope not. 70

Hovstad. It'll be in tomorrow morning.

Dr. Stockmann. Good God yes, we can't afford to waste a single day. Oh, Mr. Aslaksen, there was one thing I wanted to ask you. You must take charge of this manuscript yourself.

Aslaksen. If you wish.

Dr. Stockmann. Treat it as though it was gold. No misprints; every word is important. I'll drop back later; perhaps you'd let me look at a proof. I can't tell you how eager I am to see this thing in print—launched—!

Billing. Launched, yes! Like a thunderbolt! 80

Dr. Stockmann.—and submitted to the judgment of every intelligent citizen. Oh, you'd never guess what I've had to put up with today! I've been threatened with God knows what. They want to rob me of my elementary rights as a human being—

Billing. Your rights as a human being!

Dr. Stockmann. They want to degrade me, reduce me to the level of a beggar. They demand that I put my private interests above my most sacred and innermost convictions—

Billing. By jingo, that's going too far!

Hovstad. You can expect anything from that lot. 90

Dr. Stockmann. But they won't get far with me! I'll give it to them in black and white! I'll grapple with them every day in the *People's Tribune!* I'll sweep them with one broadside after another—!

Aslaksen. Yes, but remember—

Billing. Hurrah! It's war, it's war!

Dr. Stockmann. I'll beat them to the ground, I'll crush them, I'll flatten their defences for every honest man to see! By God I will!

Aslaksen. But do it soberly, Doctor. Act with restraint—

Billing. No, no! Don't spare your powder!

100 *Dr. Stockmann. (Continues imperturbably)* You see, it isn't just a question of the water system and the sewer. This whole community's got to be cleansed and decontaminated—

Billing. That's the very word!

Dr. Stockmann. All these skimpers and compromisers have got to be thrown out! There's got to be a clean sweep! Oh, such endless vistas have been opened up before my eyes today! I don't see my way quite clearly yet. But I will! We need fresh standard-bearers, my friends! Young men! Our advance posts must be manned by new captains!

Billing. Hear, hear!

110 *Dr. Stockmann.* As long as we stick together, it'll all happen so easily —so easily! The whole revolution will glide into existence like a ship from the stocks! Don't you agree?

Hovstad. I think we've every prospect now of getting the helm into the right hands.

Aslaksen. As long as we proceed with restraint, I don't think there can be any danger.

Dr. Stockmann. Who the hell cares about danger? I'm doing this in the name of truth and of my conscience!

Hovstad. You're a man who deserves support, Doctor.

120 *Aslaksen.* Yes, the Doctor's a true friend of the town, that's certain. I'll go further; he's a friend of society!

Billing. By jingo, Mr. Aslaksen, Dr. Stockmann is a friend of the people!

Aslaksen. I think the Property Owners' Association might be able to use that phrase.

Dr. Stockmann. (Moved, presses their hands) Thank you, my dear, good friends—thank you! It's so refreshing for me to hear this. My brother described me in vastly different terms. By God, I'll give it back to him with interest! Now I must go and see a poor devil of a 130 patient. But I'll be back! Take good care of that manuscript, Mr. Aslaksen. And for heaven's sake don't cut out any of the exclamation marks! If anything, put in a few more. Good, good. Well, goodbye! Goodbye, goodbye!

(He shakes hands with them as they accompany him to the door and he goes out.)

Hovstad. He's going to be damned useful to us.

Aslaksen. As long as he sticks to the Baths. But if he tries to go further, we'd be unwise to stay with him.

Hovstad. Hm; that all depends—

140 *Billing.* You're such a damned coward, Aslaksen!

Aslaksen. Coward? Yes, when it's a question of fighting local authorities, I am a coward, Mr. Billing. That's a lesson I have learned in the school of life. But elevate me into the field of high politics, confront me with the Government, and then see if I am a coward!

Billing. No, no, I'm sure you're not; but that's just where you're so inconsistent.

Aslaksen. Because I know my responsibilities as a citizen! Throwing stones at the government can't harm society. It doesn't bother those fellows—they stay put. But local authorities can be overthrown, and then you may get inexperience at the helm, with disastrous results 150 for property owners and the like.

Hovstad. But what about the education of people through self-government?

Aslaksen. When a man has interests to protect he can't think of everything, Mr. Hovstad.

Hovstad. Then I hope to God I never have any interests to protect.

Billing. Hear, hear!

Hovstad. I'm not a trimmer,° and I never will be.

Aslasken. A politician should never commit himself, Mr. Hovstad. And you, Mr. Billing, you ought to put a reef or two in your sails if 160 you want that job of clerk to the magistrates.

Billing. I—?

Hovstad. You, Billing?

Billing. Of course I only applied for it to put their backs up, you understand.

Aslaksen. Well, it's no business of mine. But since I'm being accused of cowardice and inconsistency, I'd like to make this clear—my political record is open for anyone to investigate. I've never changed my standpoint; apart from having learned more restraint. My heart still belongs with the people; but I don't deny that my head keeps one ear cocked 170 towards the authorities. The local ones, anyway.

(Goes into the composing-room)

Billing. Couldn't we change to some other printer, Hovstad?

Hovstad. Do you know anyone else who'd give us credit for printing and paper?

Billing. It's a damned nuisance not having any *capital!*

Hovstad. (Sits at the desk) Yes, if we only had *that*—

Billing. Ever thought of trying Dr. Stockmann?

Hovstad. (Glancing through his papers) What'd be the use of that? He hasn't a bean. 180

Billing. No; but he's got a good man behind him. Old Morten Kiil—the fellow they call the Badger—

Hovstad. (Writing) Do you really think he's got much?

Billing. By jingo, of course he has! And part of it must go to the Stockmanns—he's bound to provide for—well, the children, anyway.

158. trimmer, one who trims his sails—a compromiser.

Hovstad. (Half turns) Are you banking on that?

Billing. Banking? I never bank on anything.

Hovstad. You'd better not. And don't bank on becoming clerk to the magistrates either, because I can promise you you won't.

190 *Billing.* Do you think I don't know? *Not* to get it is just what I want! A snub like that puts you on your mettle. It gives you a fresh supply of gall, and you need that in a backwater like this, where hardly anything really infuriating ever happens.

Hovstad. (Writing) Yes, yes.

Billing. Well, they'll soon hear from me! I'll go and write that appeal for funds to the Property Owners' Association. *(Goes into the room on the right)*

Hovstad. (Sitting at the desk, chews his pen and says slowly) Hm! So that's the way the wind blows! *(There is a knock on the door.)* 200 Come in!

(Petra enters through the door upstage left.)

Hovstad. (Gets up) Why, hullo! Fancy seeing you here!

Petra. Please forgive me—

Hovstad. (Pushes forward an armchair) Won't you sit down?

Petra. No, thank you. I'm only staying a moment.

Hovstad. Is it something from your father—?

Petra. No, something from me. *(Takes a book from her coat pocket)* Here's that English novel.

Hovstad. Why are you giving it back to me?

210 *Petra.* I don't want to translate it.

Hovstad. But you promised—

Petra. I hadn't read it then. You can't have, either!

Hovstad. No—you know I don't understand English. But—

Petra. Exactly. That's why I wanted to tell you—you'll have to find something else to serialise. *(Puts the book on the table)* You can't possibly print this in the *People's Tribune.*

Hovstad. Why not?

Petra. Because it's diametrically opposed to what you believe.

Hovstad. Oh, that's the reason?

220 *Petra.* I don't think you understand. Its theme is that there's a supernatural power which takes care of all the so-called good people in this world, and works things so that in the end everything turns out well for them and all the so-called bad people get punished.

Hovstad. Yes, well, that's all right. That's just what people want to read.

Petra. But do you want to be the one who provides it for them? You don't believe a word of that! You know quite well it doesn't happen like that in real life.

Hovstad. Of course not. But an editor can't always do as he wishes. 230 One often has to bow to people's feelings in minor matters. After all, politics are the most important things in life—for a newspaper, anyway. And if I want to win people over to my views about freedom and progress, I mustn't frighten them away. If they find a moral story like this in the back pages of the newspaper they're more likely to go along with what we print on the front page. It reassures them.

Petra. Oh, really! You're not as crafty as that. I don't see you as a spider spinning webs to catch your readers!

Hovstad. (Smiles) Thank you for holding such a high opinion of me. No, actually, this was Billing's idea, not mine.

Petra. Billing's! 240

Hovstad. Yes. He was talking on those lines here the other day. He's the one who's so keen that we should publish this novel. I'd never heard of the book.

Petra. But Billing holds such progressive views—

Hovstad. Oh, there's more in Billing than meets the eye. I've just heard he's applied for the post of clerk to the magistrates.

Petra. I don't believe that, Mr. Hovstad. How could he reconcile himself to doing a thing like that?

Hovstad. You'd better ask him.

Petra. I'd never have thought that of Billing. 250

Hovstad. Wouldn't you? Does it so surprise you?

Petra. Yes. Perhaps not, though. I don't really know—

Hovstad. We journalists aren't worth much, Miss Stockmann.

Petra. How can you say that?

Hovstad. I sometimes think it.

Petra. In the ordinary run of events, perhaps not—that I can understand. But now, when you've taken up such an important cause—now surely you must feel you're worth more than most men.

Hovstad. Yes, today I do feel a bit like that.

Petra. It's true, isn't it! You do! Oh, it's a wonderful vocation you've 260 chosen! To be able to pioneer neglected truths and brave new doctrines—the mere fact of standing fearlessly forth to defend a man who's been wronged—

Hovstad. Especially when this man who's been wronged is—hm—

Petra. When he is a man of such honour and integrity?

Hovstad. (More quietly) I was about to say: especially when he is your father.

Petra. (Astounded) Mr. Hovstad!

Hovstad. Yes, Petra—Miss Petra—

Petra. Is that what seems important to you? Not the issue itself. 270 Not the truth—or the fact that this means everything to Father—

Hovstad. Yes—yes, of course—those things too—

Petra. No, thank you. You let the cat out of the bag there, Mr. Hovstad. Now I shall never believe you again—about anything.

Hovstad. Does it make you so angry that I've done this for your sake?

Petra. I'm angry because you haven't been honest with Father. You've been talking to him as though truth and the good of the people were what mattered most to you. You've been fooling both of us. You're not the man you've been pretending you are. And that I'll never for-
280 give you—never!

Hovstad. You shouldn't speak so sharply to me, Miss Petra. Least of all just now.

Petra. Why not now?

Hovstad. Because your father needs my help.

Petra. So that's the sort of man you are!

Hovstad. No, no, I didn't mean that—please believe me—

Petra. I know what to believe. Goodbye.

Aslaksen. (Hurries in furtively from the composing-room) For God's sake, Mr. Hovstad—! *(Sees Petra)* Oh, dear, that's unlucky—!

290 *Hovstad. (Goes after her)* But, Miss Petra—!

Petra. Goodbye. *(Goes)*

Aslaksen. Mr. Hovstad, listen, please!

Hovstad. Yes, yes, what is it?

Aslaksen. The Mayor's standing outside there in the composing-room!

Hovstad. The Mayor?

Aslaksen. Yes. He wants to talk to you. He came in the back way—didn't want to be seen, I suppose.

Hovstad. What can he want? No, wait, I'd better— *(Goes to the door of the composing-room, opens it, bows and invites the Mayor to enter)*

300 *Hovstad.* Keep a look out, Aslaksen, and make sure no one—

Aslaksen. Of course. *(Goes into the composing-room)*

Mayor. You weren't expecting to see me here.

Hovstad. No, frankly, I wasn't.

Mayor. (Looks round) You've done this up quite nicely. Very pleasant.

Hovstad. Oh—

Mayor. And here I am coming along and making demands on your time.

Hovstad. Not at all, sir. What can I do for you? Please allow me—*(Takes the Mayor's hat and stick and puts them on a chair)* Won't you
310 sit down?

Mayor. (Sits at the table) Thank you. *(Hovstad also sits at the table.)*

Mayor. Something—something extremely irritating has happened to me today, Mr. Hovstad.

Hovstad. Really? Of course, Your Worship has so many responsibilities—

Mayor. This particular matter concerns the medical officer at the Baths.

Hovstad. Oh—the Doctor—?

Mayor. He's written a sort of—report to the Baths Committee re-
320 garding some supposed defects in the Baths.

Hovstad. You amaze me.
Mayor. Hasn't he told you? I thought he said—
Hovstad. Oh yes, that's true, he did say something—
Aslaksen. *(From the composing-room)* I'd better have that manuscript—
Hovstad. *(Irritated)* Hm—it's there on the desk—
Aslaksen. *(Finds it)* Good.
Mayor. Why, surely that's it!
Aslaksen. Yes, this is the Doctor's article, Your Worship.
Hovstad. Oh, is this what you were talking about? 330
Mayor. The very thing. What do you think of it?
Hovstad. Of course I'm not a specialist, and I've only glanced through it—
Mayor. But you're going to print it?
Hovstad. I can't very well refuse a signed contribution—
Aslaksen. I have no say in the contents of the paper, Your Worship—
Mayor. Of course not.
Aslaksen. I only print what's put into my hands.
Mayor. Absolutely.
Aslaksen. So if you'll excuse me— *(Goes towards the composing room)* 340
Mayor. No, wait a moment, Mr. Aslaksen. With your permission, Mr. Hovstad—
Hovstad. Of course, Your Worship.
Mayor. You're an intelligent and discriminating man, Mr. Aslaksen.
Aslaksen. I'm glad Your Worship thinks so.
Mayor. And a man of wide influence in more circles than one.
Aslaksen. Oh—mostly among humble people—
Mayor. The small taxpayers are the most numerous, here as elsewhere.
Aslaksen. Yes, that's true. 350
Mayor. And I've no doubt you know how most of them feel. Don't you?
Aslaksen. Yes, I think I may say I do, Your Worship.
Mayor. Well then, since the less affluent of the citizens of this town are so laudably disposed to make this sacrifice, I—
Aslaksen. What!
Hovstad. Sacrifice—?
Mayor. It's a fine token of public spirit; a remarkably fine token. I was about to confess I hadn't expected it. But you know the mood of the people better than I do. 360
Aslaksen. But, Your Worship—
Mayor. And it will probably be no mean sacrifice that the ratepayers will be called upon to make.
Hovstad. The ratepayers?
Aslaksen. But I don't understand—surely the shareholders—?

Mayor. According to a provisional estimate the alterations that the medical officer at the Baths regards as desirable will cost some two to three hundred thousand crowns.

Aslaksen. That's a lot of money; but—

370 *Mayor.* We shall of course be forced to raise a municipal loan.

Hovstad. (Gets up) You surely don't mean that the ordinary citizens—?

Aslaksen. You mean you'd charge it on the rates! Empty the pockets of the tradespeople—?

Mayor. Well, my dear Mr. Aslaksen, where else is the money to come from?

Aslaksen. That's the business of the gentlemen who own the Baths.

Mayor. The Committee cannot see their ways towards authorising any further expenditure.

380 *Aslaksen.* Is that quite definite, Your Worship?

Mayor. I have gone into the matter very thoroughly. If the people want all these comprehensive alterations, then the people themselves will have to pay for them.

Aslaksen. But good God Almighty—oh, I beg Your Worship's pardon! —but this puts a completely different face on the situation, Mr. Hovstad.

Hovstad. It certainly does.

Mayor. The worst of the matter is that we shall be compelled to close the Baths for two to three years.

Hovstad. Close them? You mean—close them completely?

390 *Aslaksen.* For two years?

Mayor. That's how long the work will take, at the lowest calculation.

Aslaksen. But, good Heavens, we'll never be able to stand that, Your Worship! How are we property owners to live in the meantime?

Mayor. I'm afraid that's a very difficult question to answer, Mr. Aslaksen. But what do you expect us to do? Do you imagine we shall get a single visitor here if we start spreading the idea that the water is contaminated, that we are living over a cesspit, that the whole town—?

Aslaksen. And all this is just pure speculation?

400 *Mayor.* With the best will in the world I have been unable to convince myself that it is anything else.

Aslaksen. But if that's the case it's monstrous of Dr. Stockmann to have—I beg Your Worship's pardon, but—

Mayor. I deplore your observation, Mr. Aslaksen, but I'm afraid it represents the truth. My brother has unfortunately always been an impulsive man.

Aslaksen. And you still want to support him in this action, Mr. Hovstad?

Hovstad. But who could have possibly guessed that—?

Mayor. I have written a brief resumé of the situation as it appears to an impartial observer; and in it I have suggested how any possible flaws in the existing arrangements could safely be remedied by measures within the financial resources at present possessed by the Baths. 410

Hovstad. Have you that document with you, Your Worship?

Mayor. (Feels in his pocket) Yes, I brought it with me just in case you—

Aslaksen. (Quickly) Oh, my goodness, there he is!

Mayor. Who? My brother?

Hovstad. Where—where?

Aslaksen. He's just coming through the composing-room. 420

Mayor. Most unfortunate! I don't want to meet him here, and I've something else I wanted to speak to you about.

Hovstad. (Points towards the door, right) Go in there till he's gone.

Mayor, But—?

Hovstad. There's only Billing there.

Aslaksen. Quick, quick, Your Worship! He's coming now!

Mayor. Very well. But get rid of him as soon as you can.

(Goes out through the door on the right, which Aslaksen opens and closes for him)

Hovstad. Find something to do, Aslaksen. *(He sits down and writes. Aslaksen starts looking through a pile of newspapers on a chair to the right.)* 430

Dr. Stockmann. (Enters from the composing-room) Well, here I am again! *(Puts down his hat and stick)*

Hovstad. (Writing) Already, Doctor? Aslaksen, hurry up with that thing we were talking about. We're badly behind-hand today.

Dr. Stockmann. (To Aslaksen) No proofs yet, by the sound of it?

Aslaksen. (Without turning) No, surely you didn't think they'd be ready yet.

Dr. Stockmann. That's all right. I'm just impatient, as I know you'll appreciate. I can't rest till I've seen that thing in print. 440

Hovstad. Hm; it'll be a good time yet. Won't it, Aslaksen?

Aslaksen. I'm afraid so.

Dr. Stockmann. Very well, my dear friends. I'll be back later. I don't mind making the journey twice if need be! In such a vital matter, with the welfare of the whole town at stake, one mustn't grudge a little extra effort! *(Is about to go, but stops and comes back)* Oh, by the way, there's one more thing I must speak to you about.

Hovstad. I'm sorry, but couldn't it wait till another time—?

Dr. Stockmann. I can tell you in two words. It's just this. When people read my article in the paper tomorrow and discover I've been racking my brains all winter working silently for the welfare of the town— 450

Hovstad. But, Doctor—

Dr. Stockmann. I know what you're going to say! You think it was no more than my damned duty—my job as a citizen. Yes, of course—I know that as well as you do. But my fellow-citizens, you see—oh dear, those good people, they're so fond of me—

Aslaksen. Yes, the people of this town have been very fond of you, 460 Doctor, up to today.

Dr. Stockmann. Yes, and that's exactly why I'm frightened that—what I mean is—when they read this—especially the poorer people—as a clarion call bidding them take the government of their town into their own hands—

Hovstad. (Gets up) Look, Doctor, I don't want to hide anything from you—

Dr. Stockmann. Ah, something's already afoot! I might have guessed! But I don't want it! If anything like that's being organized, I—

Hovstad. Like what?

470 *Dr. Stockmann.* Well, if anything like a torchlight procession or a banquet or—a subscription for some little token of thanks is being organised, you must promise me solemnly you'll squash the idea. And you too, Mr. Aslaksen! You hear!

Hovstad. I'm sorry, Doctor, but we might as well tell you the truth now as later—

(Mrs. Stockmann, in hat and cloak, enters through the door upstage left.)

Mrs. Stockmann. (Sees the Doctor) I knew it!

Hovstad. (Goes towards her) You here too, Mrs. Stockmann?

Dr. Stockmann. What the devil do you want here, Catherine?

480 *Mrs. Stockmann.* Surely you can guess.

Hovstad. Won't you sit down? Or perhaps—?

Mrs. Stockmann. Thank you, you needn't bother. And you mustn't take offence at my coming here to fetch my husband, for I'm the mother of three children, I'd have you realise.

Dr. Stockmann. Oh really, Catherine, we know all this.

Mrs. Stockmann. Well, it doesn't seem you've much thought for your wife and children today, or you wouldn't have come here to cause all of us misery.

Dr. Stockmann. Are you quite mad, Catherine? Simply because a 490 man has a wife and children, is he to be forbidden to proclaim the truth—to be a useful and active citizen—to serve the town he lives in?

Mrs. Stockmann. Oh, Thomas, if only you'd use some restraint.

Aslaksen. That's exactly what I say. Restraint in all things.

Mrs. Stockmann. And as for you, Mr. Hovstad, it's not right for you to persuade my husband to leave his house and home and trick him into involving himself in all this—

Hovstad. I haven't tricked anyone—

Dr. Stockmann. Tricked! You think *I* allow myself to be tricked?

Mrs. Stockmann. Yes, you do. Oh, I know you're the cleverest man in the town, but you're so dreadfully easy to fool, Thomas. *(To Hovstad)* And don't forget he'll lose his job at the Baths if you print that thing he's written— 500

Aslaksen. What!

Hovstad. But Doctor—I—

Dr. Stockmann. (Laughs) Just let them try! Oh no, Catherine—they'll watch their step! You see, I have the majority behind me!

Mrs. Stockmann. Yes, that's just the trouble. They're an ugly thing to have behind you.

Dr. Stockmann. Rubbish, Catherine! You go home now and take care of the house, and let me take care of society. How can you be frightened when I feel so calm and happy? *(Rubs his hands and walks up and down)* Truth and the people will win this battle, never you fear! Oh, I can see every liberal-minded citizen in this town marching forward in an unconquerable army—! *(Stops by a chair)* What—the devil is *this?* 510

Aslaksen. (Looks at it) Oh dear!

Dr. Stockmann. The crown of authority! *(Takes the Mayor's hat carefully in his fingers and holds it in the air)*

Mrs. Stockmann. The Mayor's hat!

Dr. Stockmann. And his marshal's baton too. How in the name of Hell—? 520

Hovstad. Well—

Dr. Stockmann. Ah, I see! He's been here to talk you over! *(Laughs)* He came to the wrong men! And then he saw me in the composing room— *(Roars with laughter)* Did he run away, Mr. Aslaksen?

Aslaksen. (Quickly) Oh yes, Doctor, he ran away.

Dr. Stockmann. Ran away leaving his stick and—? Rubbish! Peter never left anything behind in his life! But where the devil have you put him? Ah, yes, of course—in there! Now, Catherine, you watch!

Mrs. Stockmann. Thomas, I beg you—! 530

Aslaksen. Don't do anything rash, Doctor!

(Dr. Stockmann has put the Mayor's hat on his head and taken his stick. Then he goes across, throws the door open and brings his hand up to the hat in salute. The Mayor enters, red with anger. Billing follows him.)

Mayor. What is the meaning of this disorderly scene?

Dr. Stockmann. A little more respect if you please, my dear Peter. I am the supreme authority in this town now. *(He walks up and down.)*

Mrs. Stockmann. (Almost in tears) Thomas, please!

540 *Mayor. (Follows him)* Give me my hat and stick!

Dr. Stockmann. (As before) You may be Chief of Police, but I'm the Mayor! I'm master of this whole town, I am!

Mayor. Take off that hat, I tell you! Remember that that hat is an official emblem—

Dr. Stockmann. Rubbish! Do you think the awakening lion of public opinion is going to let itself be frightened by a hat? We're starting a revolution tomorrow, I'd have you know! You threatened to sack me, but now I'm going to sack you—sack you from all your positions of responsibility! You think I can't? You're wrong, Peter! I have as my 550 allies the conquering forces of social revolution! Hovstad and Billing will thunder in the *People's Tribune*, and Mr. Aslaksen will march forth at the head of the entire Property Owners' Association—

Aslaksen. No, I won't, Doctor.

Dr. Stockmann. Indeed you will—!

Mayor. Aha. But perhaps Mr. Hovstad will support this uprising?

Hovstad. No, Your Worship.

Aslaksen. Mr. Hovstad isn't so mad as to ruin himself and his newspaper for the sake of an hallucination.

Dr. Stockmann. (Looks around) What the devil—?

560 *Hovstad.* You have presented your case in a false light, Doctor; and therefore I cannot support you.

Billing. No, after what His Worship has had the grace to tell me in there, I shouldn't—

Dr. Stockmann. Lies! I'll answer for the truth of my report! You just print it. I shan't be frightened to defend it.

Hovstad. I'm not printing it. I can't and I won't and I dare not print it.

Dr. Stockmann. Dare not? What nonsense is this? You're the editor, and it's the editors who rule the press.

Aslaksen. No, Doctor. It's the subscribers.

570 *Mayor.* Fortunately.

Aslaksen. It's public opinion, the educated reader, the property owners, and so forth—they're the ones who rule the press.

Dr. Stockmann. (Calmly) And all these forces are ranged against me?

Aslaksen. They are. If your report got printed, it would mean ruin for the entire community.

Dr. Stockmann. I see.

Mayor. My hat and stick! *(Dr. Stockmann takes off the hat and puts it on the table together with the stick.)*

Mayor. (Takes them both) Your little reign didn't last long.

580 *Dr. Stockmann.* It isn't over yet. *(To Hovstad)* You refuse absolutely, then, to print my report in the *People's Tribune?*

Hovstad. Absolutely. Out of consideration for your family, if for no other reason.

Mrs. Stockmann. Never you mind his family, Mr. Hovstad.

Mayor. (Takes a paper from his pocket) This will give the public full possession of the facts. It's an official statement. Mr. Hovstad—

Hovstad. (Takes the paper) Right. I'll see it's set up at once.

Dr. Stockmann. But not mine! You think you can gag me and stifle the truth! But it won't be as easy as you think. Mr. Aslaksen, take this manuscript of mine and print it immediately as a pamphlet—at my own expense! I'll publish it myself! I want four hundred copies—five—no, make it six hundred copies! 590

Aslaksen. I wouldn't give you the use of my press if you offered me gold, Doctor. I daren't. Public opinion wouldn't allow me. You won't find a printer to take it anywhere in this town.

Dr. Stockmann. Give it back to me then. *(Hovstad hands him the manuscript.)*

Dr. Stockmann. (Takes his hat and stick) I'll see the contents are made known all the same. I'll summon a public meeting and read it! All my fellow-citizens shall know the truth! 600

Mayor. You won't find anyone in this town who'll lease you a hall for such a purpose.

Aslaksen. Not one. I'm sure of that.

Billing. By jingo, you won't.

Mrs. Stockmann. This is too disgraceful! Why are they all against you?

Dr. Stockmann. (Hotly) I'll tell you why! It's because in this town all the men are old women! Like you, they just think of their families and not of the community.

Mrs. Stockmann. (Grasps his arm) Then I'll show them that an—an old woman can be a man—for once. I'm sticking with you, Thomas. 610

Dr. Stockmann. Well said, Catherine! The truth shall be told—by God it will! If I can't lease a hall, I'll hire a drummer to march through the town with me, and I'll read it out at every street corner!

Mayor. You can't be so crazy as to do that!

Dr. Stockmann. I am!

Aslaksen. You won't find a single man in the whole town who'll go with you.

Billing. No, by jingo!

Mrs. Stockmann. Don't you give in, Thomas! I'll ask the boys to go with you. 620

Dr. Stockmann. That's a splendid idea!

Mrs. Stockmann. Morten will love to do it; and so will Eilif, I'm sure.

Dr. Stockmann. Yes, and Petra too! And you, Catherine!

Mrs. Stockmann. No, no, not me. But I'll stand at the window and watch you. I'll do that.

Dr. Stockmann. (Throws his arms around her and kisses her) Thank you! Well, my fine gentlemen, let the trumpets sound! Let's see whether meanness and mediocrity have the power to gag a man who wants to clean up society!

630 *(Dr. and Mrs. Stockmann go out through the door upstage left.)*

Mayor. (Shakes his head thoughtfully) Now he's driven her mad, too!

Act IV

(A big, old-fashioned room in Captain Horster's house. In the background an open double-leaved door leads to a lobby. In the left-hand wall are three windows. Against the middle of the opposite wall has been placed a dais, on which stands a small table with two candles, a water carafe, a glass, and a bell. The room is further illuminated by bracket lamps between the windows. Downstage left stands a table with a candle on it, and a chair. Downstage right is a door, with a few chairs by it.)

(A large gathering of citizens, of all classes. Here and there, women can be seen among the crowd, and there are a few schoolboys. More and more people gradually stream in from the back, filling the room.)

A Citizen. (To another, as he bumps against him.) Hullo, Lamstad! You here too this evening?

2nd Citizen. I never miss a public meeting.

3rd Citizen. (Standing near them) Brought your whistle, I hope?

2nd Citizen. Course I have. Haven't you?

3rd Citizen. You bet! And Skipper Evensen said he'd bring a bloody great horn!

2nd Citizen. He's a card, old Evensen! *(Laughter among the Crowd)*

4th Citizen. (Joins them) I say, what's this meeting about?

10 *2nd Citizen.* Dr. Stockmann's going to deliver a lecture attacking the Mayor.

4th Citizen. But the Mayor's his brother.

1st Citizen. That don't matter. Dr. Stockmann ain't afraid of no one.

3rd Citizen. But he's in the wrong. It said so in the *People's Tribune.*

2nd Citizen. Yes, he must be in the wrong this time. The Property Owners wouldn't let him use their hall, nor the People's Club neither.

1st Citizen. He couldn't even get the hall at the Baths.

2nd Citizen. Well, what do you expect?

1st Citizen. Which one do you think we ought to support?

20 *4th Citizen.* Just keep your eye on old Aslaksen, and do as he does.

Billing. (With a portfolio under his arm, pushes his way through the crowd) Excuse me please, gentlemen! Can I get through, please? I'm reporting the meeting for the *People's Tribune.* Thank you! *(Sits down at the table, left)*

(Captain Horster escorts Mrs. Stockmann and Petra in through the door downstage right. Eilif and Morten are with them.)

Horster. I thought you might sit here. You can slip out easily if anything should happen.

Mrs. Stockmann. Do you think there'll be trouble?

Horster. One never knows, with a crowd like this. But sit down, and don't worry. 30

Mrs. Stockmann. (Sits) It was very kind of you to offer my husband this room.

Horster. Well, no one else would, so I—

Petra. (Who has sat down too) It was brave of you, too, Captain Horster.

Horster. Oh, that didn't call for much courage.

(Hovstad and Aslaksen come through the Crowd, at the same time but separately.)

Aslaksen. (Goes over to Horster) Hasn't the Doctor come yet? 40

Horster. He's waiting in there *(There is a stir among the Crowd near the door backstage.)*

Hovstad. (To Billing) There's the Mayor! See?

Billing. Yes, by jingo! So he's come after all!

(The Mayor gently pushes his way through the Crowd, greeting people politely, and stations himself against the wall on the left. A few moments later Dr. Stockmann enters through the door downstage right. He is dressed in black, with a frock coat and a white cravat. A few people clap uncertainly, but are countered by subdued hissing. Silence falls.)

Dr. Stockmann. (In a low voice) How do you feel, Catherine? 50

Mrs. Stockmann. I'm all right. *(More quietly)* Now don't lose your temper, Thomas!

Dr. Stockmann. Oh, I'll control myself, don't you worry. *(Looks at his watch, steps up onto the dais and bows)* It's a quarter past, so I'll begin—*(Takes out his manuscript)*

Aslaksen. Surely a Chairman ought to be elected first?

Dr. Stockmann. No, no, there's no need for that.

Several Men. (Shout) Yes, yes!

Mayor. I really think we should have someone in the chair.

Dr. Stockmann. But Peter, I've called this meeting to deliver a lecture! 60

Mayor. The Doctor's lecture may possibly give rise to divergent expressions of opinion.

Several Voices from the Crowd. A Chairman! A Chairman!

Hovstad. Public opinion seems to demand a Chairman.

Dr. Stockmann. (Controlling himself) Very well. Let public opinion have its way.

Aslaksen. Would His Worship the Mayor be willing to undertake that function?

70 *Three Men. (Clap)* Bravo! Hear, hear!

Mayor. For reasons which I'm sure you will appreciate, I must decline that honour. But fortunately we have among us a man whom I think we can all accept. I refer to the Chairman of the Property Owners' Association, Mr. Aslaksen.

Many Voices. Yes, yes! Good old Aslaksen! Hurrah for Aslaksen! *(Dr. Stockmann picks up his manuscript and descends from the dais.)*

Aslaksen. If my fellow-citizens want to express their trust in me, I won't refuse their call. *(Applause and cheers. Aslaksen steps up onto the dais.)*

80 *Billing. (Writes)* "Mr. Aslaksen was chosen amid acclamation..."

Aslaksen. Now that I stand here may I crave permission to say a few brief words? I'm a mild and peace-loving man who believes in sensible discretion, and in—and in discreet good sense. Everyone who knows me knows that.

Many Voices. Yes! That's right, Aslaksen!

Aslaksen. Experience in the school of life has taught me that the most valuable virtue for any citizen is restraint—

Mayor, Hear, hear!

Aslaksen. And that discretion and restraint are the best servants of

90 society. I would therefore suggest to our respected fellow-citizen who has summoned this meeting that he endeavour to keep himself within the bounds of temperance.

Drunken Man. (By the entrance door) Three cheers for the Temperance Society! Jolly good health!

A Voice. Shut your damned trap.

Many Voices. Hush, hush!

Aslaksen. No interruptions, gentlemen, please! Does anyone wish to say anything before I—?

Mayor. Mr. Chairman!

100 *Aslaksen.* Your Worship!

Mayor. As everyone here is doubtless aware, I have close ties of relationship with the present medical officer at the Baths, and would consequently have preferred not to speak this evening. But my official position on the Committee of that organization, and my anxiety for the best interests of the town, force me to table a resolution. I hope I may assume that no citizen here present would regard it as desirable that dubious and exaggerated allegations concerning the sanitary conditions at the Baths should circulate outside this town.

Many Voices. No, no, no! Certainly not! We protest!

110 *Mayor.* I therefore move that this meeting refuse the aforesaid medical officer permission to read or dilate upon his theories concerning the matter in question.

Dr. Stockmann. (Explosively) Refuse permission? What the devil—? *(Mrs. Stockmann coughs.)*

Dr. Stockmann. (Composes himself) Very well, you refuse permission.

Mayor. In my statement to the *People's Tribune* I have acquainted the public with the essential facts so that every intelligent citizen can form his own judgment. Among other things I pointed out that the medical officer's proposals—quite apart from the fact that they amount 120 to a vote of no confidence in the leading citizens of this town—will burden the ratepayers with the unnecessary expenditure of at least a hundred thousand crowns. *(Groans and a few whistles)*

Aslaksen. (Rings his bell) Order please, gentlemen! I beg leave to second His Worship's motion. I would add that in my view the Doctor has had an ulterior motive, no doubt unconscious, in stirring up this agitation. He talks about the Baths. But what he's really aiming at is a revolution. He wants to transfer authority into other hands. No one doubts the honesty of the Doctor's intentions. Heaven knows, there can be no two opinions about that! I too believe in popular self- 130 government, so long as it doesn't impose too heavy an expense upon the taxpaper. But that's just what would happen here; so I'm blowed,° if you'll excuse the expression, if I can support Dr. Stockmann in this matter. One can pay too high a price for gold; that's my opinion. *(Lively expressions of assent from all sides)*

Hovstad. I too feel impelled to explain my position. Dr. Stockmann's agitation won considerable sympathy at first, and I myself supported it as impartially as I was able. But then we found we had allowed ourselves to be misled by a false picture of the facts—

Dr. Stockmann. That's a lie! 140

Hovstad. A not completely reliable picture, then. His Worship's statement has proved that. I hope no one here doubts the liberality of my views. The *People's Tribune's* attitude on major political questions is well known to you all. But I have learned from men of discretion and experience that in local matters it is the duty of a newspaper to observe a certain caution.

Aslaksen. Exactly my feelings.

Hovstad. Now in the matter under discussion it's quite clear that Dr. Stockmann has popular opinion against him. Well, I ask you, gentlemen, what is the primary duty of an editor? Is it not to reflect 150 the opinions of his readers? Has he not been entrusted with what might be described as an unspoken mandate to advance the cause of those who hold the same views as himself, with all the eloquence of which he is capable? Or am I mistaken?

Many Voices. No, no, no! Mr. Hovstad is right!

132. *I'm blowed*, I'll be darned.

Hovstad. It has caused me much heart-searching to break with a man under whose roof I have lately been a not infrequent guest—a man who has until this day rejoiced in the undivided affection of his fellow-citizens—a man whose only, or anyway principal fault is
160 that he follows his heart rather than his head.

Scattered Voices. That's true. Hurrah for Dr. Stockmann!

Hovstad. But my duty towards society left me no alternative. And there's one further consideration which forces me to oppose him, in the hope of halting him on the inauspicious road he has now begun to tread—consideration for his family—

Dr. Stockmann. Stick to the water system and the sewer!

Hovstad. —Consideration for his wife and children he has abandoned.

Morten. Does he mean us, Mother?

Mrs. Stockmann. Hush!

170 *Aslaksen.* I shall now put His Worship's resolution to the vote.

Dr. Stockmann. Don't bother! I won't say a word about those damned Baths. No. I've something else to tell you tonight.

Mayor. (In a low voice) What the devil's this?

A Drunk Man. (Near the entrance door) I pay my taxes! So I'm entitled to express my opinion! And it's my absolute'n unintelligible opinion that—

Several Voices. Keep quiet there!

Others. He's drunk! Throw him out! *(The drunk man is removed.)*

Dr. Stockmann. Have I the floor?

180 *Aslaksen. (Rings his bell)* Dr. Stockmann has the floor.

Dr. Stockmann. A few days ago, if anyone had tried to gag me like this I'd have fought like a lion for my sacred human rights! But now that doesn't matter. Now I have more important things to talk about. *(The Crowd moves closer around him. Morten Kiil can be seen among them.)*

Dr. Stockmann. (Continues) I've been thinking a great deal these past few days. I've brooded so deeply that in the end my head began to spin—

Mayor. (Coughs) Hm—!

190 *Dr. Stockmann.* But then everything began to fall into place. I saw the whole picture of things quite clearly. And that's why I'm standing here this evening. I'm going to make a mighty revelation to you, my friends! I'm going to tell you about a discovery that is infinitely more important than the fiddling little fact that our water system is poisoned and our health baths sited above a cesspit!

Many Voices. (Shout) Leave the Baths alone! Don't talk about them! We won't listen!

Dr. Stockmann. This great discovery that I have made during these last few days is that all our spiritual sources are poisoned, and that the whole of our vaunted social system is founded upon a cesspit of lies! 200

Astonished Voices. (Mutter in low tones) What's that? What did he say?

Mayor. These are ridiculous insinuations—

Aslaksen. (His hand on the bell) I must request the speaker to moderate his language.

Dr. Stockmann. I was young when I left home, and distance, hunger, and memory threw, as it were, a brighter lustre over this place and the people who dwelt here. *(Some applause and cheers are heard.)*

Dr. Stockmann. For years I lived far up in the north. As I wandered 210 among those people who lived scattered over the mountains, I often thought it would have been better for those poor degraded creatures if they'd had a vet instead of a man like me! *(Murmurs)*

Billing. (Puts down his pen) By jingo, I've never heard the like of that—!

Hovstad. That's a filthy slander against a worthy community!

Dr. Stockmann. Wait a moment! I sat there brooding like a duck on an egg; and the chick I hatched was—the plan for these Baths. *(Clapping, and murmurs of disapproval)*

Dr. Stockmann. Then at long last fate smiled upon me and allowed 220 me to return. And then, my fellow-citizens, then I thought I had nothing left to wish for in this world. No—I had one ambition left—a burning desire to work with all my heart and soul for the welfare of my home and my community.

Mayor. (Gazing into space) You've a strange way of showing it!

Dr. Stockmann. I went around here revelling blindly in my new-found happiness. But yesterday morning—no, it was the previous night, actually—my eyes were opened, and the first thing that greeted them was the stupendous imbecility of the authorities—*(Noise, shouting, and laughter. Mrs. Stockmann coughs loudly.)* 230

Mayor. Mr. Chairman!

Aslaksen. (Rings his bell) As Chairman of this meeting, I—

Dr. Stockmann. Oh, let's not start quibbling about words, Mr. Aslaksen. I only mean that I suddenly realized how really revoltingly our politicians had behaved down there at the Baths. I can't stand politicians! They're like goats in a plantation of young trees; they destroy everything! They block the way for a free man, however much he may twist and turn—and I'd like to see them rooted out and exterminated, like other vermin—*(Commotion in the hall)*

Mayor. Mr. Chairman, are such calumnies to be permitted? 240

Aslaksen. (His hand on the bell) Dr. Stockmann—!

Dr. Stockmann. I can't understand why I'd never had a proper look at these gentlemen before. I'd had a prime example right in front of my eyes all the time—my brother Peter—procrastinating and pur-blind—! *(Laughter, confusion, and whistling. Mrs. Stockmann sits and coughs. Aslaksen rings his bell loudly.)*

The Drunk Man. (Who has come back) Are you referring to me? My name's Petersen, but don't you damned well—

Angry Voices. Throw that drunk out! Get rid of him! *(The Drunk Man* 250 *is thrown out again.)*

Mayor. Who was that person?

A Bystander. I don't know, Your Worship.

Aslaksen. The man was obviously intoxicated with German beer. Continue, Doctor; but please try to use restraint!

Dr. Stockmann. Well, my fellow-citizens, I won't say anything more about our politicians. If anyone imagines from what I've just said that I've come here this evening to immolate these gentlemen, he's wrong—quite wrong. For I cherish the comforting belief that these laggards, these survivors from a dying world, are studiously 260 cutting their own throats; they need no doctor's help to hasten their demise. And anyway, it isn't they who are the chief danger to society! They aren't the ones who are most active in poisoning the sources of our spiritual life and contaminating the ground on which we tread! It isn't they who are the most dangerous enemies of truth and freedom in our society!

Shouts from All Sides. Who, then? Who is? Name them!

Dr. Stockmann. Don't worry, I'll name them! Because this is the great discovery I've made today! *(Raises his voice)* The most dangerous enemies of truth and freedom are the majority! Yes, the solid, liberal, 270 bloody majority—they're the ones we have to fear! Now you know!

(Complete uproar. Nearly everyone is shouting, stamping, and whistling. Some of the older men exchange stolen glances and seem to be enjoying the situation. Mrs. Stockmann gets up anxiously. Eilif and Morten go threateningly over to the Schoolboys, who are making a commotion. Aslaksen rings his bell and calls for silence. Hovstad and Billing are both talking, but neither can be heard. At last silence is restored.)

Aslaksen. As Chairman I call upon the speaker to withdraw those mischievous observations.

280 *Dr. Stockmann.* Never, Mr. Aslaksen! It's the majority in this community that is depriving me of my freedom and trying to forbid me to proclaim the truth.

Hovstad. The majority is always right.

Billing. And speaks the truth, by jingo!

Dr. Stockmann. The majority is never right! Never, I tell you! That's one of those community lies that free, thinking men have got to rebel against! Who form the majority—in any country? The wise, or the fools?

I think we'd all have to agree that the fools are in a terrifying, overwhelming majority all over the world! But in the name of God it can't be right that the fools should rule the wise! *(Uproar and shouting)* 290 Yes, yes, you can shout me down! But you can't say I'm wrong! The majority has the power—unfortunately—but the majority is not right! The ones who are right are a few isolated individuals like me! The minority is always right! *(Uproar again)*

Hovstad. So Dr. Stockmann's turned aristocrat since the day before yesterday!

Dr. Stockmann. I've already said I don't want to waste words on the little flock of short-winded sheep puffing along in the rear! Life has nothing exciting left to offer them. But I'm thinking of the few, the individuals among us, who have adopted the new, fresh, burgeoning 300 truths as their watchword!

Hovstad. I see, so you've become a revolutionary!

Dr. Stockmann. Yes, Mr. Hovstad, by God I have! I intend to start a revolution against the lie that truth is a monopoly of the majority! What are these truths to which the majority clings? They're the truths which are so old that they're on the way to becoming decrepit! But when a truth's as old as that, gentlemen, it's also well on the way to becoming a lie! *(Laughter and jeers)*

Dr. Stockmann. All these majority truths are like last year's salt pork; they're hams that have gone sour and green and tainted. And 310 they're the cause of all the moral scurvy that's rotting our society!

Aslaksen. It seems to me that the honourable speaker has strayed somewhat from his text.

Mayor. I warmly endorse the Chairman's observation.

Dr. Stockmann. Oh, really, Peter, I think you must be quite mad! I'm sticking as close to my text as any man could! My whole point is precisely this, that it's the masses, the mob, this damned majority—they're the thing that's poisoning the sources of our spiritual life and contaminating the ground we walk on!

Hovstad. And the great progressive majority does this simply by 320 being sensible enough to believe in those truths which are indisputable and generally acknowledged?

Dr. Stockmann. Oh, my good Mr. Hovstad, don't talk to me about undisputed truths! There's only one indisputable truth. It is that no society can live a healthy life if it feeds on truths that are old and marrowless.

Hovstad. Instead of all this generalising why don't you give us a few examples of these old and marrowless truths on which we're living? *(Murmurs of agreement from several quarters)*

Dr. Stockmann. Oh, I could reel you off a whole list of the beastly 330 things; but to start with I'll limit myself to one "acknowledged" truth which is really a damned lie, but which Mr. Hovstad and the *People's Tribune* and all the hangers-on of the *People's Tribune* feed on all the same.

Hovstad. And that is—?

Dr. Stockmann. That is the doctrine which you have inherited from your forefathers and which you continue thoughtlessly to proclaim far and wide—the doctrine that the plebs, the masses, the mob, are the living heart of the people—that they are the people—and that the
340 common man, all those ignorant and incompetent millions, have the same right to sanction and condemn, to advise and to govern, as the few individuals who are intellectually aristocrats.

Billing. Now, really, by jingo—!

Hovstad. (Simultaneously, shouts) Mark that, fellow-citizens!

Furious Voices. Oh-ho, so we're not the people, aren't we? So it's only the aristocrats who have the right to rule?

A Worker. Throw him out if he talks like that!

Others. Chuck him through the door!

A Citizen. (Shouts) Blow that horn, Evensen! *(Loud horn-blasts are*
350 *heard. Whistles and furious uproar in the hall)*

Dr. Stockmann. (When the noise has abated somewhat) Can't you be reasonable? Can't you bear to hear the truth just for once? I'm not asking you all to agree with me immediately! But I did expect Mr. Hovstad would admit I was right once he'd given the matter a little thought. After all, Mr. Hovstad claims to be a freethinker—

Surprised Voices. (Murmur) Freethinker, did he say? What? Is Mr. Hovstad a freethinker?

Hovstad. (Shouts) Prove that, Dr. Stockmann! When have I said so in print?

360 *Dr. Stockmann. (Thinks)* No, by Jove, you're right! You've never had the guts to admit it publicly. Well, I won't corner you, Mr. Hovstad. Let me be the freethinker, then. I shall now prove to you that the masses are nothing but raw material which may, some day, be refined into individuals! *(Growls, laughter, and disturbances in the hall)*

Dr. Stockmann. Well, isn't that the way life works with the rest of creation? Look at the enormous difference there is between a breed of animal that's cultivated and one that is uncultivated! Consider dogs, with which we human beings have so much in common! Think first of a simple mongrel—one of those filthy, ragged, common curs that lope
370 along the streets and defile the walls of our houses. And then put that mongrel next to a greyhound with a distinguished pedigree, whose ancestors have been fed delicate meals for generations and have had the opportunity to listen to harmonious voices and music! Don't you think the brain of that greyhound is differently developed from that of the mongrel? You bet your life it is! It's the pups of these cultivated

animals that trainers teach to perform the most amazing tricks. A common mongrel couldn't learn to do such things if you stood it on its head! *(Noise and laughter)*

A Citizen. (Shouts) So we're dogs too now, are we?

Another. We're not animals, Doctor! 380

Dr. Stockmann. Yes, my friend, we are animals! But there aren't many aristocratic animals among us. There's a terrifying difference between men who are greyhounds and men who are mongrels. And that's what's so absurd, that Mr. Hovstad is quite at one with me as long as we're talking about four-legged animals—

Hovstad. Well, they're only beasts.

Dr. Stockmann. All right! But as soon as I start to apply the law to the ones who are two-legged, Mr. Hovstad balks at the consequences; he turns his whole philosophy upside down, and proclaims in the *People's Tribune* that the street mongrel is the champion of the menag- 390 erie. But that's how it always is, as long as a man remains possessed by this blind worship of the mob and hasn't worked his way out of spiritual bondage into aristocracy.

Hovstad. I don't want any kind of aristocracy. I come of simple peasant stock; and I'm proud that I have my roots deep down in the mob, whom you deride.

Many Workers. Hurrah for Hovstad! Hurrah, hurrah!

Dr. Stockmann. The kind of mob I'm talking about isn't only to be found at the bottom of the barrel. It swarms and mills all around us, even among the high peaks of society. Just look at your own smug, 400 sleek Mayor! My brother Peter's as good a mobster as ever walked in two shoes. *(Laughter and hisses)*

Mayor. I protest against these personal remarks.

Dr. Stockmann. (Unperturbed) And that isn't because he stems like me from a villainous old pirate from Pomerania or somewhere down there—for we do—!

Mayor. It's absurd, it's a myth! I deny it!

Dr. Stockmann. Because he thinks what his superiors think, and his opinions are the opinions he's heard them express. The men who do that are spiritually of the mob; and that's why my noble brother Peter 410 is so frighteningly unaristocratic in all essentials—and consequently so terrified of all things liberal.

Mayor. Mr. Chairman—!

Hovstad. So it's the aristocrats who are the liberals in this country? That really is a new discovery! *(Laughter among the crowd)*

Dr. Stockmann. Yes, that's part of my discovery too. And the reason is that liberality is almost exactly the same as morality. And I say it's quite indefensible of the *Tribune* day after day to proclaim the false gospel that the masses, the mob, the solid majority, have a monopoly

420 on liberality and morality, and that vice and corruption and every kind of spiritual filth are a kind of pus that oozes out of culture, just as all that beastly stuff in the Baths oozes down from the tanneries at Moelledal! *(Confusion and interruptions)*

Dr. Stockmann. (Unperturbed, laughs in his excitement) And yet this same *People's Tribune* can preach that the masses and the mob must be elevated to a higher standard of living! Good God Almighty, if what the *People's Tribune* teaches were true, then to elevate the masses would simply be to start them on the road to ruin! But luckily the idea that culture demoralises is an old inherited fairy tale. No, it's
430 stupidity, poverty, and foul living conditions that do the devil's work! In a house where the rooms aren't aired and the floors swept every day—my wife Catherine says they ought to be scrubbed, too, but there can be two opinions on that—in such a house, I say, within two or three years people lose the capacity for moral thought and moral action. Lack of oxygen debilitates the conscience. And there's a shortage of oxygen in many, many houses in this town, from the sound of things, if the whole of this damned majority can be so devoid of conscience as to want to build the prosperity of their town on a quagmire of deceit and lies.

440 *Aslaksen.* You can't cast an accusation like that against a whole community!

A Man. I appeal to the Chairman to order the speaker to stand down.

Excited Voices. Yes, yes! That's right! Make him stand down!

Dr. Stockmann. (Explodes) Then I'll shout the truth at every street corner! I'll write in the newspapers of other towns! The whole country shall be told what is happening here!

Hovstad. It sounds almost as though the Doctor wishes to destroy this town.

Dr. Stockmann. Yes, I love this town where I was born so dearly that
450 I would rather destroy it than see it flourish because of a lie!

Aslaksen. Those are strong words. *(Shouts and whistling. Mrs. Stockmann coughs in vain; the Doctor no longer hears her.)*

Hovstad. (Shouts through the uproar) The man who can want to destroy a whole community must be a public enemy!

Dr. Stockmann. (With increasing excitement) A community that lives on lies deserves to be destroyed! I say that the town that houses such a community should be levelled to the ground! All those who live by lies ought to be exterminated like vermin! You will end by contaminating the entire country! You will bring it to the pass where the whole
460 land will deserve to be laid waste! And if things go that far, then I say with all my heart: "Let the whole land be laid waste! Let the whole people be exterminated!"

A Man. That's talking like an enemy of the people!

Billing. There speaks the voice of the people, by jingo!

The Whole Crowd. (Screams) Yes, yes, yes! He's an enemy of the people! He hates his country! He hates the people!

Aslaksen. Both as a citizen and as a human being I am deeply shocked by what I have had to hear. Dr. Stockmann has shown himself in his true colours in a manner of which I should never have dreamed him capable. I fear I must support the view expressed a moment ago by respected citizens; and I move that we embody this opinion in a resolution. I suggest the following: "This meeting declares the medical officer at the Baths, Dr. Thomas Stockmann, an enemy of the people." 470

(Deafening cheers and applause. Many of the Crowd form a circle around Dr. Stockmann and whistle at him. Mrs. Stockmann and Petra have got to their feet. Morten and Eilif are fighting with the other Schoolboys, who have been whistling too. Some Adults part them.)

Dr. Stockmann. (To the people who have been whistling) You fools! I tell you—!

Aslaksen. (Rings his bell) The Doctor no longer has the floor. A formal ballot will take place; but to protect personal feelings the voting should be done in writing and anonymously. Have you any clean paper, Mr. Billing? 480

Billing. I've both blue and white here—

Aslaksen. (Descends from the dais) Good, that'll save time. Tear it into squares; like that, yes. *(To the Crowd)* Blue means no, white means yes. I'll collect the votes myself. *(The Mayor leaves the hall. Aslaksen and a couple of other Citizens go around the Crowd with the pieces of paper in hats.)*

1st Citizen. (To Hovstad) What's come over the Doctor? What's one to think? 490

Hovstad. You know how impulsive he is.

2nd Citizen. (To Billing) I say, you're a regular visitor in that house. Have you ever noticed—does the fellow drink?

Billing. I don't know what to reply, by jingo! There's always toddy on the table when anyone comes.

3rd Citizen. I think he just goes off his head now and then.

1st Man. Yes, don't they say there's madness in the family?

Billing. Could be.

4th Man. No, it's pure spite. Wants revenge for something or other. 500

Billing. He did say something the other day about a rise in salary. But he didn't get it.

All the Men. (With one voice) Ah, that explains it!

The Drunk Man. (In the thick of the Crowd) I want a blue one! And I want a white one too!

Shouts. There's the drunk man again! Throw him out!

Morten Kiil. (Comes up to Dr. Stockmann) Well, Stockmann, you see now what happens once you start playing monkey tricks?

Dr. Stockmann. I have done my duty.

510 *Morten Kiil.* What was that you were saying about the tanneries at Moelledal?

Dr. Stockmann. You heard. I said that that's where all the filth comes from.

Morten Kiil. From my tannery too?

Dr. Stockmann. I'm afraid your tannery is the worst of all.

Morten Kiil. Are you going to print that in the papers?

Dr. Stockmann. I shall hide nothing.

Morten Kiil. That'll cost you dear, Stockmann. *(Goes)*

A Fat Man. (Goes across to Horster, without greeting the Ladies)
520 Well, Captain, so you lend your house to enemies of the people?

Horster. I reckon I can do what I like with my own property.

Fat Man. Then you won't object if I do the same with mine?

Horster. What do you mean?

Fat Man. You'll hear from me tomorrow. *(Turns and goes)*

Petra. Isn't that the man who owns your ship, Captain Horster?

Horster. Yes.

Aslaksen. (With the voting papers in his hand, steps up onto the dais and rings his bell) Gentlemen, allow me to inform you of the result. With only a single dissentient vote—

530 *A Young Man.* That's the drunk man!

Aslaksen. With only one dissentient vote, and that of a man not sober, this gathering of citizens unanimously declares the medical officer of the Baths, Dr. Thomas Stockmann, an enemy of the people! *(Shouts and gestures of approval)* Long live our ancient and noble community! *(More cheers)* Long live our worthy and active Mayor, who has so loyally ignored the ties of blood! *(Cheers)* The meeting is closed. *(He steps down.)*

Billing. Three cheers for the Chairman!

Whole Crowd. Hurrah for Mr. Aslaksen! Hurrah! Hurrah!

540 *Dr. Stockmann.* My hat and coat, Petra. Captain, have you room in your ship for passengers to the new world?

Horster. For you and yours, Doctor, I'll make room.

Dr. Stockmann. (As Petra helps him on with coat) Good! Come, Catherine! Come, boys! *(He takes his wife by the arm.)*

Mrs. Stockmann. (Quietly) Thomas dear, let's go out the back way.

Dr. Stockmann. No back way for me, Catherine! *(Raises his voice)* You'll hear from your enemy of the people before he shakes the dust of this town from his feet! I'm not so forgiving as a certain person. I don't say "I forgive ye, for ye know not what ye do!"

550 *Aslaksen. (Shouts)* That comparison's a blasphemy, Dr. Stockmann!

Billing. I'll say it is, by Go—! What a dreadful thing for respectable people to hear!

A Coarse Voice. He's threatening us now!

Excited Shouts. Let's break his windows! Throw him in the fjord!

A Man. (In the Crowd) Blow your horn, Evensen! *(He imitates the sound of the horn twice. Blasts on the horn, whistles and wild cries. The Doctor goes with his family towards the door. Horster clears a way for them.)*

The Whole Crowd. (Howls after them as they go) Enemy of the people! Enemy of the people! Enemy of the people! 560

Billing. (As he puts his notes in order) I'm damned if I'll drink toddy with them tonight, by jingo! *(The Crowd swarms towards the door. The shouting spreads outside. From the street can be heard the cry:* "Enemy of the people! Enemy of the people! Enemy of the people!"*)*

Act V

(Dr. Stockmann's study. Bookshelves and cupboards containing medicine bottles along the walls. In the background is the exit to the hall; downstage left is the door to the living-room. In the wall on the right are two windows, all the panes of which are smashed. In the middle of the room stands the Doctor's desk, covered with books and papers. The room is in disorder. It is morning.)

(Dr. Stockmann, in dressing gown and slippers and with his smoking-cap on his head, is crouched down raking under one of the cupboards with an umbrella. At length he pulls out a stone.)

Dr. Stockmann. (Speaks through the open door into the living-room) Catherine, I've found another!

Mrs. Stockmann. (From the living-room) Oh, you'll find a lot more yet.

Dr. Stockmann. (Puts the stone among a heap of others on the table) I shall keep these stones as sacred relics. Eilif and Morten shall see them every day, and when they're grown up they shall inherit them from me. *(Rakes under a bookshelf)* Hasn't—what the devil's her name? —you know, the maid—hasn't she gone for the glazier yet?

Mrs. Stockmann. (Enters) He said he didn't know if he'd be able to come today. 10

Dr. Stockmann. The truth is, he doesn't dare.

Mrs. Stockmann. Yes, Randine says he daren't because of the neighbours. *(Speaks into the living-room)* What is it, Randine? Very well. *(Goes inside and returns immediately)* Here's a letter for you, Thomas.

Dr. Stockmann. Give it to me. *(Opens it and reads)* I see.

Mrs. Stockmann. Who's it from?

Dr. Stockmann. The landlord. He's giving us notice to quit.

Mrs. Stockmann. Is he really? He seems such a decent man— 20

Dr. Stockmann. (Looks at the letter) He daren't do otherwise, he says. He's very sorry, but he daren't do otherwise—his fellow-citizens—respect for public opinion—certain obligations—dare not offend certain persons of influence—

Mrs. Stockmann. There, Thomas, you see.

Dr. Stockmann. Yes, yes, I see. They're all cowards in this town; none of them dares do anything for fear of the others. *(Throws the letter on the table)* But we don't have to worry, Catherine. We're off to the new world now—

30 *Mrs. Stockmann.* Thomas, do you really think it's a good idea, this going away?

Dr. Stockmann. Am I to stay here when they've pilloried me as an enemy of the people, branded me, broken my windows? And just look at this, Catherine! They've torn my trousers, too!

Mrs. Stockmann. Oh, no! And they're your best!

Dr. Stockmann. One should never wear one's best trousers when one goes out to fight for freedom and truth. Oh, I don't mind so much about the trousers—you can always patch them up for me. It's the fact that these riff-raff dare to threaten me as though they were my
40 equals—that's the thing I can't damned well stomach!

Mrs. Stockmann. Yes, Thomas, they've behaved shockingly to you in this town. But does that mean we have to leave the country?

Dr. Stockmann. Do you think the rabble aren't just as insolent in other towns? Oh, yes, Catherine—there isn't twopence to choose between them. To hell with the curs, let them yelp—that's not the worst. The worst is that throughout this country all the people are just party slaves. Mind you, they're probably not much better in America; the majority's rampant there too, and liberal public opinion and all the rest of the rubbish. But the context is larger there, you see. They may
50 kill you, but they won't torture you slowly; they don't pin a free man in a vice like they do here. And if you want to, you can stay independent outside it all. *(Walks across the room)* If only I knew of some primaeval forest or a little South Sea island that was going cheap—

Mrs. Stockmann. But what about the boys, Thomas?

Dr. Stockmann. (Stops) How extraordinary you are, Catherine! Would you rather they grew up in a society like this? You saw for yourself last night that half the people are raving lunatics; and if the other half haven't lost their wits it's only because they're beasts that don't have any wits to lose.

60 *Mrs. Stockmann.* But, Thomas dear, you're so careless about what you say.

Dr. Stockmann. What! Don't I tell them the truth? Don't they turn every idea upside down? Don't they merge right and wrong so that they can't tell the difference? Don't they call everything a lie which I know to be true? But the maddest thing of all is that you get grown men of liberal inclinations getting together in groups and convincing themselves and other people that they're progressive thinkers! Did you ever hear the like, Catherine?

Mrs. Stockmann. Yes, yes, it's all very stupid, but—

(Petra enters from the living room.) 70

Mrs. Stockmann. Are you back from school already?

Petra. I've got the sack.

Mrs. Stockmann. The sack?

Dr. Stockmann. You too!

Petra. Mrs. Busk gave me notice. So I thought I'd better leave at once.

Dr. Stockmann. Quite right, by Heaven!

Mrs. Stockmann. Who'd have thought Mrs. Busk was such a nasty woman?

Petra. Oh, Mother, she's not nasty. It was quite obvious she didn't 80 like doing it. But she said she dared not do otherwise. So I got the sack.

Dr. Stockmann. (Laughs and rubs his hands) Dared not do otherwise! She too! Oh, that's splendid!

Mrs. Stockmann. Well, after those dreadful scenes last night, you can't—

Petra. It wasn't only that. Listen to this, Father.

Dr. Stockmann. Yes?

Petra. Mrs. Busk showed me no less than three letters she'd received this morning—

Dr. Stockmann. Anonymous, of course? 90

Petra. Yes.

Dr. Stockmann. They daren't even sign their names, Catherine.

Petra. Two of them stated that a gentleman who frequents this house announced in the Club last night that I held excessively free views on various subjects—

Dr. Stockmann. I hope you didn't deny that.

Petra. Not on your life! Mrs. Busk expresses pretty free views herself when we're alone together; but now that this has come out about me, she didn't dare to keep me.

Mrs. Stockmann. Fancy—"a gentleman who frequents this house"! 100 You see what thanks you get for your hospitality, Thomas!

Dr. Stockmann. We won't go on living in this jungle any longer. Pack the bags as quickly as you can, Catherine. The sooner we get away from here, the better.

Mrs. Stockmann. Hush—I think there's someone in the hall. Go and look, Petra.

Petra. (Opens the door) Oh, is it you, Captain Horster? Please come in.

Horster. (From the hall) Good morning. I felt I had to come along
110 and see how everything was.

Dr. Stockmann. (Shakes his hand) Thank you. It's extremely good of you.

Mrs. Stockmann. And thank you for seeing us safely back last night, Captain Horster.

Petra. How did you manage to get home again?

Horster. Oh, I managed. I'm pretty strong; and those fellows bark worse than they bite.

Dr. Stockmann. Yes, isn't it amazing what wretched cowards they are! Come here, I'll show you something. Look, here are all the stones
120 they threw through our windows. Just look at them! Upon my soul, there aren't more than two decent rocks in the whole lot; the others are just pebbles—mere gravel! And yet they stood out there howling, and swearing they'd beat the life out of me—but action—action—no, you won't see much of that in this town.

Horster. Just as well for you on this occasion, Doctor.

Dr. Stockmann. Of course! But it annoys me all the same; for if it ever comes to a serious fight, in defence of our country, you'll see, Captain Horster—public opinion'll be for safety first, and this sacred majority'll run for their lives like a flock of sheep. That's what's so
130 sad—it really hurts me to think of it—no, damn it, I'm just being stupid! They've said I'm an enemy of the people, so let me be an enemy of the people!

Mrs. Stockmann. You'll never be that, Thomas.

Dr. Stockmann. Don't be so sure, Catherine. An ugly word can be like the scratch of a needle on the lung. And that damned phrase—I can't forget it—it's got stuck down here in the pit of my stomach, and it's lying there chafing and corroding me like an acid. And there's no magnesia that will neutralise that.

Petra. You must just laugh at them, Father.

140 *Horster.* People will think differently of you in time, Doctor.

Mrs. Stockmann. Yes, Thomas, that's as sure as you're standing here.

Dr. Stockmann. Perhaps when it's too late. Well, it's their funeral! Let them live like beasts; they'll be sorry they drove a patriot into exile. When do you sail, Captain Horster?

Horster. Hm—that was what I came to talk to you about, as a matter of fact—

Dr. Stockmann. Why, has something happened to the ship?

Horster. No. It's just that I shan't be going with her.

Petra. They surely haven't given you the sack?

150 *Horster. (Smiles)* Indeed they have!

Petra. You too!

Mrs. Stockmann. There, Thomas, you see!

Dr. Stockmann. And just because I spoke the truth! Oh, if I'd ever dreamed that such a thing could happen—

Horster. Don't worry about me. I'll find a job with a company somewhere else.

Dr. Stockmann. But that boss of yours is a rich man, he's completely independent! Oh, damn, damn!

Horster. He's fair enough in the ordinary way. He said himself, he'd have liked to have kept me, if only he'd dared— 160

Dr. Stockmann. (Laughs) But he didn't dare! No, of course not!

Horster. It isn't so easy, he said, when you belong to a party—

Dr. Stockmann. That's the truest word he ever uttered! A party is like a mincing machine; it grinds everyone's brains into a pulp, and all you're left with is human sausages, all identical!

Mrs. Stockmann. Thomas, really!

Petra (To Horster) If only you hadn't seen us home, this might never have happened.

Horster. I don't regret it.

Petra. (Holds out her hand) Thank you! 170

Horster. (To Dr. Stockmann) What I wanted to say was, if you still want to go, I have thought of another way—

Dr. Stockmann. Fine; as long as we can get away quickly—

Mrs. Stockmann. Hush—wasn't that a knock at the door?

Petra. I think it's Uncle.

Dr. Stockmann. Aha! *(Shouts.)* Come in!

Mrs. Stockmann. Now, Thomas dear, do promise me—

(The Mayor enters from the hall.)

Mayor. (In the doorway) Oh, you're engaged. I'll come back later—

Dr. Stockmann. No, no. Please come in. 180

Mayor. I wanted to speak to you privately.

Mrs. Stockmann. We'll go into the living-room.

Horster. And I'll come back later.

Dr. Stockmann. No, you go in too. I want to know more about that—

Horster. Right, I'll wait, then.

(He goes with Mrs. Stockmann and Petra into the living-room.)

Mayor. (Says nothing but glances at the windows)

Dr. Stockmann. Do you find it draughty here today? Put your hat on.

Mayor. Thank you, if I may. *(Does so)* I think I caught a cold last night. I stood there shivering— 190

Dr. Stockmann. Really? I found it warm enough.

Mayor. I regret that it didn't lie within my power to prevent those nocturnal extravagances.

Dr. Stockmann. Did you come out here to tell me that?

Mayor. (Takes out a large letter) I have this document for you, from the Directors of the Baths.

Dr. Stockmann. Am I dismissed?

Mayor. From the date of writing. (*Puts the letter on the table)* It distresses us; but, frankly, we had no choice. Public opinion being 200 what it is, we didn't dare—

Dr. Stockmann. (Smiles) Didn't dare? I've heard that word before today.

Mayor. I beg you to realise your position. From now on you can't reckon on having any practice whatever in this town.

Dr. Stockmann. To hell with the practice! But what makes you so sure?

Mayor. The Property Owners' Association has drawn up a round robin which it is sending from house to house. All respectable citizens are being urged not to employ you; and I'll guarantee that not a single 210 householder will dare refuse to sign it. They just won't dare.

Dr. Stockmann. Yes, yes, I don't doubt that. But what then?

Mayor. My advice would be that you should leave town for a while—

Dr. Stockmann. Yes, I'm thinking of doing that.

Mayor. Good. Then, when you've had six months to think the matter over, you might after mature consideration, possibly reconcile yourself to issuing a short statement admitting your error and expressing your regret—

Dr. Stockmann. And then, you mean, I might get my job back?

Mayor. It's not unthinkable.

220 *Dr. Stockmann.* But what about public opinion? You daren't offend that.

Mayor. Public opinion is very fickle. And, quite frankly, it's important to us that you should publish some such admission.

Dr. Stockmann. Yes, that'd make you smack your lips, wouldn't it? But, damn it, haven't I told you already what I think of that kind of chicanery?

Mayor. Your position was somewhat stronger then. You had reason to suppose that the whole town was behind you—

Dr. Stockmann. And now they're rubbing my face in the dirt! *(Flares* 230 *up)* I don't care if I've got the devil himself and his great-grandmother on my back! Never, I tell you, never!

Mayor. A man with a family has no right to act as you're doing. You have no right, Thomas!

Dr. Stockmann. No right! There's only one thing in the world that a free man has no right to do! Do you know what that is?

Mayor. No.

Dr. Stockmann. No, of course you don't. But I'll tell you. A free man has no right to befoul himself like a beast. He has no right to get himself into the position where he feels the need to spit in his own 240 face!

Mayor. That all sounds very plausible—if only there didn't happen to exist another explanation for your stubbornness—But there does.

Dr. Stockmann. What do you mean by that?

Mayor. You know perfectly well. But as your brother, and as a man of the world, I would advise you not to put too much trust in expectations that might so easily not be fulfilled.

Dr. Stockmann. What on earth are you talking about?

Mayor. Do you seriously expect me to believe that you don't know of the arrangements that Morten Kiil has made in his will?

Dr. Stockmann. I know that what little he has is to go to a home for retired artisans. But what's that got to do with me? 250

Mayor. To begin with, it's not so little. Morten Kiil is a pretty wealthy man.

Dr. Stockmann. I had no idea—!

Mayor. Hm—hadn't you really? Then I suppose you also have no idea that a considerable proportion of his money is earmarked for your children, and that you and your wife will be able to enjoy the interest for the rest of your lives. Hasn't he told you?

Dr. Stockmann. Indeed he has not! On the contrary, he's done nothing but complain about how disgracefully overtaxed he is. But are you quite sure of this, Peter? 260

Mayor. I have it from an impeccable source.

Dr. Stockmann. But, good Heavens—that means Catherine's future is secured—and the children's too! I say, I must tell her! *(Shouts)* Catherine, Catherine!

Mayor. *(Holds him back)* Hush, don't say anything yet.

Mrs. Stockmann. *(Opens the door)* What is it?

Dr. Stockmann. Nothing, my dear. Go back in again. *(Mrs. Stockmann closes the door.)*

Dr. Stockmann. *(Paces up and down the room)* Their future secured! I can't believe it! All of them—and for life! Oh, it's a wonderful feeling to know that one's future is secured. For ever! 270

Mayor. But that's just what it isn't. Morton Kiil can revoke that will any day or hour that he chooses.

Dr. Stockmann. But he won't, my dear Peter. The Badger's much too delighted at the embarrassment I've caused to you and your worthy friends.

Mayor. *(Starts and looks searchingly at him)* Aha! So that's the explanation!

Dr. Stockmann. What do you mean? 280

Mayor. This whole thing's been a conspiracy. These violent and unprincipled accusations which you've levelled against the authorities in the name of truth were simply your price for being remembered in that vindictive old idiot's will.

Dr. Stockmann. (Almost speechless) Peter—you are the lowest bastard I have ever met in all my life!

Mayor. Things are finished between us now. Your dismissal is final. Now we have a weapon against you. *(He goes.)*

Dr. Stockmann. The filthy—damn, damn! *(Shouts)* Catherine!
290 Scrub the floors behind him! Tell her to bring in a bucket—that girl —what the devil's her name—the one who's always got a dirty nose—!

Mrs. Stockmann. (In the doorway to the living-room) Hush, hush, Thomas, please!

Petra. (Also in the doorway) Father, Grandfather's here and says can he speak to you privately?

Dr. Stockmann. Yes, of course. *(At the door)* Come in, Father.

(Morten Kiil comes in. Dr. Stockmann closes the door behind him.)

Dr. Stockmann. Well, what is it? Sit down.

Morton Kiil. No, I won't sit. *(Looks around)* Nice and cosy it looks
300 here today, Stockmann.

Dr. Stockmann. Yes, doesn't it?

Morten Kiil. Very nice. And fresh air, too! You've got enough of that oxygen you were talking about last night! Your conscience feels pretty good today, I suppose?

Dr. Stockmann. Yes, it does.

Morton Kiil. I thought it would. *(Thumps himself on the breast)* But do you know what I've got here?

Dr. Stockmann. A good conscience too, I hope.

Morten Kiil. (Snorts) No, something better than that. *(Takes out a*
310 *thick pocketbook, opens it and shows a wad of papers)*

Dr. Stockmann. (Looks at him in amazement) Shares in the Baths?

Morten Kiil. They weren't hard to come by today.

Dr. Stockmann. You mean you've been out and bought—

Morten Kiil. As many as I could afford.

Dr. Stockmann. But, my dear Mr. Kiil—the state those Baths are in now, you—!

Morten Kiil. If you act like a sensible man, you'll soon have them on their feet again.

Dr. Stockmann. You see for yourself I'm doing all I can, but—!
320 The people of this town are quite mad!

Morten Kiil. You said last night that the worst of the filth comes from my tannery. But if that were true, then my grandfather and my father before me, and I myself, have been polluting this town for generations like three angels of death. Do you think I'm going to let an imputation like that hang over my head?

Dr. Stockmann. I'm afraid it looks as though you'll have to.

Morten Kiil. No, thank you! I value my name and reputation. People call me the Badger, I'm told. A badger's a dirty beast, isn't it? Well, I'll prove them wrong. I intend to live and die clean.

Dr. Stockmann. And how are you going to go about that? 330

Morton Kiil. You're going to make me clean, Stockmann.

Dr. Stockmann. I!

Morten Kiil. Do you know what money I've used to buy these shares with? No, you can't; but I'll tell you. It's the money Catherine and Petra and the boys are going to inherit when I'm gone. I've managed to put a little aside, you see.

Dr. Stockmann. (Flares up) You mean you've spent Catherine's money on this?

Morten Kiil. Yes, now it's all invested in the Baths. So now we'll see if you're really as daft as you pretend, Stockmann. Every time you 340 say there's vermin coming out of my tannery, it'll be as though you were cutting a pound of flesh from your wife's body, and Petra's and the children. But no self-respecting husband and father would do such a thing—unless he really was mad.

Dr. Stockmann. (Walks up and down) Yes, but I *am* mad! I *am* mad!

Morten Kiil. You can't be that mad when your wife and children are at stake.

Dr. Stockmann. (Stops in front of him) Why couldn't you have come and spoken to me before you went and bought all this waste paper? 350

Morten Kiil. Actions speak louder than words.

Dr. Stockmann. (Wanders around restlessly) If only I weren't so sure—! But I *know* I'm right!

Morten Kiil. (Weighs the pocketbook in his hand) If you persist in this lunacy, these shares won't be worth much, you know. *(He puts the pocketbook back in his pocket.)*

Dr. Stockmann. But, damn it, science must be able to find some way. A preventative; or a purifier or something—

Morten Kiil. You mean something to kill these vermin?

Dr. Stockmann. Yes, or render them harmless. 360

Morten Kiil. Couldn't you try rat poison?

Dr. Stockmann. Oh, no, no! But everyone keeps saying it's just a fancy of mine. All right, then, let them have it that way. Those ignorant, narrow-minded curs denounced me as an enemy of the people, didn't they? And all but tore the clothes off my back!

Morten Kiil. And smashed your windows.

Dr. Stockmann. Yes. And then this question of my duty towards my family. I must talk to Catherine. She knows about these things.

Morten Kiil. That's a good idea. She's a sensible woman. Follow her advice. 370

Dr. Stockmann. (Turns on him) Why did you have to do such a stupid thing? Hazarding Catherine's money, and putting me in this frightful predicament! When I look at you, I feel as though I was looking at the devil himself—

Morten Kiil. Then I'd best be off. But I want your answer by two o'clock. If it's no, I'm giving these shares to the Old Folks' Home—and I'll do it today.

Dr. Stockmann. And what will Catherine get then?

Morten Kiil. Not a farthing. *(The door to the hall is opened. Hovstad*
380 *and Aslaksen are seen there.)*

Morten Kiil. Well! Look whom we have here!

Dr. Stockmann. (Stares at them) What the devil—? Do you two still dare to visit me?

Hovstad. Indeed we do.

Aslaksen. We've something we want to talk to you about.

Morten Kiil. (Whispers) Yes or no—by two o'clock!

Aslaksen. (Glances at Hovstad) Aha! *(Morten Kiil goes.)*

Dr. Stockmann. Well, what do you want? Make it short.

Hovstad. I dare say you don't feel too kindly towards us in view
390 of the stand we took at last night's meeting—

Dr. Stockmann. Stand, you call it! A fine stand indeed! You just lay down like a couple of old women! Damn the pair of you!

Hovstad. Call it what you like; we *couldn't* do otherwise.

Dr. Stockmann. You *dared* not do otherwise? Isn't that what you mean?

Hovstad. If you wish.

Aslaksen. But why didn't you tip us off? You only needed to drop a hint to Mr. Hovstad or me.

Dr. Stockmann. Hint? About what?

400 *Aslaksen.* Why you were doing it.

Dr. Stockmann. I don't understand.

Aslaksen. (Nods conspiratorially) Oh, yes you do, Dr. Stockmann.

Hovstad. There's no need to keep it secret any longer.

Dr. Stockmann. (Looks from one to the other) What the devil—?

Aslaksen. Forgive the question, but isn't your father-in-law going round the town buying up all the shares in the Baths?

Dr. Stockmann. He has bought some today; but—

Aslaksen. You'd have done wiser to employ someone else. Someone not quite so close to you.

410 *Hovstad.* And you shouldn't have done all this under your own name. Nobody need have known that the attack on the Baths came from you. You ought to have taken me into your confidence, Dr. Stockmann.

Dr. Stockmann. (Stares straight in front of him. A light seems to dawn on him, and he says as though thunderstruck.) Is it conceivable? Could such a thing really be *done?*

Aslaksen. (Smiles) Apparently. But it ought to be done with a certain subtlety, you know.

Hovstad. And there ought to be more than one person in on it. A man doesn't have so much responsibility to bear if he's in partnership.

Dr. Stockmann. (Composedly) In brief, gentlemen, what do you want? 420

Aslaksen. Mr. Hovstad can explain better than—

Hovstad. No, you tell him, Aslaksen.

Aslaksen. Well, it's just this really, that now we know how the land lies, we think we might venture to put the *People's Tribune* at your disposal.

Dr. Stockmann. You think you dare risk it? But what about public opinion? Aren't you afraid we might cause a storm?

Hovstad. We shall have to ride that storm.

Aslaksen. But you'll have to be quick on the trigger, Doctor. As soon as your campaign has done its job— 430

Dr. Stockmann. As soon as my father-in-law and I have got all the shares cheaply, you mean—?

Hovstad. It is of course principally in the cause of science that you are seeking to gain control of the Baths.

Dr. Stockmann. Of course. It was in the cause of science that I got the old Badger to come in with me on this. And then we'll tinker a bit with the water system and do a little digging on the beach, and it won't cost the ratepayers half a crown. I think we'll get away with, don't you? Eh?

Hovstad. I think so—if you have the *People's Tribune* behind you. 440

Aslaksen. In a free society the press is a power to be feared, Doctor.

Dr. Stockmann. Quite. And public opinion too. Mr. Aslaksen, you'll answer for the Property Owners' Association?

Aslaksen. The Property Owners' Association and the Temperance Society. Have no fear.

Dr. Stockmann. But, gentlemen—I blush to mention the matter, but—what consideration—er—

Hovstad. Well, of course we'd like to help you absolutely gratis. But the *People's Tribune* is going through an awkward period just now; we're having an uphill struggle, and I'm very reluctant to wind things up just 450 now, when there are such splendid causes that need our support.

Dr. Stockmann. Of course. That'd be a bitter pill for a friend of the people like you to have to swallow. *(Flares up)* But I—I am an enemy of the people! *(Strides around the room)* Where's that stick of mine? Where the devil did I put my stick?

Hovstad. What do you mean?

Aslaksen. You surely aren't thinking of—?

Dr. Stockmann. (Stops) And suppose I don't give you a penny of my shares? We rich men are pretty close with our money, you must remember. 460

Hovstad. And *you* must remember that this little business of the shares would bear more than one interpretation.

Dr. Stockmann. Yes, that'd be right up your street, wouldn't it? If I don't come to the aid of the *People's Tribune*, you'll misrepresent my motives—you'll start a witch-hunt, drive me to ground, and throttle the life out of me as a hound throttles a hare!

Hovstad. That's the law of nature. Every animal has to fight for survival, you know.

Aslaksen. Bread doesn't grow on trees. You must take it where you
470 can find it.

Dr. Stockmann. Then see if you can find any in the gutter! *(Strides around the room)* Now, by Heaven, we'll see which is the strongest animal of us three! *(Finds his umbrella)* Aha! *(Swings it)* Now—!

Hovstad. You wouldn't dare to assault us!

Aslaksen. Be careful with that umbrella!

Dr. Stockmann. Out of the window with you, Mr. Hovstad!

Hovstad. *(At the doorway to the hall)* Are you out of your mind?

Dr. Stockmann. Get through that window, Mr. Aslaksen! Jump, I tell you! Don't dally!

480 *Aslaksen.* *(Runs around the desk)* Doctor, Doctor, restrain yourself! I'm a weak man—I can't stand excitement—! *(Screams)* Help, help! *(Mrs. Stockmann, Petra, and Captain Horster enter from the living-room.)*

Mrs. Stockmann. In Heaven's name, Thomas, what's going on here?

Dr. Stockmann. *(Brandishes the umbrella)* Jump out, I tell you! Down into the gutter!

Hovstad. An unprovoked assault—I call you to witness, Captain Horster! *(Runs out through the hall)*

Mrs. Stockmann. *(Holds the Doctor)* Thomas, for mercy's sake control yourself!

490 *Aslaksen.* *(Desperate)* Restraint, Doctor! Restr—oh, dear!
(Scampers out through the living-room)

Dr. Stockmann. *(Throws away the umbrella)* Damn it, they got away after all!

Mrs. Stockmann. But what did they want?

Dr. Stockmann. I'll tell you later. I've other things to think about just now. *(Goes to the table and writes on a visiting card)* Look at this, Catherine. What do you see here?

Mrs. Stockmann. "No, no, no"—what does that mean?

Dr. Stockmann. I'll explain that later too. *(Holds out the card)* Here,
500 Petra, tell that smutty-nosed girl to run up to the Badger with this as quickly as she can. Hurry!
(Petra goes out with the card through the hall.)

Dr. Stockmann. If I haven't had all the Devil's messengers after me today, I really don't know who's left! But now I'll sharpen my pen against them until it's like a dagger! I'll dip it in gall and venom! I'll fling my inkstand against their stupid skulls!

Mrs. Stockmann. But Thomas, we're leaving!

(Petra returns.)

Dr. Stockmann. Well?

Petra. She's taken it. 510

Dr. Stockmann. Good! Leaving, did you say? No, by God, we're not! We're staying here, Catherine!

Petra. Staying?

Mrs. Stockmann. In this town?

Dr. Stockmann. Yes! This is the chosen battlefield, and it's here that the battle must be fought! And it's here that I shall win! As soon as you've sewn up those trousers of mine, I'll go into town and look for a house. We've got to have a roof over our heads when winter comes.

Horster. I can let you have my house.

Dr. Stockmann. Would you? 520

Horster. Of course. I've plenty of rooms, and I'm hardly ever there.

Mrs. Stockmann. Oh, Captain Horster, how kind of you!

Petra. Thank you!

Dr. Stockmann. (Presses his hand) Thank you, thank you! Well, that problem's behind us! I'll start my campaign this very day! Oh, Catherine, there's so much to be done! But luckily I'll be able to devote my whole time to it. Look at this. I've been sacked from the Baths—

Mrs. Stockmann. (Sighs) Ah, well. I was expecting that.

Dr. Stockmann. And they want to take away my practice too! All right, let them! At least I'll keep my poor patients—they're the ones 530 who can't pay—well, Heaven knows they're the ones who need me most. But, by God, they'll have to listen to me! I'll preach to them morning, noon, and night.

Mrs. Stockmann. Oh, Thomas, Thomas! Surely you've seen what good preaching does!

Dr. Stockmann. You really are absurd, Catherine! Am I to allow myself to be chased from the field of public opinion, and the majority and such fiddle-faddle? No, thank you! What I want is so simple and straightforward and easy! I only want to knock it into the heads of these curs that the Liberals are the most insidious enemies of freedom— 540 that party programmes strangle every new truth that deserves to live—and that expediency and self-interest turn morality and justice upside down, so that in the end life here becomes intolerable. Well, Captain Horster, don't you think I ought to be able to get people to grasp that?

Horster. I dare say. I don't really understand these things.

Dr. Stockmann. Well, you see, the real point is this! It's the party bosses—they're the ones who've got to be rooted out! A party boss is like a hungry wolf—he needs a certain number of baby lambs to devour

every year if he is to survive. Look at Hovstad and Aslaksen! How many
550 innocent and vital young idealists have they knocked on the head! Or else they mangle and maul them till they're fit for nothing but to be property owners or subscribers to the *People's Tribune! (Half sits on the table)* Come here, Catherine! Look how beautifully the sun's shining in through the windows today! And smell this glorious, fresh spring air which is being wafted in to us.

Mrs. Stockmann. Oh, my dear Thomas, if only we could live on sunshine and spring air!

Dr. Stockmann. Well, you may have to pinch and scrape a little, but we'll manage. That's the least of my worries. No, the worst is that I
560 don't know of anyone sufficiently free and unplebeian to carry on my work after me.

Petra. Oh, never mind that, Father. You'll find someone in time. Look, here are the boys!

(Eilif and Morten enter from the living-room.)

Mrs. Stockmann. Have you been given a holiday today?

Morten. No. But we had a fight with the other boys in the break, so—

Eilif. That's not true! It was the other boys who fought with us!

Morten. Yes. So I said to Dr. Roerlund I thought it would be better if we stayed at home for a few days.

570 *Dr. Stockmann. (Snaps his fingers and jumps from the table)* I've got it! By Heaven, I've got it! Neither of you shall ever set foot in that school again!

The Boys. Not go to school!

Mrs. Stockmann. But, Thomas—!

Dr. Stockmann. Never, I say! I'll teach you myself! You won't learn a damned thing—

Morten. Hurray!

Dr. Stockmann. But I'll make you free men—aristocrats! Petra, you'll have to help me.

580 *Petra.* Yes, Father, of course.

Dr. Stockmann. And we'll hold the school in the room where they branded me as an enemy of the people. But we need more pupils. I must have at least twelve to begin with.

Mrs. Stockmann. You won't find them in this town.

Dr. Stockmann. We shall see. *(To the Boys)* Do you know any street urchins—real guttersnipes—?

Eilif. Oh yes, Father, I know lots!

Dr. Stockmann. That's fine! Get hold of a few for me. I'm going to experiment with mongrels for once. They have good heads on them
590 sometimes.

Eilif. But what shall we do when we've become free men and aristocrats?

Dr. Stockmann. Then, my boys, you'll chase all these damned politicians into the Atlantic Ocean! *(Eilif looks somewhat doubtful. Morten jumps and cheers.)*

Mrs. Stockmann. Let's hope it won't be the politicians who'll chase you out, Thomas.

Dr. Stockmann. Are you quite mad, Catherine? Chase me out! Now, when I am the strongest man in town?

Mrs. Stockmann. The strongest—now? 600

Dr. Stockmann. Yes! I'll go further! I am now one of the strongest men in the whole world.

Morten. Hurrah!

Dr. Stockmann. (Lowers his voice) Hush! You mustn't talk about it yet! But I've made a great discovery!

Mrs. Stockmann. Not again!

Dr. Stockmann. Yes—yes! *(Gathers them round him and whispers to them)* The fact is, you see, that the strongest man in the world is he who stands most alone.

Mrs. Stockmann. (Smiles and shakes her head) Oh, Thomas—! 610

Petra. (Warmly, clasps his hands) Father!

Comments and Questions

Like Antigone, Dr. Stockmann in following the convictions of his conscience is forced to stand alone against the source of power, though his adversary is not a king, but the people of his community, the "compact majority." Usually a good man who acts on principle against authority or the will of the crowd ultimately commands our respect, if not our approval. There is, however, some danger, as Arthur Miller says in his essay "On Social Plays," that

"the man that is driven to question the moral chaos in which we live ends up in our estimate as a possibly commendable but definitely odd fellow, and probably as a compulsively driven neurotic . . . .In the heroic and tragic time [of ancient Greece] the act of questioning the-way-things-are implied that a quest was being carried on to discover an ultimate law or way of life which would yield excellence; in the present time the quest is that of a man made unhappy by rootlessness and, in every important modern play, by a man who is essentially a victim."

Does Ibsen present Stockmann as an "odd fellow" or a neurotic? Is he a victim? To what extent do his feelings toward his brother affect his method of handling the report on the Baths? Is he, as one critic has charged, "a classic case of blundering eccentricity" whose "ejection from society is by no means wholly unmerited"? What motivates each of his adversaries? Does Ibsen stretch probability to make them all greedy and selfish so as to rig the whole play in favor of Stockmann?

The Doctor is as impractical and impulsive at the end as he is at the beginning, but there is a change and a development in his attitudes. What are the several "discoveries" that he makes, and how do they illustrate the process of his expanding point of view? What is the significance of Petra's speech on fear of the truth? Of the scene in which Stockmann wears the mayor's hat and cane? Of the three visits in the last act? Of the veiled references to Luther ("I will fling my inkstand against their stupid skulls," p. 241, l. 506-507), and Christ (Stockmann's hope to use twelve poor boys as disciples, p. 242, l. 582-587)? Of his line at the end of Act IV, "I don't say: 'I forgive ye, for ye know not what ye do,'" p. 228, l. 548-549?

Related Reading

Jean Anouilh, *Antigone*, page 520
Friedrich Dürrenmatt, *The Visit*, page 563
Sophocles, *Antigone*, page 489
Arthur Miller, "On Social Plays," page 670

Thornton Wilder

(1897-   )

THE MATCHMAKER

Thornton Wilder is perhaps best known to the American public for his play Our Town, *written in 1938, which has already become a classic, but a live classic that is still a favorite on professional and amateur stages. He has also written several other distinguished works: two full-length plays,* The Skin of Our Teeth *(1942), and* The Matchmaker *(1954); several adaptations of plays by other dramatists; two collections of his own short plays; and six novels, most notably* The Bridge of San Luis Rey *(1927) and* Ides of March *(1948).*

The Matchmaker *is Wilder's one major excursion into farce. First produced at the Edinburgh Festival on August 23, 1954, it is a revision of his earlier play* The Merchant of Yonkers *(1938), which is based on a comedy by the Viennese Johann Nestroy,* Einen Jux will er sich machen *(1842), itself adapted from an English play,* A Day Well Spent *(1835) by John Oxenford. But the comic devices and tricks in the play date back much farther: we find some of them in the plays of Aristophanes and Plautus in classical Greece and Rome; we find them in Shakespeare, Ben Jonson, and in all the great farcical comedies of the past. A musical adaptation of* The Matchmaker *titled* Hello, Dolly! *was a glittering success on Broadway, one which may equal the successes of* Oklahoma! *and* My Fair Lady, *both musicals also adapted from well-known plays.*

Farce moves us to laugh without much concern for the realities or probabilities of the affair; the characters are recognizable stereotypes, acting, though somewhat extravagantly, as we would expect them to act. Pure farce is on the level of burlesque, slapstick, horseplay, and outrageous puns. A simple example of farce is two characters throwing custard pies at each other; in a slightly more sophisticated form an actor, playing an overly proud man, slips on a banana peel at a crucial moment. In even more sophisticated forms, farce serves beautifully for bitter satire, as in Ben Jonson's The Alchemist, *or, much less astringently, Molière's* Scapin. *It also serves for happy, positive comedy, like* The Matchmaker, *where certain human follies are revealed and corrected, if only temporarily.*

Dolly Levi, the matchmaker, says early in the play that "everything will be arranged," and when asked how, replies, "Oh, I don't know. One thing will lead to another." Somewhat crazily, it does. One might say that the play illustrates what happens when a woman like Mrs. Levi, the very spirit of Life itself, decides "to rejoin the human race." Saying more than this now would be like explaining a joke before it is told.

THE MATCHMAKER

Characters

HORACE VANDERGELDER, *a merchant of Yonkers, New York*
CORNELIUS HACKL } *clerks in his store*
BARNABY TUCKER }
MALACHI STACK
AMBROSE KEMPER, *an artist*
JOE SCANLON, *a barber*
RUDOLPH } *waiters*
AUGUST }
A CABMAN
MRS. DOLLY LEVI } *friends of Vandergelder's late wife*
MISS FLORA VAN HUYSEN }
MRS. IRENE MOLLOY, *a milliner*
MINNIE FAY, *her assistant*
ERMENGARDE, *Vandergelder's niece*
GERTRUDE, *Vandergelder's housekeeper*
MISS VAN HUYSEN'S COOK

Time: The early 80's.
Act I. *Vandergelder's house in Yonkers, New York*
Act II. *Mrs. Molloy's hat shop, New York*
Act III. *The Harmonia Gardens Restaurant on the Battery, New York*
Act IV. *Miss Van Huysen's house, New York*

Act I

Living room of Mr. Vandergelder's house, over his hay, feed and provision store in Yonkers, fifteen miles north of New York City. Articles from the store have overflowed into this room; it has not been cleaned for a long time and is in some disorder, but it is not sordid or gloomy.

There are three entrances. One at the center back leads into the principal rooms of the house. One on the back right (all the directions are from the point of view of the actors) opens on steps which descend to the street door. One on the left leads to Ermengarde's room.

In the center of the room is a trap door; below it is a ladder descending to the store below.

Behind the trap door and to the left of it is a tall accountant's desk; to the left of it is an old-fashioned stove with a stovepipe going up into the ceiling. Before the desk is a tall stool. On the right of the stage is a table with some chairs about it.

Mr. Vandergelder's Gladstone bag, packed for a journey, is beside the desk.

It is early morning.

(Vandergelder, sixty, choleric, vain and sly, wears a soiled dressing gown. He is seated with a towel about his neck, in a chair beside the desk, being shaved by Joe Scanlon. Vandergelder is smoking a cigar and holding a hand mirror. Ambrose Kemper is angrily striding about the room.)

Vandergelder. (Loudly) I tell you for the hundredth time you will never marry my niece.

Ambrose. (Thirty; dressed as an artist) And I tell you for the thousandth time that I will marry your niece; and right soon, too.

Vandergelder. Never! 10

Ambrose. Your niece is of age, Mr. Vandergelder. Your niece has consented to marry me. This is a free country, Mr. Vandergelder —not a private kingdom of your own.

Vandergelder. There are no free countries for fools, Mr. Kemper. Thank you for the honor of your visit—good morning.

Joe. (Fifty; lanky, mass of gray hair falling into his eyes) Mr. Vandergelder, will you please sit still one minute? If I cut your throat, it'll be practically unintentional.

Vandergelder. Ermengarde is not for you, nor for anybody else who can't support her. 20

Ambrose. I tell you I can support her. I make a very good living.

Vandergelder. No, sir! A living is made, Mr. Kemper, by selling something that everybody needs at least once a year. Yes, sir! And a million is made by producing something that everybody needs every day. You artists produce something that nobody needs at any time. You may sell a picture once in a while, but you'll make no living. Joe, go over there and stamp three times. I want to talk to Cornelius. *(Joe crosses to trap door and stamps three times.)*

Ambrose. Not only can I support her now, but I have considerable expectations. 30

Vandergelder. Expectations! We merchants don't do business with them. I don't keep accounts with people who promise somehow to pay something someday, and I don't allow my niece to marry such people.

Ambrose. Very well, from now on you might as well know that I regard any way we can find to get married as right and fair. Ermengarde is of age, and there's no law . . . *(Vandergelder rises and crosses toward Ambrose. Joe Scanlon follows him complainingly and tries to find a chance to cut his hair even while he is standing.)*

40 *Vandergelder.* Law? Let me tell you something, Mr. Kemper: most of the people in the world are fools. The law is there to prevent crime; we men of sense are there to prevent foolishness. It's I, and not the law, that will prevent Ermengarde from marrying you, and I've taken some steps already. I've sent her away to get this nonsense out of her head.

Ambrose. Ermengarde's . . . not here?

Vandergelder. She's gone—east, west, north, south. I thank you for the honor of your visit.

(Enter Gertrude—eighty; deaf; half blind; and very pleased with herself)

50 *Gertrude.* Everything's ready, Mr. Vandergelder. Ermengarde and I have just finished packing the trunk.

Vandergelder. Hold your tongue! *(Joe is shaving Vandergelder's throat, so he can only wave his hands vainly.)*

Gertrude. Yes, Mr. Vandergelder, Ermengarde's ready to leave. Her trunk's all marked. Care Miss Van Huysen, 8 Jackson Street, New York.

Vandergelder. (Breaking away from Joe) Hell and damnation! Didn't I tell you it was a secret?

Ambrose. (Picks up hat and coat—kisses Gertrude) Care Miss Van 60 Huysen, 8 Jackson Street, New York. Thank you very much. Good morning, Mr. Vandergelder.

(Exit Ambrose, to the street)

Vandergelder. It won't help you, Mr. Kemper—*(To Gertrude)* Deaf! And blind! At least you can do me the favor of being dumb!

Gertrude. Chk—chk! Such a temper! Lord save us! *(Cornelius puts his head up through the trap door. He is thirty-three; mock-deferential—he wears a green apron and is in his shirt-sleeves.)*

Cornelius. Yes, Mr. Vandergelder?

Vandergelder. Go in and get my niece's trunk and carry it over to 70 the station. Wait! Gertrude, has Mrs. Levi arrived yet?

(Cornelius comes up the trap door, steps into the room and closes the trap door behind him.)

Gertrude. Don't shout. I can hear perfectly well. Everything's clearly marked. *(Exit left)*

Vandergelder. Have the buggy brought round to the front of the store in half an hour.

Cornelius. Yes, Mr. Vandergelder.

Vandergelder. This morning I'm joining my lodge parade and this afternoon I'm going to New York. Before I go, I have something im-80 portant to say to you and Barnaby. Good news. Fact is—I'm going to promote you. How old are you?

Cornelius. Thirty-three, Mr. Vandergelder.

Vandergelder. What?

Cornelius. Thirty-three.

Vandergelder. That all? That's a foolish age to be at. I thought you were forty.

Cornelius. Thirty-three.

Vandergelder. A man's not worth a cent until he's forty. We just pay 'em wages to make mistakes—don't we, Joe?

Joe. You almost lost an ear on it, Mr. Vandergelder. 90

Vandergelder. I was thinking of promoting you to chief clerk.

Cornelius. What am I now, Mr. Vandergelder?

Vandergelder. You're an impertinent fool, that's what you are. Now, if you behave yourself, I'll promote you from impertinent fool to chief clerk, with a raise in your wages. And Barnaby may be promoted from idiot apprentice to incompetent clerk.

Cornelius. Thank you, Mr. Vandergelder.

Vandergelder. However, I want to see you again before I go. Go in and get my niece's trunk.

Cornelius. Yes, Mr. Vandergelder. *(Exit Cornelius, left)* 100

Vandergelder. Joe—the world's getting crazier every minute. Like my father used to say: the horses'll be taking over the world soon.

Joe. (Presenting mirror) I did what I could, Mr. Vandergelder, what with you flying in and out of the chair. *(He wipes the last of the soap from Vandergelder's face.)*

Vandergelder. Fine, fine, Joe, you do a fine job, the same fine job you've done me for twenty years. Joe . . . I've got special reasons for looking my best today . . . isn't there something a little extry you could do, something a little special? I'll pay you right up to fifty cents—see what I mean? Do some of those things you do to the young fellas. Touch 110 me up; smarten me up a bit.

Joe. All I know is fifteen cents' worth, like usual, Mr. Vandergelder; and that includes everything that's decent to do to a man.

Vandergelder. Now hold your horses, Joe—all I meant was . . .

Joe. I've shaved you for twenty years and you never asked me no such question before.

Vandergelder. Hold your horses, I say, Joe! I'm going to tell you a secret. But I don't want you telling it to that riffraff down to the barbershop what I'm going to tell you now. All I ask of you is a little extry because I'm thinking of getting married again; and this very afternoon 120 I'm going to New York to call on my intended, a very refined lady.

Joe. Your gettin' married is none of my business, Mr. Vandergelder. I done everything to you I know, and the charge is fifteen cents like it always was, and . . .*(Cornelius crosses, left to right, and exit, carrying a trunk on his shoulder. Ermengarde and Gertrude enter from left.)* I don't dye no hair, not even for fifty cents I don't!

Vandergelder. Joe Scanlon, get out!

Joe. And lastly, it looks to me like you're pretty rash to judge which is fools and which isn't fools, Mr. Vandergelder. People that's et
130 onions is bad judges of who's et onions and who ain't. Good morning, ladies; good morning, Mr. Vandergelder. *(Exit Joe)*

Vandergelder. Well, what do you want?

Ermengarde. (Twenty-four; pretty, sentimental) Uncle! You said you wanted to talk to us.

Vandergelder. Oh yes. Gertrude, go and get my parade regalia—the uniform for my lodge parade.

Gertrude. What? Oh yes. Lord have mercy!

(Exit Gertrude, back center)

Vandergelder. I had a talk with that artist of yours. He's a fool.
140 *(Ermengarde starts to cry.)* Weeping! Weeping! You can go down and weep for a while in New York where it won't be noticed. *(He sits on desk chair, puts tie round neck and calls her over to tie it for him.)* Ermengarde! I told him that when you were old enough to marry you'd marry someone who could support you. I've done you a good turn. You'll come and thank me when you're fifty.

Ermengarde. But Uncle, I love him!

Vandergelder. I tell you you don't.

Ermengarde. But I *do!*

Vandergelder. And I tell you you don't. Leave those things to me.

150 *Ermengarde.* If I don't marry Ambrose, I know I'll die.

Vandergelder. What of?

Ermengarde. A broken heart.

Vandergelder. Never heard of it. Mrs. Levi is coming in a moment to take you to New York. You are going to stay two or three weeks with Miss Van Huysen, an old friend of your mother's.

(Gertrude re-enters with coat, sash and sword. Enter from the street, right, Malachi Stack)

You're not to receive any letters except from me. I'm coming to New York myself today and I'll call on you tomorrow. *(To Malachi)* Who
160 are you?

Malachi. (Fifty. Sardonic. Apparently innocent smile; pretense of humility) Malachi Stack, your honor. I heard you wanted an apprentice in the hay, feed, provision and hardware business.

Vandergelder. An apprentice at your age?

Malachi. Yes, your honor; I bring a lot of experience to it.

Vandergelder. Have you any letters of recommendation?

Malachi. (Extending a sheaf of soiled papers) Yes, indeed, your honor! First-class recommendation.

Vandergelder. Ermengarde! Are you ready to start?

170 *Ermengarde.* Yes.

Vandergelder. Well, go and get ready some more. Ermengarde! Let me know the minute Mrs. Levi gets here.

Ermengarde. Yes, Uncle Horace. *(Ermengarde and Gertrude exit. Vandergelder examines the letters, putting them down one by one.)*

Vandergelder. I don't want an able seaman. Nor a typesetter. And I don't want a hospital cook.

Malachi. No, your honor, but it's all experience. Excuse me! *(Selects a letter)* This one is from your former partner, Joshua Van Tuyl, in Albany. *(He puts letters from table back into pocket.)*

Vandergelder. "... for the most part honest and reliable ... occasionally willing and diligent." There seems to be a certain amount of hesitation about these recommendations. 180

Malachi. Businessmen aren't writers, your honor. There's only one businessman in a thousand that can write a good letter of recommendation, your honor. Mr. Van Tuyl sends his best wishes and wants to know if you can use me in the provision and hardware business.

Vandergelder. Not so fast, not so fast! What's this "your honor" you use so much?

Malachi. Mr. Van Tuyl says you're President of the Hudson River Provision Dealers' Recreational, Musical and Burial Society. 190

Vandergelder. I am; but there's no "your honor" that goes with it. Why did you come to Yonkers?

Malachi. I heard that you'd had an apprentice that was a good-for-nothing, and that you were at your wit's end for another.

Vandergelder. Wit's end, wit's end! There's no dearth of good-for-nothing apprentices.

Malachi. That's right, Mr. Vandergelder. It's employers there's a dearth of. Seems like you hear of a new one dying every day.

Vandergelder. What's that? Hold your tongue. I see you've been a barber, and a valet too. Why have you changed your place so often? 200

Malachi. Changed my place, Mr. Vandergelder? When a man's interested in experience ...

Vandergelder. Do you drink?

Malachi. No, thanks. I've just had breakfast.

Vandergelder. I didn't ask you whether—Idiot! I asked you if you were a drunkard.

Malachi. No, sir! No! Why, looking at it from all sides I don't even like liquor.

Vandergelder. Well, if you keep on looking at it from all sides, out you go. Remember that. Here. *(Gives him remaining letters)* With all your faults, I'm going to give you a try. 210

Malachi. You'll never regret it, Mr. Vandergelder. You'll never regret it.

Vandergelder. Now today I want to use you in New York. I judge you know your way around New York?

Malachi. Do I know New York? Mr. Vandergelder, I know every hole and corner in New York.

Vandergelder. Here's a dollar. A train leaves in a minute. Take that bag to the Central Hotel on Water Street, have them save me a 220 room. Wait for me. I'll be there about four o'clock.

Malachi. Yes, Mr. Vandergelder. *(Picks up the bag, starts out, then comes back)* Oh, but first, I'd like to meet the other clerks I'm to work with.

Vandergelder. You haven't time. Hurry now. The station's across the street.

Malachi. Yes, sir. *(Away—then back once more)* You'll see, sir, you'll never regret it. . . .

Vandergelder. I regret it already. Go on. Off with you. *(Exit Malachi, right. The following speech is addressed to the audience. During it* 230 *Mr. Vandergelder takes off his dressing gown, puts on his scarlet sash, his sword and his bright-colored coat. He is already wearing light blue trousers with a red stripe down the sides.)*

Vandergelder. Ninety-nine per cent of the people in the world are fools and the rest of us are in great danger of contagion. But I wasn't always free of foolishness as I am now. I was once young, which was foolish; I fell in love, which was foolish; and I got married, which was foolish; and for a while I was poor, which was more foolish than all the other things put together. Then my wife died, which was foolish of her; I grew older, which was sensible of me; then I became a rich man, 240 which is as sensible as it is rare. Since you see I'm a man of sense, I guess you were surprised to hear that I'm planning to get married again. Well, I've two reasons for it. In the first place, I like my house run with order, comfort and economy. That's a woman's work; but even a woman can't do it well if she's merely being paid for it. In order to run a house well, a woman must have the feeling that she owns it. Marriage is a bribe to make a housekeeper think she's a householder. Did you ever watch an ant carry a burden twice its size? What excitement! What patience! What will! Well, that's what I think of when I see a woman running a house. What giant passions in those little bodies— 250 what quarrels with the butcher for the best cut—what fury at discovering a moth in a cupboard! Believe me!—if women could harness their natures to something bigger than a house and a baby carriage—tck! tck!—they'd change the world. And the second reason, ladies and gentlemen? Well, I see by your faces you've guessed it already. There's nothing like mixing with women to bring out all the foolishness in a man of sense. And that's a risk I'm willing to take. I've just turned sixty, and I've just laid side by side the last dollar of my first half million. So if I should lose my head a little, I still have enough money to buy it back. After many years' caution and hard work, I have earned a right 260 to a little risk and adventure, and I'm thinking of getting married. Yes, like all you other fools, I'm willing to risk a little security for a certain amount of adventure. Think it over. *(Exit back center)*

(Ambrose enters from the street, crosses left, and whistles softly. Ermengarde enters from left.)

Ermengarde. Ambrose! If my uncle saw you!

Ambrose. Sh! Get your hat.

Ermengarde. My hat!

Ambrose. Quick! Your trunk's at the station. Now quick! We're running away.

Ermengarde. Running away! 270

Ambrose. Sh!

Ermengarde. Where?

Ambrose. To New York. To get married.

Ermengarde. Oh, Ambrose, I can't do that. Ambrose dear—it wouldn't be proper!

Ambrose. Listen. I'm taking you to my friend's house. His wife will take care of you.

Ermengarde. But, Ambrose, a girl can't go on a train with a man. I can see you don't know anything about girls.

Ambrose. But I'm telling you we're going to get married! 280

Ermengarde. Married! But what would *Uncle* say?

Ambrose. We don't care what Uncle'd say—we're eloping.

Ermengarde. Ambrose Kemper! How can you use such an awful word!

Ambrose. Ermengarde, you have the soul of a field mouse.

Ermengarde. (Crying) Ambrose, why do you say such cruel things to me? *(Enter Mrs. Levi, from the street, right. She stands listening.)*

Ambrose. For the last time I beg you—get your hat and coat. The train leaves in a few minutes. Ermengarde, we'll get married tomorrow. . . . 290

Ermengarde. Oh, Ambrose! I see you don't understand anything about weddings. Ambrose, don't you *respect* me? . . .

Mrs. Levi. (Uncertain age; mass of sandy hair; impoverished elegance; large, shrewd but generous nature, an assumption of worldly cynicism conceals a tireless amused enjoyment of life. She carries a handbag and a small brown paper bag.) Good morning, darling girl—how are you? *(They kiss.)*

Ermengarde. Oh, good morning, Mrs. Levi.

Mrs. Levi. And who is this gentleman who is so devoted to you?

Ermengarde. This is Mr. Kemper, Mrs. Levi. Ambrose, this is . . . 300 Mrs. Levi . . . she's an old friend. . . .

Mrs. Levi. Mrs. Levi, born Gallagher. Very happy to meet you, Mr. Kemper.

Ambrose. Good morning, Mrs. Levi.

Mrs. Levi. Mr. Kemper, *the artist!* Delighted! Mr. Kemper, may I say something very frankly?

Ambrose. Yes, Mrs. Levi.

Mrs. Levi. This thing you were planning to do is a very great mistake.

310 *Ermengarde.* Oh, Mrs. Levi, please explain to Ambrose—of *course!* I want to marry him, but to *elope!* . . . How . . .

Mrs. Levi. Now, my dear girl, you go in and keep one eye on your uncle. I wish to talk to Mr. Kemper for a moment. You give us a warning when you hear your Uncle Horace coming. . . .

Ermengarde. Ye-es, Mrs. Levi. *(Exit Ermengarde, back center.)*

Mrs. Levi. Mr. Kemper, I was this dear girl's mother's oldest friend. Believe me, I am on your side. I hope you two will be married very soon, and I think I can be of real service to you. Mr. Kemper, I always go right to the point.

320 *Ambrose.* What is the point, Mrs. Levi?

Mrs. Levi. Mr. Vandergelder is a very rich man, Mr. Kemper, and Ermengarde is his only relative.

Ambrose. But I am not interested in Mr. Vandergelder's money. I have enough to support a wife and family.

Mrs. Levi. Enough? How much is enough when one is thinking about children and the future? The future is the most expensive luxury in the world, Mr. Kemper.

Ambrose. Mrs. Levi, what is the point?

Mrs. Levi. Believe me, Mr. Vandergelder wishes to get rid of Ermen-

330 garde, and if you follow my suggestions he will even permit her to marry you. You see, Mr. Vandergelder is planning to get married himself.

Ambrose. What? That monster!

Mrs. Levi. Mr. Kemper!

Ambrose. Married! To you, Mrs. Levi?

Mrs. Levi. (Taken aback) Oh, no, no . . . NO! I am merely arranging it. I am helping him find a suitable bride.

Ambrose. For Mr. Vandergelder there are no suitable brides.

Mrs. Levi. I think we can safely say that Mr. Vandergelder will be married to someone by the end of next week.

340 *Ambrose.* What are you suggesting, Mrs. Levi?

Mrs. Levi. I am taking Ermengarde to New York on the next train. I shall not take her to Miss Van Huysen's, as is planned; I shall take her to my house. I wish you to call for her at my house at five-thirty. Here is my card.

Ambrose. "Mrs. Dolly Gallagher Levi. Varicose veins reduced."

Mrs. Levi. (Trying to take back card) I beg your pardon . . .

Ambrose. (Holding card) I beg *your* pardon. "Consultations free."

Mrs. Levi. I meant to give you my other card. Here.

Ambrose. "Mrs. Dolly Gallagher Levi. Aurora Hosiery. Instruction

350 in the guitar and mandolin." You do all these things, Mrs. Levi?

Mrs. Levi. Two and two make four, Mr. Kemper—always did. So you will come to my house at five-thirty. At about six I shall take you both with me to the Harmonia Gardens Restaurant on the Battery; Mr. Vandergelder will be there and everything will be arranged.

Ambrose. How?

Mrs. Levi. Oh, I don't know. One thing will lead to another.

Ambrose. How do I know that I can trust you, Mrs. Levi? You could easily make our situation worse.

Mrs. Levi. Mr. Kemper, your situation could not possibly be worse.

Ambrose. I wish I knew what you get out of this, Mrs. Levi. 360

Mrs. Levi. That is a very proper question. I get two things: profit and pleasure.

Ambrose. How?

Mrs. Levi. Mr. Kemper, I am a woman who arranges things. At present I am arranging Mr. Vandergelder's domestic affairs. Out of it I get—shall we call it: little pickings? I need little pickings, Mr. Kemper, and especially just now, when I haven't got my train fare back to New York. You see: I am frank with you.

Ambrose. That's your profit, Mrs. Levi; but where do you get your pleasure? 370

Mrs. Levi. My pleasure? Mr. Kemper, when you artists paint a hillside or a river you change everything a little, you make thousands of little changes, don't you? Nature is never completely satisfactory and must be corrected. Well, I'm like you artists. Life as it is is never quite interesting enough for me—I'm bored, Mr. Kemper, with life as it is—and so I do things. I put my hand in here, and I put my hand in there, and I watch and I listen—and often I'm very much amused.

Ambrose. (Rises) Not in my affairs, Mrs. Levi.

Mrs. Levi. Wait, I haven't finished. There's another thing. I'm very interested in this household here—in Mr. Vandergelder and all that 380 idle, frozen money of his. I don't like the thought of it lying in great piles, useless, motionless, in the bank, Mr. Kemper. Money should circulate like rain water. It should be flowing down among the people, through dressmakers and restaurants and cabmen, setting up a little business here, and furnishing a good time there. Do you see what I mean?

Ambrose. Yes, I do.

Mrs. Levi. New York should be a very happy city, Mr. Kemper, but it isn't. My late husband came from Vienna; now there's a city that understands this. I want New York to be more like Vienna and less 390 like a collection of nervous and tired ants. And if you and Ermengarde get a good deal of Mr. Vandergelder's money, I want you to see that it starts flowing in and around a lot of people's lives. And for that reason I want you to come with me to the Harmonia Gardens Restaurant tonight.

(Enter Ermengarde)

Ermengarde. Mrs. Levi, Uncle Horace is coming.

Mrs. Levi. Mr. Kemper, I think you'd better be going. . . . *(Ambrose crosses to trap door and disappears down the ladder, closing trap as*
400 *he goes.)* Darling girl, Mr. Kemper and I have had a very good talk. You'll see: Mr. Vandergelder and I will be dancing at your wedding very soon—*(Enter Vandergelder at back. He has now added a splendid plumed hat to his costume and is carrying a standard or small flag bearing the initials of his lodge.)* Oh, Mr. Vandergelder, how handsome you look! You take my breath away. Yes, my dear girl, I'll see you soon. *(Exit Ermengarde back center)* Oh, Mr. Vandergelder, I wish Irene Molloy could see you now. But then! I don't know what's come over you lately. You seem to be growing younger every day.

Vandergelder. Allowing for exaggeration, Mrs. Levi. If a man eats
410 careful, there's no reason why he should look old.

Mrs. Levi. You never said a truer word.

Vandergelder. I'll never see fifty-five again.

Mrs. Levi. Fifty-five! Why, I can see at a glance that you're the sort that will be stamping about at a hundred—and eating five meals a day, like my Uncle Harry. At fifty-five my Uncle Harry was a mere boy. I'm a judge of hands, Mr. Vandergelder—show me your hand. *(Looks at it)* Lord in heaven! What a life line!

Vandergelder. Where?

Mrs. Levi. From *here* to *here.* It runs right off your hand. I don't
420 know where it goes. They'll have to hit you on the head with a mallet. They'll have to stifle you with a sofa pillow. You'll bury us all! However, to return to our business—Mr. Vandergelder, I suppose you've changed your mind again. I suppose you've given up all idea of getting married.

Vandergelder. (Complacently) Not at all, Mrs. Levi. I have news for you.

Mrs. Levi. News?

Vandergelder. Mrs. Levi, I've practically decided to ask Mrs. Molloy to be my wife.

Mrs. Levi. (Taken aback) You have?

430 *Vandergelder.* Yes, I have.

Mrs. Levi. Oh, you have! Well, I guess that's just about the best news I ever heard. So there's nothing more for me to do but wish you every happiness under the sun and say goodby. *(Crosses as if to leave)*

Vandergelder. (Stopping her) Well—Mrs. Levi—surely I thought—

Mrs. Levi. Well, I did have a little suggestion to make—but I won't. You're going to marry Irene Molloy, and that closes the matter.

Vandergelder. What suggestion was that, Mrs. Levi?

Mrs. Levi. Well—I *had* found *another* girl for you.

Vandergelder. Another?

440 *Mrs. Levi.* The most wonderful girl, the ideal wife.

Vandergelder. Another, eh? What's her name?

Mrs. Levi. Her name?

Vandergelder. Yes!

Mrs. Levi. (Groping for it) Err . . . er . . . her *name?*—Ernestina—Simple. *Miss* Ernestina Simple. But now of course all that's too late. After all, you're engaged—you're practically engaged to marry Irene Molloy.

Vandergelder. Oh, I ain't engaged to Mrs. Molloy!

Mrs. Levi. Nonsense! You can't break poor Irene's heart now and change to another girl. . . . When a man at your time of life calls four times on an attractive widow like that—and sends her a pot of geraniums—that's practically an engagement! 450

Vandergelder. That ain't an engagement!

Mrs. Levi. And yet—! If only you were free! I've found this treasure of a girl. Every moment I felt like a traitor to Irene Molloy—but let me tell you: I couldn't help it. I told this girl all about you, just as though you were a free man. Isn't that dreadful? The fact is: she has fallen in love with you already.

Vandergelder. Ernestina?

Mrs. Levi. Ernestina Simple. 460

Vandergelder. Ernestina Simple.

Mrs. Levi. Of course she's a very different idea from Mrs. Molloy, Ernestina is. Like her name—simple, domestic, practical.

Vandergelder. Can she cook?

Mrs. Levi. Cook, Mr. Vandergelder? I've had two meals from her hands, and—as I live—I don't know what I've done that God should reward me with such meals.

Mrs. Levi. (Continues) Her duck! Her steak!

Vandergelder. Eh! Eh! In this house we don't eat duck and steak every day, Mrs. Levi. 470

Mrs. Levi. But didn't I tell you?—that's the wonderful part about it. Her duck—what was it? Pigeon! I'm alive to tell you. I don't know how she does it. It's a secret that's come down in her family. The greatest chefs would give their right hands to know it. And the steaks? Shoulder of beef—four cents a pound. Dogs wouldn't eat. But when Ernestina passes her hands over it—! !

Vandergelder. Allowing for exaggeration, Mrs. Levi.

Mrs. Levi. No exaggeration. I'm the best cook in the world myself, and I *know* what's good.

Vandergelder. Hm. How old is she, Mrs. Levi? 480

Mrs. Levi. Nineteen, well—say twenty.

Vandergelder. Twenty, Mrs. Levi? Girls of twenty are apt to favor young fellows of their own age.

Mrs. Levi. But you don't listen to me. And you don't know the girl. Mr. Vandergelder, she has a positive horror of flighty, brainless young men. A fine head of gray hair, she says, is worth twenty shined up with goose grease. No, sir. "I like a man that's *settled*"—in so many words she said it.

Vandergelder. That's . . . that's not usual, Mrs. Levi.

490 *Mrs. Levi.* Usual? I'm not wearing myself to the bone hunting up *usual* girls to interest you, Mr. Vandergelder. Usual, indeed. Listen to me. Do you know the sort of pictures she has on her wall? Is it any of these young Romeos and Lochinvars? No!—it's Moses on the Mountain—that's what she's got. If you want to make her happy, you give her a picture of Methuselah surrounded by his grandchildren. That's my advice to you.

Vandergelder. I hope . . . hm . . . that she has some means, Mrs. Levi. I have a large household to run.

Mrs. Levi. Ernestina? She'll bring you five thousand dollars a year.

500 *Vandergelder.* Eh! Eh!

Mrs. Levi. Listen to me, Mr. Vandergelder. You're a man of sense, I hope. A man that can reckon. In the first place, she's an orphan. She's been brought up with a great saving of food. What does she eat herself? Apples and lettuce. It's what she's been used to eating and what she likes best. She saves you two thousand a year right there. Secondly, she makes her own clothes—out of old tablecloths and window curtains. And she's the best-dressed woman in Brooklyn this minute. She saves you a thousand dollars right there. Thirdly, her health is of iron—

Vandergelder. But, Mrs. Levi, that's not money in the pocket.

510 *Mrs. Levi.* We're talking about marriage, aren't we, Mr. Vandergelder? The money she saves while she's in Brooklyn is none of your affair—but if she were your wife that would be *money*. Yes, sir, that's money.

Vandergelder. What's her family?

Mrs. Levi. Her father?—God be good to him! He was the best—what am I trying to say?—the best undertaker in Brooklyn, respected, esteemed. He knew all the best people—knew them well, even before they died. So—well, that's the way it is. *(Lowering her voice, intimately)* Now let me tell you a little more of her appearance. Can you hear me:
520 as I say, a beautiful girl, beautiful, I've seen her go down the street—you know what I mean?—the young men get dizzy. They have to lean against lampposts. And she? Modest, eyes on the ground—I'm not going to tell you any more. . . . Couldn't you come to New York today?

Vandergelder. I was thinking of coming to New York this afternoon. . . .

Mrs. Levi. You were? Well now, I wonder if something could be arranged—oh, she's so eager to see you! Let me see . . .

Vandergelder. Could I . . . Mrs. Levi, could I give you a little dinner, maybe?

Mrs. Levi. Really, come to think of it, I don't see where I could get the time. I'm so busy over that wretched lawsuit of mine. Yes. If I win it, I don't mind telling you, I'll be what's called a very rich woman. I'll own half of Long Island, that's a fact. But just now I'm at my wit's end for a little help, just enough money to finish it off. My wit's end! *(She looks in her handbag. In order not to hear this, Vandergelder has a series of coughs, sneezes and minor convulsions.)* But perhaps I could arrange a little dinner; I'll see. Yes, for that lawsuit all I need is fifty dollars, and Staten Island's as good as mine. I've been trotting all over New York for you, trying to find you a suitable wife. 530

Vandergelder. Fifty dollars! ! 540

Mrs. Levi. Two whole months I've been . . .

Vandergelder. Fifty dollars, Mrs. Levi . . . is no joke. *(Producing purse)* I don't know where money's gone to these days. It's in hiding. . . . There's twenty . . . well, there's twenty-five. I can't spare no more, not now I can't.

Mrs. Levi. Well, this will help—will help somewhat. Now let me tell you what we'll do. I'll bring Ernestina to that restaurant on the Battery. You know it: the Harmonia Gardens. It's good, but it's not flashy. Now, Mr. Vandergelder, I think it'd be nice if just this once you'd order a real nice dinner. I guess you can afford it. 550

Vandergelder. Well, just this once.

Mrs. Levi. A chicken wouldn't hurt.

Vandergelder. Chicken! !—Well, just this once.

Mrs. Levi. And a little wine.

Vandergelder. Wine? Well, just this once.

Mrs. Levi. Now about Mrs. Molloy—what do you think? Shall we call that subject closed?

Vandergelder. No, not at all, Mrs. Levi, I want to have dinner with Miss . . . with Miss . . .

Mrs. Levi. Simple. 560

Vandergelder. With Miss Simple; but first I want to make another call on Mrs. Molloy.

Mrs. Levi. Dear, dear, dear! And Miss Simple? What races you make me run! Very well; I'll meet you on one of those benches in front of Mrs. Molloy's hat store at four-thirty, as usual. *(Trap door rises, and Cornelius' head appears.)*

Cornelius. The buggy's here, ready for the parade, Mr. Vandergelder.

Vandergelder. Call Barnaby. I want to talk to both of you.

Cornelius. Yes, Mr. Vandergelder.

(Exit Cornelius down trap door. Leaves trap open) 570

Mrs. Levi. Now do put your thoughts in order, Mr. Vandergelder. I can't keep upsetting and disturbing the finest women in New York City unless you mean business.

Vandergelder. Oh, I mean business all right!

Mrs. Levi. I hope so. Because, you know, you're playing a very dangerous game.

Vandergelder. Dangerous?—Dangerous, Mrs. Levi?

Mrs. Levi. Of course, it's dangerous—and there's a name for it! You're tampering with these women's affections, aren't you? And the
580 only way you can save yourself now is to be married to *someone* by the end of next week. So think that over! *(Exit center back)*

(Enter Cornelius and Barnaby, by the trap door)

Vandergelder. This morning I'm joining my lodge parade, and this afternoon I'm going to New York. When I come back, there are going to be some changes in the house here. I'll tell you what the change is, but I don't want you discussing it amongst yourselves: you're going to have a mistress.

Barnaby. (Seventeen; round-faced, wide-eyed innocence; wearing a green apron) I'm too young, Mr. Vandergelder! !

590 *Vandergelder.* Not yours! Death and damnation! Not yours, idiot—*mine! (Then realizing)* Hey! Hold your tongue until you're spoken to! I'm thinking of getting married.

Cornelius. (Crosses, hand outstretched) Many congratulations, Mr. Vandergelder, and my compliments to the lady.

Vandergelder. That's none of your business. Now go back to the store. *(The boys start down the ladder, Barnaby first.)* Have you got any questions you want to ask before I go?

Cornelius. Mr. Vandergelder—er—Mr. Vandergelder, does the chief clerk get one evening off every week?

600 *Vandergelder.* So that's the way you begin being chief clerk, is it? When I was your age I got up at five; I didn't close the shop until ten at night, and then I put in a good hour at the account books. The world's going to pieces. You elegant laddies lie in bed until six, and at nine o'clock at night you rush to close the door so fast the line of customers bark their noses. No, sir—you'll attend to the store as usual, and on Friday and Saturday nights you'll remain open until ten—now hear what I say! This is the first time I've been away from the store overnight. When I come back, I want to hear that you've run the place perfectly in my absence. If I hear of any foolishness, I'll discharge you. An evening free!
610 Do you suppose that *I* had evenings free? *(At the top of his complacency)* If I'd had evenings free, I wouldn't be what I am now!

(He marches out, right.)

Barnaby. (Watching him go) The horses nearly ran away when they saw him. What's the matter, Cornelius?

Cornelius. (Sits in dejected thought) Chief clerk! Promoted from chief clerk to chief clerk.

Barnaby. Don't you like it?

Cornelius. Chief clerk!—and if I'm good, in ten years I'll be promoted to chief clerk again. Thirty-three years old and I still don't get an evening free? When am I going to begin to live? 620

Barnaby. Well—ah . . . you can begin to live on Sundays, Cornelius.

Cornelius. That's not living. Twice to church, and old Wolf-trap's eyes on the back of my head the whole time. And as for holidays! What did we do last Christmas? All those canned tomatoes went bad and exploded. We had to clean up the mess all afternoon. Was that living?

Barnaby. (Holding his nose at the memory of the bad smell) No! ! !

Cornelius. (Rising with sudden resolution) Barnaby, how much money have you got—where you can get at it?

Barnaby. Oh—three dollars. Why, Cornelius?

Cornelius. You and I are going to New York. 630

Barnaby. Cornelius! ! ! We can't! Close the store?

Cornelius. Some more rotten-tomato cans are going to explode.

Barnaby. Holy cabooses! How do you know?

Cornelius. I know they're rotten. All you have to do is to light a match under them. They'll make such a smell that customers can't come into the place for twenty-four hours. That'll get us an evening free. We're going to New York too, Barnaby, we're going to live! I'm going to have enough adventures to last me until I'm *partner.* So go and get your Sunday clothes on.

Barnaby. Wha-a-a-t? 640

Cornelius. Yes, I mean it. We're going to have a good meal; and we're going to be in danger; and we're going to get almost arrested; and we're going to spend all our money.

Barnaby. Holy cabooses!!

Cornelius. And one more thing: we're not coming back to Yonkers until we've kissed a girl.

Barnaby. Kissed a girl! Cornelius, you can't do that. You don't know any girls.

Cornelius. I'm thirty-three. I've got to begin sometime.

Barnaby. I'm only seventeen, Cornelius. It isn't so urgent for me. 650

Cornelius. Don't start backing down now—if the worst comes to the worst and we get discharged from here, we can always join the Army.

Barnaby. Uh—did I hear you say that you'd be old Wolftrap's partner?

Cornelius. How can I help it? He's growing old. If you go to bed at nine and open the store at six, you get promoted upward whether you like it or not.

Barnaby. My! Partner.

Cornelius. Oh, there's no way of getting away from it. You and I will be Vandergelders. 660

Barnaby. I? Oh, no—I may rise a little, but I'll never be a Vandergelder.

Cornelius. Listen—everybody thinks when he gets rich he'll be a different kind of rich person from the rich people he sees around him; later on he finds out there's only one kind of rich person, and he's it.

Barnaby. Oh, but I'll—

Cornelius. No. The best of all would be a person who has all the good things a poor person has, and all the good meals a rich person has, 670 but that's never been known. No, you and I are going to be Vandergelders; all the more reason, then, for us to try and get some living and some adventure into us now—will you come, Barnaby?

Barnaby. (In a struggle with his fears, a whirlwind of words) But Wolf-trap—KRR-pt, Gertrude-KRR-pt—*(With a sudden cry of agreement)* Yes, Cornelius! *(Enter Mrs. Levi, Ermengarde and Gertrude from back center. The boys start down the ladder, Cornelius last.)*

Mrs. Levi. Mr. Hackl, is the trunk waiting at the station?

Cornelius. Yes, Mrs. Levi. *(Closes the trap door)*

Mrs. Levi. Take a last look, Ermengarde.

680 *Ermengarde.* What?

Mrs. Levi. Take a last look at your girlhood home, dear. I remember when I left my home. I gave a whinny like a young colt, and off I went. *(Ermengarde and Gertrude exit)*

Ermengarde. (As they go) Oh, Gertrude, do you think I ought to get married this way? A young girl has to be so careful! *(Mrs. Levi is alone. She addresses the audience.)*

Mrs. Levi. You know, I think I'm going to have this room with *blue* wallpaper,—yes, in blue! *(Hurries out after the others. Barnaby comes up trap door, looks off right, then lies on floor, gazing down 690 through the trap door.)*

Barnaby. All clear up here, Cornelius! Cornelius—hold the candle steady a minute—the bottom row's all right—but try the top now . . . they're swelled up like they are ready to bust! *(BANG)* Holy CABOOSES! *(BANG, BANG)* Cornelius! I can smell it up here! *(Rises and dances about, holding his nose)*

Cornelius. (Rushing up the trap door) Get into your Sunday clothes, Barnaby. We're going to New York! *(As they run out . . . there is a big explosion. A shower of tomato cans comes up from below, as—the curtain falls.)*

Act II

Mrs. Molloy's hat shop, New York City.

There are two entrances. One door at the extreme right of the back wall, to Mrs. Molloy's workroom; one at the back left corner, to the street.

The whole left wall is taken up with the show windows, filled with hats. It is separated from the shop by a low brass rail, hung with net; during the act both Mrs. Molloy and Barnaby stoop under the rail and go into the shop window. By the street door stands a large cheval glass. In the middle of the back wall is a large wardrobe or clothes cupboard, filled with ladies' coats, large enough for Cornelius to hide in. At the left, beginning at the back wall, between the wardrobe and the work-room door, a long counter extends toward the audience, almost to the footlights. In the center of the room is a large round table with a low-hanging red cloth. There are a small gilt chair by the wardrobe and two chairs in front of the counter. Over the street door and the work-room door are bells which ring when the doors are opened.

(As the curtain rises, Mrs. Molloy is in the window, standing on a box, reaching up to put hats on the stand. Minnie Fay is sewing by the counter. Mrs. Molloy has a pair of felt overshoes, to be removed later.)

Mrs. Molloy. Minnie, you're a fool. Of course I shall marry Horace Vandergelder.

Minnie. Oh, Mrs. Molloy! I didn't ask you. I wouldn't dream of asking you such a personal question.

Mrs. Molloy. Well, it's what you meant, isn't it? And there's your answer. I shall certainly marry Horace Vandergelder if he asks me. *(Crawls under window rail, into the room, singing loudly)* 10

Minnie. I know it's none of my business . . .

Mrs. Molloy. Speak up, Minnie, I can't hear you.

Minnie. . . . but do you . . . do you . . . ?

Mrs. Molloy. (Having crossed the room, is busy at the counter) Minnie, you're a fool. Say it: Do I love him? Of course, I don't love him. But I have two good reasons for marrying him just the same. Minnie, put something on that hat. It's not ugly enough. *(Throws hat over counter)*

Minnie. (Catching and taking hat to table) Not ugly enough!

Mrs. Molloy. I couldn't sell it. Put a . . . put a sponge on it.

Minnie. Why, Mrs. Molloy, you're in such a *mood* today.

Mrs. Molloy. In the first place I shall marry Mr. Vandergelder to 20 get away from the millinery business. I've hated it from the first day I had anything to do with it. Minnie, I hate hats. *(Sings loudly again)*

Minnie. Why, what's the matter with the millinery business?

Mrs. Molloy. (Crossing to window with two hats) I can no longer stand being suspected of being a wicked woman, while I have nothing to show for it. I can't stand it. *(She crawls under rail into window.)*

Minnie. Why, no one would dream of suspecting you—

Mrs. Molloy. (On her knees, she looks over the rail.) Minnie, you're 30 a fool. All millineresses are suspected of being wicked women.

Why, half the time all those women come into the shop merely to look at me.

Minnie. Oh!

Mrs. Molloy. They enjoy the suspicion. But they aren't certain. If they were *certain* I was a wicked woman, they wouldn't put foot in this place again. Do I go to restaurants? No, it would be bad for business. Do I go to balls, or theatres, or operas? No, it would be bad for business. The only men I ever meet are feather merchants.
40 *(Crawls out of window, but gazes intently into the street)* What are those two young men doing out there on that park bench? Take my word for it, Minnie, either I marry Horace Vandergelder, or I break out of this place like a fire engine. I'll go to every theatre and ball and opera in New York City. *(Returns to counter, singing again)*

Minnie. But Mr. Vandergelder's not . . .

Mrs. Molloy. Speak up, Minnie, I can't hear you.

Minnie. . . . I don't think he's attractive.

Mrs. Molloy. But what I think he is—and it's very important—I think he'd make a good fighter.

50 *Minnie.* Mrs. Molloy!

Mrs. Molloy. Take my word for it, Minnie: the best part of married life is the fights. The rest is merely so-so.

Minnie. (Fingers in ears) I won't listen.

Mrs. Molloy. Peter Molloy—God rest him!—was a fine arguing man. I pity the woman whose husband slams the door and walks out of the house at the beginning of an argument. Peter Molloy would stand up and fight for hours on end. He'd even throw things, Minnie, and there's no pleasure to equal that. When I felt tired, I'd start a good blood-warming fight and it'd take ten years off my age; now Horace Vander-
60 gelder would put up a good fight; I know it. I've a mind to marry him.

Minnie. I think they're just awful, the things you're saying today.

Mrs. Molloy. Well, I'm enjoying them myself, too.

Minnie. (At the window) Mrs. Molloy, those two men out in the street—

Mrs. Molloy. What?

Minnie. Those men. It looks as if they meant to come in here.

Mrs. Molloy. Well now, it's time some men came into this place. I give you the younger one, Minnie.

Minnie. Aren't you terrible! *(Mrs. Molloy sits on center table, while*
70 *Minnie takes off her felt overshoes.)*

Mrs. Molloy. Wait till I get my hands on that older one! Mark my words, Minnie, we'll get an adventure out of this yet. Adventure, adventure! Why does everybody have adventures except me, Minnie? Because I have no spirit, I have no gumption. Minnie, they're coming in here. Let's go into the workroom and make them wait for us for a minute.

Minnie. Oh, but Mrs. Molloy . . . my work! . . .

Mrs. Molloy. (Running to workroom) Hurry up, be quick now, Minnie! *(They go out to workroom. Barnaby and Cornelius run in from street, leaving front door open. They are dressed in the stiff discomfort of their* 80 *Sunday clothes. Cornelius wears a bowler hat, Barnaby a straw hat too large for him.)*

Barnaby. No one's here.

Cornelius. Some women were here a minute ago. I saw them. *(They jump back to the street door and peer down the street.)* That's Wolf-trap all right! *(Coming back)* Well, we've got to hide here until he passes by.

Barnaby. He's sitting down on that bench. It may be quite a while.

Cornelius. When these women come in, we'll have to make conversation until he's gone away. We'll pretend we're buying a hat. 90 How much money have you got now?

Barnaby. (Counting his money) Forty cents for the train—seventy cents for dinner—twenty cents to see the whale—and a dollar I lost—I have seventy cents.

Cornelius. And I have a dollar seventy-five. I wish I knew how much hats cost!

Barnaby. Is this an adventure, Cornelius?

Cornelius. No, but it may be.

Barnaby. I think it is. There we wander around New York all day and nothing happens; and then we come to the quietest street in the 100 whole city and suddenly Mr. Vandergelder turns the corner. *(Going to door)* I think that's an adventure. I think . . . Cornelius! That Mrs. Levi is there now. She's sitting down on the bench with him.

Cornelius. What do you know about that! We know only one person in all New York City, and there she is!

Barnaby. Even if our adventure came along now, I'd be too tired to enjoy it. Cornelius, why isn't this an adventure?

Cornelius. Don't be asking that. When you're in an adventure, you'll know it all right.

Barnaby. Maybe I wouldn't. Cornelius, let's arrange a signal for 110 you to give me when an adventure's really going on. For instance, Cornelius, you say . . . uh . . . uh . . . *pudding;* you say *pudding* to me as if it's an adventure we're in.

Cornelius. I wonder where the lady who runs this store is? What's her name again?

Barnaby. Mrs. Molloy, hats for ladies.

Cornelius. Oh yes. I must think over what I'm going to say when she comes in. *(To counter)* "Good afternoon, Mrs. Molloy, wonderful weather we're having. We've been looking everywhere for some beautiful hats." 120

Barnaby. That's fine, Cornelius!

Cornelius. "Good afternoon, Mrs. Molloy; wonderful weather . . ." We'll make her think we're very rich. *(One hand in trouser pocket, the other on back of chair)* "Good afternoon, Mrs. Molloy . . ." You keep one eye on the door the whole time. "We've been looking everywhere for . . ."

(Enter Mrs. Molloy from the workroom)

Mrs. Molloy. (Behind the counter) Oh, I'm sorry. Have I kept you waiting? Good afternoon, gentlemen.

130 *Cornelius. (Hat off)* Here, Cornelius Hackl.

Barnaby. (Hat off) Here, Barnaby Tucker.

Mrs. Molloy. I'm very happy to meet you. Perhaps I can help you. Won't you sit down?

Cornelius. Thank you, we will. *(The boys place their hats on the table, then sit down at the counter facing Mrs. Molloy.)* You see, Mrs. Molloy, we're looking for hats. We've looked everywhere. Do you know what we heard? Go to Mrs. Molloy's, they said. So we came here. Only place we *could* go . . .

Mrs. Molloy. Well, now, that's *very* complimentary.

140 *Cornelius.* . . . and we were right. Everybody was right.

Mrs. Molloy. You wish to choose some hats for a friend?

Cornelius. Yes, exactly. *(Kicks Barnaby)*

Barnaby. Yes, exactly.

Cornelius. We were thinking of five or six, weren't we, Barnaby?

Barnaby. Er—five.

Cornelius. You see, Mrs. Molloy, money's no object with us. None at all.

Mrs. Molloy. Why, Mr. Hackl . . .

Cornelius. (Rises and goes toward street door) . . . I beg your pardon,

150 what an interesting street! Something happening every minute. Passers-by, and . . . *(Barnaby runs to join him.)*

Mrs. Molloy. You're from out of town, Mr. Hackl?

Cornelius. (Coming back) Yes, ma'am—Barnaby, just keep your eye on the street, will you? You won't see that in Yonkers every day. *(Barnaby remains kneeling at street door.)*

Barnaby. Oh yes, I will.

Cornelius. Not all of it.

Mrs. Molloy. Now this friend of yours—couldn't she come in with you someday and choose her hats herself?

160 *Cornelius. (Sits at counter)* No. Oh, no. It's a surprise for her.

Mrs. Molloy. Indeed? That may be a little difficult, Mr. Hackl. It's not entirely customary.—Your friend's very interested in the street, Mr. Hackl.

Cornelius. Oh yes. Yes. He has reason to be.

Mrs. Molloy. You said you were from out of town?

Cornelius. Yes, we're from Yonkers.

Mrs. Molloy. Yonkers?

Cornelius. Yonkers . . . yes, Yonkers. *(He gazes rapt into her eyes.)* You should know Yonkers, Mrs. Molloy. Hudson River; Palisades; drives; some say it's the most beautiful town in the world; that's 170 what they say.

Mrs. Molloy. Is that so!

Cornelius. (Rises) Mrs. Molloy, if you ever had a Sunday free, I'd . . . we'd like to show you Yonkers. Y'know, it's very historic, too.

Mrs. Molloy. That's very kind of you. Well, perhaps . . . now about those hats. *(Takes two hats from under counter, and crosses to back center of the room)*

Cornelius. (Following) Is there . . . Have you a . . . Maybe Mr. Molloy would like to see Yonkers too?

Mrs. Molloy. Oh, I'm a widow, Mr. Hackl. 180

Cornelius. (Joyfully) You are! *(With sudden gravity)* Oh, that's too bad. Mr. Molloy would have enjoyed Yonkers.

Mrs. Molloy. Very likely. Now about these hats. Is your friend dark or light?

Cornelius. Don't think about that for a minute. Any hat you'd like would be perfectly all right with her.

Mrs. Molloy. Really! *(She puts one on.)* Do you like this one?

Cornelius. (In awe-struck admiration) Barnaby! *(In sudden anger)* Barnaby! Look! *(Barnaby turns; unimpressed, he laughs vaguely, and turns to door again.)* Mrs. Molloy, that's the most beautiful hat 190 I ever saw. *(Barnaby now crawls under the rail into the window.)*

Mrs. Molloy. Your friend is acting very strangely, Mr. Hackl.

Cornelius. Barnaby, stop acting strangely. When the street's quiet and empty, come back and talk to us. What was I saying? Oh yes: Mrs. Molloy, you should know Yonkers.

Mrs. Molloy. (Hat off) The fact is, I have a friend in Yonkers. Perhaps you know him. It's always so foolish to ask in cases like that, isn't it? *(They both laugh over this with increasing congeniality. Mrs. Molloy goes to counter with hats from table. Cornelius follows.)* It's a Mr. Vandergelder. 200

Cornelius. (Stops abruptly) What was that you said?

Mrs. Molloy. Then you do know him?

Cornelius. Horace Vandergelder?

Mrs. Molloy. Yes, that's right.

Cornelius. Know him! *(Looks to Barnaby)* Why, no. No!

Barnaby. No! No!

Cornelius. (Starting to glide about the room, in search of a hiding place) I beg your pardon, Mrs. Molloy—what an attractive shop you have! *(Smiling fixedly at her, he moves to the workshop door.)* And where

210 does this door lead to? *(Opens it, and is alarmed by the bell which rings above it)*

Mrs. Molloy. Why, Mr. Hackl, that's my workroom.

Cornelius. Everything here is so interesting. *(Looks under counter)* Every corner. Every door, Mrs. Molloy. Barnaby, notice the interesting doors and cupboards. *(He opens the cupboard door.)* Deeply interesting. Coats for ladies. *(Laughs)* Barnaby, make a note of the table. Precious piece of furniture, with a low-hanging cloth, I see. *(Stretches his leg under table)*

Mrs. Molloy. (Taking a hat from box left of wardrobe) Perhaps your 220 friend might like some of this new Italian straw. Mr. Vandergelder's a substantial man and very well liked, they tell me.

Cornelius. A lovely man, Mrs. Molloy.

Mrs. Molloy. Oh yes—charming, charming!

Cornelius. (Smiling sweetly) Has only one fault, as far as I know; he's hard as nails; but apart from that, as you say, a charming nature, ma'am.

Mrs. Molloy. And a large circle of friends—?

Cornelius. Yes, indeed, yes indeed—five or six.

Barnaby. Five!

230 *Cornelius.* He comes and calls on you here from time to time, I suppose.

Mrs. Molloy. (Turns from mirror where she has been putting a hat on) This summer we'll be wearing ribbons down our back. Yes, as a matter of fact I am expecting a call from him this afternoon. *(Hat off)*

Barnaby. I think . . . Cornelius! I think . . . !!

Mrs. Molloy. Now to show you some more hats—

Barnaby. Look out! *(He takes a flying leap over the rail and flings himself under the table.)*

Cornelius. Begging your pardon, Mrs. Molloy. *(He jumps into the* 240 *cupboard.)*

Mrs. Molloy. Gentlemen! Mr. Hackl! Come right out of there this minute!

Cornelius. (Sticking his head out of the wardrobe door) Help us just this once, Mrs. Molloy! We'll explain later!

Mrs. Molloy. Mr. Hackl!

Barnaby. We're as innocent as can be, Mrs. Molloy.

Mrs. Molloy. But really! Gentlemen! I can't have this! *What are you doing?*

Barnaby. Cornelius! Cornelius! Pudding?

250 *Cornelius. (A shout)* Pudding! *(They disappear.)*

(Enter from the street Mrs. Levi, followed by Mr. Vandergelder. Vandergelder is dressed in a too-bright checked suit, and wears a green derby—or bowler—hat. He is carrying a large ornate box of chocolates in one hand, and a cane in the other.)

Mrs. Levi. Irene, my darling child, how *are* you? Heaven be good to us, how well you look! *(They kiss.)*

Mrs. Molloy. But what a surprise! And Mr. Vandergelder in New York—what a pleasure!

Vandergelder. (Swaying back and forth on his heels complacently) Good afternoon, Mrs. Molloy. *(They shake hands. Mrs. Molloy brings chair from counter for him. He sits at left of table.)* 260

Mrs. Levi. Yes, Mr. Vandergelder's in New York. Yonkers lies up there—*decimated* today. Irene, we thought we'd pay you a very short call. Now you'll tell us if it's inconvenient, won't you?

Mrs. Molloy. (Placing a chair for Mrs. Levi at right of table) Inconvenient, Dolly! The idea! Why, it's sweet of you to come. *(She notices the boys' hats on the table—sticks a spray of flowers into crown of Cornelius' bowler and winds a piece of chiffon round Barnaby's panama.)*

Vandergelder. We waited outside a moment. 270

Mrs. Levi. Mr. Vandergelder thought he saw two customers coming in—two men.

Mrs. Molloy. Men! Men, Mr. Vandergelder? Why, what will you be saying next?

Mrs. Levi. Then we'll sit down for a minute or two....

Mrs. Molloy. (Wishing to get them out of the shop into the workroom) Before you sit down—*(She pushes them both.)* Before you sit down, there's something I want to show you. I want to show Mr. Vandergelder my workroom, too.

Mrs. Levi. I've seen the workroom a hundred times. I'll stay right here and try on some of these hats. 280

Mrs. Molloy. No, Dolly, you come too. I have something for you. Come along, everybody. *(Exit Mrs. Levi to workroom.)* Mr. Vandergelder, I want your advice. You don't know how helpless a woman in business is. Oh, I feel I need advice every minute from a fine business head like yours. *(Exit Vandergelder to workroom. Mrs. Molloy shouts this line and then slams the workroom door.)* Now I shut the door!! *(Exit Mrs. Molloy. Cornelius puts his head out of the wardrobe door and gradually comes out into the room, leaving door open.)*

Cornelius. Hsst! 290

Barnaby. (Pokes his head out from under the table) Maybe she wants us to go, Cornelius?

Cornelius. Certainly I won't go. Mrs. Molloy would think we were just thoughtless fellows. No, all I want is to stretch a minute.

Barnaby. What are you going to do when he's gone, Cornelius? Are we just going to run away?

Cornelius. Well... I don't know yet. I like Mrs. Molloy a lot. I wouldn't like her to think badly of me. I think I'll buy a hat. We can walk home to Yonkers, even if it takes us all night. I wonder how much hats

300 cost. Barnaby, give me all the money you've got. *(As he leans over to take the money, he sneezes. Both return to their hiding places in alarm; then emerge again.)* My, all those perfumes in that cupboard tickle my nose! But I like it in there . . . it's a woman's world, and very different.

Barnaby. I like it where I am, too; only I'd like it better if I had a pillow.

Cornelius. (Taking coat from wardrobe) Here, take one of these coats. I'll roll it up for you so it won't get mussed. Ladies don't like to have their coats mussed.

Barnaby. That's fine. Now I can just lie here and hear Mr. Vander-
310 gelder talk. *(Cornelius goes slowly above table towards cheval mirror, repeating Mrs. Molloy's line dreamily.)*

Cornelius. "This summer we'll be wearing ribbons down our back. . . ."

Barnaby. Can I take off my shoes, Cornelius? *(Cornelius does not reply. He comes to the footlights and addresses the audience, in completely simple naïve sincerity.)*

Cornelius. Isn't the world full of wonderful things. There we sit cooped up in Yonkers for years and years and all the time wonderful people like Mrs. Molloy are walking around in New York and we don't know them at all. I don't know whether—from where you're sitting—
320 you can see—well, for instance, the way *(He points to the edge of his right eye.)* her eye and forehead and cheek come together, up here. Can you? And the kind of fireworks that shoot out of her eyes all the time. I tell you right now: a fine woman is the greatest work of God. You can talk all you like about Niagara Falls and the Pyramids; they aren't in it at all. Of course, up there at Yonkers they came into the store all the time, and bought this and that, and I said, "Yes, ma'am," and "That'll be seventy-five cents, ma'am"; and I *watched* them. But today I've talked to one, equal to equal, equal to equal, and to the finest one that ever existed, in my opinion. They're so different from men!
330 Everything that they say and do is so different that you feel like laughing all the time. *(He laughs.)* Golly, they're different from men. And they're awfully mysterious, too. You never can be really sure what's going on in their heads. They have a kind of wall around them all the time—of pride and a sort of play-acting: I bet you could know a woman a hundred years without ever being really sure whether she liked you or not. This minute I'm in danger. I'm in danger of losing my job and my future and everything that people think is important; but I don't care. Even if I have to dig ditches for the rest of my life, I'll be a ditch-digger who once had a wonderful day. Barnaby!

340 *Barnaby.* Oh, you woke me up!

Cornelius. (Kneels) Barnaby, we can't go back to Yonkers yet and you know why.

Barnaby. Why not?

Cornelius. We've had a good meal. We've had an adventure. We've been in danger of getting arrested. There's only one more thing we've got to do before we go back to be successes in Yonkers.

Barnaby. Cornelius! You're never going to kiss Mrs. Molloy!

Cornelius. Maybe.

Barnaby. But she'll scream.

Cornelius. Barnaby, you don't know anything at all. You might as well know right now that everybody except us goes through life kissing right and left all the time. 350

Barnaby. (Pauses for reflection; humbly) Well, thanks for telling me, Cornelius. I often wondered.

(Enter Mrs. Levi from workroom)

Mrs. Levi. Just a minute, Irene. I must find my handkerchief. *(Cornelius, caught by the arrival of Mrs. Levi, drops to his hands and knees, and starts very slowly to crawl back to the wardrobe, as though the slowness rendered him invisible. Mrs. Levi, leaning over the counter, watches him. From the cupboard he puts his head out of it and looks pleadingly at her.)* Why, Mr. Hackl, I thought you were up in Yonkers. 360

Cornelius. I almost always am, Mrs. Levi. Oh, Mrs. Levi, don't tell Mr. Vandergelder! I'll explain everything later.

Barnaby. (Puts head out) We're terribly innocent, Mrs. Levi.

Mrs. Levi. Why, who's that?

Barnaby. Barnaby Tucker—just paying a call.

Mrs. Levi. (Looking under counter and even shaking out her skirts) Well, who else is here?

Cornelius. Just the two of us, Mrs. Levi, that's all.

Mrs. Levi. Old friends of Mrs. Molloy's, is that it? 370

Cornelius. We never knew her before a few minutes ago, but we like her a lot—don't we, Barnaby? In fact, I think she's . . . I think she's the finest person in the world. I'm ready to tell that to anybody.

Mrs. Levi. And does she think *you're* the finest person in the world?

Cornelius. Oh, no. I don't suppose she even notices that I'm alive.

Mrs. Levi. Well, I think she must notice that you're alive in that cupboard, Mr. Hackl. Well, if I were you, I'd get back into it right away. Somebody could be coming in any minute. *(Cornelius disappears. She sits unconcernedly in chair right.)*

(Enter Mrs. Molloy) 380

Mrs. Molloy. (Leaving door open and looking about in concealed alarm) Can I help you, Dolly?

Mrs. Levi. No, no, no. I was just blowing my nose.

(Enter Vandergelder from workroom)

Vandergelder. Mrs. Molloy, I've got some advice to give you about your business. *(Mrs. Molloy comes to the center of the room and puts Barnaby's hat on floor in window, then Cornelius' hat on the counter.)*

Mrs. Levi. Oh, advice from Mr. Vandergelder! The whole city should hear this.

390 *Vandergelder. (Standing in the workroom door, pompously)* In the first place, the aim of business is to make profit.

Mrs. Molloy. Is that so?

Mrs. Levi. I never heard it put so clearly before. Did you hear it?

Vandergelder. (Crossing the room to the left) You pay those girls of yours too much. You pay them as much as men. Girls like that enjoy their work. Wages, Mrs. Molloy, are paid to make people do work they don't want to do.

Mrs. Levi. Mr. Vandergelder thinks so ably. And that's exactly the way his business is run up in Yonkers.

400 *Vandergelder. (Patting her hand)* Mrs. Molloy, I'd like for you to come up to Yonkers.

Mrs. Molloy. That would be very nice. *(He hands her the box of chocolates.)* Oh, thank you. As a matter of fact, I know someone from Yonkers, someone else.

Vandergelder. (Hangs hat on the cheval mirror) Oh? Who's that? *(Mrs. Molloy puts chocolates on table and brings gilt chair forward and sits center at table facing the audience.)*

Mrs. Molloy. Someone quite well-to-do, I believe, though a little free and easy in his behavior. Mr. Vandergelder, do you know Mr. Cornelius

410 Hackl in Yonkers?

Vandergelder. I know him like I know my own boot. He's my head clerk.

Mrs. Molloy. Is that so?

Vandergelder. He's been in my store for ten years.

Mrs. Molloy. Well, I never!

Vandergelder. Where would you have known him? *(Mrs. Molloy is in silent confusion. She looks for help to Mrs. Levi, seated at right end of table.)*

Mrs. Levi. (Groping for means to help Mrs. Molloy) Err . . . blah . . .

420 err . . . bl . . . er . . . Oh, just one of those chance meetings, I suppose.

Mrs. Molloy. Yes, oh yes! One of those chance meetings.

Vandergelder. What? Chance meetings? Cornelius Hackl has no right to chance meetings. Where was it?

Mrs. Molloy. Really, Mr. Vandergelder, it's very unlike you to question me in such a way. I think Mr. Hackl is better known than you think he is.

Vandergelder. Nonsense.

Mrs. Molloy. He's in New York often, and he's very well liked.

Mrs. Levi. (Having found her idea, with decision) Well, the truth

430 might as well come out now as later. Mr. Vandergelder, Irene is quite right. Your head clerk is often in New York. Goes everywhere; has an army of friends. Everybody knows Cornelius Hackl.

Vandergelder. (Laughs blandly and sits in chair at left of table) He never comes to New York. He works all day in my store and at nine o'clock at night he goes to sleep in the bran room.

Mrs. Levi. So you think. But it's not true.

Vandergelder. Dolly Gallagher, you're crazy.

Mrs. Levi. Listen to me. You keep your nose so deep in your account books you don't know what goes on. Yes, by day, Cornelius Hackl is your faithful trusted clerk—that's true; but by night! Well, he leads a double life, that's all! He's here at the opera; at the great restaurants; in all the fashionable homes . . . why, he's at the Harmonia Gardens Restaurant three nights a week. The fact is, he's the wittiest, gayest, naughtiest, most delightful man in New York. Well, he's just *the* famous Cornelius Hackl! 440

Vandergelder. (Sure of himself) It ain't the same man. If I ever thought Cornelius Hackl came to New York, I'd discharge him.

Mrs. Levi. Who took the horses out of Jenny Lind's carriage and pulled her through the streets?

Mrs. Molloy. Who? 450

Mrs. Levi. Cornelius Hackl! Who dressed up as a waiter at the Fifth Avenue Hotel the other night and took an oyster and dropped it right down Mrs . . . *(Rises)* No, it's too wicked to tell you!

Mrs. Molloy. Oh yes, Dolly, tell it! Go on!

Mrs. Levi. No. But it *was* Cornelius Hackl.

Vandergelder. (Loud) It ain't the same man. Where'd he get the money?

Mrs. Levi. But he's very rich.

Vandergelder. (Rises) Rich! I keep his money in my own safe. He has a hundred and forty-six dollars and thirty-five cents. 460

Mrs. Levi. Oh, Mr. Vandergelder, you're killing me! Do come to your senses. He's one of *the* Hackls. *(Mrs. Molloy sits at chair right of table where Mrs. Levi has been sitting.)*

Vandergelder. The Hackls?

Mrs. Levi. They built the Raritan Canal.

Vandergelder. Then why should he work in my store?

Mrs. Levi. Well, I'll tell you. *(Sits at the center of the table, facing the audience)*

Vandergelder. (Striding about) I don't want to hear! I've got a headache! I'm going home. *It ain't the same man!!* He sleeps in my bran room. You can't get away from facts. I just made him my chief clerk. 470

Mrs. Levi. If you had any sense, you'd make him partner. *(Rises, crosses to Mrs. Molloy)* Now Irene, I can see you were as taken with him as everybody else is.

Mrs. Molloy. Why, I only met him once, very hastily.

Mrs. Levi. Yes, but I can see that you were taken with him. Now don't you be thinking of marrying him!

Mrs. Molloy. (Her hands on her cheeks) Dolly! What are you saying! Oh!

480 *Mrs. Levi.* Maybe it'd be fine. But think it over carefully. He breaks hearts like hickory nuts.

Vandergelder. Who?

Mrs. Levi. Cornelius Hackl!

Vandergelder. Mrs. Molloy, how often has he called on you?

Mrs. Molloy. Oh, I'm telling the truth. I've only seen him once in my life. Dolly Levi's been exaggerating so. I don't know where to look! *(Enter Minnie from workroom and crosses to window.)*

Minnie. Excuse me, Mrs. Molloy. I must get together that order for Mrs. Parkinson.

490 *Mrs. Molloy.* Yes, we must get that off before closing.

Minnie. I want to send it off by the errand girl. *(Having taken a hat from the window)* Oh, I almost forgot the coat. *(She starts for the wardrobe.)*

Mrs. Molloy. (Running to the wardrobe to prevent her) Oh, oh! I'll do that, Minnie! *(But she is too late. Minnie opens the right-hand cupboard door and falls back in terror, and screams.)*

Minnie. Oh, Mrs. Molloy! Help! There's a man! *(Mrs. Molloy with the following speech pushes her back to the workroom door. Minnie walks with one arm pointing at the cupboard. At the end of each of Mrs.*

500 *Molloy's sentences she repeats—at the same pitch and degree—the words—)* There's a man!

Mrs. Molloy. (Slamming cupboard door) Minnie, you imagined it. You're tired, dear. You go back in the workroom and lie down. Minnie, you're a fool; hold your tongue!

Minnie. There's a man! *(Exit Minnie to workroom)*

(Mrs. Molloy returns to the front of the stage. Vandergelder raises his stick threateningly.)

Vandergelder. If there's a man there, we'll get him out. Whoever you are, come out of there! *(Strikes table with his stick)*

510 *Mrs. Levi. (Goes masterfully to the cupboard—sweeps her umbrella around among the coats and closes each door as she does so.)* Nonsense! There's no man there. See! Miss Fay's nerves have been playing tricks on her. Come now, let's sit down again. What were you saying, Mr. Vandergelder? *(They sit, Mrs. Molloy right, Mrs. Levi center, Vandergelder left. A sneeze is heard from the cupboard. They all rise, look towards cupboard, then sit again.)* Well now . . . *(Another tremendous sneeze. With a gesture that says,* I can do no more:*)* God bless you! *(They all rise. Mrs. Molloy stands with her back to the cupboard.)*

Mrs. Molloy. (To Vandergelder) Yes, there is a man in there. I'll

520 explain it all to you another time. Thank you very much for coming to see me. Good afternoon, Dolly. Good afternoon, Mr. Vandergelder.

Vandergelder. You're protecting a man in there!

Mrs. Molloy. (With back to cupboard) There's a very simple explanation, but for the present, good afternoon. *(Barnaby now sneezes twice, lifting the table each time. Vandergelder, right of table, jerks off the tablecloth. Barnaby pulls cloth under table and rolls himself up in it. Mrs. Molloy picks up the box of chocolates, which has rolled on to the floor.)*

Mrs. Levi. Lord, the whole room's *crawling* with men! I'll never get over it. 530

Vandergelder. The world is going to pieces! I can't believe my own eyes!

Mrs. Levi. Come, Mr. Vandergelder. Ernestina Simple is waiting for us.

Vandergelder. (Finds his hat and puts it on) Mrs. Molloy, I shan't trouble you again, and *vice versa. (Mrs. Molloy is standing transfixed in front of cupboard, clasping the box of chocolates. Vandergelder snatches the box from her and goes out.)*

Mrs. Levi. (Crosses to her) Irene, when I think of all the interesting things you have in this room! *(Kisses her)* Make the most of it, dear. 540 *(Raps cupboard)* Good-by! *(Raps on table with umbrella)* Good-by! *(Exit Mrs. Levi. Mrs. Molloy opens door of cupboard. Cornelius steps out.)*

Mrs. Molloy. So that was one of your practical jokes, Mr. Hackl?

Cornelius. No, no, Mrs. Molloy!

Mrs. Molloy. Come out from under that, Barnaby Tucker, you troublemaker! *(She snatches the cloth and spreads it back on table. Minnie enters.)* There's nothing to be afraid of, Minnie, I know all about these gentlemen.

Cornelius. Mrs. Molloy, we realize that what happened here— 550

Mrs. Molloy. You think because you're rich you can make up for all the harm you do, is that it?

Cornelius. No, no!

Barnaby. (On the floor putting shoes on) No, no!

Mrs. Molloy. Minnie, this is the famous Cornelius Hackl who goes round New York tying people into knots; and that's Barnaby Tucker, another troublemaker.

Barnaby. How d'you do?

Mrs. Molloy. Minnie, choose yourself any hat and coat in the store. We're going out to dinner. If this Mr. Hackl is so rich and gay and 560 charming, he's going to be rich and gay and charming to us. He dines three nights a week at the Harmonia Gardens Restaurant, does he? Well, he's taking us there now.

Minnie. Mrs. Molloy, are you sure it's safe?

Mrs. Molloy. Minnie, hold your tongue. We're in a position to put these men into jail if they so much as squeak.

Cornelius. Jail, Mrs. Molloy?

Mrs. Molloy. Jail, Mr. Hackl. Officer Cogarty does everything I tell him to do. Minnie, you and I have been respectable for years; now we're 570 in disgrace, we might as well make the most of it. Come into the workroom with me; I know some ways we can perk up our appearances. Gentlemen, we'll be back in a minute.

Cornelius. Uh—Mrs. Molloy, I hear there's an awfully good restaurant at the railway station.

Mrs. Molloy. (High indignation) Railway station? Railway station? Certainly not! No, sir! You're going to give us a good dinner in the heart of the fashionable world. Go on in, Minnie! Don't you boys forget that you've made us lose our reputations, and now the fashionable world's the only place we can eat. *(Mrs. Molloy exits to workroom.)*

580 *Barnaby.* She's angry at us, Cornelius. Maybe we'd better run away now.

Cornelius. No, I'm going to go through with this if it kills me. Barnaby, for a woman like that a man could consent to go back to Yonkers and be a success.

Barnaby. All I know is no woman's going to make a success out of me.

Cornelius. Jail or no jail, we're going to take those ladies out to dinner. So grit your teeth.

(Enter Mrs. Molloy and Minnie from workroom dressed for the street)

Mrs. Molloy. Gentlemen, the cabs are at the corner, so forward 590 march! *(She takes a hat—which will be Barnaby's at the end of Act III —and gives it to Minnie.)*

Cornelius. Yes, ma'am. *(Barnaby stands shaking his empty pockets warningly.)* Oh, Mrs. Molloy . . . is it far to the restaurant? Couldn't we walk?

Mrs. Molloy. (Pauses a moment, then) Minnie, take off your things. We're not going.

Others. Mrs. Molloy!

Mrs. Molloy. Mr. Hackl, I don't go anywhere I'm not wanted. Good night. I'm not very happy to have met you. *(She crosses the stage as* 600 *though going to the workroom door.)*

Others. Mrs. Molloy!

Mrs. Molloy. I suppose you think we're not fashionable enough for you? Well, I won't be a burden to you. Good night, Mr. Tucker. *(The others follow her behind counter: Cornelius, Barnaby, then Minnie.)*

Cornelius. We want you to come with us more than anything in the world, Mrs. Molloy. *(Mrs. Molloy turns and pushes the three back. They are now near the center of the stage, to the right of the table, Mrs. Molloy facing the audience.)*

Mrs. Molloy. No, you don't! Look at you! Look at the pair of them, 610 Minnie! Scowling, both of them!

Cornelius. Please, Mrs. Molloy!

Mrs. Molloy. Then smile. *(To Barnaby)* Go on, smile! No, that's not enough. Minnie, you come with me and we'll get our own supper.

Cornelius. Smile, Barnaby, you lout!

Barnaby. My face can't smile any stronger than that.

Mrs. Molloy. Then do something! Show some interest. Do something lively: sing!

Cornelius. I can't sing, really I can't.

Mrs. Molloy. We're wasting our time, Minnie. They don't want us.

Cornelius. Barnaby, what can you sing? Mrs. Molloy, all we know are sad songs. 620

Mrs. Molloy. That doesn't matter. If you want us to go out with you, you've got to sing something. *(All this has been very rapid; the boys turn up to counter, put their heads together, confer and abruptly turn, stand stiffly and sing)* Tenting tonight; tenting tonight; tenting on the old camp ground. *(The four of them now repeat the refrain, softly harmonizing. At the end of the song, after a pause, Mrs. Molloy, moved, says)*

Mrs. Molloy. We'll come! *(The boys shout joyfully.)* You boys go ahead. *(Cornelius gets his hat from counter; as he puts it on he discovers the flowers on it. Barnaby gets his hat from window. They go out whistling. Minnie turns and puts her hat on at the mirror.)* Minnie, get the front door key—I'll lock the workroom. *(Mrs. Molloy goes to workroom. Minnie takes key from hook left of wardrobe and goes to Mrs. Molloy, at the workroom door. She turns her around.)* 630

Minnie. Why, Mrs. Molloy, you're crying! *(Mrs. Molloy flings her arms round Minnie.)*

Mrs. Molloy. Oh, Minnie, the world is full of wonderful things. Watch me, dear, and tell me if my petticoat's showing. *(She crosses to door, followed by Minnie, as—the curtain falls.)*

Act III

Veranda at the Harmonia Gardens Restaurant on the Battery, New York.

This room is informal and rustic. The main restaurant is indicated to be off stage back right.

There are three entrances: swinging double doors at the center of the back wall leading to the kitchen; one on the right wall (perhaps up a few steps and flanked by potted palms) to the street; one on the left wall to the staircase leading to the rooms above.

On the stage are two tables, left and right, each with four chairs. It is now afternoon and they are not yet set for dinner. Against the back wall is a large folding screen. Also against the back wall are hat and coat racks.

(As the curtain rises, Vandergelder is standing, giving orders to Rudolph, a waiter. Malachi Stack sits at table left.)

Vandergelder. Now, hear what I say. I don't want you to make any mistakes. I want a table for three.

Rudolph. (Tall "snob" waiter, alternating between cold superiority and rage. German accent) For three.

Vandergelder. There'll be two ladies and myself.

Malachi. It's a bad combination, Mr. Vandergelder. You'll regret it.

Vandergelder. And I want chicken.

10 *Malachi.* A chicken! You'll regret it.

Vandergelder. Hold your tongue. Write it down: chicken.

Rudolph. Yes, sir. Chicken Esterhazy? Chicken cacciatore? Chicken à la crème—?

Vandergelder. (Exploding) A chicken! A chicken like everybody else has. And with the chicken I want a bottle of wine.

Rudolph. Moselle? Chablis? Vouvray?

Malachi. He doesn't understand you, Mr. Vandergelder. You'd better speak louder.

Vandergelder. (Spelling) W-I-N-E.

20 *Rudolph.* Wine.

Vandergelder. Wine! And I want this table removed. We'll eat at that table alone. *(Exit Rudolph through service door at back.)*

Malachi. There are some people coming in here now, Mr. Vandergelder. *(Vandergelder goes to back right to look at the newcomers.)*

Vandergelder. What! Thunder and damnation! It's my niece Ermengarde! What's she doing here?!—Wait till I get my hands on her.

Malachi. (Running up to him) Mr. Vandergelder! You must keep your temper!

Vandergelder. And there's that rascal artist with her. Why, it's a 30 plot. I'll throw them in jail.

Malachi. Mr. Vandergelder! They're old enough to come to New York. You can't throw people into jail for coming to New York.

Vandergelder. And there's Mrs. Levi! What's she doing with them? It's a plot. It's a conspiracy! What's she saying to the cabman? Go up and hear what she's saying.

Malachi. (Listening at entrance, right) She's telling the cabman to wait, Mr. Vandergelder. She's telling the young people to come in and have a good dinner, Mr. Vandergelder.

Vandergelder. I'll put an end to this.

40 *Malachi.* Now, Mr. Vandergelder, if you lose your temper, you'll make matters worse. Mr. Vandergelder, come here and take my advice.

Vandergelder. Stop pulling my coat. What's your advice?

Malachi. Hide, Mr. Vandergelder. Hide behind this screen, and listen to what they're saying.

Vandergelder. (Being pulled behind the screen) Stop pulling at me. *(They hide behind the screen as Mrs. Levi, Ermengarde and Ambrose enter from the right. Ambrose is carrying Ermengarde's luggage.)*

Ermengarde. But I don't want to eat in a restaurant. It's not proper.

Mrs. Levi. Now, Ermengarde, dear, there's nothing wicked about eating in a restaurant. There's nothing wicked, even, about being in New York. Clergymen just make those things up to fill out their sermons. 50

Ermengarde. Oh, I wish I were in Yonkers, where *nothing* ever happens!

Mrs. Levi. Ermengarde, you're hungry. That's what's troubling you.

Ermengarde. Anyway, after dinner you must promise to take me to Aunt Flora's. She's been waiting for me all day and she must be half dead of fright.

Mrs. Levi. All right, but of course you know at Miss Van Huysen's you'll be back in your uncle's hands. 60

Ambrose. (Hands raised to heaven) I can't stand it.

Mrs. Levi. (To Ambrose) Just keep telling yourself how pretty she is. Pretty girls have very little opportunity to improve their other advantages.

Ambrose. Listen, Ermengarde! You don't want to go back to your uncle. Stop and think! That old man with one foot in the grave!

Mrs. Levi. And the other three in the cashbox.

Ambrose. Smelling of oats—

Mrs. Levi. And axle grease.

Malachi. That's not true. It's only partly true. 70

Vandergelder. (Loudly) Hold your tongue! I'm going to teach them a lesson.

Malachi. (Whisper) Keep your temper, Mr. Vandergelder. Listen to what they say.

Mrs. Levi. (Hears this; throws a quick glance toward the screen; her whole manner changes.) Oh dear, what was I saying? The Lord be praised, how glad I am that I found you two dreadful children just as you were about to break poor dear Mr. Vandergelder's heart.

Ambrose. He's got no heart to break!

Mrs. Levi. (Vainly signaling) Mr. Vandergelder's a much kinder man than you think. 80

Ambrose. Kinder? He's a wolf.

Mrs. Levi. Remember that he leads a very lonely life. Now you're going to have dinner upstairs. There are some private rooms up there, —just meant for shy timid girls like Ermengarde. Come with me. *(She pushes the young people out left, Ambrose carrying the luggage.)*

Vandergelder. (Coming forward) I'll show them! *(He sits at table right.)*

Malachi. Everybody should eavesdrop once in a while, I always say. 90 There's nothing like eavesdropping to show you that the world outside your head is different from the world inside your head.

Vandergelder. (Producing a pencil and paper) I want to write a note. Go and call that cabman in here. I want to talk to him.

Malachi. No one asks advice of a cabman, Mr. Vandergelder. They see so much of life that they have no ideas left.

Vandergelder. Do as I tell you.

Malachi. Yes, sir. Advice of a cabman! *(Exit right. Vandergelder writes his letter.)*

Vandergelder. "My dear Miss Van Huysen"—*(To audience)* Every- 100 body's dear in a letter. It's enough to make you give up writing 'em. "My dear Miss Van Huysen. This is Ermengarde and that rascal Ambrose Kemper. They are trying to run away. Keep them in your house until I come."

(Malachi returns with an enormous Cabman in a high hat and a long coat. He carries a whip.)

Cabman. (Entering) What's he want?

Vandergelder. I want to talk to you.

Cabman. I'm engaged. I'm waiting for my parties.

Vandergelder. (Folding letter and writing address) I know you are. 110 Do you want to earn five dollars?

Cabman. Eh?

Vandergelder. I asked you, do you want to earn five dollars?

Cabman. I don't know. I never tried.

Vandergelder. When those parties of yours come downstairs, I want you to drive them to this address. Never mind what they say, drive them to this address. Ring the bell: give this letter to the lady of the house: see that they get in the door and keep them there.

Cabman. I can't make people go into a house if they don't want to.

Vandergelder. (Producing purse) Can you for ten dollars?

120 *Cabman.* Even for ten dollars, I can't do it alone.

Vandergelder. This fellow here will help you.

Malachi. (Sitting at table left) Now I'm pushing people into houses.

Vandergelder. There's the address: Miss Flora Van Huysen, 8 Jackson Street.

Cabman. Even if I get them in the door I can't be sure they'll stay there.

Vandergelder. For fifteen dollars you can.

Malachi. Murder begins at twenty-five.

Vandergelder. Hold your tongue! *(To Cabman)* The lady of the house 130 will help you. All you have to do is to sit in the front hall and see that the man doesn't run off with the girl. I'll be at Miss Van Huysen's in an hour or two and I'll pay you then.

Cabman. If they call the police, I can't do anything.

Vandergelder. It's perfectly honest business. Perfectly honest.

Malachi. Every man's the best judge of his own honesty.

Vandergelder. The young lady is my niece. *(The Cabman laughs, skeptically.)* The young lady is my niece!! *(The Cabman looks at Malachi and shrugs.)* She's trying to run away with a good-for-nothing and we're preventing it.

Cabman. Oh, I know them, sir. They'll win in the end. Rivers don't run uphill. 140

Malachi. What did I tell you, Mr. Vandergelder? Advice of a cabman.

Vandergelder. (Hits table with his stick) Stack! I'll be back in half an hour. See that the table's set for three. See that nobody else eats here. Then go and join the cabman on the box.

Malachi. Yes, sir. *(Exit Vandergelder right)*

Cabman. Who's your friend?

Malachi. Friend!! That's not a friend; that's an employer I'm trying out for a few days.

Cabman. You won't like him. 150

Malachi. I can see you're in business for yourself because you talk about liking employers. No one's ever liked an employer since business began.

Cabman. Aw—!

Malachi. No, sir. I suppose you think *your horse* likes you?

Cabman. My old Clementine? She'd give her right feet for me.

Malachi. That's what all employers think. You imagine it. The streets of New York are full of cab horses winking at one another. Let's go in the kitchen and get some whiskey. I can't push people into houses when I'm sober. No, I've had about fifty employers in my life, but this is the most employer of them all. He talks to everybody as though he were paying them. 160

Cabman. I had an employer once. He watched me from eight in the morning until six at night—just sat there and watched me. Oh, dear! Even my mother didn't think I was as interesting as that.

(Cabman exits through service door.)

Malachi. (Following him off) Yes, being employed is like being loved: you know that somebody's thinking about you the whole time. *(Exits)* *(Enter right, Mrs. Molloy, Minnie, Barnaby and Cornelius)*

Mrs. Molloy. See! Here's the place I meant! Isn't it fine? Minnie, take off your things; we'll be here for hours. 170

Cornelius. (Stopping at door) Mrs. Molloy, are you sure you'll like it here? I think I feel a draught.

Mrs. Molloy. Indeed, I do like it. We're going to have a fine dinner right in this room; it's private, and it's elegant. Now we're all going to forget our troubles and call each other by our first names. Cornelius!

Call the waiter.

Cornelius. Wait—wait—I can't make a sound. I must have caught a cold on that ride. Wai—No! It won't come.

180 *Mrs. Molloy.* I don't believe you. Barnaby, you call him.

Barnaby. (Boldly) Waiter! Waiter! *(Cornelius threatens him. Barnaby runs left.)*

Minnie. I never thought I'd be in such a place in my whole life. Mrs. Molloy, is this what they call a "café."

Mrs. Molloy. (Sits at table left, facing audience) Yes, this a café. Sit down, Minnie. Cornelius, Mrs. Levi gave us to understand that every waiter in New York knew you.

Cornelius. They will. *(Barnaby sits at chair left; Minnie in chair back to audience.)*

190 *(Enter Rudolph from service door)*

Rudolph. Good evening, ladies and gentlemen.

Cornelius. (Shaking his hand) How are you, Fritz? How are you, my friend?

Rudolph. I am Rudolph.

Cornelius. Of course. Rudolph, of course. Well, Rudolph, these ladies want a little something to eat—you know what I mean? Just if you can find the time—we know how busy you are.

Mrs. Molloy. Cornelius, there's no need to be so familiar with the waiter. *(Takes menu from Rudolph)*

200 *Cornelius.* Oh, yes, there is.

Mrs. Molloy. (Passing menu across) Minnie, what do you want to eat?

Minnie. Just anything, Irene.

Mrs. Molloy. No, speak up, Minnie. What do you want?

Minnie. No, really, I have no appetite at all. *(Swings round in her chair and studies the menu, horrified at the prices)* Oh . . . Oh . . . I'd like some sardines on toast and a glass of milk.

Cornelius. (Takes menu from her) Great grindstones! What a sensible girl. Barnaby, shake Minnie's hand. She's the most sensible girl in the world. Rudolph, bring us gentlemen two glasses of beer, a loaf of

210 bread and some cheese.

Mrs. Molloy. (Takes menu) I never heard such nonsense. Cornelius, we've come here for a good dinner and a good time. Minnie, have you ever eaten pheasant?

Minnie. Pheasant? No-o-o-o!

Mrs. Molloy. Rudolph, have you any pheasant?

Rudolph. Yes, ma'am. Just in from New Jersey today.

Mrs. Molloy. Even the pheasants are leaving New Jersey. *(She laughs loudly, pushing Cornelius, then Rudolph; not from menu.)* Now, Rudolph, write this down: mock turtle soup; pheasant; mashed chest-

220 nuts; green salad; and some nice red wine. *(Rudolph repeats each item after her.)*

Cornelius. (Losing all his fears, boldly) All right, Barnaby, you watch me. *(He reads from the bill of fare.)* Rudolph, write this down: Neapolitan ice cream; hothouse peaches; champagne . . .

All. Champagne! *(Barnaby spins round in his chair.)*

Cornelius. (Holds up a finger) . . . and a German band. Have you got a German band?

Mrs. Molloy. No, Cornelius, I won't let you be extravagant. Champagne, but no band. Now, Rudolph, be quick about this. We're hungry. *(Exit Rudolph to kitchen. Mrs. Molloy crosses to right.)* Minnie, come 230 upstairs. I have an idea about your hair. I think it'd be nice in two wee horns—

Minnie. (Hurrying after her, turns and looks at the boys) Oh! Horns! *(They go out right. There is a long pause. Cornelius sits staring after them.)*

Barnaby. Cornelius, in the Army, you have to peel potatoes all the time.

Cornelius. (Not turning) Oh, that doesn't matter. By the time we get out of jail we can move right over to the Old Men's Home.

(Another waiter, August, enters from service door bearing a bottle of 240 *champagne in cooler, and five glasses. Mrs. Molloy re-enters right, followed by Minnie and stops August.)*

Mrs. Molloy. Waiter! What's that? What's that you have?

August. (Young waiter; baby face; is continually bursting into tears) It's some champagne, ma'am.

Mrs. Molloy. Cornelius; it's our champagne. *(All gather round August.)*

August. No, no. It's for His Honor the Mayor of New York and he's very impatient.

Mrs. Molloy. Shame on him! The Mayor of New York has more im- 250 portant things to be impatient about. Cornelius, open it. *(Cornelius takes the bottle, opens it and fills the glasses.)*

August. Ma'am, he'll kill me.

Mrs. Molloy. Well, have a glass first and die happy.

August. (Sits at table right, weeping) He'll kill me. *(Rudolph lays the cloth on the table, left.)*

Mrs. Molloy. I go to a public restaurant for the first time in ten years and all the waiters burst into tears. There, take that and stop crying, love. *(She takes a glass to August and pats his head, then comes back.)* Barnaby, make a toast! 260

Barnaby. (Center of the group, with naïve sincerity) I? . . . uh . . . To all the ladies in the world . . . may I get to know more of them . . . and . . . may I get to know them better. *(There is a hushed pause.)*

Cornelius. (Softly) To the ladies!

Mrs. Molloy. That's *very* sweet and *very* refined. Minnie, for that I'm going to give Barnaby a kiss.

Minnie. Oh!

Mrs. Molloy. Hold your tongue, Minnie. I'm old enough to be his mother, and—*(Indicating a height three feet from the floor)* a dear
270 wee mother I would have been too. Barnaby, this is for you from all the ladies in the world. *(She kisses him. Barnaby is at first silent and dazed, then—)*

Barnaby. Now I can go back to Yonkers, Cornelius. Pudding. Pudding. Pudding! *(He spins round and falls on his knees.)*

Mrs. Molloy. Look at Barnaby. He's not strong enough for a kiss. His head can't stand it. *(Exit August, right service door, with tray and cooler. The sound of "Les Patineurs" waltz comes from off left. Cornelius sits in chair facing audience, top of table. Minnie at left. Barnaby at right and Mrs. Molloy back to audience)* Minnie, I'm enjoying myself.
280 To think that this goes on in hundreds of places every night, while I sit at home darning my stockings. *(Mrs. Molloy rises and dances, alone, slowly about the stage.)* Cornelius, dance with me.

Cornelius. (Rises) Irene, the Hackls don't dance. We're Presbyterian.

Mrs. Molloy. Minnie, you dance with me. *(Minnie joins her. Cornelius sits again.)*

Minnie. Lovely music.

Mrs. Molloy. Why, Minnie, you dance beautifully.

Minnie. We girls dance in the workroom when you're not looking, Irene.

290 *Mrs. Molloy.* You thought I'd be angry! Oh dear, no one in the world understands anyone else in the world. *(The girls separate. Minnie dances off to her place at the table. Mrs. Molloy sits thoughtfully at table right. The music fades away.)* Cornelius! Jenny Lind and all those other ladies—do you see them all the time?

Cornelius. (Rises and joins her at table right) Irene, I've put them right out of my head. I'm interested in . . . *(Rudolph has entered by the service door. He now flings a tablecloth between them on table.)*

Mrs. Molloy. Rudolph, what are you doing?

Rudolph. A table's been reserved here. Special orders.

300 *Mrs. Molloy.* Stop right where you are. That party can eat inside. This veranda's ours.

Rudolph. I'm very sorry. This veranda is open to anybody who wants it. Ah, there comes the man who brought the order.

(Enter Malachi from the kitchen, drunk)

Mrs. Molloy. (To Malachi) Take your table away from here. We got here first, Cornelius, throw him out.

Malachi. Ma'am, my employer reserved this room at four o'clock this afternoon. You can go and eat in the restaurant. My employer said it was very important that he have a table alone.

310 *Mrs. Molloy.* No, sir. We got here first and we're going to stay here —alone, too. *(Minnie and Barnaby come forward.)*

Rudolph. Ladies and gentlemen!

Mrs. Molloy. Shut up, you! *(To Malachi)* You're an impertinent, idiotic kill-joy.

Malachi. (Very pleased) That's an insult!

Mrs. Molloy. All the facts about you are insults. *(To Cornelius)* Cornelius, do something. Knock it over! The table.

Cornelius. Knock it over. *(After a shocked struggle with himself Cornelius calmly overturns the table. August rights the table and picks up cutlery, weeping copiously.)* 320

Rudolph. (In cold fury) I'm sorry, but this room can't be reserved for anyone. If you want to eat alone, you must go upstairs. I'm sorry, but that's the rule.

Mrs. Molloy. We're having a nice dinner alone and we're going to stay here. Cornelius, knock it over. *(Cornelius overturns the table again. The girls squeal with pleasure. The waiter August again scrambles for the silver.)*

Malachi. Wait till you see my employer!

Rudolph. (Bringing screen down) Ladies and gentlemen! I'll tell you what we'll do. There's a big screen here. We'll put the screen up between the tables. August, come and help me. 330

Mrs. Molloy. I won't eat behind a screen. I won't. Minnie, make a noise. We're not animals in a menagerie. Cornelius, no screen. Minnie, there's a fight. I feel ten years younger. No screen! No screen! *(During the struggle with the screen all talk at once.)*

Malachi. (Loud and clear and pointing to entrance at right) Now you'll learn something. There comes my employer now, getting out of that cab.

Cornelius. (Coming to him, taking off his coat) Where? I'll knock him down too. *(Barnaby has gone up to right entrance. He turns and shouts clearly.)* 340

Barnaby. Cornelius, it's Wolf-trap. Yes, it is!

Cornelius. Wolf-trap! Listen, everybody. I think the screen's a good idea. Have you got any more screens, Rudolph? We could use three or four. *(He pulls the screen forward again.)*

Mrs. Molloy. Quiet down, Cornelius, and stop changing your mind. Hurry up, Rudolph, we're ready for the soup. *(During the following scene Rudolph serves the meal at the table left, as unobtrusively as possible. The stage is now divided in half. The quartet's table is at the left. Enter Vandergelder from the right. Now wears overcoat and carries the box of chocolates)* 350

Vandergelder. Stack! What's the meaning of this? I told you I wanted a table alone. What's that? *(Vandergelder hits the screen twice with his stick. Mrs. Molloy hits back twice with a spoon. The four young people sit: Barnaby facing audience, Mrs. Molloy right, Minnie left, and Cornelius back to audience.)*

Malachi. Mr. Vandergelder, I did what I could. Mr. Vandergelder, you wouldn't believe what wild savages the people of New York are. There's a woman over there, Mr. Vandergelder—civilization hasn't 360 touched her.

Vandergelder. Everything's wrong. You can't even manage a thing like that. Help me off with my coat. Don't kill me. Don't kill me. *(During the struggle with the overcoat Mr. Vandergelder's purse flies out of his pocket and falls by the screen. Vandergelder goes to the coat tree and hangs his coat up.)*

Mrs. Molloy. Speak up! I can't hear you.

Cornelius. My voice again. Barnaby, how's your throat? Can you speak?

Barnaby. Can't make a sound.

370 *Mrs. Molloy.* Oh, all right. Bring your heads together, and we'll whisper.

Vandergelder. Who are those people over there?

Malachi. Some city sparks and their girls, Mr. Vandergelder. What goes on in big cities, Mr. Vandergelder—best not think of it.

Vandergelder. Has that couple come down from upstairs yet? I hope they haven't gone off without your seeing them.

Malachi. No, sir. Myself and the cabman have kept our eyes on everything.

Vandergelder. (Sits at right of table, profile to the audience) I'll sit 380 here and wait for my guests. You go out to the cab.

Malachi. Yes, sir. *(Vandergelder unfurls newspaper and starts to read. Malachi sees the purse on the floor and picks it up.)* Eh, what's that? A purse. Did you drop something, Mr. Vandergelder?

Vandergelder. No. Don't bother me any more. Do as I tell you.

Malachi. (Stooping over. Coming center) A purse. That fellow over there must have let it fall during the misunderstanding about the screen. No, I won't look inside. Twenty-dollar bills, dozens of them. I'll go over and give it to him. *(Starts toward Cornelius, then turns and says to audience.)* You're surprised? You're surprised to see me getting 390 rid of this money so quickly, eh? I'll explain it to you. There was a time in my life when my chief interest was picking up money that didn't belong to me. The law is there to protect property, but—sure, the law doesn't care whether a property owner deserves his property or not, and the law has to be corrected. There are several thousands of people in this country engaged in correcting the law. For a while, I too was engaged in the redistribution of superfluities. A man works all his life and leaves a million to his widow. She sits in hotels and eats great meals and plays cards all afternoon and evening, with ten diamonds on her fingers. Call in the robbers! Call in the robbers! Or a 400 man leaves it to his son who stands leaning against bars all night boring a bartender. Call in the robbers! Stealing's a weakness. There are some people who say you shouldn't have any weaknesses at all—no vices. But if a man has no vices, he's in great danger of making vices out of his virtues, and there's a spectacle. We've all seen them: men who were monsters of philanthropy and women who were dragons of purity. We've seen people who told the truth, though the Heavens fall, —and the Heavens fell. No, no—nurse one vice in your bosom. Give it the attention it deserves and let your virtues spring up modestly around it. Then you'll have the miser who's no liar; and the drunkard who's the benefactor of a whole city. Well, after I'd had that weakness 410 of stealing for a while, I found another: I took to whisky—whisky took to me. And then I discovered an important rule that I'm going to pass on to you: Never support two weaknesses at the same time. It's your combination sinners—your lecherous liars and your miserly drunkards —who dishonor the vices and bring them into bad repute. So now you see why I want to get rid of this money: I want to keep my mind free to do the credit to whisky that it deserves. And my last word to you, ladies and gentlemen, is this: one vice at a time. *(Goes over to Cornelius)* Can I speak to you for a minute?

Cornelius. (Rises) You certainly can. We all want to apologize to 420 you about that screen—that little misunderstanding. *(They all rise, with exclamations of apology.)* What's your name, sir?

Malachi. Stack, sir. Malachi Stack. If the ladies will excuse you, I'd like to speak to you for a minute. *(Draws Cornelius down to front of stage)* Listen, boy, have you lost . . . ? Come here . . . *(Leads him further down, out of Vandergelder's hearing)* Have you lost something?

Cornelius. Mr. Stack, in this one day I've lost everything I own.

Malachi. There it is. *(Gives him purse)* Don't mention it.

Cornelius. Why, Mr. Stack . . . you know what it is? It's a miracle. *(Looks toward the ceiling)* 430

Malachi. Don't mention it.

Cornelius. Barnaby, come here a minute. I want you to shake hands with Mr. Stack. *(Barnaby, napkin tucked into his collar, joins them.)* Mr. Stack's just found the purse I lost, Barnaby. You know—the purse full of money.

Barnaby. (Shaking his hand vigorously) You're a wonderful man, Mr. Stack.

Malachi. Oh, it's nothing—nothing.

Cornelius. I'm certainly glad I went to church all these years. You're a good person to know, Mr. Stack. In a way. Mr. Stack, where do you 440 work?

Malachi. Well, I've just begun. I work for a Mr. Vandergelder in Yonkers. *(Cornelius is thunderstruck. He glances at Barnaby and turns to Malachi with awe. All three are swaying slightly, back and forth.)*

Cornelius. You do? It's a miracle. *(He points to the ceiling.)* Mr. Stack, I know you don't need it—but can I give you something for... for the good work?

Malachi. (Putting out his hand) Don't mention it. It's nothing. *(Starts to go left)*

450 *Cornelius.* Take that. *(Hands him a note)*

Malachi. (Taking note) Don't mention it.

Cornelius. And that. *(Another note)*

Malachi. (Takes it and moves away) I'd better be going.

Cornelius. Oh, here. And that.

Malachi. (Hands third note back) No... I might get to like them.

(Exit left. Cornelius bounds exultantly back to table.)

Cornelius. Irene, I feel a lot better about everything. Irene, I feel so well that I'm going to tell the truth.

Mrs. Molloy. I'd forgotten that, Minnie. Men get drunk so differently
460 from women. All right, what is the truth?

Cornelius. If I tell the truth, will you let me... will you let me put my arm around your waist? *(Minnie screams and flings her napkin over her face.)*

Mrs. Molloy. Hold your tongue, Minnie. All right, you can put your arm around my waist just to show it can be done in a gentlemanly way; but I might as well warn you: a corset is a corset.

Cornelius. (His arm around her; softly) You're a wonderful person, Mrs. Molloy.

Mrs. Molloy. Thank you. *(She removes his hand from around her*
470 *waist.)* All right, now that's enough. What is the truth?

Cornelius. Irene, I'm not as rich as Mrs. Levi said I was.

Mrs. Molloy. Not rich!

Cornelius. I almost never came to New York. And I'm not like she said I was,—bad. And I think you ought to know that at this very minute Mr. Vandergelder's sitting on the other side of that screen.

Mrs. Molloy. What! Well, he's not going to spoil any party of mine. So *that's* why we have been whispering? Let's forget all about Mr. Vandergelder and have some more wine. *(They start to sing softly.)* "The Sidewalks of New York."

480 *(Enter Mrs. Levi, from the street, in an elaborate dress. Vandergelder rises.)*

Mrs. Levi. Good evening, Mr. Vandergelder.

Vandergelder. Where's—where's Miss Simple?

Mrs. Levi. Mr. Vandergelder, I'll never trust a woman again as long as I live.

Vandergelder. Well? What is it?

Mrs. Levi. She ran away this afternoon and got married!

Vandergelder. She did?

Mrs. Levi. Married, Mr. Vandergelder, to a young boy of fifty.

Vandergelder. She did? 490

Mrs. Levi. Oh, I'm as disappointed as you are. I-can't-eat-a-thing-what-have-you-ordered?

Vandergelder. I ordered what you told me to, a chicken.

(Enter August. He goes to Vandergelder's table.)

Mrs. Levi. I don't think I could face a chicken. Oh, waiter. How do you do? What's your name?

August. August, ma'am.

Mrs. Levi. August, this is Mr. Vandergelder of Yonkers—Yonkers' most influential citizen, in fact. I want you to see that he's served with the best you have and served promptly. And there'll only be the two 500 of us. *(Mrs. Levi gives one set of cutlery to August. Vandergelder puts chocolate box under table.)* Mr. Vandergelder's been through some trying experiences today—what with men hidden all over Mrs. Molloy's store—like Indians in ambush.

Vandergelder. (Between his teeth) Mrs. Levi, you don't have to tell him everything about me. *(The quartet commences singing again very softly.)*

Mrs. Levi. Mr. Vandergelder, if you're thinking about getting married, you might as well learn right now you have to let women be women. Now, August, we want excellent service. 510

August. Yes, ma'am. *(Exits to kitchen)*

Vandergelder. You've managed things very badly. When I plan a thing it takes place. *(Mrs. Levi rises.)* Where are you going?

Mrs. Levi. Oh, I'd just like to see who's on the other side of that screen. *(Mrs. Levi crosses to the other side of the stage and sees the quartet. They are frightened and fall silent.)*

Cornelius. (Rising) Good evening, Mrs. Levi. *(Mrs. Levi takes no notice, but, taking up the refrain where they left off, returns to her place at the table right.)*

Vandergelder. Well, who was it? 520

Mrs. Levi. Oh, just some city sparks entertaining their girls, I guess.

Vandergelder. Always wanting to know everything; always curious about everything; always putting your nose into other people's affairs. Anybody who lived with you would get as nervous as a cat.

Mrs. Levi. What? What's that you're saying?

Vandergelder. I said anybody who lived with you would—

Mrs. Levi. Horace Vandergelder, get that idea right out of your head this minute. I'm surprised that you even mentioned such a thing. Understand once and for all that I have no intention of marrying you.

Vandergelder. I didn't mean that. 530

Mrs. Levi. You've been hinting around at such a thing for some time, but from now on put such ideas right out of your head.

Vandergelder. Stop talking that way. That's not what I meant at all.

Mrs. Levi. I hope not. I should hope not. Horace Vandergelder, you go your way. *(Points a finger)* And I'll go mine. *(Points in same direction)* I'm not some Irene Molloy, whose head can be turned by a pot of geraniums. Why, the idea of you even suggesting such a thing.

Vandergelder. Mrs. Levi, you misunderstood me.

540 *Mrs. Levi.* I certainly hope I did. If I had any intention of marrying again it would be to a far more pleasure-loving man than you. Why I'd marry Cornelius Hackl before I'd marry you. *(Cornelius raises his head in alarm. The others stop eating and listen.)* However, we won't discuss it any more. *(Enter August with a tray)* Here's August with our food. I'll serve it, August.

August. Yes, ma'am. *(Exit August)*

Mrs. Levi. Here's some white meat for you, and some giblets, very tender and very good for you. No, as I said before, you go your way and I'll go mine.—Start right in on the wine. I think you'll feel better 550 at once. However, since you brought the matter up, there's one more thing I think I ought to say.

Vandergelder. (Rising in rage) I didn't bring the matter up at all.

Mrs. Levi. We'll have forgotten all about it in a moment, but—sit down, sit down, we'll close the matter forever in just a moment, but there's one more thing I ought to say. *(Vandergelder sits down.)* It's true, I'm a woman who likes to know everything that's going on; who likes to manage things, you're perfectly right about that. But I wouldn't like to manage anything as disorderly as your household, as out of control, as untidy. You'll have to do that yourself, God helping you.

560 *Vandergelder.* It's not out of control.

Mrs. Levi. Very well, let's not say another word about it. Take some more of that squash, it's good. No, Horace, a complaining, quarrelsome, friendless soul like you is no sort of companion for me. You go your way. *(Peppers her own plate)* And I'll go mine. *(Peppers his plate)*

Vandergelder. Stop saying that.

Mrs. Levi. I won't say another word.

Vandergelder. Besides . . . I'm not those things you said I am.

Mrs. Levi. What?—Well, I guess you're friendless, aren't you? Ermengarde told me this morning you'd even quarreled with your 570 barber—a man who's held a razor to your throat for twenty years! Seems to me that that's sinking pretty low.

Vandergelder. Well, . . . but . . . my clerks, they . . .

Mrs. Levi. They like you? Cornelius Hackl and that Barnaby? Behind your back they call you Wolf-trap. *(Quietly the quartet at the other table have moved up to the screens—bringing chairs for Mrs. Molloy and Minnie. Wine glasses in hand, they overhear this conversation.)*

Vandergelder. (Blanching) They don't.

Mrs. Levi. No, Horace. It looks to me as though I were the last person in the world that liked you, and even I'm just so-so. No, for the rest 580 of my life I intend to have a good time. You'll be able to find some housekeeper who can prepare you three meals for a dollar a day—it can be done, you know, if you like cold baked beans. You'll spend your last days listening at keyholes, for fear someone's cheating you. Take some more of that.

Vandergelder. Dolly, you're a damned exasperating woman.

Mrs. Levi. There! You see? That's the difference between us. I'd be nagging you all day to get some spirit into you. You could be a perfectly charming, witty, amiable man, if you wanted to.

Vandergelder. (Rising, bellowing) I don't want to be charming. 590

Mrs. Levi. But you are. Look at you now. You can't hide it.

Vandergelder. (Sits) Listen at keyholes! Dolly, you have no right to say such things to me.

Mrs. Levi. At your age you ought to enjoy hearing the honest truth.

Vandergelder. My age! My age! You're always talking about my age.

Mrs. Levi. I don't know what your age is, but I do know that up at Yonkers with bad food and bad temper you'll double it in six months. Let's talk of something else; but before we leave the subject there's one more thing I *am* going to say.

Vandergelder. Don't! 600

Mrs. Levi. Sometimes, just sometimes, I think I'd be tempted to marry you out of sheer pity; and if the confusion in your house gets any worse I may *have* to.

Vandergelder. I haven't asked you to marry me.

Mrs. Levi. Well, *please don't.*

Vandergelder. And my house is not in confusion.

Mrs. Levi. What? With your niece upstairs in the restaurant right now?

Vandergelder. I've fixed that better than you know.

Mrs. Levi. And your clerks skipping around New York behind your 610 back?

Vandergelder. They're in Yonkers where they always are.

Mrs. Levi. Nonsense!

Vandergelder. What do you mean, nonsense?

Mrs. Levi. Cornelius Hackl's the other side of that screen this very minute.

Vandergelder. It ain't the same man!

Mrs. Levi. All right. Go on. Push it, knock it down. Go and see.

Vandergelder. (Goes to screen, pauses in doubt, then returns to his chair again) I don't believe it. 620

Mrs. Levi. All right. All right. Eat your chicken. Of course, Horace, if your affairs went from bad to worse and you became actually miserable, I might feel that it was my duty to come up to Yonkers and be of some assistance to you. After all, I was your wife's oldest friend.

Vandergelder. I don't know how you ever got any such notion. Now understand, once and for all, I have *no intention of marrying anybody.* Now, I'm tired and I don't want to talk. *(Cornelius crosses to extreme left, Mrs. Molloy following him.)*

630 *Mrs. Levi.* I won't say another word, either.

Cornelius. Irene, I think we'd better go. You take this money and pay the bill. Oh, don't worry, it's not mine.

Mrs. Molloy. No, no, I'll tell you what we'll do. You boys put on our coats and veils, and if he comes stamping over here, he'll think you're girls.

Cornelius. What! Those things!

Mrs. Molloy. Yes. Come on. *(She and Minnie take the clothes from the stand.)*

Vandergelder. (Rises) I've got a headache. I've had a bad day. I'm 640 going to Flora Van Huysen's, and then I'm going back to my hotel. *(Reaches for his purse)* So, here's the money to pay for the dinner. *(Searching another pocket)* Here's the money to pay for the . . . *(Going through all his pockets)* Here's the money . . . I've lost my purse!!

Mrs. Levi. Impossible! I can't imagine you without your purse.

Vandergelder. It's been stolen. *(Searching overcoat)* Or I left it in the cab. What am I going to do? I'm new at the hotel; they don't know me. I've never been here before. . . . Stop eating the chicken, I can't pay for it!

650 *Mrs. Levi. (Laughing gaily)* Horace, I'll be able to find some money. Sit down and calm yourself.

Vandergelder. Dolly Gallagher, I gave you twenty-five dollars this morning.

Mrs. Levi. I haven't a cent. I gave it to my lawyer. We can borrow it from Ambrose Kemper, upstairs.

Vandergelder. I wouldn't take it.

Mrs. Levi. Cornelius Hackl will lend it to us.

Vandergelder. He's in Yonkers—Waiter! *(Cornelius comes forward dressed in Mrs. Molloy's coat, thrown over his shoulder like a cape.* 660 *Mrs. Levi is enjoying herself immensely. Vandergelder again goes to back wall to examine the pockets of his overcoat.)*

Mrs. Molloy. Cornelius, is that Mr. Vandergelder's purse?

Cornelius. I didn't know it myself. I thought it was money just wandering around loose that didn't belong to anybody.

Mrs. Molloy. Goodness! That's what politicians think!

Vandergelder. Waiter! *(A band off left starts playing a polka. Barnaby comes forward dressed in Minnie's hat, coat and veil.)*

Minnie. Irene, doesn't Barnaby make a lovely girl? He just ought to stay that way. *(Mrs. Levi and Vandergelder move their table upstage while searching for the purse.)* 670

Mrs. Molloy. Why should we have our evening spoiled? Cornelius, I can teach you to dance in a few minutes. Oh, he won't recognize you.

Minnie. Barnaby, it's the easiest thing in the world. *(They move their table up against the back wall.)*

Mrs. Levi. Horace, you danced with me at your wedding and you danced with me at mine. Do you remember?

Vandergelder. No. Yes.

Mrs. Levi. Horace, you were a good dancer then. Don't confess to me that you're too old to dance. 680

Vandergelder. I'm not too old. I just don't want to dance.

Mrs. Levi. Listen to that music. Horace, do you remember the dances in the firehouse at Yonkers on Saturday nights? You gave me a fan. Come, come on! *(Vandergelder and Mrs. Levi start to dance. Cornelius dancing with Mrs. Molloy, bumps into Vandergelder, back to back. Vandergelder, turning, fails at first to recognize him, then does and roars.)*

Vandergelder. You're discharged! Not a word! You're fired! Where's that idiot, Barnaby Tucker? He's fired, too. *(The four young people, laughing, start rushing out the door to the street. Vandergelder, pointing* 690 *at Mrs. Molloy, shouts)* You're discharged!

Mrs. Molloy. (Pointing at him) You're discharged! *(Exit)*

Vandergelder. You're discharged! *(Enter from left, Ambrose and Ermengarde. To Ermengarde)* I'll lock you up for the rest of your life, young lady.

Ermengarde. Uncle! *(She faints in Ambrose's arms.)*

Vandergelder. (To Ambrose) I'll have you arrested. Get out of my sight. I never want to see you again.

Ambrose. (Carrying Ermengarde across to exit right) You can't do anything to me, Mr. Vandergelder. *(Exit Ambrose and Ermengarde)* 700

Mrs. Levi. (Who has been laughing heartily, follows the distraught Vandergelder about the stage as he continues to hunt for his purse) Well, there's your life, Mr. Vandergelder! Without niece—without clerks—without bride—and without your purse. *Will you marry me now?*

Vandergelder. No! *(To get away from her, he dashes into the kitchen. Mrs. Levi, still laughing, exclaims to the audience)*

Mrs. Levi. Damn!! *(And rushes off right. The curtain falls.)*

Act IV

Miss Flora Van Huysen's house.

This is a prosperous spinster's living room and is filled with knick-knacks, all in bright colors, and hung with family portraits, bird cages, shawls, etc.

There is only one entrance—a large double door in the center of the back wall. Beyond it one sees the hall which leads left to the street door and right to the kitchen and the rest of the house. On the left are big windows hung with lace curtains on heavy draperies. Front left is Miss Van Huysen's sofa, covered with bright-colored cushions, and behind it a table. On the right is another smaller sofa. Miss Van Huysen is lying on the sofa. The Cook is at the window, left. Miss Van Huysen, fifty, florid, stout and sentimental, is sniffing at smelling salts. Cook (enormous) holds a china mixing bowl.

Cook. No, ma'am. I could swear I heard a cab drawing up to the door.

Mrs. Van Huysen. You imagined it. Imagination. Everything in life . . . like that . . . disappointment . . . illusion. Our plans . . . our hopes . . . what becomes of them? Nothing. The story of my life. *(She sings for a moment.)*

Cook. Pray God nothing's happened to the dear girl. Is it a long journey from Yonkers?

Miss Van Huysen. No; but long enough for a thousand things to happen.

10 *Cook.* Well, we've been waiting all day. Don't you think we ought to call the police about it?

Miss Van Huysen. The police! If it's God's will, the police can't prevent it. Oh, in three days, in a week, in a year, we'll know what's happened. . . . And if anything *has* happened to Ermengarde, it'll be a lesson to *him*—that's what it'll be.

Cook. To who?

Miss Van Huysen. To that cruel uncle of hers, of course—to Horace Vandergelder, and to everyone else who tries to separate young lovers. Young lovers have enough to contend with as it is. Who should know

20 that better than I? No one. The story of my life. *(Sings for a moment, then)* There! Now I hear a cab. Quick!

Cook. No. No, ma'am. I don't see anything.

Miss Van Huysen. There! What did I tell you? Everything's imagination—illusion.

Cook. But surely, if they'd changed their plans Mr. Vandergelder would have sent you a message.

Miss Van Huysen. Oh, I know what's the matter. That poor child probably thought she was coming to another prison—to another tyrant. If she'd known that I was her friend, and a friend of all young

lovers, she'd be here by now. Oh, yes, she would. Her life shall not be 30
crossed with obstacles and disappointments as . . . Cook, a minute ago my smelling salts were on this table. Now they've completely disappeared.

Cook. Why, there they are, ma'am, right there in your hand.

Miss Van Huysen. Goodness! How did they get there? I won't inquire. Stranger things have happened!

Cook. I suppose Mr. Vandergelder was sending her down with someone?

Miss Van Huysen. Two can go astray as easily as . . . *(She sneezes.)*

Cook. God bless you! *(Runs to window)* Now, here's a carriage 40
stopping. *(The doorbell rings.)*

Miss Van Huysen. Well, open the door, Cook. *(Cook exits.)* It's probably some mistake. *(Sneezes again)* God bless you! *(Sounds of altercation off in hall)* It almost sounds as though I heard voices.

Cornelius. *(Off)* I don't want to come in. This is a free country, I tell you.

Cabman. *(Off)* Forward march!

Malachi. *(Off)* In you go. We have orders.

Cornelius. *(Off)* You can't make a person go where he doesn't want to go. 50

(Enter Malachi, followed by Cook. The Cabman bundles Barnaby and Cornelius into the room, but they fight their way back into the hall. Cornelius has lost Mrs. Molloy's coat, but Barnaby is wearing Minnie's clothes.)

Malachi. Begging your pardon, ma'am, are you Miss Van Huysen?

Miss Van Huysen. Yes, I am, unfortunately. What's all this noise about?

Malachi. There are two people here that Mr. Vandergelder said must be brought to this house and kept here until he comes. And here's his letter to you. 60

Miss Van Huysen. No one has any right to tell me whom I'm to keep in my house if they don't want to stay.

Malachi. You're right, ma'am. Everybody's always talking about people breaking into houses, ma'am; but there are more people in the world who want to break out of houses, that's what I always say. —Bring them in, Joe.

(Enter Cornelius and Barnaby being pushed by the Cabman.)

Cornelius. This young lady and I have no business here. We jumped into a cab and asked to be driven to the station and these men brought us to the house and forced us to come inside. There's been a mistake. 70

Cabman. Is your name Miss Van Huysen?

Miss Van Huysen. Everybody's asking me if my name's Miss Van Huysen. I think that's a matter I can decide for myself. Now will you all be quiet while I read this letter? . . . "This is Ermengarde and that rascal Ambrose Kemper" . . . Now I know who you two are, anyway. "They are trying to run away. . . ." Story of my life. "Keep them in your house until I come." Mr. Kemper, you have nothing to fear. *(To Cabman)* Who are you?

Cabman. I'm Joe. I stay here until the old man comes. He owes me 80 fifteen dollars.

Malachi. That's right, Miss Van Huysen, we must stay here to see they don't escape.

Miss Van Huysen. (To Barnaby) My dear child, take off your things. We'll all have some coffee. *(To Malachi and Cabman)* You two go out and wait in the hall. I'll send coffee out to you. Cook, take them *(Cook pushes Malachi and Cabman into the hall.)*

Cornelius. Ma'am, we're not the people you're expecting, and there's no reason . . .

Miss Van Huysen. Mr. Kemper, I'm not the tyrant you think I am. 90 . . . You don't have to be afraid of me. . . . I know you're trying to run away with this innocent girl. . . . All my life I have suffered from the interference of others. You shall not suffer as I did. So put yourself entirely in my hands. *(She lifts Barnaby's veil.)* Ermengarde! *(Kisses him on both cheeks)* Where's your luggage?

Barnaby. It's—uh—uh—it's . . .

Cornelius. Oh, I'll find it in the morning. It's been mislaid.

Miss Van Huysen. Mislaid! How like life! Well, Ermengarde; you shall put on some of my clothes.

Barnaby. Oh, I know I wouldn't be happy, really.

100 *Miss Van Huysen.* She's a shy little thing, isn't she? Timid little darling! . . . Cook! Put some gingerbread in the oven and get the coffee ready . . .

Cook. Yes, ma'am. *(Exits to kitchen)*

Miss Van Huysen. . . . while I go and draw a good hot bath for Ermengarde.

Cornelius. Oh, oh—Miss Van Huysen . . .

Miss Van Huysen. Believe me, Ermengarde, your troubles are at an end. You two will be married tomorrow. *(To Barnaby)* My dear, you look just like I did at your age, and your sufferings have been as 110 mine. While you're bathing, I'll come and tell you the story of my life.

Barnaby. Oh, I don't want to take a bath. I always catch cold.

Miss Van Huysen. No, dear, you won't catch cold. I'll slap you all over. I'll be back in a minute. *(Exit)*

Cornelius. (Looking out of window) Barnaby, do you think we could jump down from this window?

Barnaby. Yes—we'd kill ourselves.

Cornelius. We'll just have to stay here and watch for something to happen. Barnaby, the situation's desperate.

Barnaby. It began getting desperate about half-past four and it's been getting worse ever since. Now I have to take a bath and get 120
slapped all over.
(Enter Miss Van Huysen from kitchen)

Miss Van Huysen. Ermengarde, you've still got those wet things on. Your bath's nearly ready. Mr. Kemper, you come into the kitchen and put your feet in the oven. *(The doorbell rings. Enter Cook.)*
What's that? It's the doorbell. I expect it's your uncle.

Cook. There's the doorbell. *(At window)* It's *another* man and a girl in a cab!

Miss Van Huysen. Well, go and let them in, Cook. Now come with me, you two. Come, Ermengarde. *(Exit Cook. Miss Van* 130
Huysen drags Cornelius and the protesting Barnaby off into the kitchen.)

Cook. (Off) No, that's impossible. Come in, anyway.
(Enter Ermengarde, followed by Ambrose, carrying the two pieces of luggage)
There's some mistake. I'll tell Miss Van Huysen, but there's some mistake.

Ermengarde. But, I tell you, I *am* Mr. Vandergelder's niece; I'm Ermengarde.

Cook. Beg your pardon, Miss, but you *can't* be Miss Ermengarde.

Ermengarde. But—but—here I *am.* And that's my baggage. 140

Cook. Well, I'll tell Miss Van Huysen who you *think* you are, but she won't like it. *(Exits)*

Ambrose. You'll be all right now, Ermengarde. I'd better go before she sees me.

Ermengarde. Oh, no. You must stay. I feel so strange here.

Ambrose. I know, but Mr. Vandergelder will be here in a minute....

Ermengarde. Ambrose, you can't go. You can't leave me in this crazy house with those drunken men in the hall. Ambrose ... Ambrose, let's say you're someone else that my uncle sent down to take care of me. Let's say you're—you're Cornelius Hackl! 150

Ambrose. Who's Cornelius Hackl!

Ermengarde. You know. He's chief clerk in Uncle's store.

Ambrose. I don't want to be Cornelius Hackl! No, no, Ermengarde, come away with me now. I'll take you to my friend's house. Or I'll take you to Mrs. Levi's house.

Ermengarde. Why, it was Mrs. Levi who threw us right at Uncle Horace's face. Oh, I wish I were back in Yonkers where nothing ever happens.
(Enter Miss Van Huysen)

Miss Van Huysen. What's all this I hear? Who do you say you are? 160

Ermengarde. Aunt Flora ... don't you remember me? I'm Ermengarde.

Miss Van Huysen. And you're Mr. Vandergelder's niece?

Ermengarde. Yes, I am.

Miss Van Huysen. Well, that's very strange indeed, because he has just sent me another niece named Ermengarde. She came with a letter from him, explaining everything. Have you got a letter from him?

Ermengarde. No . . .

Miss Van Huysen. Really!—And who is this?

170 *Ermengarde.* This is Cornelius Hackl, Aunt Flora.

Miss Van Huysen. Never heard of him.

Ermengarde. He's chief clerk in Uncle's store.

Miss Van Huysen. Never heard of him. The other Ermengarde came with the man she's in love with, and that *proves* it. She came with Mr. Ambrose Kemper.

Ambrose. (Shouts) Ambrose Kemper!

Miss Van Huysen. Yes, Mr. Hackl, and Mr. Ambrose Kemper is in the kitchen there now *with his feet in the oven. (Ermengarde starts to cry. Miss Van Huysen takes her to the sofa. They both sit.)* Dear

180 child, what is your trouble?

Ermengarde. Oh, dear. I don't know what to do.

Miss Van Huysen. (In a low voice) Are you in love with this man?

Ermengarde. Yes, I am.

Miss Van Huysen. I could see it—and are people trying to separate you?

Ermengarde. Yes, they are.

Miss Van Huysen. I could see it—who? Horace Vandergelder?

Ermengarde. Yes.

Miss Van Huysen. That's enough for me. I'll put a stop to Horace

190 Vandergelder's goings on. *(Miss Van Huysen draws Ambrose down to sit on her other side.)* Mr. Hackl, think of me as your friend. Come in the kitchen and get warm. . . . *(She rises and starts to go out.)* We can decide later who everybody is. My dear, would you like a good hot bath?

Ermengarde. Yes, I would.

Miss Van Huysen. Well, when Ermengarde comes out you can go in. *(Enter Cornelius from the kitchen)*

Cornelius. Oh, Miss Van Huysen . . .

Ermengarde. Why, Mr. Hack—!!

Cornelius. (Sliding up to her, urgently) Not yet! I'll explain. I'll

200 explain everything.

Miss Van Huysen. Mr. Kemper!—Mr. Kemper! This is Mr. Cornelius Hackl. *(To Ambrose)* Mr. Hackl, this is Mr. Ambrose Kemper. *(Pause, while the men glare at one another)* Perhaps you two know one another?

Ambrose. No!

Cornelius. No, we don't.

Ambrose. (Hotly) Miss Van Huysen, I know that man is not Ambrose Kemper.

Cornelius. (Ditto) And he's not Cornelius Hackl.

Miss Van Huysen. My dear young men, what does it matter what your names are? The important thing is that you are you. *(To Ambrose)* You are alive and breathing, aren't you, Mr. Hackl? *(Pinches Ambrose's left arm)* 210

Ambrose. Ouch, Miss Van Huysen.

Miss Van Huysen. This dear child imagines she is Horace Vandergelder's niece Ermengarde.

Ermengarde. But I am.

Miss Van Huysen. The important thing is that you're all in love. Everything else is illusion. *(She pinches Cornelius' arm.)*

Cornelius. Ouch! Miss Van Huysen! 220

Miss Van Huysen. (Comes down and addresses the audience) Everybody keeps asking me if I'm Miss Van Huys . . . *(She seems suddenly to be stricken with doubt as to who she is; her face shows bewildered alarm. She pinches herself on the upper arm and is abruptly and happily relieved.)* Now, you two gentlemen sit down and have a nice chat while this dear child has a good hot bath. *(The doorbell rings. Ermengarde exits, Miss Van Huysen about to follow her, but stops. Enter Cook.)*

Cook. There's the doorbell again.

Miss Van Huysen. Well, answer it.

(She and Ermengarde exit to kitchen.) 230

Cook. (At window, very happy about all these guests) It's a cab and three ladies. I never saw such a night. *(Exit to front door)*

Miss Van Huysen. Gentlemen, you can rest easy. I'll see that Mr. Vandergelder lets his nieces marry you both.

(Enter Mrs. Levi)

Mrs. Levi. Flora, how are you?

Miss Van Huysen. Dolly Gallagher! What brings you here?

Mrs. Levi. Great Heavens, Flora, what are those two drunken men doing in your hall?

Miss Van Huysen. I don't know. Horace Vandergelder sent them to me. 240

Mrs. Levi. Well, I've brought you two girls in much the same condition. Otherwise they're the finest girls in the world. *(She goes up to the door and leads in Mrs. Molloy. Minnie follows.)* I want you to meet Irene Molloy and Minnie Fay.

Miss Van Huysen. Delighted to know you.

Mrs. Levi. Oh, I see you two gentlemen are here, too. Mr. Hackl, I was about to look for you. *(Pointing about the room) Somewhere* here.

Cornelius. No, Mrs. Levi. I'm ready to face anything now.

250 *Mrs. Levi.* Mr. Vandergelder will be here in a minute. He's downstairs trying to pay for a cab without any money.

Mrs. Molloy. (Holding Vandergelder's purse) Oh, I'll help him.

Mrs. Levi. Yes, will you, dear? You had to pay the restaurant bills. You must have hundreds of dollars there it seems.

Mrs. Molloy. This is his own purse he lost. I can't give it back to him without seeming...

Mrs. Levi. I'll give it back to him.—There, you help him with this now. *(She gives Mrs. Molloy a bill and puts the purse airily under her arm.)*

260 *Vandergelder. (Off)* Will somebody please pay for this cab?

(Mrs. Molloy exits to front door.)

Mrs. Molloy. (Off stage) I'll take care of that, Mr. Vandergelder. *(As Mr. Vandergelder enters, Malachi and the Cabman follow him in. Vandergelder carries overcoat, stick and box of chocolates.)*

Cabman. Fifteen dollars, Mr. Vandergelder.

Malachi. Hello, Mr. Vandergelder.

Vandergelder. (To Malachi) You're discharged! *(To Cabman.)* You too! *(Malachi and Cabman go out and wait in the hall.)* So I've caught up with you at last! *(To Ambrose)* I never want to see you again! *(To*

270 *Cornelius)* You're discharged! Get out of the house, both of you. *(He strikes sofa with his stick; a second after, Miss Van Huysen strikes him on the shoulder with a folded newspaper or magazine.)*

Miss Van Huysen. (Forcefully) Now then you. Stop ordering people out of my house. You can shout and carry on in Yonkers, but when you're in my house you'll behave yourself.

Vandergelder. They're both dishonest scoundrels.

Miss Van Huysen. Take your hat off. Gentlemen, you stay right where you are.

Cornelius. Mr. Vandergelder, I can explain—

280 *Miss Van Huysen.* There aren't going to be any explanations. Horace, stop scowling at Mr. Kemper and forgive him.

Vandergelder. That's not Kemper, that's a dishonest rogue named Cornelius Hackl.

Miss Van Huysen. You're crazy. *(Points to Ambrose)* That's Cornelius Hackl.

Vandergelder. I guess I know my own chief clerk.

Miss Van Huysen. I don't care what their names are. You shake hands with them both, or out you go.

Vandergelder. Shake hands with those dogs and scoundrels!

290 *Mrs. Levi.* Mr. Vandergelder, you've had a hard day. You don't want to go out in the rain now. Just for form's sake, you shake hands with them. You can start quarreling with them tomorrow.

Vandergelder. (Gives Cornelius one finger to shake) There! Don't regard that as a handshake. *(He turns to Ambrose who mockingly offers him one finger.)* Hey! I never want to see you again.
(Mrs. Molloy enters from front door.)
Mrs. Molloy. Miss Van Huysen.
Miss Van Huysen. Yes, dear?
Mrs. Molloy. Do I smell coffee?
Miss Van Huysen. Yes, dear. 300
Mrs. Molloy. Can I have some, good and black?
Miss Van Huysen. Come along, everybody. We'll all go into the kitchen and have some coffee. *(As they all go)* Horace, you'll be interested to know there are two Ermengardes in there. . . .
Vandergelder. Two!! *(Last to go is Minnie, who revolves about the room dreamily waltzing, a finger on her forehead. Mrs. Levi has been standing at one side. She now comes forward, in thoughtful mood. Minnie continues her waltz round the left sofa and out to the kitchen. Mrs. Levi, left alone, comes to the front, addressing an imaginary Ephraim.)* 310
Mrs. Levi. Ephraim Levi, I'm going to get married again. Ephraim, I'm marrying Horace Vandergelder for his money. I'm going to send his money out doing all the things you taught me. Oh, it won't be a marriage in the sense that we had one—but I shall certainly make him happy, and Ephraim—I'm tired. I'm tired of living from hand to mouth, and I'm asking your permission, Ephraim—will you give me away? *(Now addressing the audience, she holds up the purse.)* Money! Money! —it's like the sun we walk under; it can kill or cure.—Mr. Vandergelder's money! Vandergelder's never tired of saying most of the people in the world are fools, and in a way he's right, isn't he? Him- 320 self, Irene, Cornelius, myself! But there comes a moment in everybody's life when he must decide whether he'll live among human beings or not—a fool among fools or a fool alone. As for me, I've decided to live among them. I wasn't always so. After my husband's death I retired into myself. Yes, in the evenings, I'd put out the cat, and I'd lock the door, and I'd make myself a little rum toddy; and before I went to bed I'd say a little prayer, thanking God that I was independent—that no one else's life was mixed up with mine. And when ten o'clock sounded from Trinity Church tower, I fell off to sleep and I was a perfectly contented woman. And one night, after two years of this, an oak leaf 330 fell out of my Bible. I had placed it there on the day my husband asked me to marry him; a perfectly good oak leaf—but without color and without life. And suddenly I realized that for a long time I had not shed one tear; nor had I been filled with the wonderful hope that something or other would turn out well. I saw that I was like that oak leaf, and on that night I decided to rejoin the human race. Yes, we're all fools

and we're all in danger of destroying the world with our folly. But the surest way to keep us out of harm is to give us the four or five human pleasures that are our right in the world,—and that takes a little *money!*
340 The difference between a little money and no money at all is enormous —and can shatter the world. And the difference between a little money and an enormous amount of money is very slight—and that, also, can shatter the world. Money, I've always felt, money—pardon my expression—is like manure; it's not worth a thing unless it's spread about encouraging young things to grow. Anyway,—that's the opinion of the second Mrs. Vandergelder.

(Vandergelder enters with two cups of coffee. With his back, he closes both doors.)

Vandergelder. Miss Van Huysen asked me to bring you this.

350 *Mrs. Levi.* Thank you both. Sit down and rest yourself. What's been going on in the kitchen?

Vandergelder. A lot of foolishness. Everybody falling in love with everybody. I forgave 'em; Ermengarde and that artist.

Mrs. Levi. I knew you would.

Vandergelder. I made Cornelius Hackl my partner.

Mrs. Levi. You won't regret it.

Vandergelder. Dolly, you said some mighty unpleasant things to me in the restaurant tonight . . . all that about my house . . . and everything.

Mrs. Levi. Let's not say another word about it.

360 *Vandergelder.* Dolly, you have a lot of faults—

Mrs. Levi. Oh, I know what you mean.

Vandergelder. You're bossy, scheming, inquisitive . . .

Mrs. Levi. Go on.

Vandergelder. But you're a wonderful woman. Dolly, marry me.

Mrs. Levi. Horace! *(Rises)* Stop right there.

Vandergelder. I know I've been a fool about Mrs. Molloy, and that other woman. But, Dolly, forgive me and marry me. *(He goes on his knees.)*

Mrs. Levi. Horace, I don't dare. No. I don't dare.

370 *Vandergelder.* What do you mean?

Mrs. Levi. You know as well as I do that you're the first citizen of Yonkers. Naturally, you'd expect your wife to keep open house, to have scores of friends in and out all the time. Any wife of yours should be used to that kind of thing.

Vandergelder. *(After a brief struggle with himself)* Dolly, you can live any way you like.

Mrs. Levi. Horace, you can't deny it, your wife would have to be a *somebody.* Answer me: am I a somebody?

Vandergelder. You are . . . you are. Wonderful woman.

380 *Mrs. Levi.* Oh, you're partial. *(She crosses, giving a big wink at the audience, and sits on sofa right. Vandergelder follows her on his knees.)*

Horace, it won't be enough for you to load your wife with money and jewels; to insist that she be a benefactress to half the town. *(He rises and, still struggling with himself, coughs so as not to hear this.)* No, she must be a somebody. Do you really think I have it in me to be a credit to you?

Vandergelder. Dolly, everybody knows that you could do anything you wanted to do.

Mrs. Levi. I'll try. With your help, I'll try—and by the way, I found your purse. *(Holds it up)* 390

Vandergelder. Where did you—! Wonderful woman!

Mrs. Levi. It just walked into my hand. I don't know how I do it. Sometimes I frighten myself. Horace, take it. Money walks out of my hands, too.

Vandergelder. Keep it. Keep it.

Mrs. Levi. Horace! *(Half laughing, half weeping, and with an air of real affection for him)* I never thought . . . I'd ever . . . hear you say a thing like that!

(Barnaby dashes in from the kitchen in great excitement. He has discarded Minnie's clothes.) 400

Barnaby. Oh! Excuse me. I didn't know anybody was here.

Vandergelder. (Bellowing) Didn't know anybody was here. Idiot!

Mrs. Levi. (Putting her hand on Vandergelder's arm; amiably) Come in, Barnaby. Come in. *(Vandergelder looks at her a minute; then says, imitating her tone)*

Vandergelder. Come in, Barnaby. Come in.

Barnaby. Cornelius is going to marry Mrs. Molloy!

Mrs. Levi. Isn't that fine! Horace!... *(Mrs. Levi rises, and indicates that he has an announcement to make.)*

Vandergelder. Barnaby, go in and tell the rest of them that Mrs. Levi 410 has consented—

Mrs. Levi. Finally consented!

Vandergelder. Finally consented to become my wife.

Barnaby. Holy cabooses. *(Dashes back to the doorway)* Hey! Listen, everybody! Wolf-trap—I mean—Mr. Vandergelder is going to marry Mrs. Levi.

(Miss Van Huysen enters followed by all the people in this act. She is now carrying the box of chocolates.)

Miss Van Huysen. Dolly, that's the best news I ever heard. *(She addresses the audience.)* There isn't any more coffee; there isn't any 420 more gingerbread; but there are three couples in my house and they're all going to get married. And do you know, one of those Ermengardes wasn't a dear little girl at all—she was a boy! Well, that's what life is: disappointment, illusion.

Mrs. Levi. (To audience) There isn't any more coffee; there isn't any more gingerbread, and there isn't any more play—but there is

one more thing we have to do. . . . Barnaby, come here. *(She whispers to him, pointing to the audience. Then she says to the audience)* I think the youngest person here ought to tell us what the moral of the
430 play is. *(Barnaby is reluctantly pushed forward to the footlights.)*

Barnaby. Oh, I think it's about . . . I think it's about adventure. The test of an adventure is that when you're in the middle of it, you say to yourself, "Oh, now I've got myself into an awful mess; I wish I were sitting quietly at home." And the sign that something's wrong with you is when you sit quietly at home wishing you were out having lots of adventure. What we would like for you is that you have just the right amount of sitting quietly at home and just the right amount of —adventure! So that now we all want to thank you for coming tonight, and we all hope that in your lives you have just the right amount
440 of—adventure! *(The curtain falls.)*

Comments and Questions

The essays by Thornton Wilder and Barnard Hewitt included in this text offer a good deal of material for discussion. Though Wilder's essay presents his views on drama in general, it offers much that is relevant to The Matchmaker, *particularly in section III, which defines a theater of pretense, instead of one of illusion, a distinction on which Hewitt places much emphasis. What precisely is the difference? On the basis of Wilder's explanation, what dramatic conventions do you observe in* The Matchmaker? *Wilder mentions that the two functions of a convention are that "it provokes the collaborative activity of the spectator's imagination; and . . . raises the action from the specific to general." Are both functions operative in* The Matchmaker, *and if so, how?*

Hewitt questions the applicability to Wilder's play of Eric Bentley's explanation of the nature of our pleasure in watching farce. Which critic is more nearly right as far as this play is concerned? A traditional and basic distinction between farce and other forms of comedy is that comedy rises above horseplay and buffoonery, to let us laugh at our own foibles and follies in more particularized and realistic characters than farce employs. Can The Matchmaker, *then, be classified as not a simple farce, but a comedy that achieves "a generalized truth"? In answering this question, consider the degree to which we sympathize with all of the characters and understand their motivations. Observe the speeches and soliloquies which make or suggest general comments on life, such as Malachi Stack's on the virtues of possessing a single vice, and Dolly's on the right use of money.*

Related Reading

Ben Jonson, *The Alchemist* (page 354) and Molière, *Scapin* (page 311) for comparison as farcical comedies and the differing ways of playing the confidence game

Barnard Hewitt, "Thornton Wilder Says 'Yes'," page 701

Louis Kronenberger, "Some Prefatory Remarks on Comedy," page 680

(Jean-Baptiste Poquelin) Molière

(1622-1673)

SCAPIN

translated by Martin Roth

Molière, like Shakespeare, was an actor who wrote his plays for the theatrical company to which he belonged. Unlike Shakespeare, he was also the head of his troupe and usually performed the main roles. In Les Fourberies de Scapin (The Knaveries of Scapin), *which was first given on May 24, 1671, Molière had the title role. The play was not an immediate success but found its place slowly among the playwright's major works. Molière's acting troupe became the official French national theater, the Comédie Française, not long after his death in 1673 and has kept most of his plays in its repertoire over the centuries.* Scapin *has been given more than a thousand times at the Comédie Française, apart from productions in other theaters in France and elsewhere.*

On the surface it is a very simple play. It deals with two young men, Leandro and Octavio, who have fallen in love with two young ladies of whom they know very well their fathers will not approve. At the outset of the play, Octavio's father is about to return from a long voyage, intent on marrying off his son to the daughter of his friend Gerontio, Leandro's father. Both young men are threatened with imminent fireworks for their rash involvements and turn to the servant Scapin for help and advice. The rest is disguises, con games, mistaken identities, beatings, and all the other comic and farcical elements handed down from antiquity. Scapin improvises wildly, and with great resourcefulness, to save the young masters from the fury of their fathers. In the process he generally gets the short end of the stick (usually drumming on his own back), but he doggedly keeps on trying.

The clever servant was a stock character in the older comedies. Face, in Ben Jonson's The Alchemist, *is another example. The servant as such is important, of course, in an age in which all but the poor had at least one or two. They served for one's daily needs and were as little of a rarity as the car is for the middle class in America today. The servant who is cleverer than his master was a figure of comedy, because he turned the small world in which he moved upside down. His social position was the opposite of the position which his wits enabled him to hold. Such a servant could, like Face in* The Alchemist, *con "his betters" (i.e., his social superiors) out of money, or, like Scapin, he could con his old master out of his undisputed right to marry off his son as he pleased.*

European marriages, until quite recent times, were not considered something that called for love, but something that stood in need of planning by people of wisdom—that is, parents. Love had little to do with money; marriage, in the view of mature wisdom, had much to do with money, and the money was expected to come in the form of the girl's "marriage portion." Marriage, therefore, entailed dowries along with the hands of beauteous ladies, and the size of the dowry made up for what the lady lacked in beauty or youth. The converse, however, was not true; a dowerless young beauty like Hyacinth had little chance of finding a good husband, one of good family with some money. His father would see to that.

Though the intrigues of Scapin *are varied, they all have one aim: to save Leandro and his friend Octavio. There are no subplots as with Shakespeare or Jonson; no characters are introduced for their own sakes or for the sake of criticizing, or making fun of, some particular profession or class of people. The appeal of* Scapin *lies in Molière's ability to reveal human characteristics stripped of the veneer of social position, class, or background and to pare men down—not always to our comfort—to their basic traits.*

The adaptation printed here was first given at the University of Chicago in July of 1960. The translator teaches English at the University of Minnesota.

SCAPIN

Characters

ARGANTIO
OCTAVIO, *his son*
GERONTIO
LEANDRO, *his son*
ZERBINETTA, *a gypsy, loved by Leandro*
HYACINTH, *loved by Octavio*
SCAPIN, *Leandro's valet*
SYLVESTRO, *Octavio's valet*
NERINA, *Hyacinth's nurse*
CARLE, *a cheat*

Act I

Scene I. *Octavio, Sylvestro*

Octavio. Oh! Oh! Oh! Sylvestro, I'll go mad, I promise you, unless you confess that all you've been telling me is a lie. Sylvestro? You've made it up to frighten me, haven't you? No? Then I *shall* go mad. Lovers are such sensitive people; anything can upset us, but especially monstrous news like this. Now, once again, you rascal, did you really hear that my father—oh! I can hardly get the words out—is returning?

Sylvestro. Yes.

Octavio. And that he is to arrive—what a cursed day—this morning?

Sylvestro. This very morning.

Octavio. And that he's determined—the words stick in my throat—to marry me off? 10

Sylvestro. That's right.

Octavio. To Signor Gerontio's daughter?

Sylvestro. Old Gerontio.

Octavio. And this girl is being sent from Tarentum for that purpose?

Sylvestro. Yes.

Octavio. And you heard all this from my uncle?

Sylvestro. Your uncle.

Octavio. Who got it from my father, himself, in a letter?

Sylvestro. A letter. 20

Octavio. And my uncle, you say, knows all that we have been doing?

Sylvestro. Everything.

Octavio. Why don't you say something? Why do I have to pry this information out of you word by word?

Sylvestro. What more can I say? You haven't left anything out. You state each fact precisely as I heard it.

Octavio. You can at least tell me what to do in this damned predicament.

Sylvestro. To tell you the truth, I'm as dumbfounded as you. I could 30 use a little advice myself.

Octavio. I'm absolutely crucified by this cursed homecoming.

Sylvestro. You may be cursed, but I'm afraid something stronger is in store for me.

Octavio. When my father learns what has happened! . . . I can see his face now, turning redder and uglier each moment until it finally explodes with a storm of thundering castigation.

Sylvestro. Castigation is nothing; may it please Heaven to get me off so cheaply. But I shall probably pay dearly for your follies. When your storm has died down, I see a cloud of thuds and thumps that will burst 40 in a fury over my shoulders and backside.

Octavio. Oh Heaven! How shall I ever get out of this fix?

Sylvestro. You should have thought of that before you got into it.

Octavio. You'll be the death of me with your cowardly whining.

Sylvestro. You have already sealed my doom with your scatterbrained actions.

Octavio. Oh, shut up. Oh, what can I do? Whom can I turn to? Can any remedy serve me now?

Scene II. *Scapin, Octavio, Sylvestro*

Scapin. Sir, what's wrong? What's the matter? What's happened? What upsets you so? I can see that something is bothering you.

Octavio. My dear Scapin, I am lost, desperate. I'm the most unfortunate man alive.

Scapin. Why?

Octavio. You haven't heard?

Scapin. I've heard nothing.

Octavio. My father will soon be here and he wants me to get married?

Scapin. What's so disturbing about that?

10 *Octavio.* Alas! You don't understand. Lovers are always alone in this ugly world.

Scapin. But Sir, if you lovers would only tell your servants what upsets you lovers continually, we might understand more and you might moan less. Have no scruples about telling me; I'm the comforting sort and I love to meddle in the affairs of young men.

Octavio. Ah, Scapin, if you could only contrive some plan, make up some lie, to get me out of this wretched fix, I would owe more to you than to this air I breathe.

Scapin. To tell you the truth, there are very few situations I cannot straighten out when I am in my meddling mood. Heaven has endowed 20 me with a natural gift for all those delicate and sophisticated fabrications of conversation and intrigue which the vulgar call lies and deceit; I can honestly say that the world has seen few men more clever, more crafty at underhanded schemes than I. Very few have acquired more fame at this noble pastime. But, I vow, the world treats true merit so roughly these days that I have given up my good works... since my recent misfortunes.

Octavio. What misfortunes?

Scapin. A trifle, wherein I had some dealings with the law.

Octavio. The law? 30

Scapin. Yes, we had some unprofitable dealings with each other.

Sylvestro. You and the law?

Scapin. Yes, and it used me badly too, and I have been so vexed at the base ingratitude of society that I have decided never to help it again in the future. But enough of that. I'm dying to hear your story.

Octavio Alas, my story. Well, you know, Scapin, that two months ago Signor Gerontio and my father embarked on a commercial venture together?

Scapin. I know that.

Octavio. And Leandro, Gerontio's son, and I were left behind. 40

Scapin. Yes, yes, I know all that, and your father told Sylvestro to look after you, and Gerontio told me to keep an eye on Leandro, while they were gone. And I've done a splendid job of it, I must say.

Octavio. Soon after, Leandro met a young gypsy, Zerbinetta, and fell in love with her.

Scapin. I know, I know.

Octavio. Since Leandro and I are great friends, he immediately told me of his passion for the girl. He took me to see this gypsy, whom I found pretty enough, but not as pretty as he imagined her to be. From then on he talked only of her, exaggerating her beauty and manners 50 and praising her wit. He talked ecstatically of the charms of her conversation, and he would repeat everything she said, down to the least exclamation, and try to convince me even that was the most highminded utterance in the world. He sometimes quarreled with me for not being sensitive enough to the subtlety of his explanations and ceaselessly criticized my indifference before the altar of love.

Scapin. I don't see where all this talk is tending.

Octavio. One day, while we were walking to the place where this gypsy was staying, we heard a great weeping coming from a wretched house on a crowded street. We knocked, and the door was opened by a 60 woman full of sighs, who told us that we were about to witness a drama that could be paid for only by copious tears.

Scapin. Even I can't see clearly at this point.

Octavio. Curiosity urged me to witness this moving scene. Inside the parlor, we saw an old lady on her deathbed, attended by a servant and a young girl dissolved in tears—she was the most beautiful, the most touching sight imaginable as she knelt there . . .

Scapin. Ah! Ah!

Octavio. Any other girl would have been eclipsed by the double bur-
70 den of poverty and woe: she wore an old petticoat and the top of a ragged nightgown; her golden hair had fallen from its braids and was strewn over her neck and shoulders. But she shone like a star; everything that touched her was radiant . . .

Scapin. I'm beginning to see the light . . .

Octavio. Oh, Scapin, to see her as I did, even you would have been moved.

Scapin. Even without seeing her, I perceive her charms written all over my master's countenance.

Octavio. What tears dropped from those eyes! Not the ugly red kind,
80 these were light and crystalline. She was possessed of the most charming sorrow imaginable. . .

Scapin. Could you finish the catalogue some other time . . .

Octavio. Everyone around her dissolved in tears when she threw herself adoringly at the dying woman's feet; my soul was shaken by such a lovely piece of nature's work.

Scapin. And you, of course, were shaken into a state of love by this . . . piece?

Octavio. Ah, Scapin! Even a savage would have fallen in love with her.

Scapin. Obviously.

90 *Octavio.* We talked together, and I tried to ease her sorrow. After we left, I asked Leandro what he had thought of her. He answered me that she was pretty enough. His indifference stung me, and so I put him off with some casual remark; I did not wish him to see the effect she had had on me . . .

Sylvestro. If you don't cut your feelings short, we shall be hearing the end of this elegy some time tomorrow. Let me wind it up in about two words. *(To Scapin)* The girl's name was Hyacinth. Her mother died a few weeks ago. She's a pretty girl, I admit, but she is still an orphan, without connections, and my young master had the bad luck to fall in
100 love with her at first sight. Since that moment his heart has been on fire. He sighs continually: Sylvestro, I can't live unless I can make my sweet Hyacinth happy. He goes to see her every day but gets no further than the door, which the new mistress of the house, Hyacinth's governess, refuses to open to him. So there he is, my daring, dashing, desperate young master—insisting, begging, scheming, but to no effect. A friend of his who knew the girl's situation told him, that, although she was

poor, penniless, without a dowry, she was of honest stock; he can't see her unless he's willing to marry her and if he were to marry her, he must marry her debtors as well. The more obstacles one raises, the more his love grows. He held a council meeting in his mind, debated the issue 110 (he represented both sides, of course), reasoned it out, balanced it, and carefully made his decision: here he stands, a three-day-old bridegroom.

Scapin. I understand completely.

Sylvestro. Now add to this his father's unexpected return, his uncle's discovery of this secret marriage, and the other marriage which his father had already arranged with Signor Gerontio.

Octavio. And add also the poverty of my sweet wife—dear Hyacinth—and the impoverished state of my finances, without my father's support.

Scapin. Is that all? You two are like travellers who turn back because 120 you think you see a pebble in the road. Is this really what has alarmed you so? Aren't you ashamed to stop short over such trifles? The devil! From the size of your heads, one swollen with love and the other with stupidity, it's surprizing that you haven't enough brains between you (by knocking them both together), to discover some honest little scheme to set your affairs straight. The plague take all fools! How I would have loved to be commissioned to hoodwink my master . . . in the old days, before I swore never again to help people in trouble. I could have swindled him with my eyes shut. Why, when I was no bigger than that *(Gesturing)*, I had already mastered a hundred flattering phrases and 130 deceptive speeches.

Sylvestro. Oh I admit I'm stupid all right, and I haven't the talent that you have to deal with the law.

Octavio. Here is my adorable Hyacinth.

Scene III. *Hyacinth, Octavio, Scapin, Sylvestro*

Hyacinth. Octavio, look at your poor wife for the last time. Sylvestro has just told my maid, Nerina, who has told me what your uncle told Sylvestro: that your father has returned and intends to marry you to someone else. Poor, poor Hyacinth.

Octavio. But my dear, my sweet wife. The news was a surprise and a harsh blow to me as well. But, what's this? You're crying! Why these tears? Can you suspect me of any infidelity? Aren't you assured of my love?

Hyacinth. You have said you love me. And my heart tells me that you love me, now, at any rate. But how do I know that you will always love 10 me?

Octavio. But, in order to love you, must one guarantee by proofs that he will love you forever?

Hyacinth. Alas, poor Hyacinth, already he sets a term to his love. Girls are taught very early, Octavio, the difference between a man's and a woman's love, and we know how soon the fires that kindle the eyes of your sex die out. The passion that burns in male breasts is as easily extinguished as it is lit.

Octavio. But my heart is not made like other men's. And I can assure 20 you, in my case, that I will love you even after I am buried.

Hyacinth. I want to believe you when you say such comforting things, and yet I cannot forget so easily what I have been taught about men. You are a man. And a man without money. You depend upon your father, and he wants you to marry someone else. Depend on it, I shall not survive that black day.

Octavio. Never! There is not a father living that could force me to be faithless. Not a hundred fathers! I will fly Naples tonight rather than leave you. Oh how I hate the sight of this destined bride of mine. I wish there were twenty seas between us! Then don't cry. I beg you, 30 dearest Hyacinth, for your tears wound me and whenever I see you cry, tears come to my eyes as well. Surely you cannot doubt me now, after such a fiery speech.

Hyacinth. Then I'll dry my tears, if you say so.

Octavio. Don't forget that Heaven is kind to lovers.

Hyacinth. As long as it *is* kind, I shall be happy.

Scapin. (Aside) Perhaps she's as big a fool as he, perhaps she isn't. But she's damned pretty all the same.

Octavio. (Pointing to Scapin) Here is the answer to our problem, if he would only help us.

40 *Scapin.* Remember my vow sir, by all the steeples of Naples, never to meddle again; but if you were to coax me, both of you . . . perhaps . . .

Octavio. If twice will do it, I'll ask you a hundred times to guide our marriage through these rocky waters.

Scapin. And you, will you ask me too?

Hyacinth. I beg you, as he does, by all that you hold dear, to put yourself in the service of the god of love.

Scapin. So Scapin, once again the world calls you to its defense. You must bend your iron will, for the good of humanity. Now let me get to work. *(To Hyacinth)* Go now and be at ease.

50 *Scapin. (To Octavio)* And now we must teach you the proper way to greet your father.

Octavio. My father! . . . If I can stop shaking first.

Scapin. You must be firm when you first meet him. If you show any weakness, he will immediately get the upper hand and from then on treat you like a child. You must go into rigorous training for this meeting. You must practice a bold offense. You must anticipate everything he might say to you beforehand and invent unshakable answers.

Octavio. I'm really not very creative.

Scapin. Come on, I'll test you. Let's go through this scene together. Ready? Bold expression, head held high, steady gaze. 60

Octavio. Like this?

Scapin. More of everything.

Octavio. Like this?

Scapin. It will do for now. Imagine I'm your father, fresh from his voyage, and answer boldly, as if you were really talking to him.... What's this? You! Ah, you scoundrel, you swindler, you, you assassin. You vile ungrateful son of a fine upstanding father. Do you dare face me? After your scandalous behavior? After the cowardly trick you played during my absence? Is this respect, you villain? Is this love, you drunkard? Is this devotion, you milksop? Let's push it just a little 70 farther—So, you cutthroat, you sneak, you good-for-nothing. So! You had the audacity to become engaged without my consent, and then to marry secretly! Answer me, you drivelling idiot, answer me! Oh, damnit, you're folding up like a damp rag.

Octavio. It's just like listening to my father.

Scapin. Of course! And that's why it's essential that you shouldn't appear spineless.

Octavio. Let me practice being brave by myself for a while.

Scapin. Will you hold your head high? Will you stare firmly?

Octavio. I'll even try growling. 80

Sylvestro. Hold on! Here's your father now, approaching the house.

Octavio. My God! I'm done for. *(Runs off)*

Scapin Whoa, Octavio. Wait, Octavio! There he goes, running for his life. What a prize coward that boy is! We'd better calm the old man down ourselves.

Sylvestro. What shall I say to him?

Scapin. Leave the talking to me: just agree with whatever I say.

Scene IV. *Argantio, Scapin, Sylvestro*

Argantio. (Believing himself alone) Just wait 'til I get my hands on them.

Scapin. (To Sylvestro) He already knows all about it, and it's affected him so strongly that he's speaking to himself.

Argantio. (Believing himself alone) Someone will pay dearly for this.

Scapin. (To Sylvestro) Let's listen for a while.

Argantio. (Believing himself alone) I wonder how he plans to wriggle out of this, this noble marriage.

Scapin. (Aside) That will soon be figured out.

Argantio. (Believing himself alone) Would they have the nerve to 10 deny the whole affair?

Scapin. (Aside) No, that would never work.

Argantio. (Believing himself alone) Or will they try to talk their way out of it?

Scapin. (Aside) That wouldn't be too hard with a silly ass like you.

Argantio. (Believing himself alone) Will they try to distract me with fantasies?

Scapin. (Aside) Perhaps.

Argantio. (Believing himself alone) They will, will they! The nerve of
20 those scoundrels. Trying to deny the whole thing to a shrewd person like me! Trying to talk their way out of it when I know all about it! Trying to distract me! Let them try. It'll never work.

Scapin. (Aside) We'll see about that.

Argantio. (Believing himself alone) I just won't listen to a word they say. I'll hold my ears.

Scapin. (Aside) You could never cover ears that size.

Argantio. (Believing himself alone) I'll put that dog of a son in a monastery.

Scapin. (Aside) I'll smuggle women in to him.

30 *Argantio. (Believing himself alone)* As for that rogue Sylvestro, I'll beat him black and blue.

Sylvestro. (To Scapin) I would have been insulted if he had forgotten about me.

Argantio. (Noticing Sylvestro) So! So! Here you are, the faithful family retainer. You . . . you corrupter of young men!

Scapin. My dear sir, how overjoyed I am to see you again.

Argantio. Good day, Scapin. *(To Sylvestro)* How loyally you followed my orders. How dutifully my son has behaved in my absence!

Scapin. You're looking hearty sir, very fit. The sea air must agree
40 with you.

Argantio. I'm well enough. *(To Sylvestro)* Why don't you say something, you renegade, say something!

Scapin. The voyage sir, was it a success?

Argantio. Good God! Well enough, very well! Please leave me to rant in peace.

Scapin. You wish to rant?

Argantio. Yes, rant.

Scapin. At whom sir?

Argantio. (Pointing to Sylvestro) At this dog.

50 *Scapin.* Why, may I ask?

Argantio. You haven't heard what happened while I was away?

Scapin. I did hear of one or two trifles.

Argantio. What! You call it a trifle? Such unbelievable audacity, a trifle?

Scapin. A very important trifle, I heard.

Argantio. Such monstrous behavior.

Scapin. Yes, an immensely important trifle, to say the least.

Argantio. A son who marries without his father's consent.

Scapin. Well, one could put your mind at ease on that point. But I don't suppose you want to argue with an inferior. 60

Argantio. Suppose nothing. I'll argue the point at the top of my lungs with anybody who says I'm wrong. Haven't I every right to be furious?

Scapin. Most assuredly. As for myself, as soon as I heard about it, I beat a path straight to Octavio. I took your part, acted in your interest; I even went so far as to rant at your son myself. Young man, I said, in as stern a voice as I could manage—which wasn't easy, you understand, for he looked so young and intelligent and innocent. Young man, I demanded, have I (that's you sir) ever mistreated you, have I (that's you) ever refused you any benefit that a father owes his only son? Octavio, I pleaded, haven't I (that's me) continually lectured 70 you on the respect you must always pay a father whose feet you aren't worthy to kiss? Haven't I always been a loving father (you); haven't I always been a faithful servant (me). Oh, sir, you couldn't have ranted better yourself. But, would you believe it! After I had heard his explanation, I was convinced that he was not guilty as one might believe him to be on the face of it.

Argantio. What are you saying? It wasn't wrong for him to marry a nobody behind my back?

Scapin. Who are we to judge? He was driven to it by fate.

Argantio. Oh! Well! Excuse me! That makes everything all right. 80 From now on, we can lie and cheat and steal and plead as an excuse that we were driven to it by fate.

Scapin. You distort my meaning. I just meant that he found himself trapped and forced into this marriage.

Argantio. Trapped? Forced?

Scapin. Oh, sir, could you expect such an innocent to be as experienced as you? Young men are . . . young. The don't have the discrimination necessary to always do the right thing; witness Leandro, who in spite of all my good examples, has chosen a far worse bride than your son. Surely you were young once, sowed a few wild oats, tickled 90 a few ladies' . . . fancy. I've always heard that, at one time, you were quite the gallant, and got into scrapes with the gayest blades of your day, and, that, when you started an amorous escapade, you always saw it through to the end.

Argantio. There's some truth in that, I admit. But my adventures were always chivalrous; nothing as common and sordid as this, and they never cost me anything. A man may be as wicked as he pleases under those circumstances.

Scapin. What would you have done in his place? He saw a young lady who found him appealing (he gets this from you, looks that drive 100 women wild); he found her charming, paid her visits, sighed according to the latest fashion and . . . pushed just a little farther. They were found by her parents in a very compromising position, and, after a little physical persuasion, he agreed to marry her.

Sylvestro. (Aside) How easily lying comes to him!

Scapin. Should he have let them kill him? He merely preferred marriage to death.

Argantio. Why wasn't I told it happened like this?

Scapin. (Pointing to Sylvestro) Ask Sylvestro. He will back me up.

110 *Sylvestro.* It was just as he said sir, just as he said.

Scapin. Would I lie to you?

Argantio. But he should have gone to a lawyer at once and exposed this conspiracy.

Scapin. A lawyer?

Argantio. It would have made it easier for me to get this marriage annulled.

Scapin. Marriage annulled?

Argantio. Of course.

Scapin. You can't get it annulled.

120 *Argantio.* Not annulled?

Scapin. No.

Argantio. What? Not annulled? Can't I exercise a father's right to protect a son who was forced to marry at sword's point?

Scapin. He would never agree.

Argantio. Who wouldn't agree?

Scapin. Your son.

Argantio. My son?

Scapin. Your son. Would you expect him to confess that he had been afraid? to admit that he had been forced to marry? Hardly. It would 130 destroy his reputation; it would show him unworthy to be your son.

Argantio. To hell with his reputation.

Scapin. But the honor of the family. To protect that, we must tell everyone that he married because it was his choice.

Argantio. To hell with the family's honor! For my honor, for the honor of my savings, and for the honor of my worthless son, if he ever expects to get a penny of it, he will tell everyone the opposite.

Scapin. He'll never do it.

Argantio. I'll make him.

Scapin. Never.

140 *Argantio.* Then I'll disinherit him.

Scapin. You'll what?

Argantio. Dis-in-her-it-him.

Scapin. Very funny.

Argantio. What are you laughing at?

Scapin. You're going to disinherit your son.

Argantio. I won't?
Scapin. No.
Argantio. No?
Scapin. No.
Argantio. Will you stop talking in circles! What could stop me? 150
Scapin. You will prevent yourself.
Argantio. Who, me?
Scapin. Yes, you sir, I repeat, You! Yourself! You wouldn't have the heart.
Argantio. I'll get it.
Scapin. You're not serious.
Argantio. It's a subject I never joke about.
Scapin. Paternal affection will soften your heart.
Argantio. It won't soften my decision.
Scapin. Surely, it will. Oh most certainly. 160
Argantio. I tell you he will be disinherited.
Scapin. Merely noise, just words.
Argantio. Stop saying that!
Scapin. But I know you. Basically you're a good man.
Argantio. I'm not a good man; I can be a holy terror when I want to. Let's finish this conversation; it upsets my liver. *(To Sylvestro)* Go, you rogue, and find that young scamp, while I go and tell Signor Gerontio of this scandal.
Scapin. Sir, if I can be useful to you in any way, you have only to command me. 170
Argantio. Good. *(Aside)* Why am I cursed with an only son! If only the daughter that Heaven stole from me, were still beside me, she would be my heir and save me from this ruin.

Scene V. *Scapin, Sylvestro*

Sylvestro. I admit you've saved me from a beating for the moment, but as soon as your lies are discovered, I'll get one twice as bad.
Scapin. Don't worry. I have the answer to all our problems, or, at any rate, it will come to me shortly. Right now, I'm trying to think of someone I can get to impersonate . . . hold on! Sylvestro, come up here, now pull your hat down over your eyes like a hired ruffian. Stand on one leg. Your hands at your side. Glare at me a little. Now strut about like an actor playing a king. . . . Just what I want. Follow me. I have material for disguising your face and voice.
Sylvestro. I beg you, don't make me deal with the law. 10
Scapin. Come, we will share danger like brothers. And three years in the galleys, more or less, cannot frighten brave hearts like ours.

Act II

Scene I. *Argantio, Gerontio*

Gerontio. (To Argantio, entering) With a wind like this, our ship should arrive today. A sailor who was in Tarentum last week told me that our captain was preparing to set sail when he left. But after what you have told me, the arrival of my daughter will only complicate things more. This is a scandalous reason, I must say, for breaking off a solemn agreement between two gentlemen.

Argantio. Don't worry about it. I've always been a man of my word in matters of business, and I guarantee that things will go as planned. That cowardly son of mine could never stand up against me; but even
10 if he's found a heart while I've been gone, he's much too poor to risk my threat of disinheriting him.

Gerontio. But that it should have happened in the first place! I tell you Signor, and I cannot repeat it too strongly, the education of children is a very delicate matter. It requires shrewdness and great application.

Argantio. Very true. What are you getting at?

Gerontio. I'm getting at the fact that bad behavior on the part of the son always reflects a bad education on the part of the father.

Argantio. A shrewd reflection. But what are you trying to say exactly?

Gerontio. Can't you guess?

20 *Argantio.* I'd rather have you spell it out for me.

Gerontio. Very well; if you, as the boy's father, had taught your son right from wrong, he would never have played a trick like this.

Argantio. Well said, well said. If I had taught him . . . as you have taught *your* son right from wrong.

Gerontio. Exactly. It is unimaginable that my Leandro could do anything like that.

Argantio. But let us suppose for a minute that little Leandro, whom you, as the boy's father, have taught to know right from wrong as he knows day from night . . . suppose he had done something even worse
30 than Octavio. Eh?

Gerontio. What does that mean?

Argantio. That means, Signor Gerontio, that you should not be so hasty in judging others' behavior, and that those who wish to find fault with others should first see that there is nothing festering in their own closet.

Gerontio. The point of your metaphor escapes me.

Argantio. Time is a fine teacher and will soon explain it to you.

Gerontio. Have you heard some rumor about my son's behavior?

Argantio. Could be.

40 *Gerontio.* What is it?

Argantio. Your man Scapin told me about it, but I only grasped the rough outline. I was busy ranting at the time. But you could get the details from him, or probably anyone in town for that matter. Right now I have to get to a lawyer who will advise me what strategy to take to get this damn marriage annulled. Goodbye for now.

Scene II. *Gerontio, Leandro*

Gerontio. He must have made it all up to get even with me for criticizing him. He'll go to any length to avoid criticism. That must be it. My Leandro acted worse than his son? Incredible! Worse than his son? Is it possible? What could it be? What can the scoundrel have done now? Has he disgraced me? Will it cost money? The damned rogue! No, impossible, after the counsel I have given him about right and wrong. He could never act in a disgraceful manner. But, if he has? After all my counsel, to turn on me like this. The dog! What could be worse than marrying without a father's permission? What could be worse? Oh, oh, my son has ruined me! 10

Gerontio. So, there you are!

Leandro. *(Running to Gerontio to embrace him)* Father! How happy I am to see you again.

Gerontio. *(Refusing his embrace)* Slowly. Let's talk for a while first.

Leandro. Let me embrace you and . . .

Gerontio. *(Pushing him away again)* Let us go slowly, I said.

Leandro. What? You will not let me welcome you home like a son should?

Gerontio. That's right. We have something to get straightened out first. 20

Leandro. What?

Gerontio. Hold still and let me get a clear look at your face.

Leandro. What?

Gerontio. Look me straight in the eyes.

Leandro. Good Lord, are you all right?

Gerontio. Tell me about some of the things that have happened during my absence. For instance, what have you been doing?

Leandro. What would you like me to have done?

Gerontio. I didn't want you to do anything. It's you who have wanted to do it. What I want to know is what you have wanted to do so much that you have done it. 30

Leandro. But I've done nothing that you could complain of.

Gerontio. Nothing?

Leandro. Certainly not.

Gerontio. You're quite sure of that.

Leandro. I have complete faith in my innocence.

Gerontio. Scapin, however, has been telling a different story.
Leandro. Scapin?
Gerontio. Ah, ah, you blush when I mention his name.
40 *Leandro.* Scapin told you something about me?
Gerontio. Enough, I am satisfied that there is something in his story. But the street is not the place to air out family scandals. We will go into it later. I'm returning home now and expect to see you there immediately. And, you traitorous dog, if it turns out that you have disgraced me, or made a fool of me, or cost me money, I shall never call you son again . . . and you will never more look upon this kindly, smiling face.

Scene III. *Leandro, Octavio, Scapin*

Leandro. Farewell, Zerbinetta, my lovely gypsy, our love has been betrayed. And by the vilest, lowest rogue, Scapin! One who should have had a hundred reasons to conceal what I told him in the strictest confidence. And he is the first to run to my father and tell all. My God, I swear he will be punished for this treason.
Octavio. Dear Scapin, sweet Scapin, good Scapin, what do I not owe to your care and skill. What a genius you are. And I never recognized it till now. How lucky I am, to be able to persuade you to come to my aid.
Leandro. So! There you are. I am overjoyed to see you Signor Judas.
10 *Scapin.* Sir, your servant. You do me much too much honor.
Leandro. (Sword in hand) And you joke very pleasantly, for a man at the point of death. . . . Ah! Now you begin to understand.
Scapin. (Falling to his knees) Sir!
Octavio. (Putting himself between Scapin and Leandro) Leandro, have you lost your mind?
Leandro. There's no time for talking. Just step aside, Octavio, and it will soon be over.
Scapin. (To Leandro) But master . . .
Octavio. But Leandro . . .
20 *Leandro.* My honor must be satisfied.
Octavio. In the name of friendship, Leandro, do not run him through.
Scapin. In the name of honor and loyalty and love and God and life and death, do not touch me. . . . What have I done?
Leandro. (Thrusting at Scapin) Exactly that, traitor!
Octavio. (Holding him back) Gently, Leandro.
Leandro. He will live on the condition that he instantly confesses the treachery he has committed. Yes, rascal, I know the games you have been playing. Someone has just told me; although I suppose you never thought it would get back to me. Now you'd better tell me by yourself,
30 or, by God, I'll slit you from your nose to your buttocks.

Scapin. Sir, you wouldn't do that to an old man like me?

Leandro. Not if you speak.

Scapin. Certainly. Now I am supposed to have done something to you, is that right?

Leandro. Yes, you scoundrel, and your conscience will remind you only too well of what it is.

Scapin. If so, I have completely forgotten it, I assure you.

Leandro. (Advancing) You have completely forgotten it?

Octavio. (Holding him back) Leandro.

Scapin. Ah well! I will confess, since it appears that I have no choice. 40 Master, I confess . . . that it was I . . . who drank, with some friends, the flagon of Spanish wine you received as a gift some weeks ago. *(As Leandro advances again)* And if that isn't enough, I confess that it was I who tapped your brandy keg and poured water on the floor to make you think that the liquor had run out.

Leandro. You drank my wine and brandy and caused me to punish my servant, thinking it was she who had played this trick on me?

Scapin. Yes sir, and I humbly beg your pardon.

Leandro. I'm happy to hear that. But it isn't those trifles for which my sword is naked. 50

Scapin. Not that?

Leandro. No, something far more terrible which my sword and I are waiting to hear about immediately. *(Threatens him again)*

Scapin. Master, I don't remember anything else.

Leandro. You won't talk?

Scapin. Ow!!!

Octavio. Softly!

Scapin. Sir, I've just remembered something else. I confess that three weeks ago when you sent me to present a watch to your young gypsy and I returned with my clothes seeped in mud and my face full of 60 blood and told you that I had been beaten and robbed by thieves . . . I confess that I kept the watch myself.

Leandro. You kept my watch?

Scapin. Yes sir, so I could tell the time.

Leandro. Ah! I'm learning many charming things about my trusty valet. Charming! But I am waiting to hear a still more monstrous confession.

Scapin. You want me to confess again! *(Aside)* What the devil does he know?

Leandro. Quickly, I'm in a terrible hurry. 70

Scapin. Sir, as I'm a man of honor, these are the sum total of my crimes.

Leandro. Nothing else? *(Advancing on Scapin)*

Octavio. (Coming between them) Hold, Leandro, hold.

Scapin. I remember one more thing. Do you remember the ghost you thought you saw six months ago, which beat you so badly and almost caused you to break your neck by falling into a sewer as you tried to escape from him.

Leandro. Well?

80 *Scapin.* I confess, sir, that I was that ghost.

Leandro. Oh, you dog! You were that ghost?

Scapin. Yes sir, I did it to frighten you a little so that you would give up having me follow you around all night.

Leandro. Be assured that I will remember all this at the proper time and place. But what I want now is to have you confess what you told my father.

Scapin. Your father?

Leandro. Yes, my father.

Scapin. I haven't even seen him since his return.

90 *Leandro.* Not seen him?

Scapin. No sir.

Leandro. Do you swear it?

Scapin. As I'm a man of honor. Whoever told you the contrary is a knave and a liar.

Leandro. It was my father who told me this.

Scene IV. *Carle, Leandro, Octavio, Scapin*

Carle. Sir, I bring you unhappy news.

Leandro. Well?

Carle. The gypsy band threaten to take Zerbinetta away with them unless you bring the money they asked for within the next two hours. Zerbinetta herself told me this, with tears in her eyes. She said that unless the money is paid, you two would be parted forever. *(Exits)*

Leandro. In two hours. Impossible! Zerbinetta . . . My poor Scapin, what are you doing down there? Get up, my dear fellow. Here, let me help you. Now I implore you to help me meet this crisis which has just

10 arisen.

Scapin. (Walking angrily past Leandro) Now I'm poor Scapin, am I! Hang-dog Scapin becomes dear Scapin as soon as you have need of him.

Leandro. Oh please. I forgive you all that you confessed to, and worse still if you've done anything worse.

Scapin. No, no, don't pardon me for the harmless tricks I've played out of love for you; kill me for them. That's it, run me through. Draw blood. I beg of you. Nothing would make me happier now than to die on the point of your sword.

Leandro. Heavens no, don't dream of such a thing. I beg you instead

20 to forgive me and grant me life as a lover.

Scapin. No, no, stab away. Slice. Thrust.

Leandro. You are too dear to me. Consider all the years we have been together. I pray you to use your marvellous talents for a poor unfortunate man who is at his wit's ends and at times doesn't know what he is saying.

Scapin. Rip. Slash. Tear. Thrust.

Leandro. Forget that please and think instead of helping me.

Octavio. Scapin, you must do something for him.

Scapin. How can I, as a man of honor, after an insult like that?

Leandro. Forget it please, and help me.

Octavio. I plead for him also, my dear Scapin. 30

Scapin. The insult still stings like a viper at my breast.

Octavio. You must rise above revenge.

Leandro. Would you abandon me here, Scapin, to die, a hopeless lover, of a broken heart?

Scapin. To take me unaware with an insult like that.

Leandro. I did wrong, I confess it.

Scapin. To call me traitor, villain, scoundrel, Judas . . . dog!

Leandro. I am abject.

Scapin. To threaten me with a sword!

Leandro. I offer heartfelt apologies. And if going down on my knees 40 will help, you see it. Only do not abandon me like this.

Octavio. Ah, Scapin, see how low he is willing to stoop.

Scapin. Rise sir. Next time do not be so hasty.

Leandro. Do you promise to work for me?

Scapin. I'll think about it.

Leandro. But there's no time for that.

Scapin. Don't worry about time. How much money do you need to rescue your gypsy?

Leandro. Five hundred ecus.°

Scapin. And you. 50

Octavio. Two hundred pistoles.°

Scapin. I can get both those sums from your fathers. *(To Octavio)* I already have a plan to get your money. *(To Leandro)* And, as for yours, since Gerontio is incredibly miserly, it will be necessary to give it more thought. However, as you know, his supply of brains is not too great, thank God. He is as gullible as a five-year-old, and I can always make him believe exactly what I want him to. . . . Don't look offended sir, you're not in the least like him. As a matter of fact, everyone knows that your mother . . .

Leandro. That's enough! 60

Scapin. Good. Good. One must have scruples about that. It's the sort of thing one must deny. But here comes Octavio's father. I'll be-

49. ecus, a French gold coin of considerable value. ***51. pistoles,*** a valuable Spanish gold coin.

gin with him. Get off, both of you, and let me work in peace. *(To Octavio)* And you, tell your valet Sylvestro to come instantly to play his role. *(Alone)* After I get their money for them, there will be time to plan my revenge on Gerontio. It must be especially severe. I have two scores against him. He almost got me killed with his stories about me; and of all the villainy I am capable of, he had to spread tales that weren't even true.

Scene V. *Argantio, Scapin*

Scapin. (Aside) He's still fuming about the marriage.

Argantio. (Believing himself alone) To have so little consideration. To rush into such an expensive marriage. Oh, oh, the young fools.

Scapin. Your servant, sir.

Argantio. Good day, Scapin.

Scapin. I imagine that you're still thinking about your son's marriage.

Argantio. Yes, my blood has not stopped boiling since our interview this morning.

Scapin. Ah sir, life is beset with obstacles, and the wisest of us should
10 be constantly prepared for them. I heard, as a youth, an ancient proverb which has stayed with me all my life.

Argantio. So?

Scapin. It went like this: No matter how short a time the head of a family has been away from home, it is wise to go over in his mind all the possible misfortunes he may witness on his return. He should imagine his house burned, his money stolen, his wife dead, his son maimed for life, his daughter seduced in the most ugly manner; and he should consider himself extremely lucky if any of these things has *not* happened on his return. I have always followed this strategy, being in
20 my own way a minor philosopher; and I have never returned home from an errand without expecting to find my master beside himself with rage, to have him rant at me, insult me, kick me in the backside or hammer me with blows; and whatever he fails to do, I account to my good fortune.

Argantio. But I cannot suffer this marriage calmly! I have just come from the lawyers where we discussed means to have it annulled.

Scapin. I wish that you would take my advice and try anything rather than go to the law. You know how trials drag on interminably, and how, no matter what the justice of your case is, a clever lawyer can always
30 contrive to make it seem unjust.

Argantio. I can see your point, and I shiver when I think of the money a long suit can cost, but what other way is there?

Scapin. I think I've found one. Your troubles have touched me so deeply that I've thought of nothing since I saw you last, but ways to ease your discontent. In general, my love for fathers of all descriptions ... (I, alas, was never blessed with this responsibility) ... makes me take any ingratitude on the part of their sons as a personal affront; but, in particular, I have always felt a special inclination for you.

Argantio. That's very kind of you, Scapin, I'm sure.

Scapin. Listen then: I've just run across the brother of the girl 40 Octavio married. He's a professional soldier, and much worse, I suspect. You know, one of these husky, roaring fellows with a low brow, and a swollen red face veined from heavy drinking. The kind of brute that swears enough in a day for a whole regiment in a week, flashes his sword at people who so much as look at him when they pass. He was born and bred to slaughter, always talks of breaking men in two, and would think no more of killing a man than of drinking his health. I led him up to the subject of this marriage and showed him how easily you could get it annulled. Octavio had been forced into it in the first place. I made him see how well your suit would look in court, with you posing 50 as the injured father. I told him how many judges you could buy with your money and how many jurors you could persuade with your influential friends. In other words, I have convinced him that opposing your suit would leave him empty-handed whereas settling in private might net him a tidy sum. And a great risk I ran too, for his sword was thrusting out at me all the time. Anyway, he agreed to break off this marriage provided you would make it worth his while.

Argantio. What did the blackguard want?

Scapin. Oh, unheard of sums to begin with.

Argantio. Such as? 60

Scapin. He said he wouldn't even consider less than five or six hundred pistoles.

Argantio. Five or six hundred devils blast his black soul! What kind of fool does he take me for?

Scapin. That's what I told him. I rejected all such extravagant demands; I convinced him at length that you were not that kind of fool, and would never pay that much. At length, after much bickering, he made his final proposition. "Soon," he said, "I must rejoin my regiment. I am in the process of getting my equipment together, and my immediate needs cause me to give in to you, despite my better sense. I must have 70 a horse, and I can't get a decent one for under sixty pistoles."

Argantio. Well, if it's a matter of sixty pistoles, they're his.

Scapin. "And," says he, "a harness and a set of pistols, another twenty pistoles."

Argantio. Sixty pistoles for a horse; harness and pistols, twenty pistoles; that makes eighty in all.

Scapin. Exactly.

Argantio. It's too much, but, so be it. I agree to that sum.

Scapin. "And my valet will need a horse," he says, "that's at least
80 thirty pistoles."

Argantio. What the devil. Let his valet walk, or he'll find himself on foot as well.

Scapin. But sir . . .

Argantio. Why, the man is impertinent.

Scapin. But how can you expect him to ride when his valet must stumble after him on foot?

Argantio. Let them ride each other for all I care.

Scapin. For God's sake, sir, don't balk at trifles. Anything rather than the courts. Give freely, for he is saving you from the claws of
90 justice.

Argantio. (Pause) Very well then, thirty more pistoles.

Scapin. "Then there's a small question of a mule to carry . . ."

Argantio. Damn the mule and the master. It's too much. I'll go to court.

Scapin. But sir, think a minute.

Argantio. I go no higher.

Scapin. But master, a little mule . . . ?

Argantio. No, I prefer a trial. Besides you said a minute ago that I could easily win.

100 *Scapin.* That was said in order to knock his price down. You and I know how corrupt the legal system is.

Argantio. Corrupt or not, I will not be blackmailed. I'll go to court.

Scapin. Sir, what are you saying? Think of what your decision involves. Consider the subtleties of the judiciary: The bewildering array of higher and lower courts: justices of the peace, circuit courts, probate courts, supreme and superior courts, ultrasuperior courts, courts of taxes, claims patent appeals, errors, surrogates, lead, silver and gold. You would have to go through them all. Consider the long and tedious delays. Think of those beasts of prey grinning at you from be-
110 neath their freshly-curled wigs as you move within reach of their claws: bailiffs, attorneys, barristers, advocates, receivers and assessors, public prosecutors, deputy public-prosecutors, deputy deputy public-prosecutors, and judges, and, for each of them, an army of clerks, secretaries and assistants. Any one of them, on the slightest whim, can damage the best case in the world. Consider: the bailiff can serve a false writ and you are condemned before you can even open your mouth; your attorneys may reach an agreement with your opponents and sell you out for ready cash; your advocate may also sell out and not appear when he is scheduled to plead your case, or, if he does, he may make
120 an absurd defense, he may talk for hours without ever getting to the point; the register may be bribed to hold you in contempt of court; the

recorder's clerk may conveniently lose your exhibits, or the recorder himself may record only the testimony injurious to your case. But even if, by taking extreme precautions, throwing money around as if it were air, you avoid these pitfalls, you will find to your amazement that your judges have been swayed by any loudmouthed fellow with an opinion about the case, or by their mistresses as they prepared for bed the night before. Sir, I beg of you, if you can possibly do it, save yourself from this legal hell. To have to plead a case in court is to be truly damned. The thought of a lawsuit would send me flying to the Indies. 130

Argantio. What was the price of that mule again?

Scapin. Sir, for the mule, his horse, his valet's horse, the harness and the brace of pistols, and a trifle more to settle his bill with his innkeeper, he asks only two hundred pistoles.

Argantio. Two hundred pistoles?

Scapin. Not a penny more.

Argantio. (Angrily walking offstage) I'm going. I'm going. To the courts . . .

Scapin. But think . . .

Argantio. . . . to plead. 140

Scapin. . . . of what you're getting yourself into.

Argantio. . . . my case and damn the inconvenience.

Scapin. But going to court costs *money.* Money for processes, subpoenas, summons, money for registration, attorneys, exhibition of documents. Money for conferences and consultations, pleas, discovery interrogatories. *Money!* Money for depositions, money for settlements, money for decrees, money for rolls, money for writs: writs of assistance, mandamus, certiorari, quo warrantus—not to mention the gifts it will be necessary to present to the right people. Give this fellow his money and you are through with it. Think only of the money 150 you save . . .

Argantio. But two hundred pistoles?

Scapin. Yes. But you come out ahead on it. I've made a rough calculation of the expense of a lawsuit, and I find that by giving this man two hundred pistoles you'll make a clear one hundred fifty pistoles profit, let alone the worries, the time and the agitation you will spare yourself. Were it only to avoid the insult and embarrassment of being made a fool in public by these tricky lawyers, I would gladly pay three hundred pistoles.

Argantio. Let those damned lawyers try and make fun of me. 160

Scapin. Do as you like, but if I were about to suffer the curse of a trial I'd flee the country, I swear.

Argantio. I'm not going to give him two hundred pistoles.

Scapin. As you wish, sir. But here comes the man now.

Scene VI. *Argantio, Scapin, Sylvestro (Disguised as a hired ruffian)*

Sylvestro. Hey Scapin, where is this bird Argantio, Octavio's father?
Scapin. Why do you ask?
Sylvestro. Someone just told me that he's taking me to court to break off my sister's marriage. By the King's whiskers!
Scapin. As to that, I couldn't say, but I do know that he refused to pay two hundred pistoles you asked. He said it was too much.
Sylvestro. Damn his eyes! Damn his thick head! Damn his weak guts! If I find him, I'll break him in two even though the law break me in turn. By my mother's grey beard. *(Argantio hides behind Scapin.)*
10 *Scapin.* Sir, Octavio's father has courage; if he were here he would snap his fingers at your threats.
Argantio. Shut up, you fool. What are you trying to do to me?
Sylvestro. He would! He would! Damn his fat head! If he were here right now . . . thrust . . . a sword in his bloated guts. By my sweetheart's wart! *(Follow through with appropriate motions; seeing Argantio)* Who is this fellow?
Scapin. Not him, sir, certainly not him.
Sylvestro. Maybe it's one of his friends.
Argantio. Oh, no, sir. I'm his worst enemy.
20 *Sylvestro.* His worst enemy?
Argantio. Yes, oh dear, how I hate the man. Nasty old Argantio, fat old Argantio.
Sylvestro. By my father's drawers, I'm delighted to meet you. An enemy of that fat coward Argantio, eh?
Scapin. Of course, of course, I'll answer for him.
Sylvestro. (Roughly seizing Argantio's hand) Put it there, put it here. By the Queen's mattress! I give you my word and swear to you by my honor and the sword that I carry and by all the vows I know that before the sun sets I will please you by ridding the world of this scum Argantio.
30 Trust me.
Scapin. But sir, violence is severely punished in Naples.
Sylvestro. I laugh at the law. I have nothing to lose. By my bottle!
Scapin. But Argantio is always prepared for trouble, and he has relatives, friends and servants who will rally to his defense.
Argantio. Don't provoke this fine young man, you fool!
Sylvestro. That adds spice to the kill, by God, spice to the slaughter. *(Holding his sword in his hand)* Hah, head! Hah, guts! If I could meet him this minute with all his friends. If he were only here before me with thirty supporters. If he would only appear armed to the teeth. Hah,
40 throat! *(Putting himself on guard)* What, you dogs, you have the boldness to attack the best swordfighter in Naples! Well then, by God, die! *(Thrusting out on all sides as if he were fighting an army)* No quarter.

Take that. Hold. Thrust. Good foot, good eye. Ah, rogues! Ah, scum! Drink your fill of my flashing steel. Stand fast, cowards, no flinching! Here we go! Thrust at this one! Now this one! *(Turning himself so he faces Scapin and Argantio)* Now this one. And this one. What, you draw back? Stand fast, damn you, stand your ground!

Scapin. Lower your sword, please sir, we're not the enemy.

Sylvestro. That's what they get who try to play tricks on me.

(Exit) 50

Scapin. See all these bodies scattered around. They were all killed over your two hundred pistoles. Hoard your money well, sir; I wish you good fortune.

Argantio. (Trembling) Scapin!

Scapin. What is King Midas' wish?

Argantio. I have decided to give him the two hundred pistoles.

Scapin. I'm delighted to hear it, for your sake.

Argantio. Let us find him; I have the money on me.

Scapin. You'd better give me the money. It wouldn't be advisable for him to see you again in his frame of mind, particularly since you 60 just passed yourself off as one of *your* own worst enemies. Besides, seeing you trembling in front of him might make him decide to ask for more.

Argantio. You're right, but I would like to see where my money goes.

Scapin. You don't trust me?

Argantio. No, no, but . . .

Scapin. That's the last straw. Sir, make up your mind, either I am a thief or I'm an honest man, one or the other. Why should I deceive you when you have seen, in what just passed, that I have no other interest than serving you because you are my master's friend? If you can't trust 70 me, then I wash my hands of the whole business, and you can search from now to doomsday for someone to handle your affairs as honestly as I.

Argantio. Here, take it please.

Scapin. No, don't give me your money. I am far too unworthy to be entrusted with an affair of this magnitude.

Argantio. My God, man, take it.

Scapin. No, I repeat, don't trust me. How do you know that I'm not going to cheat you of your money?

Argantio. Take it, take it, don't say another word. But be sure to 80 get some kind of security from him.

Scapin. Leave it to me.

Argantio. I'll wait for you at my house.

Scapin. I'll not fail to be there. *(Alone)* That's one of them. Now I must look for the other. Ah, here he comes now. It seems that Heaven leads them in turn to my net.

Scene VII. *Gerontio, Scapin*

Scapin. (Pretending not to see Gerontio) Oh God! What an unforeseen catastrophe! Oh, miserable father! Poor, poor Gerontio, what will you do now!

Gerontio. (Aside) What is he saying about me with such downcast eyes?

Scapin. Can anyone tell me where Signor Gerontio is, immediately?

Gerontio. Here I am, Scapin.

Scapin. (Running about the stage madly without hearing or seeing Gerontio) Where can he be? He must hear of this misfortune immedi-
10 ately.

Gerontio. (Running after Scapin) What is it? What is it?

Scapin. In vain do I run everywhere in my mad search for him.

Gerontio. (Shouting) But here I am!

Scapin. He must be hidden in some secret place.

Gerontio. (Catching up with Scapin) Hey, are you blind? Can't you see me?

Scapin. Master, master, is there no way to find you?

Gerontio. I've been in front of you for an hour. What's the matter?

Scapin. Master! *(Out of breath)*

20 *Gerontio.* What?

Scapin. Master! Your son! *(Out of breath)*

Gerontio. Yes, yes. My son . . .

Scapin. Has met with a strange misfortune.

Gerontio. What, what?

Scapin. I found him a while ago, very sad because of something you had said to him. He kept mumbling that I was responsible for it; that I had betrayed him. Anyway, thinking to divert him, I walked him down to the harbor. There, among a great spectacle of ships and sailors, our eyes were attracted by a Turkish galley. A handsome Turk invited us
30 aboard. We boarded the ship and were fed some of the sweetest fruits I have ever tasted, and drank the most exquisite wine in the world.

Gerontio. What is so catastrophic in all that?

Scapin. Wait, master. Here we are on board, eating and drinking. Suddenly the ship begins to move. We're sailing away from port! The young Turk dumps me in a skiff and orders me to tell you that if you don't send him five hundred ecus immediately, he will carry your son away to Algiers.

Gerontio. Good Heavens! This is terrible! Catastrophic! Five hundred ecus!

40 *Scapin.* Yes master, and, moreover, I have only two hours in which to get back to him with the money.

Gerontio. Bastard of a Turk, to ruin me like this.

Scapin. The time grows short, sir. You must think, quickly, of some way to save a son whom you love so tenderly from slavery.

Gerontio. Go Scapin, go tell this Turk I'll call the police.

Scapin. The police on the open sea? You're joking!

Gerontio. What the devil did he board the galley for?

Scapin. Misfortune happens to everyone sir; you can never explain why.

Gerontio. In this dreadful emergency, Scapin, I'm counting on you to be a loyal servant. 50

Scapin. How can I help sir?

Gerontio. You must go to the Turk and tell him to send back my son. Tell him that you will take my son's place while I try to scrape up the money.

Scapin. Think of what you're saying! Do you think even a Turk is stupid enough to exchange a servant for an heir?

Gerontio. What the devil did he board the galley for?

Scapin. He couldn't have foreseen this. Think master, he has only given me two hours. 60

Gerontio. You say that he's asking for . . .

Scapin. Five hundred ecus.

Gerontio. Five hundred ecus! He has no soul!

Scapin. Certainly, but a Turkish soul.

Gerontio. Does he know how much five hundred ecus are worth?

Scapin. Yes sir, he knows they are worth fifteen hundred pounds.

Gerontio. Does this heathen think that fifteen hundred pounds can be picked from trees?

Scapin. Turks are very unreasonable men.

Gerontio. What the devil did he board the galley for? 70

Scapin. True, true. But one can't foresee everything. Please master, hurry.

Gerontio. Very well, here is the key to my strong box.

Scapin. Good.

Gerontio. Open it.

Scapin. Very well.

Gerontio. On the left side you will find another large key which opens the door to the attic.

Scapin. Yes.

Gerontio. In the attic you will find a large trunk full of old clothes. Take them all, sell them to the dealers and ransom my son. 80

Scapin. (Giving him back the key) Are you joking? I won't even get a hundred francs for that junk; you know how little time we've got.

Gerontio. But what the devil did he board the galley for?

Scapin. We're wasting time. Leave the galley where it is; think of the time flying by. You risk losing your son forever. Alas, poor master,

poor Leandro, I may never see you again; while I stand here talking you lie rotting in your chains on your way to Algiers. But God will witness that I have done all I could for you, and that if you must die in slavery,
90 there is no one to blame but a father who doesn't love you.

Gerontio. Wait, Scapin, I'll go and raise the money.

Scapin. Hurry then, I tremble for fear we hear the hour strike before we are ready.

Gerontio. I'm off right now to get the four hundred ecus.

Scapin. Five hundred ecus!

Gerontio. Five hundred ecus!

Scapin. Yes.

Gerontio. What the devil did he board that galley for?

Scapin. Right, right. But hurry.

100 *Gerontio.* Wasn't there any other street you could have taken?

Scapin. Yes, but do be quick.

Gerontio. Ah, damnable galley.

Scapin. *(Aside)* That galley catches in his throat.

Gerontio. Scapin, I just remembered that I have the money on me—I never dreamed I'd lose it so quickly. *(Taking out his purse and giving it to Scapin but holding onto it)* Here, go ransom my son.

Scapin. *(Holding out his hand)* Yes sir.

Gerontio. *(Not letting go of the purse)* But tell that Turk he's a scoundrel.

110 *Scapin.* *(Trying to get the purse)* Yes.

Gerontio. *(Not letting go of the purse)* A dirty Heathen.

Scapin. *(Still trying to get the purse)* Yes.

Gerontio. *(Again)* A man without a soul, a thief.

Scapin. Let me be off.

Gerontio. *(Again)* He hasn't a shred of right to this money.

Scapin. Yes.

Gerontio. *(Again)* He owes me five hundred ecus.

Scapin. Very good.

Gerontio. *(Again)* If I ever catch him, I'll collect with interest.

120 *Scapin.* Yes.

Gerontio. *(Putting his purse back in his pocket and walking off)* Good, now go ransom my son.

Scapin. *(Running after Gerontio)* Wait, master.

Gerontio. What?

Scapin. Where is the money to pay for him?

Gerontio. Didn't I give it to you?

Scapin. No. You put it back in your pocket.

Gerontio. Ah, it's sadness which affects my mind.

Scapin. So I see.

130 *Gerontio.* What the devil did he board the galley for? Ah, damnable galley! Traitorous Turk! Devil take the whole race.

Scapin. (Alone) He still can't accept the loss of five hundred ecus; but we're still not even. I will collect in another kind of coin for the lies he told Leandro about me.

Scene VIII. *Leandro, Octavio, Scapin*

Octavio. Ho there, Scapin, have your efforts in my behalf been successful?

Leandro. Have you helped me in my efforts to rescue my love?

Scapin. (To Octavio) Two hundred pistoles, courtesy of Signor Argantio.

Octavio. You fill me with joy!

Scapin. (To Leandro) As for you, I could do nothing.

Leandro. (Walking away) So I must die. If Zerbinetta is taken away from me, I have nothing to live for.

Scapin. Wait a minute. What are you rushing away for! 10

Leandro. (Returning) What else can I do but end my miserable life.

Scapin. Here's your money.

Leandro. You have given me back my life.

Scapin. But take it on one condition, that I am allowed to revenge myself on your father for the lies he spread concerning me and no matter what I do, you will neither interfere nor tell him about it.

Leandro. Whatever you wish.

Scapin. You swear it before a witness.

Leandro. Yes.

Scapin. Then here are five hundred ecus. 20

Leandro. Let us hurry and ransom the one I adore.

Act III

Scene I. *Hyacinth, Scapin, Sylvestro, Zerbinetta*

Sylvestro. Here is the house where you ladies must wait until your lovers join you.

Hyacinth. (To Zerbinetta) Nothing could be more welcome than your companionship. I have long wished that the love and friendship that unites the men we love should mark our relationship as well.

Zerbinetta. It pleases me. I am not one to withdraw when one forces friendship upon me.

Scapin. But if one were to force a little love upon you?

Zerbinetta. Then I would have to think again. There is too much at risk with love for a girl to lower her defenses. 10

Sylvestro. Do I still detect mistrust of Leandro in your words? Surely his repeated efforts to buy you from the gypsies is proof of his love.

Zerbinetta. I trust him as a friend, no more. You may think of me as a light-hearted gypsy, but I think deeply about many things. I think about marriage. I know that I shall be abused by Leandro if I let him think that a mere exchange of money is sufficient to guarantee my love. I expect more. In exchange for my love I must have security and ceremony.

Scapin. He will go as far as you want him to; he's that much in love with you. Besides, if his intentions weren't honorable, do you think you'd see a man of character like me mixed up in this affair?

Zerbinetta. There will be trouble from his father.

Scapin. That's my concern, not yours.

Hyacinth. That is another bond to cement our friendship. Both of us are threatened by the fathers of the men we love.

Zerbinetta. You have this advantage. You at least know who your parents are, and can hope to find them again, and that would turn your marriage into a blessed event. I cannot even imagine who my parents were. Nothing about me can please a father who thinks only of money. Beauty, affection, merit, mean nothing to a narrow-minded miser.

Hyacinth. You're right, true merit is always opposed. Love could be so sweet; life could be a dream, but there are always obstacles. The course of true love . . .

Scapin. No, you're wrong. A calm and peaceful love is like a stagnant pool. Happiness soon becomes a bore. A life must have crises and . . . climaxes. The difficulties you complain of increase passion and make pleasure more intense.

Zerbinetta. Let's not discuss this any longer. I hate deep subjects. Besides everyone knows that a secure marriage is God's greatest gift to man. But Scapin, you can make my pleasure more intense by telling me again how you wheedled money out of that old miser Gerontio. You will be well paid by seeing the joy such a story gives me.

Scapin. Let Sylvestro do it; he was my partner in crime. I'm busy planning revenge on the old man, which will certainly make my pleasure more intense.

Sylvestro. Why take this chance of undoing all we have gained so far?

Scapin. Easy victories bore me; the real pleasure is in pulling off something outrageous.

Sylvestro. If you want my advice, you'll leave well enough alone.

Scapin. The only advice I listen to is mine.

Sylvestro. What a diabolical sense of humor you have.

Scapin. No more diabolical than your conscience.

Sylvestro. I just don't like to see you go around looking for a beating.

Scapin. Just as long as it lands on my back, and not yours.

Sylvestro. Yes, it's your back; do with it as you will.

Scapin. The threat of a beating never stopped me yet. I hate those cowardly backs which, twitching and cringing before a blow actually falls, live in constant fear.

Zerbinetta. But we still have need of you.

Scapin. Never shall it be said that Scapin allowed someone to slander him with impunity, particularly when it wasn't true. 60

Scene II. *Gerontio, Scapin*

Gerontio. Scapin, is my son free?

Scapin. Your son, sir, is in a safe place. He is free from harm. But not you, sir. You, sir, run a great risk just being out in the street. What has persuaded you to leave the security of your home?

Gerontio. What?

Scapin. At this moment, there is someone looking all over town for you.

Gerontio. Me?

Scapin. You.

Gerontio. Who?

Scapin. The brother of the girl Octavio married. He thinks it was you that persuaded Argantio to break up the marriage. He thinks that you are robbing him and his sister of some easy money, and he is furious about it. He's worked himself into a frenzy and believes that only by taking your life can he avenge the stain on his family. His friends are scouring the city, asking everyone if they have seen you. They were thick as fleas on the streets as I made my way here. Soldiers of his regiment are blocking the streets, going into houses, surrounding all the avenues leading to your house. Whatever you do—go home, don't go home, hide, don't hide, go right, go left—you are lost. 10

Gerontio. Scapin, what will I do? 20

Scapin. I don't know. I can't think. I'm trembling from head to foot myself out of sympathy for you. It's a bad business . . . but . . . wait *(Pretends to scout around to see that no one is coming)*

Gerontio. What is it?

Scapin. No, no, it was nothing.

Gerontio. Isn't there anything you can do for me?

Scapin. No, it's too risky. What if they should find out and come looking for me?

Gerontio. But, Scapin, I'm your master. I have cared for you all these years. You can't leave me like this. Ask anything of me, and if I can spare it, it's yours. 30

Scapin. It's no use. I can't be callous, I can't be cruel even though I should pay for it with my life. My affection for you is too deep to allow me to desert you.

Gerontio. I won't be ungrateful. No, not I. You shall have this suit of clothes as recompense, when I have worn it a bit longer.

Scapin. Listen, here is the best plan I know. You must hide yourself in this sack. *(Gerontio, frightened by some noises he hears, tries to scramble into the sack before it's opened.)*

40 *Scapin.* Wait a minute. No one is there. Once you are in, don't move or cry out under any circumstances. I'll carry you on my back through enemy lines, and if anyone questions me I'll tell them I'm carrying . . . manure, so they won't look inside. Once in your house, we'll set up a barricade and send for help.

Gerontio. A wonderful plan. You're a genius, Scapin.

Scapin. I'll have you home in no time *(Aside)* and laid up for a week.

Gerontio. What did you say?

Scapin. I said that they could seek and seek and never find you. Get in. Now take care not to show yourself or wiggle about, whatever may 50 occur.

Gerontio. I'm capable of anything when my life is at stake.

Scapin. Hurry, hide yourself. Here's one of those cutthroats. *(Changing his voice)* Where's Gerontio, I want to kill him first—Don't move—I'll find him even if he's hiding in hell—Don't show yourself—Hey, the man with the sack; here's a louis° for you if you take me to Gerontio—You're looking for Signor Gerontio, sir?—No, death is looking for him—Then why are you looking for him, sir?—Because, my little friend, I'm going to beat him to death—Oh, sir, you can't treat a gentleman in such an undignified manner—Gentleman! That fat fool—I must ask 60 you to speak more civilly, sir—Oh, so you're a friend of his? Then take this beating for him. *(Beats the sack several times)*—Pass that on to him for me—*(Scapin cries as if he were being beaten.)* Ah, ew, ow, sir . . . oh, oh, sir, no more . . . ow, ow, little softer. Oh, oh, oh, oh—take him that from me—damned bully, oh, I ache all over.

Gerontio. *(Sticking his head out)* You ache?

Scapin. Ah, sir, I'm black and blue from that beating, your beating. My shoulders ache terribly.

Gerontio. But it was my shoulders he was beating.

Scapin. No sir, it was my back.

70 *Gerontio.* I felt those blows land on me. I still do.

Scapin. No, no. It was only the small end of his club that you felt.

Gerontio. You should have stood away from the sack while you were being beaten.

Scapin. *(Pushing his head down)* Down. Here comes another armed stranger. I'm out of breath, running all day after Gerontio, not a glimpse of him.—Hide yourself, well—Can you tell me where he is?—I don't

55. louis, a French gold coin.

know where he is, sir—Tell me quickly, my good man. I don't want much with him—just a few dozen strokes of my stick and three or four little sword thrusts—I assure you, sir, I don't know where he is—What's moving in that bag?—That's only manure, sir—Then you won't mind if I run 80 my sword through it?—You'll damage my manure—Then you won't mind if I look inside—I will defend my manure, sir, with my life—Oh, you will, then maybe this club will teach you to answer questions properly *(Beats the sack, cries as if he were being beaten)* oh, ew, ow. No more, I beg you, ah, ah, oh, oh, oh, oh,—Next time, answer quickly, let this be a lesson to you—The devil take him and his brute of a club.

Gerontio. (Sticking his head out) I'm broken into bits.

Scapin. I'm bruised and beaten.

Gerontio. I'm aching all over.

Scapin. I can hardly move. 90

Gerontio. What was he beating me for?

Scapin. (Pushing him down again) No time for talk, here are half a dozen soldiers coming down the street—*(Imitates many voices)* Find him. Look everywhere. Overlook nothing. Run all over town. Don't forget any corner where he might be hiding. Poke your nose into every alley. Where shall we go now? Down that way. No, over here. Here, left. No, right. No. Yes. Sirs, don't look at me like that. Keep away from me. Don't raise your clubs. Don't . . . *(Gerontio raises his head from the sack and sees the trick.)*—Tell us where he is or we'll leave you bleeding in the street—I'll suffer rather than turn my master over to you—You had 100 your chance—Do what you will—You're asking for it then, take this—Oh, ah, ew *(As he is about to strike, Gerontio gets out, Scapin runs away.)*

Gerontio. (Hobbling about) Son of a whore! Cousin of a toad! You, you, you fish!

Scene III. *Gerontio, Zerbinetta*

Zerbinetta. (Laughing, not seeing Gerontio) I must catch my breath!

Gerontio. (Cursing, not seeing Zerbinetta) I'll twist your gullet!

Zerbinetta. (Laughing, not seeing Gerontio) That story was so funny! That old man was such a fool to be tricked like that!

Gerontio. It's funny, is it? A fool, am I? Who do you think you are, laughing at me?

Zerbinetta. I wasn't laughing at you.

Gerontio. You were laughing at the moon, I suppose. What right does a young girl like you have to make fun of me?

Zerbinetta. Who's making fun of you? 10

Gerontio. Then why do you come along laughing at me?

Zerbinetta. Why I'm laughing has nothing to do with you. I'm laughing at a story I was told. *(Laughs)* A very funny story. I've never heard anything as funny as this story of a trick a son played on his father in order to get money.

Gerontio. A son? A father? Money?

Zerbinetta. Let me tell you about it. It's bubbling up inside me, and I just have to share my laughter with someone. *(Through all these speeches Zerbinetta laughs continually.)* There can be no harm in 20 telling it because the whole town will soon know it anyway. As you can see, I'm a gypsy. People don't like us, but then we don't like them. They never think about deeper things. My story is a very old one. A young man of this town fell in love with me. Since I belonged to the gypsies he found he would have to buy me from them. And being a well-brought-up, a refined, a sophisticated young man, naturally he had no money. In order to pay for me he had to have money. His father who is just swollen with wealth, is, however, a miser, a mean, heartless, nasty old man. As I said, it's the oldest story in the world. The father's name is . . . oh, what was his name? Oh dear, give me a little help. Who has 30 the reputation of being the biggest miser in Naples?

Gerontio. I wouldn't know, I'm sure.

Zerbinetta. His name is "roono" . . . "runtio" . . . "orontio" . . . No, it begins with "Ge" . . . That's it, Gerontio. Oh, you do know him. Well, that's the villain of my story. It was his meanness, his miserliness, his nastiness I was referring to. To get on with my story. The gypsies decided to leave Naples today and it looked as if my young man would lose me forever. But luckily, his servant was just the man to help us. There's no mistaking his name—I could never forget it—Scapin. An incredibly clever man. One cannot praise him highly enough.

40 *Gerontio. (Aside)* Son of a whore, lover of sheep—that's the praises he'll get from me.

Zerbinetta. Here's the strategy he used to dupe the old man. I can't think of it without breaking into laughter. He found the old miser and told him that his son had been kidnapped by Turks. Can you imagine anyone stupid enough to swallow that? Turks! And that they demanded a ransom of five hundred ecus—just what the gypsies asked for me.

Gerontio. The swine.

Zerbinetta. Imagine this old man, in agony, trying to decide which 50 he loved more, his son or five hundred ecus. Five hundred ecus were like five hundred stabs in the heart to him. It was like giving away part of his body. And in his miserly desperation he hit upon the most ridiculous, but cheap, ways of recovering his son. He wanted to send a policeman after them—at sea. He asked the servant to take the son's place while he tried to get the money—as if he ever would. He finally decided, with great benevolence, to sell, in order to raise the money, four or five old suits that weren't even worth thirty ecus.

Gerontio. The damned dog.

Zerbinetta. The servant kept repeating that it was urgent, but this old fool kept stalling and squirming to the refrain of "What the devil did he board that galley for?" "Oh damnable galley," "Oh treacherous Turk." Finally after he had tried every dodge—but, you aren't even smiling at my story. What do you think of it? 60

Gerontio. I think that the young man is an insolent son who will be severely punished by his father. I think that the gypsy is an impertinent slut who goes around seducing proper young men. And I think that the servant is an . . . there are no more names for him! . . . who will be sent to the gallows, by Gerontio, before the sun rises again.

Scene IV. *Sylvestro, Zerbinetta*

Sylvestro. What were you talking to Gerontio for? Did you know it was he?

Zerbinetta. I was beginning to suspect it from the way he was acting. And I've been telling him without knowing it, the whole story of how he was tricked.

Sylvestro. Oh, no!

Zerbinetta. I was so delighted with it myself, I was burning to tell it to someone. But what does it matter? Let him burn. I don't see how things could be much worse for us anyway.

Sylvestro. Like all women, you have a big mouth. We never should have told you about it in the first place. 10

Zerbinetta. Like all men, you have to brag about your exploits. You would have told it to someone who would have told it to Gerontio.

Scene V. *Argantio, Sylvestro*

Argantio. (From the back) Ho, Sylvestro.

Sylvestro. (To Zerbinetta) Get back in the house. Here's my master.

Argantio. Ah, you thief. You had it all arranged. Ah, you had it all arranged. You, Scapin, and my son. Ah, all arranged to swindle me. Did you think I would stand for it when I found out?

Sylvestro. Scapin cheated you sir? I'm sorry to hear that. Surely you don't think I had anything to do with it.

Argantio. We'll look into that later. Later, you dog. Oh, I'm in such a mood! Mark my words, no one will get away with anything.

Scene VI. *Argantio, Gerontio, Sylvestro*

Gerontio. My dear Argantio, I'm disgraced. I am the whole town's laughing stock.

Argantio. They won't have time to laugh at you; they'll be too busy laughing at me.
Gerontio. Scapin robbed me of five hundred ecus.
Argantio. Scapin robbed me of two hundred pistoles.
Gerontio. Not only did he rob me, he beat me as well.
Both. (On the point of tears) The dog will pay for this.
Sylvestro. (Aside) Thank God, I was in disguise. I'll simply deny
10 the whole thing.
Gerontio. But that isn't all that oppresses me. Misfortunes follow fast upon each other. I was expecting to welcome my daughter today. But I have just heard that her ship has foundered.
Argantio. What a great misfortune. But why was she in Tarentum in the first place? Why didn't she stay here with you?
Gerontio. There were reasons. Family interests, finances, many things forced me to keep this second marriage a secret. Until now. And it's too late. But who is this?

Scene VII. *Argantio, Gerontio, Nerina, Sylvestro*

Gerontio. Why, it's her nurse.
Nerina. (Throwing herself at his feet) Oh Signor Pandolpho!
Gerontio. Call me Gerontio. That name is no longer necessary.
Nerina. A false name? That name has caused us weeks of misery. No wonder we couldn't find you in Naples.
Gerontio. Where are my wife and daughter?
Nerina. Your daughter, sir, is not far from here. But before I let you see her, I must tell you that she is married. *(Throwing herself at his knees again)* Oh sir, what else could we do—alone and penniless
10 in a strange town, without any hope of finding you again.
Gerontio. Married?
Nerina. Yes.
Gerontio. To whom?
Nerina. A young man named Octavio.
Gerontio. Incredible! I can't believe it!
Argantio. My Octavio!
Gerontio. Take me to her immediately.
Nerina. She is right inside this house.
Gerontio. After you, after you. After me Argantio, after me.
20 *Sylvestro. (Alone)* Well, how lucky can you get?

Scene VIII. *Scapin, Sylvestro*

Scapin. Pssst, Sylvestro. Have they all gone?
Sylvestro. Listen stranger, I have two things to say to you. The first is for information only. Hyacinth is really Gerontio's daughter and

luck has brought about what you with your fabulous skill could never accomplish. The second is: Leave Naples while you still can and forget that you ever knew me.

Scapin. What a coward you are. Threats of punishment never harmed me yet. Mere words, clouds that pass far over one's head.

Sylvestro. You look out for yourself. Those sons are going to get in the good graces of their fathers and leave you for the scapegoat. 10

Scapin. I'll figure out a way to make them all happy without any danger to ourselves.

Sylvestro. To yourself, my ex-friend. Go away, I hear someone coming.

Scene IX. *Argantio, Gerontio, Hyacinth, Nerina, Sylvestro*

Gerontio. Come, my darling little daughter, let us go home. My joy would be perfect now, if only your mother were here with you.

Argantio. Here comes that handsome son of mine.

Scene X.*(Plus) Octavio, Zerbinetta*

Argantio. My son, my darling boy, come and let us celebrate your marriage.

Octavio. Never, father. Don't speak of marriage to me. I will no longer keep any secrets from you. It is time you knew . . .

Argantio. Yes, but don't you know . . .

Octavio. I know all that I need to know.

Argantio. Listen, Signor Gerontio's daughter . . .

Octavio. . . . will never be anything to me.

Gerontio. But she . . .

Octavio. (To Gerontio) Pardon me, sir. I have nothing against your daughter, but fate has led me to another. 10

Sylvestro. (To Octavio) Oh, listen to them.

Octavio. You shut up. I'm through listening to people.

Argantio. (To Octavio) Your wife . . .

Octavio. No father, this is my wife *(Crossing to Hyacinth)* and I will die before I surrender her. Yes, I defy all of you. Take a good look at her and then do what you will. But here is the only woman I could ever love. I will always love her. I couldn't love anyone else.

Argantio. Then take her, for God's sake! The fool can only stick to that one point. 20

Hyacinth. (Pointing to Gerontio) This is my father, Octavio, I've found him at last.

Gerontio. Let's go home. We can talk at length there.

Hyacinth. (Indicating Zerbinetta) Oh father, I forgot my friend. I beg you not to separate me from her. Once you know her you will love her as I do.

Gerontio. You want me to take your brother's mistress home with me; moreover, a girl who slandered me to my face?

Zerbinetta. Forgive me sir. I would never have spoken if I had known 30 who you were. I only knew you by your reputation.

Gerontio. What reputation?

Hyacinth. Father, let me answer for her virtue. The love Leandro has for her is one you can be proud of.

Gerontio. That may be. But he wants to marry her—a nobody, a vagabond.

Scene XI. *(Plus) Leandro*

Leandro. Before you insult her further, Father, hear what I have to say. I have just discovered that Zerbinetta is really the daughter of a fine old family of Naples. The gypsies told me this when I paid the ransom money. They kidnapped her at the age of four. They gave me this bracelet which was the only ornament found on her when they took her.

Argantio. Let me see that. That's my bracelet! That's my daughter! It's my bracelet! That's the bracelet my daughter was wearing . . . when I lost her . . . at the age of four . . .

10 *Gerontio.* Your daughter?

Argantio. Yes, this is she. And now I see the resemblance which makes me sure. My daughter . . .

Hyacinth. What an extraordinary coincidence.

Scene XII. *(Plus) Carle*

Carle. Sirs, I come to report a tragic accident.

Gerontio. What now?

Carle. (Crying) Scapin.

Gerontio. The man I'm going to see hanged?

Carle. There's no need for that now. As he was passing under a building, a flower pot fell on his head and broke his skull. He's dying. He begged, with his last breath, to be carried here so that he might speak to you before he died.

Argantio. Where is he?

10 *Carle.* Here he comes.

Scene XIII. *(Plus) Scapin*

Scapin. (Carried by two men, his head in bandages, acting as though it were broken) Oh sirs, you see me . . . oh, ah, you see me very close to death. Oh! I couldn't die without begging forgiveness of everyone

I may have innocently offended. It's the Christian thing to do. Oh! Yes, before breathing my last, I beg you to forgive a dying man, particularly you, Signor Argantio, and you, Signor Gerontio.

Argantio. Well, I forgive you; go and die in peace.

Scapin. (To Gerontio) It's you sir, that I have offended most by beating. . . .

Gerontio. Don't mention it. I pardon you also. 10

Scapin. That was going too far, to beat you. . . .

Gerontio. Forget it.

Scapin. But, in dying, I am haunted by those blows that . . .

Gerontio. Good God, be silent and die.

Scapin. Those miserable blows that I . . .

Gerontio. Quiet, I tell you. I forgive you. I've forgotten it, now go.

Scapin. What kindness, what generosity. But, is it from the heart that you forgive me for the blows. . . .

Gerontio. With all my heart. Speak of it no more. I forgive you everything. Now die. 20

Scapin. Ah, this forgiveness brings some of my old vigor back to me.

Gerontio. But I pardon you only on the condition that you die.

Scapin. What? But sir . . .

Gerontio. Recover and I take it back.

Scapin. Oh, ah. Death hovers over me. I feel it approaching.

Argantio. Signor Gerontio, in honor of this happy ending, pardon him unconditionally.

Gerontio. Very well.

Argantio. Let us go and dine together, in order to taste our delights the better. 30

Scapin. As for me, let me be carried to the foot of the table. I shall await death there.

Comments and Questions

The opening scenes of a play generally comprise what is called "the exposition," setting forth the who, what, where and when, at times as directly as a news report. The exposition in Scapin *is very direct and very simple: Octavio attempts, with considerable misgivings, to digest some information, evidently just supplied by his servant Sylvestro. You might compare this exposition to that of some other plays: the quarrel, for example, among the principal characters of* The Alchemist *in which they gradually, and with great heat, disclose their backgrounds and what led them to their present positions; or the fleeing captain's dramatic intrusion into Raina's bedroom in* Arms and the Man. *You might compare the value of the direct exposition to the indirect. The exposition in* Scapin *reveals a young man, about to be married off against his will by his own father in the best seventeenth-century manner. Then Scapin enters and, for the first of many times, promises with sublime confidence to set everything right. Most of the fun of the play lies in this tragically misplaced self-confidence and its results.*

Note, also, that Scapin's arrival actually interrupts the exposition, which continues afterwards with the rest of the story about Gerontio and his son Leandro. To give the whole explanation in one sweep would have been too much for the audience to absorb.

Leandro's story runs parallel to that of Octavio; the classic French dramatists liked the neatness of such arrangements. What other parallels in plot development, or among the characters, do you find in Scapin?

Contrasts are important too, especially because of the many parallels: Scapin's tone of quiet confidence stands in contrast to the lyric effusions of Octavio. How would you characterize Hyacinth's speeches in Act I, Scene III in contrast to these two? Are there any marks—in speech, in attitude, in character generally—to distinguish between some of those who are paired off, such as the two heavies, Argantio and Gerontio?

Molière uses a wide variety of comic effects, ranging from the subtle irony of romantic exuberance in young lovers to farcical beatings. What other variants of humor can you find?

Scapin, the central manipulator of the plot, can be compared to either Subtle or Face in The Alchemist, *or Mrs. Levi in* The Matchmaker. *Which of these does Scapin resemble more, and why?*

And, finally, the student should consider, in the case of Scapin, *or in all these, how a man sets himself up to be conned. What do we do to lure the Scapins of this world into action?*

Related Reading

Ben Jonson, *The Alchemist*, page 354
Thornton Wilder, *The Matchmaker*, page 248
Louis Kronenberger, "Some Prefatory Words on Comedy," page 680

Ben Jonson

(1572-1637)

THE ALCHEMIST

Playwrights take their cues from life; thus, many have been attracted to the subject of the swindler and the swindled, and comic writers have delighted in it as a way to make us laugh at human weaknesses in both ourselves and in others.

Ben Jonson's comedy The Alchemist *basically plays upon the pleasure of watching the swindling of a company of fools: a gambling clerk, a greedy merchant, a country bumpkin and his sister, a knight, and two Puritan clergymen. The swindlers are the sly servant Face (a perfect name for a man of so many faces) and the charlatan alchemist Subtle with his accomplice Dol Common (both are what their names imply). Face is the helper and contact man who finds the gulls; Dol plays various roles assigned her, from The Queen of the Fairies to a prostitute; Subtle is the lead man, who plays not only the alchemist but also the astrologer, procurer, fortune teller, and even marriage counselor.*

Alchemists were the scientists of the Middle Ages and the early Renaissance, before the methods of observing nature and natural causes led to the development of what we now consider a science. Their methods were largely those of magic, their formulas the abracadabra of the supernatural. Alchemists were involved in looking for panaceas—universal remedies for all ailments; they experimented with turning base metals into gold.

In the time of Shakespeare and Ben Jonson, alchemy was still a respectable profession. Queen Elizabeth employed the alchemist and astrologer John Dee, to whom Jonson refers; the Hapsburg Emperor Rudolf II was himself a practitioner; King James I, Jonson's sovereign, was a well-known student of magic and black arts. But more often than not, alchemists in the early seventeenth century were simply clever con men who knew the terms and rituals of that murky science and knew even better how to establish themselves in a profitable business. Subtle is such a latter-day alchemist.

Along with the pleasure in watching deserving gulls being conned, Jonson's play offers other delights: characters unwittingly exposing their private weaknesses to the world—Sir Epicure Mammon and Deacon Ananias being especially capable in this line since they have most to expose; the comic use of alchemical lingo, both real and imaginary, and often in rather risqué puns; the disguises, hurried exits, and sudden crises; the comic situations themselves, as when Dapper the clerk is undressed in a mock ritual so that the con men can discover all the money he has hidden in pockets, shoes, and locket; the spirited activity necessary to keep the customers separated; and finally, all the events in the play converging in a comic crisis.

Jonson is not merely offering an amusing comedy allowing laughter from a safe distance at *the assembled fools and* with *the swindlers, but is rather satirizing, that is, attacking through ridicule, certain human tendencies. Thus, though comedy always allows us to look down from our "normal" rather self-satisfied position at characters who represent human weaknesses, it forces us finally to look to ourselves, and sometimes, in comedies like* The Alchemist, *to see ourselves, not without some apprehension and distaste.*

The Alchemist *was registered, as was required by law, in 1610, and was performed in that year in London, probably in November when the theaters reopened after having been closed for four months because of the plague. In 1612 the play was given at court before King James I. The famous eighteenth-century British actor David Garrick adapted the play in a highly successful version which made Abel Drugger the star part, a kind of freedom often taken by the famous stage stars of the eighteenth and nineteenth centuries.*

The Argument

T he sickness hot,° a master quit, for fear,
H is house in town, and left one servant there;
E ase him corrupted, and gave means to know
A Cheater and his punk;° who, now brought low,
L eaving their narrow practice, were become
C ozeners° at large; and only wanting some
H ouse to set up, with him they here contract,
E ach for a share, and all begin to act.
M uch company they draw, and much abuse,°
I n casting figures,° telling fortunes, news, 10
S elling of flies,° flat bawdry, with the stone,°
T ill it, and they, and all in fume are gone.

Prologue

Fortune, that favours fools, these two short hours
  We wish away, both for your sakes and ours,
Judging spectators; and desire, in place,
  To the author justice, to ourselves but grace.
Our scene is London, 'cause we would make known,
  No country's mirth is better than our own:
No clime breeds better matter for your whore,
  Bawd, squire, impostor, many persons more,
Whose manners, now called humours, feed the stage;
  And which have still been subject for the rage 10
Or spleen of comic writers. Though this pen
  Did never aim to grieve, but better men;
Howe'er the age he lives in doth endure
  The vices that she breeds, above their cure.
But when the wholesome remedies are sweet,
  And in their working gain and profit meet,
He hopes to find no spirit so much diseased,
  But will with such fair correctives be pleased;
For here he doth not fear who can apply.
  If there be any that will sit so nigh 20
Unto the stream, to look what it doth run,
  They shall find things, they'd think or wish were done:
They are so natural follies, but so shown,
  As even the doers may see, and yet not own.

1. ***The sickness hot,*** *the plague raging.* *4.* ***punk,*** whore. *6.* ***Cozeners,*** swindlers, con men. *9.* ***abuse,*** *i.e.,* practice abuse. *10.* ***casting figures,*** making horoscopes. *11.* ***flies,*** familiar spirits. ***stone,*** Philosopher's stone, a substance supposedly capable of transforming baser metals into gold.

THE ALCHEMIST

Characters

SUBTLE, *the Alchemist*
FACE, *the House-keeper*
DOL COMMON, *their colleague*
DAPPER, *a Lawyer's clerk*
DRUGGER, *a Tobacco-man*
LOVEWIT, *Master of the House*
SIR EPICURE MAMMON, *a Knight*
PERTINAX SURLY, *a Gamester*
TRIBULATION WHOLESOME, *a Pastor of Amsterdam*
ANANIAS, *a Deacon there*
KASTRIL, *the angry boy*
DAME PLIANT, *his sister, a Widow*
Neighbors, Officers

Scene: *London*

Act I

Scene I. *A room in Lovewit's house*

(Enter Face in a captain's uniform, Subtle with a vial, and Dol Common. Face and Subtle are quarrelling.)

Face. Believe 't, I will.
Subtle. Thy worst. I fart at thee.
Dol. Have you your wits? why, gentlemen! for love—
Face. Sirrah, I'll strip you—
Subtle. Out at my—What to do? Lick figs.°
Face. Rogue, rogue!—out of all your sleights.°
Dol. Nay, look ye! Sovereign, general, are you madmen?
Subtle. O, let the wild sheep loose. I'll gum your silks
With good strong water, an° you come.
Dol. Will you have
The neighbors hear you? Will you betray all?
Hark! I hear somebody.
Face. Sirrah—
Subtle. I shall mar
10 All that the tailor has made if you approach.

3. Lick figs, allusion to an obscene kiss in Rabelais' *Pantagruel*, Book IV ch. 45. ***4. sleights,*** tricks. ***7. an,*** if.

Face. You most notorious whelp, you insolent slave,
Dare you do this?
Subtle. Yes, faith; yes, faith.
Face. Why, who
Am I, my mongrel, who am I?
Subtle. I'll tell you,
Since you know not yourself.
Face. Speak lower, rogue.
Subtle. Yes, you were once (time's not long past) the good,
Honest, plain, livery-three-pound-thrum,° that kept
Your master's worship's house here in the Friars,°
For the vacations—
Face. Will you be so loud?
Subtle. Since, by my means, translated° suburb-captain.
Face. By your means, doctor dog?
Subtle. Within man's memory, 20
All this I speak of.
Face. Why, I pray you, have I
Been countenanced by you, or you by me?
Do but collect, sir, where I met you first.
Subtle. I do not hear well.
Face. Not of this, I think it.
But I shall put you in mind, sir: at Pie-corner,
Taking your meal of steam in, from cooks' stalls,
Where, like the father of hunger, you did walk
Piteously costive,° with your pinched-horn-nose,
And your complexion of the Roman wash,°
Stuck full of black and melancholic worms, 30
Like powder-corns shot at the artillery-yard.
Subtle. I wish you could advance your voice a little.
Face. When you went pinned up in the several rags
You had raked and picked from dunghills, before day;
Your feet in mouldy slippers, for your kibes;°
A felt of rug, and a thin threaden cloak,
That scarce would cover your no-buttocks—
Subtle. So, sir!
Face. When all your alchemy, and your algebra,
Your minerals, vegetals, and animals,°
Your conjuring, cozening,° and your dozen of trades, 40

16. livery . . . thrum, underpaid drudge. ***17. Friars. Blackfriars,*** a fashionable district in London. ***19. translated,*** transformed into. ***28. costive,*** with a cramped stomach. ***29. Roman wash,*** sallow. ***35. kibes,*** chilblains. ***36. felt of rug,*** hat of the coarsest material. ***39. minerals . . . animals,*** the alchemists' terms for the three "kingdoms" of matter. ***40. cozening,*** swindling.

Could not relieve your corpse with so much linen
Would make you tinder, but to see a fire;
I gave you countenance, credit for your coals,
Your stills, your glasses, your materials;
Built you a furnace, drew you customers,
Advanced all your black arts; lent you, beside,
A house to practise in—

Subtle. Your master's house!

Face. Where you have studied the more thriving skill
Of bawdry since.

Subtle. Yes, in your master's house.
50 You and the rats here kept possession.
Make it not strange.° I know you were one could keep
The buttery-hatch still locked, and save the chippings,°
Sell the dole beer to aqua-vitæ men,°
The which, together with your Christmas vails°
At post-and-pair,° your letting out of counters,°
Made you a pretty stock, some twenty marks,
And gave you credit to converse with cobwebs,
Here, since your mistress' death hath broke up house.

Face. You might talk softlier, rascal.

Subtle. No, you scarab,
60 I'll thunder you in pieces: I will teach you
How to beware to tempt a Fury again
That carries tempest in his hand and voice.

Face. The place has made you valiant.

Subtle. No, your clothes.
Thou vermin, have I ta'en thee out of dung,
So poor, so wretched, when no living thing
Would keep thee company, but a spider or worse?
Raised thee from brooms, and dust, and watering-pots,
Sublimed thee, and exalted thee, and fixed thee
In the third region, called our state of grace?
70 Wrought thee to spirit, to quintessence,° with pains
Would twice have won me the philosopher's work?
Put thee in words and fashion, made thee fit
For more than ordinary fellowships?
Given thee thy oaths, thy quarrelling dimensions,
Thy rules to cheat at horse-race, cock-pit, cards,
Dice, or whatever gallant tincture° else?
Made thee a second in mine own great art?

51. Make . . . strange, don't pretend you forget. ***52. chippings,*** waste bread, usually given to the poor. ***53. Sell . . . men,*** sell the beer intended for the poor to liquor dealers. ***54. vails,*** tips, gifts. ***55. post-and-pair,*** a card game. ***counters,*** chips (rented to card players). ***68-70. Sublimed . . . quintessence,*** alchemical jargon. ***76. tincture,*** status.

And have I this for thanks? Do you rebel?
Do you fly out in the projection?°
Would you be gone now?
Dol. Gentlemen, what mean you? 80
Will you mar all?
Subtle. Slave, thou hadst had no name—
Dol. Will you undo yourselves with civil war?
Subtle. Never been known, past *equi clibanum*,°
The heat of horse-dung, under ground, in cellars,
Or an ale-house darker than deaf John's; been lost
To all mankind, but laundresses and tapsters,
Had not I been.
Dol. Do you know who hears you, sovereign?
Face. Sirrah—
Dol. Nay, general, I thought you were civil.
Face. I shall turn desperate, if you grow thus loud.
Subtle. And hang thyself, I care not.
Face. Hang thee, collier, 90
And all thy pots and pans, in picture, I will,
Since thou hast moved me—
Dol. (Aside) O, this'll o'erthrow all.
Face. Write thee up bawd in Paul's,° have all thy tricks
Of cozening with a hollow coal, dust, scrapings,
Searching for things lost, with a sieve and shears,
Erecting figures in your rows of houses,°
And taking in of shadows with a glass,
Told in red letters; and a face cut for thee,
Worse than Gamaliel Ratsey's.°
Dol. Are you sound?
Have you your senses, masters?
Face. I will have 100
A book, but barely reckoning thy impostures,
Shall prove a true philosopher's stone to printers.
Subtle. Away, you trencher-rascal!
Face. Out, you dog-leech!
The vomit of all prisons—
Dol. Will you be
Your own destructions, gentlemen?
Face. Still spewed out
For lying too heavy on the basket.°
Subtle. Cheater!

79. in the projection, with success so near (application of alchemical lingo to their present situation). ***83. equi clibanum,*** (translated in the next line). ***93. Paul's,*** St. Paul's Church. ***96. Erecting . . . houses,*** an astrological trick. ***99. Gamaliel Ratsey,*** a highwayman hanged in 1605. ***106. lying . . . basket,*** eating more than his share of rations.

Face. Bawd!
Subtle. Cow-herd!
Face. Conjurer!
Subtle. Cutpurse!
Face. Witch!
Dol. O me!
We are ruined, lost! Have you no more regard
To your reputations? Where's your judgment? 'Slight,
110 Have yet some care of me, of your republic°—
Face. Away, this brach!° I'll bring thee, rogue, within
The statute of sorcery, tricesimo tertio
Of Harry the Eighth:° ay, and perhaps thy neck
Within a noose, for laundering gold and barbing it.°
Dol. You'll bring your head within a cockscomb,° will you? *(She catches Face's sword, and breaks Subtle's glass.)*
And you, sir, with your menstrue!°—gather it up.
'Sdeath, you abominable pair of stinkards,
Leave off your barking, and grow one again,
Or, by the light that shines, I'll cut your throats.
120 I'll not be made a prey unto the marshal
For ne'er a snarling dog-bolt of you both.
Have you together cozened all this while,
And all the world, and shall it now be said,
You've made most courteous shift to cozen yourselves?
(To Face) You will accuse him! You will bring him in
Within the statute! Who shall take your word?
A whoreson, upstart, apocryphal captain,
Whom not a Puritan in Blackfriars will trust
So much as for a feather; *(To Subtle)* And you, too,
130 Will give the cause, forsooth! You will insult,
And claim a primacy in the divisions!°
You must be chief! As if you only had
The powder to project° with, and the work
Were not begun out of equality!
The venture tripartite! All things in common!
Without priority! Sdeath! You perpetual curs,
Fall to your couples again, and cozen kindly,
And heartily, and lovingly, as you should,
And lose not the beginning of a term,

110. republic, fraternity (of cheats). ***111. brach,*** bitch. ***112-113. statute . . . Eighth,*** law of the thirty-third year of King Henry VIII (against witchcraft). ***114. laundering . . . it,*** clipping gold coinage. ***115. cockscomb,*** rope. ***116. menstrue,*** liquid which dissolves solids. ***131. primacy . . . divisions,*** first choice in the loot. ***133. powder to project,*** *i.e.,* to make the philosopher's stone.

Or, by this hand, I shall grow factious° too, 140
And take my part, and quit you.
Face. 'Tis his fault;
He ever murmurs, and objects his pains,
And says, the weight of all lies upon him.
Subtle. Why, so it does.
Dol. How does it? Do not we
Sustain our parts?
Subtle. Yes, but they are not equal.
Dol. Why, if your part exceed today, I hope
Ours may tomorrow match it.
Subtle. Ay, they *may.*
Dol. May, murmuring mastiff! Ay, and do. Death on me!
Help me to throttle him. *(Seizes Subtle by the throat)*
Subtle. Dorothy! Mistress Dorothy!
'Ods precious, I'll do anything. What do you mean? 150
Dol. Because of your fermentation and cibation?
Subtle. Not I, by heaven—
Dol. Your Sol and Luna—help me. *(To Face)*
Subtle. Would I were hanged then! I'll conform myself.
Dol. Will you, sir? Do so then, and quickly: swear.
Subtle. What should I swear?
Dol. To leave your faction, sir,
And labour kindly in the common work.
Subtle. Let me not breathe if I meant aught beside.
I only used those speeches as a spur
To him.
Dol. I hope we need no spurs, sir. Do we?
Face. 'Slid, prove today who shall shark best.
Subtle. Agreed. 160
Dol. Yes, and work close and friendly.
Subtle. 'Slight, the knot
Shall grow the stronger for this breach, with me.
(They shake hands.)
Dol. Why, so, my good baboons! Shall we go make
A sort of sober, scurvy, precise neighbours,
That scarce have smiled twice since the king° came in,
A feast of laughter at our follies? Rascals,
Would run themselves from breath, to see me ride,°
Or you to have but a hole to thrust your heads in,
For which you should pay ear-rent?° No, agree.

140. factious, cantankerous. ***165. the king,*** James I, king since 1603. ***167. ride,*** be carted off as a whore. ***168-169. hole . . . ear-rent,*** to be put in the pillory and have your ears cut off.

170 And may Don Provost° ride a feasting long,
In his old velvet jerkin and stained scarfs,
My noble sovereign, and worthy general,
Ere we contribute a new crewel garter
To his most worsted worship.

Subtle. Royal Dol!
Spoken like Claridiana,° and thyself.

Face. For which at supper, thou shalt sit in triumph,
And not be styled Dol Common, but Dol Proper,
Dol Singular: the longest cut at night,
Shall draw thee for his Dol Particular. *(Bell rings without)*

Subtle. Who's that? One rings. To the window, Dol:—*(Exit Dol)*
180 pray heaven,
The master do not trouble us this quarter.

Face. O, fear not him. While there dies one a week
Of the plague, he's safe from thinking toward London.
Beside, he's busy at his hop-yards now;
I had a letter from him. If he do,
He'll send such word for airing of the house
As you shall have sufficient time to quit it:
Though we break up a fortnight, 'tis no matter.°
(Re-enter Dol)

Subtle. Who is it, Dol?

Dol. A fine young quodling.°

Face. O,
190 My lawyer's clerk, I lighted on last night,
In Holborn, at the Dagger. He would have
(I told you of him) a familiar,°
To rifle with at horses, and win cups.

Dol. O, let him in.

Subtle. Stay. Who shall do't?

Face. Get you
Your robes on; I will meet him, as going out.

Dol. And what shall I do?

Face. Not be seen; away! *(Exit Dol)*
Seem you very reserved.

Subtle. Enough. *(Exit)*

Face. (Aloud and retiring) God be with you, sir,
I pray you let him know that I was here:
His name is Dapper. I would gladly have stayed, but—

170. Don Provost, the hangman received the clothes of the people he executed. ***175. Claridiana,*** heroine of a popular romance. ***188. Though . . . matter,*** we can safely stay another two weeks. ***189. quodling,*** green youth. ***192. familiar,*** a familiar spirit, to serve Dapper.

Scene II. *The same*

(Face, alone)

Dapper. (Within) Captain, I am here.

Face. Who's that?—He's come, I think, doctor.

(Enter Dapper)

Good faith, sir, I was going away.

Dapper. In truth
I am very sorry, captain.

Face. But I thought
Sure I should meet you.

Dapper. Ay, I am very glad.
I had a scurvy writ or two to make,
And I had lent my watch last night to one
That dines today at the sheriff's, and so was robbed
Of my pass-time.

(Re-enter Subtle in his velvet cap and gown)

Is this the cunning-man?

Face. This is his worship.

Dapper. Is he a doctor?

Face. Yes.

Dapper. And have you broke with him,° captain?

Face. Ay.

Dapper. And how? 10

Face. Faith, he does make the matter, sir, so dainty,°
I know not what to say.

Dapper. Not so, good captain.

Face. Would I were fairly rid of it, believe me.

Dapper. Nay, now you grieve me, sir. Why should you wish so?
I dare assure you, I'll not be ungrateful.

Face. I cannot think you will, sir. But the law
Is such a thing—and then he says, Read's° matter
Falling so lately.

Dapper. Read! he was an ass,
And dealt, sir, with a fool.

Face. It was a clerk,° sir.

Dapper. A clerk!

Face. Nay, hear me, sir. You know the law 20
Better, I think—

10. broke . . . him, told him. ***11. make . . . dainty,*** has such scruples. ***17. Read's,*** in 1608 Dr. Simon Read was indicted for invoking spirits. ***19. clerk,*** Read dealt with a law clerk (like Dapper).

Dapper. I should, sir, and the danger:
You know, I showed the statute to you.
Face. You did so.
Dapper. And will I tell then? By this hand of flesh,
Would it might never write good court-hand more,
If I discover. What do you think of me,
That I am a chiaus?
Face. What's that?
Dapper. The Turk,° was here—
As one would say, do you think I am a Turk?
Face. I'll tell the doctor so.
Dapper. Do, good sweet captain.
Face. Come, noble doctor, pray thee let's prevail;
30 This is the gentleman, and he is no chiaus.
Subtle. Captain, I have returned you all my answer.
I would do much, sir, for your love—But this
I neither may, nor can.
Face. Tut, do not say so.
You deal now with a noble fellow, doctor,
One that will thank you richly; and he is no chiaus:
Let that, sir, move you.
Subtle. Pray you, forbear—
Face. He has
Four angels° here.
Subtle. You do me wrong, good sir.
Face. Doctor, wherein? To tempt you with these spirits?
Subtle. To tempt my art and love, sir, to my peril.
40 'Fore heaven, I scarce can think you are my friend,
That so would draw me to apparent danger.
Face. I draw you! A horse draw you, and a halter,
You, and your flies together—
Dapper. Nay, good captain.
Face. That know no difference of men.
Subtle. Good words, sir.
Face. Good deeds, sir, doctor dogs'-meat. 'Slight, I bring you
No cheating Clim o' the Cloughs' or Claribels,
That look as big as five-and-fifty, and flush;°
And spit out secrets like hot custard—
Dapper. Captain!
Face. Nor any melancholic underscribe,
50 Shall tell the vicar; but a special gentle,
That is the heir to forty marks a year,

26. Turk, a Turkish interpreter (chiaus) had recently cheated some traders. ***37. angels,*** gold coins. ***47. five . . . flush,*** winning hand in primero, a card game.

Consorts with the small poets of the time,
Is the sole hope of his old grandmother;
That knows the law, and writes you six fair hands,
Is a fine clerk, and has his ciphering perfect.
Will take his oath o' the Greek Testament,
If need be, in his pocket; and can court
His mistress out of Ovid.
Dapper. Nay, dear captain—
Face. Did you not tell me so?
Dapper. Yes; but I'd have you
Use master doctor with some more respect. 60
Face. Hang him, proud stag, with his broad velvet head!—
But for your sake, I'd choke ere I would change
An article of breath with such a puck-fist!°
Come, let's be gone. *(Going)*
Subtle. Pray you, let me speak with you.
Dapper. His worship calls you, captain.
Face. I am sorry
I e'er embarked myself in such a business.
Dapper. Nay, good sir; he did call you.
Face. Will he take then?
Subtle. First, hear me—
Face. Not a syllable, unless you take.
Subtle. Pray ye, sir—
Face. Upon no terms but an *assumpsit.*°
Subtle. Your humour must be law. *(He takes the money.)*
Face. Why now, sir, talk. 70
Now I dare hear you with mine honour. Speak.
So may this gentleman too.
Subtle. Why, sir— *(Offering to whisper to Face.)*
Face. No whispering.
Subtle. 'Fore heaven, you do not apprehend the loss
You do yourself in this.
Face. Wherein? for what?
Subtle. Marry, to be so importunate for one
That, when he has it, will undo you all:
He'll win up all the money in the town.
Face. How?
Subtle. Yes, and blow up gamester after gamester,
As they do crackers in a puppet-play.
If I do give him a familiar, 80
Give you him all you play for; never set° him:

63. puck-fist, puff ball, i.e., empty boaster. ***69. assumpsit,*** acceptance (legal term). ***81. set,*** bet against.

For he will have it.
Face. You're mistaken, doctor.
Why, he does ask one but for cups and horses,
A rifling fly; none of your great familiars.
Dapper. Yes, captain, I would have it for all games.
Subtle. I told you so.
Face. (Taking Dapper aside) 'Slight, that is a new business!
I understood you, a tame bird, to fly
Twice in a term, or so, on Friday nights,
When you had left the office; for a nag
Of forty or fifty shillings.
90 *Dapper.* Ay, 'tis true, sir;
But I do think, now, I shall leave the law,
And therefore—
Face. Why, this changes quite the case.
Do you think that I dare move him?
Dapper. If you please, sir;
All's one to him, I see.
Face. What! For that money?
I cannot with my conscience; nor should you
Make the request, methinks.
Dapper. No, sir, I mean
To add consideration.
Face. Why then, sir,
I'll try. *(Goes to Subtle. They speak apart.)* Say, that it were for all games, doctor?
Subtle. I say then, not a mouth shall eat for him
100 At any ordinary,° but on the score,°
That is a gaming mouth, conceive me.
Face. Indeed!
Subtle. He'll draw you all the treasure of the realm,
If it be set him.
Face. Speak you this from art?
Subtle. Ay, sir, and reason too, the ground of art.
He is of the only best complexion,
The queen of Fairy loves.
Face. What! Is he?
Subtle. Peace.
He'll overhear you. Sir, should she but see him—
Face. What?
Subtle. Do not you tell him.
Face. Will he win at cards too?
Subtle. The spirits of dead Holland, living Isaac,°

100. ordinary, restaurant. ***on the score,*** on credit. ***109. Holland . . . Isaac,*** alchemists.

You'd swear, were in him; such a vigorous luck 110
As cannot be resisted. 'Slight, he'll put
Six of your gallants to a cloak,° indeed.
Face. A strange success, that some man shall be born to!
Subtle. He hears you, man—
Dapper. Sir, I'll not be ingrateful.
Face. Faith, I have confidence in his good nature:
You hear, he says he will not be ingrateful.
Subtle. Why, as you please; my venture follows yours.
Face. Troth, do it, doctor; think him trusty, and make him.
He may make us both happy in an hour;
Win some five thousand pound, and send us two on't. 120
Dapper. Believe it, and I will, sir.
Face. And you shall, sir.
You have heard all? *(To Dapper)*
Dapper. No, what was't? Nothing, I, sir. *(Face takes him aside.)*
Face. Nothing!
Dapper. A little, sir.
Face. Well, a rare star
Reigned at your birth.
Dapper. At mine, sir! No.
Face. The doctor
Swears that you are—
Subtle. Nay, captain, you'll tell all now.
Face. Allied to the queen of Fairy.
Dapper. Who! That I am?
Believe it, no such matter—
Face. Yes, and that
You were born with a caul° on your head.
Dapper. Who says so?
Face. Come,
You know it well enough, though you dissemble it.
Dapper. I' fac', I do not; you are mistaken.
Face. How! 130
Swear by your fac', and in a thing so known
Unto the doctor? How shall we, sir, trust you
In the other matter; can we ever think,
When you have won five or six thousand pound,
You'll send us shares in't by this rate?
Dapper. By Jove, sir,
I'll win ten thousand pound, and send you half.
In faith's no oath.

112. cloak, i.e., strip them bare. ***126. caul,*** a lucky sign. ***130. fac',*** faith.

Subtle. No, no, he did but jest.
Face. Go to. Go thank the doctor: he's your friend,
To take it so.
Dapper. I thank his worship.
Face. So!
Another angel.
Dapper. Must I?
140 *Face.* Must you! 'slight,
What else is thanks? Will you be trivial?—Doctor, *(Dapper gives him the money.)*
When must he come for his familiar?
Dapper. Shall I not have it with me?
Subtle. O, good sir!
There must a world of ceremonies pass;
You must be bathed and fumigated first:
Besides, the queen of Fairy does not rise
Till it be noon.
Face. Not if she danced to-night.
Subtle. And she must bless it.
Face. Did you never see
Her royal grace yet?
Dapper. Whom?
Face. Your aunt of Fairy?
150 *Subtle.* Not since she kissed him in the cradle, captain;
I can resolve you that.
Face. (Aside to Dapper)
Well, see her grace.
Whate'er it cost you, for a thing that I know.
It will be somewhat hard to compass; but,
However, see her. You are made, believe it,
If you can see her. Her grace is a lone woman,
And very rich; and if she take a fancy,
She will do strange things. See her, at any hand.
'Slid, she may hap to leave you all she has:
It is the doctor's fear.
Dapper. How will't be done, then?
160 *Face.* Let me alone, take you no thought. Do you
But say to me, "Captain, I'll see her grace."
Dapper. "Captain, I'll see her grace."
Face. Enough. *(One knocks without.)*
Subtle. Who's there?
Anon.°—*(Aside to Face)* Conduct him forth by the back way.
—Sir, against one o'clock prepare yourself;

163. Anon, in a moment.

Till when you must be fasting; only take
Three drops of vinegar in at your nose,
Two at your mouth, and one at either ear;
Then bathe your fingers' ends and wash your eyes,
To sharpen your five senses, and cry *hum*
Thrice, and then *buz* as often; and then come. *(Exit)* 170

Face. Can you remember this?

Dapper. I warrant you.

Face. Well then, away. It is but your bestowing
Some twenty nobles 'mong her grace's servants,
And put on a clean shirt. You do not know
What grace her grace may do you in clean linen.

(Exeunt Face and Dapper)

Scene III. *The same*

Subtle. (Within as if speaking to clients) Come in! Good wives, I pray you forbear me now;
Troth, I can do you no good till afternoon—
(Enter Subtle, followed by Drugger)

Subtle. What is your name, say you? Abel Drugger?

Drugger. Yes, sir.

Subtle. A seller of tobacco?

Drugger. Yes, sir.

Subtle. Umph!
Free of the grocers?°

Drug. Ay, an't please you.

Subtle. Well—
Your business, Abel?

Drugger. This, an't please your worship;
I am a young beginner, and am building
Of a new shop, an't like your worship, just
At corner of a street:—Here is the plot on't—
And I would know by art, sir, of your worship, 10
Which way I should make my door, by necromancy,
And where my shelves; and which should be for boxes,
And which for pots. I would be glad to thrive, sir:
And I was wished° to your worship by a gentleman,
One Captain Face, that says you know men's planets,
And their good angels, and their bad.

Subtle. I do,
If I do see them—
(Enter Face)

5. Free . . . grocers, or member of the grocers' guild. ***14. wished,*** recommended.

Face. What! my honest Abel?
Thou art well met here.
Drugger. Troth, sir, I was speaking,
Just as your worship came here, of your worship:
20 I pray you speak for me to master doctor.
Face. He shall do anything. Doctor, do you hear?
This is my friend, Abel, an honest fellow;
He lets me have good tobacco, and he does not
Sophisticate it with sack-lees° or oil,
Nor washes it in muscadel and grains,
Nor buries it in gravel, under ground,
Wrapped up in greasy leather, or pissed clouts:
But keeps it in fine lily pots, that, opened,
Smell like conserve of roses, or French beans.
30 He has his maple block, his silver tongs,
Winchester pipes, and fire of juniper:°
A neat, spruce, honest fellow, and no goldsmith.°
Subtle. He's a fortunate fellow, that I am sure on.
Face. Already, sir, have you found it? Lo thee, Abel!
Subtle. And in right way toward riches—
Face. Sir!
Subtle. This summer
He will be of the clothing of his company,°
And next spring called to the scarlet;° spend what he can.
Face. What, and so little beard?
Subtle. Sir, you must think,
He may have a receipt to make hair come.
40 But he'll be wise, preserve his youth, and fine for it;
His fortune looks for him another way.
Face. 'Slid, doctor, how canst thou know this so soon?
I am amused at that.
Subtle. By a rule, captain,
In metoposcopy, which I do work by;
A certain star in the forehead, which you see not.
Your chestnut or your olive-coloured face
Does never fail; and your long ear doth promise.
I knew't, by certain spots, too, in his teeth,
And on the nail of his mercurial finger.
Face. Which finger's that?
50 *Subtle.* His little finger. Look.
You were born upon a Wednesday?
Drugger. Yes, indeed, sir.

24. Sophisticate . . . sack-lees, adulterate it with the dregs of sack, a white wine. ***30-31. He . . . juniper,*** tools for shredding and lighting tobacco. ***32. goldsmith,*** usurer. ***36. clothing . . . company,*** be a full member of his guild. ***37. scarlet,*** be made sheriff.

Subtle. The thumb, in chiromancy, we give Venus;
The forefinger to Jove; the midst to Saturn;
The ring to Sol; the least to Mercury,
Who was the lord, sir, of his horoscope,
His house of life being Libra; which foreshowed
He should be a merchant, and should trade with balance.
Face. Why, this is strange! Is it not, honest Nab?
Subtle. There is a ship now coming from Ormus,
That shall yield him such a commodity 60
Of drugs—This is the west, and this the south? *(Pointing to the plan)*
Drugger. Yes, sir.
Subtle. And those are your two sides?
Drugger. Ay, sir.
Subtle. Make me your door then, south; your broad side, west:
And on the east side of your shop, aloft,
Write Mathlai, Tarmiel, and Baraborat;
Upon the north part, Rael, Velel, Thiel.
They are the names of those Mercurial spirits
That do fright flies from boxes.
Drugger. Yes, sir.
Subtle. And
Beneath your threshold, bury me a loadstone
To draw in gallants that wear spurs: the rest, 70
They'll seem to follow.
Face. That's a secret, Nab!
Subtle. And, on your stall, a puppet, with a vise
And a court-fucus,° to call city-dames:
You shall deal much with minerals.
Drugger. Sir, I have.
At home, already—
Subtle. Ay, I know you have arsenic,
Vitriol, sal-tartar, argaile, alkali,
Cinoper: I know all.—This fellow, captain,
Will come, in time, to be a great distiller,
And give a say°—I will not say directly,
But very fair—at the philosopher's stone. 80
Face. Why, how now, Abel! is this true?
Drugger. (Aside to Face) Good captain,
What must I give?
Face. Nay, I'll not counsel thee.
Thou hear'st what wealth (he says, spend what thou canst),
Thou'rt like to come to.
Drugger. I would give him a crown.

73. *court-fucus,* cosmetic. **79. *give a say,*** make an attempt.

Face. A crown! and toward such a fortune? Heart,
Thou shalt rather give him thy shop. No gold about thee?
Drugger. Yes, I have a portague,° I have kept this half-year.
Face. Out on thee, Nab! 'Slight, there was such an offer—
Shalt keep't no longer, I'll give't him for thee.
90 Doctor, Nab prays your worship to drink this, and swears
He will appear more grateful, as your skill
Does raise him in the world.
Drugger. I would entreat
Another favour of his worship.
Face. What is't, Nab?
Drugger. But to look over, sir, my almanac,
And cross out my ill-days, that I may neither
Bargain, nor trust upon them.
Face. That he shall, Nab:
Leave it, it shall be done, against afternoon.
Subtle. And a direction for his shelves.
Face. Now, Nab,
Art thou well pleased, Nab?
Drugger. 'Thank, sir, both your worships.
Face. Away.
(Exit Drugger)
100 Why, now, you smoaky persecutor of nature!
Now do you see, that something's to be done,
Beside your beech-coal, and your corrosive waters,
Your crosslets, crucibles, and cucurbites?°
You must have stuff, brought home to you, to work on:
And yet you think, I am at no expense
In searching out these veins, then following them,
Then trying them out. 'Fore God, my intelligence
Costs me more money than my share oft comes to,
In these rare works.
Subtle. You're pleasant, sir.—How now!

Scene IV. *The same*

(Face, Subtle. Enter Dol)
Subtle. What says my dainty Dolkin?
Dol. Yonder fish-wife
Will not away. And there's your giantess,
The bawd of Lambeth.

87. portague, a valuable gold coin. ***102-103. Corrosive . . . cucubrites,*** "corrosive" water and various crucibles were part of the alchemist's equipment.

Subtle. Heart, I cannot speak with them.
Dol. Not afore night, I have told them in a voice,
Thorough the trunk, like one of your familiars.
But I have spied Sir Epicure Mammon—
Subtle. Where?
Dol. Coming along, at far end of the lane,
Slow of his feet, but earnest of his tongue
To one that's with him.
Subtle. Face, go you and shift.°
Dol, you must presently make ready too. *(Exit Face)* 10
Dol. Why, what's the matter?
Subtle. O, I did look for him
With the sun's rising: marvel he could sleep.
This is the day I am to perfect for him
The magisterium, our great work, the stone;
And yield it, made, into his hands: of which
He has, this month, talked as he were possessed.
And now he's dealing pieces on't away.
Methinks I see him entering ordinaries
Dispensing for the pox, and plaguy houses,
Reaching his dose, walking Moorfields for lepers, 20
And offering citizens' wives pomander°-bracelets,
As his preservative, made of the elixir;
Searching the spittle,° to make old bawds young;
And the highways, for beggars to make rich.
I see no end of his labours. He will make
Nature ashamed of her long sleep: when art,
Who's but a step-dame, shall do more than she,
In her best love to mankind, ever could,
If his dream last, he'll turn the age to gold. *(Exeunt)*

Act II

Scene I. *An outer room in Lovewit's house*

(Enter Sir Epicure Mammon and Surly)
Mammon. Come on, sir. Now you set your foot on shore
In *Novo Orbe,*° here's the rich Peru:
And there within, sir, are the golden mines,
Great Solomon's Ophir! He was sailing to't
Three years, but we have reached it in ten months.

9. shift, change. ***21. pomander,*** a perfume ball used to ward off infection. ***23. spittle,*** hospital. ***2. Novo Orbe,*** The New World.

This is the day wherein, to all my friends,
I will pronounce the happy word, *Be rich;*
This day you shall be spectatissimi.°
You shall no more deal with the hollow die,
10 Or the frail card. No more be at charge of keeping
The livery-punk° for the young heir, that must
Seal, at all hours, in his shirt: no more,
If he deny, have him beaten to't, as he is
That brings him the commodity. No more
Shall thirst of satin, or the covetous hunger
Of velvet entrails° for a rude-spun cloak,
To be displayed at Madam Augusta's, make
The sons of Sword and Hazard° fall before
The golden calf, and on their knees, whole nights,
20 Commit idolatry with wine and trumpets:
Or go a feasting after drum and ensign.
No more of this. You shall start up young viceroys,
And have your punks and punkettees, my Surly.
And unto thee I speak it first, *Be rich.*
Where is my Subtle, there? Within, ho!

Face. (Within) Sir,
He'll come to you by and by.

Mammon. That is his fire-drake,
His Lungs, his Zephyrus, he that puffs his coals,
Till he firk° nature up, in her own centre.
You are not faithful,° sir. This night I'll change
30 All that is metal in my house to gold:
And, early in the morning, will I send
To all the plumbers and the pewterers,
And buy their tin and lead up; and to Lothbury
For all the copper.

Surly. What, and turn that, too?

Mammon. Yes, and I'll purchase Devonshire and Cornwall,
And make them perfect Indies! You admire now?

Surly. No, faith.

Mammon. But when you see th' effects of the Great Medicine,
Of which one part projected on a hundred
40 Of Mercury, or Venus, or the moon,
Shall turn it to as many of the sun;°
Nay, to a thousand, so *ad infinitum:*
You will believe me.

8. spectatissimi, most eminent. ***11. livery-punk,*** prostitute (used to swindle a young heir to a fortune). ***16. entrails,*** lining. ***18. sons . . . Hazard,*** highwaymen and gamblers. ***28. firk,*** stir. ***29. faithful,*** a believer. ***41. sun,*** i.e., turn mercury etc. into gold.

Surly. Yes, when I see't, I will.
But if my eyes do cozen me so, and I
Giving them no occasion, sure I'll have
Them out next day.
Mammon. Ha! why?
Do you think I fable with you? I assure you,
He that has once the flower of the sun,
The perfect ruby, which we call elixir,
Not only can do that, but by its virtue, 50
Can confer honour, love, respect, long life;
Give safety, valour, yea, and victory,
To whom he will. In eight and twenty days,
I'll make an old man of fourscore, a child.
Surly. No doubt; he's that already.
Mammon. Nay, I mean,
Restore his years, renew him, like an eagle,
To the fifth age; make him get sons and daughters,
Young giants; as our philosophers have done,
The ancient patriarchs, afore the flood,
But taking, once a week, on a knife's point, 60
The quantity of a grain of mustard of it;
Become stout Marses, and beget young Cupids.
Surly. The decayed vestals of Pickt-hatch° would thank you,
That keep the fire alive there.
Mammon. 'Tis the secret
Of nature naturized 'gainst all infections,
Cures all diseases coming of all causes;
A month's grief in a day, a year's in twelve;
And, of what age soever, in a month:
Past all the doses of your drugging doctors.
I'll undertake, withal, to fright the plague 70
Out of the kingdom in three months.
Surley. And I'll
Be bound, the players shall sing your praises then,
Without their poets.°
Mammon. Sir, I'll do't. Meantime,
I'll give away so much unto my man,
Shall serve the whole city with preservative
Weekly; each house his dose, and at the rate—
Surly. As he that built the Water-work does with water?
Mammon. You are incredulous.

63. Pickt-hatch, a London district unlikely to contain many vestals (virgins). ***72-73. players . . . poets,*** as the theaters were closed because of the plague, the actors would praise him if he frightened the plague away.

Surly. Faith, I have a humour,
I would not willingly be gulled. Your stone
Cannot transmute me.
80 *Mammon.* Pertinax my Surly,
Will you believe antiquity? Records?
I'll show you a book where Moses, and his sister,
And Solomon have written of the art;
Ay, and a treatise penned by Adam—
Surly. How!
Mammon. Of the philosopher's stone, and in High Dutch.
Surly. Did Adam write, sir, in High Dutch?
Mammon. He did;
Which proves it was the primitive tongue.
Surly. What paper?
Mammon. On cedar board.
Surly. O that, indeed, they say,
Will last 'gainst worms.
Mammon. 'Tis like your Irish wood,
90 'Gainst cobwebs. I have a piece of Jason's fleece too,
Which was no other than a book of alchemy,
Writ in large sheepskin, a good fat ram-vellum.
Such was Pythagoras' thigh, Pandora's tub,
And all that fable of Medea's charms,
The manner of our work; the bulls, our furnace,
Still breathing fire; our argent-vive,° the dragon:
The dragon's teeth, mercury sublimate,
That keeps the whiteness, hardness, and the biting;
And they are gathered into Jason's helm,
100 The alembic, and then sowed in Mars his field,
And thence sublimed so often, till they're fixed.
Both this, the Hesperian garden, Cadmus' story,
Jove's shower, the boon of Midas, Argus'° eyes,
Boccace his Demogorgon,° thousands more,
All abstract riddles of our stone.—How now!

Scene II. *(The same)*

(Mammon, Surly. Enter Face, as a Servant)
Mammon. Do we succeed? Is our day come? And holds it?
Face. The evening will set red upon you, sir;
You have colour for it, crimson: the red ferment

90-103. Jason . . . Argus, in his exuberance Mammon draws on the authority of Greek mythology to confirm his huge expectations. ***96. argent-vive,*** quicksilver. ***104. Demogorgon,*** ancestor of all the Gods according to Boccacio.

Has done his office; three hours hence prepare you
To see projection.°
Mammon. Pertinax, my Surly.
Again I say to thee, aloud, *be rich.*
This day thou shalt have ingots; and tomorrow
Give lords the affront.—Is it, my Zephyrus, right?
Blushes the bolt's-head?°
Face. Like a wench with child, sir,
That were but now discovered to her master. 10
Mammon. Excellent witty Lungs!—My only care is
Where to get stuff enough now, to project on;
This town will not half serve me.
Face. No, sir! buy
The covering off of churches.
Mammon. That's true.
Face. Yes.
Let them stand bare, as do their auditory;
Or cap them new with shingles.
Mammon. No, good thatch:
Thatch will lie light upon the rafters, Lungs.—
Lungs, I will manumit thee from the furnace;
I will restore thee thy complexion, Puff,
Lost in the embers; and repair this brain, 20
Hurt with the fume of the metals.
Face. I have blown, sir,
Hard, for your worship; thrown by many a coal,
When 'twas not beech; weighed those I put in, just,
To keep your heat still even. These bleared eyes
Have waked to read your several colours, sir,
Of the pale citron, the green lion, the crow,
The peacock's tail, the plumed swan.°
Mammon. And lastly,
Thou hast descried the flower, the *sanguis agni?*
Face. Yes, sir.
Mammon. Where's master?
Face. At his prayers, sir, he;
Good man, he's doing his devotions 30
For the success.
Mammon. Lungs, I will set a period
To all thy labours; thou shalt be the master
Of my seraglio.

5. projection, casting (of the philosopher's stone). ***9. bolt's-head,*** retort. ***15. auditory,*** congregation (in church). ***26-27. pale . . . swan,*** alchemical jargon for various colors.

Face. Good, sir.
Mammon. But do you hear?
I'll geld you, Lungs.
Face. Yes, sir.
Mammon. For I do mean
To have a list of wives and concubines
Equal with Solomon, who had the stone
Alike with me; and I will make me a back
With the elixir that shall be as tough
As Hercules, to encounter fifty a night.—
Thou'rt sure thou saw'st it blood?
40 *Face.* Both blood and spirit, sir.
Mammon. I will have all my beds blown up, not stuft;
Down is too hard: and then, mine oval room
Filled with such pictures as Tiberius took
From Elephantis, and dull Aretine°
But coldly imitated. Then, my glasses
Cut in more subtle angles, to disperse
And multiply the figures, as I walk
Naked between my succubae.° My mists
I'll have of perfume, vapoured 'bout the room,
50 To lose our selves in; and my baths, like pits
To fall into; from whence we will come forth
And roll us dry in gossamer and roses.—
Is it arrived at ruby?—Where I spy
A wealthy citizen, or [a] rich lawyer,
Have a sublimed pure wife, unto that fellow
I'll send a thousand pound to be my cuckold.
Face. And I shall carry it?
Mammon. No. I'll have no bawds
But fathers and mothers: they will do it best,
Best of all others. And my flatterers
60 Shall be the pure and gravest of divines,
That I can get for money. My mere fools,
Eloquent burgesses, and then my poets
The same that writ so subtly of the fart,
Whom I will entertain still for that subject.
The few that would give out themselves to be
Court and town-stallions, and, each-where, bely°
Ladies who are known most innocent, for them,
Those will I beg, to make me eunuchs of:

44. Aretine, a writer of lewd verses. ***48. succubae,*** concubines. ***66. bely,*** a pun: "lie with," and "slander."

And they shall fan me with ten ostrich tails
A-piece, made in a plume to gather wind. 70
We will be brave, Puff, now we have the med'cine.
My meat shall all come in, in Indian shells,
Dishes of agate set in gold, and studded
With emeralds, sapphires, hyacinths, and rubies.
The tongues of carps, dormice, and camels' heels,
Boiled in the spirit of sol, and dissolved pearl
(Apicius' diet, 'gainst the epilepsy)
And I will eat these broths with spoons of amber,
Headed with diamond and carbuncle.
My foot-boy shall eat pheasants, calvered salmons, 80
Knots, godwits, lampreys: I myself will have
The beards of barbel served, instead of salads;
Oiled mushrooms; and the swelling unctuous paps
Of a fat pregnant sow, newly cut off,
Drest with an exquisite and poignant sauce;
For which, I'll say unto my cook, *There's gold,*
Go forth, and be a knight.°

Face. Sir, I'll go look
A little, how it heightens.

(*Exit*)

Mammon. Do.—My shirts
I'll have of taffeta-sarsnet, soft and light
As cobwebs; and for all my other raiment, 90
It shall be such as might provoke the Persian,
Were he to teach the world riot anew.
My gloves of fishes and birds' skins, perfumed
With gums of paradise, and Eastern air—

Surly. And do you think to have the stone with this?

Mammon. No, I do think to have all this with the stone.

Surly. Why, I have heard he must be *homo frugi,*°
A pious, holy, and religious man,
One free from mortal sin, a very virgin.

Mammon. That makes it, sir; he is so: but I buy it; 100
My venture brings it me. He, honest wretch,
A notable, superstitious, good soul,
Has worn his knees bare, and his slippers bald,
With prayer and fasting for it: and, sir, let him
Do it alone, for me, still. Here he comes.
Not a profane word afore him; 'tis poison.—

86-87. There's . . . knight, an allusion to King James' practice of selling knighthoods. ***97. homo frugi,*** a frugal man.

Scene III. *The same*

(Mammon, Surly. Enter Subtle)
Mammon. Good morrow, father.
Subtle. Gentle son, good morrow,
And to your friend there. What is he is with you?
Mammon. An heretic, that I did bring along,
In hope, sir, to convert him.
Subtle. Son, I doubt
You're covetous, that thus you meet your time
In the just° point, prevent° your day at morning.
This argues something worthy of a fear
Of importune and carnal appetite.
Take heed you do not cause the blessing leave you,
10 With your ungoverned haste. I should be sorry
To see my labours, now even at perfection,
Got by long watching and large patience,
Not prosper where my love and zeal hath placed them.
Which (heaven I call to witness, with your self,
To whom I have poured my thoughts) in all my ends,
Have looked no way, but unto public good,
To pious uses, and dear charity
Now grown a prodigy with men. Wherein
If you, my son, should now prevaricate,
20 And to your own particular lusts employ
So great and catholic a bliss, be sure
A curse will follow, yea, and overtake
Your subtle and most secret ways.
Mammon. I know, sir;
You shall not need to fear me; I but come
To have you confute this gentleman.
Surly. Who is,
Indeed, sir, somewhat costive of belief
Toward your stone; would not be gulled.
Subtle. Well, son,
All that I can convince him in, is this,
The work is done, bright Sol is in his robe.
30 We have a med'cine of the triple soul,
The glorified spirit. Thanks be to heaven,
And make us worthy of it!—Ulen Spiegel!°
Face. (Within) Anon, sir.

6. *just,* exact. ***prevent,*** anticipate, i.e., come too early. **32. *Ulen Spiegel!*** Till Eulenspiegel, the knavish hero of a popular German book.

Subtle. Look well to the register.
And let your heat still lessen by degrees,
To the aludels.
Face. (Within) Yes, sir.
Subtle. Did you look
On the bolt's head yet?
Face. (Within) Which? On D, sir?
Subtle. Ay;
What's the complexion?
Face. (Within) Whitish.
Subtle. Infuse vinegar,
To draw his volatile substance and his tincture:
And let the water in glass E be filtered.
And put into the gripe's egg. Lute him well; 40
And leave him closed *in balneo*.
Face. (Within) I will, sir.
Surly. What a brave language here is! next to canting.
Subtle. I have another work you never saw, son,
That three days since past the philosopher's wheel,
In the lent heat of Athanor; and's become
Sulphur of Nature.
Mammon. But 'tis for me?
Subtle. What need you?
You have enough in that is perfect.
Mammon. O, but—
Subtle. Why, this is covetise!
Mammon. No, I assure you,
I shall employ it all in pious uses,
Founding of colleges and grammar schools, 50
Marrying young virgins, building hospitals,
And now and then a church.
(Re-enter Face)
Subtle. How now!
Face. Sir, please you,
Shall I not change the filter?
Subtle. Marry, yes;
And bring me the complexion of glass B. *(Exit Face)*
Mammon. Have you another?
Subtle. Yes, son; were I assured
Your piety were firm, we would not want
The means to glorify it: but I hope the best.
I mean to tinct C in sand-heat tomorrow,
And give him imbibition.
Mammon. Of white oil?

60 *Subtle*. No, sir, of red. F is come over the helm too,
I thank my maker, in St. Mary's bath,
And shows *lac virginis*. Blessed be heaven!
I sent you of his fæces there calcined:
Out of that calx, I have won the salt of mercury.
Mammon. By pouring on your rectified water?
Subtle. Yes, and reverberating in Athanor.
(Re-enter Face)
How now! what colour says it?
Face. The ground black, sir.
Mammon. That's your crow's head?
Surly. Your cock's-comb's, is it not?
Subtle. No, 'tis not perfect. Would it were the crow!
That work wants something.
70 *Surly*. *(Aside)* O, I looked for this,
The hay's a pitching.
Subtle. Are you sure you loosed them
In their own menstrue?
Face. Yes, sir, and then married them,
And put them in a bolt's-head nipped to digestion,
According as you bade me, when I set
The liquor of Mars to circulation
In the same heat.
Subtle. The process then was right.
Face. Yes, by the token, sir, the retort brake,
And what was saved was put into the pelican,
And signed with Hermes' seal.
Subtle. I think 'twas so.
We should have a new amalgama.
80 *Surly*. *(Aside)* O, this ferret
Is rank as any polecat.
Subtle. But I care not;
Let him even die; we have enough beside,
In embrion. He has his white shirt on?
Face. Yes, sir,
He's ripe for inceration, he stands warm,
In his ash-fire. I would not you should let
Any die now, if I might counsel, sir,
For luck's sake to the rest: it is not good.
Mammon. He says right.
Surly. *(Aside)* Ah, are you bolted?
Face. Nay, I know't, sir,
I have seen the ill fortune. What is some three ounces
Of fresh materials?

Mammon. Is't no more?
Face. No more, sir, 90
Of gold, to amalgam with some six of mercury.
Mammon. Away, here's money. What will serve?
Face. Ask him, sir.
Mammon. How much?
Subtle. Give him nine pound: you may give him ten.
Surly. Yes, twenty, and be cozened, do.
Mammon. There 'tis. *(Gives Face the money)*
Subtle. This needs not; but that you will have it so,
To see conclusions of all: for two
Of our inferior works are at fixation,
A third is in ascension. Go your ways.
Have you set the oil of luna in kemia?
Face. Yes, sir.
Subtle. And the philosopher's vinegar?°
Face. Ay. *(Exit)* 100
Surly. We shall have a salad!
Mammon. When do you make projection?
Subtle. Son, be not hasty, I exalt our med'cine,
By hanging him *in balneo vaporoso*,
And giving him solution; then congeal him;
And then dissolve him; then again congeal him;
For look, how oft I iterate the work,
So many times I add unto his virtue.
As if at first one ounce convert a hundred,
After his second loose, he'll turn a thousand;
His third solution, ten; his fourth, a hundred; 110
After his fifth, a thousand thousand ounces
Of any imperfect metal, into pure
Silver or gold, in all examinations,
As good as any of the natural mine.
Get you your stuff here against afternoon,
Your brass, your pewter, and your andirons.
Mammon. Not those of iron?
Subtle. Yes, you may bring them too;
We'll change all metals.
Surly. I believe you in that.
Mammon. Then I may send my spits?
Subtle. Yes, and your racks.

35-100. Subtle uses alchemical jargon to impress Mammon. Surly interpolates sarcastic comments.

120 *Surly.* And dripping-pans, and pot-hangers, and hooks?
Shall he not?
Subtle. If he please.
Surly. —To be an ass.
Subtle. How, sir!
Mammon. This gentleman you must bear withal:
I told you he had no faith.
Surly. And little hope, sir;
But much less charity, should I gull myself.
Subtle. Why, what have you observed, sir, in our art,
Seems so impossible?
Surly. But your whole work, no more.
That you should hatch gold in a furnace, sir,
As they do eggs in Egypt!
Subtle. Sir, do you
Believe that eggs are hatched so?
Surly. If I should?
130 *Subtle.* Why, I think that the greater miracle.
No egg but differs from a chicken more
Than metals in themselves.
Surly. That cannot be.
The egg's ordained by nature to that end,
And is a chicken *in potentia.*
Subtle. The same we say of lead and other metals,
Which would be gold if they had time.
Mammon. And that
Our art doth further.
Subtle. Ay, for 'twere absurd
To think that nature in the earth bred gold
Perfect in the instant: something went before.
There must be remote matter.
140 *Surly.* Ay, what is that?
Subtle. Marry,° we say—
Mammon. Ay, now it heats: stand, father,
Pound him to dust.
Subtle. It is, of the one part,
A humid exhalation, which we call
Materia liquida, or the unctuous water;
On the other part, a certain crass and viscous
Portion of earth; both which, concorporate,
Do make the elementary matter of gold;
Which is not yet *propria materia*,

141. *Marry*, by Mary, a mild oath.

But common to all metals and all stones;
For, where it is forsaken of that moisture, 150
And hath more dryness, it becomes a stone:
Where it retains more of the humid fatness,
It turns to sulphur, or to quicksilver,
Who are the parents of all other metals.
Nor can this remote matter suddenly
Progress so from extreme unto extreme,
As to grow gold, and leap o'er all the means.
Nature doth first beget the imperfect, then
Proceeds she to the perfect. Of that airy
And oily water, mercury is engendered; 160
Sulphur of the fat and earthy part; the one,
Which is the last, supplying the place of male,
The other, of the female, in all metals.
Some do believe hermaphrodeity,
That both do act and suffer. But these two
Make the rest ductile, malleable, extensive.
And even in gold they are; for we do find
Seeds of them by our fire, and gold in them;
And can produce the species of each metal
More perfect thence, than nature doth in earth. 170
Beside, who doth not see in daily practice
Art can beget bees, hornets, beetles, wasps,
Out of the carcases and dung of creatures;
Yea, scorpions of an herb, being rightly placed?
And these are living creatures, far more perfect
And excellent than metals.

Mammon. Well said, father!
Nay, if he take you in hand, sir, with an argument,
He'll bray° you in a mortar.

Surly. Pray you, sir, stay.
Rather than I'll be brayed, sir, I'll believe
That Alchemy is a pretty kind of game, 180
Somewhat like tricks o' the cards, to cheat a man
With charming.

Subtle. Sir?

Surly. What else are all your terms,
Whereon no one of your writers 'grees with other?
Of your elixir, your *lac virginis*,
Your stone, your med'cine, and your chrysosperm,
Your sal, your sulphur, and your mercury,

178. bray, crush.

Your oil of height, your tree of life, your blood,
Your marchesite, your tutie, your magnesia,
Your toad, your crow, your dragon, and your panther;
190 Your sun, your moon, your firmament, your adrop,
Your lato, azoch, zernich, chibrit, heautarit,
And then your red man, and your white woman,
With all your broths, your menstrues, and materials
Of piss and egg-shells, women's terms, man's blood,
Hair of the head, burnt clouts, chalk, merds, and clay,
Powder of bones, scalings of iron, glass,
And worlds of other strange ingredients,
Would burst a man to name?°

Subtle. And all these named,
Intending but one thing; which art our writers
Used to obscure their art.

200 *Mammon.* Sir, so I told him,
Because the simple idiot should not learn it,
And make it vulgar.

Subtle. Was not all the knowledge
Of the Egyptians written in mystic symbols?
Speak not the scriptures oft in parables?
Are not the choicest fables of the poets,
That were the fountains and first springs of wisdom,
Wrapt in perplexed allegories?

Mammon. I urged that,
And cleared to him, that Sisyphus was damned
To roll the ceaseless stone, only because
He would have made ours common. *(Dol appears at the door.)*
210 Who is this?

Subtle. God's precious!—What do you mean? Go in, good lady,
Let me entreat you. *(Dol retires.)*—Where's this varlet?
(Re-enter Face)

Face. Sir.

Subtle. You very knave! do you use me thus?

Face. Wherein, sir?

Subtle. Go in and see, you traitor. Go! *(Exit Face)*

Mammon. Who is it, sir?

Subtle. Nothing, sir; nothing.

Mammon. What's the matter, good sir?
I have not seen you thus distempered: who is't?

Subtle. All arts have still had, sir, their adversaries;
But ours the most ignorant.—

182-198. Surly knows the language of alchemy as well as Subtle.

(Re-enter Face)

What now?

Face. 'Twas not my fault, sir; she would speak with you.

Subtle. Would she, sir! Follow me. *(Exit)*

Mammon. (Stopping him) Stay, Lungs.

Face. I dare not, sir. 220

Mammon. Stay, man; what is she?

Face. A lord's sister, sir.

Mammon. How! pray thee, stay.

Face. She's mad, sir, and sent hither—

He'll be mad too.—

Mammon. I warrant thee.—

Why sent hither?

Face. Sir, to be cured.

Subtle. (Within) Why, rascal!

Face. Lo you!—Here, sir! *(Exit)*

Mammon. 'Fore God, a Bradamante,° a brave piece.

Surly. Heart, this is a bawdy-house! I'll be burnt else.

Mammon. O, by this light, no: do not wrong him. He's

Too scrupulous that way: it is his vice.

No, he's a rare physician, do him right,

An excellent Paracelsian,° and has done 230

Strange cures with mineral physic. He deals all

With spirits, he; he will not hear a word

Of Galen;° or his tedious recipes—

(Re-enter Face)

How now, Lungs!

Face. Softly, sir; speak softly. I meant

To have told your worship all. This must not hear.

Mammon. No, he will not be gulled; let him alone.

Face. You're very right, sir; she is a most rare scholar,

And is gone mad with studying Broughton's° works.

If you but name a word touching the Hebrew,

She falls into her fit, and will discourse 240

So learnedly of genealogies,

As you would run mad too, to hear her, sir.

Mammon. How might one do to have conference with her, Lungs?

Face. O, divers have run mad upon the conference:

I do not know, sir. I am sent in haste

To fetch a vial.

Surly. Be not gulled, Sir Mammon.

225. Bradamante, heroine in an Italian play. ***230. Paracelsian,*** Paracelsus was a famous sixteenth-century alchemist. ***233. Galen,*** a famous physician in ancient Greece. ***238. Broughton,*** a Biblical scholar, hardly the man any lady would read.

Mammon. Wherein? Pray ye, be patient.
Surly. Yes, as you are,
And trust confederate knaves and bawds and whores.
Mammon. You are too foul, believe it.—Come here, Ulen,
One word.
Face. I dare not, in good faith. *(Going)*
250 *Mammon.* Stay, knave.
Face. He is extreme angry that you saw her, sir.
Mammon. Drink that. *(Gives him money)* What is she when she's out of her fit?
Face. O, the most affablest creature, sir! so merry!
So pleasant! She'll mount you up, like quicksilver,
Over the helm; and circulate like oil,
A very vegetal:° discourse of state,
Of mathematics, bawdry, anything—
Mammon. Is she no way accessible? no means,
No trick to give a man a taste of her—wit—
Or so?
Subtle. (Within) Ulen!
260 *Face.* I'll come to you again, sir. *(Exit)*
Mammon. Surly, I did not think one of your breeding
Would traduce personages of worth.
Surly. Sir Epicure,
Your friend to use; yet still loth to be gulled:
I do not like your philosophical bawds.
Their stone is lechery enough to pay for,
Without this bait.
Mammon. Heart, you abuse yourself.
I know the lady, and her friends, and means,
The original of this disaster. Her brother
Has told me all.
Surly. And yet you never saw her
Till now!
270 *Mammon.* O yes, but I forgot. I have, believe it,
One of the treacherousest memories, I do think,
Of all mankind.
Surly. What call you her brother?
Mammon. My lord—
He will not have his name known, now I think on't.
Surly. A very treacherous memory!
Mammon. On my faith—

256. vegetal, charmer.

Surly. Tut, if you have it not about you, pass it,
Till we meet next.
Mammon. Nay, by this hand, 'tis true.
He's one I honour, and my noble friend;
And I respect his house.
Surly. Heart! can it be
That a grave sir, a rich, that has no need,
A wise sir, too, at other times, should thus, 280
With his own oaths, and arguments, make hard means
To gull himself? And this be your elixir,
Your *lapis mineralis*, and your lunary,
Give me your honest trick yet at primero,
Or gleek;° and take your *lutum sapientis*,
Your *menstruum simplex!*° I'll have gold before you,
And with less danger of the quicksilver,
Or the hot sulphur.
(Re-enter Face)
Face. Here's one from Captain Face, sir, *(To Surly)*
Desires you meet him in the Temple-church,
Some half-hour hence, and upon earnest business. 290
Sir, *(Whispers to Mammon)* if you please to quit us now; and come
Again within two hours, you shall have
My master busy examining of the works;
And I will steal you in unto the party,
That you may see her converse.—Sir, shall I say
You'll meet the captain's worship?
Surly. Sir, I will.— *(Walks aside)*
But, by attorney, and to a second purpose.
Now, I am sure it is a bawdy-house;
I'll swear it, were the marshal here to thank me:
The naming this commander doth confirm it. 300
Don Face! why, he's the most authentic dealer
In these commodities, the superintendent
To all the quainter traffickers in town!
He is the visitor, and does appoint
Who lies with whom, and at what hour; what price;
Which gown, and in what smock; what fall; what tire.°
Him will I prove, by a third person, to find
The subtleties of this dark labyrinth:
Which if I do discover, dear Sir Mammon,

283-285. The Latin is alchemical jargon. ***primero*** and ***gleek*** are card games. ***306. fall . . . tire,*** collar and headgear.

310 You'll give your poor friend leave, though no philosopher,
To laugh: for you that are, 'tis thought, shall weep.
Face. Sir, he does pray you'll not forget.
Surly. I will not, sir.
Sir Epicure, I shall leave you. *(Exit)*
Mammon. I follow you straight.
Face. But do so, good sir, to avoid suspicion.
This gentleman has a parlous head.
Mammon. But wilt thou, Ulen,
Be constant to thy promise?
Face. As my life, sir.
Mammon. And wilt thou insinuate what I am, and praise me,
And say I am a noble fellow?
Face. O, what else, sir?
And that you'll make her royal with the stone,
320 An empress; and yourself King of Bantam.°
Mammon. Wilt thou do this?
Face. Will I, sir!
Mammon. Lungs, my Lungs!
I love thee.
Face. Send your stuff, sir, that my master
May busy himself about projection.
Mammon. Thou'st witched me, rogue: take, go. *(Gives him money)*
Face. Your jack,° and all, sir.
Mammon. Thou art a villain—I will send my jack,
And the weights too. Slave, I could bite thine ear.
Away, thou dost not care for me.
Face. Not I, sir!
Mammon. Come, I was born to make thee, my good weasel,
Set thee on a bench, and have thee twirl a chain
With the best lord's vermin of them all.
330 *Face.* Away, sir.
Mammon. A count, nay, a count palatine—
Face. Good sir, go.
Mammon. Shall not advance thee better: no, nor faster. *(Exit)*

Scene IV. *The same*

(Face. Enter Subtle and Dol)
Subtle. Has he bit? has he bit?
Face. And swallowed, too, my Subtle.
I have given him line, and now he plays, in faith.

320. *Bantam,* a fabulously rich Eastern kingdom. **324. *jack,*** turnspit (for roasting).

Subtle. And shall we twitch him?
Face. Thorough both the gills.
A wench is a rare bait, with which a man
No sooner's taken, but he straight firks mad.
Subtle. Dol, my Lord What'ts'hum's sister, you must now
Bear yourself *statelich.*°
Dol. O, let me alone.
I'll not forget my race, I warrant you.
I'll keep my distance, laugh and talk aloud;
Have all the tricks of a proud scurvy lady, 10
And be as rude's her woman.
Face. Well said, sanguine!°
Subtle. But will he send his andirons?
Face. His jack too,
And's iron shoeing-horn; I have spoke to him. Well,
I must not lose my wary gamester yonder.
Subtle. O, Monsieur Caution, that will not be gulled?
Face. Ay, if I can strike a fine hook into him, now!—
The Temple-church, there I have cast mine angle.
Well, pray for me. I'll about it. *(Knocking without)*
Subtle. What, more gudgeons!°
Dol, scout, scout! *(Dol goes to the window.)* Stay, Face, you must go to the door.
'Pray God it be my anabaptist—Who is't, Dol? 20
Dol. I know him not: he looks like a gold-end-man.°
Subtle. 'Ods so! 'tis he, he said he would send—what call you him?
The sanctified elder, that should deal
For Mammon's jack and andirons. Let him in.
Stay, help me off, first, with my gown. *(Exit Face with the gown)* Away,
Madam, to your withdrawing chamber. *(Exit Dol)* Now,
In a new tune, new gesture, but old language.—
This fellow is sent from one negotiates with me
About the stone too, for the holy brethren
Of Amsterdam, the exiled saints, that hope 30
To raise their discipline by it. I must use him
In some strange fashion now, to make him admire me.

Scene V. *The same*

(Subtle. Enter Ananias)
Subtle. Where is my drudge? *(Aloud)*

7. *statelich,* in a dignified manner. **11. *sanguine,*** red cheeks. **18. *gudgeons,*** dupes.
21. *gold-end-man,* buyer of odds and ends of gold.

(Enter Face)

Face. Sir!

Subtle. Take away the recipient,

And rectify your menstrue from the phlegma.

Then pour it on the Sol, in the cucurbite,

And let them macerate together.

Face. Yes, sir.

And save the ground?

Subtle. No: *terra damnata*

Must not have entrance in the work.—Who are you?

Ananias. A faithful brother,° if it please you.

Subtle. What's that?

A Lullianist? a Ripley?° *Filius artis?*

Can you sublime and dulcify? Calcine?

10 Know you the sapor pontic? Sapor stiptic?

Or what is homogene, or heterogene?

Ananias. I understand no heathen language, truly.

Subtle. Heathen! You Knipperdoling?° Is Ars sacra,

Or chrysopœia, or spagyrica,

Or the pamphysic, or panarchic knowledge,

A heathen language?

Ananias. Heathen Greek, I take it.

Subtle. How! Heathen Greek?

Ananias. All's heathen but the Hebrew.

Subtle. Sirrah my varlet, stand you forth and speak to him

20 Like a philosopher: answer in the language.

Name the vexations, and the martyrizations

Of metals in the work.

Face. Sir, putrefaction,

Solution, ablution, sublimation,

Cohobation, calcination, ceration, and

Fixation.

Subtle. This is heathen Greek, to you, now!—

And when comes vivification?

Face. After mortification.

Subtle. What's cohobation?

Face. 'Tis the pouring on

Your *aqua regis*, and then drawing him off,

To the trine circle of the seven spheres.

Subtle. What's the proper passion of metals?

7. faithful brother, a Puritan. ***8. Lullianist, Ripley,*** Subtle deliberately misunderstands Ananias and asks if he is a faithful brother of the alchemists. ***13. Knipperdoling,*** a Puritan (Anabaptist) leader.

Face. Malleation.
Subtle. What's your *ultimum supplicium auri?*
Face. Antimonium. 30
Subtle. This is heathen Greek to you!—And what's your mercury?
Face. A very fugitive, he will be gone, sir.
Subtle. How know you him?
Face. By his viscosity,
His oleosity, and his suscitability.
Subtle. How do you sublime him?
Face. With the calce of egg-shells,
White marble, talc.
Subtle. Your magisterium now,
What's that?
Face. Shifting, sir, your elements,
Dry into cold, cold into moist, moist into hot,
Hot into dry.
Subtle. This is heathen Greek to you still!
Your *lapis philosophicus?*
Face. 'Tis a stone, 40
And not a stone; a spirit, a soul, and a body:
Which if you do dissolve, it is dissolved;
If you coagulate, it is coagulated;
If you make it to fly, it flieth.
Subtle. Enough. *(Exit Face)*
This is heathen Greek to you! What are you, sir?
Ananias. Please you, a servant of the exiled brethren,
That deal with widows' and with orphans' goods,
And make a just account unto the saints:
A deacon.
Subtle. O, you are sent from Master Wholesome,
Your teacher?
Ananias. From Tribulation Wholesome, 50
Our very zealous pastor.
Subtle. Good! I have
Some orphans' goods to come here.
Ananias. Of what kind, sir?
Subtle. Pewter and brass, andirons and kitchen-ware.
Metals, that we must use our med'cine on:
Wherein the brethren may have a penn'orth
For ready money.
Ananias. Were the orphans' parents
Sincere professors?
Subtle. Why do you ask?

Ananias. Because
We then are to deal justly, and give, in truth,
Their utmost value.
Subtle. 'Slid, you'd cozen else,
60 An if their parents were not of the faithful!—
I will not trust you, now I think on it,
Till I have talked with your pastor. Have you brought money
To buy more coals?
Ananias. No, surely.
Subtle. No? How so?
Ananias. The brethren bid me say unto you, sir,
Surely, they will not venture any more
Till they may see projection.
Subtle. How!
Ananias. You've had
For the instruments, as bricks, and lome, and glasses,
Already thirty pound; and for materials,
They say, some ninety more: and they have heard since,
70 That one, at Heidelberg, made it of an egg,
And a small paper of pin-dust.
Subtle. What's your name?
Ananias. My name is Ananias.
Subtle. Out, the varlet
That cozened the apostles! Hence, away!
Flee, mischief! had your holy consistory
No name to send me, of another sound,
Than wicked Ananias? Send your elders
Hither, to make atonement for you, quickly,
And give me satisfaction; or out goes
The fire; and down the alembecs, and the furnace,
80 *Piger Henricus*, or what not. Thou wretch!
Both *sericon* and *bufo* shall be lost,
Tell them. All hope of rooting out the bishops,
Or the anti-Christian hierarchy shall perish,
If they stay threescore minutes: the aqueity,
Terreity, and sulphureity
Shall run together again, and all be annulled,
Thou wicked Ananias!

(Exit Ananias)

This will fetch them,
And make them haste towards their gulling more.
A man must deal like a rough nurse, and fright
90 Those that are froward, to an appetite.

Scene VI. *The same*

(Subtle. Enter Face in his uniform, followed by Drugger)

Face. He's busy with his spirits, but we'll upon him.
Subtle. How now! What mates,° what Bayards° have we here?
Face. I told you he would be furious.—Sir, here's Nab
Has brought you another piece of gold to look on;
—We must appease him. Give it me,—and prays you,
You would devise—what is it, Nab?
Drugger. A sign, sir.
Face. Ay, a good lucky one, a thriving sign, doctor.
Subtle. I was devising now.
Face. (Aside to Subtle) Slight, do not say so,
He will repent he gave you any more—
What say you to his constellation, doctor, 10
The balance?
Subtle. No, that way is stale and common.
A townsman born in Taurus, gives the bull,
Or the bull's head: in Aries, the ram,
A poor device! No, I will have his name
Formed in some mystic character; whose radii,
Striking the senses of the passers-by,
Shall, by a virtual° influence, breed affections,
That may result upon the party owns it:
As thus—
Face. Nab!
Subtle. He first shall have a *bell*, that's *Abel;*
And by it standing one whose name is *Dee,*° 20
In a *rug* gown, there's *D*, and *Rug*, that's *drug*:
And right anenst him a dog snarling *er;*
There's Drugger, Abel Drugger. That's his sign.
And here's now mystery and hieroglyphic!
Face. Abel, thou art made.
Drugger. Sir, I do thank his worship.
Face. Six of thy legs° more will not do it, Nab.
He has brought you a pipe of tobacco, doctor.
Drugger. Yes, sir;
I have another thing I would impart—
Face. Out with it, Nab.
Drugger. Sir, there is lodged, hard by me,

2. mates, wretches. ***Bayards,*** blind fools. ***17. virtual,*** virtuous. ***20. Dee,*** Dr. John Dee, a famous astrologer. ***26. legs,*** bows.

A rich young widow—
30 *Face.* Good! a bona roba?°
Drugger. But nineteen at the most.
Face. Very good, Abel.
Drugger. Marry, she's not in fashion yet; she wears
A hood, but 't stands a cop.°
Face. No matter, Abel.
Drugger. And I do now and then give her a fucus°—
Face. What! dost thou deal, Nab?
Subtle. I did tell you, captain.
Drugger. And physic too, sometime, sir; for which she trusts me
With all her mind. She's come up here of purpose
To learn the fashion.
Face. Good (his match too!)—On, Nab.
Drugger. And she does strangely long to know her fortune.
40 *Face.* 'Ods lid, Nab, send her to the doctor, hither.
Drugger. Yes, I have spoke to her of his worship already;
But she's afraid it will be blown abroad,
And hurt her marriage.
Face. Hurt it! 'tis the way
To heal it, if 'twere hurt; to make it more
Followed and sought. Nab, thou shalt tell her this.
She'll be more known, more talked of; and your widows
Are ne'er of any price till they be famous;
Their honour is their multitude of suitors.
Send her, it may be thy good fortune. What!
Thou dost not know.
50 *Drugger.* No, sir, she'll never marry
Under a knight: her brother has made a vow.
Face. What! and dost thou despair, my little Nab,
Knowing what the doctor has set down for thee,
And seeing so many of the city dubbed?°
One glass of thy water, with a madam I know,
Will have it done, Nab. What's her brother, a knight?
Drugger. No, sir, a gentleman newly warm in his land, sir,
Scarce cold in his one and twenty, that does govern
His sister here; and is a man himself
60 Of some three thousand a year, and is come up
To learn to quarrel, and to live by his wits,
And will go down again, and die in the country.

30. bona roba, good-looking girl. ***33. cop,*** i.e., she does not wear her widow's hood fashionably. ***34. fucus,*** cosmetic, make-up. ***54. dubbed,*** another allusion to James I and his indiscriminate distribution of knighthoods.

Face. How! to quarrel?
Drugger. Yes, sir, to carry quarrels,
As gallants do; to manage them by line.
Face. 'Slid, Nab, the doctor is the only man
In Christendom for him. He has made a table,
With mathematical demonstrations,
Touching the art of quarrels: he will give him
An instrument to quarrel by. Go, bring them both,
Him and his sister. And, for thee, with her 70
The doctor happ'ly may persuade. Go to:
'Shalt give his worship a new damask suit
Upon the premises.
Subtle. O, good captain!
Face. He shall;
He is the honestest fellow, doctor. Stay not,
No offers; bring the damask, and the parties.
Drugger. I'll try my power, sir.
Face. And thy will too, Nab.
Subtle. 'Tis good tobacco, this! What is't an ounce?
Face. He'll send you a pound, doctor.
Subtle. O no.
Face. He will do't.
It is the goodest soul!—Abel, about it.
Thou shalt know more anon. Away, be gone. *(Exit Drugger)* 80
A miserable rogue, and lives with cheese,
And has the worms. That was the cause, indeed,
Why he came now: he dealt with me in private,
To get a medicine for them.
Subtle. And shall, sir. This works.
Face. A wife, a wife for one on us, my dear Subtle!
We'll even draw lots, and he that fails, shall have
The more in goods, the other has in tail.
Subtle. Rather the less. For she may be so light
She may want grains.
Face. Ay, or be such a burden
A man would scarce endure her, for the whole. 90
Subtle. Faith, best let's see her first, and then determine.
Face. Content: but Dol must have no breath on't.
Subtle. Mum.
Away you, to your Surly yonder, catch him.
Face. Pray God I have not staid too long.
Subtle. I fear it.

(Exeunt)

Act III

Scene I. *The lane before Lovewit's house*

(Enter Tribulation Wholesome and Ananias)

Tribulation. These chastisements are common to the saints,
And such rebukes we of the Separation°
Must bear with willing shoulders, as the trials
Sent forth to tempt our frailties.

Ananias. In pure zeal,
I do not like the man; he is a heathen,
And speaks the language of Canaan, truly.

Tribulation. I think him a profane person indeed.

Ananias. He bears
The visible mark of the beast in his forehead.
And for his stone, it is a work of darkness,
10 And with philosophy blinds the eyes of man.

Tribulation. Good brother, we must bend unto all means,
That may give furtherance to the holy cause.

Ananias. Which his cannot: the sanctified cause
Should have a sanctified course.

Tribulation. Not always necessary:
The children of perdition are oft-times
Made instruments even of the greatest works.
Beside, we should give somewhat to man's nature,
The place he lives in, still about the fire,
And fume of metals, that intoxicate
20 The brain of man, and make him prone to passion.
Where have you greater atheists than your cooks?
Or more profane, or choleric, than your glass-men?
More anti-Christian than your bell-founders?
What makes the devil so devilish, I would ask you,
Satan, our common enemy, but his being
Perpetually about the fire, and boiling
Brimstone and arsenic? We must give, I say,
Unto the motives, and the stirrers up
Of humours in the blood. It may be so,
30 When as the work is done, the stone is made,
This heat of his may turn into a zeal,
And stand up for the beauteous discipline
Against the menstruous° cloth and rag of Rome.
We must await his calling, and the coming

2. *Separation,* the Dissenters. **33. *menstruous,*** polluted.

Of the good spirit. You did fault to upbraid him
With the brethren's blessing of Heidelberg, weighing
What need we have to hasten on the work,
For the restoring of the silenced saints,°
Which ne'er will be but by the philosopher's stone.
And so a learned elder, one of Scotland, 40
Assured me; *aurum potabile*° being
The only med'cine for the civil magistrate,
T' incline him to a feeling of the cause;
And must be daily used in the disease.
Ananias. I have not edified more. truly, by man;
Not since the beautiful light first shone on me:
And I am sad my zeal hath so offended.
Tribulation. Let us call on him then.
Ananias. The motion's good,
And of the spirit; I will knock first. *(Knocks)* Peace be within!
(The door is opened, and they enter.)

Scene II. *A room in Lovewit's house*

(Enter Subtle, followed by Tribulation and Ananias)
Subtle. O, are you come? 'Twas time. Your threescore minutes
Were at last thread, you see; and down had gone
Furnus acediæ, turris circulatorius:
Limbec, bolt's-head, retort, and pelican
Had all been cinders. Wicked Ananias!
Art thou returned? Nay, then it goes down yet.
Tribulation. Sir, be appeased; he is come to humble
Himself in spirit, and to ask your patience,
If too much zeal hath carried him aside
From the due path.
Subtle. Why, this doth qualify! 10
Tribulation. The brethren had no purpose, verily,
To give you the least grievance; but are ready
To lend their willing hands to any project
The spirit and you direct.
Subtle. This qualifies more!
Tribulation. And for the orphans' goods, let them be valued
Or what is needful else to the holy work,
It shall be numbered; here, by me, the saints
Throw down their purse before you.

38. silenced saints, the dissenting clergy, not allowed to preach. ***41. aurum potabile,*** a golden medicine, i.e., a bribe.

Subtle. This qualifies most!
Why, thus it should be, now you understand.
20 Have I discoursed so unto you of our stone,
And of the good that it shall bring your cause?
Showed you (beside the main of hiring forces
Abroad, drawing the Hollanders, your friends,
From the Indies, to serve you, with all their fleet)
That even the med'cinal use shall make you a faction,
And party in the realm? As, put the case,
That some great man in state, he have the gout,
Why, you but send three drops of your elixir,
You help him straight: there you have made a friend.
30 Another has the palsy or the dropsy,
He takes of your incombustible stuff,
He's young again: there you have made a friend.
A lady that is past the feat of body,
Though not of mind, and hath her face decayed
Beyond all cure of paintings, you restore,
With the oil of talc: there you have made a friend;
And all her friends. A lord that is a leper,
A knight that has the bone-ache, or a squire
That hath both these, you make them smooth and sound,
40 With a bare fricace° of your med'cine: still
You increase your friends.
Tribulation. Ay, 'tis very pregnant.
Subtle. And then the turning of this lawyer's pewter
To plate at Christmas—
Ananias. Christ-tide,° I pray you.
Subtle. Yet, Ananias!
Ananias. I have done.
Subtle. Or changing
His parcel gilt to massy gold. You cannot
But raise you friends. Withal, to be of power
To pay an army in the field, to buy
The King of France out of his realms, or Spain
Out of his Indies. What can you not do
50 Against lords spiritual or temporal,
That shall oppose you?
Tribulation. Verily, 'tis true.
We may be temporal lords ourselves, I take it.
Subtle. You may be anything, and leave off to make
Long-winded exercises; or suck up

40. fricace, rubbing. ***43. christ-tide,*** the Puritans avoided the word *mass* as being Roman Catholic.

Your *ha!* and *hum!* in a tune. I not deny,
But such as are not graced in a state,
May, for their ends, be adverse in religion,
And get a tune to call the flock together:
For, to say sooth, a tune does much with women
And other phlegmatic people; it is your bell. 60
Ananias. Bells are profane; a tune may be religious.
Subtle. No warning with you? Then farewell my patience.
'Slight, it shall down; I will not be thus tortured.
Tribulation. I pray you, sir.
Subtle. All shall perish. I have spoke it.
Tribulation. Let me find grace, sir, in your eyes; the man
He stands corrected: neither did his zeal,
But as your self, allow a tune somewhere.
Which now, being toward° the stone, we shall not need.
Subtle. No, nor your holy vizard,° to win widows
To give you legacies; or make zealous wives 70
To rob their husbands for the common cause:
Nor take the start of bonds broke but one day,
And say they were forfeited by providence.
Nor shall you need o'er night to eat huge meals,
To celebrate your next day's fast the better;
The whilst the brethren and the sisters humbled,
Abate the stiffness of the flesh. Nor cast
Before your hungry hearers scrupulous bones;
As whether a Christian may hawk or hunt,
Or whether matrons of the holy assembly 80
May lay their hair out, or wear doublets,
Or have that idol, starch, about their linen.
Ananias. It is indeed an idol.
Tribulation. Mind him not, sir.
I do command thee, spirit (of zeal, but trouble),
To peace within him! Pray you, sir, go on.
Subtle. Nor shall you need to libel 'gainst the prelates,
And shorten so your ears° against the hearing
Of the next wire-drawn grace. Nor of necessity
Rail against plays, to please the alderman
Whose daily custard you devour; nor lie 90
With zealous rage till you are hoarse. Not one
Of these so singular arts. Nor call yourselves
By names of Tribulation, Persecution,
Restraint, Long-patience, and such like, affected

68. being toward, nearing possession of. ***69. vizard,*** face; the rest of Subtle's speech and his next outline the sanctimonious and opportunistic side of Puritanism. ***87. shorten . . . ears,*** be condemned to have your ears cut off.

By the whole family or wood of you,
Only for glory, and to catch the ear
Of the disciple.

Tribulation. Truly, sir, they are
Ways that the godly brethren have invented,
For propagation of the glorious cause,
100 As very notable means, and whereby also
Themselves grow soon, and profitably famous.

Subtle. O, but the stone, all's idle to't! Nothing!
The art of angels, nature's miracle,
The divine secret that doth fly in clouds
From east to west: and whose tradition
Is not from men, but spirits.

Ananias. I hate traditions;
I do not trust them—

Tribulation. Peace!

Ananias. They are popish all.
I will not peace: I will not—

Tribulation. Ananias!

Ananias. Please the profane, to grieve the godly; I may not.

110 *Subtle.* Well, Ananias, thou shalt overcome.

Tribulation. It is an ignorant zeal that haunts him, sir:
But truly else a very faithful brother,
A botcher,° and a man by revelation
That hath a competent knowledge of the truth.

Subtle. Has he a competent sum there in the bag
To buy the goods within? I am made guardian,
And must, for charity and conscience' sake,
Now see the most be made for my poor orphan;
Though I desire the brethren, too, good gainers:
120 There they are within. When you have viewed and bought them,
And taken the inventory of what they are,
They are ready for projection; there's no more
To do: cast on the med'cine, so much silver
As there is tin there, so much gold as brass,
I'll give it you in by weight.

Tribulation. But how long time,
Sir, must the saints expect yet?

Subtle. Let me see,
How's the moon now? Eight, nine, ten days hence,
He will be silver potate; then three days
Before he citronise. Some fifteen days,
130 The magisterium will be perfected.

113. botcher, tailor.

Ananias. About the second day of the third week,
In the ninth month?
Subtle. Yes, my good Ananias.
Tribulation. What will the orphans' goods arise to, think you?
Subtle. Some hundred marks, as much as filled three cars,
Unladed now: you'll make six millions of them—
But I must have more coals laid in.
Tribulation. How?
Subtle. Another load,
And then we have finished. We must now increase
Our fire to *ignis ardens*, we are past
Fimus equinus, balnei, cineris,
And all those lenter heats. If the holy purse 140
Should with this draught fall low, and that the saints
Do need a present sum, I have a trick
To melt the pewter, you shall buy now instantly,
And with a tincture make you as good Dutch dollars
As any are in Holland.
Tribulation. Can you so?
Subtle. Ay, and shall bide the third examination.
Ananias. It will be joyful tidings to the brethren.
Subtle. But you must carry it secret.
Tribulation. Ay; but stay,
This act of coining, is it lawful?
Ananias. Lawful?
We know no magistrate. Or, if we did, 150
This is foreign coin.
Subtle. It is no coining, sir.
It is but casting.
Tribulation. Ha! you distinguish well:
Casting of money may be lawful.
Ananias. 'Tis, sir.
Tribulation. Truly, I take it so.
Subtle. There is no scruple,
Sir, to be made of it; believe Ananias:
This case of conscience he is studied in.
Tribulation. I'll make a question of it to the brethren.
Ananias. The brethren shall approve it lawful, doubt not.
Where shall it be done?
Subtle. For that we'll talk anon. *(Knock without)*
There's some to speak with me. Go in, I pray you, 160
And view the parcels. That's the inventory.
I'll come to you straight.
(Exeunt Tribulation and Ananias)
Who is it?—Face! appear.

Scene III. *The same*

(Subtle. Enter Face in his uniform)

Subtle. How now! good prize?

Face. Good pox! Yond' costive cheater°
Never came on.

Subtle. How then?

Face. I have walked the round
Till now, and no such thing.

Subtle. And have you quit him?

Face. Quit him! An hell would quit him too, he were happy.
'Slight! would you have me stalk like a mill-jade,°
All day, for one that will not yield us grains?
I know him of old.

Subtle. O, but to have gulled him,
Had been a mastery.

Face. Let him go, black boy!
And turn thee, that some fresh news may possess thee.
10 A noble count, a don of Spain (my dear
Delicious compeer, and my party°-bawd),
Who is come hither private for his conscience
And brought munition with him, six great slops,°
Bigger than three Dutch hoys,° beside round trunks,
Furnished with pistolets, and pieces of eight,°
Will straight be here, my rogue, to have thy bath,
(That is the colour,°) and to make his battery
Upon our Dol, our castle, our cinqueport,
Our Dover pier,° our what thou wilt. Where is she?
20 She must prepare perfumes, delicate linen,
The bath in chief, a banquet, and her wit,
For she must milk his epididymis.
Where is the doxy?

Subtle. I'll send her to thee:
And but despatch my brace of little John Leydens,°
And come again myself.

Face. Are they within then?

Subtle. Numbering the sum.

Face. How much?

Subtle. A hundred marks, boy.
(Exit)

1. cheater, Surly. ***5. mill-jade,*** the broken-down horses, condemned to circle in order to grind corn. ***11. party,*** partner. ***13. slops,*** large breeches. ***14. hoys,*** ships. ***15. pistolets . . . eight,*** Spanish coins. ***17. colour,*** pretext. ***18-19. cinque port . . . pier,*** The five (cinque) major ports on the southeast coast of England, including Dover. ***24. John Leydens,*** Puritans.

Face. Why, this is a lucky day. Ten pounds of Mammon!
Three of my clerk! A portague of my grocer!
This of the brethren! Beside reversions
And states to come, in the widow, and my count! 30
My share today will not be bought for forty—
(Enter Dol)
Dol. What?
Face. Pounds, dainty Dorothy! Art thou so near?
Dol. Yes; say, lord general, how fares our camp?
Face. As with the few that had entrenched themselves
Safe, by their discipline, against a world, Dol,
And laughed within those trenches, and grew fat
With thinking on the booties, Dol, brought in
Daily by their small parties. This dear hour,
A doughty don is taken with my Dol;
And thou mayst make his ransom what thou wilt 40
My Dousabel;° he shall be brought here fettered
With thy fair looks, before he sees thee; and thrown
In a down-bed, as dark as any dungeon;
Where thou shalt keep him waking with thy drum;
Thy drum, my Dol, thy drum; till he be tame
As the poor blackbirds were in the great frost,
Or bees are with a bason; and so hive him
In the swan-skin coverlid and cambric sheets,
Till he work honey and wax, my little God's-gift.
Dol. What is he, general?
Face. An adalantado,° 50
A grandee, girl. Was not my Dapper here yet?
Dol. No.
Face. Nor my Drugger?
Dol. Neither.
Face. A pox on them,
They are so long a furnishing! such stinkards
Would not be seen upon these festival days.—
(Re-enter Subtle)
How now! have you done?
Subtle. Done. They are gone: the sum
Is here in bank, my Face. I would we knew
Another chapman who would buy them outright.
Face. 'Slid, Nab shall do't against he have the widow,
To furnish household.
Subtle. Excellent, well thought on:
Pray God he come.

41. *Dousabel*, sweetheart. **50. *adalantado*,** governor of a province.

60 *Face.* I pray he keep away
Till our new business be o'erpast.
Subtle. But, Face,
How camst thou by this secret don?
Face. A spirit
Brought me the intelligence in a paper here,
As I was conjuring yonder in my circle
For Surly; I have my flies abroad. Your bath
Is famous, Subtle, by my means. Sweet Dol,
You must go tune your virginal, no loosing
Of the least time. And, do you hear? good action.
Fish, like a flounder; kiss, like a scallop, close;
70 Tickle him with thy mother tongue. His great
Verdugoship° has not a jot of language;
So much the easier to be cozened, my Dolly.
He will come here in a hired coach, obscure,
And our own coachman, whom I have sent as guide,
No creature else. *(One knocks.)* Who's that? *(Exit Dol)*
Subtle. It is not he?
Face. O no, not yet this hour.
(Re-enter Dol)
Subtle. Who is't?
Dol. Dapper,
Your clerk.
Face. God's will then, Queen of Fairy,
On with your tire; *(Exit Dol)* and, doctor, with your robes.
Let's despatch him for God's sake.
Subtle. 'Twill be long.
80 *Face.* I warrant you, take but the cues I give you,
It shall be brief enough. *(Goes to the window)* 'Slight, here are more!
Abel, and I think the angry boy, the heir,
That fain would quarrel.
Subtle. And the widow?
Face. No,
Not that I see. Away! *(Exit Subtle)*

Scene IV. *The same*

(Face. Enter Dapper)
Face. O, sir, you are welcome.
The doctor is within a moving for you;

71. Verdugoship, Face is unlikely to know the meaning (executioner).

I have had the most ado to win him to it!—
He swears you'll be the darling of the dice:
He never heard her highness dote till now.
Your aunt has given you the most gracious words
That can be thought on.
  Dapper. Shall I see her grace?
  Face. See her, and kiss her too.—
(Enter Drugger, followed by Kastril)
What honest Nab!
Hast brought the damask?
  Drugger. No, sir; here's tobacco.
  Face. 'Tis well done, Nab; thou'lt bring the damask too?
  Drugger. Yes. Here's the gentleman, captain, Master Kastril, 10
I have brought to see the doctor.
  Face. Where's the widow?
  Drugger. Sir, as he likes, his sister, he says, shall come.
  Face. O, is it so? Good time. Is your name Kastril, sir?
  Kastril. Ay, and the best of the Kastrils, I'd be sorry else,
By fifteen hundred a year.° Where is this doctor?
My mad tobacco-boy here tells me of one
That can do things. Has he any skill?
  Face. Wherein, sir?
  Kastril. To carry a business, manage a quarrel fairly,
Upon fit terms.
  Face. It seems, sir, you're but young
About the town, that can make that a question! 20
  Kastril. Sir, not so young but I have heard some speech
Of the angry boys, and seen them take tobacco;
And in his shop; and I can take it too.
And I would fain be one of them, and go down
And practice in the country.
  Face. Sir, for the duello,
The doctor, I assure you, shall inform you,
To the least shadow of a hair; and show you
An instrument he has of his own making,
Wherewith, no sooner shall you make report
Of any quarrel, but he will take the height on't 30
Most instantly, and tell in what degree
Of safety it lies in, or mortality.
And how it may be borne, whether in a right line,
Or a half circle; or may else be cast
Into an angle blunt, if not acute:

15. by . . .year, i.e., he has £1,500 more than any other member of the family.

And this he will demonstrate. And then, rules
To give and take the lie by.
Kastril. How! to take it?
Face. Yes, in oblique he'll show you, or in circle;
But never in diameter. The whole town
40 Study his theorems, and dispute them ordinarily°
At the eating academies.
Kastril. But does he teach
Living by the wits too?
Face. Anything whatever.
You cannot think that subtlety but he reads it.
He made me a captain. I was a stark pimp,
Just of your standing, 'fore I met with him;
It's not two months since. I'll tell you his method:
First, he will enter you at some ordinary.
Kastril. No, I'll not come there: you shall pardon me.
Face. For why, sir?
Kastril. There's gaming there, and tricks.
Face. Why, would you be
A gallant, and not game?
50 *Kastril.* Ay, 'twill spend a man.
Face. Spend you! It will repair you when you are spent.
How do they live by their wits there, that have vented
Six times your fortunes?
Kastril. What, three thousand a year!
Face. Ay, forty thousand.
Kastril. Are there such?
Face. Ay, sir,
And gallants yet. Here's a young gentleman
Is born to nothing,—*(Points to Dapper)* forty marks a year
Which I count nothing:—he is to be initiated,
And have a fly of the doctor. He will win you
By unresistible luck, within this fortnight,
60 Enough to buy a barony. They will set him
Upmost, at the groom porters,° all the Christmas:
And for the whole year through at every place
Where there is play, present him with the chair,
The best attendance, the best drink, sometimes
Two glasses of Canary, and pay nothing;
The purest linen and the sharpest knife,
The partridge next his trencher: and somewhere

40. ordinarily, a pun on the "ordinary" restaurant (or eating academy). ***61. groom porters,*** officer of the royal household in charge of gambling.

The dainty bed, in private, with the dainty.
You shall have your ordinaries bid for him,
As playhouses for a poet; and the master 70
Pray him aloud to name what dish he affects,
Which must be buttered shrimps: and those that drink
To no mouth else, will drink to his, as being
The goodly president mouth of all the board.
Kastril. Do you not gull one?
Face. 'Ods my life! Do you think it?
You shall have a cast° commander, (can but get
In credit with a glover, or a spurrier,°
For some two pair of either's ware aforehand,)
Will, by most swift posts, dealing with him,
Arrive at competent means to keep himself, 80
His punk, and naked boy, in excellent fashion,
And be admired for't.
Kastril. Will the doctor teach this?
Face. He will do more, sir: when your land is gone,
(As men of spirit hate to keep earth long),
In a vacation,° when small money is stirring,
And ordinaries suspended till the term,
He'll show a perspective,° where on one side
You shall behold the faces and the persons
Of all sufficient young heirs in town,
Whose bonds are current for commodity;° 90
On the other side, the merchants' forms, and others,
That without help of any second broker,
Who would expect a share, will trust such parcels:
In the third square, the very street and sign
Where the commodity dwells, and does but wait
To be delivered, be it pepper, soap,
Hops, or tobacco, oatmeal, woad, or cheeses.
All which you may so handle, to enjoy
To your own use, and never stand obliged.
Kastril. In faith! is he such a fellow?
Face. Why, Nab here knows him. 100
And then for making matches for rich widows,
Young gentlewomen, heirs, the fortunat'st man!
He's sent to, far and near, all over England,
To have his counsel, and to know their fortunes.
Kastril. God's will, my suster shall see him.

76. cast, cashiered. ***77. spurrier,*** maker of spurs. ***85. vacation,*** i.e., of the courts of law. ***87. perspective,*** an ingeniously devised picture. ***90. commodity,*** a fraud in which the borrower had to take part of his loan in over-priced goods.

Face. I'll tell you, sir,
What he did tell me of Nab. It's a strange thing—
By the way, you must eat no cheese, Nab, it breeds melancholy,
And that same melancholy breeds worms but pass it:—
He told me, honest Nab here was never at tavern
But once in his life.

110 *Drugger.* Truth, and no more I was not.

Face. And then he was so sick—

Drugger. Could he tell you that too?

Face. How should I know it?

Drugger. In troth, we had been a shooting,
And had a piece of fat ram-mutton to supper,
That lay so heavy on my stomach—

Face. And he has no head
To bear any wine; for what with the noise of the fiddlers,
And care of his shop, for he dares keep no servants—

Drugger. My head did so ache—

Face. And he was fain to be brought home,
The doctor told me: and then a good old woman—

Drugger. Yes, faith, she dwells in Seacoal-lane,—did cure me,
120 With sodden ale, and pellitory° of the wall
Cost me but twopence. I had another sickness
Was worse than that.

Face. Ay, that was with the grief
Thou took'st for being cessed° at eighteenpence,
For the waterwork.

Drugger. In truth, and it was like
To have cost me almost my life.

Face. Thy hair went off?

Drugger. Yes, sir; 'twas done for spite.

Face. Nay, so says the doctor.

Kastril. Pray thee, tobacco-boy, go fetch my suster;
I'll see this learned boy before I go;
And so shall she.

Face. Sir, he is busy now:
130 But if you have a sister to fetch hither,
Perhaps your own pains may command her sooner;
And he by that time will be free.

Kastril. I go. *(Exit)*

Face. Drugger, she's thine: the damask!—*(Exit Drugger)* Subtle and I
Must wrestle for her. *(Aside)* Come on, Master Dapper,
You see how I turn clients here away,

120. pellitory, an herb. ***123. cessed,*** assessed.

To give your cause dispatch; have you performed
The ceremonies were enjoined you?
Dapper. Yes, of the vinegar,
And the clean shirt.
Face. 'Tis well: that shirt may do you
More worship than you think. Your aunt's a-fire,
But that she will not show it, to have a sight of you. 140
Have you provided for her grace's servants?
Dapper. Yes, here are six score Edward shillings.
Face. Good!
Dapper. And an old Harry's sovereign.
Face. Very good!
Dapper. And three James shillings, and an Elizabeth groat,
Just twenty nobles.
Face. O, you are too just.
I would you had had the other noble in Maries.
Dapper. I have some Philip and Maries.°
Face. Ay, those same
Are best of all: where are they? Hark, the doctor.

Scene V. *The same*

(Face, Dapper. Enter Subtle, disguised like a priest of Fairy with a strip of cloth)
Subtle. (In a feigned voice) Is yet her grace's cousin come?
Face. He is come.
Subtle. And is he fasting?
Face. Yes.
Subtle. And hath cried hum?
Face. Thrice, you must answer.
Dapper. Thrice.
Subtle. And as oft buz?
Face. If you have, say.
Dapper. I have.
Subtle. Then, to her cuz,
Hoping that he hath vinegared his senses,
As he was bid, the Fairy queen dispenses,
By me, this robe, the petticoat of fortune;
Which that he straight put on, she doth importune.
And though to fortune near be her petticoat,
Yet nearer is her smock, the queen doth note: 10

147. Philip and Maries, coins minted in the reign of Mary Tudor (1550-1558) and King Philip of Spain.

And therefore, even of that a piece she hath sent,
Which, being a child, to wrap him in was rent;
And prays him for a scarf he now will wear it,
With as much love as then her grace did tear it,
About his eyes, *(They blind him with the rag.)* to show he is fortunate.
And, trusting unto her to make his state,
He'll throw away all worldly pelf about him;
Which that he will perform, she doth not doubt him.
Face. She need not doubt him, sir. Alas, he has nothing
20 But what he will part withal as willingly,
Upon her grace's word—throw away your purse—
As she would ask it:—handkerchiefs and all—
She cannot bid that thing but he'll obey.—
If you have a ring about you, cast it off,
Or a silver seal at your wrist; her grace will send *(He throws it away, as they bid him.)*
Her fairies here to search you, therefore deal
Directly° with her highness: if they find
That you conceal a mite, you are undone.
Dapper. Truly, there's all.
Face. All what?
Dapper. My money; truly.
30 *Face.* Keep nothing that is transitory about you.
(Aside to Subtle) Bid Dol play music.—Look, the elves are come. *(Dol plays on the cittern within.)*
To pinch you, if you tell not truth. Advise you. *(They pinch him.)*
Dapper. O! I have a paper with a spur-ryal° in't.
Face. *Ti, ti.*
They knew't, they say.
Subtle. *Ti, ti, ti, ti.* He has more yet.
Face. Ti, ti-ti-ti. I' the other pocket?
Subtle. *Titi, titi, titi, titi, titi.*
They must pinch him or he will never confess, they say. *(They pinch him again.)*
Dapper. O, O!
Face. Nay, pray you, hold; he is her grace's nephew,
Ti, ti, ti? What care you? good faith, you shall care.—
Deal plainly, sir, and shame the fairies. Show
You are innocent.
40 *Dapper.* By this good light, I have nothing.
Subtle. Ti, ti, ti, ti, to, ta. He does equivocate she says:
Ti, ti do ti, ti ti do, ti da; and swears by the *light* when he is blinded.

27. *Directly*, correctly. **33. *spur-ryal*,** a gold coin.

Dapper. By this good *dark*, I have nothing but a half-crown
Of gold about my wrist, that my love gave me;
And a leaden heart I wore since she forsook me.
Face. I thought 'twas something. And would you incur
Your aunt's displeasure for these trifles? Come,
I had rather you had thrown away twenty half-crowns. *(Takes it off)*
You may wear your leaden heart still.—
(Enter Dol, hastily)
How now!
Subtle. What news, Dol?
Dol. Yonder's your knight, Sir Mammon. 50
Face. 'Ods lid, we never thought of him till now!
Where is he?
Dol. Here hard by. He's at the door.
Subtle. And you are not ready now! Dol, get his suit.
(Exit Dol)
He must not be sent back.
Face. O, by no means.
What shall we do with this same puffin° here,
Now he's on the spit?
Subtle. Why, lay him back awhile,
With some device.
(Re-enter Dol with Face's clothes)
—*Ti, ti, ti, ti, ti, ti*, Would her grace speak with me?
I come.—Help, Dol!° *(Knocking without)*
Face. *(Speaks through the keyhole)*—Who's there? Sir Epicure,
My master's in the way. Please you to walk
Three or four turns, but till his back be turned, 60
And I am for you.—Quickly, Dol!
Subtle. Her grace
Commends her kindly to you, Master Dapper.
Dapper. I long to see her grace.
Subtle. She now is set
At dinner in her bed, and she has sent you
From her own private trencher, a dead mouse,
And a piece of gingerbread, to be merry withal,
And stay your stomach, lest you faint with fasting:
Yet if you could hold out till she saw you, she says,
It would be better for you.
Face. Sir, he shall
Hold out, an 'twere this two hours, for her highness; 70

55. puffin, gull. ***58. help dol,*** i.e., to get into his proper clothes, as part of the frantic activity of the end of Act III.

I can assure you that. We will not lose
All we have done.—
Subtle. He must not see, nor speak
To anybody, till then.
Face. For that we'll put, sir,
A stay in his mouth.
Subtle. Of what?
Face. Of gingerbread.
Make you it fit. He that hath pleased her grace
Thus far, shall not now crinkle° for a little.—
Gape, sir, and let him fit you. *(They thrust a gag of gingerbread into his mouth.)*
Subtle. Where shall we now
Bestow him?
Dol. In the privy.°
Subtle. Come along, sir,
I must now show you Fortune's privy lodgings.
Face. Are they perfumed, and his bath ready?
80 *Subtle.* All:
Only the fumigation's somewhat strong.
Face. *(Speaking through the keyhole)* Sir Epicure, I am yours, sir, by and by.
(Exeunt with Dapper)

Act IV

Scene I. *A room in Lovewit's house*

(Enter Face and Mammon)
Face. O, sir, you're come in the only finest time.—
Mammon. Where's master?
Face. Now preparing for projection, sir.
Your stuff will be all changed shortly.
Mammon. Into gold?
Face. To gold and silver, sir.
Mammon. Silver I care not for.
Face. Yes, sir, a little to give beggars.
Mammon. Where's the lady?
Face. At hand here. I have told her such brave things of you,
Touching your bounty and your noble spirit—
Mammon. Hast thou?

76. crinkle, shirk. **77-78. Where . . . privy,** these are hurried asides while they conduct Dapper out.

Face. As she is almost in her fit to see you.
But, good sir, no divinity in your conference,
For fear of putting her in rage.—
Mammon. I warrant thee. 10
Face. Six men will not hold her down. And then,
If the old man should hear or see you—
Mammon. Fear not.
Face. The very house, sir, would run mad. You know it,
How scrupulous he is, and violent,
'Gainst the least act of sin. Physic or mathematics,
Poetry, state,° or bawdry, as I told you,
She will endure, and never startle; but
No word of controversy.
Mammon. I am schooled, good Ulen.
Face. And you must praise her house, remember that,
And her nobility.
Mammon. Let me alone: 20
No herald, no, nor antiquary, Lungs,
Shall do it better. Go.
Face. *(Aside)* Why, this is yet
A kind of modern happiness, to have
Dol Common for a great lady. *(Exit)*
Mammon. Now, Epicure,
Heighten thyself, talk to her all in gold;
Rain her as many showers as Jove did drops
Unto his Danaë; show the god a miser,
Compared with Mammon. What! the stone will do't.
She shall feel gold, taste gold, hear gold, sleep gold;
Nay, we will *concumbere*° gold: I will be puissant, 30
And mighty in my talk to her.—
(Re-enter Face with Dol richly dressed)
Here she comes.—
Face. To him, Dol, suckle him.—This is the noble knight
I told your ladyship—
Mammon. Madam, with your pardon,
I kiss your vesture.
Dol. Sir, I were uncivil
If I would suffer that; my lip to you, sir.
Mammon. I hope my lord your brother be in health, lady.
Dol. My lord my brother is, though I no lady, sir.
Face. *(Aside)* Well said, my Guinea bird.°
Mammon. Right noble madam—

16. state, politics. ***30. concumbere***, fornicate. ***38. Guinea bird***, prostitute.

Face. (Aside) O, we shall have most fierce idolatry.
Mammon. 'Tis your prerogative.
40 *Dol.* Rather your courtesy.
Mammon. Were there nought else to enlarge your virtues to me,
These answers speak your breeding and your blood.
Dol. Blood we boast none, sir; a poor baron's daughter.
Mammon. Poor! and gat you? Profane not. Had your father
Slept all the happy remnant of his life
After that act, lain but there still, and panted,
He'd done enough to make himself, his issue,
And his posterity noble.
Dol. Sir, although
We may be said to want the gilt and trappings,
50 The dress of honour, yet we strive to keep
The seeds and the materials.
Mammon. I do see
The old ingredient, virtue, was not lost,
Nor the drug money used to make your compound.
There is a strange nobility in your eye,
This lip, that chin! Methinks you do resemble
One of the Austriac princes.
Face. (Aside) Very like!
Her father was an Irish costermonger.
Mammon. The house of Valois just had such a nose,
And such a forehead yet the Medici
Of Florence boast.
60 *Dol.* Troth, and I have been likened
To all these princes.
Face. (Aside) I'll be sworn, I heard it.
Mammon. I know not how! it is not any one,
But even the very choice of all their features.
Face. (Aside) I'll in, and laugh. *(Exit)*
Mammon. A certain touch, or air,
That sparkles a divinity beyond
An earthly beauty!
Dol. O, you play the courtier.
Mammon. Good lady, give me leave—
70 *Dol.* In faith, I may not,
To mock me, sir.
Mammon. To burn in this sweet flame;
The phœnix never knew a nobler death.
Dol. Nay, now you court the courtier, and destroy
What you would build. This art, sir, in your words,
Calls your whole faith in question.

Mammon. By my soul—
Dol. Nay, oaths are made of the same air, sir.
Mammon. Nature
Never bestowed upon mortality
A more unblamed,° a more harmonious feature;
She played the step-dame in all faces else:
Sweet madam, let me be particular°—
Dol. Particular, sir! I pray you know your distance.
Mammon. In no ill sense, sweet lady; but to ask
How your fair graces pass the hours? I see 80
You're lodged here, in the house of a rare man,
An excellent artist; but what's that to you?
Dol. Yes, sir; I study here the mathematics,
And distillation.°
Mammon. O, I cry your pardon.
He's a divine instructor! can extract
The souls of all things by his art; call all
The virtues, and the miracles of the sun,
Into a temperate furnace; teach dull nature
What her own forces are. A man, the emperor
Has courted above Kelly;° sent his medals 90
And chains, to invite him.
Dol. Ay, and for his physic, sir—
Mammon. Above the art of Æsculapius,
That drew the envy of the thunderer!°
I know all this, and more.
Dol. Troth, I am taken, sir,
Whole with these studies, that contemplate nature.
Mammon. It is a noble humour; but this form
Was not intended to so dark a use.
Had you been crooked, foul, of some coarse mould,
A cloister had done well; but such a feature
That might stand up the glory of a kingdom, 100
To live recluse! is a mere solœcism,
Though in a nunnery. It must not be.
I muse,° my lord your brother will permit it:
You should spend half my land first, were I he.
Does not this diamond better on my finger
Than in the quarry?
Dol. Yes.

75. unblamed, unblemished. ***77. particular,*** personal. ***84. distillation,*** chemistry. ***90. Kelly,*** Edward Kelly, an alchemist employed by the Emperor Rudolph II. ***93. thunderer,*** Zeus. ***103. muse,*** am amazed.

Mammon. Why, you are like it.
You were created, lady, for the light.
Here, you shall wear it; take it, the first pledge
Of what I speak, to bind you to believe me.
Dol. In chains of adamant?
110 *Mammon.* Yes, the strongest bands.
And take a secret too.—Here, by your side,
Doth stand this hour the happiest man in Europe.
Dol. You are contented, sir?
Mammon. Nay, in true being,
The envy of princes and the fear of states.
Dol. Say you so, Sir Epicure?
Mammon. Yes, and thou shalt prove it,
Daughter of honour. I have cast mine eye
Upon thy form, and I will rear this beauty
Above all styles.
Dol. You mean no treason, sir?
Mammon. No, I will take away that jealousy.°
120 I am the lord of the philosopher's stone,
And thou the lady.
Dol. How, sir! have you that?
Mammon. I am the master of the mastery.
This day the good old wretch here of the house
Has made it for us: now he's at projection.
Think therefore thy first wish now, let me hear it;
And it shall rain into thy lap, no shower,
But floods of gold, whole cataracts, a deluge,
To get a nation on thee.
Dol. You are pleased, sir,
To work on the ambition of our sex.
130 *Mammon.* I'm pleased the glory of her sex should know,
This nook here of the Friars is no climate
For her to live obscurely in, to learn
Physic and surgery, for the constable's wife
Of some odd hundred° in Essex; but come forth,
And taste the air of palaces; eat, drink
The toils of empirics,° and their boasted practice;
Tincture of pearl, and coral, gold, and amber;
Be seen at feasts and triumphs; have it asked,
What miracle she is; set all the eyes
140 Of court a-fire, like a burning glass,

119. jealousy, suspicion. ***134. hundred,*** township. ***136. empirics,*** alchemists.

And work them into cinders, when the jewels
Of twenty states adorn thee, and the light
Strikes out the stars! that, when thy name is mentioned,
Queens may look pale; and we but showing our love,
Nero's Poppæa may be lost in story!
Thus will we have it.

Dol. I could well consent, sir.
But in a monarchy, how will this be?
The prince will soon take notice, and both seize
You and your stone, it being a wealth unfit
For any private subject.

Mammon. If he knew it. 150

Dol. Yourself do boast it, sir.

Mammon. To thee, my life.

Dol. O, but beware, sir! You may come to end
The remnant of your days in a loathed prison,
By speaking of it.

Mammon. 'Tis no idle fear.
We'll therefore go with all, my girl, and live
In a free state, where we will eat our mullets,
Soused in high-country wines, sup pheasants' eggs,
And have our cockles boiled in silver shells;
Our shrimps to swim again, as when they lived,
In a rare butter made of dolphins' milk, 160
Whose cream does look like opals; and with these
Delicate meats set ourselves high for pleasure,
And take us down again, and then renew
Our youth and strength with drinking the elixir,
And so enjoy a perpetuity
Of life and lust! And thou shalt have thy wardrobe
Richer than nature's, still to change thyself,
And vary oftener, for thy pride, than she,
Or art, her wise and almost-equal servant.

(Re-enter Face)

Face. Sir, you are too loud. I hear you every word 170
Into the laboratory. Some fitter place;
The garden, or great chamber above. How like you her?

Mammon. Excellent, Lungs! There's for thee. *(Gives him money)*

Face. But do you hear?
Good sir, beware, no mention of the rabbins.

Mammon. We think not on them.

(Exeunt Mammon and Dol)

Face. O, it is well, sir.—Subtle!

Scene II. *The same*

(Face. Enter Subtle)

Face. Dost thou not laugh?

Subtle. Yes; are they gone?

Face. All's clear.

Subtle. The widow is come.

Face. And your quarrelling disciple?

Subtle. Ay.

Face. I must to my captainship again then.

Subtle. Stay, bring them in first.

Face. So I meant. What is she?
A bonnibel?°

Subtle. I know not.

Face. We'll draw lots:
You'll stand to that?

Subtle. What else?

Face. O, for a suit,°
To fall now like a curtain, flap!

Subtle. To the door, man.

Face. You'll have the first kiss, because I am not ready. *(Exit)*

Subtle. Yes, and perhaps hit you through both the nostrils.°

Face. (Within) Who would you speak with?

Kastril. (Within) Where's the captain?

10 *Face. (Within)* Gone, sir,
About some business.

Kastril. (Within) Gone!

Face. (Within) He'll return straight.
But, master doctor, his lieutenant, is here.

(Enter Kastril, followed by Dame Pliant)

Subtle. Come near, my worshipful boy, my *terræ fili.*
That is, my boy of land; make thy approaches:
Welcome; I know thy lusts, and thy desires,
And I will serve and satisfy them. Begin,
Charge me from thence, or thence, or in this line;
Here is my centre: ground thy quarrel.

Kastril. You lie.

Subtle. How, child of wrath and anger! the loud lie?
For what, my sudden boy?

20 *Kastril.* Nay, that look you to,
I am aforehand.°

5. *bonnibel,* bonnie belle. **6. *suit,*** Face wishes he were dressed as captain instead of servant.
9. *hit . . . nostrils,* put your nose out of joint. **21. *I am aforehand,*** I challenged you first.

Subtle. O, this is no true grammar,
And as ill logic! You must render causes, child,
Your first and second intentions, know your canons
And your divisions, moods, degrees, and differences,
Your predicaments, substance, and accident,
Series extern and intern, with their causes,
Efficient, material, formal, final,
And have your elements perfect?
Kastril. What is this?
The angry tongue he talks in?
Subtle. That false precept
Of being aforehand, has deceived a number, 30
And made them enter quarrels oftentimes
Before they were aware; and afterward,
Against their wills.
Kastril. How must I do then, sir?
Subtle. I cry this lady mercy; she should first
Have been saluted. *(Kisses her)* I do call you lady,
Because you are to be one ere 't be long,
My soft and buxom widow.
Kastril. Is she, in faith?
Subtle. Yes, or my art is an egregious liar.
Kastril. How know you?
Subtle. By inspection on her forehead,
And subtlety of her lip, which must be tasted 40
Often to make a judgment. *(Kisses her again)* 'Slight, she melts
Like a myrobolane.° Here is yet a line,
In *rivo frontis*,° tells me he is no knight.
Dame Pliant. What is he then, sir?
Subtle. Let me see your hand.
O, your *linea fortunæ* makes it plain;
And *stella* here *in monte Veneris*.
But, most of all, *junctura annularis*.°
He is a soldier, or a man of art, lady,
But shall have some great honour shortly.
Dame Pliant. Brother,
He's a rare man, believe me!
(Re-enter Face, in his uniform)
Kastril. Hold your peace. 50
Here comes the other rare man.—'Save you, captain.
Face. Good Master Kastril! Is this your sister?

42. myrobolane, candy. ***43. rivo frontis,*** frontal vein. ***45-47.*** Subtle, now a palmist, examines her line of fortune, root of the thumb and joint of the ring finger.

Kastril. Ay, sir.
Please you to kiss her, and be proud to know her.
Face. I shall be proud to know you, lady. *(Kisses her)*
Dame Pliant. Brother,
He calls me lady too.
Kastril. Ay, peace: I heard it. *(Takes her aside)*
Face. The count is come.
Subtle. Where is he?
Face. At the door.
Subtle. Why, you must entertain him.
Face. What will you do
With these the while?
Subtle. Why, have them up, and show them
Some fustian book, or the dark glass.
Face. 'Fore God,
60 She is a delicate dabchick! I must have her. *(Exit)*
Subtle. (Aside) Must you! Ay, if your fortune will, you must.—
Come, sir, the captain will come to us presently:
I'll have you to my chamber of demonstrations,
Where I'll show you both the grammar and logic,
And rhetoric of quarrelling; my whole method
Drawn out in tables; and my instrument,
That hath the several scales upon't, shall make you
Able to quarrel at a straw's-breadth by moonlight.
And, lady, I'll have you look in a glass,
70 Some half an hour, but to clear your eyesight,
Against° you see your fortune; which is greater
Than I may judge upon the sudden, trust me. *(Exeunt)*

Scene III. *The same*

(Enter Face)
Face. Where are you, doctor?
Subtle. (Within) I'll come to you presently.
Face. I will have this same widow, now I have seen her,
On any composition.
(Enter Subtle)
Subtle. What do you say?
Face. Have you disposed of them?
Subtle. I have sent them up.
Face. Subtle, in troth, I needs must have this widow.

71. Against, so that.

Subtle. Is that the matter?
Face. Nay, but hear me.
Subtle. Go to.
If you rebel once, Dol shall know it all:
Therefore be quiet, and obey your chance.
Face. Nay, thou art so violent now. Do but conceive,
Thou art old, and canst not serve—
Subtle. Who cannot? I? 10
'Slight, I will serve her with thee, for a—
Face. Nay,
But understand: I'll give you composition.°
Subtle. I will not treat with thee. What! sell my fortune?
'Tis better than my birthright. Do not murmur:
Win her, and carry her. If you grumble, Dol
Knows it directly.
Face. Well, sir, I am silent.
Will you go help to fetch in Don in state? *(Exit)*
Subtle. I follow you, sir. *(Aside)* We must keep Face in awe,
Or he will overlook us like a tyrant.
(Re-enter Face, introducing Surly disguised as a Spaniard)
Brain of a tailor! who comes here? Don John! 20
Surly. Señores, beso las manos a vuestras mercedes.°
Subtle. Would you had stooped a little and kissed our anos.
Face. Peace, Subtle.
Subtle. Stab me; I shall never hold, man.
He looks in that deep ruff like a head in a platter,
Served in by a short cloak upon two trestles.
Face. Or what do you say to a collar of brawn,° cut down
Beneath the souse,° and wriggled° with a knife?
Subtle. 'Slud, he does look too fat to be a Spaniard.
Face. Perhaps some Fleming or some Hollander got him
In d'Alva's° time; Count Egmont's° bastard.
Subtle. Don, 30
Your scurvy, yellow, Madrid face is welcome.
Surly. Gratia.°
Subtle. He speaks out of a fortification.
Pray God he has no squibs° in those deep sets.
Surly. Por dios, señores, muy linda casa!°

12. composition, recompense. ***21. Señores . . . mercedes,*** "Gentlemen, I kiss your graces' hands." Subtle's Spanish, not always perfect, is given in this scene as Jonson wrote it. ***26. brawn,*** roll of boar's flesh. ***27. souse,*** ear. **wriggled,** slashed. ***30. Alva,*** a famous general and Spanish governor of the Netherlands; ***Egmont,*** a Flemish patriot executed by Alva. ***32. Gratia,*** thanks. ***33. squibs,*** firecrackers. ***sets,*** plaits (of his collar). ***34. Por . . . casa,*** by God, gentlemen, a very fine house.

Subtle. What says he?
Face. Praises the house, I think;
I know no more but his action.
Subtle. Yes, the *casa.*
My precious Diego, will prove fair enough
To cozen you in. Do you mark? You shall
Be cozened, Diego.
Face. Cozened, do you see,
My worthy Donzel,° cozened.
40 *Surly.* *Entiendo.*°
Subtle. Do you intend it? So do we, dear Don.
Have you brought pistolets, or portagues,
My solemn Don? *(To Face)* Dost thou feel any? *(Face feels his pockets.)*
Full.
Subtle. You shall be emptied, Don, pumped and drawn
Dry, as they say.
Face. Milked, in troth, sweet Don.
Subtle. See all the monsters; the great lion of all, Don.
Surly. Con licencia, se puede ver a esta señora?°
Subtle. What talks he now?
Face. Of the señora.
Subtle. O, Don,
This is the lioness, which you shall see
Also, my Don.
50 *Face.* 'Slid, Subtle, how shall we do?
Subtle. For what?
Face. Why, Dol's employed, you know.
Subtle. That's true.
'Fore heaven I know not: he must stay, that's all.
Face. Stay! that he must not by no means.
Subtle. No! why?
Face. Unless you'll mar all. 'Slight, he'll suspect it;
And then he will not pay, not half so well.
This is a travelled punk-master, and does know
All the delays; a notable hot rascal,
And looks already rampant.
Subtle. 'Sdeath, and Mammon
Must not be troubled.
Face. Mammon! in no case.
Subtle. What shall we do then?
60 *Face.* Think: you must be sudden.°

40. Donzel, "little Don." ***Entiendo,*** I understand. ***47. Con . . . señora,*** if you please, may I see the lady? ***60. sudden,*** quick.

Surly. Entiendo que la señora es tan hermosa, que codicio tan a verla, como la bien aventuranza de mi vida.°

Face. Mi vida! 'Slid, Subtle, he puts me in mind of the widow.
What dost thou say to draw her to't, ha!
And tell her 'tis her fortune? All our venture
Now lies upon't. It is but one man more,
Which on his chance to have her: and beside,
There is no maidenhead to be feared or lost.
What dost thou think on't, Subtle?

Subtle. Who, I? why—

Face. The credit of our house too is engaged. 70

Subtle. You made me an offer for my share erewhile.
What wilt thou give me, in faith?

Face. O, by that light
I'll not buy now. You know your doom° to me.
Even take your lot, obey your chance, sir; win her,
And wear her—out for me.

Subtle. 'Slight, I'll not work her then.

Face. It is the common cause; therefore bethink you.
Dol else must know it, as you said.

Subtle. I care not.

Surly. Señores, porque se tarda tanto?°

Subtle. Faith, I am not fit, I am old.

Face. That's now no reason, sir.

Surly. Puede ser de hacer burla de mi amor?° 80

Face. You hear the Don too? by this air I call,
And loose the hinges. Dol!

Subtle. A plague of hell—

Face. Will you then do?

Subtle. You're a terrible rogue!
I'll think of this. Will you, sir, call the widow?

Face. Yes, and I'll take her too with all her faults,
Now I do think on't better.

Subtle. With all my heart, sir;
Am I discharged of the lot?

Face. As you please.

Subtle. Hands. *(They shake hands.)*

Face. Remember now, that upon any change,
You never claim her.

Subtle. Much good joy and health to you, sir,
Marry a whore! Fate, let me wed a witch first. 90

61-62. Entiendo . . . vida, I hear that the lady is so beautiful that I am as eager to see her as the good fortune of my life. ***73. Doom,*** agreement. ***78. Señores . . . tanto,*** Gentlemen, why do you delay so long? ***80. Puede . . . amor,*** could it be that you are making a joke of my love?

Surly. Por estas honradas barbas° —
Subtle. He swears by his beard.
Dispatch, and call the brother too.
(Exit Face)
Surly. Tengo duda, señores, que no me hagan alguna traicion.°
Subtle. How, issue on? yes, *præsto, señor.* Please you
Enthratha the *chambratha,* worthy don:
Where if you please the fates, in your *bathada,*
You shall be soaked, and stroked and tubbed and rubbed,
And scrubbed, and fubbed,° dear don, before you go.
You shall in faith, my scurvy baboon don,
100 Be curried, clawed, and flawed, and tawed,° indeed.
I will the heartlier go about it now,
And make the widow a punk so much the sooner,
To be revenged on this impetuous Face:
The quickly doing of it is the grace.
(Exeunt Subtle and Surly)

Scene IV. *Another room in the same*

(Enter Face, Kastril, and Dame Pliant)
Face. Come, lady: I knew the doctor would not leave
Till he had found the very nick of her fortune.
Kastril. To be a countess, say you?
Face. A Spanish countess, sir.
Dame Pliant. Why, is that better than an English countess?
Face. Better! 'Slight, make you that a question, lady?
Kastril. Nay, she is a fool, captain, you must pardon her.
Face. Ask from your courtier to your inns-of-court-man,
To your mere milliner; they will tell you all,
Your Spanish jennet is the best horse; your Spanish
10 Stoop is the best garb; your Spanish beard
Is the best cut; your Spanish ruffs are the best
Wear; your Spanish pavin the best dance;
Your Spanish titillation in a glove
The best perfume: and for your Spanish pike,
And Spanish blade, let your poor captain speak.—
Here comes the doctor.
(Enter Subtle with a paper)
Subtle. My most honoured lady,
For so I am now to style you, having found

91. Por . . . barbas, by this honored beard. ***93. Tengo . . . traicion,*** I fear, gentlemen, that you are playing me a foul trick. ***98. fubbed,*** cheated. ***100. tawed,*** soaked.

By this my scheme, you are to undergo
An honourable fortune very shortly,
What will you say now, if some—
Face. I have told her all, sir, 20
And her right worshipful brother here, that she shall be
A countess; do not delay them, sir; a Spanish countess.
Subtle. Still, my scarce-worshipful captain, you can keep
No secret! Well, since he has told you, madam,
Do you forgive him, and I do.
Kastril. She shall do that, sir;
I'll look to it, 'tis my charge.
Subtle. Well then: nought rests
But that she fit her love now to her fortune.
Dame Pliant. Truly I shall never brook a Spaniard.
Subtle. No?
Dame Pliant. Never since eighty-eight° could I abide them,
And that was some three years afore I was born, in truth. 30
Subtle. Come, you must love him, or be miserable;
Choose which you will.
Face. By this good rush, persuade her,
She will cry strawberries° else within this twelve month.
Subtle. Nay, shads and mackerel, which is worse.
Face. Indeed, sir!
Kastril. God's lid, you shall love him, or I'll kick you.
Dame Pliant. Why,
I'll do as you will have me, brother.
Kastril. Do,
Or by this hand I'll maul you.
Face. Nay, good sir,
Be not so fierce.
Subtle. No, my enraged child;
She will be ruled. What, when she comes to taste
The pleasures of a countess! to be courted— 40
Face. And kissed, and ruffled!
Subtle. Ay, behind the hangings.
Face. And then come forth in pomp!
Subtle. And know her state!
Face. Of keeping all the idolaters of the chamber
Barer to her, than at their prayers!
Subtle. Is served
Upon the knee!

29. eighty-eight, 1588, the year of the Armada. ***33. cry strawberries,*** become a street seller.

Face. And has her pages, ushers,
Footmen, and coaches—
Subtle. Her six mares—
Face. Nay, eight!
Subtle. To hurry her through London, to the Exchange,
Bethlem,° the China-houses—
Face. Yes, and have
The citizens gape at her, and praise her tires,°
50 And my lord's goose-turd bands,° that rides with her!
Kastril. Most brave! By this hand, you are not my suster
If you refuse.
Dame Pliant. I will not refuse, brother.
(Enter Surly)
Surly. Que es esto, señores, que non se venga?
Esta tardanza me mata!°
Face. It is the count come:
The doctor knew he would be here, by his art.
Subtle. En gallanta madama, Don! gallantissima!
Surly. Por todos los dioses, la mas acabada hermosura, que he visto en ma vida!°
Face. Is't not a gallant language that they speak?
60 *Kastril.* An admirable language! Is't not French?
Face. No, Spanish, sir.
Kastril. It goes like law French,
And that, they say, is the courtliest language.
Face. List, sir.
Surly. El sol ha perdido su lumbre, con el resplandor que trae esta dama! Valgame dios!°
Face. He admires your sister.
Kastril. Must not she make curtsy.
Subtle. 'Ods will, she must go to him, man, and kiss him!
It is the Spanish fashion, for the women
To make first court.
Face. 'Tis true he tells you, sir:
His art knows all.
Surly. *Porque no se acude?*°
Kastril. He speaks to her, I think.
70 *Face.* That he does, sir.
Surly. Por el amor de dios, que es esto que se tarda?°

48. Bethlem, visits to Bethlehem Hospital, the lunatic asylum of London, were a favorite entertainment. ***49. tires,*** hats. ***50. goose-turd bands,*** servants in yellowish green liveries. ***53-54. Que . . . mata,*** Why is it, gentlemen, that she does not come? The delay is killing me. ***58. Por . . . vida,*** By all the gods, the most accomplished beauty that I have seen in my life. ***63-64. El . . . dios,*** The sun has lost his light with the splendor this lady brings, so help me God! ***69. Porque . . . acude,*** Why don't you come closer? ***71. Por . . . tarda,*** For the love of God, why does she delay?

Kastril. Nay, see: she will not understand him! Gull, Noddy.
Dame Pliant. What say you, brother?
Kastril. Ass, my suster,
Go kuss him, as the cunning man would have you;
I'll thrust a pin in your buttocks else.
Face. O no, sir.
Surly. Señora mia, mi persona muy indigna esta a llegar a tanta hermosura.°
Face. Does he not use her bravely?
Kastril. Bravely, in faith!
Face. Nay, he will use her better.
Kastril. Do you think so?
Surly. Señora, si sera servida, entremos.° *(Exit with Dame Pliant)* 80
Kastril. Where does he carry her?
Face. Into the garden, sir;
Take you no thought: I must interpret for her.
Subtle. (Aside to Face who goes out) Give Dol the word.
(To Kastril) —Come, my fierce child, advance,
We'll to our quarrelling lesson again.
Kastril. Agreed.
I love a Spanish boy with all my heart.
Subtle. Nay, and by this means, sir, you shall be brother
To a great count.
Kastril. Ay, I knew that at first.
This match will advance the house of the Kastrils.
Subtle. 'Pray God your sister prove but pliant!
Kastril. Why,
Her name is so, by her other husband.
Subtle. How! 90
Kastril. The Widow Pliant. Knew you not that?
Subtle. No, faith, sir;
Yet, by erection of her figure,° I guessed it.
Come, let's go practise.
Kastril. Yes, but do you think, doctor,
I e'er shall quarrel well?
Subtle. I warrant you. *(Exeunt)*

Scene V. *Another room in the same*

(Enter Dol in her fit of raving, followed by Mammon)
Dol. For after Alexander's death°—

76. Señora . . . hermosura, My lady, my person is unworthy to draw near to such beauty. ***80. Señora . . . entremos,*** Madam, if it is convenient, let us enter. ***92. figure,*** her horoscope, as well as a pun. ***1.*** Dol's ravings are random items from a book by the aforementioned scholar Broughton.

Mammon. Good lady—
Dol. That Perdiccas and Antigonus were slain,
The two that stood, Seleuc' and Ptolomy—
Mammon. Madam—
Dol. Made up the two legs, and the fourth beast,
That was Gog-north and Egypt-south: which after
Was called Gog iron-leg and South iron-leg—
Mammon. Lady—
Dol. And then Gog-horned. So was Egypt, too:
Then Egypt clay-leg, and Gog clay-leg—
Mammon. Sweet madam—
Dol. And last Gog-dust, and Egypt-dust, which fall
10 *In the last link of the fourth chain. And these*
Be stars in story, which none see, or look at—
Mammon. What shall I do?
Dol. *For,* as he says, *except*
We call the rabbins, and the heathen Greeks—
Mammon. Dear lady—
Dol. *To come from Salem, and from Athens,*
And teach the people of Great Britain—
(Enter Face hastily, in his servant's dress)
Face. What's the matter, sir?
Dol. To speak the tongue of Eber and Javan—
Mammon. O,
She's in her fit.
Dol. *We shall know nothing—*
Face. Death, sir,
We are undone!
Dol. *Where then a learned linguist*
Shall see the ancient used communion
Of vowels and consonants—
20 *Face.* My master will hear!
Dol. A wisdom, which Pythagoras held most high—
Mammon. Sweet honourable lady!
Dol. *To comprise*
All sounds of voices, in few marks of letters.
Face. Nay, you must never hope to lay her now. *(They all speak together.)*
25 *Dol. And so we may arrive by Talmud skill,*
And profane Greek, to raise the building up
Of Helen's house against the Ismaelite,
King of Thogarma, and his habergions
Brimstony, blue, and fiery; and the force

Of king Abaddon, and the beast of Cittim; 30
Which rabbi David Kimchi, Onkelos,
And Aben Ezra do interpret Rome.
Face. How did you put her into't?
Mammon. Alas, I talked° 25A
Of a fifth monarchy I would erect
With the philosopher's stone, by chance, and she
Falls on the other four straight.
Face. Out of Broughton!
I told you so. 'Slid, stop her mouth.
Mammon. Is't best?
Face. She'll never leave else. If the old man hear her, 30A
We are but fæces, ashes.
Subtle. (Within) What's to do there?
Face. O, we are lost! Now she hears him, she is quiet.
(Enter Subtle; they run different ways.)
Mammon. Where shall I hide me!
Subtle. How! what sight is here?
Close deeds of darkness, and that shun the light!
Bring him again. Who is he? What, my son!
O, I have lived too long.
Mammon. Nay, good, dear father,
There was no unchaste purpose.
Subtle. Not? and flee me
When I come in?
Mammon. That was my error.
Subtle. Error?
Guilt, guilt, my son; give it the right name. No marvel
If I found check in our great work within, 40
When such affairs as these were managing!
Mammon. Why, have you so?
Subtle. It has stood still this half hour:
And all the rest of our less works gone back.
Where is the instrument of wickedness,
My lewd false drudge?
Mammon. Nay, good sir, blame not him;
Believe me, 'twas against his will or knowledge:
I saw her by chance.
Subtle. Will you commit more sin,
To excuse a varlet?
Mammon. By my hope, 'tis true, sir.

25A. lines 25 to 32 and 25A to 32A are spoken at the same time.

Subtle. Nay, then I wonder less, if you, for whom
50 The blessing was prepared, would so tempt heaven,
And lose your fortunes.
Mammon. Why, sir?
Subtle. This will retard
The work a month at least.
Mammon. Why, if it do,
What remedy? But think it not, good father:
Our purposes were honest.°
Subtle. As they were,
So the reward will prove. *(A great crack and noise within)*
—How now! ay me!
God and all saints be good to us.—
(Re-enter Face)
What's that?
Face. O, sir, we are defeated! all the works
Are flown *in fumo*, every glass is burst;
Furnace and all rent down, as if a bolt
60 Of thunder had been driven through the house.
Retorts, receivers, pelicans, bolt-heads,
All struck in shivers! *(Subtle falls down as in a swoon.)*
Help, good sir! alas,
Coldness and death invades him. Nay, Sir Mammon,
Do the fair offices of a man! You stand,
As you were readier to depart than he. *(One knocks.)*
Who's there? My lord her brother is come.
Mammon. Ha, Lungs!
Face. His coach is at the door. Avoid his sight,
For he's as furious as his sister's mad.
Mammon. Alas!
Face. My brain is quite undone with the fume, sir,
70 I never must hope to be mine own man again.
Mammon. Is all lost, Lungs? Will nothing be preserved
Of all our cost?
Face. Faith, very little, sir;
A peck of coals or so, which is cold comfort, sir.
Mammon. O, my voluptuous mind! I am justly punished.
Face. And so am I, sir.
Mammon. Cast from all my hopes—
Face. Nay, certainties, sir.
Mammon. By mine own base affections.
Subtle. *(Seeming to come to himself)* O, the curst fruits of vice and lust!

54. honest, chaste.

Mammon. Good father,
It was my sin. Forgive it.
Subtle. Hangs my roof
Over us still, and will not fall, O justice,
Upon us, for this wicked man!
Face. Nay, look, sir, 80
You grieve him now with staying in his sight.
Good sir, the nobleman will come too, and take you,
And that may breed a tragedy.
Mammon. I'll go.
Face. Ay, and repent at home, sir. It may be,
For some good penance you may have it yet;
A hundred pound to the box at Bethlem—
Mammon. Yes.
Face. For the restoring such as—have their wits.
Mammon. I'll do't.
Face. I'll send one to you to receive it.
Mammon. Do.
Is no projection left?
Face. All flown, or stinks, sir.
Mammon. Will nought be saved that's good for med'cine, think'st thou? 90
Face. I cannot tell, sir. There will be perhaps
Something about the scraping of the shards,
Will cure the itch—though not your itch of mind, sir. *(Aside)*
It shall be saved for you, and sent home. Good sir,
This way for fear the lord should meet you. *(Exit* Mammon)
Subtle. (Raising his head) Face!
Face. Ay.
Subtle. Is he gone?
Face. Yes, and as heavily
As all the gold he hoped for were in his blood.
Let us be light though.
Subtle. (Leaping up) Ay, as balls, and bound
And hit our heads against the roof for joy:
There's so much of our care now cast away. 100
Face. Now to our don.
Subtle. Yes, your young widow by this time
Is made a countess, Face; she's been in travail
Of a young heir for you.
Face. Good, sir.
Subtle. Off with your case,°

103. case, his dress as Lungs, the servant.

And greet her kindly, as a bridegroom should,
After these common hazards.
Face. Very well, sir.
Will you go fetch Don Diego off the while?
Subtle. And fetch him over too, if you'll be pleased, sir.
Would Dol were in her place, to pick his pockets now!
Face. Why, you can do't as well, if you would set to't.
I pray you prove your virtue.°
110 *Subtle.* For your sake, sir. *(Exeunt)*

Scene VI. *Another room in the same*

(Enter Surly and Dame Pliant)
Surly. Lady, you see into what hands you are fallen;
'Mongst what a nest of villains! and how near
Your honour was to have catched a certain clap,
Through your credulity, had I but been
So punctually forward, as place, time,
And other circumstances would have made a man;
For you're a handsome woman: would you were wise too!
I am a gentleman come here disguised,
Only to find the knaveries of this citadel;
10 And where I might have wronged your honour, and have not,
I claim some interest in your love. You are,
They say, a widow, rich; and I'm a bachelor,
Worth nought: your fortunes may make me a man,
As mine have preserved you a woman. Think upon it,
And whether I have deserved you or no.
Dame Pliant. I will, sir.
Surly. And for these household-rogues, let me alone
To treat with them.
(Enter Subtle)
Subtle. How doth my noble Diego,
And my dear madam countess? Hath the count
Been courteous, lady? liberal and open?
20 Donzel, methinks you look melancholic,
After your coitum, and scurvy; truly
I do not like the dulness of your eye;
It hath a heavy cast, 'tis upsee Dutch,°
And says you are a lumpish whoremaster.
Be lighter, and I will make your pockets so. *(He falls to picking of them.)*
Surly. *(Throws open his cloak)* Will you, don bawd and pick-purse?
(Strikes him down) How now! Reel you?

110. virtue, power. ***23. upsee Dutch,*** in the Dutch manner.

Stand up, sir, you shall find, since I am so heavy,
I'll give you equal weight.
Subtle. Help! murder!
Surly. No, sir,
There's no such thing intended. A good cart
And a clean whip shall ease you of that fear. 30
I am the Spanish don *that should be cozened,*
Do you see? *Cozened?* Where's your Captain Face,
That parcel-broker, and whole-bawd, all rascal?
(Enter Face in his uniform)
Face. How, Surly!
Surly. O, make your approach, good captain.
I have found from whence your copper rings and spoons
Come now, wherewith you cheat abroad in taverns.
'Twas here you learned t'anoint your boot with brimstone,
Then rub men's gold on't for a kind of touch,
And say 'twas naught, when you had changed the colour,
That you might have't for nothing. And this doctor, 40
Your sooty, smoky-bearded compeer, he
Will close you so much gold, in a bolt's-head,
And, on a turn, convey in the stead another
With sublimed mercury, that shall burst in the heat,
And fly out all *in fumo!* Then weeps Mammon;
Then swoons his worship. *(Face slips out.)* Or, he is the Faustus,
That casteth figures and can conjure, cures
Plagues, piles, and pox, by the ephemerides,°
And holds intelligence with all the bawds
And midwives of three shires: while you send in— 50
Captain!—what! is he gone?—damsels with child,
Wives that are barren, or the waiting-maid
With the green sickness. *(Seizes Subtle as he is retiring)*—Nay, sir, you must tarry,
Though he be scaped; and answer by the ears, sir.

Scene VII. *The same*

(Re-enter Face with Kastril, Surly and Subtle)
Face. Why, now's the time, if ever you will quarrel
Well, as they say, and be a true-born child:
The doctor and your sister both are abused.
Kastril. Where is he? Which is he? He is a slave,
Whatever he is, and the son of a whore.—Are you

48. *ephemerides*, astrological almanacs.

The man, sir, I would know?
Surly. I should be loth, sir,
To confess so much.
Kastril. Then you lie in your throat.
Surly. How!
Face. (To Kastril) A very arrant rogue, sir, and a cheater,
Employed here by another conjurer
10 That does not love the doctor, and would cross him
If he knew how.
Surly. Sir, you are abused.
Kastril. You lie:
And 'tis no matter.
Face. Well said, sir! He is
The impudent'st rascal—
Surly. You are indeed. Will you hear me, sir?
Face. By no means: bid him be gone.
Kastril. Begone, sir, quickly.
Surly. This is strange!—Lady, do you inform your brother.
Face. There is not such a foist° in all the town. *(Aside)*
The doctor had him presently; and finds yet
The Spanish count will come here.—Bear up, Subtle.
Subtle. Yes, sir, he must appear within this hour.
20 *Face.* And yet this rogue would come in a disguise,
By the temptation of another spirit,
To trouble our art, though he could not hurt it!
Kastril. Ay,
I know—Away, *(To his sister)* you talk like a foolish mauther.°
Surly. Sir, all is truth she says.
Face. Do not believe him, sir.
He is the lying'st swabber! Come your ways, sir.
Surly. You are valiant out of company!
Kastril. Yes, how then, sir?
(Enter Drugger with a piece of damask)
Face. Nay, here's an honest fellow too that knows him,
And all his tricks. *(Aside to Drugger)* Make good what I say, Abel,
This cheater would have cozened thee of the widow.
30 He owes this honest Drugger here seven pound,
He has had on him in twopenny'orths of tobacco.
Drugger. Yes, sir. And he has damned himself three terms to pay me.
Face. And what does he owe for lotium?
Drugger. Thirty shillings, sir;
And for six syringes.

16. foist, rogue. ***23. mauther,*** wench.

Surly. Hydra of villainy!
Face. Nay, sir, you must quarrel him out of the house.
Kastril. I will
—Sir, if you get not out of doors, you lie;
And you are a pimp.
Surly. Why, this is madness, sir,
Not valour in you; I must laugh at this.
Kastril. It is my humour; you are a pimp and a trig.°
And an *Amadis de Gaul,* or a Don Quixote. 40
Drugger. Or a knight of the curious coxcomb, do you see?
(Enter Ananias)
Ananias. Peace to the household!
Kastril. I'll keep peace for no man.
Ananias. Casting of dollars is concluded lawful.
Kastril. Is he the constable?
Subtle. Peace, Ananias.
Face. No, sir.
Kastril. Then you are an otter, and a shad, a whit,
A very tim.°
Surly. You'll hear me, sir?
Kastril. I will not.
Ananias. What is the motive?
Subtle. Zeal in the young gentleman,
Against his Spanish slops.
Ananias. They are profane,
Lewd, superstitious, and idolatrous breeches.
Surly. New rascals!
Kastril. Will you be gone, sir?
Ananias. Avoid, Satan! 50
Thou art not of the light! That ruff of pride
About thy neck betrays thee; and is the same
With that which the unclean birds, in seventy-seven,
Were seen to prank it with on divers coasts:
Thou look'st like antichrist, in that lewd hat.
Surly. I must give way.
Kastril. Be gone, sir.
Surly. But I'll take
A course with you—
Ananias. Depart, proud Spanish fiend!
Surly. Captain and doctor.
Ananias. Child of perdition!

39. trig, fool. ***45-46. otter . . . tim,*** Kastril draws on the animal kingdom to express his rage.

Kastril. Hence, sir!— . *(Exit Surly)*
Did I not quarrel bravely?
Face. Yes, indeed, sir.
60 *Kastril.* Nay, an I give my mind to't, I shall do't.
Face. O, you must follow, sir, and threaten him tame:
He'll turn again else.
Kastril. I'll re-turn him then. *(Exit)*
Face. Drugger, this rogue prevented us, for thee:
We had determined that thou should'st have come
In a Spanish suit, and have carried her so; and he,
A brokerly slave, goes, puts it on himself.
Hast brought the damask?
Drugger. Yes, sir.
Face. Thou must borrow
A Spanish suit. Hast thou no credit with the players?
Drugger. Yes, sir; did you never see me play the Fool?
70 *Face.* I know not, Nab:—thou shalt, if I can help it.—*(Aside)*
Hieronimo's° old cloak, ruff, and hat will serve;
I'll tell thee more when thou bring'st them.
(Exit Drugger. Subtle hath whispered with Ananias this while.)
Ananias. Sir, I know.
The Spaniard hates the brethren, and hath spies
Upon their actions: and that this was one
I make no scruple.—But the holy synod
Have been in prayer and meditation for it;
And 'tis revealed no less to them than me,
That casting of money is most lawful.
Subtle. True.
But here I cannot do it: if the house
80 Should chance to be suspected, all would out,
And we be locked up in the Tower for ever,
To make gold there for the state, never come out;
And then are you defeated.
Ananias. I will tell
This to the elders and the weaker brethren,
That the whole company of the separation
May join in humble prayer again.
Subtle. And fasting.
Ananias. Yea, for some fitter place. The peace of mind
Rest with these walls! *(Exit)*
Subtle. Thanks, courteous Ananias.

71. Hieronimos, chief character in the popular play *The Spanish Tragedy*.

Face. What did he come for?
Subtle. About casting dollars,
Presently out of hand. And so I told him, 90
A Spanish minister came here to spy,
Against the faithful!—
Face. I conceive. Come, Subtle,
Thou art so down upon the least disaster!
How wouldst thou have done, if I had not helped thee out?
Subtle. I thank thee, Face, for the angry boy, in faith.
Face. Who would have looked it should have been that rascal
Surly? He had dyed his beard and all. Well, sir.
Here's damask come to make you a suit.
Subtle. Where's Drugger?
Face. He is gone to borrow me a Spanish habit;
I'll be the count now.
Subtle. But where's the widow? 100
Face. Within, with my lord's sister; Madam Dol
Is entertaining her.
Subtle. By your favour, Face,
Now she is honest, I will stand again.°
Face. You will not offer it?
Subtle. Why?
Face. Stand to your word,
Or—here comes Dol. She knows—
Subtle. You're tyrannous still.
(Enter Dol hastily)
Face. —Strict for my right.—How now, Dol! Hast told her,
The Spanish count will come?
Dol. Yes; but another is come,
You little looked for!
Face. Who's that?
Dol. Your master;
The master of the house.
Subtle. How, Dol!
Face. She lies,
This is some trick. Come, leave your quiblins,° Dorothy. 110
Dol. Look out and see. *(Face goes to the window.)*
Subtle. Art thou in earnest?
Dol. 'Slight,
Forty of the neighbors are about him, talking.

103. Now . . . again, now that she has remained chaste, I want her again. ***110. quiblins,*** quibbles.

Face. 'Tis he, by this good day.
Dol. 'Twill prove ill day
For some on us.
Face. We are undone, and taken.
Dol. Lost, I'm afraid.
Subtle. You said he would not come,
While there died one a week within the liberties.°
Face. No: 'twas within the walls.
Subtle. Was't so! cry you mercy.
I thought the liberties. What shall we do now, Face?
Face. Be silent: not a word, if he call or knock.
120 I'll into mine old shape again and meet him,
Of Jeremy, the butler. In the meantime,
Do you two pack up all the goods and purchase°
That we can carry in the two trunks. I'll keep him
Off for today, if I cannot longer: and then
At night, I'll ship you both away to Ratcliff,
Where we will meet tomorrow, and there we'll share.
Let Mammon's brass and pewter keep the cellar;
We'll have another time for that. But, Dol,
Prithee go heat a little water quickly;
130 Subtle must shave me. All my captain's beard
Must off, to make me appear smooth Jeremy.
You'll do it?
Subtle. Yes, I'll shave you as well as I can.
Face. And not cut my throat, but trim me?
Subtle. You shall see, sir.
(Exeunt)

Act V

Scene I. *Before Lovewit's door*

(Enter Lovewit, with several of the Neighbors)
Lovewit. Has there been such resort,° say you?
1st Neighbor. Daily, sir.
2nd Neighbor. And nightly, too.
3rd Neighbor. Ay, some as brave as lords.
4th Neighbor. Ladies and gentlewomen.
5th Neighbor. Citizens' wives.
1st Neighbor. And knights.

116. liberties, districts just outside the walls of London. ***122. purchase,*** loot. ***1. resort,*** traffic.

6th Neighbor. In coaches.
2nd Neighbor. Yes, and oyster-women.
1st Neighbor. Beside other gallants.
3rd Neighbor. Sailors' wives.
4th Neighbor. Tobacco men.
5th Neighbor. Another Pimlico!°
Lovewit. What should my knave advance,
To draw this company? He hung out no banners
Of a strange calf with five legs to be seen,
Or a huge lobster with six claws?
6th Neighbor. No, sir.
3rd Neighbor. We had gone in then, sir.
Lovewit. He has no gift 10
Of teaching in the nose° that ever I knew of.
You saw no bills set up that promised cure
Of agues, or the tooth-ache?
2nd Neighbor. No such thing, sir!
Lovewit. Nor heard a drum struck for baboons or puppets?
5th Neighbor. Neither, sir.
Lovewit. What device should he bring forth now?
I love a teeming wit as I love my nourishment:
Pray God he have not kept such open house,
That he had sold my hangings, and my bedding!
I left him nothing else. If he have eat them,
A plague of the moth, say I! Sure he has got 20
Some bawdy pictures to call all this ging;°
The Friar and the Nun; or the new motion
Of the knight's courser covering the parson's mare;
Or't may be, he has the fleas that run at tilt
Upon a table, or some dog to dance.
When saw you him?
1st Neighbor. Who, sir, Jeremy?
2nd Neighbor. Jeremy butler?
We saw him not this month.
Lovewit. How!
4th Neighbor. Not these five weeks, sir.
6th Neighbor. These six weeks at the least.
Lovewit. You amaze me, neighbors!
5th Neighbor. Sure, if your worship know not where he is,
He's slipt away.
6th Neighbor. Pray God he be not made away. 30

6. Pimlico, a popular suburban summer resort. ***11. Of . . .nose,*** preaching like a Puritan. ***21. ging,*** crowd.

Lovewit. Ha! it's no time to question, then. *(Knocks at the door)*
6th Neighbor. About
Some three weeks since I heard a doleful cry,
As I sat up a mending my wife's stockings.
Lovewit. 'Tis strange that none will answer! Did'st thou hear
A cry, sayst thou?
6th Neighbor. Yes, sir, like unto a man
That had been strangled an hour, and could not speak.
2nd Neighbor. I heard it too, just this day three weeks, at two o'clock
Next morning.
Lovewit. These be miracles, or you make them so!
A man an hour strangled, and could not speak,
And both you heard him cry?
40 *3rd Neighbor.* Yes, downward, sir.
Lovewit. Thou art a wise fellow. Give me thy hand, I pray thee.
What trade art thou on?
3rd Neighbor. A smith, an't please your worship.
Lovewit. A smith! Then lend me thy help to get this door open.
3rd Neighbor. That I will presently, sir, but fetch my tools— *(Exit)*
1st Neighbor. Sir, best to knock again afore you break it.

Scene II. *The same*

(Lovewit, Neighbors)
Lovewit. (Knocks again) I will.
(Enter Face in his butler's livery)
Face. What mean you, sir?
1st, 2nd, 4th Neighbor. O, here's Jeremy!
Face. Good sir, come from the door.
Lovewit. Why, what's the matter?
Face. Yet farther, you are too near yet.
Lovewit. In the name of wonder,
What means the fellow!
Face. The house, sir, has been visited.
Lovewit. What, with the plague? Stand thou then farther.
Face. No, sir,
I had it not.
Lovewit. Who had it then? I left
None else but thee in the house.
Face. Yes, sir, my fellow,
The cat that kept the buttery, had it on her
A week before I spied it; but I got her
10 Conveyed away in the night: and so I shut
The house up for a month—

Lovewit. How!
Face. Purposing then, sir,
To have burnt rose-vinegar, treacle, and tar,
And have made it sweet, that you should ne'er have known it;
Because I knew the news would but afflict you, sir.
Lovewit. Breathe less, and farther off! Why this is stranger:
The neighbors tell me all here that the doors
Have still been open—
Face. How, sir!
Lovewit. Gallants, men and women,
And of all sorts, tag-rag, been seen to flock here
In threaves,° these ten weeks, as to a second Hogsden,°
In days of Pimlico and Eye-bright.°
Face. Sir, 20
Their wisdoms will not say so.
Lovewit. Today they speak
Of coaches and gallants; one in a French hood
Went in, they tell me; and another was seen
In a velvet gown at the window: divers more
Pass in and out.
Face. They did pass through the doors then,
Or walls, I assure their eye-sights, and their spectacles;
For here, sir, are the keys, and here have been,
In this my pocket, now above twenty days!
And for before, I kept the fort alone there.
But that 'tis yet not deep in the afternoon, 30
I should believe my neighbors had seen double
Through the black pot, and made these apparitions!
For, on my faith to your worship, for these three weeks
And upwards, the door has not been opened.
Lovewit. Strange!
1st Neighbor. Good faith, I think I saw a coach.
2nd Neighbor. And I too,
I'd have been sworn.
Lovewit. Do you but think it now?
And but one coach?
4th Neighbor. We cannot tell, sir: Jeremy
Is a very honest fellow.
Face. Did you see me at all?
1st Neighbor. No; that we are sure on.
2nd Neighbor. I'll be sworn on that.

19. threaves, droves. ***Hogsden,*** Hoxton, the suburb in which Pimlico was located. ***20. Eye-bright,*** a popular tavern.

40 *Lovewit.* Fine rogues to have your testimonies built on!
(Re-enter third Neighbor, with his tools)
3rd Neighbor. Is Jeremy come!
1st Neighbor. O yes; you may leave your tools;
We were deceived, he says.
2nd Neighbor. He has had the keys;
And the door has been shut these three weeks.
3rd Neighbor. Like enough.
Lovewit. Peace, and get hence, you changelings.
(Enter Surly and Mammon)
Face. (Aside) Surly come!
And Mammon made acquainted! They'll tell all.
How shall I beat them off? What shall I do?
Nothing's more wretched than a guilty conscience.

Scene III. *The same*

(Surly, Mammon, Lovewit, Face, Neighbors)
Surly. No, sir, he was a great physician. This,
It was no bawdy-house, but a mere chancel!
You knew the lord and his sister.
Mammon. Nay, good Surly.—
Surly. The happy word, Be rich—
Mammon. Play not the tyrant.—
Surly. Should be today pronounced to all your friends.
And where be your andirons now? And your brass pots,
That should have been golden flagons, and great wedges?
Mammon. Let me but breathe. What, they have shut their doors,
Methinks! *(He and Surly knock.)*
Surly. Ay, now 'tis holiday with them.
Mammon. Rogues.
Cozeners, impostors, bawds!
10 *Face.* What mean you, sir?
Mammon. To enter if we can.
Face. Another man's house!
Here is the owner, sir; turn you to him,
And speak your business.
Mammon. Are you, sir, the owner?
Lovewit. Yes, sir.
Mammon. And are those knaves within your cheaters!
Lovewit. What knaves, what cheaters?
Mammon. Subtle and his Lungs.
Face. The gentleman is distracted, sir! No lungs
Nor lights have been seen here these three weeks, sir,

Within these doors, upon my word.
  Surly. Your word,
Groom arrogant!
  Face. Yes, sir, I am the housekeeper,
And know the keys have not been out of my hands. 20
  Surly. This is a new face.°
  Face. You do mistake the house, sir:
What sign was't at?
  Surly. You rascal! This is one
Of the confederacy. Come, let's get officers,
And force the door.
  Lovewit. Pray you stay, gentlemen.
  Surly. No, sir, we'll come with warrant.
  Mammon. Ay, and then
We shall have your doors open. *(Exeunt Mammon and Surly)*
  Lovewit. What means this?
  Face. I cannot tell, sir.
  1st Neighbor. These are two of the gallants
That we do think we saw.
  Face. Two of the fools!
You talk as idly as they. Good faith, sir,
I think the moon has crazed 'em all.—*(Aside)* O me, 30
(Enter Kastril)
The angry boy come too! He'll make a noise,
And ne'er away till he have betrayed us all.
  Kastril. (Knocking) What rogues, bawds, slaves, you'll open the door, anon!
Punk, cockatrice,° my suster! By this light
I'll fetch the marshal to you. You are a whore
To keep your castle.
  Face. Who would you speak with, sir?
  Kastril. The bawdy doctor, and the cozening captain,
And puss my suster.
  Lovewit. This is something, sure.
  Face. Upon my trust, the doors were never open, sir.
  Kastril. I have heard all their tricks told me twice over, 40
By the fat knight and the lean gentleman.
  Lovewit. Here comes another.
(Enter Ananias and Tribulation)
  Face. Ananias too!
And his pastor!
  Tribulation. (Beating at the door) The doors are shut against us.

21. *face*, Surly makes an unintentional pun. **34. *cockatrice*,** prostitute.

Ananias. Come forth, you seed of sulphur, sons of fire!
Your stench it is broke forth; abomination
Is in the house.
Kastril. Ay, my suster's there.
Ananias. The place,
It is become a cage of unclean birds.
Kastril. Yes, I will fetch the scavenger, and the constable.
Tribulation. You shall do well.
Ananias. We'll join to weed them out.
50 *Kastril.* You will not come then, punk devise,° my suster!
Ananias. Call her not sister; she's a harlot verily.
Kastril. I'll raise the street.
Lovewit. Good gentlemen, a word.
Ananias. Satan avoid, and hinder not our zeal!
(Exeunt Ananias, Tribulation and Kastril)
Lovewit. The world's turned Bethlem.
Face. These are all broke loose,
Out of St. Katherine's, where they use to keep
The better sort of mad-folks.
1st Neighbor. All these persons
We saw go in and out here.
2nd Neighbor. Yes, indeed, sir.
3rd Neighbor. These were the parties.
Face. Peace, you drunkards! Sir,
I wonder at it. Please you to give me leave
60 To touch the door; I'll try an the lock be changed.
Lovewit. It mazes me!
Face. (Goes to the door) Good faith, sir, I believe
There's no such thing: 'tis all *deceptio visus.*°—
(Aside) Would I could get him away.
Dapper. (Within) Master captain! Master doctor!
Lovewit. Who's that?
Face. (Aside) Our clerk within, that I forgot!—I know not, sir.
Dapper. (Within) For God's sake, when will her grace be at leisure?
Face. Ha!
Illusions, some spirit of the air!—*(Aside)* His gag is melted,
And now he sets out the throat.°
Dapper. (Within) I am almost stifled—
Face. (Aside) Would you were together.
Lovewit. 'Tis in the house.
Ha! list.

50. punk devise, you perfect whore. ***62. deceptio visus,*** an optical illusion. ***67. he . . . throat,*** he shouts off his mouth.

Face. Believe it, sir, in the air.
Lovewit. Peace, you.
Dapper. *(Within)* Mine aunt's grace does not use me well.
Subtle. *(Within)* You fool, 70
Peace, you'll mar all.
Face. *(Speaks through the keyhole, while Lovewit advances to the door unobserved.)* Or you will else, you rogue.
Lovewit. O, is it so? Then you converse with spirits!—
Come, sir. No more of your tricks, good Jeremy.
The truth, the shortest way.
Face. Dismiss this rabble, sir.—
(Aside) What shall I do? I am catched.
Lovewit. Good neighbors,
I thank you all. You may depart. *(Exeunt Neighbors)*—Come, sir,
You know that I am an indulgent master;
And therefore conceal nothing. What's your medicine,
To draw so many several sorts of wild fowl?
Face. Sir, you were wont to affect mirth and wit— 80
But here's no place to talk on't in the street.
Give me but leave to make the best of my fortune,
And only pardon me the abuse of your house:
It's all I beg. I'll help you to a widow,
In recompense, that you shall give me thanks for,
Will make you seven years younger, and a rich one.
'Tis but your putting on a Spanish cloak:
I have her within. You need not fear the house;
It was not visited.
Lovewit. But by me, who came
Sooner than you expected.
Face. It is true, sir. 90
'Pray you forgive me.
Lovewit. Well: let's see your widow. *(Exeunt)*

Scene IV. *A room in the same*

(Enter Subtle, leading in Dapper, with his eyes bound as before)
Subtle. How! you have eaten your gag?
Dapper. Yes, faith, it crumbled
Away in my mouth.
Subtle. You have spoiled all then.
Dapper. No!
I hope my aunt of Fairy will forgive me.
Subtle. Your aunt's a gracious lady; but in troth
You were to blame.

Dapper. The fume did overcome me,
And I did do't to stay my stomach. Pray you
So satisfy her grace.
(Enter Face in his uniform)
Here comes the captain.
Face. How now! Is his mouth down?
Subtle. Ay, he has spoken!
Face. A pox, I heard him, and you too. He's undone then.—
10 *(Aside to Subtle)* I have been fain to say, the house is haunted
With spirits, to keep churl° back.
Subtle. And hast thou done it?
Face. Sure, for this night.
Subtle. Why, then triumph and sing
Of Face so famous, the precious king
Of present wits.
Face. Did you not hear the coil
About the door?
Subtle. Yes, and I dwindled° with it.
Face. Show him his aunt, and let him be dispatched:
I'll send her to you. *(Exit Face)*
Subtle. Well, sir, your aunt her grace
Will give you audience presently, on my suit,
And the captain's word that you did not eat your gag
In any contempt of her highness. *(Unbinds his eyes)*
20 *Dapper.* Not I, in troth, sir.
(Enter Dol like the Queen of Fairy)
Subtle. Here she is come. Down on your knees and wriggle:
She has a stately presence. *(Dapper kneels and shuffles towards her.)*
Good! Yet nearer,
And bid, God save you!
Dapper. Madam!
Subtle. And your aunt.
Dapper. And my most gracious aunt, God save your grace.
Dol. Nephew, we thought to have been angry with you;
But that sweet face of yours hath turned the tide,
And made it flow with joy, that ebbed of love.
Arise, and touch our velvet gown.
Subtle. The skirts,
And kiss them. So!
Dol. Let me now stroke that head.
30 *Much, nephew, shalt thou win, much shalt thou spend;*
Much shalt thou give away, much shalt thou lend.

11. churl, i.e., Lovewit. ***15. dwindled,*** shook.

Subtle. (Aside) Ay, much! indeed.—Why do you not thank her grace?
Dapper. I cannot speak for joy.
Subtle. See, the kind wretch!
Your grace's kinsman right.
Dol. (To Subtle) Give me the bird.
Here is your fly in a purse, about your neck, cousin:
Wear it, and feed it about this day se'en-night,
On your right wrist—
Subtle. Open a vein with a pin,
And let it suck but once a week; till then,
You must not look on't.
Dol. No: and, kinsman,
Bear yourself worthy of the blood you come on.° 40
Subtle. Her grace would have you eat no more Woolsack pies,
Nor Dagger° frumety.°
Dol. Nor break his fast
In Heaven and Hell.°
Subtle. She's with you everywhere!
Nor play with costermongers, at mumchance, traytrip,
God-make-you-rich° (when as your aunt has done it);
But keep
The gallant'st company, and the best games—
Dapper. Yes, sir.
Subtle. Gleek and primero; and what you get, be true to us.
Dapper. By this hand, I will.
Subtle. You may bring us a thousand pound
Before tomorrow night, if but three thousand
Be stirring, an you will.
Dapper. I swear I will then. 50
Subtle. Your fly will learn you all games.
Face. (Within) Have you done there?
Subtle. Your grace will command him no more duties?
Dol. No:
But come, and see me often. *(To Subtle)* I may chance
To leave him three or four hundred chests of treasure,
And some twelve thousand acres of fairy land,
If he game well and comely with good gamesters.
Subtle. There's a kind aunt: kiss her departing part.—
But you must sell your forty mark a year now.
Dapper. Ay, sir, I mean.
Subtle. Or, give it away; pox on't!
Dapper. I'll give it mine aunt. I'll go and fetch the writings. *(Exit)* 60

40. *on,* of. **41-42. *Woolsack, Dagger,*** names of taverns. ***frumety,*** wheat boiled in milk.
43. *Heaven, Hell,* more taverns. **44-45. *mumchance . . . rich,*** games of chance.

Subtle. 'Tis well; away.
(Re-enter Face)
Face. Where's Subtle?
Subtle. Here: what news?
Face. Drugger is at the door, go take his suit,
And bid him fetch a parson presently.
Say he shall marry the widow. Thou shalt spend
A hundred pound by° the service! *(Exit Subtle)* Now, Queen Dol,
Have you packed up all?
Dol. Yes.
Face. And how do you like
The Lady Pliant?
Dol. A good dull innocent.
(Re-enter Subtle)
Subtle. Here's your Hieronimo's cloak and hat.
Face. Give me them.
Subtle. And the ruff too?
Face. Yes; I'll come to you presently. *(Exit)*
70 *Subtle.* Now he is gone about his project, Dol,
I told you of, for the widow.
Dol. 'Tis direct
Against our articles.
Subtle. Well, we will fit him, wench.
Hast thou gulled her of her jewels or her bracelets?
Dol. No; but I will do it.
Subtle. Soon at night, my Dolly,
When we are shipped, and all our goods aboard,
Eastward for Ratcliff, we will turn our course
To Brainford, westward, if thou sayst the word,
And take our leaves of this o'erweening rascal,
This peremptory Face.
Dol. Content; I'm weary of him.
80 *Subtle.* Thou'st cause, when the slave will run a wiving, Dol,
Against the instrument that was drawn between us.
Dol. I'll pluck his bird° as bare as I can.
Subtle. Yes, tell her
She must by any means address some present
To the cunning man, make him amends for wronging
His art with her suspicion; send a ring,
Or chain of pearl; she will be tortured else
Extremely in her sleep, say, and have strange things
Come to her. Wilt thou?

65. by, for. ***82. his bird,*** i.e., Dame Pliant.

Dol. Yes.
Subtle. My fine flitter-mouse,
My bird of the night! We'll tickle it at the Pigeons,°
When we have all, and may unlock the trunks, 90
And say, this's mine, and thine; and thine, and mine. *(They kiss.)*
(Re-enter Face)
Face. What now! a billing?
Subtle. Yes, a little exalted
In the good passage of our stock-affairs.
Face. Drugger has brought his parson; take him in, Subtle,
And send Nab back again to wash his face.
Subtle. I will: and shave himself? *(Exit)*
Face. If you can get him.
Dol. You are hot upon it, Face, whate'er it is!
Face. A trick that Dol shall spend ten pound a month by.
(Re-enter Subtle)
Is he gone?
Subtle. The chaplain waits you in the hall, sir.
Face. I'll go bestow him. *(Exit)*
Dol. He'll now marry her instantly.° 100
Subtle. He cannot yet, he is not ready. Dear Dol,
Cozen her of all thou canst. To deceive him
Is no deceit, but justice, that would break
Such an inextricable tie as ours was.
Dol. Let me alone to fit him.
(Re-enter Face)
Face. Come, my venturers,
You have packed up all? Where be the trunks? Bring forth.
Subtle. Here.
Face. Let us see them. Where's the money?
Subtle. Here,
In this.
Face. Mammon's ten pound; eight score before:
The brethren's money this. Drugger's and Dapper's.
What paper's that?
Dol. The jewel of the waiting maid's, 110
That stole it from her lady, to know certain—
Face. If she should have precedence of her mistress.
Dol. Yes.
Face. What box is that?
Subtle. The fish-wives' rings, I think,

89. Pigeons, a tavern in Brainford. ***100. He'll . . . instantly,*** Dol believes that Face is betraying them at this moment by the widow.

And the ale-wives' single money. Is't not, Dol?
Dol. Yes; and the whistle that the sailor's wife
Brought you to know an her husband were with Ward.°
Face. We'll wet it tomorrow; and our silver beakers
And tavern cups. Where be the French petticoats
And girdles and hangers?
Subtle. Here, in the trunk,
And the bolts of lawn.
120 *Face.* Is Drugger's damask there,
And the tobacco?
Subtle. Yes.
Face. Give me the keys.
Dol. Why you the keys?
Subtle. No matter, Dol; because
We shall not open them before he comes.
Face. 'Tis true, you shall not open them, indeed;
Nor have them forth, do you see? Not forth, Dol.
Dol. No!
Face. No, my smock-rampant. The right is, my master
Knows all, has pardoned me, and he will keep them.
Doctor, 'tis true—you look—for all your figures:
I sent for him, indeed. Wherefore, good partners,
130 Both he and she be satisfied; for here
Determines° the indenture tripartite
'Twixt Subtle, Dol, and Face. All I can do
Is to help you over the wall, on the back-side,
Or lend you a sheet to save your velvet gown, Dol.
Here will be officers presently, bethink you
Of some course suddenly to scape the dock;
For thither you will come else. *(A knock)* Hark you, thunder.
Subtle. You are a precious fiend!
Officer. (Without) Open the door.
Face. Dol, I am sorry for thee, in faith; but hear'st thou?
140 It shall go hard but I will place thee somewhere:
Thou shalt have my letter to Mistress Amo—
Dol. Hang you!
Face. Or Madam Cæsarean.°
Dol. Pox upon you, rogue.
Would I had but time to beat thee!
Face. Subtle,
Let's know where you set up next; I will send you

114. single money, small change. ***116. Ward,*** a famous pirate. ***131. determines,*** ends.
141-142. Amo, Caesarean, Madams of brothels.

A customer now and then, for old acquaintance.
What new course have you?
Subtle. Rogue, I'll hang myself;
That I may walk a greater devil than thou,
And haunt thee in the flock-bed and the buttery.° *(Exeunt)*

Scene V. *An outer room in the same*

(Enter Lovewit in the Spanish dress, with the Parson. Loud knocking at the door)

Lovewit. What do you mean, my masters?
Mammon. (Without) Open your door,
Cheaters, bawds, conjurers.
Officer. (Without) Or we will break it open.
Lovewit. What warrant have you?
Officer. (Without) Warrant enough, sir, doubt not,
If you'll not open it.
Lovewit. Is there an officer there?
Officer. (Without) Yes, two or three for failing.°
Lovewit. Have but patience,
And I will open it straight.
(Enter Face, as butler)
Face. Sir, have you done?
Is it a marriage? Perfect?
Lovewit. Yes, my brain.
Face. Off with your ruff and cloak then; be yourself, sir.
Surly. (Without) Down with the door.
Kastril. (Without) 'Slight, ding° it open.
Lovewit. (Opening the door) Hold,
Hold, gentlemen what means this violence? 10
(Mammon, Surly, Kastril, Ananias, Tribulation, and Officers rush in.)
Mammon. Where is this collier?
Surly. And my Captain Face?
Mammon. These day owls.
Surly. That are birding in men's purses.
Mammon. Madam Suppository.
Kastril. Doxy, my suster.
Ananias. Locusts
Of the foul pit.
Tribulation. Profane as Bel and the Dragon.
Ananias. Worse than the grasshoppers, or the lice of Egypt.

148. flock-bed . . . buttery, in bed and board. ***5. for failing,*** for fear of failing, i.e., for good measure. ***9. ding,*** break.

Lovewit. Good gentlemen, hear me. Are you officers,
And cannot stay this violence?
lst Officer. Keep the peace.
Lovewit. Gentlemen, what is the matter? Whom do you seek?
Mammon. The chemical cozener.
Surly. And the captain pander.
Kastril. The nun my suster.
Mammon. Madam Rabbi.
20 *Ananias.* Scorpions,
And caterpillars.
Lovewit. Fewer at once, I pray you.
lst Officer. One after another, gentlemen, I charge you,
By virtue of my staff.
Ananias. They are the vessels
Of pride, lust, and the cart.
Lovewit. Good zeal, lie still
A little while.
Tribulation. Peace, Deacon Ananias.
Lovewit. The house is mine here, and the doors are open;
If there be any such persons as you seek for,
Use your authority, search on of God's name.
I am but newly come to town, and finding
30 This tumult 'bout my door, to tell you true,
It somewhat mazed me; till my man here, fearing
My more displeasure, told me he had done
Somewhat an insolent part, let out my house
(Belike presuming on my known aversion
From any air of the town while there was sickness),
To a doctor and a captain: who, what they are
Or where they be, he knows not.
Mammon. Are they gone?
Lovewit. You may go in and search, sir. *(Mammon, Ananias, and Tribulation go in.)* Here I find
The empty walls worse than I left them, smoked,
40 A few cracked pots, and glasses, and a furnace;
The ceiling filled with poesies of the candle,
And "Madam with a dildo"° writ on the walls.
Only one gentlewoman I met here
That is within, that said she was a widow—
Kastril. Ay, that's my suster; I'll go thump her. Where is she? *(Goes in)*
Lovewit. And should have married a Spanish count, but he,

42. *Madam . . . dildo,* probably a line from an obscene song.

When he came to't, neglected her so grossly,
That I, a widower, am gone through with her.
Surly. How! have I lost her then?
Lovewit. Were you the don, sir?
Good faith, now she does blame you extremely, and says 50
You swore, and told her you had taken the pains
To dye your beard, and umber o'er your face,
Borrowed a suit, and ruff, all for her love:
And then did nothing. What an oversight
And want of putting forward, sir, was this!
Well fare an old harquebusier° yet,
Could prime his powder, and give fire, and hit,
All in a twinkling!
(Re-enter Mammon)
Mammon. The whole nest are fled!
Lovewit. What sort of birds were they?
Mammon. A kind of choughs,°
Or thievish daws, sir, that have picked my purse 60
Of eight score and ten pounds within these five weeks,
Beside my first materials; and my goods,
That lie in the cellar, which I am glad they have left,
I may have home yet.
Lovewit. Think you so, sir?
Mammon. Ay.
Lovewit. By order of law, sir, but not otherwise.
Mammon. Not mine own stuff!
Lovewit. Sir, I can take no knowledge
That they are yours, but by public means.
If you can bring certificate that you were gulled of them,
Or any formal writ out of a court,
That you did cozen yourself, I will not hold them. 70
Mammon. I'll rather lose them.
Lovewit. That you shall not, sir,
By me, in troth; upon these terms, they are yours.
What, should they have been, sir, turned into gold, all?
Mammon. No.
I cannot tell.—It may be they should.—What then?
Lovewit. What a great loss in hope have you sustained!
Mammon. Not I, the commonwealth has.
Face. Ay, he would have built
The city new; and made a ditch about it
Of silver, should have run with cream from Hogsden;

56. harquebusier, musketeer. ***59. choughs,*** crows.

That every Sunday in Moorfields the younkers,
80 And tits and tom-boys should have fed on, gratis.
Mammon. I will go mount a turnip-cart, and preach
The end of the world within these two months. Surly,
What! in a dream?
Surly. Must I needs cheat myself,
With that same foolish vice of honesty!
Come, let us go and hearken out the rogues:
That Face I'll mark for mine, if e'er I meet him.
Face. If I can hear of him, sir, I'll bring you word
Unto your lodging; for in troth, they were strangers
To me; I thought them honest as myself, sir.
(Exeunt Mammon and Surly)
(Re-enter Ananias and Tribulation)
90 *Tribulation.* 'Tis well, the saints shall not lose all yet. Go
And get some carts—
Lovewit. For what, my zealous friends?
Ananias. To bear away the portion of the righteous
Out of this den of thieves.
Lovewit. What is that portion?
Ananias. The goods sometimes the orphans', that the brethren
Bought with their silver pence.
Lovewit. What, those in the cellar,
The knight Sir Mammon claims?
Ananias. I do defy
The wicked Mammon, so do all the brethren,
Thou profane man! I ask thee with what conscience
Thou canst advance that idol against us,
100 That have the seal?° Were not the shillings numbered
That made the pounds; were not the pounds told out
Upon the second day of the fourth week,
In the eighth month, upon the table dormant,
The year of the last patience of the saints,
Six hundred and ten?
Lovewit. Mine earnest vehement botcher,
And deacon also, I cannot dispute with you:
But if you get you not away the sooner,
I shall confute you with a cudgel.
Ananias. Sir!
Tribulation. Be patient, Ananias.
Ananias. I am strong,
110 And will stand up, well girt, against an host
That threaten Gad in exile.

100. seal, i.e., as God's people.

Lovewit. I shall send you
To Amsterdam, to your cellar.
Ananias. I will pray there,
Against thy house. May dogs defile thy walls,
And wasps and hornets breed beneath thy roof,
This seat of falsehood, and this cave of cozenage!
(Exeunt Ananias and Tribulation)

(Enter Drugger)
Lovewit. Another too?
Drugger. Not I, sir, I am no brother.
Lovewit. (Beats him) Away, you Harry Nicholas!° do you talk?
(Exit Drugger)

Face. No, this was Abel Drugger. *(To the Parson)* Good sir, go,
And satisfy him; tell him all is done:
He staid too long a washing of his face. 120
The doctor, he shall hear of him at Westchester;
And of the captain, tell him, at Yarmouth, or
Some good port-town else, lying for a wind. *(Exit Parson)*
If you can get off the angry child now, sir—
(Enter Kastril, dragging in his sister)
Kastril. Come on, you ewe, you have matched most sweetly, have you not?
Did not I say, I would never have you tupped
But by a dubbed boy,° to make you a lady-tom?
'Slight, you are a mammet!° O, I could touse° you now.
Death, mun° you marry with a pox!
Lovewit. You lie, boy;
As sound as you; and I'm aforehand with you.
Kastril. Anon! 130
Lovewit. Come, will you quarrel? I will feize° you, sirrah;
Why do you not buckle to your tools?
Kastril. Od's light,
This is a fine old boy as e'er I saw!
Lovewit. What, do you change your copy now? Proceed;
Here stands my dove:° stoop° at her if you dare.
Kastril. 'Slight, I must love him! I cannot choose in faith,
An I should be hanged for't! Suster, I protest,
I honour thee for this match.
Lovewit. O, do you so, sir?
Kastril. Yes, an thou canst take tobacco and drink, old boy,
I'll give her five hundred pound more to her marriage, 140
Than her own state.

117. Harry Nicholas, an Anabaptist and founder of the extremist sect "The Family of Love." ***127. dubbed boy,*** a knight. ***128. mammet,*** puppet. ***touse,*** beat. ***129. mun,*** must. ***131. feize,*** scare. ***135. dove,*** i.e., Dame Pliant. ***stoop,*** swoop ("Kastril" means "young hawk").

Lovewit. Fill a pipe full, Jeremy.
Face. Yes; but go in and take it, sir.
Lovewit. We will.
I will be ruled by thee in anything, Jeremy.
Kastril. 'Slight, thou art not hide-bound, thou art a jovy° boy!
Come, let us in, I pray thee, and take our whiffs.
Lovewit. Whiff in with your sister, brother boy. *(Exeunt Kastril and Dame Pliant)* That master
That had received such happiness by a servant,
In such a widow, and with so much wealth,
Were very ungrateful, if he would not be
150 A little indulgent to that servant's wit,
And help his fortune, though with some small strain
Of his own candour. *(Advancing)* Therefore, gentlemen,
And kind spectators, if I have outstript
An old man's gravity, or strict canon, think
What a young wife and a good brain may do;
Stretch age's truth sometimes, and crack it too.
Speak for thyself, knave.
Face. So I will, sir. *(Advancing to the front of the stage)*
Gentlemen,
My part a little fell in this last scene,
Yet 'twas decorum.° And though I am clean
160 Got off from Subtle, Surly, Mammon, Dol,
Hot Ananias, Dapper, Drugger, all
With whom I traded; yet I put myself
On you, that are my country:° and this pelf,
Which I have got, if you do quit me, rests
To feast you often, and invite new guests. *(Exeunt)*

Comments and Questions

The editors suggest that after reading the play, you study carefully Professor Knoll's "How to Read The Alchemist," *and then reread the play following closely his discussion of the organization of the plot and its meaning. Try to test Knoll's reading of the play against your own observations, taking care to give reasons, as he does. Does he convince you that "the plotting is really quite straightforward" and that* "The Alchemist *is a religious not a social tract, directed against the*

144. jovy, jovial. ***159. decorum,*** according to the rules of drama. ***163. country,*** i.e., jury.

impious, not against the anti-social"? Are there other difficulties in the play he does not mention? Could or should Jonson have simplified the play by cutting out some of the characters or deleting some of the actions?

Some further considerations are offered by the following questions. Is Jonson's satire directed more to the dupers or to the duped, or to both equally? Who is more nearly the main character, or protagonist, Subtle or Face? What implied comment is made by the fact that Face is not punished, that, in fact, though he has lost a battle, he will probably win the war? Does Face for all the roles he plays come to believe in any one of them? That is, does he suffer from the sin of pride in the same way the other characters do, or is his real pride in his native wit, his clever ability to make the best of any situation? How do he, Subtle, and Dol adapt their methods to the personalities and desires of each of their customers?

Explain the appropriateness of the characters' names. Is there any attempt to make them representative of society or of the degrees of religious pride Knoll writes of? If you were directing the play, how would you differentiate between the characters in costuming and mannerisms? Take your clues from Jonson.

Related Reading

Molière, *Scapin*, page 311
Thornton Wilder, *The Matchmaker*, page 248
Oscar G. Brockett, "The Elizabethan Theater," page 656
Robert Knoll, "How to Read *The Alchemist*," page 712
Louis Kronenberger, "Some Prefatory Words on Comedy," page 680

Robert Lowell

(1917-)

MY KINSMAN, MAJOR MOLINEUX

Robert Lowell, heir to the talent of a distinguished family, is one of the foremost living American poets. Born in Boston, he attended Harvard and then Kenyon College in Ohio, from which he graduated in 1940, the same year he became a convert to Roman Catholicism. During World War II he served six months of a year's sentence in a conscientious objectors' camp. In 1947 he won the Pulitzer Prize for his second volume of poems, Lord Weary's Castle. *He has taught at Kenyon, Boston University, and Harvard, and has been Consultant in Poetry to the Library of Congress. Puritan, Boston Brahmin, Catholic, scholar, individualist, conservative formalist, and innovator, Lowell in his complexities and contradictions, in his moral idealism and indignation with the world as it is, is molded firmly in the pattern of American literary and intellectual traditions.*

His short plays, My Kinsman, Major Molineux, *based on the story by Nathaniel Hawthorne, and* Benito Cereno, *on the story by Herman Melville, opened under the title* The Old Glory *on November 1, 1964 at the American Place Theatre in New York. Though Lowell's first attempts at playwriting were not a popular success, his efforts were highly rated by most critics. It would be difficult to find stories that seem more intractable to dramatic presentation than these two, but with a poetic flair and a sure instinct for theatre, Lowell recreated them as his own and still managed to retain the metaphorical splendor and symbolic overtones of the originals, much as Anouilh did with Sophocles'* Antigone.

Lowell had prepared himself well in both the subjects and methods of The Old Glory. *Readers of Lowell's poetry were not surprised that he turned to stories by Hawthorne and Melville, since their sin-haunted and dark Puritan temperaments, along with that of the Puritan divine Jonathan Edwards, have always attracted Lowell; he has long been engrossed in history and in the American past, including the history of his own family (as recorded in his book* Life Studies*). In a manner that can be compared to T.S. Eliot's and Ezra Pound's, many of Lowell's poems make use of situations, phrases, and passages from earlier writings to create distinctive, original poems that illuminate the falling off of the present by reminding us of the glory of the past. Further, Lowell has translated Racine's tragic drama* Phèdre *and has adapted and re-created the poems of a wide selection of poets from Homer to the contemporary Russian Boris Pasternak, which he has collected in his volume titled* Imitations.

In order to visualize the staging of My Kinsman, Major Molineux, *the reader must exercise his imagination to the fullest. Sights, sounds, and movements are especially important in this play, since it is largely by them, rather than by language alone, that Lowell has been able to capture the tone and meaning of the story. Neither the set nor the acting is realistic. The ferryman must remind us of Charon, the mythological figure who ferries souls to the kingdom of the dead. The city of Boston is represented by only five miniature houses with man-sized doors painted impressionistically on stage flats "in the style of a primitive New England sampler." The costuming and make-up are both typical of the time and place and suggestive of other meanings. Robin and his brother wear simple deerskin country clothes; the prostitute, a scarlet petticoat; the British soldiers, their brilliant redcoats; while the citizens of Boston wear combinations of black, gray, or white clothes and powdered wigs and have their faces covered with chalk-white make-up and masks. The gestures of the actors are deliberate and highly stylized; songs and dances are part of the action; symbolic props are numerous: for example, the Union Jack and the Lion and Unicorn emblem of the British, the rattlesnake flag of the rebelling citizens, and the changing masks of Colonel Greenough.*

Lowell is reputed to have called the play "a political cartoon." It is like one, or a caricature, and at the same time is reminiscent of the elaborate spectacles performed at the English court in the seventeenth century called masques (many of the best of them by Ben Jonson) and of a long tradition in the theater of mime and symbolic costuming. Everything in the play—staging, costuming, gesture, language—serves also to give it the quality of a parable, or brief moral tale, here pointing out the trials of a youthful rustic innocent as he seeks advancement in the city of Boston from his powerful kinsman. He is grimly forewarned by the ferryman that he is entering "the city of the dead." His innocence is to be tested in the nightmare of rebellion, confusion, and enigmas he discovers there. Does he pass the test, or is his innocence corrupted?

MY KINSMAN, MAJOR MOLINEUX

Characters

ROBIN
BOY, *his brother*
FERRYMAN
1ST REDCOAT
2ND REDCOAT
FIRST BARBER
TAVERN KEEPER
MAN WITH PEWTER MUG
CLERGYMAN
PROSTITUTE
COLONEL GREENOUGH
MAN IN PERIWIG
WATCHMAN
MAJOR MOLINEUX
CITIZENS OF BOSTON

Scene: *Boston, just before the American Revolution*

To the left of the stage, Robin, a young man barely eighteen, in a coarse grey coat, well-worn but carefully repaired, leather breeches, blue yarn stockings, and a worn three-cornered hat. He carries a heavy oak-sapling cudgel and has a wallet slung over his shoulder. Beside him, his brother, a boy of ten or twelve, dressed in the same respectable but somewhat rustic manner. On the far left of the stage, the triangular prow of a dory; beside it, a huge Ferryman holding an upright oar. He has a white curling beard. His dress, although eighteenth century, half suggests that he is Charon. Lined across the stage and in the style of a primitive New England sampler, are dimly seen five miniature houses: a barber shop, a tavern, a white church, a shabby brick house with a glass bay window, and a pillared mansion, an official's house, on its cornice the golden lion and unicorn of England. The houses are miniature, but their doors are man-size. Only Robin, his Brother, and the Ferryman are lit up.

Robin. Here's my last crown, your double price
for ferrying us across the marsh
at this ungodly hour.
Ferryman. A crown!
Do you want me to lose my soul?
Do you see King George's face?

judging us on this silver coin?
I have no price.
Robin. You asked for double.
Ferryman. I'll take the crown for your return trip. *(Takes the coin)*
No one returns.
Robin. No one?
Ferryman. No one.
10 Legs go round in circles here.
This is the city of the dead.
Robin. What's that?
Ferryman. I said this city's Boston,
No one begs here. Are you deaf? *(The little houses on stage light up, then dim out.)*
Robin. (To the Ferryman) Show me my kinsman's mansion. You must know him—Major Molineux,
the most important man in town.
Ferryman. The name's familiar . . . Molineux . . .
Wasn't he mixed up with the French?
20 He's never at home now. If you'll wait
here, you'll meet him on his rounds.
All our important people drift
sooner or later to my ferry landing,
and stand here begging for the moon.
You'll see your cousin. You're well-placed.
Robin. I know it. My kinsman's a big man here.
He told me he would make my fortune;
I'll be a partner in his firm,
either here or in London.
Ferryman. Settle
30 for London, that's your city, Boy.
Majors are still sterling silver across
the waters. All the English-born
suddenly seem in love with London.
Your cousin's house here is up for sale.
Robin. He cares for England. *Rule Britannia,*
that's the tune he taught me. I'm
surprised he's leaving.
Ferryman. He's surprised!
He seemed to belong here once. He wished
to teach us *Rule Britannia,* but
40 we couldn't get it through our heads.
He gave us this to keep us singing. *(The Ferryman holds up a boiled lobster.)*
Robin. You're joking, it's a lobster.

Ferryman. No.
Look, it's horny, boiled and red,
It is the Major's spitting image. *(On the other side of the stage, Two British Redcoats are seen marching slowly in step with shouldered muskets.* Rule Britannia *played faintly.)*
Ferryman. (Pointing to Soldiers) Here are the Major's chicken lobsters.
Robin. Our soldiers!
Ferryman. We call them lobsterbacks. 50
They are the Major's privates. Wherever
they are gathered together, he is present.
You'll feel his grip behind their claws.
What are you going to do now:
run home to Deerfield, take a ship
for England, Boy, or chase the soldiers?
Robin. Why, I'm staying here. I like
soldiers. They make me feel at home.
They kept the Frenchmen out of Deerfield.
They'll tell me where my kinsman lives. 60
Ferryman. The French are finished. The British
are the only Frenchmen left.
Didn't you say your cousin's name
was Molineux?
Robin. He's Norman Irish.
Why are you leaving?
Ferryman. Money. The soldiers
make me pay them for the pleasure
of shuttling them across the marsh.
Run, Boy, and catch those soldiers' scarlet
coat-tails, while they're still around. *(The Ferryman goes off pushing his boat; Robin and the Boy advance towards the soldiers.)* 70
Robin. I need your help, Sirs.
First Soldier. (Smiling) We are here
for service, that's our unpleasant duty.
Robin. I liked the way
the soldiers smiled. I wonder how
anyone could distrust a soldier.
Boy. We've lost our guide.
Robin. We'll find another.
Boy. Why did that boatman gnash his teeth
at Cousin Major?
Robin. He was cold.
That's how big city people talk.
Let's walk. We're here to see the city. 80

(As Robin and the Boy start moving, the miniature houses light up one by one and then go dark. A Barber comes out of the barber shop; he holds a razor, and a bowl of suds. A Tavern Keeper enters holding a newspaper.)

Barber. (Cutting away the suds with his razor)
That's how we shave a wig.

Tavern Keeper. You mean
a Tory.

Barber. Shave them to the bone!

Tavern Keeper. (Pointing to newspaper) Here's the last picture of
90 King George;
He's passed another tax on tea.

Barber. Health to the King, health to the King!
Here's rum to drown him in the tea! *(Drenches the newspaper with his mug; a Clergyman, white-wigged, all in black, comes out of the church.)*

Clergyman. What an ungodly hour! The city's
boiling. All's rum and revolution.
We have an everlasting city,
but here in this unsteady brightness,
nothing's clear, unless the Lord
100 enlighten us and show the winner! *(A Prostitute comes out of the bay-window house. She wears a red skirt and a low, full-bosomed white blouse.)*

Prostitute. Here in the shadow of the church,
I save whatever God despises—
Whig or Tory, saint or sinner,
I'm their refuge from the church.

(The pillared mansion lights up. A man comes out in a blue coat and white trousers like General Washington's. He wears a grayish mask covered with pocks. His forehead juts out and divides in a double bulge.
110 *His nose is a yellow eagle's beak. His eyes flash like fire in a cave. He looks at himself in a mirror.)*

Man with Mask. My mind's on fire. This fire will burn
the pocks and paleness from my face.
Freedom has given me this palace.
I'll go and mingle with the mob. *(Now the houses are dark. Robin rubs his eyes in a daze, stares into the darkness, then turns to his brother.)*

Boy. Who are these people, Brother Robin?
We're in the dark and far from Deerfield.

Robin. We're in the city, little brother.
120 Things will go smoother when we find
our kinsman, Major Molineux.

Boy. Our kinsman isn't like these people.
He is a loyal gentleman.

Robin. We'll see. He swore he'd make my fortune,
and teach you Latin.
Boy. I want something.
Robin. Let's see the city.
Boy. I want a flintlock.
(A man enters from the right. He wears a full gray periwig, a wide-skirted coat of dark cloth and silk stockings rolled up above the knees. He carries a polished cane which he digs angrily into the ground at every step. "Hem, hem," he says in a sepulchral voice as he walks over 130
to the barber shop. The two barbers appear, one with a razor, the other with a bowl of suds.)
Man in Periwig. Hem! Hem!
Robin. Good evening, honored sir.
Help us. We come from out of town.
Man in Periwig. A good face and a better shoulder!
Hem, hem! I see you're not from Boston.
We need good stock in Boston. You're lucky!
meeting me here was providential.
I'm on the side of youth. Hem, hem!
I'll be your guiding lamp in Boston. 140
Where do you come from?
Robin. Deerfield.
Man in Periwig. Deerfield!
Our bulwark from the savages!
Our martyred village! He's from Deerfield,
Barber. We can use his muscle.
Barber. You can feel it.
Man in Periwig. (Seeing the Boy)
Look, a child!
Barber. Shall I shave him?
Man in Periwig. Yes, shave him.
Shave him and teach him to beat a drum.
Boy. I want a flintlock.
Man in Periwig. A gun! You scare me!
Come on Apollo, we must march.
We'll put that shoulder to the wheel. 150
Come, I'll be your host in Boston.
Robin. I have connections here, a kinsman . . .
Man in Periwig. Of course you have connections here.
They will latch on to you like fleas.
This is your town! Boy! With that leg
You will find kinsmen on the moon.
Robin. My kinsman's Major Molineux.
Man in Periwig. Your kinsman's Major Molineux!

Let go my coat cuff, Fellow. I have
160 authority, authority!
Hem! Hem! Respect your betters. Your leg
will be acquainted with the stocks
by peep of day! You fellows help me!
Barber, this man's molesting me!
First Barber. (Closing in) Don't hit His Honor, Boy!
Second Barber. His Honor
is a lover of mankind!
Boy. Brain him with your cudgel, Robin!
Robin. Come, Brother, we will see the city;
they're too many of them and one has a razor. *(Robin and the Boy back*
170 *off. Barber shop goes dark.)*
Boy. Who was that fellow, Brother Robin?
Robin. He is some snotty, county clerk,
chipping and chirping at his betters.
He isn't worth the Major's spit.
Boy. You should have brained him with your stick.
Robin. Let's go, now. We must see the city
and try to find our kinsman's house.
I am beginning to think he's out
of town. Look, these men will help us. *(The tavern lights up. A sign*
180 *with King George III's head hangs in front. There's a poster nailed to*
the door. The Man with the Mask strolls over and sits in the chair.)
Crowd. Health to the rattlesnake. A health
to Colonel Greenough! He's our man!
Man with Mask. A shine, men, you must shine my shoes
so bright King George will see his face
flash like a guinea on the toe.
Crowd. Health to the rattlesnake!
Tavern Keeper. (Turning to Robin)
You boys
are from the country, I presume.
I envy you, you're seeing Boston
190 for the first time. Fine town, there's lots
to hold you, English monuments,
docks, houses, and a fleet of tea-ships
begging for buyers. I trust you'll stay;
nobody ever leaves this city.
Robin. We come from Deerfield.
Tavern Keeper. Then you'll stay;
no Indians scalp us in our beds;
our only scalper is this man here. *(General laughter)*

Robin. Our massacre was eighty years
ago.° We're not frontiersmen now,
we've other things to talk about. 200
Barber. He has other things to talk about.
This boy's a gentleman. He is
no redskin in a coonskin cap.
Robin. I'm on our village council. I've
read Plutarch.
Tavern Keeper.
You are an ancient Roman.
You'll find you like our commonwealth.
I crave the honor of your custom.
I've whiskey, gin and rum and beer,
and a spruce beer for your brother.
Boy. I want a real beer.
Barber. Give them beer. *(Shouting)* 210
Tavern Keeper. Two real beers for the Deerfield boys,
they have the fighting Deerfield spirit.
Robin. I'm sure you'll trust me for your money.
I have connections here in Boston,
my kinsman's Major Molineux.
I spent our money on this journey.
Man. His kinsman's Major Molineux;
sometimes a boy is short of money! *(Laughter)*
Man. (Bringing out a silver Liberty Bowl) I've something stronger
than beer. 220
Here is the Bowl of Liberty.
The Major dropped this lobster in
the bowl. It spikes the drink. *(Man puts down his mug and lifts a lobster out of bowl. Cheers)*
Robin. I know
the lobster is a British soldier.
Man. Yes, there they are. *(The two redcoats march on stage as before. Silence. The Man with the Mask starts writing on a bench. The soldiers saunter over to him.)*
First Soldier. What are you writing, Colonel Greenough?
Man with Mask. My will.
First Soldier. Things aren't that desperate. 230
Man with Mask. I'm adding up my taxes, Redcoat.

198-199. Our massacre was eighty years ago. The Deerfield Massacre took place on February 29, 1704. In a strategic position on the western frontier of the Massachusetts colony, Deerfield was often attacked by the Indians and French. In the massacre, fifty citizens were killed, 111 were taken prisoner, and 137 escaped.

Just counting up the figures kills me.
My bankers say I'm burning money.
I can't afford your bed and board
and livery, Soldiers. We'll have to part.
Second Soldier. I've had enough. We ought to throw
them all in jail.
First Soldier. Go easy.
Robin. (Walking shyly up to Soldiers)
Sir,
240 I need your guidance, I'm looking for
my kinsman, Major Molineux.
First Soldier. Watch your words!
Second Soldier. Damn your insolence!
First Soldier. We'll haul you to the Major's court. *(Shots and screams off stage. Soldiers leave on the run.)*
Man. (Pointing to Robin) He's one of us.
Second Man. He is a spy.
Crowd. Both boys are spies or Tories.
Tavern Keeper. (Drawing Robin over to the poster)
Look,
do you see this poster? It says,
"Indentured servant, Jonah Mudge:
ran from his master's house, blue vest,
250 oak cudgel, leather pants, small brother,
and his master's third best hat.
Pound sterling's offered any man
who nabs and lodges him in jail."
Trudge off, Young Man, you'd better trudge!
Crowd. Trudge, Jonah Mudge, you'd better trudge!
Boy. They're drunk. You'd better hit them, Robin.
Robin. They'd only break my stick and brains.
Boy. For God's sake stand and be a man!
Robin. No, they're too many, little brother.
260 Come, I feel like walking.
We haven't seen the city yet. *(Lights go off. Robin and Boy stand alone.)*
Boy. We haven't seen our kinsman, Robin.
I can't see anything.
Robin. You'd think
the Major's name would stand us for
a beer. It's a funny thing, Brother, naming
our kinsman, Major Molineux,
sets all these people screaming murder.
Even the soldiers. *(The house with the bay-window lights up. A woman's red skirt and bare shoulders are clearly visible through the window. She is singing.)*

Woman. Soldiers, sailors.
Whig and Tories, saints and sinners,
I'm your refuge from despair. 270
Robin. (Knocks) Sweet, pretty mistress, help me. I
am tired and lost. I'm looking for
my kinsman, Major Molineux.
You have bright eyes.
Woman. I know your kinsman.
Everybody is my kinsman here.
Robin. Yes, I am sure. You have kind eyes.
My kinsman is a blood relation.
Woman. You're my blood relation too then.
What a fine back and leg you have!
You're made right.
Robin. Oh, I will be made 280
when I find my kinsman. You
must know him, he's a man of some
importance in your city, Lady.
Woman. The Major dwells here.
Robin. You're thinking of some other major,
Lady; mine is something more
important than a major, he's
a sort of royal governor,
and a man of fortune. Molineux
tea ships sail from here to China. 290
He has a gilded carriage, twenty
serving men, two flags of England
flying from his lawn. You could hide
your little house behind a sofa
in his drawing-room.
Woman. I know,
your kinsman is a man of parts,
that's why he likes to camp here. Sometimes
his greatness wearies him. These days
even kings draw in their horns,
and mingle with the common people. 300
Listen, you'll hear him snoring by
the roof.
Robin.
I hear a hollow sound.
My kinsman must be happy here.
I envy him this hideaway.
Woman. You mean to say you envy him
the mistress of his house. Don't worry,
a kinsman of the Major's is

my kinsman. I knew you right away.
You have your kinsman's leg and shoulders.
310 He wears an old three-cornered hat
and leather small-clothes here in the rain.
Why, you *are* the good old gentleman,
only you're young! What is this cloth?
You've good material on your leg. *(The Woman feels the cloth of Robin's trousers.)*

Robin. It's deerskin. I'm from Deerfield, Lady.

Woman. You must be starved. I'll make you happy.

Robin. I'll wait here on your doorstep, Lady.
Run up and tell the Major that
320 his Deerfield cousins are in town.

Woman. The Major'd kill me, if I woke him.
You see, he spilled a little too much
rum in his tea.

Robin. I'll leave a note then. I must go,
my little brother needs some sleep. *(Woman takes Robin's hat and twirls it on her finger.)*
What are you doing with my hat?

Woman. I'm showing you our Boston rites
of hospitality. The Major
330 would kill me, if I turned you out
on such a night. I even have
a downstairs bedroom for your brother.
I find a playroom comes in handy.

Boy. I want to go with Robin.

Woman. Oh, dear,
children keep getting me in trouble.
We have a law. *(A bell is heard off stage.)*
Mother of God! *(The Woman ducks into her house. Her light goes out.)*

Boy. Why did the lady slam her door?

Robin. The bell reminded her of something.
340 She has to catch up on her sleep.

Boy. Has the Major left his mansion?
Is he really sleeping here?

Robin. How can I tell you? Everyone
answers us in riddles.

Boy. She said,
the Major dwells here.

Robin. That's her city
way of being friendly, Brother.

Boy. Robin, the Major could afford
to buy the lady better clothes.
She was almost naked.

Robin. She
was dressed unwisely.
Boy. Isn't Eve 350
almost naked in our Bible?
Robin. Don't ask so many questions, brother.
I wish I knew the naked truth. *(A Watchman enters, dishevelled and yawning. He holds a lantern with a bell tied to it and a spiked staff.)*
Watchman. Stop, we don't allow this sort
of talk about the Bible here.
Robin. You are mistaken, Sir. I said
I wished I knew the naked truth.
Watchman. You're in New England. Here we fine
mothers for bearing naked children. 360
You're leading this child into perdition.
We have a fine for that. What's in
your wallet, Boy?
Robin. Nothing.
Watchman. Nothing! You've been inside then!
Robin. Watchman, I'm looking for my kinsman.
Watchman. And you thought you'd find him in this house
Doing his martial drill.
Robin. You know him!
My kinsman's Major Molineux.
I see you know him, he will pay you 370
if you will lead us to his house.
Watchman. (Singing)
Your aunt's the lord high sheriff,
your uncle is King George;
if you can't pay the tariff,
the house will let you charge.
Robin. I asked for Major Molineux.
Watchman. Keep asking! We are cleaning house.
The Major's lost a lot of money
lately, buying bad real estate.
He can't afford his country cousins. 380
Move, you filthy, sucking hayseed!
or I'll spike you with my stick!
Boy. Why don't you hit him, brother?
Watchman. I'll have
you in the stocks by daybreak, Boy.
Robin. We'll go, Sir. I'm your countryman
learning the customs of the city.
Watchman. (Goes off singing)
Baggy buttocks, baggy buttocks,
The Queen of England's willing

To serve you for a shilling
And stick you in the stocks.
390 *Robin.* We're learning
how to live. The man was drunk.
Boy. Our Deerfield watchmen only drink
at Communion. Something's wrong,
these people need new blood.
Robin. Perhaps
they'll get it. Here's a clergyman,
he'll tell us where to find our kinsman. *(The Clergyman comes across the stage. He is awkwardly holding a large English flag on a staff.)*
Robin. Help me, I beg you, Reverend Sir,
I'm from Deerfield, I'm looking for
400 my kinsman, Major Molineux.
No one will tell me where he lives.
Clergyman. I have just left the Major's house.
He is my patron and example.
A good man—it's a pity though
he's so outspoken; other good men
misunderstand the Major's meaning.
He just handed me this British
flag to put above my pulpit—
a bit outspoken!
Robin. Our country's flag, Sir!
410 *Clergyman.* Yes, a bit outspoken. Come
I'll lead you to your kinsman's house. *(The Man with the Mask strides hurriedly across the stage, and unrolls a rattlesnake flag, which he hands to the Clergyman, who has difficulty in managing the two flags.)*
Man with Mask. I have a present for you, Parson:
our Rattlesnake. "Don't tread on me!"
it says. I knew you'd want to have one.
Hang it up somewhere in church;
there's nothing like the Rattlesnake
for raising our declining faith.
Clergyman. I thank you, Sir.
420 *Man with Mask.* You'd better hurry.
Think of the man who had no garment
for the wedding.° Things are moving. *(Man with Mask hurries off stage.)*
Clergyman. (To himself) God help us, if we lose! *(Turns to go)*
Robin. Sir, you're leaving! You promised me
you'd lead me to my kinsman's house.
Please, let me help you with the flags.

421-422. had no garment for the wedding. See Christ's parable teaching that "many are called but few chosen." Matthew 22: 1-14.

Clergyman. I'll see you later. I have to hurry.
I have a sick parishioner,
a whole sick parish! I have a notion
one of these flags will cure us. Which? 430
Everyone's so emphatic here.
If you should meet your kinsman, tell him
I'm praying for him in my church.

(Clergyman goes out. A loud "hem, hem" is heard. The Man in the Periwig comes jauntily forward followed by the two barbers. He goes to the house with the bay-window and raps with his cane. The light inside the house goes on. A rattlesnake flag has been nailed to the door. No one sees Robin and the Boy.)

First Barber. Look, Your Honor, Mrs. Clark
has taken on the Rattlesnake. 440
Man in Periwig. Good, this pricks my fainting courage.
"Don't tread on me!" That's rather odd
for Mrs. Clark.
First Barber. Come on, your Honor.
Second Barber. There's always a first time.
First Barber. Then a second.
Man in Periwig. Thank God, I've but one life to give
my country.°
Lay on, Macduff! I owe this to
my reputation, boys.
First Barber. He owes
his reputation to the boys. 450
Second Barber. Between the devil and the deep
blue sea, Your Honor!
First Barber. His Honor likes
the sea. Everyone loves a sailor.
Man in Periwig. Hurry! I'm in torture! Open!
I have authority hem, hem! *(Man in Periwig knocks loudly. The Woman stands in doorway.)*
Woman. (Singing)
Where is my boy in leather pants,
who gives a woman what she wants?
Man in Periwig. (Singing in falsetto)
Woman, I have a royal Crown
your countryman gave the ferryman 460
a-standing on the strand;
but money goes from hand to hand:
the crown is on the town,

446-447. Thank God, I've but one life to give my country. Compare Nathan Hale's dying statement: "I only regret that I have but one life to lose for my country."

the money's mine, I want to dine.
Whatever we do is our affair,
the breath of freedom's in the air.

First Barber. The lady's ballast's in the air.

Second Barber. Two ten pound tea chests. The lady needs a little uplift from the clergy.

470 *Man in Periwig.* I'm breaking on the foamy breakers!
Help! help!
I wish my lady had a firm,
hard-chested figure like a mast,
but what has love to do with fact?
A lover loves his nemesis;
the patriotic act. *(The Man in the Periwig gives the lady the crown and passes in. The lights go out.)*

Barber. Once to every man and nation
comes the time a gentleman
480 wants to clear his reputation.

Tavern Keeper. Once to every man and nation
comes the time a man's a man.°

Barber. His Honor's perished on the blast. *(The Barber saunters off along with Tavern Keeper. The Boy turns to Robin, who is lost in thought.)*

Robin. I think the Major
has left. By watching I have learned
to read the signs. The Rattlesnake
means Major Molineux is out.
490 A British flag means he's at home.

Boy. You talk in riddles like the town.

Robin. Say what you mean; mean what you say:
that's how we used to talk in Deerfield.
It's not so simple here in the city. *(The pillared mansion lights up. Robin and the Boy approach it. The Lion and Unicorn of England are gone. Instead, a large Rattlesnake flag is showing.)*
Brother, we've reached our destination.
This is our kinsman's house. I know it
from the steel engraving that
500 he gave us when he came to Deerfield.
Our journey's over. Here's our mansion.

Boy. Robin, it has a Rattlesnake.

Robin. That means the Major's not at home. *(The Man with the Mask comes out of the mansion. Half his face is now fiery red, the other half is still mottled.)*

481-482. Once to every man and nation comes the time a man's a man. Adaptations of lines from James Russell Lowell's "The Present Crisis": "Once to every man and nation comes the moment to decide, In the strife of Truth with Falsehood, for the good or evil side."

Man with Mask. I am the man on horseback.
Robin. No,
you're walking, Sir.
Man with Mask. I am a king.
Robin. The king's in England. You must be sick.
Have you seen your face? Half's red,
the other half is pocked and mottled. 510
Man with Mask. Oh I'm as healthy as the times.
I am an image of this city.
Do you see this colored handkerchief? *(Man with Mask draws out a small British flag.)*
Robin. Our British flag, Sir.
Man with Mask. Yes, it doesn't
help my illness any more,
when I try to cool my burning brow,
or blow my nose on it.
Robin. I know
a man who used to own this house.
Let's see if he's still here. Perhaps, 520
my friend can help to heal your sickness.
Man with Mask. My face will be entirely red soon;
then I'll be well. Who is your friend?
Robin. A kinsman, Major Molineux.
Man with Mask. I have a fellow feeling for him.
The Major used to own this house:
now it's mine. I'm taking over,
I've just signed the final deed.
Do you see my nameplate on the gate?
Robin. The Rattlesnake?
Man with Mask. The Rattlesnake. 530
Robin. If I pick up the Rattlesnake,
will it help me find my kinsman?
I think he needs my help. We are
his last relations in the world.
Man with Mask. The last shall be the first, my Boy.
Robin. What do you mean? You talk like Christ.
Man with Mask. The first shall be the last, my Boy.°
The Major has a heavy hand;
we have been beaten to the ground.
Robin. My kinsman has an open hand. 540
Man with Mask. Ridden like horses, fleeced like sheep,
worked like cattle, clothed and fed

537. The first shall be the last. "But many that are first shall be last; and the last shall be first." Matthew 19:30.

like hounds and hogs!
Robin. I want to find him.
Man with Mask. Whipping-posts, gibbets, bastinadoes
and the rack! I must be moving.
Robin. Wait, I'll take up the Rattlesnake.
Please, help me find my kinsman. *(Robin takes hold of the Man with the Mask's shoulder. The Man steps back and draws his sword.)*
Man with Mask. Move!
You've torn my cloak. You'd better keep
a civil tongue between your teeth.
I have a mission. *(Robin raises his cudgel. He and the Man with the Mask stand a moment facing each other.)*
550 *Boy.* Brain him, Robin.
Mangle the bastard's bloody face.
He doesn't like our kinsman, Robin.
Robin. I only asked for information.
Man with Mask. For information! Information
is my trade. I was a lawyer
before I learned the pleasures of
the military life. The Major
was my first teacher. Now I know you!
I met you at the tavern. You
560 were short of cash then. Take this crown:
drink to the Major, then a health
to Greenough, and the Rattlesnake.
To Greenough!
Robin. You're a fighter.
Man with Mask. I hate war, wars leave us where
they find us, don't they, boy?
Let's talk about my health.
Robin. Where can
I find my kinsman?
Man with Mask. He owned this house.
Men used to find him here all day,
before the storms disturbed his judgment.
570 He's out now ranging through the town,
looking for new accommodations.
Wait here. You'll meet him on his walk. *(Strides off singing)*
The king is in his counting house;
we're counting up his money.
Boy. Why was that fellow's face half red now?
He's changing color.
Robin. I don't know.
He is someone out of "Revelations"—

Hell revolting on its jailers. *(The church lights up a little. Robin walks over to it, and looks in a window.)*
Our church is empty, brother. Moonbeams 580
are trembling on the snow-pure pews,
the altar's drowned in radiant fog,
a single restless ray has crept
across the open Bible. *(Turns to a gravestone by the church)*
I'm lonely.
What's this? A gravestone? A grave? Whose grave?
I think the Major must have died:
everything tells me he is gone
and nothing is forever.
(Turns back to the church)
Brother,
the moon's the only worshipper! *(The Clergyman comes out of the church. He lays a white clay pipe on the steps and holds up a little* 590 *colored celluloid whirligig.)*

Clergyman. The wind has died.

Cast of the original production of My Kinsman, Major Molineux *at the American Place Theatre, New York, 1964.*

Robin. What are you doing?
Clergyman. I'm playing with this whirligig,
and waiting to see which way the wind
will veer. It's quite amusing, Son,
trying to guess the whims of the wind.
I am waiting for a sign.
A strange thing for a modern churchman.
Robin. My father says the Church is a rock.
600 *Clergyman.* Yes, yes, a rock is blind. That's why
I've shut my eyes.
Robin. I see my father. He's the Deerfield
minister, and Church of England.
You remind me of my father.
Clergyman. Be careful, son. Call no man father:
that's what we tell the Roman clergy;
sometimes I think we go too far,
they get their people out for Mass.
Robin. Father. When I shut
610 my eyes, I dream I'm back in Deerfield.
The people sit in rows below
the old oak; a horseman stops to water
his horse and to refresh his soul.
I hear my father holding forth
thanksgiving, hope and all the mercies—
Clergyman. Those village
pastors! Once they used to preach
as if the world were everlasting;
each Sunday was longer than a summer!
That's gone now. We have competition:
620 taverns, papers, politics
and trade. It takes a wolfhound now
to catch a flock!
Robin. Why are you waiting
for the wind?
Clergyman. *(Taking up two little flags)*
Do you see
these two flags? One's the Union Jack,
the other is the Rattlesnake.
The wind will tell me which to fly.
Robin. I'm thinking of the absent one.
My kinsman, Major Molineux
is absent. The storms have hurt his house
630 lately. No one will help me find him.
Clergyman. Perhaps the wind will blow him back.

Robin. I met a strange man, Colonel Greenough;
Half of his face was red, and half
was pocked. He said, "Wait here, and you
will meet your kinsman on his walk."
Clergyman. You'd better wait here then. That red
and pocked man tends to speak the truth.
Robin. Why was his face two-colors, Father?
Clergyman. He is an image of the city.
If his whole face turns red as blood, 640
We'll have to fly the Rattlesnake.
Robin. Say more about my kinsman, Father.
You said he was your friend and patron.
Clergyman. Poor Molineux! he served the clergy
somewhat better than this city.
He had a special pew, you know.
He used to set a grand example.
Robin. He used to! You speak as if he were dead!
Clergyman. Men blamed me, but I liked to watch
his red coat blazing like the sunset 650
at Sunday morning service here.
He was an easy-going fellow
a lover of life, no Puritan.
He had invention, used to send
two six-foot Privates here to help
with the collection. Yes, I had
to like him. He had his flaws, of course.
Robin. A red coat blazing like the sunrise,
that's how the Major was in Deerfield;
the gold lion of England shone 660
on his gilded carriage. He had a little
white scar like a question mark
on his right cheek. He got it killing
Frenchmen. He seemed to hold the world
like a gold ball in the palm of his hand.
Ours for the asking! All! We are
his last relations in the world!
Clergyman. No one will dispute your claim.
Robin. The Major said he was the King's
intelligence in Massachusetts. 670
Clergyman. No one will dispute his claim.
What shall we do with people? They
get worse and worse, but God improves.
God was green in Moses' time;
little by little though, he blossomed.

First came the prophets, then our Lord,
and then the Church.
Robin. The Church?
Clergyman. The Church
gets more enlightened every day.
We've learned to disregard the Law
680 and look at persons. Who is my neighbor?
Anyone human is my neighbor. Sometimes
my neighbor is a man from Sodom. *(Great noise of shouting. All former characters, except the Man with the Mask, parade across the stage. Most of them wave Rattlesnake flags.)*
Robin. Father, I see two clergymen,
they're waving flags.
Clergyman. I see my sign. *(Snaps the whirligig with his thumb)*
Look, the wind has risen! Wherever
the spirit calls me, I must follow.
Crowd. Hurrah for the Republic!
690 Down with Major Molineux! *(The People sing a verse of Yankee Doodle and draw Colonel Greenough on stage in a red, white and blue cart. He stands up and draws his sword. One can see that his face is now entirely red.)*
Man with Mask. The die is cast! I say, the die is cast.
Robin. Look at the Colonel,
his whole face is red as blood!
Man with Mask. Major Molineux is coming.
Clergyman. Are you sure we're strong enough?
Man with Mask. Every British soldier in Boston
is killed or captured.
Crowd. Don't tread on me!
700 Don't tread on me! Don't tread on me!
Robin. What can I do to help my kinsman?
Clergyman. Swap your flag and save your soul.
Robin. I want to save my kinsman, Father.
Clergyman. No, no, Son, do as I do. Here, hold
this flag a moment, while I speak.
(The Clergyman hands Robin his Rattlesnake flag, tosses away the whirligig, breaks his clay pipe, then takes a chair and stands on it while he addresses the Crowd with both hands raised. Throughout the crowd scene, Robin stands unconsciously holding the flag and suf-
710 *fering.)*
How long, how long now, Men of Boston!
You've faced the furious tyrant's trident,
you've borne the blandishments of Sodom.
The Day of Judgment is at hand,

now we'll strip the scarlet whore,
King George shall swim in scarlet blood.
now Nebuchadnezzar shall eat grass and die.
How long! How long! O Men of Boston,
behave like men, if you are men! *(The people cheer and take the Clergyman on their shoulders.)* 720
You've drawn the sword, Boys, throw away
the scabbard!

(The Clergyman draws a sword and throws down the scabbard. Many of the people, including the Prostitute, draw swords and throw the scabbards rattling across the stage. They draw Major Molineux on stage in a red cart. He is partly tarred and feathered; one cheek is bleeding; his red British uniform is torn; he shakes with terror.)

Robin. Oh my kinsman, my dear kinsman,
they have wounded you!

Man with Mask. Throw the boy from Deerfield out, 730
he has no garment for our wedding.

Clergyman. No, let him stay, he is just a boy.

(Robin, unthinking, holds the flag in front of him, while his eyes are fixed in horror and pity on the figure of the Major. The Boy, unconsciously, too, mingles among the Crowd without thinking. Someone asks him to give some dirt to throw at the Major, and he unthinkingly picks up some from a basket and hands it to the Tavern Keeper, who throws it at the Major.)

Robin. (With a loud cry, but unconsciously waving the flag in his grief) Oh my poor kinsman, you are hurt! 740

Crowd. Don't tread on me! Don't tread on me! *(The Major slowly staggers to his feet. Slowly he stretches out his right arm and points to Robin.)*

Major Molineux. Et tu, Brute!

Tavern Keeper. The Major wants to teach us Latin. *(The Crowd laughs, and Robin, once more without thinking, laughs too, very loudly. Tavern Keeper goes up to the Major and hands him a Rattlesnake flag.)*
You're out of step, Sir. Here's your flag. *(The Major lurches a few steps from the cart, grinds the Rattlesnake underfoot, then turns and addresses the crowd.)* 750

Major Molineux. Long live King George! Long live King George!
I'll sing until you cut my tongue out!

Crowd. Throw the Major in the river,
in the river, in the river! *(With a grating sound, the Ferryman appears*

717. now Nebuchadnezzar shall eat grass and die. For this earthly pride, the powerful Babylonian king Nebuchadnezzar at the command of heaven "was driven from men, and did eat grass as oxen," until he acknowledged the everlasting power of God. Daniel 4: 28-33.

at the side of the stage, pushing the prow of his dory. The Major staggers towards the Ferryman.)

Major Molineux. (To Ferryman) Help me in my trouble. Let me cross the river to my King! *(The Ferryman stiffens. The Man with*
760 *the Mask throws him a silver crown.)*

Man with Mask. Ferryman, here's a silver crown,
take him or leave him, we don't care.

Ferryman. (Still more threatening) The crown's no longer currency. *(The Ferryman kicks the crown into the water.)*

Major Molineux. Boatman, you rowed me here in state;
save me, now that I'm fallen!

Ferryman. There's no returning on my boat.

Major Molineux. (Stretching out his hands and grappling the Ferryman) Save me in the name of God! *(The Ferryman pushes the Major*
770 *off and hits him on the head with his oar. The Major screams, and lies still.)*

Ferryman. He's crossed the river into his kingdom;
all tyrants must die as this man died. *(One by one, the principal characters come up and look at the Major.)*

Clergyman. He's dead. He had no time to pray.
I wish he'd called me. O Lord, remember
his past kindness to the Church;
all tyrants must die as this man died.

Man in Periwig. (Taking the Major's empty scabbard) I have the
780 Major's sword of office;
hem, hem, I have authority.

First Barber. His Honor has the hollow scabbard.

Man in Periwig. They build men right in England. Take him
all in all, he was a man;
all tyrants must die as this man died.

Tavern Keeper. (Holding a poster) Look, this poster says the town
of Boston offers a thousand guineas
to anyone who kills the Major.
I'll take his wallet for the cause.
790 All tyrants must die as this man died.

Prostitute. (Taking the Major's hat) I'll need this hat to hide my head.
They build men right in England. Take him
all in all, he was a man;
all tyrants must die as this man died.

Man with Mask. (Plunging his sword in the Major) Sic semper tyrannis!°

Ferryman. His fare is paid now;

795-796. Sic semper tyrannis! Literally, "Thus always to tyrants!"

the Major's free to cross the river. *(The Ferryman loads Major Molineux's body on his boat, and pushes off.)*

Clergyman. (Coming up to Man with Mask)

Your hand! I want
to shake your hand, Sir. A great day!

Man with Mask. Great and terrible! There's nothing 800
I can do about it now. *(Turns to Robin)*
Here, boy, here's the Major's sword;
perhaps, you'll want a souvenir. *(Crowd starts to leave. Robin and Boy alone)*

Boy. The Major's gone. We'll have to go
Back home. There's no one here to help us.

Robin. Yes, Major Molineux is dead. *(Starts sadly towards the river)*

Crowd. Long live the Republic! Long live the Republic!

Boy. Look, Robin, I have found a flintlock. *(Robin looks wistfully at the crowd, now almost entirely gone. He pauses and then answers in a daze.)* 810

Robin. A flintlock?

Boy. Well, that's all I came to Boston for, I guess.
Let's go, I see the ferryman.

Robin. (Still inattentive) I'm going. *(Robin takes his brother's hand and turns firmly towards the city.)*

Boy. We are returning to the city! *(All the people are gone now, the lights start to go out. A red sun shows on the river.)*

Robin. Yes, brother, we are staying here.
Look, the lights are going out, 820
the red sun's moving on the river.
Where will it take us to? . . . It's strange
to be here on our own—and free.

Boy. (Sighting along his flintlock) Major Molineux is dead.

Robin. Yes, Major Molineux is dead.

Comments and Questions

In Lowell's play there are two lines of action. One deals with the preparation and successful completion of the Boston colonists' revolt against the power of the Crown, represented by Major Molineux; the other with the achievement of independence by a young, untried country boy. Since the political humiliation and murder of the protector he seeks makes possible Robin's freedom, one level of action complements and fuses into the other. The old order of the Major is crushed; Robin is the reborn hero. The Redcoats are replaced by the deerskin suit and the cudgel of the backwoods villager, the pioneer of a new free land. But from the first scene we are grimly reminded that freedom is not gained without a price. What is that price? The following questions should help to lead you to some answers.

In the face of all the spirited rebellious activity in Boston, what does the Ferryman mean in the first scene when he calls it "the city of the dead?" What other significant warnings or predictions does he give at the time? Characterize the more important people Robin meets in his search for the Major; most of them, since they are nameless and not highly individualized, are representative and symbolic: the Barber, Tavern Keeper, Clergyman, Watchman, and the Man in the Periwig; but the Prostitute, who also appears as The Woman and as Mrs. Clark, and The Man in the Mask, who seems both human (as Colonel Greenough) and non-human (as "the image of the city" and possibly the devil himself) are equally symbolic. Although the Major appears only briefly, he is very important. Is he a tyrant or a scapegoat? Are his humiliation and death to be at all deplored? Are any of his virtues or vices reflected in any of the other characters? The most enigmatic figure is The Man in the Mask; what is the significance of the changing masks he wears; is he perhaps the most useful guide for Robin; what is the meaning of his final remark to the clergyman:

"Great and terrible! There's nothing
I can do about it now"?

Finally, trace step by step Robin's progress from dependent innocence to independent awareness. What are his more notable virtues? What precisely does he learn, and what price does he pay?

Lowell's play is a reading, an interpretation, of Hawthorne's complex and ambiguous story, which itself has been open to several, even diametrically opposed, interpretations. The short story and the play, of course, are distinct and autonomous forms, but a comparison of the same story in both forms tells us a good deal about the limitations imposed upon each and the unique power of each to move us in certain ways. If the play is good, it stands on its own merits, and the reader need not know Hawthorne's story. Hence, you might first consider the play on its own terms, as the questions above have asked you to do. But since the purpose here is to direct you to consider what a play is, it will help to compare as closely as we can how in this one case a short story "becomes" a play, or more accurately, is adapted (not copied) for dramatic performance.

The essay "Some Thoughts on Playwrighting" by Thornton Wilder, who is both a prominent novelist and dramatist, offers several useful dis-

tinctions between the arts of fiction and drama that should help you explain some of the specific changes Lowell makes. A few of the important changes in plotting are the addition of Robin's younger brother and the clergyman, the omission of the "cheerful" man, having the Major killed instead of escorted out of town, and having Robin make a definite decision at the end to stay in the city. Lowell also gives The Man in the Mask a name, makes several of the characters more simply and pointedly symbolic, and adds several visual symbols, like the flags, the lobster, the whirligig, and the clay pipe. Which of these changes might be explained by Wilder's distinctions?

It soon becomes clear, however, that not all of these changes can be explained by the special demands of stage presentation. Other changes are determined by how Lowell read and used Hawthorne's story for his own purposes. Because the play is adapted from the narrative to the dramatic form, and designed for a public rather than a private audience, it is necessarily both an interpretation and a simplification of the story. Which of the changes and modifications Lowell makes serve best to clarify his theme or unifying idea? Consider Lowell's adaptation in light of your own interpretation of Hawthorne's story.

Related Reading

Nathaniel Hawthorne, "My Kinsman, Major Molineux," page 725
Thornton Wilder, "Some Thoughts on Playwrighting," page 644

Sophocles

(496-406 B.C.)

ANTIGONE

translated by Michael Townsend

Tragedy is a complex dramatic form that is difficult, if not impossible, to define satisfactorily. One can say that tragedy continues to be defined, for each age modifies the meaning of tragic action and the tragic character which it has inherited. Initially, the student of the play might well be satisfied with Maxwell Anderson's definition (pp. 663-669) as it may be qualified by close readings of the Antigone *by Sophocles and its retelling, some two thousand years later, by Jean Anouilh. We might only add here a sentence from Edith Hamilton's splendid book* The Greek Way: *"Tragedy's one essential," she writes, "is a soul that can feel greatly. Given such a one and any catastrophe may be tragic. But the earth may be removed and the mountains be carried into the midst of the sea, and if only the small and shallow are confounded, tragedy is absent."*

Antigone *was produced in Athens about 441 B.C., when Sophocles was in his middle fifties, as part of the annual spring festival honoring the god Dionysus. The conditions of production and performance at that time are outlined in the essay by Raymond Williams, on page 652 of this text. The play is a part of the series of three plays dramatizing the fortunes of Oedipus, King of Thebes, and his children. Though in the sequence of the legend* Antigone *is the final play, it was written first,* Oedipus the King *being written twenty-two years later, and the middle play,* Oedipus at Colonus, *thirty-seven years later when Sophocles was ninety-one.*

Oedipus, under a curse placed by the god Apollo on his father, was fated to murder his father and marry his mother, events which inevitably come to pass in spite of the efforts of Laius and Oedipus to prevent them. Oedipus the King *deals with the anguished discovery of Oedipus that he has not escaped his fate; his wife-mother, Jocasta, commits suicide, and Oedipus inflicts blindness and exile on himself. After his wanderings and death, depicted in* Oedipus at Colonus, *his daughters, Antigone and Ismene, who had accompanied him, return to Thebes to find that their brothers Eteocles and Polynices have quarrelled over the throne and that Eteocles has exiled Polynices. With the support of the powerful King of Argos and five other foreign princes, Polynices returns to fight for his succession. He and his brother meet in combat and slay each other. The Argive army retreats, and Creon, the brother-in-law of Oedipus, becomes king and decrees that the enemy dead, including Polynices, cannot be allowed the rite of burial, and thus their souls cannot enter Hades, the Greek abode of death.*

At this point, Antigone *begins. The reader should be cautioned that in Sophoclean tragedy the main characters are not merely pawns or puppets of righteous gods or predestined fate, as the summary of the legend might imply. They are first of all human beings who quite humanly confront life, whether or not they are initially aware of their destiny. The reader must also keep in mind that Antigone lives under the shadow of her father's sins, as the Chorus reminds her, but it is not her father's sins alone which bring her to an early grave. The case is rather this: a passionate, headstrong girl, her spirit affronted by the blasphemy of her uncle's edict, deliberately defies his law, knowing her death is certain, though she is unaware of all the other consequences. Her performing the burial ritual springs the action of the plot, which then moves with the swift force of destined events until the arrogant King is brought to a tragic awareness of the inviolability of divine law. What makes Sophocles' plays and much of Greek tragedy still vital to the modern audience is largely the fact that though the protagonists may live under the threat of a god-directed doom, their characters still determine their fates.*

ANTIGONE

Characters

ANTIGONE
ISMENE
CREON
GUARD
HAEMON
TEIRESIAS
BOY
MESSENGER
EURYDICE
SERVANT
CHORUS

Antigone. My darling sister Ismene, we have had
A fine inheritance from Oedipus.
God has gone through the whole range of sufferings
And piled them all on us,—grief upon grief,
Humiliation upon humiliation.
And now this latest thing that our dictator
Has just decreed . . . you heard of it? Or perhaps
You haven't noticed our enemies at work.
Ismene. No news, either good or bad, has come
To me, Antigone: nothing since the day 10
We were bereaved of our two brothers. No,
Since the withdrawal of the Argive army
Last night, I've heard nothing about our loved ones
To make me glad or sad.
Antigone. I thought as much.
That's why I brought you out, outside the gate,
So we could have a talk here undisturbed.
Ismene. You've something on your mind. What is it then?
Antigone. Only that our friend Creon has decided
To discriminate between our brothers' corpses.
Eteocles he buried with full honors 20
To light his way to hell in a blaze of glory.
But poor dear Polynices,—his remains
Are not allowed a decent burial.
He must be left unmourned, without a grave,
A happy hunting ground for birds
To peck for tidbits. This ukase applies
To you,—and me of course. What's more, friend Creon

Is on his way here now to supervise
Its circulation in person. And don't imagine
30 He isn't serious,—the penalty
For disobedience is to be stoned to death.
So, there you have it. You're of noble blood.
Soon you must show your mettle,—if you've any.
Ismene. Oh my fire-eating sister, what am I
Supposed to do about it, if this is the case?
Antigone. Just think it over—if you'll give a hand . . .
Ismene. In doing what? What do you have in mind?
Antigone. Just helping me do something for the corpse.
Ismene. You don't intend to bury him? It's forbidden.
40 *Antigone.* He is my brother, and yours. My mind's made up.
You please yourself.
Ismene. But Creon has forbidden. . . .
Antigone. What Creon says is quite irrelevant.
He is my brother. I will bury him.
Ismene. Oh God.
Have you forgotten how our father died,
Despised and hated? How he turned
Detective to discover his own crimes,
Then stabbed his own eyes out with his own hands?
And then Jocasta, who was both together
50 His mother and his wife,
Hanged herself with a rope? Next, our two brothers
Became each other's murderers. We are left,
We two. How terrible if we as well
Are executed for disobeying
The lawful orders of the head of state.
Oh please remember,—we are women, aren't we?
We shouldn't take on men. In times of crisis
It is the strongest men who take control.
We must obey their orders, however harsh.
60 So, while apologizing to the dead,
Regretting that I act under constraint,
I will comply with my superior's orders.
Sticking one's neck out would be merely foolish.
Antigone. Don't think I'm forcing you. In fact, I wouldn't
Have your assistance if you offered it.
You've made your bed; lie on it. I intend
To give my brother burial. I'll be glad
To die in the attempt,—if it's a crime,
Then it's a crime that God commands. I then
70 Could face my brother as a friend and look

Him in the eyes. Why shouldn't I make sure
I get on with the dead rather than with
The living? There is all eternity
To while away below. And as for you,
By all means be an atheist if you wish.
Ismene. I'm not. I'm simply powerless to act
Against this city's laws.
Antigone. That's your excuse.
Good-bye. I'm going now to make a grave
For our brother, whom I love.
Ismene. Oh, dear.
I'm terribly afraid for you.
Antigone. Don't make a fuss 80
On my account,—look after your own skin.
Ismene. At least then promise me that you will tell
No one of this; and I'll keep quiet too.
Antigone. For God's sake don't do that,—you're sure to be
Far more unpopular if you keep quiet.
No; blurt it out, please do.
Ismene. You're very cheerful.
Antigone. That is because I'm helping those I know
That I should help.
Ismene. I only hope you can,
But it's impossible.
Antigone. Must I hang back
From trying, just because you say I can't? 90
Ismene. If it's impossible, you shouldn't try
At all.
Antigone. If that's your line, you've earned my hatred
And that of our dead brother too, by rights.
Oh, kindly let me go my foolish way,
And take the consequences. I will suffer
Nothing worse than death in a good cause.
Ismene. All right then, off you go. I'm bound to say
You're being very loyal, but very silly.
Chorus. At last it has dawned, the day that sees 100
The force that rode from Argos driven
Back upon its road again
With headlong horses on a looser rein.

Roused by Polynices to aid his claim,
Like an eagle screaming,
With snow-tipped wings and bloody claws
And mouth agape, it wheeled about our fortress doors.

But Thebes, a hissing snake, fought back.
The god of fire could get no grip
110 Upon our crown of walls. That bird of prey,
Its beak balked of our blood, has turned away.

God hates presumption. When he saw
Those men in ostentatious force
And clash of gold advancing,
He singled out one man all set
To shout the victory cry upon the parapet,
And flung at him a lightning bolt, to curtail his prancing.°

Covered in flame he dropped
Down like an empty balance and drummed the earth;
120 He who before had breathed
The winds of hate against us. In many a foray and rout,
War, a runaway horse, was hitting out.

Seven enemy kings at seven gates,
Fighting at equal odds,
Left their arms as trophies to Theban gods.

Elsewhere, the hated pair,
Sons of the same mother,
Crossed their swords in combat and killed each other.

But now that Victory has smiled on us,
130 Let us forget the war, and dance
At every temple all night long. And let
Bacchus° be king in Thebes, until the strong earth reels.

Ah, here comes Creon, our ruler,—in haste.
Something new has developed.
He has something afoot . . .
Else why has he summoned us to council?
Creon. Well, friends, our city has passed through stormy weather.
But now God has restored an even keel.
Why have I summoned you? Because I know
140 That you were at all times loyal to Laius.

112-117. A reference to Capaneus, one of the six kings leading Polynices' attack upon the Seven Gates of Thebes. Though he boasted he would enter Thebes in spite of Zeus himself, Zeus struck him dead with a thunderbolt as he was climbing the wall of the city. ***132. Bacchus,*** Greek god of wine and patron of the drama; also called Dionysus.

And afterwards, when Oedipus put things right,
Then ruined them again, you showed
Your steadiness throughout his sons' dispute.
Well, now they're dead; and so, by due succession,
The power of the crown passes to me.
You cannot possibly judge a ruler's worth
Until he exercises the power he's got.
I've no time for the man who has full powers
Yet doesn't use them to enact good measures,
But adopts a timid policy of "do nothing." 150
Those aren't my principles. I'm not the man
To sit quietly by and watch my country
Sliding towards the precipice of ruin.
Nor can I be a friend to my country's foes.
This I believe—and God may witness it—
Our safety is bound up with that of our country. Therefore
All other loyalties are subject to
Our country's interests.
By such measures I'll make this city great;—
Measures like those that I have just enacted 160
Concerning Oedipus' sons. That Eteocles
Who died while fighting in his country's service,
Is to be buried with ceremonial honors.
But Polynices,—whose intention was
To fight his way back from exile, burn to the ground
His mother city and the temples of
His family's gods, to slaughter out of hand
And to enslave his fellow citizens—
He's not to have a grave or any mourning.
His corpse is to be left, a grim warning, 170
Pecked at by birds and worried by the dogs.
That is my policy. A malefactor mustn't
Have the same treatment as the loyal man.
I intend to see our country's friends rewarded
When they are dead, as well as while they live.

Chorus. We understand the attitude you take
Towards these men. It's true your word is law,
And you can legislate for living and dead....

Creon. What do you think then of this new enactment?

Chorus. If I were younger, I might criticize.... 180

Creon. No turning back. The guard is set on the corpse.

Chorus. What are the penalties for disobeying?

Creon. The penalty is death. As simple as that.

Chorus. That ought to stop them. Who'd be such a fool?

Creon. You'd be surprised. Men led astray by hopes
Of gain will risk even their lives for money.
Guard. Sir, here I am. I can't pretend I'm puffed
From running here with all possible speed.
I kept changing my mind on the way.
190 One moment I was thinking, "What's the hurry?
You're bound to catch it when you get there." Then:
"What are you dithering for? You'll get it hot
And strong if Creon finds out from someone else."
Torn by these doubts I seem to have taken my time.
So what should be a short journey has become
A long one. Anyway I have arrived.
And now I'm going to tell you what I came
To tell you, even if you've heard it. See,
I've made up my mind to expect the worst.
200 We can't avoid what's coming to us, can we?
Creon. Well then, what puts you in such deep despair?
Guard. First I must make a statement—about myself.
I didn't do it, and didn't see who did it.
So I'm quite in the clear, you understand.
Creon. For God's sake tell me what it is, and then
Get out.
Guard. All right, all right. It amounts to this.
Somebody's buried the body, thrown earth on it,
And done the necessary purifications.
210 *Creon.* Someone has been a damn fool. Who was it?
Guard. Dunno. There were no spade-marks in the earth.
The ground was hard and dry, and so there was
No sign of the intruder.
See, when the man who had the first day watch
Told us about it, we had the shock of our lives.
The corpse had not been buried in a grave.
But enough dust was thrown on to avoid
The curse unburied bodies suffer from.
There wasn't even a sign of any dog
220 That might have come and scuffed the dust upon him.
Then everyone started shouting. Each man blamed
His mate. We very nearly came to blows.
Everyone claimed that one of the others had done it,
And tried to prove that he himself was blameless.
To prove their innocence, some said they were
Prepared to pick up red-hot coals or walk
Through fire. While others swore on oath,
By a catalog of gods, they didn't do it
And weren't accomplices in any form.

When our investigations made no progress, 230
In the end one man came out with a sobering speech.
We couldn't answer him, though what he said
Was none too pleasant.
He said we mustn't try to hush it up,
But tell you everything. His view prevailed.
Who was to bring the news? We tossed for it.
I was the lucky person. I can tell you,
I don't like being the bearer of bad news.
Chorus. I think I see the hand of God in this,
Bringing about the body's burial. 240
Creon. Shut up, before I lose my temper.
You may be old, try not to be foolish as well.
How can you say God cares about this corpse?
Do you suppose God feels obliged to him
For coming to burn down his temples and
His statues, in defiance of his laws?
Ever noticed God being kind to evildoers?
No. Certain hostile elements in the city
Who don't like discipline and resent my rule,
Are in on this. They've worked upon the guards 250
By bribes. There is no human institution
As evil as money. Money ruins nations,
And makes men refugees. Money corrupts
The best of men into depravity.
The people who have done this thing for money
Will get what's coming to them. Listen here,
I swear to you by God who is my judge,
That if you and your friends do not divulge
The name of him who did the burying
One hell won't be enough for you. You'll all 260
Be hanged up and flogged until you tell.
That ought to teach you to be more selective
About what you get your money from.
Guard. Am I dismissed?
Or may I speak?
Creon. I thought I made it plain
I couldn't stand your talk.
Guard. Where does it hurt you,—
Your ears, or in your mind?
Creon. What do you mean?
What does it matter where you give me pain?
Guard. The guilty party bothers you deep down.
But my offense is only at ear level.
Creon. My dear good man, you're much too talkative. 270

Guard. I may be that, but I am not your culprit.
Creon. I think you are, and that you did it for money.
Guard. Oh God! I tell you your suspicions are wrong.
Creon. Suspicion he calls it! Look here, if you
Don't tell me who the culprits are, you'll find
That ill-gotten gains are not without their drawbacks.
Guard. Good luck to you, I hope you find the man.
In any case I won't be in a hurry
To come back here again. I thank my stars
280 That I have saved my skin. I didn't expect to.
Chorus. Many amazing things exist, and the most amazing is man.
He's the one, when the gale-force winds
Blow and the big waves
Tower and topple on every side,
Cruises over the deep on the gray tide.

He's the one that to and fro
Over the clods year after year
Wends with his horses and ploughing gear,
Works to his will the untiring Earth, the greatest of gods.

290 He traps the nitwit birds, and the wild
Beasts in their lairs. The ocean's myriad clan
In woven nets he catches,—ingenious man.

He has devised himself shelter against
The rigors of frost and the pelting weather.
Speech and science he's taught himself,
And the city's political arts for living together.

For incurable diseases he has found a cure;
By his inventiveness defying
Every eventuality there can be,—except dying.

300 But the most brilliant gifts
Can be misapplied.
On his moral road
Man swerves from side to side.

God and the government ordain
Just laws; the citizen
Who rules his life by them
Is worthy of acclaim.

But he that presumes
To set the law at naught
Is like a stateless person, 310
Outlawed, beyond the pale.

With such a man I'd have
No dealings whatsoever.
In public and in private
He'd get the cold shoulder.

What's this? What on earth?
My God. Can it be? Yes, Antigone.
Your father before, now you!
Is it so, you were caught disobeying the law?
How could you have been so stupid? 320

Guard. Here she is. She is the one,—the one that did it.
We caught her in the act. Where's Creon gone?

Chorus. There, by good luck he's coming out right now.

Creon. Soon as I leave the house, some trouble starts.
What's happening?

Guard. Well, well, I never thought
That I'd be coming back here again so soon,
Considering how you swore at me just now.
But here I am, in spite of what I said.
I'm bringing in this girl. I caught her tending
The grave. I caught her, no one else. And so 330
I hand her over to you to stand her trial.
And now I reckon I'm entitled to beat it.

Creon. Give me full details, with the circumstances.

Guard. This girl was burying him. As simple as that.

Creon. I trust you understand what you are saying.

Guard. I saw her burying the corpse you said
Was not permitted to be buried. Clear enough?

Creon. Tell me precisely how you saw and caught her.

Guard. It was like this. When we got back,
With your threats still smarting in our ears, 340
We swept all the dust from off the corpse,
And laid the moldering thing completely bare.
Then we went and sat on the high ground to windward,
To avoid the smell. And everyone gave hell
To the man who was on duty, to keep him up
To scratch. We watched till midday, when the sun
Is hottest. Suddenly a squall came on,—
A whirlwind with a thunderstorm; it ripped

The leaves from every tree in all the plain.
350 The air was full of it; we had to keep
Our eyes tight shut against the wrath of heaven.
At last, when all was over, there we see
The girl, —crying like a bird that finds
Its nest empty of chicks,—her having seen
The corpse uncovered. Then she started cursing
Whoever did it. Next she goes and fetches
Dust in her hands; and from a jug she pours
A set of three libations on the corpse.
When we saw that of course we jumped straight up
360 And grabbed the girl. She took it very calmly.
We charged her with this crime and the previous one,
And she admitted them. So I'm half glad,
Half sorry. Glad that I am out of danger,
But sorry someone that I like's in trouble.
However, main thing is that I'm all right.

Creon. You, with your eyes fixed on the ground.
Do you admit the charges or deny them?

Antigone. I don't deny the charges. I admit them.

Creon. (To Guard) All right, clear off. Consider yourself lucky
370 To be absolved of guilt.
(To Antigone) Now tell me, briefly,—I don't want a speech.
You knew about my edict which forbade this?

Antigone. Of course I knew. You made it plain enough.

Creon. You took it on yourself to disobey?

Antigone. Sorry, who made this edict? Was it God?
Isn't a man's right to burial decreed
By divine justice? I don't consider your
Pronouncements so important that they can
Just . . . overrule the unwritten laws of heaven.
380 You are a man, remember.
These divine laws are not just temporary measures.
They stand forever. I would have to face
Them when I died. And I will die, without
Your troubling to arrange it. So, what matter
If I must die before my time? I'd welcome
An early death, living as I do now.
What I can't stand is passively submitting
To my own brother's body being unburied.
I dare say you think I'm being silly.
390 Perhaps you're not so very wise yourself.

Chorus. She's difficult, just like her father was.
She doesn't realize when to give in.

Creon. I know these rigid temperaments. They're the first
To break. The hardest-tempered steel
Will shatter at a blow. The highest-mettled
Horses are broken in with a small bit.
That's what is needed, discipline. This girl
Knew damned well she was kicking over the traces,
Breaking the law. And now when she has done it,
She boasts about it, positively gloats. 400
If she gets away with this behavior,
Call me a woman and call her a man.
I don't care if she is my sister's daughter.
I don't care if she's closer to me than all
My family. She and her sister won't get off.
I'll execute them.
Oh yes, her as well.
She's in it too. Go get her. She's inside.
I saw her in there muttering, half-balmy.
It is her conscience. She can't hide her guilt.
At least she doesn't try to justify it. 410
Antigone. Won't my death be enough? Do you want more?
Creon. No, that will do, as far as I'm concerned.
Antigone. Then why not do it now? Our wills conflict
Head-on. No chance of reconciliation.
I can't think of a finer reason for dying,—
Guilty of having buried my own brother.
These men are on my side. But they daren't say so.
Creon. That's where you're wrong. You're quite alone in this.
Antigone. They're on my side. They're forced to cringe to you.
Creon. These men obey. But you and you alone 420
Decide to disobey. Aren't you ashamed?
Antigone. Ashamed? Ashamed of what? Ashamed of being
Loyal to my own family, my own brother?
Creon. Eteocles was also your own brother.
Antigone. Indeed he was. Of course he was my brother.
Creon. Then why were you so disloyal to him?
Antigone. If he were living now, he'd back me up.
Creon. For treating his brother no differently from him!
Antigone. It was his brother that died, not just some servant.
Creon. Died while commanding an invading force! 430
But Eteocles died fighting for his country.
Antigone. That doesn't affect the laws of burial.
Creon. You can't treat friend and enemy the same.
Antigone. Who knows what the rules are among the dead?
Creon. Your enemy doesn't become your friend by dying.

Antigone. If we must have these groupings, let me say
I'll join anyone in loving, but not in hating.
Creon. All right then, die, and love them both in hell.
I'm not here to be shoved around by a woman.
440 *Chorus.* Oh, look, by the gate, here's Ismene.
She's crying because of her sister.
What a shame this heavy cloud of grief
Should spoil her attractive appearance.
Creon. And now for you. You who've been skulking quiet,
Injecting your slow poison like a viper.
Imagine my not noticing,—I've been rearing
Two furies in my house, ready to bite
The hand that fed them. Just you tell me now—
Will you confess you were party to this burial,
450 Or will you swear you had no knowledge of it?
Ismene. I did it, if she did it. I'm involved.
I'm in with her and bear my share of blame.
Antigone. That's quite unjustified. You didn't want
To help me, and I didn't let you join me.
Ismene. You are in trouble. May I then not make
Myself your comrade in adversity?
Antigone. The dead know who it was that did the deed.
You took no action. Your speeches don't impress me.
Ismene. How can you, being my sister, deny my wish
460 To die with you for Polynices' sake?
Antigone. Don't go and die as well as me, and don't
Lay claim to what you haven't done. I'm going
To die. One death's enough.
Ismene. Will life be worth
Living to me, left all alone without you?
Antigone. May I suggest an object of affection?
Creon. He is your uncle, after all.
Ismene. Why do you try to hurt me? What's the point?
Antigone. I may make fun of you, but I feel this deeply.
Ismene. I only want to know how I can help you.
470 *Antigone.* Well, save yourself then. I don't grudge you that.
Ismene. I don't want that. I want to die with you.
Antigone. You chose to live; I chose to die, remember?
Ismene. I didn't express my innermost convictions.
Antigone. You sounded pretty convinced at the time.
Ismene. I still maintain that we two share the guilt.
Antigone. Don't worry. You won't die. But I've already
Sacrificed my life to help the dead.
Creon. These girls! One of them's been mad all her life.
And now the other one's gone balmy too.

Ismene. But, sir, however sensible one is, 480
Adversity is bound to affect one's judgment.
Creon. Well, it has yours! You join this criminal,
And identify yourself with her misdeeds . . .
Ismene. There is no life left for me without her.
Creon. Forget about her. She's as good as dead.
Ismene. So you would execute your own son's bride?
Creon. Plenty of other women in the world.
Ismene. But they were so well suited to each other.
Creon. I won't have my son marrying a bitch.
Antigone. Poor Haemon! See how much your father cares. 490
Creon. Oh, go to hell,—you and your marriage with you.
Ismene. You really intend to take her from your son?
Creon. I won't stop the marriage. Death will stop it.
Ismene. There's no way out? It is fixed that she dies?
Creon. Of course it's fixed. Stop wasting time.
You servants, take her in. It's very important
To keep women strictly disciplined.
That's the deterrent. Even the bravest people
Will step down quick when they see death loom up.
Chorus. Happy the man whose life is uneventful. 500
For once a family is cursed by God,
Disasters come like earthquake tremors, worse
With each succeeding generation.

It's like when the sea is running rough
Under stormy winds from Thrace.
The black ooze is stirred up from the sea-bed,
And louder and louder the waves crash on shore.

Look now at the last sunlight that sustains
The one surviving root of Oedipus' tree,—
The sword of death is drawn to hack it down. 510

And all through nothing more than intemperate language.
All through nothing more than hasty temper.

What power on earth can resist
Your strength, O God? You stand supreme,
Untouched by sleep that makes all else feel old,
Untired by the passing years that wear all else away.

I know one rule that has stood,
And will stand, forever.
That nothing in our life can be exempt
From the universal forces that make for ruin. 520

Hope, that tramps all roads, may help at times.
More often, it deludes weak-minded men.
They never notice, till they feel the fire.

It is a wise saying, that
When God is set against you,
You welcome the path to ruin,—but not for long.

Here comes Haemon, your youngest son.
I expect he's grieved about his bride,
And this sudden bar to his marriage.
530 *Creon.* There's one way of finding out for certain.
My son, you've heard about this public decree.
Have you come here in a spirit of indignation
About your bride, or are you going to be
Loyal to me whatever I'm involved in?
Haemon. I am your son. So while your policies
Are just, you have my full obedience.
I certainly wouldn't consider any marriage
As important as the right leadership by you.
Creon. Good, good. Your heart is in the right place. Nothing
540 Should come before your loyalty to your father.
Why else do fathers pray for well-behaved sons?
They do things together. Work together against
Their common enemy. Vie with each
Other in being good friends to their friends.
As for the man who brings up useless sons,
He's got himself a load of trouble,—all
His enemies laugh at them, a bad team.
Never get carried away by a woman, son.
Sex isn't everything. If she's a bitch,
550 You'll feel a coldness as she lies beside you.
Can there be anything worse than giving your love
To a bitch that doesn't deserve it? No, reject her,
And let her go and find a husband in hell.
Now that I've caught her flagrantly disobeying
When everybody else has toed the line,
The eyes of the nation are on me. I must stay
True to my principles. I must execute her.
I don't give a damn for all her talk
About family ties. If I allow
560 My own relations to get out of control,
That gives the cue to everybody else.
People who are loyal members of their families

Will be good citizens too. But if a person
Sets himself up above the law and tries
To tell his rulers what they ought to do,—
You can't expect me to approve of that.
Once a man has authority, he must be obeyed,—
In big things and in small, in every act,
Whether just or not so just. I tell you this,
The well-disciplined man is good 570
At giving orders and at taking them too.
In war, in a crisis, he's the sort of man
You like to have beside you. On the other hand,
There's nothing so disastrous as anarchy.
Anarchy means an ill-disciplined army,
A rabble that will break into a panic rout.
What follows? Plundered cities, homeless people.
A disciplined army loses few men;
Discipline pulls them through to victory.
We can't go about kowtowing to women. 580
If I must lose my throne, let it be a man
That takes it from me. I can't have people saying
My will has been defeated by a woman.
Chorus. I think your observations very just,
In general . . . though perhaps I'm old and silly.
Haemon. Father, don't you agree,—
Of all God's gifts, good sense is far the best.
I'm sure I'd be the last person to deny
That what you said is true. Yet there may be
A lot of justice in the opposite view. 590
I've one advantage over you,—I know
Before you what the people think about you,
Especially criticism. You're so held in awe
That people dare not say things to your face.
But I am able to hear their secret talk.
The people feel sorry for Antigone.
They say it isn't equitable she must die
A horrible death for such a noble action.
They say that she in fact deserves special
Honor for refusing to allow 600
The body of her brother to be left
Unburied for dogs and birds to pull to pieces.
That is their secret opinion, and it's gaining ground.
Of course I want your rule to be a success.
There's nothing more important to me than that.
Such feeling is mutual, between father and son,—

One's glad to see the other doing well.
Don't be too single-minded, then. Don't think
You have a complete monopoly of the truth.
610 Isn't it true that people who refuse
To see any other point of view but theirs
Often get shown up and discredited?
However acute one is, there's no disgrace
In being able to learn, being flexible.
In winter, when the streams turn into torrents,
You can see the trees that try to resist the water
Get rooted out and killed. But those that bend
A little, manage to survive the flood.
In a gale at sea if you cram on full sail,
620 You'll soon have the waves breaking aboard
And bowling over all the furniture.
Why not relax and change your mind for once?
Perhaps at my age I should not express
An opinion, but I would like to say this:—
Not everyone can be right on every issue,
But the next best thing is to take notice of
And learn from the judicious thoughts of others.

Chorus. Yes, everyone can learn. You, sir, can learn
From him,—and he of course from you. There's much
630 Of substance in the arguments on both sides.

Creon. Am I to stand here and be lectured to
By a kid? A man of my experience!

Haemon. I'm not suggesting anything illegal.
I may be young, but judge me by the facts.

Creon. The facts are, you're encouraging my detractors.

Haemon. I'm not encouraging anything that's wrong.

Creon. You seem to have caught Antigone's disease.

Haemon. The people of Thebes don't call it a disease.

Creon. Must I ask their permission for everything?

640 *Haemon.* You're talking like an adolescent now.

Creon. Am I the king of Thebes, or am I not?

Haemon. It takes more than one person to make a nation.

Creon. But a nation is personified in its ruler.

Haemon. In that case Thebes has got no population.

Creon. I take it you are siding with this woman.

Haemon. It is your interests I have at heart.

Creon. You show it by arguing against me?

Haemon. Because I think you're making a mistake.

Creon. Must I let my authority be undermined?

650 *Haemon.* Yes, rather your authority than God's.

Creon. What character! Subservient to a woman.
Haemon. Subservient to what I think is right.
Creon. You've done nothing but back Antigone up.
Haemon. Not only her, but God, and you as well.
Creon. Don't try to butter me up, you ladies' man.
Haemon. You like to talk, but you're not prepared to listen.
Creon. This woman will not live to marry you.
Haemon. Then she won't be the only one to die.
Creon. Oh, oh. Threats is it now? You've got a nerve.
Haemon. I'm trying to show you that you're being perverse. 660
Creon. You will regret you tried to schoolmaster me.
Haemon. If you weren't my father, I'd say you were deranged.
Creon. What's that? I've had enough of your abuse.
By heaven, I swear I'll make you suffer for it.
Take that hell-cat away. You'll watch her die.
Ha, she will die in front of her bridegroom's nose.
Haemon. I won't give you that satisfaction.
I won't be around when she dies.
You must find other friends to condone your madness.
You will never set eyes on me again. 670
Chorus. He's rushed off in a really furious temper.
He's young,—I fear he may do something rash.
Creon. Let him.
Who does he think he is, God almighty?
In any case, he won't save these girls from death.
Chorus. You don't mean to execute them both?
Creon. No, no. You're right. Not her that wasn't involved.
Chorus. What sort of execution do you intend?
Creon. I'll take her to a deserted spot
And bury her alive in a trench. 680
She'll have enough food to avoid the curse,—
The people mustn't suffer because of her.
There she can pray to the god she likes so much,—
The god of death. Perhaps he'll save her life.
Either that, or she'll find out too late
That corpses are more trouble than they're worth.
Chorus. What is it that nestles in
The soft cheeks of a girl,
And pervades the deep sea and the teeming earth,
And persecutes god and man, a force 690
Irresistible? We call it Love.
A man possessed by Love loses control.
Love drives the law-abiding into crime;
And sets a family against itself.

So here a lovely girl's appealing glance
Has prevailed, and destroyed the bonds of blood.
For Love makes mock of time-honored laws
Ordaining loyalty from son to father.

And grief also is irresistible.
700 The tears come to my eyes,—I cannot stop them;
Seeing Antigone go to such a bed,
The bed that puts all mortal things to sleep.
Antigone. Take a good look. With life still strong in me,
I'm going on my last journey, seeing
For the last time the bright rays of the sun.

Unmarried, never having heard my wedding song,
Death takes me to the dark riverbanks to be his bride.
Chorus. You have one glorious consolation.
By your own choice you go down to death
710 Alive, not wasted by disease,
Nor hacked by instruments of war.
Antigone. I shall go to sleep like Niobe.°
I know her story well. On Mount Sipylus
The rock grew, like ivy, round her and weighed her down.
And now the rain and snow
Make tears that run across her stony face.
Chorus. There's no comparison. For she was born
Of divine parentage. You would be lucky
To share the fate of mythical heroines.
720 *Antigone.* Are you getting at me? Wait till I'm dead.
I'm going to die,—do I merit no respect?
O my city, O my friends, rich householders,
O river Dirce,° with the sacred grove
Of Thebes the Charioteer,° I call you all
To witness that I die with nobody
To shed a tear for me, the victim
Of an unjust law. Who'd like to go with me
To an eerie heap of stones, a tomb that is no tomb,
A no-man's land between the living and the dead?

712. Niobe, the wife of an earlier king of Thebes, boasted of her fourteen children to Leto, who had only two children by Zeus. Leto's children, Apollo and Artemis, punished Niobe by killing all of her children. The inconsolable Niobe returned to her home upon Mount Sipylus, and though turned into a stone by Zeus, she continued to weep. ***723. river Dirce,*** a spring or fountain near Thebes named after the cruel wife of the Theban king Lycus. She was punished by being tied to a bull, which dragged her over rocks and precipices until the gods took pity and changed her into a fountain. ***724. Thebes the Charioteer,*** literally, the Thebes of many chariots.

Chorus. You tried to do the right thing by your brother. 730
You stepped boldly towards the altar of Justice,
But somehow stumbled. I fear you must suffer
For your father's sins.

Antigone. Don't speak of it again. It's only too well known,—
My father's fate. To think how much
Our family was admired, in generations past.
Then came successive strokes of doom. My mother's
Marriage to her son, the union
From which I came, to end like this.
My brother, dishonored, drags me down with him. 740
And so I go to join my stricken family in hell.

Chorus. We respect what you did for your brother.
But there's no question that the orders
Of those in authority must be obeyed.
You were self-willed. That has been your undoing.

Antigone. I see I have no friends to say good-bye.
No friends, no tears for me, no marriage to look back on.
Never again to see the face of the sun.

Creon. If I don't stop this blubbering, we'll be here
All night. Stop wasting time. Take her away. 750
As my instructions state, you are to place
Her in the vaulted trench, and brick it in.
It's up to her then,—either live or die.
My hands are clean in this. I've merely
Deprived her of all contact with the living.

Antigone. This stone dugout, half tomb, half bridal-chamber,
Will house me now for good. By this road
I go below to Queen Persephone's kingdom,°
To see again so many of my family.
As I am the latest recruit, so is my fate 760
By far the cruelest. And I've not used
My life's full span.
At least I can look forward to a warm
Welcome from my dear mother and father and
My brother Eteocles. When they were dead,
I washed them and prepared them for the grave
With my own hands, and poured libations over them.
But now, for doing the same to Polynices,
This is my reward. Because Creon thinks
I have committed an act of brazen defiance. 770

758. Queen Persephone's kingdom, that is, Hades. Persephone was the wife of Pluto, king of the underworld, the kingdom of death.

For this I'm being dragged off by force,
Deprived of my chance to marry and raise children.
I'm to be buried alive, not very pleasant. . . .
I just want to ask, what moral law
Have I disobeyed? But what's the point
Of appealing to God? Or asking
Help from my fellow humans? It appears
That virtue is to be repaid by malice.
If that is God's idea of what is right,
780 Then I apologize; I made a mistake.
But if Creon is wrong, I only hope
He isn't treated any better than me.
Chorus. A hurricane of passionate conviction
Still sweeps her mind.
Creon. Don't stand about, you lot; or else . . .
Hurry, and off with her.
Antigone. Oh, right before me now. Death.
Chorus. If you had any hopes, I should forget them.
Your punishment is fixed. There's no appeal.
790 *Antigone.* This is it. The time has come.
For doing what was right,
I'm dragged away to death.
And Thebes, city where I was born,
And you my friends, the rich people of Thebes,
Will you judge between us?
You might at least look and remember.
Chorus. My poor child, what must be
Must be. Console yourself,
Such things have happened before.

800 There's nothing that can win the fight
Against the force of destiny;
Not wealth, or military might,
Or city walls, or ships that breast the sea.

Lycurgus, king of Thrace, tried to stop
The bacchanal women° and their torchlit orgies.
For his vindictive rage,
He lost his liberty with his temper, locked
By Bacchus in a mountain cave
To let his anger simmer down.

805. bacchanal women, tempestuous votaries of Bacchus (i.e., Dionysus), usually referred to as the Maenads.

In Salmydessus on the Euxine Sea, 810
The two sons of Phineus lost their eyes.
In their stepmother's° hand, a pointed shuttle...
And their blood on her nails cried out for vengeance.

But their mother was jailed in a cavern
Under a steep mountain far away.
She was Cleopatra, the North Wind's daughter.
A god's daughter, but fate weighed her down.
(Enter Teiresias, led by a boy)
Teiresias. Councillors of Thebes, I have come,—
A man with four eyes, half of them blind...
Creon. It's old Teiresias.° What's up, old fellow? 820
Teiresias. Listen, and I will tell you. I'm no liar...
Creon. I've never suggested that. Quite the reverse.
Teiresias. By doing so, you were able to save Thebes.
Creon. True, I have found what you have said most useful.
Teiresias. Listen to me. You're on the razor's edge.
Creon. What's wrong? The way you talk gives me a turn.
Teiresias. You may think nothing's wrong. But my skill
Says differently.
I went to my accustomed place
Of augury, where there's a wide view of 830
The sky, to observe the birds. There I heard
An unprecedented din of birds, barbarous,
Confused, as though some madness stung them into
Screaming. I heard them fighting with their claws;
The noise was unmistakable, their wings
Whirring... and I felt fear. Immediately
I tried the burnt sacrifices, but
They gave no flame. Only a damp vapor
Smoldered and spat. The gall burst in the fire,
Exposing the thighbones bare of fat. 840
The boy saw all this and told it me.
Thus I interpret. These signs portend evil
For Thebes; and the trouble stems from your policy.
Why? Because our altars are polluted
By flesh brought by dogs and birds, pickings
From Polynices' corpse. Small wonder that
The gods won't accept our sacrifices.

812. stepmother's. Eidothea, second wife of Phineus, king of a Thracian kingdom, blinded and imprisoned her two stepsons and held captive their mother, Cleopatra, who, as the text says, was the daughter of Boreas, or the North Wind. ***820. Teiresias,*** one of the most famous legendary Greek prophets and seers who had lived as both male and female. He appears often in Greek literature, most notably in Homer's *Odyssey* and Sophocles' *Oedipus, the King*.

My son, I ask you to consider well
What you are doing. We all make mistakes.
850 The wise man, having made an error of judgment,
Will seek a remedy, not keep grinding on.
Obstinacy isn't far removed from folly.
The man is dead. No need to persecute him.
You can give way, with good grace, to a corpse.
He has died once, why try to kill him again?
I'm saying this because I wish you well.
A bit of sound advice is always welcome.

Creon. Money! Must everyone set their cap at me
Because of money? Even you augurers
860 Have formed a corporation to exploit me.
For years now I have been traded about
By your gang in the open market like
A piece of merchandise. All right, rake in
The cash, pile up the wealth of Lydia
And all the gold of India in bribes.
You'll never persuade me to bury that corpse.
Not even if the eagles of Zeus decide
To carry off its flesh in their claws
And place it right on their master's throne.
870 I refuse for the simple reason that
It's quite impossible for any man
To throw pollution on the gods. They are
Inviolate. But certain gifted men
That I could mention do not seem to mind
A little sharp practice, in the matter
Of telling a lie or two, strictly for cash.

Teiresias. Well!
Can there exist a man who doesn't know . . .

Creon. Watch out, here comes another resounding cliché!

880 *Teiresias.* . . . Good sense is a man's most precious attibute?

Creon. And bad judgment is a great encumbrance?

Teiresias. It's an encumbrance you have plenty of.

Creon. . . . No.
You started it, but I won't insult a "seer."

Teiresias. You've done that already,—accused me of lying.

Creon. The whole lot of you seers are on the make.

Teiresias. Kings also have been known to make their pile.

Creon. Are you implying some reflection on me?

Teiresias. You wouldn't be king now, but for me.

890 *Creon.* You're good at your job. But you've gone crooked.

Teiresias. Much more of this, and you'll make me reveal . . .

Creon. Reveal away. But straight, and not for bribes.

Teiresias. You'll wish you had bribed me not to speak . . .
Creon. Don't try to pull the wool over my eyes.
Teiresias. The sun won't run its course for many days
Before you have to repay a corpse of your own,
One of your own children as recompense.
One body that belongs to this world
You have locked up in a tomb. Another body
That rightly should be in the underworld 900
You have forcibly retained here on earth.
Because of this, the Furies° have been waiting
To pay you back in your own coin. And so
It won't be long before your house is full
Of grief; I can see men and women crying.
Make up your own mind whether I've been bribed
To say this. Yes, it hurts. But you provoked me.
My boy, take me home. I'm not so young,—
I dare not be around when he explodes.
I only hope he learns from this to show 910
A little sense and keep a civil tongue.
Chorus. That was a horrible prophecy.
I'm bound to say I've never known him wrong
In any of his predictions.
Creon. Yes, I know,
I know. I can't pretend that I'm not worried.
The consequences of giving in are terrible.
But if I hold out, I court disaster.
Chorus. The right decision now is vitally important.
Creon. What should I do then? Tell me what to do.
Chorus. You'll have to go and set Antigone free, 920
And give the exposed corpse a burial.
Creon. Is that your real opinion? To give in?
Chorus. And waste no time about it, for the wrath
Of God will not be slow to catch you up.
Creon. Can't fight against what's destined. It is hard,
But I'll change my mind. You servants,—
Pick-axes, hurry, and come with me. I must
Personally undo what I have done.
I shouldn't have tried being unorthodox.
I'll stick by the established laws in the future. 930
Chorus. We call on Bacchus, god of many names,
And god of many places.
You were once a little child

902. *Furies,* three frightening female spirits, often called the Erinyes or Eumenides, who mercilessly sought justice for unavenged crimes.

In Thebes here, the darling of your mother's eye.
Your father was Zeus, lord of the thundering sky;
But your mother was Semele, a Theban girl.

Are you among the rich cities
Of Italy? Or presiding
Over the cosmopolitan crowds
940 That throng the Eleusinian Games?°

Perhaps the firebrand lights your face
Between the twin peaks of Mount Parnassus,°
Where the nymphs of Castaly
And Corycus walk free.

Perhaps you hear the songs of poets
Where the ivy wreathes the crags
On Nysa,° looking over green
Vineyards clustering on the plain.

But this is your home,—the oil-like waters
950 Of Ismene River,° and the fields
Where the dragon's teeth were sown.
This is your mother city, Thebes.
This is the city you honor most.
If ever you heard us before, come to us now.
Our nation is in the grip of a dread disease.
Hasten to help us, speed to doctor our pain
Over the slopes of Parnes Hill° or over the roaring seas.
Messenger. Citizens of Thebes, who knows how long
Their luck will last? Whether you're up or down,
960 It's all pure chance. You can't predict what's coming.
Take Creon now. I thought he was doing well,—
The savior of his country, king of Thebes,
And the proud father of a lovely family.
He's lost the lot. Oh, yes, he's wealthy still;
But wealth can't buy you happiness. What's the use
Of money without the means of enjoying it?

940. Eleusinian Games, secret religious fertility rituals celebrated every spring at Eleusis, a city northwest of Athens. Initiates were assured of a happy existence in the after life. ***942. Mount Parnassus,*** a mountain in central Greece sacred to Apollo and the Muses. Castaly is a river on the mountain; Corycus, a cave and grove at its foot; both were sacred places. ***947. Nysa,*** a mountain where Bacchus spent his early life before going to Thebes. The exact location is unknown, since various mountains were called Nysa, notably in Thrace and Lydia. ***950. Ismene River,*** a river winding through Thebes. ***957. Parnes Hill,*** a mountain range beginning in northwest Attica and merging with Mt. Cythaeron in Boeotia.

His wealth's no more to him than a puff of smoke.
You can't say Creon lives; he's just a walking corpse.
Chorus. About Creon's family, is there bad news then?
Messenger. They're dead. And those that live deserve to die. 970
Chorus. How did they die? Who's dead? Why can't you tell me?
Messenger. Haemon is dead. Committed suicide.
Chorus. He killed himself? His father didn't do it?
Messenger. Suicide, because Creon had murdered her.
Chorus. Teiresias' prophecy was all too true.
Messenger. That's what has happened. Now it's up to you.
Chorus. Here is Eurydice, Creon's wife, poor woman.
Why is she coming out? Perhaps she's heard. . . .
Eurydice. As I was going out, I heard you talking.
I was opening the door when I heard it, 980
Some more bad news about my children. I fainted,
But my maids held me up. Tell me about it.
I am quite used to suffering.
Messenger. I'll tell you everything, my dear mistress.
I was there, you know. No sense in glossing things over;
You've got to hear it sometime.
I went with my master, your husband, to the place
Where Polynices' corpse was exposed,
Cruelly torn by dogs. We said prayers
Placating Hecate° and Pluto; then we washed 990
The body to purify it, gathered branches
Of olive, and cremated him or what
Was left of him. We piled him up a mound
Of his mother-earth; then went to get
Antigone. While we were on the way,
Somebody heard a sound of crying coming
From the stone chamber. He went up to Creon
And told him of it. Creon hurried on.
As we got near, the sound was all around us,—
Impossible to tell whose it was. 1000
But Creon, in a voice breaking with grief,
Said, "Dare I prophesy? These yards of ground
Will prove the bitterest journey of my life.
It's faint, but it's my son's voice. Hurry, men,
Get round the tomb, pull back the stones, and look
Inside. Is it Haemon's voice, or do the gods
Delude me?" At the far end of the tomb
We saw Antigone hanging by the neck

990. Hecate, a powerful goddess of the underworld.

In a noose of linen. He was hugging her
1010 And talking bitterly of their marriage and
His father's action. Creon saw him and
Cried out and ran in, shouting, "Oh my son,
What is this? What possessed you? Why are you trying
To kill yourself? Come out now, please, I beg you."
His son made no reply, just looked at him
Savagely with a look of deep contempt.
Then he suddenly drew his sword, evaded Creon,
Held it out, and plunged the blade into his ribs.
He collapsed against Antigone's arms which were
1020 Still warm, and hugged her. Then his blood came coughing,
And covered all her white cheeks with scarlet.
So now he lies, one corpse upon another;
And thus their marriage is consummated,—in hell.
It only goes to show good sense is best,
When all this tragedy comes from one rash action.

Chorus. What a strange thing. Eurydice has gone,
Without saying a word.

Messenger. It is surprising.
I dare say she's too well-bred to go
Showing her grief in public. I expect
1030 She's gone to have a good cry inside.

Chorus. Perhaps. Noisy grief is a bad thing.
But this extraordinary silence is ominous.

Messenger. You're right. Let's go in then, and find out.
She may have had her mind on something rash.

Chorus. Who's coming? Creon with
The body of his son.
If truth be told, he is
Himself the murderer.

Creon. Wrong! How could I have been so wrong?
1040 And these deaths I caused—you have seen them—
In my own family by my stubbornness.
Oh my son, so young, to die so young,
And all because of me!

Chorus. It's a bit late to find out you were wrong.

Creon. I know that. God has taken his revenge,
Leapt on my head and beaten me
And trampled on the only joy I had.
And all the years that I have labored—wasted.

Servant. My lord, what you see before your eyes,—
1050 It isn't all. You'd better come inside.

Creon. What fresh disaster could I suffer now?

Servant. Your wife, the mother of this corpse is dead.
Only a moment ago, she stabbed herself.
Creon. Oh death, can I never wash it away?
Why are you destroying me? What
Is your message now? Why stab me again?
My wife dead too?
Servant. See for yourself. They've brought the body out.
Creon. Oh.
Another blow. What else has fate in store? 1060
My wife, my son.
Servant. Stabbed herself by the altar, and so passed on.
But first she bewailed Megareus' death,
Her first son, that was; then Haemon's death.
And her last words were curses on your head.
Creon. Now I'm afraid. Why wasn't I killed?
Why didn't somebody kill me, stab me to death?
Servant. Before she died she made a point of planting
The guilt of these two deaths squarely on you.
Creon. How did she die? How did she kill herself? 1070
Servant. I told you. Stabbed herself. Under the heart.
Soon as she heard about her son's death.
Creon. Nobody else to share the blame. Just me . . .
I killed you. I killed you, my dear.
Servants, carry me in, away from all this.
I wish I weren't alive.
Chorus. Try to forget it. It is the only way.
Creon. I invite Death. Do you only come uninvited?
Come and take me. I cannot bear to live.
Chorus. No time for such thoughts now. You're still in charge. 1080
You've got to see about these corpses, or
We'll all be polluted.
Creon. I meant what I said.
Chorus. No use in such prayers. You'll get what's destined.
Creon. Lead me away, a wreck, a useless wreck.
I'll keep out of the way. I killed them both.
Everything has crumbled. I feel
A huge weight on my head.
Chorus. Who wants happiness? The main
Requirement is to be sensible.
This means not rebelling against 1090
God's law, for that is arrogance.
The greater your arrogance, the heavier God's revenge.
All old men have learned to be sensible;
But their juniors will not take the lesson as proved.

Comments and Questions

There are no villains in this tragedy. Antigone acts out of love for her brother and her faith that she is right in God's eyes. Creon acts out of devotion to the state, thinking only of its welfare and glory. Once Antigone and the King are in conflict, there is no turning back or giving in, though Creon does relent when it is too late. But theirs is a deeper and more poignant conflict than one between defenders of God and the state. In light of the terrifying consequences of their struggle, they truly show themselves to be members of the same proud and doomed family. In their stubbornness and pride they are alike, for they both act alone, rejecting all help or advice from those who love them. But there is an important difference between them. Creon loses control, defending his position at the expense of reason, for he will not "be shoved around by a woman" or a mere child like Haemon. At the end, he can only condemn himself as a "useless wreck," destined to live in lonely misery. Antigone, as she is led off to her living tomb "to join [her] *stricken family in hell," understandably bemoans her fate but achieves dignity in her womanly realization that she has "not used* [her] *life's full span" and has been denied marriage and children, and in her leaving the elders with the haunting question, "Will you judge between us?" Unlike Creon, she understands herself, is willing to leave her fate to the gods she defends, and can still proudly claim respect from the Chorus for her dying alone, "the victim of an unjust law." The Chorus has earlier told her she is paying the price of her father's sins, and Creon has alleged she glories in her crime. To what extent are these explanations accurate?*

The use of the Chorus is one convention of the Greek stage that is unfamiliar to modern audiences. Greek drama began as a religious ritual in choric dances and chants. In time, one member stepped out to speak, then two, and finally, with Sophocles, three, each assuming a number of roles. Typically, the Chorus performed several functions, such as singer of religious songs or odes, sometimes designed to indicate the passage of time between scenes; it acts as collective spokesman for the author or the townspeople, or both. Various playwrights used the Chorus differently. Euripides, for example, used it mostly for incidental songs between scenes, while Sophocles makes full dramatic use of it. In Antigone *the songs or odes between scenes both directly and indirectly relate to the issues in the play. One of the most famous passages in Sophocles is the choric ode beginning "Many amazing things exist, and the most amazing is man" (p. 496). The singing of this gives time for the guard to leave and return with Antigone, but in what other ways is it related to the action or theme of the play? Most importantly, in* Antigone *the Chorus serves as a character in the play, acting as a single voice to represent the elders of Thebes and to remind the characters of established moral and religious truths. In this role, the Chorus has to be evaluated much like the other characters in the play. Do you notice any shift in its responses to the actions of Antigone and Creon? Do some of its remarks seem trite or superficially conventional? Do its comments, and especially its final judgments on Antigone and Creon, adequately explain the full significance of the play's action?*

The extensive use of messengers is another convention of ancient Greek drama. Their basic functions are to save time by bringing news from places other than the single setting characteristic in Greek plays, and, in deference to another convention of the time, to avoid representing scenes of horror, like suicides and murders, on stage. Observe, though, that Sophocles' messengers are not mere reporters but have personalities of their own. The comic guard in the early scenes is the prototype of a long line of functional minor characters who bring comic relief in tragedies, the most famous perhaps being the drunken porter in Shakespeare's Macbeth.

Related Reading

Jean Anouilh, *Antigone*, page 520
Maxwell Anderson, "The Essence of Tragedy," page 663
Raymond Williams, "*Antigone* by Sophocles," page 652

Jean Anouilh

(1910-   )

ANTIGONE

translated by Lewis Galantière

From Corneille and Racine in the seventeenth century to Giraudoux, Cocteau, Sartre, and Anouilh in the twentieth, French playwrights have been drawn to ancient Greek drama, particularly to the tragedies. Anouilh, one of the finest contemporary French dramatists, has been notably successful in using Greek tragic myths to explore imaginatively the moral and philosophical predicament of modern man. In his plays Eurydice, Medea, Antigone, *and the fragment* Orestes, *all written in the early nineteen-forties, Anouilh re-created the Greek models along the lines of his own tragic vision. Perhaps the most remarkable of these is Antigone, which was written in 1942, when there seemed no end to the German victories in World War II. France was occupied territory and the collaborationist Vichy government tried hard to make Frenchmen say "Yes" to life—King Creon's phrase in the play—or at least to their German overlords. Surprisingly, the play was passed by the German censor and had its first performance in Paris in February, 1944. The audience had no doubts about the topical meaning of Antigone's valiant opposition to the repressive measures Creon takes in the name of public order and safety. The play ran for five hundred performances under the Nazis and, after a brief interruption, in the liberated city.*

Anouilh probably went as far as he dared by giving the play a contemporary setting, a Thebes with automobiles and night clubs, and actors wearing simple evening clothes. Though he denied having any political intentions in the play, he could not have been blind to its implications or to the fact that his audience would be almost as unified in their political, as the ancient Greek audience had been in their religious, emotions.

The major problems in adapting classical tragedy in this century are that going to the theater is no longer a part of religious ritual, and that there is no longer a universal faith in heavenly powers against which man can test his fate. Today man seems to struggle against a fragmented and diminished world of the spirit, and because Anouilh and many of his contemporaries are acutely aware of man's spiritual condition, usually defined as one of loneliness and alienation under the threat of annihilation, they have had, so to speak, to write tragedies without God.

In the France of the nineteen-forties, Anouilh might have felt it necessary to turn to the Greek tragic myths as a kind of symbolic veil for his subjects, which, if told directly, would certainly have been suppressed. But looking beneath the surface of his Antigone *and reading it now, separated from the charged atmosphere in which it was first produced, we can see that his concerns are more philosophical than political, and that he achieved a remarkable approximation of the possibilities of Sophoclean tragedy on the modern stage.*

ANTIGONE

Characters

CHORUS
ANTIGONE
NURSE
ISMENE
HAEMON
CREON
FIRST GUARD *(Jonas)*
SECOND GUARD *(a Corporal)*
THIRD GUARD
MESSENGER
PAGE
EURYDICE

(Antigone, her hands clasped round her knees, sits on the top step. The Three Guards sit on the steps, in a small group, playing cards. The Chorus stands on the top step. Eurydice sits on the top step, just left of center, knitting. The Nurse sits on the second step, left of Eurydice. Ismene stands in front of arch, left, facing Haemon, who stands left of her. Creon sits in the chair at right end of the table, his arm over the shoulder of his Page who sits on the stool beside his chair. The Messenger is leaning against the downstage portal of the right arch. The curtain rises slowly; then the Chorus turns and moves downstage.)

Chorus. Well, here we are.

These people are about to act out for you the story of Antigone.

That thin little creature sitting by herself, staring straight ahead, seeing nothing, is Antigone. She is thinking. She is thinking that the instant I finish telling you who's who and what's what in this play, she will burst forth as the tense, sallow, willful girl whose family would never take her seriously and who is about to rise up alone against Creon, her uncle, the King.

Another thing that she is thinking is this: she is going to die. Antigone is young. She would much rather live than die. But there is no help for it. When your name is Antigone, there is only one part you can play; and she will have to play hers through to the end.

From the moment the curtain went up, she began to feel that inhuman forces were whirling her out of this world, snatching her away from her sister Ismene, whom you see smiling and chatting with that young man; from all of us who sit or stand here, looking at her, not in the least upset ourselves—for we are not doomed to die tonight. *(Chorus turns and indicates Haemon.)*

The young man talking to Ismene—to the gay and beautiful Ismene —is Haemon. He is the King's son, Creon's son. Antigone and he are engaged to be married. You wouldn't have thought she was his type. He likes dancing, sports, competition; he likes women, too. Now look at Ismene again. She is certainly more beautiful than Antigone. She is the girl you'd think he'd go for. Well . . . there was a ball one night. Ismene wore a new evening frock. She was radiant. Haemon danced every dance with her. And yet, that same night, before the dance was over, suddenly he went in search of Antigone, found her sitting alone —like that, with her arms clasped round her knees—and asked her to marry him. We still don't know how it happened. It didn't seem to surprise Antigone in the least. She looked up at him out of those solemn eyes of hers, smiled sort of sadly and said "yes." That was all. The band struck up another dance. Ismene, surrounded by a group of young men, laughed out loud. And . . . well, here is Haemon expecting to marry Antigone. He won't, of course. He didn't know, when he asked her, that the earth wasn't meant to hold a husband of Antigone, and that this princely distinction was to earn him no more than the right to die sooner than he might otherwise have done. *(Chorus turns toward Creon.)*

That gray-haired, powerfully built man sitting lost in thought, with his little page at his side, is Creon, the King. His face is lined. He is tired. He practices the difficult art of a leader of men. When he was younger, when Oedipus was King and Creon was no more than the King's brother-in-law, he was different. He loved music, bought rare manuscripts, was a kind of art patron. He would while away whole afternoons in the antique shops of this city of Thebes. But Oedipus died. Oedipus' sons died. Creon had to roll up his sleeves and take over the kingdom. Now and then, when he goes to bed weary with the day's work, he wonders whether this business of being a leader of men is worth the trouble. But when he wakes up, the problems are there to be solved; and like a conscientious workman, he does his job.

Creon has a wife, a Queen. Her name is Eurydice. There she sits, the old lady with the knitting, next to the Nurse who brought up the two girls. She will go on knitting all through the play, till the time comes for her to go to her room and die. She is a good woman, a worthy, loving soul. But she is no help to her husband. Creon has to face the music alone. Alone with his Page, who is too young to be of any help.

The others? Well, let's see. *(He points toward the Messenger.)*

That pale young man leaning against the wall is the Messenger. Later on he will come running in to announce that Haemon is dead. He has a premonition of catastrophe. That's what he is brooding over. That's why he won't mingle with the others.

As for those three red-faced card players—they are the guards. One smells of garlic, another of beer; but they're not a bad lot. They have wives they are afraid of, kids who are afraid of them; they're bothered by the little day-to-day worries that beset us all. At the same time—they are policemen: eternally innocent, no matter what crimes are committed; eternally indifferent, for nothing that happens can matter to them. They are quite prepared to arrest anybody at all, including Creon himself, should the order be given by a new leader.

70 That's the lot. Now for the play.

Oedipus, who was the father of the two girls, Antigone and Ismene, had also two sons, Eteocles and Polynices. After Oedipus died, it was agreed that the two sons should share his throne, each to reign over Thebes in alternate years. *(Gradually, the lights on the stage have been dimmed.)*

But when Eteocles, the elder son, had reigned a full year, and time had come for him to step down, he refused to yield up the throne to his younger brother. There was civil war. Polynices brought up allies—six foreign princes; and in the course of the war he and his foreigners 80 were defeated, each in front of one of the seven gates of the city. The two brothers fought, and they killed one another in single combat just outside the city walls. Now Creon is King. *(Chorus is leaning, at this point, against the left proscenium arch. By now the stage is dark, with only the cyclorama bathed in dark blue. A single spot lights up the face of Chorus.)*

Creon has issued a solemn edict that Eteocles, with whom he had sided, is to be buried with pomp and honours, and that Polynices is to be left to rot. The vultures and the dogs are to bloat themselves on his carcass. Nobody is to go into mourning for him. No gravestone is to be 90 set up in his memory. And above all, any person who attempts to give him religious burial will himself be put to death. *(While Chorus has been speaking, the characters have gone out one by one. Chorus disappears through the left arch.)*

(It is dawn, gray and ashen, in a house asleep. Antigone steals in from out-of-doors, through the arch, right. She is carrying her sandals in her hand. She pauses, looking off through the arch, taut, listening, then turns and moves across downstage. As she reaches the table, she sees the Nurse approaching through the arch, left. She runs quickly toward the exit. As she reaches the steps, the Nurse enters through arch and 100 *stands still when she sees Antigone.)*

Nurse. Where have you been?

Antigone. Nowhere. It was beautiful. The whole world was gray when I went out. And now—you wouldn't recognize it. It's like a post card: all pink, and green, and yellow. You'll have to get up earlier, Nurse, if you want to see a world without color.

Nurse. It was still pitch black when I got up. I went to your room, for I thought you might have flung off your blanket in the night. You weren't there.

Antigone. (Comes down the steps) The garden was lovely. It was still asleep. Have you ever thought how lovely a garden is when it is not yet thinking of men? 110

Nurse. You hadn't slept in your bed. I couldn't find you. I went to the back door. You'd left it open.

Antigone. The fields were wet. They were waiting for something to happen. The whole world was breathless, waiting. I can't tell you what a roaring noise I seemed to make alone on the road. It bothered me that whatever was waiting wasn't waiting for me. I took off my sandals and slipped into a field. *(She moves down to the stool and sits.)*

Nurse. (Kneels at Antigone's feet to chafe them and put on the sandals) You'll do well to wash your feet before you go back to bed, Miss. 120

Antigone. I'm not going back to bed.

Nurse. Don't be a fool! You get some sleep! And me, getting up to see if she hasn't flung off her blanket; and I find her bed cold and nobody in it!

Antigone. Do you think that if a person got up every morning like this, it would be just as thrilling every morning to be the first girl out-of-doors? *(Nurse puts Antigone's left foot down, lifts her other foot and chafes it.)*

Nurse. Morning my grandmother! It was night. It still is. And now, my girl, you'll stop trying to squirm out of this and tell me what you were up to. Where've you been? 130

Antigone. That's true. It was still night. There wasn't a soul out of doors but me, who thought that it was morning. Don't you think it's marvelous—to be the first person who is aware that it is morning?

Nurse. Oh, my little flibbertigibbet! Just can't imagine what I'm talking about, can she? Go on with you! I know that game. Where have you been, wicked girl?

Antigone. (Soberly) No. Not wicked.

Nurse. You went out to meet someone, didn't you? Deny it if you can.

Antigone. Yes. I went out to meet someone. 140

Nurse. A lover?

Antigone. Yes, Nurse. Yes, the poor dear. I have a lover.

Nurse. (Stands up; bursting out) Ah, that's very nice now, isn't it? Such goings on! You, the daughter of a king, running out to meet lovers. And we work our fingers to the bone for you, we slave to bring you up like young ladies! *(She sits on chair, right of table.)* You're all alike, all of you. Even you—who never used to stop to primp in front of a looking glass, or smear your mouth with rouge, or dindle and dandle to make the boys ogle you, and you ogle back. How many times I'd say to myself, "Now that one, now: I wish she was a little more of a coquette—always wearing the same dress, her hair tumbling round her face. One thing's sure," I'd say to myself, "none of the boys will look at her while Ismene's about, all curled and cute and tidy and trim. 150

I'll have this one on my hands for the rest of my life." And now, you see? Just like your sister, after all. Only worse: a hypocrite. Who is the lad? Some little scamp, eh? Somebody you can't bring home and show to your family, and say, "Well, this is him, and I mean to marry him and no other." That's how it is, is it? Answer me!

Antigone. (Smiling faintly) That's how it is. Yes, Nurse.

160 *Nurse.* Yes, says she! God save us! I took her when she wasn't that high. I promised her poor mother I'd make a lady of her. And look at her! But don't you go thinking this is the end of this, my young'un. I'm only your nurse and you can play deaf and dumb with me; I don't count. But your Uncle Creon will hear of this! That, I promise you.

Antigone. (A little weary) Yes. Creon will hear of this.

Nurse. And we'll hear what he has to say when he finds out that you go wandering alone o' nights. Not to mention Haemon. For the girl's engaged! Going to be married! Going to be married, and she hops out of bed at four in the morning to meet somebody else in a field. Do you 170 know what I ought to do to you? Take you over my knee the way I used to do when you were little.

Antigone. Please, Nurse, I want to be alone.

Nurse. And if you so much as speak of it, she says she wants to be alone!

Antigone. Nanny, you shouldn't scold, dear. This isn't a day when you should be losing your temper.

Nurse. Not scold, indeed! Along with the rest of it, I'm to like it. Didn't I promise your mother? What would she say if she was here? "Old Stupid!" That's what she'd call me. "Old Stupid. Not to know how 180 to keep my little girl pure! Spend your life making them behave, watching over them like a mother hen, running after them with mufflers and sweaters to keep them warm, and eggnogs to make them strong; and then at four o'clock in the morning, you who always complained you never could sleep a wink, snoring in your bed and letting them slip out into the bushes." That's what she'd say, your mother. And I'd stand there, dying of shame if I wasn't dead already. And all I could do would be not to dare look her in the face; and "That's true," I'd say. "That's all true what you say, Your Majesty."

Antigone. Nanny, dear. Dear Nanny. Don't cry. You'll be able to 190 look Mamma in the face when it's your time to see her. And she'll say, "Good morning, Nanny. Thank you for my little Antigone. You did look after her so well." She knows why I went out this morning.

Nurse. Not to meet a lover?

Antigone. No. Not to meet a lover.

Nurse. Well, you've a queer way of teasing me, I must say! Not to know when she's teasing me! *(Rises to stand behind Antigone)* I must be getting awfully old, that's what it is. But if you loved me, you'd tell me the truth. You'd tell me why your bed was empty when I went along to tuck you in. Wouldn't you?

Antigone. Please, Nanny, don't cry any more. *(Antigone turns partly toward Nurse, puts an arm up to Nurse's shoulder. With her other hand, Antigone caresses Nurse's face.)* There now, my sweet red apple. Do you remember how I used to rub your cheeks to make them shine? My dear, wrinkled red apple! I didn't do anything tonight that was worth sending tears down the little gullies of your dear face. I am pure, and I swear that I have no other lover than Haemon. If you like, I'll swear that I shall never have any other lover than Haemon. Save your tears, Nanny, save them, Nanny dear; you may still need them. When you cry like that, I become a little girl again; and I mustn't be a little girl today. *(Antigone rises and moves upstage.)* 200 210

(Ismene enters through arch, left. She pauses in front of arch.)

Ismene. Antigone! What are you doing up at this hour? I've just been to your room.

Nurse. The two of you, now! You're both going mad, to be up before the kitchen fire has been started. Do you like running about without a mouthful of breakfast? Do you think it's decent for the daughters of a king? *(She turns to Ismene.)* And look at you, with nothing on, and the sun not up! I'll have you both on my hands with colds before I know it.

Antigone. Nanny dear, go away now. It's not chilly, really. Summer's here. Go and make us some coffee. Please, Nanny, I'd love some coffee. It would do me so much good. 220

Nurse. My poor baby! Her head's swimming, what with nothing on her stomach, and me standing here like an idiot when I could be getting her something hot to drink. *(Exit Nurse)*

(A pause)

Ismene. Aren't you well?

Antigone. Of course I am. Just a little tired. I got up too early. *(Antigone sits on a chair, suddenly tired.)*

Ismene. I couldn't sleep, either. 230

Antigone. Ismene, you ought not to go without your beauty sleep.

Ismene. Don't make fun of me.

Antigone. I'm not, Ismene, truly. This particular morning, seeing how beautiful you are makes everything easier for me. Wasn't I a miserable little beast when we were small? I used to fling mud at you, and put worms down your neck. I remember tying you to a tree and cutting off your hair. Your beautiful hair! How easy it must be never to be unreasonable with all that smooth silken hair so beautifully set round your head.

Ismene. *(Abruptly)* Why do you insist upon talking about other things? 240

Antigone. (Gently) I am not talking about other things.

Ismene. Antigone, I've thought about it a lot.

Antigone. Have you?

Ismene. I thought about it all night long. Antigone, you're mad.

Antigone. Am I?

Ismene. We cannot do it.

Antigone. Why not?

Ismene. Creon will have us put to death.

250 *Antigone.* Of course he will. That's what he's here for. He will do what he has to do, and we will do what we have to do. He is bound to put us to death. We are bound to go out and bury our brother. That's the way it is. What do you think we can do to change it.

Ismene. (Releases Antigone's hand; draws back a step) I don't want to die.

Antigone. I'd prefer not to die, myself.

Ismene. Listen to me, Antigone. I thought about it all night. I'm older than you are. I always think things over, and you don't. You are impulsive. You get a notion in your head and you jump up and do the thing
260 straight off. And if it's silly, well, so much the worse for you. Whereas, *I* think things out.

Antigone. Sometimes it is better not to think too much.

Ismene. I don't agree with you! *(Antigone looks at Ismene, then turns and moves to chair behind table. Ismene leans on end of table top, toward Antigone.)* Oh, I know it's horrible. And I pity Polynices just as much as you do. But all the same, I sort of see what Uncle Creon means.

Antigone. I don't want to "sort of see" anything.

Ismene. Uncle Creon is the king. He has to set an example!

270 *Antigone.* But I am not the king; and I don't have to set people examples. Little Antigone gets a notion in her head—the nasty brat, the willful, wicked girl; and they put her in a corner all day, or they lock her up in the cellar. And she deserves it. She shouldn't have disobeyed!

Ismene. There you go, frowning, glowering, wanting your own stubborn way in everything. Listen to me. I'm right oftener than you are.

Antigone. I don't want to be right!

Ismene. At least you can try to understand.

Antigone. Understand! The first word I ever heard out of any of you
280 was that word "understand." Why didn't I "understand" that I must not play with water—cold, black, beautiful flowing water—because I'd spill it on the palace tiles. Or with earth, because earth dirties a little girl's frock. Why didn't I "understand" that nice children don't eat out of every dish at once; or give everything in their pockets to beggars; or run in the wind so fast that they fall down; or ask for a

drink when they're perspiring; or want to go swimming when it's either too early or too late, merely because they happen to feel like swimming. Understand! I don't want to understand. There'll be time enough to understand when I'm old. . . . If I ever *am* old. But not now.

Ismene. He is stronger than we are, Antigone. He is the king. And 290 the whole city is with him. Thousands and thousands of them, swarming through all the streets of Thebes.

Antigone. I am not listening to you.

Ismene. His mob will come running, howling as it runs. A thousand arms will seize our arms. A thousand breaths will breathe into our faces. Like one single pair of eyes, a thousand eyes will stare at us. We'll be driven in a tumbrel through their hatred, through the smell of them and their cruel, roaring laughter. We'll be dragged to the scaffold for torture, surrounded by guards with their idiot faces all bloated, their animal hands clean-washed for the sacrifice, their 300 beefy eyes squinting as they stare at us. And we'll know that no shrieking and no begging will make them understand that we want to live, for they are like slaves who do exactly as they've been told, without caring about right or wrong. And we shall suffer, we shall feel pain rising in us until it becomes so unbearable that we *know* it must stop. But it won't stop; it will go on rising and rising, like a screaming voice. Oh, I can't, I can't, Antigone! *(A pause)*

Antigone. How well have you thought it all out.

Ismene. I thought of it all night long. Didn't you?

Antigone. Oh, yes. 310

Ismene. I'm an awful coward, Antigone.

Antigone. So am I. But what has that to do with it?

Ismene. But, Antigone! Don't you want to go on living?

Antigone. Go on living! Who was it that was always the first out of bed because she loved the touch of the cold morning air on her bare skin? Who was always the last to bed because nothing less than infinite weariness could wean her from the lingering night? Who wept when she was little because there were too many grasses in the meadow, too many creatures in the field, for her to know and touch them all?

Ismene. (Clasps Antigone's hands, in a sudden rush of tenderness) 320 Darling little sister!

Antigone. (Repulsing her) No! For heaven's sake! Don't paw me! And don't let us start sniveling! You say you've thought it all out. The howling mob—the torture—the fear of death. . . . They've made up your mind for you. Is that it?

Ismene. Yes.

Antigone. All right. They're as good excuses as any.

Ismene. Antigone, be sensible. It's all very well for men to believe in ideas and die for them. But you are a girl!

330 *Antigone.* Don't I know I'm a girl? Haven't I spent my life cursing the fact that I was a girl?

Ismene. (With spirit) Antigone! You have everything in the world to make you happy. All you have to do is reach out for it. You are going to be married; you are young; you are beautiful—

Antigone. I am not beautiful.

Ismene. Yes, you are! Not the way other girls are. But it's always you that the little boys turn to look back at when they pass us in the street. And when you go by, the little girls stop talking. They stare and stare at you, until we've turned a corner.

340 *Antigone. (A faint smile)* "Little boys—little girls."

Ismene. (Challengingly) And what about Haemon? *(A pause)*

Antigone. I shall see Haemon this morning. I'll take care of Haemon. You always said I was mad; and it didn't matter how little I was or what I wanted to do. Go back to bed now, Ismene. The sun is coming up, and, as you see, there is nothing I can do today. Our brother Polynices is as well guarded as if he had won the war and were sitting on his throne. Go along. You are pale with weariness.

Ismene. What are you going to do?

Nurse. (Calls from off-stage) Come along, my dove. Come to break-
350 fast.

Antigone. I don't feel like going to bed. However, if you like, I'll promise not to leave the house till you wake up. Nurse is getting me breakfast. Go and get some sleep. The sun is just up. Look at you: you can't keep your eyes open. Go.

Ismene. And you will listen to reason, won't you? You'll let me talk to you about this again? Promise?

Antigone. I promise. I'll let you talk. I'll let all of you talk. Go to bed, now. *(Ismene goes to arch; exit)*
Poor Ismene!

360 *Nurse. (Enters through arch, speaking as she enters)* Come along, my dove. I've made you some coffee and toast and jam. *(She turns towards arch as if to go out.)*

Antigone. I'm not really hungry. Nurse. *(Nurse stops, looks at Antigone, then moves behind her.)*

Nurse. (Very tenderly) Where is your pain?

Antigone. Nowhere, Nanny dear. But you must keep me warm and safe, the way you used to do when I was little. Nanny! Stronger than all fever, stronger than any nightmare, stronger than the shadow of the cupboard that used to snarl at me and turn into a dragon on the bedroom
370 wall. Stronger than the thousand insects gnawing and nibbling in the silence of the night. Stronger than the night itself, with the weird hooting of the night birds that frightened me even when I couldn't hear them. Nanny, stronger than death. Give me your hand, Nanny, as if I were ill in bed, and you sitting beside me.

Nurse. My sparrow, my lamb! What is it that's eating your heart out?

Antigone. Oh, it's just that I'm a little young still for what I have to go through. But nobody but you must know that.

Nurse. (Places her other arm around Antigone's shoulder) A little young for what, my kitten? 380

Antigone. Nothing in particular, Nanny. Just—all this. Oh, it's so good that you are here. I can hold your callused hand, your hand that is so prompt to ward off evil. You are very powerful, Nanny.

Nurse. What is it you want me to do for you, my baby?

Antigone. There isn't anything to do, except put your hand like this against my cheek. *(She places the Nurse's hand against her cheek. A pause, then, as Antigone leans back, her eyes shut.)* There! I'm not afraid any more. Not afraid of the wicked ogre, nor of the sandman, nor of the dwarf who steals little children. *(A pause. Antigone resumes on another note.)* Nanny . . . 390

Nurse. Yes?

Antigone. My dog, Puff . . .

Nurse. (Straightens up, draws her hand away) Well?

Antigone. Promise me that you will never scold her again.

Nurse. Dogs that dirty up a house with their filthy paws deserve to be scolded.

Antigone. I know. Just the same, promise me.

Nurse. You mean you want me to let her make a mess all over the place and not say a thing?

Antigone. Yes, Nanny. 400

Nurse. You're asking a lot. The next time she wets my living-room carpet, I'll—

Antigone. Please, Nanny, I beg of you!

Nurse. It isn't fair to take me on my weak side, just because you look a little peaked today. . . . Well, have it your own way. We'll mop up and keep our mouth shut. You're making a fool of me, though.

Antigone. And promise me that you will talk to her. That you will talk to her often.

Nurse. (Turns and looks at Antigone) Me, talk to a dog!

Antigone. Yes. But mind you: you are not to talk to her the way 410 people usually talk to dogs. You're to talk to her the way I talk to her.

Nurse. I don't see why both of us have to make fools of ourselves. So long as you're here, one ought to be enough.

Antigone. But if there was a reason why I couldn't go on talking to her—

Nurse. (Interrupting) Couldn't go on talking to her! And why couldn't you go on talking to her? What kind of poppycock—?

Antigone. And if she got too unhappy, if she moaned and moaned, waiting for me with her nose under the door as she does when I'm

420 out all day, then the best thing, Nanny, might be to have her mercifully put to sleep.

Nurse. Now what *has* got into you this morning?

(Haemon enters through arch.)

Running around in the darkness, won't sleep, won't eat—*(Antigone sees Haemon.)*—and now it's her dog she wants killed. I never.

Antigone. (Interrupting) Nanny! Haemon is here. Go inside, please. And don't forget that you've promised me.

(Nurse goes to arch; exit. Antigone rises.)

Haemon, Haemon! Forgive me for quarreling with you last night.
430 *(She crosses quickly to Haemon and they embrace.)* Forgive me for everything. It was all my fault. I beg you to forgive me.

Haemon. You know that I've forgiven you. You had hardly slammed the door, your perfume still hung in the room, when I had already forgiven you. *(He holds her in his arms and smiles at her. Then draws slightly back)* You stole that perfume. From whom?

Antigone. Ismene.

Haemon. And the rouge? and the face powder? and the frock? Whom did you steal them from?

Antigone. Ismene.

440 *Haemon.* And in whose honor did you get yourself up so elegantly?

Antigone. I'll tell you everything. *(She draws him closer.)* Oh, darling, what a fool I was! To waste a whole evening! A whole, beautiful evening!

Haemon. We'll have other evenings, my sweet.

Antigone. Perhaps we won't.

Haemon. And other quarrels, too. A happy love is full of quarrels, you know.

Antigone. A happy love, yes. Haemon, listen to me.

Haemon. Yes?

Antigone. Don't laugh at me this morning. Be serious.

450 *Haemon.* I am serious.

Antigone. And hold me tight. Tighter than you have ever held me. I want all your strength to flow into me.

Haemon. There! With all my strength. *(A pause)*

Antigone. (Breathless) That's good. *(They stand for a moment, silent and motionless.)* Haemon! I wanted to tell you. You know—the little boy we were going to have when we were married?

Haemon. Yes?

Antigone. I'd have protected him against everything in the world.

Haemon. Yes, dearest.

460 *Antigone.* Oh, you don't know how I should have held him in my arms and given him my strength. He wouldn't have been afraid of anything, I swear he wouldn't. Not of the falling night, nor of the terrible noonday sun, nor of all the shadows, or all the walls in the world. Our little boy,

Haemon! His mother wouldn't have been very imposing: her hair wouldn't always have been brushed; but she would have been strong where he was concerned, so much stronger than all those real mothers with their real bosoms and their aprons around their middle. You believe that, don't you, Haemon?

Haemon. (Soothingly) Yes, yes, my darling.

Antigone. And you believe me when I say that you would have had a real wife? 470

Haemon. Darling, you are my real wife.

Antigone. (Pressing against him and crying out) Haemon, you loved me! You did love me that night, didn't you? You're sure of it!

Haemon. (Rocking her gently) What night, my sweet?

Antigone. And you are very sure, aren't you, that that night, at the dance, when you came to the corner where I was sitting, there was no mistake? It was me you were looking for? It wasn't another girl? And you're sure that never, not in your most secret heart of hearts, have you said to yourself that it was Ismene you ought to have asked to marry you? 480

Haemon.(Reproachfully) Antigone, you are idiotic. You might give me credit for knowing my own mind. It's you I love, and no one else.

Antigone. But you love me as a woman—as a woman wants to be loved, don't you? Your arms around me aren't lying, are they? Your hands, so warm against my back—they're not lying? This warmth that's in me; this confidence, this sense that I am safe, secure, that flows through me as I stand here with my cheek in the hollow of your shoulder: they are not lies, are they?

Haemon. Antigone, darling, I love you exactly as you love me. With all of myself. *(They kiss.)* 490

Antigone. I'm sallow, and I'm scrawny. Ismene is pink and golden. She's like a fruit.

Haemon. Look here, Antigone—

Antigone. Ah, dearest, I am ashamed of myself. But this morning, this special morning, I must know. Tell me the truth! I beg you to tell me the truth! When you think about me, when it strikes you suddenly that I am going to belong to you—do you have the feeling that—that a great empty space is being hollowed out inside you, that there is something inside you that is just—dying? 500

Haemon. Yes, I do, I do. *(A pause)*

Antigone. That's the way I feel. And another thing. I wanted you to know that I should have been very proud to be your wife—the woman whose shoulder you would put your hand on as you sat down to table, absentmindedly, as upon a thing that belonged to you. *(After a moment, draws away from him. Her tone changes.)* There! Now I have two things more to tell you. And when I have told them to you, you must go away instantly, without asking any questions. However strange they may seem to you. However much they may hurt you. Swear that you will!

510 *Haemon. (Beginning to be troubled)* What are these things that you are going to tell me?

Antigone. Swear, first, that you will go away without one word. Without so much as looking at me. *(She looks at him, wretchedness in her face.)* You hear me, Haemon. Swear it, please. This is the last mad wish that you will ever have to grant me. *(A pause)*

Haemon. I swear it, since you insist. But I must tell you that I don't like this at all.

Antigone. Please, Haemon. It's very serious. You must listen to me and do as I ask. First, about last night, when I came to your house.
520 You asked me a moment ago why I wore Ismene's dress and rouge. It was because I was stupid. I wasn't very sure that you loved me as a woman; and I did it—because I wanted you to want me. I was trying to be more like other girls.

Haemon. Was *that* the reason? My poor . . .

Antigone. Yes. And you laughed at me. And we quarreled; and my awful temper got the better of me and I flung out of the house. . . . The real reason was that I wanted you to take me; I wanted to be your wife before—

Haemon. Oh, my darling—

530 *Antigone. (Shuts him off)* You swore you wouldn't ask any questions. You swore, Haemon. *(Turns her face away and goes on in a hard voice)* As a matter of fact, I'll tell you why. I wanted to be your wife last night because I love you that way very—very strongly. And also because —oh, my darling, my darling, forgive me; I'm going to cause you quite a lot of pain. *(She draws away from him.)* I wanted it also because I shall never, never be able to marry you, never! *(Haemon is stupefied and mute; then he moves a step towards her.)* Haemon! You took a solemn oath! You swore! Leave me quickly! Tomorrow the whole thing will be clear to you. Even before tomorrow: this afternoon. If you
540 please, Haemon, go now. It is the only thing left that you can do for me if you still love me. *(A pause as Haemon stares at her. Then he turns and goes out through the arch. Antigone stands motionless, then moves to a chair at end of table and lets herself gently down on it. In a mild voice, as of calm after storm)* Well, it's over for Haemon, Antigone. *(Ismene enters through arch, pauses for a moment in front of it when she sees Antigone, then crosses behind table.)*

Ismene. I can't sleep. I'm terrified. I'm so afraid that, even though it is daylight, you'll still try to bury Polynices. Antigone, little sister, we all want to make you happy—Haemon, and Nurse, and I, and Puff
550 whom you love. We love you, we are alive, we need you. And you remember what Polynices was like. He was our brother, of course. But

he's dead; and he never loved you. He was a bad brother. He was like an enemy in the house. He never thought of you. Why should you think of him? What if his soul does have to wander through endless time without rest or peace? Don't try something that is beyond your strength. You are always defying the world, but you're only a girl, after all. Stay at home tonight. Don't try to do it, I beg you. It's Creon's doing, not ours.

Antigone. You are too late, Ismene. When you first saw me this morning, I had just come in from burying him. 560

(Exit Antigone through arch)

(The lighting, which by this time has reached a point of early morning sun, is quickly dimmed out, leaving the stage bathed in a light blue color. Ismene runs out after Antigone. On Ismene's exit the lights are brought up suddenly to suggest a later period of the day. Creon and Page enter through curtain upstage. Creon stands on the top step; his Page stands at his right side.)

Creon. A private of the guards, you say? One of those standing watch over the body? Show him in.

(The Page crosses to arch; exit. Creon moves down to end of table. 570 *Page re-enters, preceded by the First Guard, livid with fear. Page remains on upstage side of arch. Guard salutes.)*

Guard. Private Jonas, Second Battalion.

Creon. What are you doing here?

Guard. It's like this, sir. Soon as it happened, we said: "Got to tell the chief about this before anybody else spills it. He'll want to know right away." So we tossed a coin to see which one would come up and tell you about it. You see, sir, we thought only one man had better come, because, after all, you don't want to leave the body without a guard. Right? I mean, there's three of us on duty, guarding the body. 580

Creon. What's wrong about the body?

Guard. Sir, I've been seventeen years in the service. Volunteer. Wounded three times. Two mentions. My record's clean. I know my business and I know my place. I carry out orders. Sir, ask any officer in the battalion; they'll tell you. "Leave it to Jonas. Give him an order: he'll carry it out." That's what they'll tell you, sir. Jonas, that's me —that's my name.

Creon. What's the matter with you, man? What are you shaking for?

Guard. By rights it's the corporal's job, sir. I've been recommended for a corporal, but they haven't put it through yet. June, it was supposed 590 to go through.

Creon. (Interrupts) Stop chattering and tell me why you are here. If anything has gone wrong, I'll break all three of you.

Guard. Nobody can say we didn't keep our eye on that body. We had the two-o'clock watch—the tough one. You know how it is, sir. It's

nearly the end of the night. Your eyes are like lead. You've got a crick in the back of your neck. There's shadows, and the fog is beginning to roll in. A fine watch they give us! And me, seventeen years in the service. But we was doing our duty all right. On our feet, all of us. Any-
600 body says we were sleeping is a liar. First place, it was too cold. Second place—*(Creon makes a gesture of impatience.)* Yes, sir. Well, I turned around and looked at the body. We wasn't only ten feet away from it, but that's how I am. I was keeping my eye on it. *(Shouts)* Listen, sir, I was the first man to see it! Me! They'll tell you. I was the one let out that yell!

Creon. What for? What was the matter?

Guard. Sir, the body! Somebody had been there and buried it. *(Creon comes down a step on the stair. The Guard becomes more frightened.)* It wasn't much, you understand. With us three there, it couldn't have
610 been. Just covered over with a little dirt, that's all. But enough to hide it from the buzzards.

Creon. By God, I'll—! *(He looks intently at the Guard.)* You are sure that it couldn't have been a dog, scratching up the earth?

Guard. Not a chance, sir. That's kind of what we hoped it was. But the earth was scattered over the body just like the priests tell you you should do it. Whoever did that job knew what he was doing, all right.

Creon. Who could have dared? *(He turns and looks at the Guard.)* Was there anything to indicate who might have done it?

Guard. Not a thing, sir. Maybe we heard a footstep—I can't swear
620 to it. Of course we started right in to search, and the corporal found a shovel, a kid's shovel no bigger than that, all rusty and everything. Corporal's got the shovel for you. We thought maybe a kid did it.

Creon. (To himself) A kid! *(He looks away from the Guard.)* I broke the back of the rebellion; but like a snake, it is coming together again. Polynices' friends, with their gold, blocked by my orders in the banks of Thebes. The leaders of the mob, stinking of garlic and allied to envious princes. And the temple priests, always ready for a bit of fishing in troubled waters. A kid! I can imagine what he is like, their kid: a baby-faced killer, creeping in the night with a toy shovel under his jacket.
630 *(He looks at his Page.)* Though why shouldn't they have corrupted a real child? Very touching! Very useful to the party, an innocent child. A martyr. A real white-faced baby of fourteen who will spit with contempt at the guards who kill him. A free gift to their cause: the precious, innocent blood of a child on my hands. *(He turns to the Guard.)* They must have accomplices in the Guard itself. Look here, you. Who knows about this?

Guard. Only us three, sir. We flipped a coin, and I came right over.

Creon. Right. Listen, now. You will continue on duty. When the relief squad comes up, you will tell them to return to barracks. You will

uncover the body. If another attempt is made to bury it, I shall expect 640
you to make an arrest and bring the person straight to me. And you will keep your mouths shut. Not one word of this to a human soul. You are all guilty of neglect of duty, and you will be punished; but if the rumor spreads through Thebes that the body received burial, you will be shot—all three of you.

Guard. (Excitedly) Sir, we never told nobody, I swear we didn't! Anyhow, I've been up here. Suppose my pals spilled it to the relief; I couldn't have been with them and here too. That wouldn't be my fault if they talked. Sir, I've got two kids. You're my witness, sir, it couldn't have been me. I was here with you. I've got a witness! If 650
anybody talked, it couldn't have been me! I was—

Creon. (Interrupting) Clear out! If the story doesn't get around, you won't be shot. *(The Guard salutes, turns, and exits at the double. Creon turns and paces upstage, then comes down to end of the table.)* A child! *(He looks at Page.)* Come along, my lad. Since we can't hope to keep this to ourselves, we shall have to be the first to give out the news. And after that, we shall have to clean up the mess. *(Page crosses to side of Creon. Creon puts his hand on Page's shoulder.)* Would you be willing to die for me? Would you defy the Guard with your little shovel? *(Page looks up at Creon.)* Of course you would. You would do it, too. 660
(A pause. Creon looks away from Page and murmurs.) A child! *(Creon and Page go slowly upstage center to top step. Page draws aside the curtain, through which exit Creon with Page behind him.)*

(As soon as Creon and Page have disappeared, Chorus enters and leans against the upstage portal or arch, left. The lighting is brought up to its brightest point to suggest mid-afternoon. Chorus allows a pause to indicate that a crucial moment has been reached in the play, then moves slowly downstage, center. He stands for a moment silent, reflecting, and then smiles faintly.)

Chorus. The spring is wound up tight. It will uncoil of itself. That 670
is what is so convenient in tragedy. The least little turn of the wrist will do the job. Anything will set it going: a glance at a girl who happens to be lifting her arms to her hair as you go by; a feeling when you wake up on a fine morning that you'd like a little respect paid to you today, as if it were as easy to order as a second cup of coffee; one question too many, idly thrown out over a friendly drink—and the tragedy is on.

The rest is automatic. You don't need to lift a finger. The machine is in perfect order; it has been oiled ever since time began, and it runs without friction. Death, treason, and sorrow are on the march; and they move in the wake of storm, of tears, of stillness. Every kind of stillness. 680
The hush when the executioner's ax goes up at the end of the last act. The unbreathable silence when, at the beginning of the play, the two lovers, their hearts bared, their bodies naked, stand for the first time

face to face in the darkened room, afraid to stir. The silence inside you when the roaring crowd acclaims the winner—so that you think of a film without a sound track, mouths agape and no sound coming out of them, a clamor that is no more than a picture; and you, the victor, already vanquished, alone in the desert of your silence. That is tragedy.

Tragedy is clean, it is restful, it is flawless. It has nothing to do with melodrama—with wicked villains, persecuted maidens, avengers, sudden revelations, and eleventh-hour repentances. Death, in a melo-
690 drama, is really horrible because it is never inevitable. The dear old father might so easily have been saved; the honest young man might so easily have brought in the police five minutes earlier.

In a tragedy, nothing is in doubt and everyone's destiny is known. That makes for tranquillity. There is a sort of fellow-feeling among characters in a tragedy: he who kills is as innocent as he who gets killed: it's all a matter of what part you are playing. Tragedy is restful; and the reason is that hope, that foul, deceitful thing, has no part
700 in it. There isn't any hope. You're trapped. The whole sky has fallen on you, and all you can do about it is to shout.

Don't mistake me: I said "shout": I did not say groan, whimper, complain. That, you cannot do. But you can shout aloud; you can get all those things said that you never thought you'd be able to say—or never even knew you had it in you to say. And you don't say these things because it will do any good to say them: you know better than that. You say them for their own sake; you say them because you learn a lot from them.

In melodrama you argue and struggle in the hope of escape. That
710 is vulgar; it's practical. But in tragedy, where there is no temptation to try to escape, argument is gratuitous: it's kingly. *(Voices of the Guards and scuffling sound heard through the archway. Chorus looks in that direction; then, in a changed tone:)*

The play is on. Antigone has been caught. For the first time in her life, little Antigone is going to be able to be herself.

(Exit Chorus through arch. A pause, while the offstage voices rise in volume, then the First Guard enters, followed by Second and Third Guards, holding the arms of Antigone and dragging her along. The First Guard, speaking as he enters, crosses swiftly to end of the table.
720 *The Two Guards and Antigone stop downstage.)*

First Guard. (Recovered from his fright) Come on, now, Miss, give it a rest. The chief will be here in a minute and you can tell him about it. All I know is my orders. I don't want to know what you were doing there. People always have excuses; but I can't afford to listen to them, see. Why, if we had to listen to all the people who want to tell us what's the matter with this country, we'd never get our work done. *(To the Guards)* You keep hold of her and I'll see that she keeps her face shut.

Antigone. They are hurting me. Tell them to take their dirty hands off me. 730

First Guard. Dirty hands, eh? The least you can do is try to be polite, Miss. Look at me: I'm polite.

Antigone. Tell them to let me go. I shan't run away. My father was King Oedipus. I am Antigone.

First Guard. King Oedipus' little girl! Well, well, well! Listen, Miss, the night watch never picks up a lady but they say, you better be careful: I'm sleeping with the police commissioner. *(The Guards laugh.)*

Antigone. I don't mind being killed, but I don't want them to touch me.

First Guard. And what about stiffs, and dirt, and such like? You 740 wasn't afraid to touch them, was you? "Their dirty hands!" Take a look at your own hands. *(Antigone, handcuffed, smiles despite herself as she looks down at her hands. They are grubby.)* You must have lost your shovel, didn't you? Had to go at it with your fingernails the second time, I'll bet. By God, I never saw such nerve! I turn my back for about five seconds; I ask a pal for a chew; I say "thanks"; I get the tobacco stowed away in my cheek—the whole thing don't take ten seconds; and there she is, clawing away like a hyena. Right out in broad daylight! And did she scratch and kick when I grabbed her! Straight for my eyes with them nails she went. And yelling something fierce about, "I 750 haven't finished yet; let me finish!" She ain't got all her marbles!

Second Guard. I pinched a nut like that the other day. Right on the main square she was, hoisting up her skirts and showing her behind to anybody that wanted to take a look.

First Guard. Listen, we're going to get a bonus out of this. What do you say we throw a party, the three of us?

Second Guard. At the old woman's? Behind Market Street?

Third Guard. Suits me. Sunday would be a good day. We're off duty Sunday. What do you say we bring our wives?

First Guard. No. Let's have some fun this time. Bring your wife, 760 there's always something goes wrong. First place, what do you do with the kids? Bring them, they always want to go to the can just when you're right in the middle of a game of cards or something. Listen, who would have thought an hour ago that us three would be talking about throwing a party now? The way I felt when the old man was interrogating me, we'd be lucky if we got off with being docked a month's pay. I want to tell you, I was scared.

Second Guard. You sure we're going to get a bonus?

First Guard. Yes. Something tells me this is big stuff.

Third Guard. (To Second Guard) What's-his-name, you know—in 770 the Third Battalion? He got an extra month's pay for catching a firebug.

Second Guard. If we get an extra month's pay, I vote we throw the party at the Arabian's.

First Guard. You're crazy! He charges twice as much for liquor as anybody else in town. Unless you want to go upstairs, of course. Can't do that at the old woman's.

Third Guard. Well, we can't keep this from our wives, no matter how you work it out. You get an extra month's pay, and what happens? Everybody in the battalion knows it, and your wife knows it too. They might even line up the battalion and give it to you in front of everybody, so how could you keep your wife from finding out?

First Guard. Well, we'll see about that. If they do the job out in the barrack yard—of course that means women, kids, everything.

Antigone. I should like to sit down, if you please. *(A pause, as the First Guard thinks it over.)*

First Guard. Let her sit down. But keep hold of her. *(The two Guards start to lead her toward the chair at end of table. The curtain upstage opens, and Creon enters, followed by his Page. First Guard turns and moves upstage a few steps, sees Creon.)* 'Tenshun! *(The three Guards salute. Creon, seeing Antigone handcuffed to Third Guard, stops on the top step, astonished.)*

Creon. Antigone! *(To the First Guard)* Take off those handcuffs! *(First Guard crosses above table to left of Antigone.)* What is this? *(Creon and his Page come down off the steps.)*

(First Guard takes key from his pocket and unlocks the cuff on Antigone's hand. Antigone rubs her wrist as she crosses below table toward chair at end of table. Second and Third Guards step back to front of arch. First Guard turns upstage toward Creon.)

First Guard. The watch, sir. We all came this time.

Creon. Who is guarding the body?

First Guard. We sent for the relief. *(Creon comes down.)*

Creon. But I gave orders that the relief was to go back to barracks and stay there! *(Antigone sits on chair at left of table.)* I told you not to open your mouth about this!

First Guard. Nobody's said anything, sir. We made this arrest, and brought the party in, the way you said we should.

Creon. *(To Antigone)* Where did these men find you?

First Guard. Right by the body.

Creon. What were you doing near your brother's body? You knew what my orders were.

First Guard. What was she doing? Sir, that's why we brought her in. She was digging up the dirt with her nails. She was trying to cover up the body all over again.

Creon. Do you realize what you are saying?

First Guard. Sir, ask these men here. After I reported to you, I went back, and first thing we did, we uncovered the body. The sun was coming up and it was beginning to smell, so we moved it up on a little rise to get him in the wind. Of course, you wouldn't expect any trouble in broad daylight. But just the same, we decided one of us had better keep his eye peeled all the time. About noon, what with the 820 sun and the smell, and as the wind dropped and I wasn't feeling none too good, I went over to my pal to get a chew. I just had time to say "thanks" and stick it in my mouth, when I turned round and there she was, clawing away at the dirt with both hands. Right out in broad daylight! Wouldn't you think when she saw me come running she'd stop and leg it out of there? Not her! She went right on digging as fast as she could, as if I wasn't there at all. And when I grabbed her, she scratched and bit and yelled to leave her alone, she hadn't finished yet, the body wasn't all covered yet, and the like of that.

Creon. (To Antigone) Is this true? 830

Antigone. Yes, it is true.

First Guard. We scraped the dirt off as fast as we could, then we sent for the relief and we posted them. But we didn't tell them a thing, sir. And we brought in the party so's you could see her. And that's the truth, so help me God.

Creon. (To Antigone) And was it you who covered the body the first time? In the night?

Antigone. Yes, it was. With a toy shovel we used to take to the seashore when we were children. It was Polynices' own shovel; he had cut his name in the handle. That was why I left it with him. But these men 840 took it away; so the next time, I had to do it with my hands.

First Guard. Sir, she was clawing away like a wild animal. Matter of fact, first minute we saw her, what with the heat haze and everything, my pal says, "That must be a dog," he says. "Dog!" I says, "that's a girl, that is!" And it was.

Creon. Very well. *(Turns to the Page)* Show these men to the anteroom. *(The Page crosses to the arch, stands there, waiting. Creon moves behind the table. To the First Guard)* You three men will wait outside. I may want a report from you later.

First Guard. Do I put the cuffs back on her, sir? 850

Creon. No. *(The three Guards salute, do an about-turn, and exeunt through arch, right. Page follows them out. A pause)* Had you told anybody what you meant to do?

Antigone. No.

Creon. Did you meet anyone on your way—coming or going?

Antigone. No, nobody.

Creon. Sure of that, are you?

Antigone. Perfectly sure.

Creon. Very well. Now listen to me. You will go straight to your room. When you get there, you will go to bed. You will say that you 860 are not well and that you have not been out since yesterday. Your nurse will tell the same story. *(He looks toward arch, through which the Guards have gone out.)* And I'll get rid of those three men.

Antigone. Uncle Creon, you are going to a lot of trouble for no good reason. You must know that I'll do it all over again tonight. *(A pause. They look one another in the eye.)*

Creon. Why did you try to bury your brother?

Antigone. I owed it to him.

Creon. I had forbidden it.

870 *Antigone.* I owed it to him. Those who are not buried wander eternally and find no rest. If my brother were alive, and he came home weary after a long day's hunting, I should kneel down and unlace his boots, I should fetch him food and drink, I should see that his bed was ready for him. Polynices is home from the hunt. I owe it to him to unlock the house of the dead in which my father and my mother are waiting to welcome him. Polynices has earned his rest.

Creon. Polynices was a rebel and a traitor, and you know it.

Antigone. He was my brother.

Creon. You heard my edict. It was proclaimed throughout Thebes.

880 You read my edict. It was posted up on the city walls.

Antigone. Of course I did.

Creon. You knew the punishment I decreed for any person who attempted to give him burial.

Antigone. Yes, I knew the punishment.

Creon. Did you by any chance act on the assumption that a daughter of Oedipus, a daughter of Oedipus' stubborn pride, was above the law?

Antigone. No, I did not act on that assumption.

Creon. Because if you had acted on that assumption, Antigone, you would have been deeply wrong. Nobody has a more sacred obligation

890 to obey the law than those who make the law. You are a daughter of lawmakers, a daughter of kings, Antigone. You must observe the law.

Antigone. Had I been a scullery maid washing my dishes when that law was read aloud to me, I should have scrubbed the greasy water from my arms and gone out in my apron to bury my brother.

Creon. What nonsense! If you had been a scullery maid, there would have been no doubt in your mind about the seriousness of that edict. You would have known that it meant death; and you would have been satisfied to weep for your brother in your kitchen. But you! You thought that because you come of the royal line, because you were my niece

900 and were going to marry my son, I shouldn't dare have you killed.

Antigone. You are mistaken. Quite the contrary. I never doubted for an instant that you would have me put to death. *(A pause, as Creon stares fixedly at her)*

Creon. The pride of Oedipus! Oedipus and his headstrong pride all over again. I can see your father in you—and I believe you. Of course you thought that I should have you killed! Proud as you are, it seemed to you a natural climax in your existence. Your father was like that. For him as for you human happiness was meaningless; and mere human misery was not enough to satisfy his passion for torment. *(He sits on stool behind the table.)* You come of people for whom the human vestment is a kind of straitjacket: it cracks at the seams. You spend your lives wriggling to get out of it. Nothing less than a cosy tea party with death and destiny will quench your thirst. The happiest hour of your father's life came when he listened greedily to the story of how, unknown to himself, he had killed his own father and dishonored the bed of his own mother. Drop by drop, word by word, he drank in the dark story that the gods had destined him first to live and then to hear. How avidly men and women drink the brew of such a tale when their names are Oedipus—and Antigone! And it is so simple, afterwards, to do what your father did, to put out one's eyes and take one's daughter begging on the highways. 910 920

Let me tell you, Antigone: those days are over for Thebes. Thebes has a right to a king without a past. My name, thank God, is only Creon. I stand here with both feet firm on the ground; with both hands in my pockets; and I have decided that so long as I am king—being less ambitious than your father was—I shall merely devote myself to introducing a little order into this absurd kingdom; if that is possible.

Don't think that being a king seems to me romantic. It is my trade; a trade a man has to work at every day; and like every other trade, it isn't all beer and skittles. But since it is my trade, I take it seriously. And if, tomorrow, some wild and bearded messenger walks in from some wild and distant valley—which is what happened to your dad—and tells me that he's not quite sure who my parents were, but thinks that my wife Eurydice is actually my mother, I shall ask him to do me the kindness to go back where he came from; and I shan't let a little matter like that persuade me to order my wife to take a blood test and the police to let me know whether or not my birth certificate was forged. Kings, my girl, have other things to do than to surrender themselves to their private feelings. *(He looks at her and smiles.)* Hand you over to be killed! *(He rises, moves to end of table and sits on the top of table.)* I have other plans for you. You're going to marry Haemon; and I want you to fatten up a bit so that you can give him a sturdy boy. Let me assure you that Thebes needs that boy a good deal more than it needs your death. You will go to your room, now, and do as you have been told; and you won't say a word about this to anybody. Don't fret about the guards: I'll see that their mouths are shut. And don't annihilate me with those eyes. I know that you think I am a brute, and I'm sure you must consider me very prosaic. But the fact is, I have always been fond of you, stubborn though you always were. Don't forget that 930 940

950 the first doll you ever had came from me. *(A pause. Antigone says nothing, rises, and crosses slowly below the table toward the arch. Creon turns and watches her; then)* Where are you going?

Antigone. (Stops downstage. Without any show of rebellion) You know very well where I am going.

Creon. (After a pause) What sort of game are you playing?

Antigone. I am not playing games.

Creon. Antigone, do you realize that if, apart from those three guards, a single soul finds out what you have tried to do, it will be impossible for me to avoid putting you to death? There is still a chance 960 that I can save you; but only if you keep this to yourself and give up your crazy purpose. Five minutes more, and it will be too late. You understand that?

Antigone. I must go and bury my brother. Those men uncovered him.

Creon. What good will it do? You know that there are other men standing guard over Polynices. And even if you did cover him over with earth again, the earth would again be removed.

Antigone. I know all that. I know it. But that much, at least, I can do. And what a person can do, a person ought to do. *(Pause)*

970 *Creon.* Tell me, Antigone, do you believe all that flummery about religious burial? Do you really believe that a so-called shade of your brother is condemned to wander for ever homeless if a little earth is not flung on his corpse to the accompaniment of some priestly abracadabra? Have you ever listened to the priests of Thebes when they were mumbling their formula? Have you ever watched those dreary bureaucrats while they were preparing the dead for burial—skipping half the gestures required by the ritual, swallowing half their words, hustling the dead into their graves out of fear that they might be late for lunch?

Antigone. Yes, I have seen all that.

980 *Creon.* And did you never say to yourself as you watched them, that if someone you really loved lay dead under the shuffling, mumbling ministrations of the priests, you would scream aloud and beg the priests to leave the dead in peace?

Antigone. Yes, I've thought all that.

Creon. And you still insist upon being put to death—merely because I refuse to let your brother go out with that grotesque passport; because I refuse his body the wretched consolation of that mass-production jibber-jabber, which you would have been the first to be embarrassed by if I had allowed it. The whole thing is absurd!

990 *Antigone.* Yes, it's absurd.

Creon. Then why, Antigone, why? For whose sake? For the sake of them that believe in it? To raise them against me?

Antigone. No.

Creon. For whom then if not for them and not for Polynices either?

Antigone. For nobody. For myself. *(A pause as they stand looking at one another)*

Creon. You must want very much to die. You look like a trapped animal.

Antigone. Stop feeling sorry for me. Do as I do. Do your job. But if you are a human being, do it quickly. That is all I ask of you. I'm not going to be able to hold out for ever. 1000

Creon. (Takes a step toward her) I want to save you, Antigone.

Antigone. You are the king, and you are all-powerful. But that you cannot do.

Creon. You think not?

Antigone. Neither save me nor stop me.

Creon. Prideful Antigone! Little Oedipus!

Antigone. Only this can you do: have me put to death.

Creon. Have you tortured, perhaps?

Antigone. Why would you do that? To see me cry? To hear me beg for mercy? Or swear whatever you wish, and then begin over again? *(A pause)* 1010

Creon. You listen to me. You have cast me for the villain in this little play of yours, and yourself for the heroine. And you know it, you damned little mischief-maker! But don't you drive me too far! If I were one of your preposterous little tyrants that Greece is full of, you would be lying in a ditch this minute with your tongue pulled out and your body drawn and quartered. But you can see something in my face that makes me hesitate to send for the guards and turn you over to them. Instead, I let you go on arguing; and you taunt me, you take the offensive. *(He grasps her left wrist.)* What are you driving at, you she devil? 1020

Antigone. Let me go. You are hurting my arm.

Creon. (Gripping her tighter) I will not let you go.

Antigone. (Moans) Oh!

Creon. I was a fool to waste words. I should have done this from the beginning. *(He looks at her.)* I may be your uncle—but we are not a particularly affectionate family. Are we, eh? *(Through his teeth, as he twists)* Are we? *(Creon propels Antigone round below him to his side.)* What fun for you, eh? To be able to spit in the face of a king who has all the power in the world; a man who has done his own killing in his day; who has killed people just as pitiable as you are—and who is still soft enough to go to all this trouble in order to keep you from being killed. *(A pause)* 1030

Antigone. Now you are squeezing my arm too tightly. It doesn't hurt any more. *(Creon stares at her, then drops her arm.)*

Creon. I shall save you yet. *(He goes below the table to the chair at end of table, takes off his coat, and places it on the chair.)* God knows, I have things enough to do today without wasting my time on an insect

1040 like you. There's plenty to do, I assure you, when you've just put down a revolution. But urgent things can wait. I am not going to let politics be the cause of your death. For it is a fact that this whole business is nothing but politics: the mournful shade of Polynices, the decomposing corpse, the sentimental weeping, and the hysteria that you mistake for heroism—nothing but politics.

Look here. I may not be soft, but I'm fastidious. I like things clean, shipshape, well scrubbed. Don't think that I am not just as offended as you are by the thought of that meat rotting in the sun. In the evening, when the breeze comes in off the sea, you can smell it in the palace, 1050 and it nauseates me. But I refuse even to shut my window. It's vile; and I can tell you what I wouldn't tell anybody else: it's stupid, monstrously stupid. But the people of Thebes have got to have their noses rubbed into it a little longer. My God! If it was up to me, I should have had them bury your brother long ago as a mere matter of public hygiene. I admit that what I am doing is childish. But if the featherheaded rabble I govern are to understand what's what, that stench has got to fill the town for a month!

Antigone. (Turns to him) You are a loathsome man!

Creon. I agree. My trade forces me to be. We could argue whether 1060 I ought or ought not to follow my trade; but once I take on the job, I must do it properly.

Antigone. Why do you do it at all?

Creon. My dear, I woke up one morning and found myself King of Thebes. God knows, there were other things I loved in life more than power.

Antigone. Then you should have said no.

Creon. Yes, I could have done that. Only, I felt that it would have been cowardly. I should have been like a workman who turns down a job that has to be done. So I said yes.

1070 *Antigone.* So much the worse for you, then. I didn't say yes. I can say no to anything I think vile, and I don't have to count the cost. But because you said yes, all that you can do, for all your crown and your trappings, and your guards—all that you can do is to have me killed.

Creon. Listen to me.

Antigone. If I want to. I don't have to listen to you if I don't want to. You've said your *yes.* There is nothing more you can tell me that I don't know. You stand there, drinking in my words. *(She moves behind chair.)* Why is it that you don't call your guards? I'll tell you why. You want to hear me out to the end; that's why.

1080 *Creon.* You amuse me.

Antigone. Oh, no, I don't. I frighten you. That is why you talk about saving me. Everything would be so much easier if you had a docile, tongue-tied little Antigone living in the palace. I'll tell you something,

Uncle Creon: I'll give you back one of your own words. You are too fastidious to make a good tyrant. But you are going to have to put me to death today, and you know it. And that's what frightens you. God! Is there anything uglier than a frightened man!

Creon. Very well. I am afraid, then. Does that satisfy you? I am afraid that if you insist upon it, I shall have to have you killed. And I don't want to. 1090

Antigone. I don't have to do things that I think are wrong. If it comes to that, you didn't really want to leave my brother's body unburied, did you? Say it! Admit that you didn't.

Creon. I have said it already.

Antigone. But you did it just the same. And now, though you don't want to do it, you are going to have me killed. And you call that being a king!

Creon. Yes, I call that being a king.

Antigone. Poor Creon! My nails are broken, my fingers are bleeding, my arms are covered with the welts left by the paws of your guards— 1100 but I am a queen!

Creon. Then why not have pity on me, and live? Isn't your brother's corpse, rotting there under my windows, payment enough for peace and order in Thebes? My son loves you. Don't make me add your life to the payment. I've paid enough.

Antigone. No, Creon! You said yes, and made yourself king. Now you will never stop paying.

Creon. But God in heaven! Won't you try to understand me! I'm trying hard enough to understand you! There had to be one man who said yes. Somebody had to agree to captain the ship. She had sprung 1110 a hundred leaks; she was loaded to the water line with crime, ignorance, poverty. The wheel was swinging with the wind. The crew refused to work and were looting the cargo. The officers were building a raft, ready to slip overboard and desert the ship. The mast was splitting, the wind was howling, the sails were beginning to rip. Every man jack on board was about to drown—and only because the only thing they thought of was their own skins and their cheap little day-to-day traffic. Was that a time, do you think, for playing with words like yes and no? Was that a time for a man to be weighing the pros and cons, wondering if he wasn't going to pay too dearly later on; if he wasn't going to lose 1120 his life, or his family, or his touch with other men? You grab the wheel, you right the ship in the face of a mountain of water. You shout an order, and if one man refuses to obey, you shoot straight into the mob. Into the mob, I say! The beast as nameless as the wave that crashes down upon your deck; as nameless as the whipping wind. The thing that drops when you shoot may be someone who poured you a drink the night before; but it has no name. And you, braced at the wheel, you have no name, either. Nothing has a name—except the ship, and the storm. *(A pause as he looks at her)* Now do you understand?

1130 *Antigone.* I am not here to understand. That's all very well for you. I am here to say no to you, and die.

Creon. It is easy to say no.

Antigone. Not always.

Creon. It is easy to say no. To say yes, you have to sweat and roll up your sleeves and plunge both hands into life up to the elbows. It is easy to say no, even if saying no means death. All you have to do is to sit still and wait. Wait to go on living; wait to be killed. That is the coward's part. *No* is one of your man-made words. Can you imagine a world in which trees say *no* to the sap? In which beasts say *no* to 1140 hunger or to propagation? Animals are good, simple, tough. They move in droves, nudging one another onwards, all traveling the same road. Some of them keel over, but the rest go on; and no matter how many may fall by the wayside, there are always those few left that go on bringing their young into the world, traveling the same road with the same obstinate will, unchanged from those who went before.

Antigone. Animals, eh, Creon! What a king you could be if only men were animals! *(A pause. Creon turns and looks at her.)*

Creon. You despise me, don't you? *(Antigone is silent. Creon goes on, as if to himself.)* Strange. Again and again, I have imagined my-1150 self holding this conversation with a pale young man I have never seen in the flesh. He would have come to assassinate me, and would have failed. I would be trying to find out from him why he wanted to kill me. But with all my logic and all my powers of debate, the only thing I could get out of him would be that he despised me. Who would have thought that the white-faced boy would turn out to be you? And that the debate would arise out of something so meaningless as the burial of your brother?

Antigone. (Repeats contemptuously) Meaningless!

Creon. (Earnestly, almost desperately) And yet, you must hear me 1160 out. My part is not an heroic one, but I shall play my part. I shall have you put to death. Only, before I do, I want to make one last appeal. I want to be sure that you know what you are doing as well as I know what I am doing. Antigone, do you know what you are dying for? Do you know the sordid story to which you are going to sign your name in blood, for all time to come?

Antigone. What story?

Creon. The story of Eteocles and Polynices, the story of your brothers. You think you know it, but you don't. Nobody in Thebes knows that story but me. And it seems to me, this afternoon, that you have a right 1170 to know it too. *(A pause as Antigone moves to chair and sits)* It's not a pretty story. *(He turns, gets stool from behind the table and places it between the table and the chair.)* You'll see. *(He looks at her for a moment.)* Tell me, first. What do you remember about your brothers? They were older than you, so they must have looked down on you. And I imagine that they tormented you—pulled your pigtails, broke your dolls, whispered secrets to each other to put you in a rage.

Antigone. They were big and I was little.

Creon. And later on, when they came home wearing evening clothes, smoking cigarettes, they would have nothing to do with you; and you thought they were wonderful. 1180

Antigone. They were boys and I was a girl.

Creon. You didn't know why, exactly, but you knew that they were making your mother unhappy. You saw her in tears over them; and your father would fly into a rage because of them. You heard them come in, slamming doors, laughing noisily in the corridors—insolent, spineless, unruly, smelling of drink.

Antigone. (Staring outward) Once, it was very early and we had just got up. I saw them coming home, and hid behind a door. Polynices was very pale and his eyes were shining. He was so handsome in his evening clothes. He saw me, and said: "Here, this is for you"; and he 1190 gave me a big paper flower that he had brought home from his night out.

Creon. And of course you still have that flower. Last night, before you crept out, you opened a drawer and looked at it for a time, to give yourself courage.

Antigone. Who told you so?

Creon. Poor Antigone! With her night club flower. Do you know what your brother was?

Antigone. Whatever he was, I know that you will say vile things about him.

Creon. A cheap, idiotic bounder, that is what he was. A cruel, vicious 1200 little voluptuary. A little beast with just wit enough to drive a car faster and throw more money away than any of his pals. I was with your father one day when Polynices, having lost a lot of money gambling, asked him to settle the debt; and when your father refused, the boy raised his hand against him and called him a vile name.

Antigone. That's a lie!

Creon. He struck your father in the face with his fist. It was pitiful. Your father sat at his desk with his head in his hands. His nose was bleeding. He was weeping with anguish. And in a corner of your father's study, Polynices stood sneering and lighting a cigarette. 1210

Antigone. That's a lie. *(A pause)*

Creon. When did you last see Polynices alive? When you were twelve years old. *That's* true, isn't it?

Antigone. Yes, that's true.

Creon. Now you know why. Oedipus was too chicken-hearted to have the boy locked up. Polynices was allowed to go off and join the Argive army. And as soon as he reached Argos, the attempts upon your father's life began—upon the life of an old man who couldn't make up his mind to die, couldn't bear to be parted from his kingship. One 1220 after another, men slipped into Thebes from Argos for the purpose of assassinating him, and every killer we caught always ended by confessing who had put him up to it, who had paid him to try it. And it wasn't only Polynices. That is really what I am trying to tell you. I want you to know what went on in the back room, in the kitchen of politics; I want you to know what took place in the wings of this drama in which you are burning to play a part.

Yesterday, I gave Eteocles a State funeral, with pomp and honors. Today, Eteocles is a saint and a hero in the eyes of all Thebes. The whole city turned out to bury him. The schoolchildren emptied their 1230 saving boxes to buy wreaths for him. Old men, orating in quavering, hypocritical voices, glorified the virtues of the great-hearted brother, the devoted son, the loyal prince. I made a speech myself; and every temple priest was present with an appropriate show of sorrow and solemnity in his stupid face. And military honors were accorded the dead hero.

Well, what else could I have done? People had taken sides in the civil war. Both sides couldn't be wrong; that would be too much. I couldn't have made them swallow the truth. Two gangsters was more of a luxury than I could afford. *(He pauses for a moment.)* And this is 1240 the whole point of my story. Eteocles, that virtuous brother, was just as rotten as Polynices. That great-hearted son had done his best, too, to procure the assassination of his father. That loyal prince had also offered to sell out Thebes to the highest bidder.

Funny, isn't it? Polynices lies rotting in the sun while Eteocles is given a hero's funeral and will be housed in a marble vault. Yet I have absolute proof that everything that Polynices did, Eteocles had plotted to do. They were a pair of blackguards—both engaged in selling out Thebes, and both engaged in selling out each other; and they died like the cheap gangsters they were, over a division of the spoils.

1250 But, as I told you a moment ago, I had to make a martyr of one of them. I sent out to the holocaust for their bodies; they were found clasped in one another's arms—for the first time in their lives, I imagine. Each had been spitted on the other's sword, and the Argive cavalry had trampled them down. They were mashed to a pulp, Antigone. I had the prettier of the two carcasses brought in and gave it a State funeral; and I left the other to rot. I don't know which was which. And I assure you, I don't care. *(Long silence, neither looking at the other)*

Antigone. (In a mild voice) Why do you tell me all this?

Creon. Would it have been better to let you die a victim to that 1260 obscene story?

Antigone. It might have been. I had my faith.

Creon. What are you going to do now?

Antigone. (Rises to her feet in a daze) I shall go up to my room.

Creon. Don't stay alone. Go and find Haemon. And get married quickly.

Antigone. (In a whisper) Yes.

Creon. All this is really beside the point. You have your whole life ahead of you—and life is a treasure.

Antigone. Yes.

Creon. And you were about to throw it away. Don't think me fatuous 1270 if I say that I understand you; and that at your age I should have done the same thing. A moment ago, when we were quarreling, you said I was drinking in your words. I was. But it wasn't you I was listening to; it was a lad named Creon who lived here in Thebes many years ago. He was thin and pale, as you are. His mind, too, was filled with thoughts of self-sacrifice. Go and find Haemon. And get married quickly, Antigone. Be happy. Life flows like water, and you young people let it run away through your fingers. Shut your hands; hold on to it, Antigone. Life is not what you think it is. Life is a child playing around your feet, a tool you hold firmly in your grip, a bench you sit down upon in the 1280 evening, in your garden. People will tell you that that's not life, that life is something else. They will tell you that because they need your strength and your fire, and they will want to make use of you. Don't listen to them. Believe me, the only poor consolation that we have in our old age is to discover that what I have just said to you is true. Life is nothing more than the happiness that you get out of it.

Antigone. (Murmurs, lost in thought) Happiness . . .

Creon. (Suddenly a little self-conscious) Not much of a word, is it?

Antigone. (Quietly) What kind of happiness do you foresee for me? Paint me the picture of your happy Antigone. What are the unim- 1290 portant little sins that I shall have to commit before I am allowed to sink my teeth into life and tear happiness from it? Tell me: to whom shall I have to lie? Upon whom shall I have to fawn? To whom must I sell myself? Whom do you want me to leave dying, while I turn away my eyes?

Creon. Antigone, be quiet.

Antigone. Why do you tell me to be quiet when all I want to know is what I have to do to be happy? This minute; since it is this very minute that I must make my choice. You tell me that life is so wonderful. I want to know what I have to do in order to be able to say that myself. 1300

Creon. Do you love Haemon?

Antigone. Yes, I love Haemon. The Haemon I love is hard and young, faithful and difficult to satisfy, just as I am. But if what I love in Haemon is to be worn away like a stone step by the tread of the thing you call life, the thing you call happiness, if Haemon reaches the point where he stops growing pale with fear when I grow pale, stops thinking that I must have been killed in an accident when I am five minutes late, stops feeling that he is alone on earth when I laugh and he doesn't know why—if he too has to learn to say yes to everything—why, no, then, 1310 no! I do not love Haemon!

Creon. You don't know what you are talking about!

Antigone. I do know what I am talking about! Now it is you who have stopped understanding. I am too far away from you now, talking to you from a kingdom you can't get into, with your quick tongue and your hollow heart. *(Laughs)* I laugh, Creon, because I see you suddenly as you must have been at fifteen: the same look of impotence in your face and the same inner conviction that there was nothing you couldn't do. What has life added to you, except those lines in your face, and that fat on your stomach?

1320 *Creon.* Be quiet, I tell you!

Antigone. Why do you want me to be quiet? Because you know that I am right? Do you think I can't see in your face that what I am saying is true? You can't admit it, of course; you have to go on growling and defending the bone you call happiness.

Creon. It is your happiness, too, you little fool!

Antigone. I spit on your happiness! I spit on your idea of life—that life that must go on, come what may. You are all like dogs that lick everything they smell. You with your promise of a humdrum happiness —provided a person doesn't ask too much of life. I want everything of 1330 life, I do; and I want it now! I want it total, complete: otherwise I reject it! I will *not* be moderate. I will *not* be satisfied with the bit of cake you offer me if I promise to be a good little girl. I want to be sure of everything this very day; sure that everything will be as beautiful as when I was a little girl. If not, I want to die!

Creon. Scream on, daughter of Oedipus! Scream on, in your father's own voice!

Antigone. In my father's own voice, yes! We are of the tribe that asks questions, and we ask them to the bitter end. Until no tiniest chance of hope remains to be strangled by our hands. We are of the 1340 tribe that hates your filthy hope, your docile, female hope; hope, your whore—

Creon. (Grasps her by her arms) Shut up! If you could see how ugly you are, shrieking those words!

Antigone. Yes, I am ugly! Father was ugly, too. *(Creon releases her arms, turns, and moves away. Stands with his back to Antigone)* But Father became beautiful. And do you know when? *(She follows him to behind the table.)* At the very end. When all his questions had been answered. When he could no longer doubt that he *had* killed his own father; that he *had* gone to bed with his own mother. When all hope

was gone, stamped out like a beetle. When it was absolutely certain 1350
that nothing, nothing could save him. Then he was at peace; then he could smile, almost; then he became beautiful. . . . Whereas you! Ah, those faces of yours, you candidates for election to happiness! It's you who are the ugly ones, even the handsomest of you—with that ugly glint in the corner of your eyes, that ugly crease at the corner of your mouths. Creon, you spoke the word a moment ago: the kitchen of politics. You look it and you smell of it.

Creon. (Struggles to put his hand over her mouth) I order you to shut up! Do you hear me?

Antigone. You order me? Cook! Do you really believe that you can 1360
give me orders?

Creon. Antigone! The anteroom is full of people! Do you want them to hear you?

Antigone. Open the doors! Let us make sure that they can hear me!

Creon. By God! You shut up, I tell you!

(Ismene enters through arch.)

Ismene. (Distraught) Antigone!

Antigone. (Turns to Ismene) You, too? What do you want?

Ismene. Oh, forgive me, Antigone. I've come back. I'll be brave. I'll go with you now. 1370

Antigone. Where will you go with me?

Ismene. (To Creon) Creon! If you kill her, you'll have to kill me too.

Antigone. Oh, no, Ismene. Not a bit of it. I die alone. You don't think I'm going to let you die with me after what I've been through? You don't deserve it.

Ismene. If you die, I don't want to live. I don't want to be left behind, alone.

Antigone. You chose life and I chose death. Now stop blubbering. You had your chance to come with me in the black night, creeping on your hands and knees. You had your chance to claw up the earth with 1380
your nails, as I did; to get yourself caught like a thief, as I did. And you refused it.

Ismene. Not any more. I'll do it alone tonight.

Antigone. (Turns round toward Creon) You hear that, Creon? The thing is catching! Who knows but that lots of people will catch the disease from me! What are you waiting for? Call in your guards! Come on, Creon! Show a little courage! It only hurts for a minute! Come on, cook!

Creon. (Turns toward arch and calls) Guard!

(Guards enter through arch.) 1390

Antigone. (In a great cry of relief) At last, Creon!

(Chorus enters through left arch.)

Creon. (To the Guards) Take her away! *(Creon goes up on top step.)*

(Guards grasp Antigone by her arms, turn and hustle her toward the arch, right, and exeunt. Ismene mimes horror, backs away toward the arch, left, then turns and runs out through the arch. A long pause, as Creon moves slowly downstage)

Chorus. (Behind Creon. Speaks in a deliberate voice) You are out of your mind, Creon. What have you done?

1400 *Creon. (His back to Chorus)* She had to die.

Chorus. You must not let Antigone die. We shall carry the scar of her death for centuries.

Creon. She insisted. No man on earth was strong enough to dissuade her. Death was her purpose, whether she knew it or not. Polynices was a mere pretext. When she had to give up that pretext, she found another one—that life and happiness were tawdry things and not worth possessing. She was bent upon only one thing: to reject life and to die.

Chorus. She is a mere child, Creon.

Creon. What do you want me to do for her? Condemn her to live?

1410 *Haemon. (Calls from offstage)* Father!

(Haemon enters through arch, right. Creon turns toward him.)

Creon. Haemon, forget Antigone. Forget her, my dearest boy.

Haemon. How can you talk like that?

Creon. (Grasps Haemon by the hands) I did everything I could to save her, Haemon. I used every argument. I swear I did. The girl doesn't love you. She could have gone on living for you; but she refused. She wanted it this way; she wanted to die.

Haemon. Father! The guards are dragging Antigone away! You've got to stop them! *(He breaks away from Creon.)*

1420 *Creon. (Looks away from Haemon)* I can't stop them. It's too late. Antigone has spoken. The story is all over Thebes. I cannot save her now.

Chorus. Creon, you must find a way. Lock her up. Say that she has gone out of her mind.

Creon. Everybody will know it isn't so. The nation will say that I am making an exception of her because my son loves her. I cannot.

Chorus. You can still gain time, and get her out of Thebes.

Creon. The mob already knows the truth. It is howling for her blood. I can do nothing.

1430 *Haemon.* But, Father, you are master in Thebes!

Creon. I am master under the law. Not above the law.

Haemon. You cannot let Antigone be taken from me. I am your son!

Creon. I cannot do anything else, my poor boy. She must die and you must live.

Haemon. Live, you say! Live a life without Antigone? A life in which I am to go on admiring you as you busy yourself about your kingdom, make your persuasive speeches, strike your attitudes? Not without Antigone. I love Antigone. I will not live without Antigone!

Creon. Haemon—you will have to resign yourself to life without Antigone. *(He moves to left of Haemon.)* Sooner or later there comes a day of sorrow in each man's life when he must cease to be a child and take up the burden of manhood. That day has come for you. 1440

Haemon. (Backs away a step) That giant strength, that courage. That massive god who used to pick me up in his arms and shelter me from shadows and monsters—was that you, Father? Was it of you I stood in awe? Was that man you?

Creon. For God's sake, Haemon, do not judge me! Not you, too!

Haemon. (Pleading now) This is all a bad dream, Father. You are not yourself. It isn't true that we have been backed up against a wall, forced to surrender. We don't have to say *yes* to this terrible thing. You are still king. You are still the father I revered. You have no right to desert me, to shrink into nothingness. The world will be too bare, I shall be too alone in the world, if you force me to disown you. 1450

Creon. The world *is* bare, Haemon, and you *are* alone. You must cease to think your father all-powerful. Look straight at me. See your father as he is. That is what it means to grow up and be a man.

Haemon. (Stares at Creon for a moment) I tell you that I will not live without Antigone. *(Turns and goes quickly out through arch)*

Chorus. Creon, the boy will go mad.

Creon. Poor boy! He loves her. 1460

Chorus. Creon, the boy is wounded to death.

Creon. We are all wounded to death.

(First Guard enters through arch, right, followed by Second and Third Guards pulling Antigone along with them.)

First Guard. Sir, the people are crowding into the palace!

Antigone. Creon, I don't want to see their faces. I don't want to hear them howl. You are going to kill me; let that be enough. I want to be alone until it is over.

Creon. Empty the palace! Guards at the gates!

(Creon quickly crosses toward the arch; exit. Two Guards release Antigone; exeunt behind Creon. Chorus goes out through arch, left. The lighting dims so that only the area about the table is lighted. The cyclorama is covered with a dark blue color. The scene is intended to suggest a prison cell, filled with shadows and dimly lit. Antigone moves to stool and sits. The First Guard stands upstage. He watches Antigone, and as she sits, he begins pacing slowly downstage, then upstage. A pause) 1470

Antigone. (Turns and looks at the Guard) It's you, is it?

Guard. What do you mean, me?

Antigone. The last human face that I shall see. *(A pause as they look at each other, then Guard paces upstage, turns, and crosses behind table.)* Was it you that arrested me this morning? 1480

Guard. Yes, that was me.

Antigone. You hurt me. There was no need for you to hurt me. Did I act as if I was trying to escape?

Guard. Come on now, Miss. It was my business to bring you in. I did it. *(A pause. He paces to and fro upstage. Only the sound of his boots is heard.)*

Antigone. How old are you?

1490 *Guard.* Thirty-nine.

Antigone. Have you any children?

Guard. Yes. Two.

Antigone. Do you love your children?

Guard. What's that got to do with you? *(A pause. He paces upstage and downstage.)*

Antigone. How long have you been in the Guard?

Guard. Since the war. I was in the army. Sergeant. Then I joined the Guard.

Antigone. Does one have to have been an army sergeant to get into 1500 the Guard?

Guard. Supposed to be. Either that or on special detail. But when they make you a guard, you lose your stripes.

Antigone. (Murmurs) I see.

Guard. Yes. Of course, if you're a guard, everybody knows you're something special; they know you're an old N.C.O. Take pay, for instance. When you're a guard you get your pay, and on top of that you get six months' extra pay, to make sure you don't lose anything by not being a sergeant any more. And of course you do better than that. You get a house, coal, rations, extras for the wife and kids. If you've got two 1510 kids, like me, you draw better than a sergeant.

Antigone. (Barely audible) I see.

Guard. That's why sergeants, now, they don't like guards. Maybe you noticed they try to make out they're better than us? Promotion, that's what it is. In the army, anybody can get promoted. All you need is good conduct. Now in the Guard, it's slow, and you have to know your business—like how to make out a report and the like of that. But when you're an N.C.O. in the Guard, you've got something that even a sergeant-major ain't got. For instance—

Antigone. (Breaking him off) Listen.

1520 *Guard.* Yes, Miss.

Antigone. I'm going to die soon. *(The Guard looks at her for a moment, then turns and moves away.)*

Guard. For instance, people have a lot of respect for guards, they have. A guard may be a soldier, but he's kind of in the civil service, too.

Antigone. Do you think it hurts to die?

Guard. How would I know? Of course, if somebody sticks a saber in your guts and turns it round, it hurts.

Antigone. How are they going to put me to death?

Guard. Well, I'll tell you. I heard the proclamation all right. Wait a minute. How did it go now? *(He stares into space and recites from memory.)* "In order that our fair city shall not be pol-luted with her sinful blood, she shall be im-mured—immured." That means, they shove you in a cave and wall up the cave. 1530

Antigone. Alive?

Guard. Yes. . . . *(He moves away a few steps.)*

Antigone. (Murmurs) O tomb! O bridal bed! Alone! *(Antigone sits there, a tiny figure in the middle of the stage. You would say she felt a little chilly. She wraps her arms round herself.)*

Guard. Yes! Outside the southeast gate of the town. In the Cave of Hades. In broad daylight. Some detail, eh, for them that's on the job! First they thought maybe it was a job for the army. Now it looks like it's going to be the Guard. There's an outfit for you! Nothing the Guard can't do. No wonder the army's jealous. 1540

Antigone. A pair of animals.

Guard. What do you mean, a pair of animals?

Antigone. When the winds blow cold, all they need do is to press close against one another. I am all alone.

Guard. Is there anything you want? I can send out for it, you know.

Antigone. You are very kind. *(A pause. Antigone looks up at the Guard.)* Yes, there is something I want. I want you to give someone a letter from me, when I am dead. 1550

Guard. How's that again? A letter?

Antigone. Yes, I want to write a letter; and I want you to give it to someone for me.

Guard. (Straightens up) Now, wait a minute. Take it easy. It's as much as my job is worth to go handing out letters from prisoners.

Antigone. (Removes a ring from her finger and holds it out toward him) I'll give you this ring if you will do it.

Guard. Is it gold? *(He takes the ring from her.)*

Antigone. Yes, it is gold. 1560

Guard. (Shakes his head) Uh-uh. No can do. Suppose they go through my pockets. I might get six months for a thing like that. *(He stares at the ring, then glances off right to make sure that he is not being watched.)* Listen, tell you what I'll do. You tell me what you want to say, and I'll write it down in my book. Then, afterwards, I'll tear out the pages and give them to the party, see? If it's in my handwriting, it's all right.

Antigone. (Winces) In your handwriting? *(She shudders slightly.)* No. That would be awful. The poor darling! In your handwriting.

Guard. (Offers back the ring) O.K. It's no skin off my nose.

Antigone. (Quickly) Of course, of course. No, keep the ring. But hurry. Time is getting short. Where is your notebook? *(The Guard* 1570 *pockets the ring, takes his notebook and pencil from his pocket, puts his foot up on chair, and rests the notebook on his knee, licks his pencil.)* Ready? *(He nods.)* Write, now. "My darling . . ."

Guard. (Writes as he mutters) The boy friend, eh?

Antigone. "My darling. I wanted to die, and perhaps you will not love me any more . . ."

Guard. (Mutters as he writes) ". . . will not love me any more."

Antigone. "Creon was right. It is terrible to die."

1580 *Guard. (Repeats as he writes)* ". . . terrible to die."

Antigone. "And I don't even know what I am dying for. I am afraid . . ."

Guard. (Looks at her) Wait a minute! How fast do you think I can write?

Antigone. (Takes hold of herself) Where are you?

Guard. (Reads from his notebook) "And I don't even know what I am dying for."

Antigone. No. Scratch that out. Nobody must know that. They have no right to know. It's as if they saw me naked and touched me, after I was dead. Scratch it all out. Just write: "Forgive me."

1590 *Guard. (Looks at Antigone)* I cut out everything you said there at the end, and I put down, "Forgive me"?

Antigone. Yes. "Forgive me, my darling. You would all have been so happy except for Antigone. I love you."

Guard. (Finishes the letter) ". . . I love you." *(He looks at her.)* Is that all?

Antigone. That's all.

Guard. (Straightens up, looks at notebook) Damn funny letter.

Antigone. I know.

Guard. (Looks at her) Who is it to? *(A sudden roll of drums begins and*
1600 *continues until after Antigone's exit. The First Guard pockets the notebook and shouts at Antigone.)* O.K. That's enough out of you! Come on! *(At the sound of the drum roll, Second and Third Guards enter through the arch. Antigone rises. Guards seize her and exeunt with her. The lighting moves up to suggest late afternoon. Chorus enters.)*

Chorus. And now it is Creon's turn. *(Messenger runs through the arch, right.)*

Messenger. The Queen . . . the Queen! Where is the Queen?

Chorus. What do you want with the Queen? What have you to tell the Queen?

1610 *Messenger.* News to break her heart. Antigone had just been thrust into the cave. They hadn't finished heaving the last block of stone into place when Creon and the rest heard a sudden moaning from the tomb. A hush fell over us all, for it was not the voice of Antigone. It was Haemon's voice that came forth from the tomb. Everybody looked at Creon; and he howled like a man demented: "Take away the stones!

Take away the stones!" The slaves leaped at the wall of stones, and Creon worked with them, sweating and tearing at the blocks with his bleeding hands. Finally a narrow opening was forced, and into it slipped the smallest guard.

Antigone had hanged herself by the cord of her robe, by the red and golden twisted cord of her robe. The cord was round her neck like a child's collar. Haemon was on his knees, holding her in his arms and moaning, his face buried in her robe. More stones were removed, and Creon went into the tomb. He tried to raise Haemon to his feet. I could hear him begging Haemon to rise to his feet. Haemon was deaf to his father's voice, till suddenly he stood up of his own accord, his eyes dark and burning. Anguish was in his face, but it was the face of a little boy. He stared at his father. Then suddenly he struck him—hard; and he drew his sword. Creon leaped out of range. Haemon went on staring at him, his eyes full of contempt—a glance that was like a knife, and that Creon couldn't escape. The King stood trembling in the far corner of the tomb, and Haemon went on staring. Then, without a word, he stabbed himself and lay down beside Antigone, embracing her in a great pool of blood. 1620 1630

(A pause as Creon and Page enter through arch on the Messenger's last words. Chorus and the Messenger both turn to look at Creon; then exit the Messenger through curtain.)

Creon. I have had them laid out side by side. They are together at last, and at peace. Two lovers on the morrow of their bridal. Their work is done. 1640

Chorus. But not yours, Creon. You have still one thing to learn. Eurydice, the Queen, your wife—

Creon. A good woman. Always busy with her garden, her preserves, her sweaters—those sweaters she never stopped knitting for the poor. Strange, how the poor never stop needing sweaters. One would almost think that was all they needed.

Chorus. The poor in Thebes are going to be cold this winter, Creon. When the Queen was told of her son's death, she waited carefully until she had finished her row, then put down her knitting calmly—as she did everything. She went up to her room, her lavender-scented room, with its embroidered doilies and its pictures framed in plush; and there, Creon, she cut her throat. She is laid out now in one of those two old-fashioned twin beds, exactly where you went to her one night when she was still a maiden. Her smile is still the same, scarcely a shade more melancholy. And if it were not for that great red blot on the bed linen by her neck, one might think she was asleep. 1650

Creon. (In a dull voice) She, too. They are all asleep. *(Pause)* It must be good to sleep.

Chorus. And now you are alone, Creon.

1660 *Creon.* Yes, all alone. *(To Page)* My lad.

Page. Sir?

Creon. Listen to me. They don't know it, but the truth is the work is there to be done, and a man can't fold his arms and refuse to do it. They say it's dirty work. But if we didn't do it, who would?

Page. I don't know, sir.

Creon. Of course you don't. You'll be lucky if you never find out. In a hurry to grow up, aren't you?

Page. Oh, yes, sir.

Creon. I shouldn't be if I were you. Never grow up if you can help 1670 it. *(He is lost in thought as the hour chimes.)* What time is it?

Page. Five o'clock, sir.

Creon. What have we on at five o'clock?

Page. Cabinet meeting, sir.

Creon. Cabinet meeting. Then we had better go along to it.

(Exeunt Creon and Page slowly through arch, left, and Chorus moves downstage.)

Chorus. And there we are. It is quite true that if it had not been for Antigone they would all have been at peace. But that is over now. And they are all at peace. All those who were meant to die have died: those 1680 who believed one thing, those who believed the contrary thing, and even those who believed nothing at all, yet were caught up in the web without knowing why. All dead: stiff, useless, rotting. And those who have survived will now begin quietly to forget the dead: they won't remember who was who or which was which. It is all over. Antigone is calm tonight, and we shall never know the name of the fever that consumed her. She has played her part. *(Three Guards enter, resume their places on steps as at the rise of the curtain, and begin to play cards.)*

A great melancholy wave of peace now settles down upon Thebes, upon the empty palace, upon Creon, who can now begin to wait for 1690 his own death.

Only the guards are left, and none of this matters to them. It's no skin off their noses. They go on playing cards. *(Chorus walks toward the arch, left, as the curtain falls.)*

Comments and Questions

Anouilh, like Sophocles, is less interested in highly individualized characters, presented with all the fastidiousness of the psychological realist (like Ibsen, say), than he is in representing characters who help illustrate and define the dilemma of man as he seeks some meaning to his life and in the universe outside of himself. In Anouilh's play the struggle between Antigone and Creon is a reflection of the conflict between the rights of the individual and of the state, and this conflict, as dramatized in the play, should be carefully defined. But there are also deeper and broader conflicts between two basic attitudes toward life. How are such conflicts resolved? Is it accurate to say that Creon wins and Antigone loses? Characterize the attitude and comments of the Chorus.

What is Antigone seeking? Does she foresee the consequences? What is Creon seeking? Explain the motive behind his explanation to Antigone regarding the burials of her brothers (p. 548, lines 1227-1257). Why does he offer her a reprieve? Why must she refuse? Is Creon a good statesman? Is he a more or less sympathetic character than Antigone? How do you explain Creon's reactions at the end to the slaughter he has helped bring about? What is the significance of Creon's remarks to the page boy in the final scene of the play? To what extent are the inevitable conflicts between youth and age, between passionate feelings and public responsibilities, a part of the tragedy? Or, to what extent can we accept passionate protest, and to what extent can a "sense of public responsibility" merely serve as an escape or an excuse for the wielding of power?

Readers of Sophocles' Antigone *will want to study the differences in tragic vision between the two plays, as well as, of course, all the important changes Anouilh makes, which should be listed and explained. Professor Pronko's article on page 719 contains useful leads. Why does Anouilh place more emphasis than Sophocles on Antigone's youth and her need for love and affection, as evidenced in the scenes with the nurse and Haemon? Is she a more pitiable and a more tragic figure than Sophocles' Antigone? Do you think Anouilh's Creon is a more sympathetic character than Sophocles'? Do Anouilh's changes succeed in making Sophocles' play more tragic for a contemporary audience? Why do you think Anouilh adapted an old play instead of writing an original play of his own?*

Related Reading

Sophocles, *Antigone*, page 489
Maxwell Anderson, "The Essence of Tragedy," page 663
Leonard Pronko, "Anouilh's *Antigone*," page 719
Arthur Miller, "On Social Plays," page 670

Friedrich Dürrenmatt

(1921-)

THE VISIT

translated and adapted by Maurice Valency

In his postscript to The Visit, *the Swiss playwright Friedrich Dürrenmatt says:* "The Visit *is the story of an action which takes place in a small town in Central Europe. It is told by someone who feels himself at no great remove from the people involved, and who is not so sure he would have acted differently." By implication Dürrenmatt therefore invited the audience to judge if they would have acted differently. If, after reading (or seeing) this explosively challenging play, the reader feels unsure of his own possible response, he should consider events in recent history: a world shaped, or misshaped, by two world wars, the incongruities of warlike peace, and the realizations this kind of peace has brought to most men. As never before, we see events and actions on a global scale and are aware both of individual insignificance and the fantastic controls that shape our lives. We are aware of power: the power of money, of thought control, of ultimate, total destruction. We know that millions can be held in a political or economic or psychological vise so complete that Julius Caesar or Napoleon would never have imagined it. We know that men cannot only be brainwashed, to use a recent term for an old habit, but can be made to participate actively in their own brainwashing.*

Life in such a world is absurd and grotesque, and Dürrenmatt writes in his essay "Problems of the Theatre," that "the world (hence the stage which represents this world) is for me something monstrous, a riddle of misfortunes which must be accepted but before which one must not capitulate." The world is now one, he contends, without "tragic heroes, but only vast tragedies staged by world butchers and produced by slaughtering machines." Tragedy in the classical Greek or Shakespearian sense is therefore no longer possible in our time, because we can no longer conceive of the old heroes in modern life and because the modern audience is no longer a community, that is, a society more or less unified in spirit and beliefs. (Arthur Miller's essay "Of Social Plays," reprinted in this volume, also takes up this issue.) Dürrenmatt is convinced that under these conditions comedy, usually of a serious or bitter sort, becomes the playwright's best tactic to engross his audience, to provide "the mousetrap in which the public is easily caught." In that mousetrap the writer hopes to bring us face to face with ideas we usually prefer to avoid.

The Visit *begins amusingly enough; by the end of Act I, though, the tone has changed, and thereafter the abyss of moral horror opens, a horror resulting from human weakness rather than willful choice, and from primitive urges glossed over by civilization.*

Dürrenmatt combines old and new forms and techniques in his play. In structure the play follows traditional forms; in Act I the action slowly builds like a fire until the conflict is fully revealed at the end; in Act II the issue is forced to its crisis and reaches its turning point, the point at which only one course of action remains; and in Act III the action is brought to its resolution. The act endings and dramatic confrontations remind one of a "well-made" play of the nineteenth century, but for some of his effects and materials Dürrenmatt goes back all the way to the ancient Greeks. The citizens of Güllen, particularly in the last act, are reminiscent of the chorus in Sophoclean tragedy, and Madame Claire Zachanassian is not unlike a deus ex machina, literally "the god of the machine," a device sometimes used in Greek plays whereby a character portraying a god is lowered to the stage on a platform operated by a rope and pulley in order to dispense divine justice. But there the analogy ends, for Madame Zachanassian's justice is mercilessly twentieth century.

Other reminders of ancient legends used in Greek tragedy are evident in Dürrenmatt's adapting, with significant variations, the ritual of a community periodically transferring its guilt and suffering onto an innocent victim or scapegoat. We find undertones of the myths of the plague-ridden land regenerated by a suffering king or hero, of avenging deities or furies, or of brutally vengeful heroines like Medea or Clytemnestra. But, again, the parallels also point out the differences: no longer do we find the classical tragedy that portrayed a world temporarily dislocated by forces of evil eventually to be subdued. As in another contemporary work along the lines of Dürrenmatt's world view, William Golding's Lord of the Flies, we cannot come away with the view that evil is the aberration; instead we discover that it is the rule.

Dürrenmatt pairs these variants of ancient ideas with modern techniques. The staging is impressionistic, the sets merely suggest time and place. Scene dissolves into scene without the lowering of a curtain, thereby giving the play the fluidity of a film. Like in a film, music is used to reinforce the mood of the action.

The original title of the play, first produced in 1956, is Der Besuch der Alten Dame (The Visit of the Old Lady). The version printed here is an adaptation, considerably modified in its techniques and subdued in its language over the original, but essentially the same in theme and structure. It was first given in New York City on May 5, 1958, at the Lunt-Fontanne Theater, with Lynn Fontanne and Alfred Lunt in the leading roles.

THE VISIT

Characters

HOFBAUER, *First Man*
HELMESBERGER, *Second Man*
WECHSLER, *Third Man*
VOGEL, *Fourth Man*
PAINTER
STATION MASTER
BURGOMASTER
TEACHER
PASTOR
ANTON SCHILL
CLAIRE ZACHANASSIAN
CONDUCTOR
PEDRO CABRAL
BOBBY
POLICEMAN
FIRST GRANDCHILD
SECOND GRANDCHILD
MIKE
MAX
FIRST BLIND MAN
SECOND BLIND MAN
ATHLETE
FRAU BURGOMASTER
FRAU SCHILL
DAUGHTER
SON
DOCTOR NÜSSLIN
FRAU BLOCK, *First Woman*
TRUCK DRIVER
REPORTER
CAMERAMAN
TOWNSMAN
TOWNSMAN

(The action of the play takes place in and around the little town of Güllen, somewhere in Europe.)

(There are three acts.)

Act I

(A railway-crossing bell starts ringing. Then is heard the distant sound of a locomotive whistle. The curtain rises.)

(The scene represents, in the simplest possible manner, a little town somewhere in Central Europe. The time is the present. The town is shabby and ruined, as if the plague had passed there. Its name, Güllen, is inscribed on the shabby signboard which adorns the façade of the railway station. This edifice is summarily indicated by a length of rusty iron paling, a platform parallel to the proscenium, beyond which one imagines the rails to be, and a baggage truck standing by a wall on 10 *which a torn timetable, marked* "Fahrplan," *is affixed by three nails. In the station wall is a door with a sign:* "Eintritt Verboten."° *This leads to the Station Master's office.)*

(Left of the station is a little house of gray stucco, formerly white-washed. It has a tile roof, badly in need of repair. Some shreds of travel posters still adhere to the windowless walls. A shingle hanging over the entrance, left, reads: "Männer." *On the other side the shingle reads:* "Damen." *Along the wall of the little house there is a wooden bench, backless, on which four men are lounging cheerlessly, shabbily dressed, with cracked shoes. A fifth man is busied with paintpot and* 20 *brush. He is kneeling on the ground, painting a strip of canvas with the words:* "Welcome, Clara.")

(The warning signal rings uninterruptedly. The sound of the approaching train comes closer and closer. The Station Master issues from his office, advances to the center of the platform and salutes.)

(The train is heard thundering past in a direction parallel to the footlights, and is lost in the distance. The men on the bench follow its passing with a slow movement of their heads, from left to right.)

First Man. The "Emperor." Hamburg-Naples.

Second Man. Then comes the "Diplomat."

30 *Third Man.* Then the "Banker."

Fourth Man. And at eleven twenty-seven the "Flying Dutchman." Venice-Stockholm.

First Man. Our only pleasure—watching trains. *(The station bell rings again. The Station Master comes out of his office and salutes another train. The men follow its course, right to left.)*

Fourth Man. Once upon a time the "Emperor" and the "Flying Dutchman" used to stop here in Güllen. So did the "Diplomat," the "Banker" and the "Silver Comet."

Second Man. Now it's only the local from Kaffigen and the twelve-40 forty from Kalberstadt.

Third Man. The fact is, we're ruined.

First Man. What with the Wagonworks shut down . . .

Second Man. The Foundry finished . . .

11. *Eintritt Verboten*, no entrance.

Fourth Man. The Golden Eagle Pencil Factory all washed up . . .
First Man. It's life on the dole.
Second Man. Did you say life?
Third Man. We're rotting.
First Man. Starving.
Second Man. Crumbling.
Fourth Man. The whole damn town. *(The station bell rings.)* 50
Third Man. Once we were a center of industry.
Painter. A cradle of culture.
Fourth Man. One of the best little towns in the country.
First Man. In the world.
Second Man. Here Goethe slept.
Fourth Man. Brahms composed a quartet.
Third Man. Here Berthold Schwarz invented gunpowder.°
Painter. And I once got first prize at the Dresden Exhibition of Contemporary Art. What am I doing now? Painting signs. *(The station bell rings. The Station Master comes out. He throws away a cigarette* 60 *butt. The men scramble for it.)*
First Man. Well, anyway, Madame Zachanassian will help us.
Fourth Man. If she comes . . .
Third Man. If she comes.
Second Man. Last week she was in France. She gave them a hospital.
First Man. In Rome she founded a free public nursery.
Third Man. In Leuthenau, a bird sanctuary.
Painter. They say she got Picasso to design her car.
First Man. Where does she get all that money?
Second Man. An oil company, a shipping line, three banks and five 70 railways—
Fourth Man. And the biggest string of geisha houses in Japan.
(From the direction of the town come the Burgomaster, the Pastor, the Teacher and Anton Schill. The Burgomaster, the Teacher and Schill are men in their fifties. The Pastor is ten years younger. All four are dressed shabbily and are sad-looking. The Burgomaster looks official. Schill is tall and handsome, but graying and worn; nevertheless a man of considerable charm and presence. He walks directly to the little house and disappears into it.)
Painter. Any news, Burgomaster? Is she coming? 80
All. Yes, is she coming?
Burgomaster. She's coming. The telegram has been confirmed. Our distinguished guest will arrive on the twelve-forty from Kalberstadt. Everyone must be ready.
Teacher. The mixed choir is ready. So is the children's chorus.

57. *invented gunpowder,* the invention of gunpowder is claimed for many men in many places.

Burgomaster. And the church bell, Pastor?

Pastor. The church bell will ring. As soon as the new bell ropes are fitted. The man is working on them now.

Burgomaster. The town band will be drawn up in the market place 90 and the Athletic Association will form a human pyramid in her honor—the top man will hold the wreath with her initials. Then lunch at the Golden Apostle. I shall say a few words.

Teacher. Of course.

Burgomaster. I had thought of illuminating the town hall and the cathedral, but we can't afford the lamps.

Painter. Burgomaster—what do you think of this? *(He shows the banner.)*

Burgomaster. (Calls) Schill! Schill!

Teacher. Schill! *(Schill comes out of the little house.)*

100 *Schill.* Yes, right away. Right away.

Burgomaster. This is more in your line. What do you think of this?

Schill. (Looks at the sign) No, no, no. That certainly won't do, Burgomaster. It's much too intimate. It shouldn't read: "Welcome, Clara." It should read: "Welcome, Madame . . ."

Teacher. Zachanassian.

Burgomaster. Zachanassian.

Schill. Zachanassian.

Painter. But she's Clara to us.

First Man. Clara Wäscher.

110 *Second Man.* Born here.

Third Man. Her father was a carpenter. He built this. *(All turn and stare at the little house.)*

Schill. All the same . . .

Painter. If I . . .

Burgomaster. No, no, no. He's right. You'll have to change it.

Painter. Oh, well, I'll tell you what I'll do. I'll leave this and I'll put "Welcome, Madame Zachanassian" on the other side. Then if things go well, we can always turn it around.

Burgomaster. Good idea. *(To Schill)* Yes?

120 *Schill.* Well, anyway, it's safer. Everything depends on the first impression. *(The train bell is heard. Two clangs. The Painter turns the banner over and goes to work.)*

First Man. Hear that? The "Flying Dutchman" has just passed through Leuthenau.

Fourth Man. Eleven-twenty.

Burgomaster. Gentlemen, you know that the millionairess is our only hope.

Pastor. Under God.

Burgomaster. Under God. Naturally. Schill, we depend entirely 130 on you.

Schill. Yes, I know. You keep telling me.

Burgomaster. After all, you're the only one who really knew her.

Schill. Yes, I knew her.

Pastor. You were really quite close to one another, I hear, in those days.

Schill. Close? Yes, we were close, there's no denying it. We were in love. I was young—good-looking, so they said—and Clara—you know, I can still see her in the great barn coming toward me—like a light out of the darkness. And in the Konradsweil Forest she'd come running to meet me—barefooted—her beautiful red hair streaming 140 behind her. Like a witch. I was in love with her, all right. But you know how it is when you're twenty.

Pastor. What happened?

Schill. *(Shrugs)* Life came between us.

Burgomaster. You must give me some points about her for my speech. *(He takes out his notebook.)*

Schill. I think I can help you there.

Teacher. Well, I've gone through the school records. And the young lady's marks were, I'm afraid to say, absolutely dreadful. Even in deportment. The only subject in which she was even remotely passable 150 was natural history.

Burgomaster. Good in natural history. That's fine. Give me a pencil. *(He makes a note.)*

Schill. She was an outdoor girl. Wild. Once, I remember, they arrested a tramp, and she threw stones at the policeman. She hated injustice passionately.

Burgomaster. Strong sense of justice. Excellent.

Schill. And generous . . .

All. Generous?

Schill. Generous to a fault. Whatever little she had, she shared— 160 so good-hearted. I remember once she stole a bag of potatoes to give to a poor widow.

Burgomaster. *(Writing in notebook)* Wonderful generosity—

Teacher. Generosity.

Burgomaster. That, gentlemen, is something I must not fail to make a point of.

Schill. And such a sense of humor. I remember once when the oldest man in town fell and broke his leg, she said, "Oh, dear, now they'll have to shoot him."

Burgomaster. Well, I've got enough. The rest, my friend, is up to you. 170 *(He puts the notebook away.)*

Schill. Yes, I know, but it's not so easy. After all, to part a woman like that from her millions—

Burgomaster. Exactly. Millions. We have to think in big terms here.

Teacher. If she's thinking of buying us off with a nursery school—

All. Nursery school!

Pastor. Don't accept.

Teacher. Hold out.

Schill. I'm not so sure that I can do it. You know, she may have for-
180 gotten me completely.

Burgomaster. (He exchanges a look with the Teacher and the Pastor.) Schill, for many years you have been our most popular citizen. The most respected and the best loved.

Schill. Why, thank you . . .

Burgomaster. And therefore I must tell you—last week I sounded out the political opposition, and they agreed. In the spring you will be elected to succeed me as Burgomaster. By unanimous vote. *(The others clap their hands in approval.)*

Schill. But, my dear Burgomaster—!

190 *Burgomaster.* It's true.

Teacher. I'm a witness. I was at the meeting.

Schill. This is—naturally, I'm terribly flattered—It's a completely unexpected honor.

Burgomaster. You deserve it.

Schill. Burgomaster! Well, well—! *(Briskly)* Gentlemen, to business. The first chance I get, of course, I shall discuss our miserable position with Clara.

Teacher. But tactfully, tactfully—

Schill. What do you take me for? We must feel our way. Everything
200 must be correct. Psychologically correct. For example, here at the railway station, a single blunder, one false note, could be disastrous.

Burgomaster. He's absolutely right. The first impression colors all the rest. Madame Zachanassian sets foot on her native soil for the first time in many years. She sees our love and she sees our misery. She remembers her youth, her friends. The tears well up into her eyes. Her childhood companions throng about her. I will naturally not present myself like this, but in my black coat with my top hat. Next to me, my wife. Before me, my two grandchildren all in white, with roses. My God, if it only comes off as I see it! If only it comes off. *(The station*
210 *bell begins ringing.)* Oh, my God! Quick! We must get dressed.

First Man. It's not her train. It's only the "Flying Dutchman."

Pastor. (Calmly) We have still two hours before she arrives.

Schill. For God's sake, don't let's lose our heads. We still have a full two hours.

Burgomaster. Who's losing their heads? *(To First and Second Man)* When her train comes, you two, Helmesberger and Vogel, will hold up the banner with "Welcome Madame Zachanassian." The rest will applaud.

Third Man. Bravo! *(He applauds.)*

Burgomaster. But, please, one thing—no wild cheering like last year with the government relief committee. It made no impression at all and we still haven't received any loan. What we need here is a feeling of genuine sincerity. That's how we greet with full hearts our beloved sister who has been away from us so long. Be sincerely moved, my friends, that's the secret; be sincere. Remember you're not dealing with a child. Next a few brief words from me. Then the church bell will start pealing— 220

Pastor. If he can fix the ropes in time. *(The station bell rings.)*

Burgomaster.—Then the mixed choir moves in. And then—

Teacher. We'll form a line down here. 230

Burgomaster. Then the rest of us will form in two lines leading from the station—*(He is interrupted by the thunder of the approaching train. The men crane their heads to see it pass. The Station Master advances to the platform and salutes. There is a sudden shriek of air brakes. The train screams to a stop. The four men jump up in consternation.)*

Painter. But the "Flying Dutchman" never stops!

First Man. It's stopping.

Second Man. In Güllen!

Third Man. In the poorest— 240

First Man. The dreariest—

Second Man. The lousiest—

Fourth Man. The most God-forsaken hole between Venice and Stockholm.

Station Master. It cannot stop! *(The train noises stop. There is only the panting of the engine.)*

Painter. It's stopped! *(The Station Master runs out.)*

Offstage Voices. What's happened? Is there an accident? *(A hubbub of offstage voices, as if the passengers on the invisible train were alighting)*

Claire. (Offstage) Is this Güllen? 250

Conductor. (Offstage) Here, here, what's going on?

Claire. (Offstage) Who the hell are you?

Conductor. (Offstage) But you pulled the emergency cord, madame!

Claire. (Offstage) I always pull the emergency cord.

Station Master. (Offstage) I must ask you what's going on here.

Claire. (Offstage) And who the hell are you?

Station Master. (Offstage) I'm the Station Master, madame, and I must ask you—

Claire. (Enters) No!

(From the right Claire Zachanassian appears. She is an extraordinary woman. She is in her fifties, red-haired, remarkably dressed, with a face as impassive as that of an ancient idol, beautiful still, and with a singular grace of movement and manner. She is simple and unaffected, 260

yet she has the haughtiness of a world power. The entire effect is striking to the point of the unbelievable. Behind her comes her fiancé, Pedro Cabral, tall, young, very handsome, and completely equipped for fishing, with creel and net, and with a rod case in his hand. An excited Conductor follows.)

Conductor. But, madame, I must insist! You have stopped "The 270 Flying Dutchman." I must have an explanation.

Claire. Nonsense. Pedro.

Pedro. Yes, my love?

Claire. This is Güllen. Nothing has changed. I recognize it all. There's the forest of Konradsweil. There's a brook in it full of trout, where you can fish. And there's the roof of the great barn. Ha! God! What a miserable blot on the map.

(She crosses the stage and goes off with Pedro.)

Schill. My God! Clara!

Teacher. Claire Zachanassian!

280 *All.* Claire Zachanassian!

Burgomaster. And the town band? The town band! Where is it?

Teacher. The mixed choir! The mixed choir!

Pastor. The church bell! The church bell!

Burgomaster. (To the First Man) Quick! My dress coat. My top hat. My grandchildren. Run! Run! *(First Man runs off. The Burgomaster shouts after him.)* And don't forget my wife! *(General panic. The Third Man and Fourth Man hold up the banner, on which only part of the name has been painted: "Welcome Mad—" Claire and Pedro re-enter, right.)*

290 *Conductor. (Mastering himself with an effort)* Madame. The train is waiting. The entire international railway schedule has been disrupted. I await your explanation.

Claire. You're a very foolish man. I wish to visit this town. Did you expect me to jump off a moving train?

Conductor. (Stupefied) You stopped the "Flying Dutchman" because you wished to visit the town?

Claire. Naturally.

Conductor. (Inarticulate) Madame!

Station Master. Madame, if you wished to visit the town, the twelve-300 forty from Kalberstadt was entirely at your service. Arrival in Güllen, one-seventeen.

Claire. The local that stops at Loken, Beisenbach and Leuthenau? Do you expect me to waste three-quarters of an hour chugging dismally through this wilderness?

Conductor. Madame, you shall pay for this!

Claire. Bobby, give him a thousand marks. *(Bobby, her butler, a man in his seventies, wearing dark glasses, opens his wallet. The townspeople gasp.)*

Conductor. (Taking the money in amazement) But, madame!

Claire. And three thousand for the Railway Widows' Relief Fund. 310

Conductor. (With the money in his hands) But we have no such fund, madame.

Claire. Now you have. *(The Burgomaster pushes his way forward.)*

Burgomaster. (He whispers to the Conductor and Teacher.) The lady is Madame Claire Zachanassian.

Conductor. Claire Zachanassian? Oh, my God! But that's naturally quite different. Needless to say, we would have stopped the train if we'd had the slightest idea. *(He hands the money back to Bobby.)* Here, please. I couldn't dream of it. Four thousand. My God!

Claire. Keep it. Don't fuss. 320

Conductor. Would you like the train to wait, madame, while you visit the town? The administration will be delighted. The cathedral porch. The town hall—

Claire. You may take the train away. I don't need it any more.

Station Master. All aboard! *(He puts his whistle to his lips. Pedro stops him.)*

Pedro. But the press, my angel. They don't know anything about this. They're still in the dining car.

Claire. Let them stay there. I don't want the press in Güllen at the moment. Later they will come by themselves. *(To Station Master)* And 330 now what are you waiting for?

Station Master. All aboard! *(The Station Master blows a long blast on his whistle. The train leaves. Meanwhile, the First Man has brought the Burgomaster's dress coat and top hat. The Burgomaster puts on the coat, then advances slowly and solemnly.)*

Conductor. I trust madame will not speak of this to the administration. It was a pure misunderstanding. *(He salutes and runs for the train as it starts moving.)*

Burgomaster. (Bows) Gracious lady, as Burgomaster of the town of Güllen, I have the honor—*(The rest of the speech is lost in the roar of* 340 *the departing train. He continues speaking and gesturing, and at last bows amid applause as the train noises end.)*

Claire. Thank you, Mr. Burgomaster. *(She glances at the beaming faces, and lastly at Schill, whom she does not recognize. She turns upstage.)*

Schill. Clara!

Claire. (Turns and stares) Anton?

Schill. Yes. It's good that you've come back.

Claire. Yes. I've waited for this moment. All my life. Ever since I left Güllen. 350

Schill. (A little embarrassed) That is very kind of you to say, Clara.

Claire. And have you thought about me?

Schill. Naturally. Always. You know that.

Claire. Those were happy times we spent together.
Schill. Unforgettable. *(He smiles reassuringly at the Burgomaster.)*
Claire. Call me by the name you used to call me.
Schill. *(Whispers)* My kitten.
Claire. What?
Schill. *(Louder)* My kitten.
360 *Claire.* And what else?
Schill. Little witch.
Claire. I used to call you my black panther. You're gray now, and soft.
Schill. But you are still the same, little witch.
Claire. I am the same? *(She laughs.)* Oh, no, my black panther, I am not at all the same.
Schill. *(Gallantly)* In my eyes you are. I see no difference.
Claire. Would you like to meet my fiancé? Pedro Cabral. He owns an enormous plantation in Brazil.
Schill. A pleasure.
370 *Claire.* We're to be married soon.
Schill. Congratulations.
Claire. He will be my eighth husband. *(Pedro stands by himself downstage, right.)* Pedro, come here and show your face. Come along, darling—come here! Don't sulk. Say hello.
Pedro. Hello.
Claire. A man of few words! Isn't he charming? A diplomat. He's interested only in fishing. Isn't he handsome, in his Latin way? You'd swear he was a Brazilian. But he's not—he's a Greek. His father was a White Russian. We were betrothed by a Bulgarian priest. We plan to
380 be married in a few days here in the cathedral.
Burgomaster. Here in the cathedral? What an honor for us!
Claire. No. It was my dream, when I was seventeen, to be married in Güllen cathedral. The dreams of youth are sacred, don't you think so, Anton?
Schill. Yes, of course.
Claire. Yes, of course. I think so, too. Now I would like to look at the town. *(The mixed choir arrives, breathless, wearing ordinary clothes with green sashes.)* What's all this? Go away. *(She laughs.)* Ha! Ha! Ha!
Teacher. Dear lady—*(He steps forward, having put on a sash also.)*
390 Dear lady, as Rector of the high school and a devotee of that noble muse, Music, I take pleasure in presenting the Güllen mixed choir.
Claire. How do you do?
Teacher. Who will sing for you an ancient folk song of the region, with specially amended words—if you will deign to listen.
Claire. Very well. Fire away.
(The Teacher blows a pitch pipe. The mixed choir begins to sing the ancient folk song with the amended words. Just then the station bell starts ringing. The song is drowned in the roar of the passing express.

The Station Master salutes. When the train has passed, there is applause.) 400

Burgomaster. The church bell! The church bell! Where's the church bell? *(The Pastor shrugs helplessly.)*

Claire. Thank you, Professor. They sang beautifully. The little blond bass—no, not that one—the one with the big Adam's apple—was most impressive. *(The Teacher bows. The Policeman pushes his way professionally through the mixed choir and comes to attention in front of Claire Zachanassian.)* Now, who are you?

Policeman. (Clicks heels) Police Chief Schultz. At your service.

Claire. (She looks him up and down.) I have no need of you at the moment. But I think there will be work for you by and by. Tell me, do 410 you know how to close an eye from time to time?

Policeman. How else could I get along in my profession?

Claire. You might practice closing both.

Schill. (Laughs) What a sense of humor, eh?

Burgomaster. (Puts on the top hat) Permit me to present my grandchildren, gracious lady. Hermine and Adolphine. There's only my wife still to come. *(He wipes the perspiration from his brow, and replaces the hat. The little girls present the roses with elaborate curtsies.)*

Claire. Thank you, my dears. Congratulations, Burgomaster. Extraordinary children. *(She plants the roses in Pedro's arms. The Burgo-* 420 *master secretly passes his top hat to the Pastor, who puts it on.)*

Burgomaster. Our pastor, madame. *(The Pastor takes off the hat and bows.)*

Claire. Ah. The pastor. How do you do? Do you give consolation to the dying?

Pastor. (A bit puzzled) That is part of my ministry, yes.

Claire. And to those who are condemned to death?

Pastor. Capital punishment has been abolished in this country, madame.

Claire. I see. Well, it could be restored, I suppose. *(The Pastor hands* 430 *back the hat. He shrugs his shoulders in confusion.)*

Schill. (Laughs) What an original sense of humor! *(All laugh, a little blankly.)*

Claire. Well, I can't sit here all day—I should like to see the town. *(The Burgomaster offers his arm.)*

Burgomaster. May I have the honor, gracious lady?

Claire. Thank you, but these legs are not what they were. This one was broken in five places.

Schill. (Full of concern) My kitten!

Claire. When my airplane bumped into a mountain in Afghanistan. 440 All the others were killed. Even the pilot. But as you see, I survived. I don't fly any more.

Schill. But you're as strong as ever now.

Claire. Stronger.

Burgomaster. Never fear, gracious lady. The town doctor has a car.

Claire. I never ride in motors.

Burgomaster. You never ride in motors?

Claire. Not since my Ferrari crashed in Hong Kong.

Schill. But how do you travel, then, little witch? On a broom?

450 *Claire.* Mike—Max! *(She claps her hands. Two huge bodyguards come in, left, carrying a sedan chair. She sits in it.)* I travel this way —a bit antiquated, of course. But perfectly safe. Ha! Ha! Aren't they magnificent? Mike and Max. I bought them in America. They were in jail, condemned to the chair. I had them pardoned. Now they're condemned to my chair. I paid fifty thousand dollars apiece for them. You couldn't get them now for twice the sum. The sedan chair comes from the Louvre. I fancied it so much that the President of France gave it to me. The French are so impulsive, don't you think so, Anton? Go! *(Mike and Max start to carry her off.)*

460 *Burgomaster.* You wish to visit the cathedral? And the old town hall?

Claire. No. The great barn. And the forest of Konradsweil. I wish to go with Anton and visit our old haunts once again.

The Pastor. Very touching.

Claire. (To the butler) Will you send my luggage and the coffin to the Golden Apostle?

Burgomaster. The coffin?

Claire. Yes. I brought one with me. Go!

Teacher. Hip-hip—

All. Hurrah! Hip-hip, hurrah! Hurrah! *(They bear her off in the direction of the town. The Townspeople burst into cheers. The church bell rings.)*

470

Burgomaster. Ah, thank God—the bell at last.

(The Policeman is about to follow the others, when the two Blind Men appear. They are not young, yet they seem childish—a strange effect. Though they are of different height and features, they are dressed exactly alike, and so create the effect of being twins. They walk slowly, feeling their way. Their voices, when they speak, are curiously high and flutelike, and they have a curious trick of repetition of phrases.)

First Blind Man. We're in—

480 *Both Blind Men.* Güllen.

First Blind Man. We breathe—

Second Blind Man. We breathe—

Both Blind Men. We breathe the air, the air of Güllen.

Policeman. (Startled) Who are you?

First Blind Man. We belong to the lady.

Second Blind Man. We belong to the lady. She calls us—

First Blind Man. Kobby.

Second Blind Man. And Lobby.

Policeman. Madame Zachanassian is staying at the Golden Apostle.

First Blind Man. We're blind. 490

Second Blind Man. We're blind.

Policeman. Blind? Come along with me, then. I'll take you there.

First Blind Man. Thank you, Mr. Policeman.

Second Blind Man. Thanks very much.

Policeman. Hey! How do you know I'm a policeman, if you're blind?

Both Blind Men. By your voice. By your voice.

First Blind Man. All policemen sound the same.

Policeman. You've had a lot to do with the police, have you, little men?

First Blind Man. Men he calls us! 500

Both Blind Men. Men!

Policeman. What are you then?

Both Blind Men. You'll see. You'll see. *(The Policeman claps his hands suddenly. The Blind Men turn sharply toward the sound. The Policeman is convinced they are blind.)*

Policeman. What's your trade?

Both Blind Men. We have no trade.

Second Blind Man. We play music.

First Blind Man. We sing.

Second Blind Man. We amuse the lady. 510

First Blind Man. We look after the beast.

Second Blind Man. We feed it.

First Blind Man. We stroke it.

Second Blind Man. We take it for walks.

Policeman. What beast?

Both Blind Men. You'll see—you'll see.

Second Blind Man. We give it raw meat.

First Blind Man. And she gives us chicken and wine.

Second Blind Man. Every day—

Both Blind Men. Every day. 520

Policeman. Rich people have strange tastes.

Both Blind Men. Strange tastes—strange tastes. *(The Policeman puts on his helmet.)*

Policeman. Come along, I'll take you to the lady. *(The two Blind Men turn and walk off.)*

Both Blind Men. We know the way—we know the way.

(The station and the little house vanish. A sign representing the Golden Apostle descends. The scene dissolves into the interior of the inn. The Golden Apostle is seen to be in the last stages of decay. The walls are cracked and moldering, and the plaster is falling from the ancient 530 *lath. A table represents the café of the inn. The Burgomaster and the*

Teacher sit at this table, drinking a glass together. A procession of Townspeople, carrying many pieces of luggage, passes. Then comes a coffin, and last, a large box covered with a canvas. They cross the stage from right to left.)

Burgomaster. Trunks. Suitcases. Boxes. *(He looks up apprehensively at the ceiling.)* The floor will never bear the weight. *(As the large covered box is carried in, he peers under the canvas, then draws back.)* Good God!

540 *Teacher.* Why, what's in it?

Burgomaster. A live panther. *(They laugh. The Burgomaster lifts his glass solemnly.)* Your health, Professor. Let's hope she puts the Foundry back on its feet.

Teacher. (Lifts his glass) And the Wagonworks.

Burgomaster. And the Golden Eagle Pencil Factory. Once that starts moving, everything else will go. *Prosit. (They touch glasses and drink.)*

Teacher. What does she need a panther for?

Burgomaster. Don't ask me. The whole thing is too much for me.
550 The Pastor had to go home and lie down.

Teacher. (Sets down his glass) If you want to know the truth, she frightens me.

Burgomaster. (Nods gravely) She's a strange one.

Teacher. You understand, Burgomaster, a man who for twenty-two years has been correcting the Latin compositions of the students of Güllen is not unaccustomed to surprises. I have seen things to make one's hair stand on end. But when this woman suddenly appeared on the platform, a shudder tore through me. It was as though out of the clear sky all at once a fury descended upon us, beating its black
560 wings—

(The Policeman comes in. He mops his face.)

Policeman. Ah! Now the old place is livening up a bit!

Burgomaster. Ah, Schultz, come and join us.

Policeman. Thank you. *(He calls.)* Beer!

Burgomaster. Well, what's the news from the front?

Policeman. I'm just back from Schiller's barn. My God! What a scene! She had us all tiptoeing around in the straw as if we were in church. Nobody dared to speak above a whisper. And the way she carried on! I was so embarrassed I let them go to the forest by them-
570 selves.

Burgomaster. Does the fiancé go with them?

Policeman. With his fishing rod and his landing net. In full marching order. *(He calls again.)* Beer!

Burgomaster. That will be her seventh husband.

Teacher. Her eighth.

Burgomaster. But what does she expect to find in the Konradsweil forest?

Policeman. The same thing she expected to find in the old barn, I suppose. The—the—

Teacher. The ashes of her youthful love. 580

Policeman. Exactly.

Teacher. It's poetry.

Policeman. Poetry.

Teacher. Sheer poetry! It makes one think of Shakespeare, of Wagner. Of Romeo and Juliet. *(The Second Man comes in as a waiter. The Policeman is served his beer.)*

Burgomaster. Yes, you're right. *(Solemnly)* Gentlemen, I would like to propose a toast. To our great and good friend, Anton Schill, who is even now working on our behalf.

Policeman. Yes! He's really working. 590

Burgomaster. Gentlemen, to the best-loved citizen of this town. My successor, Anton Schill!

(They raise their glasses. At this point an unearthly scream is heard. It is the black panther howling offstage. The sign of the Golden Apostle rises out of sight. The lights go down. The inn vanishes. Only the wooden bench, on which the four men were lounging in the opening scene, is left on the stage, downstage right. The procession comes on upstage. The two bodyguards carry in Claire's sedan chair. Next to it walks Schill. Pedro walks behind, with his fishing rod. Last come the two Blind Men and the butler. Claire alights.) 600

Claire. Stop! Take my chair off somewhere else. I'm tired of looking at you *(The bodyguards and the sedan chair go off.)* Pedro darling, your brook is just a little further along down that path. Listen. You can hear it from here. Bobby, take him and show him where it is.

Both Blind Men. We'll show him the way—we'll show him the way.

(They go off, left. Pedro follows. Bobby walks off, right.)

Claire. Look, Anton. Our tree. There's the heart you carved in the bark long ago.

Schill. Yes. It's still there.

Claire. How it has grown! The trunk is black and wrinkled. Why, 610 its limbs are twice what they were. Some of them have died.

Schill. It's aged. But it's there.

Claire. Like everything else. *(She crosses, examining other trees.)* Oh, how tall they are. How long it is since I walked here, barefoot over the pine needles and the damp eaves. Look, Anton. A fawn.

Schill. Yes, a fawn. It's the season.

Claire. I thought everything would be changed. But it's all just as we left it. This is the seat we sat on years ago. Under these branches you kissed me. And over there under the hawthorn, where the moss

620 is soft and green, we would lie in each other's arms. It is all as it used to be. Only we have changed.

Schill. Not so much, little witch. I remember the first night we spent together, you ran away and I chased you till I was quite breathless—

Claire. Yes.

Schill. Then I was angry and I was going home, when suddenly I heard you call and I looked up, and there you were sitting in a tree, laughing down at me.

Claire. No. It was in the great barn. I was in the hayloft.

Schill. Were you?

630 *Claire.* Yes. What else do you remember?

Schill. I remember the morning we went swimming by the waterfall, and afterwards we were lying together on the big rock in the sun, when suddenly we heard footsteps and we just had time to snatch up our clothes and run behind the bushes when the old pastor appeared and scolded you for not being in school.

Claire. No. It was the schoolmaster who found us. It was Sunday and I was supposed to be in church.

Schill. Really?

Claire. Yes. Tell me more.

640 *Schill.* I remember the time your father beat you, and you showed me the cuts on your back, and I swore I'd kill him. And the next day I dropped a tile from a roof top and split his head open.

Claire. You missed him.

Schill. No!

Claire. You hit old Mr. Reiner.

Schill. Did I?

Claire. Yes. I was seventeen. And you were not yet twenty. You were so handsome. You were the best-looking boy in town. *(The two Blind Men begin playing mandolin music offstage, very softly.)*

650 *Schill.* And you were the prettiest girl.

Claire. We were made for each other.

Schill. So we were.

Claire. But you married Mathilde Blumhard and her store, and I married old Zachanassian and his oil wells. He found me in a whorehouse in Hamburg. It was my hair that entangled him, the old golden beetle.

Schill. Clara!

Claire. *(She claps her hands.)* Bobby! A cigar. *(Bobby appears with a leather case. He selects a cigar, puts it in a holder, lights it, and*
660 *presents it to Claire.)*

Schill. My kitten smokes cigars!

Claire. Yes. I adore them. Would you care for one?

Schill. Yes, please. I've never smoked one of those.

Claire. It's a taste I acquired from old Zachanassian. Among other things. He was a real connoisseur.

Schill. We used to sit on this bench once, you and I, and smoke cigarettes. Do you remember?

Claire. Yes. I remember.

Schill. The cigarettes I bought from Mathilde.

Claire. No. She gave them to you for nothing. 670

Schill. Clara—don't be angry with me for marrying Mathilde.

Claire. She had money.

Schill. But what a lucky thing for you that I did!

Claire. Oh?

Schill. You were so young, so beautiful. You deserved a far better fate than to settle in this wretched town without any future.

Claire. Yes?

Schill. If you had stayed in Güllen and married me, your life would have been wasted, like mine..

Claire. Oh? 680

Schill. Look at me. A wretched shopkeeper in a bankrupt town!

Claire. But you have your family.

Schill. My family! Never for a moment do they let me forget my failure, my poverty.

Claire. Mathilde has not made you happy?

Schill. *(Shrugs)* What does it matter?

Claire. And the children?

Schill. *(Shakes his head)* They're so completely materialistic. You know, they have no interest whatever in higher things.

Claire. How sad for you. *(A moment's pause, during which only the faint tinkling of the music is heard)* 690

Schill. Yes. You know, since you went away my life has passed by like a stupid dream. I've hardly once been out of this town. A trip to a lake years ago. It rained all the time. And once five days in Berlin. That's all.

Claire. The world is much the same everywhere.

Schill. At least you've seen it.

Claire. Yes. I've seen it.

Schill. You've lived in it.

Claire. I've lived in it. The world and I have been on very intimate terms. 700

Schill. Now that you've come back, perhaps things will change.

Claire. Naturally. I certainly won't leave my native town in this condition.

Schill. It will take millions to put us on our feet again.

Claire. I have millions.

Schill. One, two, three.

Claire. Why not?

Schill. You mean—you will help us?

710 *Claire.* Yes. *(A woodpecker is heard in the distance.)*

Schill. I knew it—I knew it. I told them you were generous. I told them you were good. Oh, my kitten, my kitten. *(He takes her hand. She turns her head away and listens.)*

Claire. Listen! A woodpecker.

Schill. It's all just the way it was in the days when we were young and full of courage. The sun high above the pines. White clouds, piling up on one another. And the cry of the cuckoo in the distance. And the wind rustling the leaves, like the sound of surf on a beach. Just as it was years ago. If only we could roll back time and be together always.

720 *Claire.* Is that your wish?

Schill. Yes. You left me, but you never left my heart. *(He raises her hand to his lips.)* The same soft little hand.

Claire. No, not quite the same. It was crushed in the plane accident. But they mended it. They mend everything nowadays.

Schill. Crushed? You wouldn't know it. See, another fawn.

Claire. The old wood is alive with memories.

(Pedro appears, right, with a fish in his hand.)

Pedro. See what I've caught, darling. See? A pike. Over two kilos.

(The Blind Men appear onstage.)

730 *Both Blind Men. (Clapping their hands)* A pike! A pike! Hurrah! Hurrah!

(As the Blind Men clap their hands, Claire and Schill exit, and the scene dissolves. The clapping of hands is taken up on all sides. The townspeople wheel in the walls of the café. A brass band strikes up a march tune. The door of the Golden Apostle descends. The townspeople bring in tables and set them with ragged tablecloths, cracked china and glassware. There is a table in the center, upstage, flanked by two tables perpendicular to it, right and left. The Pastor and the Burgomaster come in. Schill enters. Other townspeople filter in, left and 740 right. One, the Athlete, is in gymnastic costume. The applause continues.)

Burgomaster. She's coming! *(Claire enters upstage, center, followed by Bobby.)* The applause is meant for you, gracious lady.

Claire. The band deserves it more than I. They blow from the heart. And the human pyramid was beautiful. You, show me your muscles. *(The Athlete kneels before her.)* Superb. Wonderful arms, powerful hands. Have you ever strangled a man with them?

Athlete. Strangled?

Claire. Yes. It's perfectly simple. A little pressure in the proper place, and the rest goes by itself. As in politics.

750 *(The Burgomaster's wife comes up, simpering.)*

Burgomaster. (Presents her) Permit me to present my wife, Madame Zachanassian.

Claire. Annette Dummermuth. The head of our class.

Burgomaster. (He presents another sour-looking woman.) Frau Schill.

Claire. Mathilde Blumhard. I remember the way you used to follow Anton with your eyes, from behind the shop door. You've grown a little thin and dry, my poor Mathilde.

Schill. My daughter, Ottilie.

Claire. Your daughter... 760

Schill. My son, Karl.

Claire. Your son. Two of them!

(The town Doctor comes in, right. He is a man of fifty, strong and stocky, with bristly black hair, a mustache and a saber cut on his cheek. He is wearing an old cutaway.)

Doctor. Well, well, my old Mercedes got me here in time after all!

Burgomaster. Dr. Nüsslin, the town physician. Madame Zachanassian.

Doctor. Deeply honored, madame. *(He kisses her hand. Claire studies him.)* 770

Claire. It is you who signs the death certificates?

Doctor. Death certificates?

Claire. When someone dies.

Doctor. Why certainly. That is one of my duties.

Claire. And when the heart dies, what do you put down? Heart failure?

Schill. (Laughing) What a golden sense of humor!

Doctor. Bit grim, wouldn't you say?

Schill. (Whispers) Not at all, not at all. She's promised us a million.

Burgomaster. (Turns his head) What? 780

Schill. A million!

All. (Whisper) A million! *(Claire turns toward them.)*

Claire. Burgomaster.

Burgomaster. Yes?

Claire. I'm hungry. *(The girls and the waiter fill glasses and bring food. There is a general stir. All take their places at the tables.)* Are you going to make a speech? *(The Burgomaster bows. Claire sits next to the Burgomaster. The Burgomaster rises, tapping his knife on his glass. He is radiant with good will. All applaud.)*

Burgomaster. Gracious lady and friends. Gracious lady, it is now many years since you first left your native town of Güllen, which was founded by the Elector Hasso and which nestles in the green slope between the forest of Konradsweil and the beautiful valley of Pückenried. Much has taken place in this time, much that is evil. 790

Teacher. That's true.

Burgomaster. The world is not what it was; it has become harsh and bitter, and we too have had our share of harshness and bitterness.

But in all this time, dear lady, we have never forgotten our little Clara. *(Applause)* Many years ago you brightened the town with your pretty 800 face as a child, and now once again you brighten it with your presence. *(Polite applause)* We haven't forgotten you, and we haven't forgotten your family. Your mother, beautiful and robust even in her old age— *(He looks for his notes on the table.)*—although unfortunately taken from us in the bloom of her youth by an infirmity of the lungs. Your respected father, Siegfried Wäscher, the builder, an example of whose work next to our railway station is often visited—*(Schill covers his face.)*—that is to say, admired—a lasting monument of local design and local workmanship. And you, gracious lady, whom we remember as a golden-haired—*(He looks at her.)*—little red-headed sprite romping 810 about our peaceful streets—on your way to school—which of us does not treasure your memory? *(He pokes nervously at his notebook.)* We well remember your scholarly attainments—

Teacher. Yes.

Burgomaster. Natural history . . . Extraordinary sense of justice . . . And, above all, your supreme generosity. *(Great applause)* We shall never forget how you once spent the whole of your little savings to buy a sack of potatoes for a poor starving widow who was in need of food. Gracious lady, ladies and gentlemen, today our little Clara has become the world-famous Claire Zachanassian who has founded 820 hospitals, soup kitchens, charitable institutes, art projects, libraries, nurseries and schools, and now that she has at last once more returned to the town of her birth, sadly fallen as it is, I say in the name of all her loving friends who have sorely missed her: Long live our Clara!

All. Long live our Clara! *(Cheers. Music. Fanfare. Applause. Claire rises.)*

Claire. Mr. Burgomaster. Fellow townsmen. I am greatly moved by the nature of your welcome and the disinterested joy which you have manifested on the occasion of my visit to my native town. I was not 830 quite the child the Burgomaster described in his gracious address . . .

Burgomaster. Too modest, madame.

Claire. In school I was beaten—

Teacher. Not by me.

Claire. And the sack of potatoes which I presented to Widow Boll, I stole with the help of Anton Schill, not to save the old trull from starvation, but so that for once I might sleep with Anton in a real bed instead of under the trees of the forest. *(The townspeople look grave, embarrassed.)* Nevertheless, I shall try to deserve your good opinion. In memory of the seventeen years I spent among you, I am prepared 840 to hand over as a gift to the town of Güllen the sum of one billion marks. Five hundred million to the town, and five hundred million to be divided per capita among the citizens. *(There is a moment of dead silence.)*

Burgomaster. A billion marks?

Claire. On one condition. *(Suddenly a movement of uncontrollable joy breaks out. People jump on chairs, dance about, yell excitedly. The Athlete turns handsprings in front of the speaker's table.)*

Schill. Oh, Clara, you astonishing, incredible, magnificent woman! What a heart! What a gesture! Oh—my little witch! *(He kisses her hand.)* 850

Burgomaster. (Holds up his arms for order.) Quiet! Quiet, please! On one condition, the gracious lady said. Now, madame, may we know what that condition is?

Claire. I will tell you. In exchange for my billion marks, I want justice. *(Silence)*

Burgomaster. Justice, madame?

Claire. I wish to buy justice.

Burgomaster. But justice cannot be bought, madame.

Claire. Everything can be bought.

Burgomaster. I don't understand at all. 860

Claire. Bobby, step forward. *(The butler goes to the center of the stage. He takes off his dark glasses and turns his face with a solemn air.)*

Bobby. Does anyone here present recognize me?

Frau Schill. Hofer! Hofer!

All. Who? What's that?

Teacher. Not Chief Magistrate Hofer?

Bobby. Exactly. Chief Magistrate Hofer. When Madame Zachanassian was a girl, I was presiding judge at the criminal court of Güllen. I served there until twenty-five years ago, when Madame 870 Zachanassian offered me the opportunity of entering her service as butler. I accepted. You may consider it a strange employment for a member of the magistracy, but the salary—*(Claire bangs the mallet on the table.)*

Claire. Come to the point.

Bobby. You have heard Madame Zachanassian's offer. She will give you a billion marks—when you have undone the injustice that she suffered at your hands here in Güllen as a girl. *(All murmur.)*

Burgomaster. Injustice at our hands? Impossible!

Bobby. Anton Schill . . . 880

Schill. Yes?

Bobby. Kindly stand. *(Schill rises. He smiles, as if puzzled. He shrugs.)*

Schill. Yes?

Bobby. In those days, a bastardy case was tried before me. Madame Claire Zachanassian, at that time called Clara Wäscher, charged you with being the father of her illegitimate child. *(Silence)* You denied the charge. And produced two witnesses in your support.

Schill. That's ancient history. An absurd business. We were children. Who remembers?

890 *Claire.* Where are the blind men?

Both Blind Men. Here we are. Here we are. *(Mike and Max push them forward.)*

Bobby. You recognize these men, Anton Schill?

Schill. I never saw them before in my life. What are they?

Both Blind Men. We've changed. We've changed.

Bobby. What were your names in your former life?

First Blind Man. I was Jacob Hueblein. Jacob Hueblein.

Second Blind Man. I was Ludwig Sparr. Ludwig Sparr.

Bobby. (To Schill) Well?

900 *Schill.* These names mean nothing to me.

Bobby. Jacob Hueblein and Ludwig Sparr, do you recognize the defendant?

First Blind Man. We're blind.

Second Blind Man. We're blind.

Schill. Ha-ha-ha!

Bobby. By his voice?

Both Blind Men. By his voice. By his voice.

Bobby. At that trial, I was the judge. And you?

Both Blind Men. We were the witnesses.

910 *Bobby.* And what did you testify on that occasion?

First Blind Man. That we had slept with Clara Wäscher.

Second Blind Man. Both of us. Many times.

Bobby. And was it true?

First Blind Man. No.

Second Blind Man. We swore falsely.

Bobby. And why did you swear falsely?

First Blind Man. Anton Schill bribed us.

Second Blind Man. He bribed us.

Bobby. With what?

920 *Both Blind Men.* With a bottle of schnapps.

Bobby. And now tell the people what happened to you. *(They hesitate and whimper.)* Speak!

First Blind Man. (In a low voice) She tracked us down.

Bobby. Madame Zachanassian tracked them down. Jacob Hueblein was found in Canada. Ludwig Sparr in Australia. And when she found you, what did she do to you?

Second Blind Man. She handed us over to Mike and Max.

Bobby. And what did Mike and Max do to you?

First Blind Man. They made us what you see. *(The Blind Men cover*
930 *their faces. Mike and Max push them off.)*

Bobby. And there you have it. We are all present in Güllen once again. The plaintiff. The defendant. The two false witnesses. The judge. Many years have passed. Does the plaintiff have anything further to add?

Claire. There is nothing to add.

Bobby. And the defendant?

Schill. Why are you doing this? It was all dead and buried.

Bobby. What happened to the child that was born?

Claire. (In a low voice) It lived a year.

Bobby. And what happened to you? 940

Claire. I became a whore.

Bobby. Why?

Claire. The judgment of the court left me no alternative. No one would trust me. No one would give me work.

Bobby. So. And now, what is the nature of the reparation you demand?

Claire. I want the life of Anton Schill. *(Frau Schill springs to Anton's side. She puts her arms around him. The children rush to him. He breaks away.)*

Frau Schill. Anton! No! No! 950

Schill. No— No— She's joking. That happened long ago. That's all forgotten.

Claire. Nothing is forgotten. Neither the mornings in the forest, nor the nights in the great barn, nor the bedroom in the cottage, nor your treachery at the end. You said this morning that you wished that time might be rolled back. Very well—I have rolled it back. And now it is I who will buy justice. You bought it with a bottle of schnapps. I am willing to pay one billion marks. *(The Burgomaster stands up, very pale and dignified.)*

Burgomaster. Madame Zachanassian, we are not in the jungle. 960 We are in Europe. We may be poor, but we are not heathens. In the name of the town of Güllen, I decline your offer. In the name of humanity. We shall never accept. *(All applaud wildly. The applause turns into a sinister rhythmic beat. As Claire rises, it dies away. She looks at the crowd, then at the Burgomaster.)*

Claire. Thank you, Burgomaster. *(She stares at him a long moment.)* I can wait. *(She turns and walks off. Curtain.)*

Act II

(The façade of the Golden Apostle, with a balcony on which chairs and a table are set out. To the right of the inn is a sign which reads: "Anton Schill, Handlung." *Under the sign the shop is represented by a broken counter. Behind the counter are some shelves with tobacco, cigarettes and liquor bottles. There are two milk cans. The shop door*

is imaginary, but each entrance is indicated by a doorbell with a tinny sound.)

(It is early morning.)

(Schill is sweeping the shop. The Son has a pan and brush and also sweeps. The Daughter is dusting. They are singing "The Happy Wanderer.")

Schill. Karl—*(Karl crosses with a dustpan. Schill sweeps dust into the pan. The doorbell rings. The Third Man appears, carrying a crate of eggs.)*

Third Man. 'Morning.

Schill. Ah, good morning, Wechsler.

Third Man. Twelve dozen eggs, medium brown. Right?

Schill. Take them, Karl. *(The Son puts the crate in a corner.)* Did they deliver the milk yet?

Son. Before you came down.

Third Man. Eggs are going up again, Herr Schill. First of the month. *(He gives Schill a slip to sign.)*

Schill. What? Again? And who's going to buy them?

Third Man. Fifty pfennig a dozen.

Schill. I'll have to cancel my order, that's all.

Third Man. That's up to you, Herr Schill. *(Schill signs the slip.)*

Schill. There's nothing else to do. *(He hands back the slip.)* And how's the family?

Third Man. Oh, scraping along. Maybe now things will get better.

Schill. Maybe.

Third Man. (Going) 'Morning.

Schill. Close the door. Don't let the flies in. *(The children resume their singing.)* Now, listen to me, children. I have a little piece of good news for you. I didn't mean to speak of it yet awhile, but well, why not? Who do you suppose is going to be the next Burgomaster? Eh? *(They look up at him.)* Yes, in spite of everything. It's settled. It's official. What an honor for the family, eh? Especially at a time like this. To say nothing of the salary and the rest of it.

Son. Burgomaster!

Schill. Burgomaster. *(The Son shakes him warmly by the hand. The Daughter kisses him.)* You see, you don't have to be entirely ashamed of your father. *(Silence)* Is your mother coming down to breakfast soon?

Daughter. Mother's tired. She's going to stay upstairs.

Schill. You have a good mother, at least. There you are lucky. Oh, well, if she wants to rest, let her rest. We'll have breakfast together, the three of us. I'll fry some eggs and open a tin of the American ham. This morning we're going to breakfast like kings.

Son. I'd like to, only—I can't.

Schill. You've got to eat, you know. 50

Son. I've got to run down to the station. One of the laborers is sick. They said they could use me.

Schill. You want to work on the rails in all this heat? That's no work for a son of mine.

Son. Look, Father, we can use the money.

Schill. Well, if you feel you have to. *(The Son goes to the door. The Daughter moves toward Schill.)*

Daughter. I'm sorry, Father. I have to go too.

Schill. You too? And where is the young lady going, if I may be so bold? 60

Daughter. There may be something for me at the employment agency.

Schill. Employment agency?

Daughter. It's important to get there early.

Schill. All right. I'll have something nice for you when you get home.

Son and Daughter. (Salute) Good day, Burgomaster.

(The Son and Daughter go out.)

Lynn Fontanne as Claire, Alfred Lunt as Schill, in the original American production of The Visit *at the Lunt-Fontanne Theatre, New York, 1958.*

(The First Man comes into Schill's shop. Mandolin and guitar music are heard offstage.)

70 *Schill.* Good morning, Hofbauer.

First Man. Cigarettes. *(Schill takes a pack from the shelf.)* Not those. I'll have the green today.

Schill. They cost more.

First Man. Put it in the book.

Schill. What?

First Man. Charge it.

Schill. Well, all right, I'll make an exception this time—seeing it's you, Hofbauer. *(Schill writes in his cash book.)*

First Man. (Opening the pack of cigarettes) Who's that playing 80 out there?

Schill. The two blind men.

First Man. They play well.

Schill. To hell with them.

First Man. They make you nervous? *(Schill shrugs. The First Man lights a cigarette.)* She's getting ready for the wedding, I hear.

Schill. Yes. So they say.

(Enter the First and Second Woman. They cross to the counter.)

First Woman. Good morning, good morning.

Second Woman. Good morning.

90 *First Man.* Good morning.

Schill. Good morning, ladies.

First Woman. Good morning, Herr Schill.

Second Woman. Good morning.

First Woman. Milk please, Herr Schill.

Schill. Milk.

Second Woman. And milk for me too.

Schill. A liter of milk each. Right away.

First Woman. Whole milk, please, Herr Schill.

Schill. Whole milk?

100 *Second Woman.* Yes. Whole milk, please.

Schill. Whole milk, I can only give you half a liter each of whole milk.

First Woman. All right.

Schill. Half a liter of whole milk here, and half a liter of whole milk here. There you are.

First Woman. And butter please, a quarter kilo.

Schill. Butter, I haven't any butter. I can give you some very nice lard?

First Woman. No. Butter.

110 *Schill.* Goose fat? *(The First Woman shakes her head.)* Chicken fat?

First Woman. Butter.

Schill. Butter. Now, wait a minute, though. I have a tin of imported butter here somewhere. Ah. There you are. No, sorry, she asked first, but I can order some for you from Kalberstadt tomorrow.

Second Woman. And white bread.

Schill. White bread. *(He takes a loaf and a knife.)*

Second Woman. The whole loaf.

Schill. But a whole loaf would cost . . .

Second Woman. Charge it.

Schill. Charge it? 120

First Woman. And a package of milk chocolate.

Schill. Package of milk chocolate—right away.

Second Woman. One for me, too, Herr Schill.

Schill. And a package of milk chocolate for you, too.

First Woman. We'll eat it here, if you don't mind.

Schill. Yes, please do.

Second Woman. It's so cool at the back of the shop.

Schill. Charge it?

Women. Of course.

Schill. All for one, one for all. 130

(The Second Man enters.)

Second Man. Good morning.

The Two Women. Good morning.

Schill. Good morning, Helmesberger.

Second Man. It's going to be a hot day.

Schill. Phew!

Second Man. How's business?

Schill. Fabulous. For a while no one came, and now all of a sudden I'm running a luxury trade.

Second Man. Good! 140

Schill. Oh, I'll never forget the way you all stood by me at the Golden Apostle in spite of your need, in spite of everything. That was the finest hour of my life.

First Man. We're not heathens, you know.

Second Man. We're behind you, my boy; the whole town's behind you.

First Man. As firm as a rock.

First Woman. *(Munching her chocolate)* As firm as a rock, Herr Schill.

Both Women. As firm as a rock.

Second Man. There's no denying it—you're the most popular man in town. 150

First Man. The most important.

Second Man. And in the spring, God willing, you will be our Burgomaster.

First Man. Sure as a gun.

All. Sure as a gun.

(Enter Pedro with fishing equipment and a fish in his landing net)

Pedro. Would you please weigh my fish for me?

Schill. (Weighs it) Two kilos.

Pedro. Is that all?

160 *Schill.* Two kilos exactly.

Pedro. Two kilos! *(He gives Schill a tip and exits.)*

Second Woman. The fiancé.

First Woman. They're to be married this week. It will be a tremendous wedding.

Second Woman. I saw his picture in the paper.

First Woman. (Sighs) Ah, what a man!

Second Man. Give me a bottle of schnapps.

Schill. The usual?

Second Man. No, cognac.

170 *Schill.* Cognac? But cognac costs twenty-two marks fifty.

Second Man. We all have to splurge a little now and again—

Schill. Here you are. Three Star.

Second Man. And a package of pipe tobacco.

Schill. Black or blond?

Second Man. English.

Schill. English! But that makes twenty-three marks eighty.

Second Man. Chalk it up.

Schill. Now, look. I'll make an exception this week. Only, you will have to pay me the moment your unemployment check comes in. I
180 don't want to be kept waiting. *(Suddenly)* Helmesberger, are those new shoes you're wearing?

Second Man. Yes, what about it?

Schill. You too, Hofbauer. Yellow shoes! Brand new!

First Man. So?

Schill. (To the women) And you. You all have new shoes! New shoes!

First Woman. A person can't walk around forever in the same old shoes.

Second Woman. Shoes wear out.

Schill. And the money. Where does the money come from?

190 *First Woman.* We got them on credit, Herr Schill.

Second Woman. On credit.

Schill. On credit? And where all of a sudden do you get credit?

Second Man. Everybody gives credit now.

First Woman. You gave us credit yourself.

Schill. And what are you going to pay with? Eh? *(They are all silent. Schill advances upon them threateningly.)* With what? Eh? With what? With what?

(Suddenly he understands. He takes his apron off quickly, flings it on the counter, gets his jacket, and walks off with an air of determination.

Now the shop sign vanishes. The shelves are pushed off. The lights go up on the balcony of the Golden Apostle, and the balcony unit itself moves forward into the optical center. Claire and Bobby step out on the balcony. Claire sits down. Bobby serves coffee.) 200

Claire. A lovely autumn morning. A silver haze on the streets and a violet sky above. Count Holk would have liked this. Remember him, Bobby? My third husband?

Bobby. Yes, madame.

Claire. Horrible man!

Bobby. Yes, madame.

Claire. Where is Monsieur Pedro? Is he up yet? 210

Bobby. Yes, madame. He's fishing.

Claire. Already? What a singular passion!

(Pedro comes in with the fish.)

Pedro. Good morning, my love.

Claire. Pedro! There you are.

Pedro. Look, my darling. Four kilos!

Claire. A jewel! I'll have it grilled for your lunch. Give it to Bobby.

Pedro. Ah—it is so wonderful here! I like your little town.

Claire. Oh, do you?

Pedro. Yes. These people, they are all so—what is the word? 220

Claire. Simple, honest, hard-working, decent.

Pedro. But, my angel, you are a mind reader. That's just what I was going to say—however did you guess?

Claire. I know them.

Pedro. Yet when we arrived it was all so dirty, so—what is the word?

Claire. Shabby.

Pedro. Exactly. But now everywhere you go, you see them busy as bees, cleaning their streets—

Claire. Repairing their houses, sweeping—dusting—hanging new curtains in the windows—singing as they work. 230

Pedro. But you astonishing, wonderful woman! You can't see all that from here.

Claire. I know them. And in their gardens—I am sure that in their gardens they are manuring the soil for the spring.

Pedro. My angel, you know everything. This morning on my way fishing I said to myself, look at them all manuring their gardens. It is extraordinary—and it's all because of you. Your return has given them a new—what is the word?

Claire. Lease on life?

Pedro. Precisely. 240

Claire. The town was dying, it's true. But a town doesn't have to die. I think they realize that now. People die, not towns. Bobby! *(Bobby appears.)* A cigar.

(The lights fade on the balcony, which moves back upstage. Somewhat to the right, a sign descends. It reads: "Polizei." *The Policeman pushes a desk under it. This, with the bench, becomes the police station. He places a bottle of beer and a glass on the desk, and goes to hang up his coat offstage. The telephone rings.)*

Policeman. Schultz speaking. Yes, we have a couple of rooms for
250 the night. No, not for rent. This is not the hotel. This is the Güllen police station. *(He laughs and hangs up. Schill comes in. He is evidently nervous.)*

Schill. Schultz.

Policeman. Hello, Schill. Come in. Sit down. Beer?

Schill. Please. *(He drinks thirstily.)*

Policeman. What can I do for you?

Schill. I want you to arrest Madame Zachanassian.

Policeman. Eh?

Schill. I said I want you to arrest Madame Zachanassian.

260 *Policeman.* What the hell are you talking about?

Schill. I ask you to arrest this woman at once.

Policeman. What offense has the lady committed?

Schill. You know perfectly well. She offered a billion marks—

Policeman. And you want her arrested for that? *(He pours beer into his glass.)*

Schill. Schultz! It's your duty.

Schultz. Extraordinary! Extraordinary idea! *(He drinks his beer.)*

Schill. I'm speaking to you as your next Burgomaster.

Policeman. Schill, that's true. The lady offered us a billion marks.
270 But that doesn't entitle us to take police action against her.

Schill. Why not?

Policeman. In order to be arrested, a person must first commit a crime.

Schill. Incitement to murder.

Policeman. Incitement to murder is a crime. I agree.

Schill. Well?

Policeman. And such a proposal—if serious—constitutes an assault.

Schill. That's what I mean.

Policeman. But her offer can't be serious.

280 *Schill.* Why?

Policeman. The price is too high. In a case like yours, one pays a thousand marks, at the most two thousand. But not a billion! That's ridiculous. And even if she meant it, that would only prove she was out of her mind. And that's not a matter for the police.

Schill. Whether she's out of her mind or not, the danger to me is the same. That's obvious.

Policeman. Look, Schill, you show us where anyone threatens your life in any way—say, for instance, a man points a gun at you—and we'll be there in a flash.

Schill. (Gets up) So I'm to wait till someone points a gun at me? 290

Policeman. Pull yourself together, Schill. We're all for you in this town.

Schill. I wish I could believe it.

Policeman. You don't believe it?

Schill. No. No, I don't. All of a sudden my customers are buying white bread, whole milk, butter, imported tobacco. What does it mean?

Policeman. It means business is picking up.

Schill. Helmesberger lives on the dole; he hasn't earned anything in five years. Today he bought French cognac.

Policeman. I'll have to try your cognac one of these days. 300

Schill. And shoes. They all have new shoes.

Policeman. And what have you got against new shoes? I'm wearing a new pair myself. *(He holds out his foot.)*

Schill. You too?

Policeman. Why not? *(He pours out the rest of his beer.)*

Schill. Is that Pilsen you're drinking now?

Policeman. It's the only thing.

Schill. You used to drink the local beer.

Policeman. Hogwash. *(Radio music is heard offstage.)*

Schill. Listen. You hear? 310

Policeman. "The Merry Widow." Yes.

Schill. No. It's a radio.

Policeman. That's Bergholzer's radio.

Schill. Bergholzer!

Policeman. You're right. He should close his window when he plays it. I'll make a note to speak to him. *(He makes a note in his notebook.)*

Schill. And how can Bergholzer pay for a radio?

Policeman. That's his business.

Schill. And you, Schultz, with your new shoes and your imported beer—how are you going to pay for them? 320

Policeman. That's my business. *(His telephone rings. He picks it up.)* Police Station, Güllen. What? What? Where? Where? How? Right, we'll deal with it. *(He hangs up.)*

Schill. (He speaks during the Policeman's telephone conversation.) Schultz, listen. No. Schultz, please—listen to me. Don't you see they're all . . . Listen, please. Look, Schultz. They're all running up debts. And out of these debts comes this sudden prosperity. And out of this prosperity comes the absolute need to kill me.

Policeman. (Putting on his jacket) You're imagining things.

330 *Schill.* All she has to do is to sit on her balcony and wait.

Policeman. Don't be a child.

Schill. You're all waiting.

Policeman. (Snaps a loaded clip into the magazine of a rifle) Look, Schill, you can relax. The police are here for your protection. They know their job. Let anyone, any time, make the slightest threat to your life, and all you have to do is let us know. We'll do the rest . . . Now, don't worry.

Schill. No, I won't.

Policeman. And don't upset yourself. All right?

340 *Schill.* Yes. I won't. *(Then suddenly, in a low tone)* You have a new gold tooth in your mouth!

Policeman. What are you talking about?

Schill. (Taking the Policeman's head in his hands, and forcing his lips open) A brand new, shining gold tooth.

Policeman. (Breaks away and involuntarily levels the gun at Schill) Are you crazy? Look, I've no time to waste. Madame Zachanassian's panther's broken loose.

Schill. Panther?

Policeman. Yes, it's at large. I've got to hunt it down.

350 *Schill.* You're not hunting a panther and you know it. It's me you're hunting! *(The Policeman clicks on the safety and lowers the gun.)*

Policeman. Schill! Take my advice. Go home. Lock the door. Keep out of everyone's way. That way you'll be safe. Cheer up! Good times are just around the corner! *(The lights dim in this area and light up on the balcony. Pedro is lounging in a chair. Claire is smoking.)*

Pedro. Oh, this little town oppresses me.

Claire. Oh, does it? So you've changed your mind?

Pedro. It is true, I find it charming, delightful—

Claire. Picturesque.

360 *Pedro.* Yes. After all, it's the place where you were born. But it is too quiet for me. Too provincial. Too much like all small towns everywhere. These people—look at them. They fear nothing, they desire nothing, they strive for nothing. They have everything they want. They are asleep.

Claire. Perhaps one day they will come to life again.

Pedro. My God—do I have to wait for that?

Claire. Yes, you do. Why don't you go back to your fishing?

Pedro. I think I will. *(Pedro turns to go.)*

Claire. Pedro.

370 *Pedro.* Yes, my love?

Claire. Telephone the president of Hambro's Bank. Ask him to transfer a billion marks to my current account.

Pedro. A billion? Yes, my love.

(He goes. The lights fade on the balcony. A sign is flown in. It reads: "Rathaus."° *The Third Man crosses the stage, right to left, wheeling a new television set on a hand truck. The counter of Schill's shop is transformed into the Burgomaster's office. The Burgomaster comes in. He takes a revolver from his pocket, examines it and sets it down on the desk. He sits down and starts writing. Schill knocks.)*

Burgomaster. Come in. 380

Schill. I must have a word with you, Burgomaster.

Burgomaster. Ah, Schill. Sit down, my friend.

Schill. Man to man. As your successor.

Burgomaster. But of course. Naturally. *(Schill remains standing. He looks at the revolver.)*

Schill. Is that a gun?

Burgomaster. Madame Zachanassian's black panther's broken loose. It's been seen near the cathedral. It's as well to be prepared.

Schill. Oh, yes. Of course.

Burgomaster. I've sent out a call for all able-bodied men with fire- 390 arms. The streets have been cleared. The children have been kept in school. We don't want any accidents.

Schill. (Suspiciously) You're making quite a thing of it.

Burgomaster. (Shrugs) Naturally. A panther is a dangerous beast. Well? What's on your mind? Speak out. We're old friends.

Schill. That's a good cigar you're smoking, Burgomaster.

Burgomaster. Yes. Havana.

Schill. You used to smoke something else.

Burgomaster. Fortuna.

Schill. Cheaper. 400

Burgomaster. Too strong.

Schill. A new tie? Silk?

Burgomaster. Yes. Do you like it?

Schill. And have you also bought new shoes?

Burgomaster. (Brings his feet out from under the desk) Why, yes. I ordered a new pair from Kalberstadt. Extraordinary! However did you guess?

Schill. That's why I'm here. *(The Third Man knocks.)*

Burgomaster. Come in.

Third Man. The new typewriter, sir. 410

Burgomaster. Put it on the table. *(The Third Man sets it down and goes.)* What's the matter with you? My dear fellow, aren't you well?

Schill. It's you who don't seem well, Burgomaster.

Burgomaster. What do you mean?

Schill. You look pale.

375. *Rathaus,* City Hall.

Burgomaster. I?

Schill. Your hands are trembling. *(The Burgomaster involuntarily hides his hands.)* Are you frightened?

Burgomaster. What have I to be afraid of?

420 *Schill.* Perhaps this sudden prosperity alarms you.

Burgomaster. Is prosperity a crime?

Schill. That depends on how you pay for it.

Burgomaster. You'll have to forgive me, Schill, but I really haven't the slightest idea what you're talking about. Am I supposed to feel like a criminal every time I order a new typewriter?

Schill. Do you?

Burgomaster. Well, I hope you haven't come here to talk about a new typewriter. Now, what was it you wanted?

Schill. I have come to claim the protection of the authorities.

430 *Burgomaster.* Ei! Against whom?

Schill. You know against whom.

Burgomaster. You don't trust us?

Schill. That woman has put a price on my head.

Burgomaster. If you don't feel safe, why don't you go to the police?

Schill. I have just come from the police.

Burgomaster. And?

Schill. The chief has a new gold tooth in his mouth.

Burgomaster. A new—? Oh, Schill, really! You're forgetting. This is Güllen, the town of humane traditions. Goethe slept here. Brahms com-
440 posed a quartet. You must have faith in us. This is a law-abiding community.

Schill. Then arrest this woman who wants to have me killed.

Burgomaster. Look here, Schill. God knows the lady has every right to be angry with you. What you did there wasn't very pretty. You forced two decent lads to perjure themselves and had a young girl thrown out on the streets.

Schill. That young girl owns half the world. *(A moment's silence)*

Burgomaster. Very well, then, we'll speak frankly.

Schill. That's why I'm here.

450 *Burgomaster.* Man to man, just as you said. *(He clears his throat.)* Now—after what you did, you have no moral right to say a word against this lady. And I advise you not to try. Also—I regret to have to tell you this—there is no longer any question of your being elected Burgomaster.

Schill. Is that official?

Burgomaster. Official.

Schill. I see.

Burgomaster. The man who is chosen to exercise the high post of Burgomaster must have, obviously, certain moral qualifications. Qualifications which, unhappily, you no longer possess. Naturally, you may count on the esteem and friendship of the town, just as before. That goes without saying. The best thing will be to spread the mantle of silence over the whole miserable business. 460

Schill. So I'm to remain silent while they arrange my murder? *(The Burgomaster gets up.)*

Burgomaster. (Suddenly noble) Now, who is arranging your murder? Give me the names and I will investigate the case at once. Unrelentingly. Well? The names?

Schill. You.

Burgomaster. I resent this. Do you think we want to kill you for money? 470

Schill. No. You don't want to kill me. But you want to have me killed.

(The lights go down. The stage is filled with men prowling about with rifles, as if they were stalking a quarry. In the interval the Policeman's bench and the Burgomaster's desk are shifted somewhat, so that they will compose the setting for the sacristy. The stage empties. The lights come up on the balcony.)

(Claire appears)

Claire. Bobby, what's going on here? What are all these men doing with guns? Whom are they hunting?

Bobby. The black panther has escaped, madame. 480

Claire. Who let him out?

Bobby. Kobby and Lobby, madame.

Claire. How excited they are! There may be shooting?

Bobby. It is possible, madame.

(The lights fade on the balcony. The sacristan comes in. He arranges the set, and puts the altar cloth on the altar. Then Schill comes on. He is looking for the Pastor. The Pastor enters, left. He is wearing his gown and carrying a rifle.)

Schill. Sorry to disturb you, Pastor.

Pastor. God's house is open to all. *(He sees that Schill is staring at the gun.)* Oh, the gun? That's because of the panther. It's best to be prepared. 490

Schill. Pastor, help me.

Pastor. Of course. Sit down. *(He puts the rifle on the bench.)* What's the trouble?

Schill. (Sits on the bench) I'm frightened.

Pastor. Frightened? Of what?

Schill. Of everyone. They're hunting me down like a beast.

Pastor. Have no fear of man, Schill. Fear God. Fear not the death of the body. Fear the death of the soul. Zip up my gown behind, Sacristan. 500

Schill. I'm afraid, Pastor.

Pastor. Put your trust in heaven, my friend.

Schill. You see, I'm not well. I shake. I have such pains around the heart. I sweat.

Pastor. I know. You're passing through a profound psychic experience.

Schill. I'm going through hell.

Pastor. The hell you are going through exists only within yourself. 510 Many years ago you betrayed a girl shamefully, for money. Now you think that we shall sell you just as you sold her. No, my friend, you are projecting your guilt upon others. It's quite natural. But remember, the root of our torment lies always within ourselves, in our hearts, in our sins. When you have understood this, you can conquer the fears that oppress you; you have weapons with which to destroy them.

Schill. Siemethofer has bought a new washing machine.

Pastor. Don't worry about the washing machine. Worry about your immortal soul.

Schill. Stockers has a television set.

520 *Pastor.* There is also great comfort in prayer. Sacristan, the bands. *(Schill crosses to the altar and kneels. The sacristan ties on the Pastor's bands.)* Examine your conscience, Schill. Repent. Otherwise your fears will consume you. Believe me, this is the only way. We have no other. *(The church bell begins to peal. Schill seems relieved.)* Now I must leave you. I have a baptism. You may stay as long as you like. Sacristan, the Bible, Liturgy and Psalter. The child is beginning to cry. I can hear it from here. It is frightened. Let us make haste to give it the only security which this world affords.

Schill. A new bell?

530 *Pastor.* Yes. Its tone is marvelous, don't you think? Full. Sonorous.

Schill. (Steps back in horror) A new bell! You too, Pastor? You too? *(The Pastor clasps his hands in horror. Then he takes Schill into his arms.)*

Pastor. Oh, God, God forgive me. We are poor, weak things, all of us. Do not tempt us further into the hell in which you are burning. Go, Schill, my friend, go, my brother, go while there is time.

(The Pastor goes.)

(Schill picks up the rifle with a gesture of desperation. He goes out with it. As the lights fade, men appear with guns. Two shots are fired 540 *in the darkness. The lights come up on the balcony, which moves forward.)*

Claire. Bobby! What was that shooting? Have they caught the panther?

Bobby. He is dead, madame.

Claire. There were two shots.

Bobby. The panther is dead, madame.

Claire. I loved him. *(Waves Bobby away)* I shall miss him.

(The Teacher comes in with two little girls, singing. They stop under the balcony.)

Teacher. Gracious lady, be so good as to accept our heartfelt condolences. Your beautiful panther is no more. Believe me, we are deeply pained that so tragic an event should mar your visit here. But what could we do? The panther was savage, a beast. To him our human laws could not apply. There was no other way—*(Schill appears with the gun. He looks dangerous. The girls run off, frightened. The Teacher follows the girls.)* Children—children—children! 550

Claire. Anton, why are you frightening the children? *(He works the bolt, loading the chamber, and raises the gun slowly.)*

Schill. Go away, Claire—I warn you. Go away.

Claire. How strange it is, Anton! How clearly it comes back to me! The day we saw one another for the first time, do you remember? I was on a balcony then. It was a day like today, a day in autumn without a breath of wind, warm as it is now—only lately I am always cold. You stood down there and stared at me without moving. I was embarrassed. I didn't know what to do. I wanted to go back into the darkness of the room, where it was safe, but I couldn't. You stared up at me darkly, almost angrily, as if you wished to hurt me, but your eyes were full of passion. *(Schill begins to lower the rifle involuntarily.)* Then, I don't know why, I left the balcony and I came down and stood in the street beside you. You didn't greet me, you didn't say a word, but you took my hand and we walked together out of the town into the fields, and behind us came Kobby and Lobby, like two dogs, sniveling and giggling and snarling. Suddenly you picked up a stone and hurled it at them, and they ran yelping back into the town, and we were alone. *(Schill has lowered the rifle completely. He moves forward toward her, as close as he can come.)* That was the beginning, and everything else had to follow. There is no escape. *(She goes in and closes the shutters. Schill stands immobile. The Teacher tiptoes in. He stares at Schill, who doesn't see him. Then he beckons to the children.)* 560 570

Teacher. Come, children, sing. Sing. *(They begin singing. He creeps behind Schill and snatches away the rifle. Schill turns sharply. The Pastor comes in.)* 580

Pastor. Go, Schill—go!

(Schill goes out. The children continue singing, moving across the stage and off. The Golden Apostle vanishes. The crossing bell is heard. The scene dissolves into the railway-station setting, as in Act One. But there are certain changes. The timetable marked "Fahrplan" *is now new, the frame freshly painted. There is a new travel poster on the station wall. It has a yellow sun and the words:* "Reist in den Süden."° *On the*

589. *Reist in den Süden,* travel to the South.

590 *other side of the Fahrplan is another poster with the words:* "Die Passionsspiele Oberammergau."° *The sound of passing trains covers the scene change. Schill appears with an old valise in his hand, dressed in a shabby trench coat, his hat on his head. He looks about with a furtive air, walking slowly to the platform. Slowly, as if by chance, the townspeople enter, from all sides. Schill hesitates, stops.)*

Burgomaster. (From upstage, center) Good evening, Schill.

Schill. Good evening.

Policeman. Good evening.

Schill. Good evening.

600 *Painter. (Enters)* Good evening.

Schill. Good evening.

Doctor. Good evening.

Schill. Good evening.

Burgomaster. So you're taking a little trip?

Schill. Yes. A little trip.

Policeman. May one ask where to?

Schill. I don't know.

Painter. Don't know?

Schill. To Kalberstadt.

610 *Burgomaster. (With disbelief, pointing to the valise)* Kalberstadt?

Schill. After that—somewhere else.

Painter. Ah. After that somewhere else.

(The Fourth Man walks in.)

Schill. I thought maybe Australia.

Burgomaster. Australia!

All. Australia!

Schill. I'll raise the money somehow.

Burgomaster. But why Australia?

Policeman. What would you be doing in Australia?

620 *Schill.* One can't always live in the same town, year in, year out.

Painter. But Australia—

Doctor. It's a risky trip for a man of your age.

Burgomaster. One of the lady's little men ran off to Australia . . .

All. Yes.

Policeman. You'll be much safer here.

Painter. Much! *(Schill looks about him in anguish, like a beast at bay.)*

Schill. (Low voice) I wrote a letter to the administration at Kaffigen.

Burgomaster. Yes? And? *(They are all intent on the answer.)*

630 *Schill.* They didn't answer. *(All laugh.)*

590-591. Die Passionsspiele Oberammergau, the Oberammergau Passion Play. The German village of Oberammergau continues the tradition of the medieval play depicting the life and death of Jesus. It is now a major tourist attraction.

Doctor. Do you mean to say you don't trust your old friends? That's not very flattering, you know.

Burgomaster. No one's going to do you any harm here.

Doctor. No harm here.

Schill. They didn't answer because our postmaster held up my letter.

Painter. Our postmaster? What an idea.

Burgomaster. The postmaster is a member of the town council.

Policeman. A man of the utmost integrity.

Doctor. He doesn't hold up letters. What an idea! *(The crossing bell starts ringing.)* 640

Station Master. (Announces) Local to Kalberstadt! *(The townspeople all cross down to see the train arrive. Then they turn, with their backs to the audience, in a line across the stage. Schill cannot get through to reach the train.)*

Schill. (In a low voice) What are you all doing here? What do you want of me?

Burgomaster. We don't like to see you go.

Doctor. We've come to see you off. *(The sound of the approaching train grows louder.)*

Schill. I didn't ask you to come. 650

Policeman. But we have come.

Doctor. As old friends.

All. As old friends. *(The Station Master holds up his paddle. The train stops with a screech of brakes. We hear the engine panting offstage.)*

Voice. (Offstage) Güllen!

Burgomaster. A pleasant journey.

Doctor. And long life!

Painter. And good luck in Australia!

All. Yes, good luck in Australia. *(They press around him jovially. He stands motionless and pale.)* 660

Schill. Why are you crowding me?

Policeman. What's the matter now? *(The Station Master blows a long blast on his whistle.)*

Schill. Give me room.

Doctor. But you have plenty of room. *(They all move away from him.)*

Policeman. Better get aboard, Schill.

Schill. I see. I see. One of you is going to push me under the wheels.

Policeman. Oh, nonsense. Go on, get aboard.

Schill. Get away from me, all of you. 670

Burgomaster. I don't know what you want. Just get on the train.

Schill. No. One of you will push me under.

Doctor. You're being ridiculous. Now, go on, get on the train.

Schill. Why are you all so near me?

Doctor. The man's gone mad.

Station Master. 'Board! *(He blows his whistle. The engine bell clangs. The train starts.)*

Burgomaster. Get aboard, man. Quick. *(The following speeches are spoken all together until the train noises fade away.)*

680 *Doctor.* The train's starting.

All. Get aboard, man. Get aboard. The train's starting.

Schill. If I try to get aboard, one of you will hold me back.

All. No, no.

Burgomaster. Get on the train.

Schill. (In terror, crouches against the wall of the Station Master's office) No—no—no. No. *(He falls on his knees. The others crowd around him. He cowers on the ground, abjectly. The train sounds fade away.)* Oh, no—no—don't push me, don't push me!

Policeman. There. It's gone off without you. *(Slowly they leave him.*
690 *He raises himself up to a sitting position, still trembling. A Truck Driver enters with an empty can.)*

Truck Driver. Do you know where I can get some water? My truck's boiling over. *(Schill points to the station office.)* Thanks. *(He enters the office, gets the water and comes out. By this time, Schill is erect.)* Missed your train?

Schill. Yes.

Truck Driver. To Kalberstadt?

Schill. Yes.

Truck Driver. Well, come with me. I'm going that way.

700 *Schill.* This is my town. This is my home. *(With strange new dignity)* No, thank you. I've changed my mind. I'm staying.

Truck Driver. (Shrugs) All right.

(He goes out. Schill picks up his bag, looks right and left, and slowly walks off. Curtain.)

Act III

(Music is heard. Then the curtain rises on the interior of the old barn, a dim, cavernous structure. Bars of light fall across the shadowy forms, shafts of sunlight from the holes and cracks in the walls and roof. Overhead hang old rags, decaying sacks, great cobwebs. Extreme left is a ladder leading to the loft. Near it, an old haycart. Left, Claire Zachanassian is sitting in her gilded sedan chair, motionless, in her magnificent bridal gown and veil. Near the chair stands an old keg.)

Bobby. (Comes in, treading carefully) The doctor and the teacher from the high school to see you, madame.

10 *Claire. (Impassive)* Show them in. *(Bobby ushers them in as if they were entering a hall of state. The two grope their way through the litter.*

At last they find the lady, and bow. They are both well dressed in new clothes, but are very dusty.)

Bobby. Dr. Nüsslin and Professor Müller.

Doctor. Madame.

Claire. You look dusty, gentlemen.

Doctor. (Dusts himself off vigorously) Oh, forgive us. We had to climb over an old carriage.

Teacher. Our respects.

Doctor. A fabulous wedding. 20

Teacher. Beautiful occasion.

Claire. It's stifling here. But I love this old barn. The smell of hay and old straw and axle grease—it is the scent of my youth. Sit down. All this rubbish—the haycart, the old carriage, the cask, even the pitchfork—it was all here when I was a girl.

Teacher. Remarkable place. *(He mops his brow.)*

Claire. I thought the pastor's text was very appropriate. The lesson a trifle long.

Teacher. I Corinthians 13.°

Claire. Your choristers sang beautifully, Professor. 30

Teacher. Bach. From the *St. Matthew Passion.*

Doctor. Güllen has never seen such magnificence! The flowers! The jewels! And the people.

Teacher. The theatrical world, the world of finance, the world of art, the world of science . . .

Claire. All these worlds are now back in their Cadillacs, speeding toward the capital for the wedding reception. But I'm sure you didn't come here to talk about them.

Doctor. Dear lady, we should not intrude on your valuable time. Your husband must be waiting impatiently. 40

Claire. No, no, I've packed him off to Brazil.

Doctor. To Brazil, madame?

Claire. Yes. For his honeymoon.

Teacher and Doctor. Oh! But your wedding guests?

Claire. I've planned a delightful dinner for them. They'll never miss me. Now what was it you wished to talk about?

Teacher. About Anton Schill, madame.

Claire. Is he dead?

Teacher. Madame, we may be poor. But we have our principles.

Claire. I see. Then what do you want? 50

Teacher. (He mops his brow again.) The fact is, madame, in anticipation of your well-known munificence, that is, feeling that you would

29. I. Corinthians 13:13: "But now abideth faith, hope, love, these three; and the greatest of these is love."

give the town some sort of gift, we have all been buying things. Necessities . . .

Doctor. With money we don't have. *(The Teacher blows his nose.)*

Claire. You've run into debt?

Doctor. Up to here.

Claire. In spite of your principles?

Teacher. We're human, madame.

60 *Claire.* I see.

Teacher. We have been poor for a long time. A long, long time.

Doctor. *(He rises.)* The question is, how are we going to pay?

Claire. You already know.

Teacher. *(Courageously)* I beg you, Madame Zachanassian, put yourself in our position for a moment. For twenty-two years I've been cudgeling my brains to plant a few seeds of knowledge in this wilderness. And all this time, my gallant colleague, Dr. Nüsslin, has been rattling around in his ancient Mercedes, from patient to patient, trying to keep these wretches alive. Why? Why have we spent our lives in this
70 miserable hole? For money? Hardly. The pay is ridiculous.

Doctor. And yet, the professor here has declined an offer to head the high school in Kalberstadt.

Teacher. And Dr. Nüsslin has refused an important post at the University of Erlangen. Madame, the simple fact is, we love our town. We were born here. It is our life.

Doctor. That's true.

Teacher. What has kept us going all these years is the hope that one day the community will prosper again as it did in the days when we were young.

80 *Claire.* Good.

Teacher. Madame, there is no reason for our poverty. We suffer here from a mysterious blight. We have factories. They stand idle. There is oil in the valley of Pückenried.

Doctor. There is copper under the Konradsweil Forest. There is power in our streams, in our waterfalls.

Teacher. We are not poor, madame. If we had credit, if we had confidence, the factories would open, orders and commissions would pour in. And our economy would bloom together with our cultural life. We would become once again like the towns around us, healthy and
90 prosperous.

Doctor. If the Wagonworks were put on its feet again—

Teacher. The Foundry.

Doctor. The Golden Eagle Pencil Factory.

Teacher. Buy these plants, madame. Put them in operation once more, and I swear to you, Güllen will flourish and it will bless you. We don't need a billion marks. Ten million, properly invested, would give us back our life, and incidentally return to the investor an excellent dividend. Save us, madame. Save us, and we will not only bless you, we will make money for you.

Claire. I don't need money. 100

Doctor. Madame, we are not asking for charity. This is business.

Claire. It's a good idea . . .

Doctor. Dear lady! I knew you wouldn't let us down.

Claire. But it's out of the question. I cannot buy the Wagonworks. I already own them.

Doctor. The Wagonworks?

Teacher. And the Foundry?

Claire. And the Foundry.

Doctor. And the Golden Eagle Pencil Factory?

Claire. Everything. The valley of Pückenried with its oil, the forest 110 of Konradsweil with its ore, the barn, the town, the streets, the houses, the shops, everything. I had my agents buy up this rubbish over the years, bit by bit, piece by piece, until I had it all. Your hopes were an illusion, your vision empty, your self-sacrifice a stupidity, your whole life completely senseless.

Teacher. Then the mysterious blight—

Claire. The mysterious blight was I.

Doctor. But this is monstrous!

Claire. Monstrous. I was seventeen when I left this town. It was winter. I was dressed in a sailor suit and my red braids hung down my 120 back. I was in my seventh month. As I walked down the street to the station, the boys whistled after me, and someone threw something. I sat freezing in my seat in the Hamburg Express. But before the roof of the great barn was lost behind the trees, I had made up my mind that one day I would come back . . .

Teacher. But, madame—

Claire. (She smiles.) And now I have. *(She claps her hands.)* Mike. Max. Take me back to the Golden Apostle. I've been here long enough. *(Mike and Max start to pick up the sedan chair. The Teacher pushes Mike away.)* 130

Teacher. Madame. One moment. Please. I see it all now. I had thought of you as an avenging fury, a Medea, a Clytemnestra—but I was wrong. You are a warm-hearted woman who has suffered a terrible injustice, and now you have returned and taught us an unforgettable lesson. You have stripped us bare. But now that we stand before you naked, I know you will set aside these thoughts of vengeance. If we made you suffer, you too have put us through the fire. Have mercy, madame.

Claire. When I have had justice. Mike! *(She signals to Mike and Max to pick up the sedan chair. They cross the stage. The Teacher bars the way.)* 140

Teacher. But, madame, one injustice cannot cure another. What good will it do to force us into crime? Horror succeeds horror, shame is piled on shame. It settles nothing.

Claire. It settles everything. *(They move upstage toward the exit. The Teacher follows.)*

Teacher. Madame, this lesson you have taught us will never be forgotten. We will hand it down from father to son. It will be a monument more lasting than any vengeance. Whatever we have been, in the future we shall be better because of you. You have pushed us to
150 the extreme. Now forgive us. Show us the way to a better life. Have pity, madame—pity. That is the highest justice. *(The sedan chair stops.)*

Claire. The highest justice has no pity. It is bright and pure and clear. The world made me into a whore; now I make the world into a brothel. Those who wish to go down, may go down. Those who wish to dance with me, may dance with me. *(To her porters)* Go.

(She is carried off.)

(The lights black out. Downstage, right, appears Schill's shop. It has a new sign, a new counter. The doorbell, when it rings, has an impressive
160 *sound. Frau Schill stands behind the counter in a new dress. The First Man enters, left. He is dressed as a prosperous butcher, a few bloodstains on his snowy apron, a gold watch chain across his open vest.)*

First Man. What a wedding! I'll swear the whole town was there. Cigarettes.

Frau Schill. Clara is entitled to a little happiness after all. I'm happy for her. Green or white?

First Man. Turkish. The bridesmaids! Dancers and opera singers. And the dresses! Down to here.

Frau Schill. It's the fashion nowadays.

170 *First Man.* Reporters! Photographers! From all over the world! *(In a low voice)* They will be here any minute.

Frau Schill. What have reporters to do with us? We are simple people, Herr Hofbauer. There is nothing for them here.

First Man. They're questioning everybody. They're asking everything. *(The First Man lights a cigarette. He looks up at the ceiling.)* Footsteps.

Frau Schill. He's pacing the room. Up and down. Day and night.

First Man. Haven't seen him all week.

Frau Schill. He never goes out.

180 *First Man.* It's his conscience. That was pretty mean, the way he treated poor Madame Zachanassian.

Frau Schill. That's true. I feel very badly about it myself.

First Man. To ruin a young girl like that—God doesn't forgive it. *(Frau Schill nods solemnly with pursed lips. The butcher gives her a level glance.)* Look, I hope he'll have sense enough to keep his mouth shut in front of the reporters.

Frau Schill. I certainly hope so.

First Man. You know his character.

Frau Schill. Only too well, Herr Hofbauer.

First Man. If he tries to throw dirt at our Clara and tell a lot of lies, how she tried to get us to kill him, which anyway she never meant— 190

Frau Schill. Of course not.

First Man. —Then we'll really have to do something! And not because of the money—*(He spits.)* But out of ordinary human decency. God knows Madame Zachanassian has suffered enough through him already.

Frau Schill. She has indeed.

(The Teacher comes in. He is not quite sober.)

Teacher. (Looks about the shop) Has the press been here yet?

First Man. No. 200

Teacher. It's not my custom, as you know, Frau Schill—but I wonder if I could have a strong alcoholic drink?

Frau Schill. It's an honor to serve you. Herr Professor. I have a good Steinhäger. Would you like to try a glass?

Teacher. A very small glass. *(Frau Schill serves bottle and glass. The Teacher tosses off a glass.)*

Frau Schill. Your hand is shaking, Herr Professor.

Teacher. To tell the truth, I have been drinking a little already.

Frau Schill. Have another glass. It will do you good. *(He accepts another glass.)* 210

Teacher. Is that he up there, walking?

Frau Schill. Up and down. Up and down.

First Man. It's God punishing him.

(The Painter comes in with the Son and the Daughter.)

Painter. Careful! A reporter just asked us the way to this shop.

First Man. I hope you didn't tell him.

Painter. I told him we were strangers here. *(They all laugh. The door opens. The Second Man darts into the shop.)*

Second Man. Look out, everybody! The press! They are across the street in your shop, Hofbauer. 220

First Man. My boy will know how to deal with them.

Second Man. Make sure Schill doesn't come down, Hofbauer.

First Man. Leave that to me. *(They group themselves about the shop.)*

Teacher. Listen to me, all of you. When the reporters come I'm going to speak to them. I'm going to make a statement. A statement to the world on behalf of myself as Rector of Güllen High School and on behalf of you all, for all your sakes.

Painter. What are you going to say?

Teacher. I shall tell the truth about Claire Zachanassian.

230 *Frau Schill.* You're drunk, Herr Professor; you should be ashamed of yourself.

Teacher. I should be ashamed? You should all be ashamed!

Son. Shut your trap. You're drunk.

Daughter. Please, Professor—

Teacher. Girl, you disappoint me. It is your place to speak. But you are silent and you force your old teacher to raise his voice. I am going to speak the truth. It is my duty and I am not afraid. The world may not wish to listen, but no one can silence me. I'm not going to wait—I'm going over to Hofbauer's shop now.

240 *All.* No, you're not. Stop him. Stop him. *(They all spring at the Teacher. He defends himself. At this moment, Schill appears through the door upstage. In contrast to the others, he is dressed shabbily in an old black jacket, his best.)*

Schill. What's going on in my shop? *(The townsmen let go of the Teacher and turn to stare at Schill.)* What's the trouble, Professor?

Teacher. Schill, I am speaking out at last! I am going to tell the press everything.

Schill. Be quiet, Professor.

Teacher. What did you say?

250 *Schill.* Be quiet.

Teacher. You want me to be quiet?

Schill. Please.

Teacher. But, Schill, if I keep quiet, if you miss this opportunity—they're over in Hofbauer's shop now . . .

Schill. Please.

Teacher. As you wish. If you too are on their side, I have no more to say.

(The doorbell jingles. A Reporter comes in.)

Reporter. Is Anton Schill here? *(Moves to Schill)* Are you Herr

260 Schill?

Schill. What?

Reporter. Herr Schill.

Schill. Er—no. Herr Schill's gone to Kalberstadt for the day.

Reporter. Oh, thank you. Good day. *(He goes out.)*

Painter. (Mops his brow) Whew! Close shave.

(He follows the Reporter out.)

Second Man. (Walking up to Schill) That was pretty smart of you to keep your mouth shut. You know what to expect if you don't.

(He goes.)

270 *First Man.* Give me a Havana. *(Schill serves him.)* Charge it. You bastard!

(He goes. Schill opens his account book.)

Frau Schill. Come along, children—

(Frau Schill, the Son and the Daughter go off, upstage.)

Teacher. They're going to kill you. I've known it all along, and you too, you must have known it. The need is too strong, the temptation too great. And now perhaps I too will join against you. I belong to them and, like them, I can feel myself hardening into something that is not human—not beautiful.

Schill. It can't be helped. 280

Teacher. Pull yourself together, man. Speak to the reporters; you've no time to lose. *(Schill looks up from his account book.)*

Schill. No. I'm not going to fight any more.

Teacher. Are you so frightened that you don't dare open your mouth?

Schill. I made Claire what she is, I made myself what I am. What should I do? Should I pretend that I'm innocent?

Teacher. No, you can't. You are as guilty as hell.

Schill. Yes.

Teacher. You are a bastard.

Schill. Yes. 290

Teacher. But that does not justify your murder. *(Schill looks at him.)* I wish I could believe that for what they're doing—for what they're going to do—they will suffer for the rest of their lives. But it's not true. In a little while they will have justified everything and forgotten everything.

Schill. Of course.

Teacher. Your name will never again be mentioned in this town. That's how it will be.

Schill. I don't hold it against you.

Teacher. But I do. I will hold it against myself all my life. That's 300 why—*(The doorbell jingles. The Burgomaster comes in. The Teacher stares at him, then goes out without another word.)*

Burgomaster. Good afternoon, Schill. Don't let me disturb you. I've just dropped in for a moment.

Schill. I'm just finishing my accounts for the week. *(A moment's pause)*

Burgomaster. The town council meets tonight. At the Golden Apostle. In the auditorium.

Schill. I'll be there.

Burgomaster. The whole town will be there. Your case will be dis- 310 cussed and final action taken. You've put us in a pretty tight spot, you know.

Schill. Yes. I'm sorry.

Burgomaster. The lady's offer will be rejected.

Schill. Possibly.

Burgomaster. Of course, I may be wrong.

Schill. Of course.

Burgomaster. In that case—are you prepared to accept the judgment of the town? The meeting will be covered by the press, you know.

320 *Schill.* By the press?

Burgomaster. Yes, and the radio and the newsreel. It's a very ticklish situation. Not only for you—believe me, it's even worse for us. What with the wedding, and all the publicity, we've become famous. All of a sudden our ancient democratic institutions have become of interest to the world.

Schill. Are you going to make the lady's condition public?

Burgomaster. No, no, of course not. Not directly. We will have to put the matter to a vote—that is unavoidable. But only those involved will understand.

330 *Schill.* I see.

Burgomaster. As far as the press is concerned, you are simply the intermediary between us and Madame Zachanassian. I have whitewashed you completely.

Schill. That is very generous of you.

Burgomaster. Frankly, it's not for your sake, but for the sake of your family. They are honest and decent people.

Schill. Oh—

Burgomaster. So far we've all played fair. You've kept your mouth shut and so have we. Now can we continue to depend on you? Be-

340 cause if you have any idea of opening your mouth at tonight's meeting, there won't be any meeting.

Schill. I'm glad to hear an open threat at last.

Burgomaster. We are not threatening you. You are threatening us. If you speak, you force us to act—in advance.

Schill. That won't be necessary.

Burgomaster. So if the town decides against you?

Schill. I will accept their decision.

Burgomaster. Good. *(A moment's pause)* I'm delighted to see there is still a spark of decency left in you. But—wouldn't it be better if

350 we didn't have to call a meeting at all? *(He pauses. He takes a gun from his pocket and puts it on the counter.)* I've brought you this.

Schill. Thank you.

Burgomaster. It's loaded.

Schill. I don't need a gun.

Burgomaster. *(He clears his throat.)* You see? We could tell the lady that we had condemned you in secret session and you had anticipated our decision. I've lost a lot of sleep getting to this point, believe me.

Schill. I believe you.

Burgomaster. Frankly, in your place, I myself would prefer to take

360 the path of honor. Get it over with, once and for all. Don't you agree?

For the sake of your friends! For the sake of our children, your own children—you have a daughter, a son—Schill, you know our need, our misery.

Schill. You've put me through hell, you and your town. You were my friends, you smiled and reassured me. But day by day I saw you change—your shoes, your ties, your suits—your hearts. If you had been honest with me then, perhaps I would feel differently toward you now. I might even use that gun you brought me. For the sake of my friends. But now I have conquered my fear. Alone. It was hard, but it's done. And now you will have to judge me. And I will accept your judgment. For me that will be justice. How it will be for you, I don't know. *(He turns away.)* You may kill me if you like. I won't complain, I won't protest, I won't defend myself. But I won't do your job for you either. 370

Burgomaster. (Takes up his gun) There it is. You've had your chance and you won't take it. Too bad. *(He takes out a cigarette.)* I suppose it's more than we can expect of a man like you. *(Schill lights the Buromaster's cigarette.)* Good day.

Schill. Good day. *(The Burgomaster goes. Frau Schill comes in, dressed in a fur coat. The Daughter is in a new red dress. The Son has a new sports jacket.)* What a beautiful coat, Mathilde! 380

Frau Schill. Real fur. You like it?

Schill. Should I? What a lovely dress, Ottilie!

Daughter. C'est très chic, n'est-ce-pas?°

Schill. What?

Frau Schill. Ottilie is taking a course in French.

Schill. Very useful. Karl—whose automobile is that out there at the curb?

Son. Oh, it's only an Opel. They're not expensive.

Schill. You bought yourself a car? 390

Son. On credit. Easiest thing in the world.

Frau Schill. Everyone's buying on credit now, Anton. These fears of yours are ridiculous. You'll see. Clara has a good heart. She only means to teach you a lesson.

Daughter. She means to teach you a lesson, that's all.

Son. It's high time you got the point, Father.

Schill. I get the point. *(The church bells start ringing.)* Listen. The bells of Güllen. Do you hear?

Son. Yes, we have four bells now. It sounds quite good.

Daughter. Just like Gray's Elegy. 400

Schill. What?

Frau Schill. Ottilie is taking a course in English literature.

384. C'est très chic, n'est-ce-pas? That's very smart, isn't it?

Schill. Congratulations! It's Sunday. I should very much like to take a ride in your car. Our car.

Son. You want to ride in the car?

Schill. Why not? I want to ride through the Konradsweil Forest. I want to see the town where I've lived all my life.

Frau Schill. I don't think that will look very nice for any of us.

Schill. No—perhaps not. Well, I'll go for a walk by myself.

410 *Frau Schill.* Then take us to Kalberstadt, Karl, and we'll go to a cinema.

Schill. A cinema? It's a good idea.

Frau Schill. See you soon, Anton.

Schill. Good-bye, Ottilie. Good-bye, Karl. Good-bye, Mathilde.

Family. Good-bye *(They go out.)*

Schill. Good-bye. *(The shop sign flies off. The lights black out. They come up at once on the forest scene.)* Autumn. Even the forest has turned to gold. *(Schill wanders down to the bench in the forest. He sits. Claire's voice is heard.)*

420 *Claire. (Offstage)* Stop. Wait here. *(Claire comes in. She gazes slowly up at the trees, kicks at some leaves. Then she walks slowly down center. She stops before a tree, glances up the trunk.)* Bark-borers. The old tree is dying. *(She catches sight of Schill.)*

Schill. Clara.

Claire. How pleasant to see you here. I was visiting my forest. May I sit by you?

Schill. Oh, yes. Please do. *(She sits next to him.)* I've just been saying good-bye to my family. They've gone to the cinema. Karl has bought himself a car.

430 *Claire.* How nice.

Schill. Ottilie is taking French lessons. And a course in English literature.

Claire. You see? They're beginning to take an interest in higher things.

Schill. Listen. A finch. You hear?

Claire. Yes. It's a finch. And a cuckoo in the distance. Would you like some music?

Schill. Oh, yes. That would be very nice.

Claire. Anything special?

440 *Schill.* "Deep in the Forest."

Claire. Your favorite song. They know it. *(She raises her hand. Offstage, the mandolin and guitar play the tune softly.)*

Schill. We had a child?

Claire. Yes.

Schill. Boy or girl?

Claire. Girl.

Schill. What name did you give her?

Claire. I called her Genevieve.

Schill. That's a very pretty name.

Claire. Yes. 450

Schill. What was she like?

Claire. I saw her only once. When she was born. Then they took her away from me.

Schill. Her eyes?

Claire. They weren't open yet.

Schill. And her hair?

Claire. Black, I think. It's usually black at first.

Schill. Yes, of course. Where did she die, Clara?

Claire. In some family. I've forgotten their name. Meningitis, they said. The officials wrote me a letter. 460

Schill. Oh, I'm so very sorry, Clara.

Claire. I've told you about our child. Now tell me about myself.

Schill. About yourself?

Claire. Yes. How I was when I was seventeen in the days when you loved me.

Schill. I remember one day you waited for me in the great barn. I had to look all over the place for you. At last I found you lying in the haycart with nothing on and a long straw between your lips . . .

Claire. Yes. I was pretty in those days.

Schill. You were beautiful, Clara. 470

Claire. You were strong. The time you fought with those two railway men who were following me, I wiped the blood from your face with my red petticoat. *(The music ends.)* They've stopped.

Schill. Tell them to play "Thoughts of Home."

Claire. They know that too. *(The music plays.)*

Schill. Here we are, Clara, sitting together in our forest for the last time. The town council meets tonight. They will condemn me to death, and one of them will kill me. I don't know who and I don't know where. Clara, I only know that in a little while a useless life will come to an end. *(He bows his head on her bosom. She takes him in her arms.)* 480

Claire. (Tenderly) I shall take you in your coffin to Capri. You will have your tomb in the park of my villa, where I can see you from my bedroom window. White marble and onyx in a grove of green cypress. With a beautiful view of the Mediterranean.

Schill. I've always wanted to see it.

Claire. Your love for me died years ago, Anton. But my love for you would not die. It turned into something strong, like the hidden roots of the forest; something evil, like white mushrooms that grow unseen in the darkness. And slowly it reached out for your life. Now I have you. You are mine. Alone. At last, and forever, a peaceful ghost in a silent 490 house. *(The music ends.)*

Schill. The song is over.

Claire. Adieu, Anton. *(Claire kisses Anton, a long kiss. Then she rises.)*

Schill. Adieu.

(She goes. Schill remains sitting on the bench. A row of lamps descends from the flies. The townsmen come in from both sides, each bearing his chair. A table and chairs are set upstage, center. On both sides sit the townsmen. The Policeman, in a new uniform, sits on the bench behind Schill. All the townsmen are in new Sunday clothes. Around them are technicians of all sorts, with lights, cameras and other equipment. The townswomen are absent. They do not vote. The Burgomaster takes his place at the table, center. The Doctor and the Pastor sit at the same table, at his right, and the Teacher in his academic gown, at his left.)

Burgomaster. (At a sign from the radio technician, he pounds the floor with his wand of office.) Fellow citizens of Güllen, I call this meeting to order. The agenda: there is only one matter before us. I have the honor to announce officially that Madame Claire Zachanassian, daughter of our beloved citizen, the famous architect Siegfried Wäscher, has decided to make a gift to the town of one billion marks. Five hundred million to the town, five hundred million to be divided per capita among the citizens. After certain necessary preliminaries, a vote will be taken, and you, as citizens of Güllen, will signify your will by a show of hands. Has anyone any objection to this mode of procedure? The pastor? *(Silence)* The police? *(Silence)* The town health official? *(Silence)* The Rector of Güllen High School? *(Silence)* The political opposition? *(Silence)* I shall then proceed to the vote—*(The Teacher rises. The Burgomaster turns in surprise and irritation.)* You wish to speak?

Teacher. Yes.

Burgomaster. Very well. *(He takes his seat. The Teacher advances. The movie camera starts running.)*

Teacher. Fellow townsmen. *(The photographer flashes a bulb in his face.)* Fellow townsmen. We all know that by means of this gift, Madame Claire Zachanassian intends to attain a certain object. What is this object? To enrich the town of her youth, yes. But more than that, she desires by means of this gift to re-establish justice among us. This desire expressed by our benefactress raises an all-important question. Is it true that our community harbors in its soul such a burden of guilt?

Burgomaster. Yes! True!

Second Man. Crimes are concealed among us.

Third Man. (He jumps up.) Sins!

Fourth Man. (He jumps up also.) Perjuries.

Painter. Justice!

Townsmen. Justice! Justice!

Teacher. Citizens of Güllen, this, then, is the simple fact of the case. We have participated in an injustice. I thoroughly recognize the material advantages which this gift opens to us—I do not overlook the fact that it is poverty which is the root of all this bitterness and evil. Nevertheless, there is no question here of money.

Townsmen. No! No!

Teacher. Here there is no question of our prosperity as a community, or our well-being as individuals—The question is—must be—whether or not we wish to live according to the principles of justice, those principles for which our forefathers lived and fought and for which they died, those principles which form the soul of our Western culture. 540

Townsmen. Hear! Hear! *(Applause)*

Teacher. (Desperately, realizing that he is fighting a losing battle, and on the verge of hysteria) Wealth has meaning only when benevolence comes of it, but only he who hungers for grace will receive grace. Do you feel this hunger, my fellow citizens, this hunger of the spirit, or do you feel only that other profane hunger, the hunger of the body? That is the question which I, as Rector of your high school, now propound to you. Only if you can no longer tolerate the presence of evil among you, only if you can in no circumstances endure a world in which injustice exists, are you worthy to receive Madame Zachanassian's billion and fulfill the condition bound up with this gift. If not—*(Wild applause. He gestures desperately for silence.)* If not, then God have mercy on us! *(The townsmen crowd around him, ambiguously, in a mood somewhat between threat and congratulation. He takes his seat, utterly crushed, exhausted by his effort. The Burgomaster advances and takes charge once again. Order is restored.)* 550 560

Burgomaster. Anton Schill—*(The Policeman gives Schill a shove. Schill gets up.)* Anton Schill, it is through you that this gift is offered to the town. Are you willing that this offer should be accepted? *(Schill mumbles something.)*

Radio Reporter. (Steps to his side) You'll have to speak up a little, Herr Schill.

Schill. Yes.

Burgomaster. Will you respect our decision in the matter before us?

Schill. I will respect your decision.

Burgomaster. Then I proceed to the vote. All those who are in accord with the terms on which this gift is offered will signify the same by raising their right hands. *(After a moment, the Policeman raises his hand. Then one by one the others. Last of all, very slowly, the Teacher)* All against? The offer is accepted. I now solemnly call upon you, fellow townsmen, to declare in the face of all the world that you take this action, not out of love for worldly gain . . . 570

Townsmen. (In chorus) Not out of love for worldly gain . . .

Burgomaster. But out of love for the right.

Townsmen. But out of love for the right.

580 *Burgomaster. (Holds up his hand, as if taking an oath)* We join together, now, as brothers . . .

Townsmen. (Hold up their hands) We join together, now, as brothers . . .

Burgomaster. To purify our town of guilt . . .

Townsmen. To purify our town of guilt . . .

Burgomaster. And to reaffirm our faith . . .

Townsmen. And to reaffirm our faith . . .

Burgomaster. In the eternal power of justice.

Townsmen. In the eternal power of justice. *(The lights go off sud-*
590 *denly.)*

Schill. (A scream) Oh, God!

Voice. I'm sorry, Herr Burgomaster. We seem to have blown a fuse. *(The lights go on.)* Ah—there we are. Would you mind doing that last bit again?

Burgomaster. Again?

The Cameraman. (Walks forward) Yes, for the newsreel.

Burgomaster. Oh, the newsreel. Certainly.

The Cameraman. Ready now? Right.

Burgomaster. And to reaffirm our faith . . .

600 *Townsmen.* And to reaffirm our faith . . .

Burgomaster. In the eternal power of justice.

Townsmen. In the eternal power of justice.

The Cameraman. (To his assistant) It was better before, when he screamed "Oh, God." *(The assistant shrugs.)*

Burgomaster. Fellow citizens of Güllen, I declare this meeting adjourned. The ladies and gentlemen of the press will find refreshments served downstairs, with the compliments of the town council. The exits lead directly to the restaurant.

The Cameraman. Thank you. *(The newsmen go off with alacrity.*
610 *The townsmen remain on the stage. Schill gets up.)*

Policeman. (Pushes Schill down) Sit down.

Schill. Is it to be now?

Policeman. Naturally, now.

Schill. I thought it might be best to have it at my house.

Policeman. It will be here.

Burgomaster. Lower the lights. *(The lights dim.)* Are they all gone?

Voice. All gone.

Burgomaster. The gallery?

Second Voice. Empty.

620 *Burgomaster.* Lock the doors.

The Voice. Locked here.

Second Voice. Locked here.

Burgomaster. Form a lane. *(The men form a lane. At the end stands the Athlete in elegant white slacks, a red scarf around his singlet.)* Pastor. Will you be so good? *(The Pastor walks slowly to Schill.)*

Pastor. Anton Schill, your heavy hour has come.

Schill. May I have a cigarette?

Pastor. Cigarette, Burgomaster.

Burgomaster. Of course. With pleasure. And a good one. *(He gives his case to the Pastor, who offers it to Schill. The Policeman lights the cigarette. The Pastor returns the case.)* 630

Pastor. In the words of the prophet Amos—

Schill. Please—*(He shakes his head.)*

Pastor. You're no longer afraid?

Schill. No. I'm not afraid.

Pastor. I will pray for you.

Schill. Pray for us all. *(The Pastor bows his head.)*

Burgomaster. Anton Schill, stand up! *(Schill hesitates.)*

Policeman. Stand up, you swine!

Burgomaster. Schultz, please. 640

Policeman. I'm sorry. I was carried away. *(Schill gives the cigarette to the Policeman. Then he walks slowly to the center of the stage and turns his back on the audience.)* Enter the lane.

(Schill hesitates a moment. He goes slowly into the lane of silent men. The Athlete stares at him from the opposite end. Schill looks in turn at the hard faces of those who surround him, and sinks slowly to his knees. The lane contracts silently into a knot as the men close in and crouch over. Complete silence. The knot of men pulls back slowly, coming downstage. Then it opens. Only the Doctor is left in the center of the stage, kneeling by the corpse, over which the Teacher's gown has been spread. The Doctor rises and takes off his stethoscope.) 650

Pastor. Is it all over?

Doctor. Heart failure.

Burgomaster. Died of joy.

All. Died of joy.

(The townsmen turn their backs on the corpse and at once light cigarettes. A cloud of smoke rises over them. From the left comes Claire Zachanassian, dressed in black, followed by Bobby. She sees the corpse. Then she walks slowly to center stage and looks down at the body of Schill.) 660

Claire. Uncover him. *(Bobby uncovers Schill's face. She stares at it a long moment. She sighs.)* Cover his face.

(Bobby covers it. Claire goes out, up center. Bobby takes the check from his wallet, holds it out peremptorily to the Burgomaster, who walks over from the knot of silent men. He holds out his hand for the check. The lights fade. At once the warning bell is heard, and the scene dissolves

into the setting of the railway station. The gradual transformation of the shabby town into a thing of elegance and beauty is now accomplished. The railway station glitters with neon lights and is surrounded
670 *with garlands, bright posters and flags. The townsfolk, men and women, now in brand new clothes, form themselves into a group in front of the station. The sound of the approaching train grows louder. The train stops.)*

Station Master. Güllen-Rome Express. All aboard, please.

(The church bells start pealing. Men appear with trunks and boxes, a procession which duplicates that of the lady's arrival, but in inverse order. Then come the Two Blind Men, then Bobby, and Mike and Max carrying the coffin. Lastly Claire. She is dressed in modish black. Her head is high, her face as impassive as that of an ancient idol. The pro-
680 *cession crosses the stage and goes off. The people bow in silence as the coffin passes. When Claire and her retinue have boarded the train, the Station Master blows a long blast.)*
'Bo—ard!

(He holds up his paddle. The train starts and moves off slowly, picking up speed. The crowd turns slowly, gazing after the departing train in complete silence. The train sounds fade. The curtain falls slowly.)

Comments and Questions

In the first act Dürrenmatt prepares the mousetrap in which he intends to catch the conscience of the audience. As the dramatist depends upon our immediate response as well as upon our memory, every action, every speech, every prop must function as a live, active detail, telling us both directly and by implication not only what is happening at the moment but also, even if obscurely, what is to come. As the first act moves through its four scenes, the comedy of the townspeople's greedy expectations and of Claire's arrival acquires increasingly ominous undertones which culminate in the shock of the revelation of the dark purpose of her visit. Several references are made to arouse our curiosity and concern. Explain the meaning of the references to Konradsweil, the presence of the coffin, the panther, the blind men, and Mike and Max.

You might observe that as in life our responses are not uniform but are being constantly modified as events warrant. For example, consider the Burgomaster's morally indignant and noble response to Claire's announcement of her mission in light of our knowledge gained in the first scene that the citizens of Güllen are guilty of at least a modest duplicity in the courting of Claire's good opinion. Consider further that the re-

mark, so serious when made, is in retrospect by the end of the play to become grimly comic, an ironic comment upon a tendency in people to say what they are supposed to and to act as they have to. What other similar ironies can you find being prepared in the first act?

In the second and third acts we come to understand more clearly what the townspeople, the apparent victims of some powerful law of human nature, are about to do. "We're human" is the teacher's only excuse for their actions. The highly typed characters (except possibly Schill), and the stylized language (as that of the blind men or the choral responses in the final scene) and the ritual-like action in much of the play (as at the ends of Acts II and III) strengthen the impression that the citizens are following an established and predictable pattern. Certainly, Claire has no doubts her mission will succeed; she has merely to place the bait in the trap she has carefully set. Slowly Schill sees she will get what she wants. Why does he not escape?

Claire's assurance and Schill's acceptance of his fate lead to several interpretive questions posed by the play. What makes Claire so certain her premeditated revenge will succeed? To what extent is she responsible for making the world a brothel? Does she bear more or less responsibility for making it so than the townspeople do or than Schill does? If Güllen can be said to represent the "monstrous world" Dürrenmatt claims we live in, what comment does he make through community leaders like the teacher, burgomaster, and pastor on the social institutions designed to maintain morality and justice? Are there any suggested parallels between Schill's crime and that of the townspeople? How do the townspeople justify their destruction of Schill? Are there any clues in the play that they will have to pay for selling out to "the stone goddess"? Has the old order of "humane traditions" ("Goethe slept here. Brahms composed a quartet.") been overthrown? In fact, has such a tradition ever exerted any real control over human drives? Does the play offer any assurance that man will ever withstand a really basic corruptive influence, that he will ever have hopes that are not illusory, or a life that is not "completely senseless"?

Dürrenmatt once wrote that he admires Thornton Wilder's managing to create in his audiences the feeling that they were participating in their own psychoanalysis. Does this play create such a feeling in you? Possibly another way to phrase the question is to ask how successfully do you think Dürrenmatt springs his trap upon the audience?

Contrast the handling of the theme of justice in The Visit *and the* Antigone *plays. Compare Schill and Dr. Stockmann in* An Enemy of the People *as scapegoats. Compare the view of the world implicit in* The Visit, Christopher Columbus, *Anouilh's* Antigone, *and* Hughie.

Related Reading

Maxwell Anderson, "The Essence of Tragedy," page 663
Henrik Ibsen, *An Enemy of the People*, page 174
Arthur Miller, "On Social Plays," page 670

Michel de Ghelderode

(1898-1962)

CHRISTOPHER COLUMBUS

translated by George Hauger

Public recognition came late to the Belgian poet and dramatist Michel de Ghelderode. He began to publish his work shortly after he reached the age of twenty and continued to produce plays, poems, and essays until the time of his death, but fame did not come until the nineteen-fifties. Then, almost at once, the strange world created by this eccentric and somewhat withdrawn man seemed important, first to fellow writers, and eventually to an increasingly large public. Ghelderode has come to be recognized as one of the forerunners of the Theater of the Absurd.

Absurd, as the word is used in describing some of this contemporary theater, does not mean ridiculous. Rather, it means senseless, out of tune with rational thinking. The present world is one in which tremendous breakthroughs in medicine and technology promise to carry us into a new era—physiologically, psychologically, and materially. At the same time we live in the age of genocide and of instant total destruction. Our age has lost the certainties and underlying basic assumptions, which man used to have, and with which he was able to explain the universe to himself. Albert Camus, in The Myth of Sisyphus, *said that a world that can be explained by reasoning is a familiar world, even if the reasoning is faulty. Our world is no longer subject to reasoning, however, and man is like a stranger in it.*

Ben Jonson and Molière castigate the follies of the world. They see the world as an ordered universe, however, in which disorder can be pointed to with the aim of exposing and thereby perhaps correcting it. Man is not a stranger in this world; on the contrary, it is he who forms its center and gives it its reason. If, on the other hand, the world is considered as basically irrational, then a man who attempts to act reasonably is a stranger in it, because the world is not subject to his reason.

The world of Christopher Columbus *is one in which that rational man is surrounded by men who spout familiar phrases, which, as we listen to them, become demonstrably irrational. Ghelderode's macabre, farcical world is not one which contains some fools, but one which is basically foolish. His Columbus is a seer—a visionary who knows that his visions, if made into reality, will bring only evil. As Ghelderode describes the situation, Columbus' object is not to discover America but to find the perfect sphere, with undertones of the Garden of Eden.*

To make his symbolic points, Ghelderode draws on the techniques of surrealism, developing a dream-like world in which he can disregard historical events and setting, and freely introduce fictional characters, anachronisms, and the supernatural. This freedom enables him to comment on the role of civilization, on human accomplishments, failings, and delusions, and to make these, rather than the individual human being, the center of the play.

CHRISTOPHER COLUMBUS

(Christophe Colomb)
A Dramatic Fairy Tale
in Three Scenes
(1927)

Characters

CHRISTOPHER COLUMBUS
THE CROWD MAN
THE REPORTER
FRIEND
THE SLEEPWALKER
THE LEARNED MAN
THE MINISTER
THE KING
FOLIAL
THE WOMAN
THE LOOKOUT
THE HELMSMAN
MONTEZUMA
THE ANGEL AZURET
VISQUOSINE
THE POET
ADMIRAL DEATH
THE AMERICAN
BUFFALO BILL
Sailors, Indians, A Bombardon Player, A Big-Drum Beater, A Ballerina, Three Indian Dancers.

Note for the Director
(Dances, lights, music, some acrobatics, pathos, absurdity, tragedy, a message for those who like them. This play is spectacle and enchantment, and plays swiftly, without pause, in the perspective of dream.)
The Author

Scene I. A plain wall on which there are some trite posters, one of which reads:
IS THE EARTH ROUND?
FIERCE CONTROVERSY!

(When the curtain goes up, Columbus is alone, sitting on his suitcase and occupied in blowing soap bubbles. He is lost in delight and wrapped in thought.)

Columbus. Bubbles! Little spheres! It's a strange sign that I should still be playing, at my age. My thoughts shape themselves into spheres and fly away. Where do they go? *(He blows bubbles.)* Geometry causes deep emotion in me. I can't explain. I blow bubbles. They justify themselves and vanish. *(More bubbles)* Little spheres, logical, perfect! Sphere, ideal volume, shape of my dream, one must be like a child to understand you. *(He puts his clay pipe in his pocket and ponders.)* I am haunted by the horizon, tormented by distances. I am full of anguish, as at the onset of love, and my face is no doubt lit up with madness. Do traces of an ancient knowledge still linger in me? I have a recollection of a lost world. I do not know. I know nothing. Tomorrow I shall know, and I shall no longer be in anguish; but I shall be less happy. *(He takes out his pipe and begins to blow bubbles again.)* All of one's actions must be carried out with great seriousness. One must be born, brought up, and disappear with simplicity. *(More bubbles)* I am going to leave without a good-by, perhaps never to return, and I have no boat. Nevertheless, I pass my last night on this continent without giving a thought to the journey. I am not disillusioned; but people are insolent, and the air smells of the charnel house. *(Bubbles)* I must go, for what fate will society appoint for me if I go on blowing bubbles, bubbles that I cannot explain? I must go under the cloak of my mysteriousness, letting people think I have designs. I am going to enter a great silence, a long darkness. I am going to sail upon supernatural waters. It is a good thing for a man to busy himself. . . .

(No more soapy water. He clutches his forehead.)

(Someone arrives, walking on the wall.)

The Reporter. Christopher Columbus?

Columbus. I have an uncommon name that sounds like a famous one.

The Reporter. Bubbles, Columbus? You make such lovely ones!

Columbus. Bubbles? . . . Yes . . . *(He stirs his pipe in the empty cup. Magnesium flash)* Eh?

The Reporter. Thank you.

Columbus. (Standing) Who are you?

The Reporter. The press. The earth is round, isn't it?

Columbus. I am a little mad.

The Reporter. You are extraordinary.

Columbus. For having found out that the earth is round?

The Reporter. For daring to maintain it. Men like you are sensational, and that's what's wanted—sensational men.

Columbus. Broadcast it throughout the universe, go on. I'm tired.

The Reporter. Nothing would go, you know. I am the organizer of public emotions. Nothing would go—neither the comet nor the coming of the Antichrist—so I announced a new heaven and a new earth. Speak, Columbus: the time has come.

Columbus. The wind seems good.

The Reporter. Are you convinced?

50 *Columbus.* I have faith in the stars.

The Reporter. The stars? Indeed, what a lovely night! *(Magnesium flash)* Your face at those words . . . You were sublime.

Columbus. I wasn't thinking of anything.

The Reporter. (Annoyed) Oh! *(Friendly)* So, it's round? *(With some excitement)* It's stupid. It's tragic. You realize that this will upset people's habits?

Columbus. (Who has had enough) It's only tragic for idiots. As for habits, people will acquire others. *(Bowing to The Reporter)* And the sphere, calmly indifferent, harmonious and satisfied with itself, makes 60 great fun of our observations.

The Reporter. A joke? . . . *(Aside)* Well, that was his chance to make his mark.

(The Reporter goes; but someone else has already come as Columbus tightens the straps of his case.)

Friend. Good evening! Fastening up your case, Columbus?

Columbus. Where have I seen you?

Friend. We were at school together. You weren't very well up in geography, old chap. Do you persist in maintaining that it's round?

Columbus. They'll finish up by making me doubt it.

70 *Friend.* After all, why shouldn't it be round? Here's five francs. *(He throws a coin which Columbus catches in the air.)*

Columbus. Charity?

Friend. An investment. I am a financier, God forgive me. I'm putting five francs into your venture. Who knows? . . . But if it is round, if you find the alleged new land, remember that henceforth you will have to play the part of civilizer, and that you can't civilize without the help and the backing of Finance. These five francs are symbolic, a token of the confidence Finance places in your genius. What do they prove?—your lack of aptitude for geography! Good-by. *(He goes.)*

80 *Columbus. (Picks up his case and looks around, trying to decide in which direction to make off)* A little solitude, oh my spirit, a little solitude. . . . *(He is going off when a man in a nightshirt appears on the wall. The man carries a lighted candle and a suitcase. Columbus seems rooted to the spot.)*

The Sleepwalker. A little solitude that I may reflect on your roundness. . . . For it is round. I maintain that it must be round. Sphere on which I walk. . . .

Columbus. What are you trying to make out? Impostor! I alone can declare that it is round.

90 *The Sleepwalker.* It is round, just as I am pointed.

Columbus. And who told you it was round?

The Sleepwalker. (Ambiguously) Revelation, revelation. . . . It's no longer a mystery. And that is why I am going. . . .

Columbus. (Alarmed) Have you a boat? Where are you going?

The Sleepwalker. Elsewhere . . . where my spirit, full of sails, of compasses, and of routes, leads me. My spirit dances on the waves. But I shall return to the very place from which I set out, because the earth is round.

Columbus. They know; but they only know in their dreams, and they wake up ignorant. 100

The Sleepwalker. (Going out) Bubble . . . bubble . . . bubble . . .

Columbus. And when they wake up, I shall know the salt kiss of the high seas. It's time I went. *(Determined)* A ship, ahoy! a ship?

(Two men have come in, one to the right, one to the left. One is dressed like a Minister in an operetta, the other like a fairground astrologer.)

The Minister. A ship!

The Learned Man. Give him a ship!

Columbus. Supporters?

The Minister. It would be wise to give you a ship, that's all.

The Learned Man. Science agrees. 110

Columbus. I beg your pardon?

The Minister. (Beginning a speech) Political sagacity . . .

Columbus. Excuse me, the ship . . . *(An alarm clock rings loudly. Columbus opens his case, takes out the clock, and goes pale. The other two take out their watches.)* My moment already? It gains: it always gains. It's a present from my mother. *(Thoughtful)* What time will it be on the other side of the world? A homing pigeon or a bottle in the sea will no doubt one day tell you what sort of dawn I have seen breaking. *(He winds the alarm clock and puts it back in his case. The Minister has put on a compassionate air.)* 120

The Minister. Are you accessible to reason, Columbus? Let us be frank. Among its many tasks the State has to look after those of its citizens who indulge in strange behavior. No one knows what these people may lead us to, either for good or ill. The State does not like initiative, either. That is a monopoly which it claims for itself. The State does not willingly encourage innovators and discoverers. The State likes to bide its time. However, in your case, the State has made an unusual decision—neither to encourage nor to discourage you in anything: it will remain strictly neutral, while expressing the wish to see you succeed. If you do not succeed, your example will serve as a 130 warning to youth; if you do succeed, we shall appoint a commission to consider a suitable way of rewarding you. In any case, we insist on your going, if only for the sake of public opinion. The State will always be able to turn your adventure to some account. You understand, don't you? You are intelligent. *(Columbus bows. The Learned Man presses forward.)*

The Learned Man. The learned societies have decided to bestow their kindly attention and their sympathy on you, as on one of their members. It was officially agreed that the earth was flat. You maintain 140 that you will demonstrate that that is not so. Our assemblies will continue to uphold the idea of platitude. In the event of your theory turning out correct, remember that our assemblies venture to foresee that the earth could be spherical or cubic. *(Confidentially)* Let me know first, so that I can write about it. You understand? You are . . .

Columbus. (Courteously) I am of modest origin and of average intelligence. I did not suspect that the State and the learned assemblies would attach any importance to my voyage, which is a journey of convenience. The true motive for this journey is that I am weary. If I discover the new world, I shall not come back to say so. If I discover 150 nothing, ask the laconic fishes for my address. Your confidence is delightful to me; but . . . the smallest boat would have been more to my purpose. *(The Minister and The Learned Man stand sadly. They are getting ready to justify themselves when a bugle sounds. Minister and savant, bowing and scraping and loudly crying* "The King!" *go out backward.)*

Columbus. The King? *(The King arrives. He has a golden crutch and a fantastic crown, and is followed by his fool, Folial, who is in motley.)* I've had enough of interviews. The ship?

Folial. It's yours. Thank His Majesty.

160 *Columbus.* It was my due.

The King. Pooh! It was to please the Queen. The Queen is an odd individual.

Columbus. I am deeply moved.

The King. As far as I am concerned, I give you the boat willingly. It saves me the trouble of shutting you up. Set off quickly and sail toward oblivion. My subjects talk of nothing but the Eden you want to discover—as if my kingdom wasn't Eden! What do you think about it, Folial?

Folial. Let the people have filth and mirages. Promise them Eden.

170 *Columbus.* And if I discover Eden?

The King. That will be because God wishes to bless my reign by your act. Haven't I given you the boat? *(He ponders.)* Columbus, it has always been men of your kind who have spoiled my life. Artists, in a way. I have my reasons for admiring them and for not thinking much of them. Is that not so, Folial?

Folial. Sire, great minds don't understand little things.

The King. Still, I have need of them. You see there would be difficulty in writing the chronicle of my reign. And, after all, it wouldn't be a bad thing if you discovered this Eden—which we would make into a well-managed colony. 180

Columbus. Sire, by my holy scapular, I shall find this Eden, which you shall make a tribute to the Queen. Thank you. . . . I see the ship. What memorable phrase can I pronounce?

Folial. This is a historic evening; but it is for you, Sire, to speak royally. Come!

The King. (Warmly) Hail, Columbus! You who are sound in body and mind; what an ailing world it is. Find a new world. I reign over a neurasthenic kingdom. Happy are you to possess the sea, mighty misanthrope! As for me . . .

Columbus. Are you troubled? 190

The King. I am moved. You have a ship. I have only a throne. *(He grasps Columbus' hand.)* I lied to you. It was I, not the Queen, who gave you this ship. And, no, my kingdom is not Eden. Ah, you farsighted traveler . . . *(The fool weeps.)* Shut up, Folial. It's your job to be gay.

Folial. And yours to be courteous.

The King. You are right. *(He too weeps.)*

Columbus. I would have liked to have gone without tears.

The King. Indeed. Dignity, Folial.

Folial. This is a historic evening. *(The over-all dressing of the ship appears across the stage, enlivening it with multicolored flags.)* 200

Columbus. Thank you for the ship. *(A murmuring begins.)* It's no good, it makes your heart swell. One may as well empty the vase . . . *(A Woman enters and begins to cross the stage.)* Not so fast!

The Woman. What?

Columbus. You are my mother, and no mistake.

The Woman. So what?

Columbus. Good-by, Mother. *(He kisses her, wipes away a tear, takes several steps, then comes back.)* I made a mistake. You are my fiancée. Good-by, darling. *(He kisses her, wipes away another tear, and makes off.)* 210

The Woman. That suits me better.

Columbus. (Coming back) Pardon?

The Woman. Go ahead.

Columbus. You are my country!

The Woman. Come to my arms, you confused young man. Give me children.

Columbus. Out strumpet! *(He pushes her out.)*

The Woman. Tramp!

The King. I don't get it.

Columbus. Tramp! that's a title. My eyes are dry. At last I am pure. 220 At last I am alone.

(A gangway is slid on the stage. Columbus begins to climb it. The King waves good-by with his handkerchief. The crowd arrives—that is,

a single actor who gives the impression of many people in tumult.)

The Crowd Man. There he is! Good luck! Bravo!

Columbus. (Modestly acknowledging) Here I am.

The Crowd Man. Stupendous! Stupid! Right! Wrong! Where is he? Him? Yes! No! Encore! Daredevil! Opportunist! Martyr!

Columbus. Well, get it over with, go on.

230 *The Crowd Man.* Speech!

Columbus. I haven't prepared anything.

The King. Be a good fellow, Columbus.

Columbus. People . . .

The Reporter. (Coming into view on the wall) Hasn't this chap gone yet?

The Crowd Man. He is speaking. He has spoken. Marvelous! Bravo!

Columbus. I have little to say, and much to do.

The Crowd Man. He's beginning again. We've had enough.

The Reporter. Is he going? Much to do, did you say?

240 *Columbus.* Make my testament, for example. Here it is. O King, O people . . . Having destroyed a surface and created a volume, I make light of the critics who maintain that the object of my life is to make an egg stand on end. Excuse me for adding nothing more, and for appearing absent-minded. I see things from above. Yes, I am from another world. I do not belong to yours. I am setting out for another world. But you must realize that it is not my ambition to discover one. It is a much more serious matter. I have a taste for unhappiness. I am fleeing the reasonable nations. *(He makes a gesture with his hand, and goes.)*

250 *The Crowd Man.* The departure! Lovely! Thrilling!

Voice of Columbus. Ocean, old friend . . .

The Crowd Man. Up the navy! *(Some national fanfare or other sounds somewhere. A clamor breaks out and dies away.)*

The King. Let's get to hell. It's dismal. . . .

(He goes, with his fool at his heels.)

The Crowd Man. (Wildly) The boat! He's off! Good luck! Fair winds! Out of sight! Done with!

(He rushes off as fast as his legs will carry him.)

The Reporter. (Still on the wall, finishing his notes) Carrying away

260 hope . . . launching out toward hope. . . .

(He goes, singing.)

A little ship was on the sea. . . . *(Curtain)*

Scene II

(A sailing ship seen in cross section. The audience is looking from the poop forward. Red and green lights on the deck (practical), white lights in the rigging, where The Lookout is in position. Columbus sits at a table in the hold. This narrow place is bathed in bluish light. At the

back, toward the prow, are the quarters where the sleeping crew is. Ropes and ladders run up and down almost everywhere.)

The Lookout. Nothing to report, nothing, still nothing! Gulfs and darkness to port, gulfs and darkness to starboard, gulfs and darkness at the zenith, gulfs and darkness at the nadir. The stars are dead, except for one with a peculiar glitter. . . . 10

Columbus. Mine!

The Lookout. Night . . . Is it night? Silence . . . Is it silence? The sea and its gulfs. . . . Horrible! The sea . . .

Columbus. The orchestral sea whose melody escapes me. Our Lady of the Mariners, protect my ship! They are asleep. The winds are bearing us along. Unexpectedly, I came across strange scents in the breeze. This is the sea of delusions. *(One of the sleeping sailors begins to struggle.)*

The Sleeper. Shipwreck!

Columbus. Sleep, sailors. This ship is a cradle. Bye, bye, sailor, bye, 20 bye. . . . *(He sings softly.)* A little ship was on the sea. . . .

Voices of Sleepers. No, not that! It's too sad. We want to go home. We want a love song or something funny. . . .

Columbus. (Authoritatively) What? Sleep! I order it! You will awaken in the new world. There's no danger, except to your brains. Men without mystery! The little ship has its destiny. Get to bed, Captain's orders! *(He fills his pipe and smokes.)*

The Lookout. No moon. White moon in the sky at my birth! Laughing moon! Me, I weep.

Columbus. Put on a diving suit, my spirit, and slip under the waters. 30 turn about in the currents, swim among the flowers of the deep, loiter among the worm-eaten stage setting of old disasters, follow the trail of the drowned nonchalants, those who were drowned on voyage, like my voyage, without design, without timetable. Good *Nautilus* protect you, my little ship, my absurd boat! May God direct the winds and the sails! The sea is absolute. I am all the time moved. . . .

The Lookout. It is warm. There are fanfares sounding beneath the waves.

Columbus. This is my ship's record book, a collection of monologues. *(He begins to write.)* 40

The Lookout. A lighthouse? No. Lights? One, two . . . No. *(Pause)* Lord have mercy on us! Christ have mercy on us! Holy Trinity have mercy . . . *(His voice dies away.)*

Voices of Sleepers. Sleep. There are flies. Sailor's sorrow. The accordion has pegged out. More music, more hope. Where are we? Thirst, thirst! See my little girl again, ah!

Columbus. Fever . . . *(He stands.)*

Voices of Sleepers. She's called Julie. Hang him from the yardarm. Eden has seven springs. *(The voices become incoherent. Sound of an*

50 *accordion)* In Europe! Enough lies! Are you asleep, Jack? The captain's in the drink! *(Various kinds of grunts)*

Columbus. (Shrugs his shoulders and says forcibly) If they knew that this world is at hand! *(The voices grow still.)*

The Lookout. Perfumes . . . birds . . .

Columbus. In the old days, monks lost themselves on the ocean and discovered the supposedly unknown lands, whose maps they drew. Nature was so lovely there, and life so sweet, that they thought they had found the Biblical paradise. *(Dead silence around)* Strange flowers, oils, palms, gold nuggets! Gold, gold everywhere, rivers of gold, cities 60 of gold, gold and feasting, wines, tall lascivious women! Feasting and sacrifice! Purple wine and blood! It is understood that no one ever works there. What rapture! It will be Eden indeed which those companions in fortune who maintain their courage and patience will share out between them. They have no idea of the orgies that threaten, of the sins, the dreadful sins that they will commit. And they have doubts about me? They suspect my genius? Blind men who allow themselves to be led astray by the legends of a deluded Middle Ages! Nightmares of pitch and foam, waters of terror, the mouths of hell, the gruesome vessel that sails in the height of the storm, with its crew of the dead! They 70 have read the tales of Edgar Allan Poe. All of that, the chaos, the gymnastic octopuses, the hordes of leviathans, the submarine craters, is tremendously literary—and quite beside the point. Let them sleep and dream in their guileless perversity. I am guiding the boat across enchanted waters. Their awakening will be marvelous. Poor ragtime sailors! *(He goes to the crew's quarters, spits in it, and comes back.)*

The Lookout. Dawn's going to break.

Columbus. Fools! I strongly doubt whether the dawn will bring you the promised land. And if, by that chance which no one calls to mind in the event of success, I should discover this world whose whereabouts 80 I do not know, nor even whether it exists, all would be finished for me, the adventure and its adorable anguish. *(The peaceful snoring of the sailors is heard, then silence. Someone sings.)* Not very good, this artist. *(A porthole, at the left, is pushed open from outside, allowing the face of a sixty-year-old female, purple and bloated after long immersion, to appear in profile.)*

Visquosine. Love?

Columbus. Of course! *(He catches sight of the head and starts.)* What a horror! *(He goes to the porthole.)* What do you want?

Visquosine. Permission, nice Captain, to render the hits from my 90 repertoire in honor of your gallant crew.

Columbus. Who are you?

Visquosine. Visquosine, the famous siren with the voice of the Atlantic.

Columbus. What do you sing that is really bewitching?

Visquosine. You shall hear . . . . *(She begins to sing raucously.)*

I am a pretty little fish,
Sticky, lithe, and naughty,
And unto those who live in hope
I sing of love at forty. *(Gurgling and ogling, she continues.)*
I charm the lonely bachelor . . . 100

Columbus. Really? *(He throws a handful of coins in her face.)* Swim off and don't let's have any more, you boiled-beef beauty.

Visquosine. What an insult to my art. *(Sob)* I shall drown myself at daybreak. *(She squirts a jet of water from her mouth at Columbus and disappears from the porthole.)*

Columbus. Here it is, daybreak, a difficult moment. *(He sits and writes.)* Another dawn. I hope that it lasts. We are somewhere. My crew is a little disturbed and its spirit is not of the best. As for myself, it is a matter of indifference whether I sail on or under the waters, or in the clouds, toward the paradise. I sail. And, in truth, I am afraid to 110 see the end of the ocean. My delusion is dear to me. I would not like the earth to be round, because it is pleasant to go nowhere and to be conscious of being nothing, to be lost to the eyes of men. Sailing for a hundred years and a hundred years more, I shall find the Eden that is at the center of myself, perfect silence, perfect solitude. I shall know the happiness that is without words. I shall be a crab or a whiff of this perfume that has caught my senses. I write in . . . *(The Lookout gives a tremendous yawn. Columbus yawns similarly.)* in this book that I ask God to forgive this inexpressible desire of not-being. . . . *(The deck is caressed by a pink light. Pause. Columbus is going to doze off; but there* 120 *is a cautious knocking in the timbers.)* Come in! *(He waits.)* Whoever knocks and doesn't come in can't be a thing of flesh. Are you there, spirit?

Voice of the Angel Azuret. One knock for Yes. Lift the trap.

Columbus. The classic scene of the stowaway revealing his presence! *(He lifts a trap and a mournful and insipid creature comes into view. He is very true to type. He wears a clerical gown and has wings rigged up at his shoulder blades.)* Good evening, sir, or madame. I'll settle your hash for you. You're just another useless mouth to feed, so I'm going to pitch you overboard. 130

The Angel Azuret. I don't eat, and water doesn't disagree with me. I am amphibious, from the Greek *amphi* and *bios*. What pleasure would you get from throwing me in the sea if I didn't die from it?

Columbus. None. Name and profession?

The Angel Azuret. Azuret, guardian angel.

Columbus. And you guard . . . ?

The Angel Azuret. You, Columbus.

Columbus. (Shakes hands) Pleased to meet... *(Puzzled)* One is always being watched, spied on.... *(Pause)* What have we to tell each
140 other in particular? You know everything. That is annoying.

The Angel Azuret. I am an excellent guardian, but you can set yourself at rest: I have a lamentable memory. If I have had the indelicacy to show myself, it is because of curiosity. Are you really going to discover America?

Columbus. I imagine so.

The Angel Azuret. Look out for the consequences. I have it on good authority that the Jesuits have their eyes on these future territories. And the Jesuits, you know...

Columbus. Are the enemy. Thank you. *(Voices in the crew's quarters*
150 *are heard.)* Hide yourself, my dear angel. It can't be comfortable down there? Go back, for if my men saw your gown, they could make a mistake. As a matter of fact, are you a boy or a girl?

The Angel Azuret. Nasty little devil! *(He disappears through the trap.)*

Columbus. Wouldn't it be that angel who, in the end, gave me this ship? *(He goes back and sits at the table. His head nods. Sleep lays hold of him. He resists.)* Fatigue! I saw a Jesuit wearing a black robe and with wings on his back. I heard cries....

The Lookout. Land!

Columbus. I dreamed that the lookout shouted....

160 *The Lookout.* Land! I see land!

Columbus. (Coming back to reality, leaps to his feet and climbs nimbly to the deck) What? Ahoy! Flying sailor, below!

The Lookout. (Clattering down to the deck) I saw it, Captain, and I'm still trembling from it....

Columbus. You saw?

The Lookout. Captain...

Columbus. Sleep! *(He makes hypnotic passes. The Lookout immediately stiffens.)* Up the mast! Keep watch!

The Lookout. I sleep... up the mast... keep watch....

170 *Columbus.* And when you sight America, for that is what it is, you will keep your trap shut. To your post! *(The Lookout climbs in the rigging and disappears.)* Helmsman!

The Helmsman. (Coming) Captain...

Columbus. Sleep! *(Hypnotic passes. The Helmsman stiffens.)* When you sight America, you will turn about and set her head toward Europe. Fall out! *(The Helmsman goes.)* To hell with America! I say, to hell with it! *(He goes down into the hold. There is a murmur of voices from the crew's quarters.)* I have had a narrow escape. And one mustn't think of going back to Europe. We shall go to the devil. This is the real
180 voyage! I have got plenty of liquor aboard. Farewell, America! You were too easy to discover.... *(He stations himself near the crew's quarters and listens to the voices which have become very clear.)*

First Voice. Eat.
Second Voice. Eat what?
First Voice. The captain.
Third Voice. How old is the captain?
Second Voice. Not eat, drink.
First Voice. Drink what?
Third Voice. That is the question.
Columbus. (In a loud voice) Whisky. *(He takes a flat flask from his pocket.)* Very good whisky! Oh, solace of clowns and navigators! *(He drinks. The deck grows light. Muffled music with a persistent rhythm begins in the distance. In the hold, the shaven heads of the sailors, looking as though they have been cut off, appear in line above the partition of the crew's quarters. Their eyes are like those of attentive dogs, and their tongues are hanging out. Columbus walks about and takes nips of his whisky.)* Everyone to his illusion. Mine is harsh, unalterable, more beautiful than art, than love. Magic figures, my dear illusion, what is your name? $V=\frac{4}{3}\pi R^3$! Sphere, I call you forth like a woman, and I wed your finished shape. I slip along your insensible sides. But you, Earth, are no longer the ideal sphere. I shall leave you for another

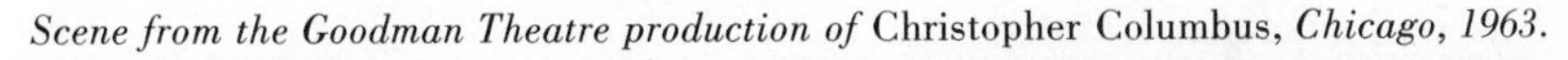
Scene from the Goodman Theatre production of Christopher Columbus, *Chicago, 1963.*

where I shall be alone, a more advanced sphere. . . . *(The rhythm has become obsessive. The night is gone at last.)*

Voice. Land!

Columbus. Calamity! He wasn't asleep, the shammer! Sleepers, it's over. All on deck. *(The sailors leap from their quarters and scatter about the ship, but gaudy, bawling Indians appear everywhere on deck —an invasion of magnificent feathers. They dance to the rhythm of the music and excitedly embrace the astounded sailors. Columbus goes*
210 *on deck.)* What is this show, this carnival? And what about your orders, helmsman?

The Sailors. The new world! Victory!

Columbus. (Dominating the tumult and the situation) Let us get things clear! Are we really in America, savage gentlemen?

Montezuma. (Gorgeous, comes forward and bows) In South America, to be exact.

Columbus. I have no luck. You speak English?

Montezuma. It is an elegant language. Would you rather have French?

Columbus. It doesn't matter. We were made to understand each
220 other. How ornamental you are! But, tell me, what are your intentions? Have you come to cut our throats?

Montezuma. I ask *you* that. We are peacefully celebrating your arrival, as we do every time a navigator discovers America.

Columbus. Then I am not the first?

Montezuma. Alas, Christopher Columbus!

Columbus. And you know my name?

Montezuma. The oracles told it to me. We were awaiting your arrival. The oracles also revealed that there was a lot of whisky in the hold.

Columbus. I had a presentiment that you were superior to and con-
230 temptuous of our civilization?

Montezuma. So what? We despise your civilization, but not whisky. No fibs, friend. You come to civilize us. That is in order. It will soon be done—I mean that we shall be exterminated. What does it matter? It is written on our oldest stones. In you, we celebrate the agents of destiny. We dance our death among our out-of-date pyramids and our tarnished suns. Perish our plumes and our millenial wisdom! You understand? We need whisky in order to despair better.

Columbus. Exterminate you, you lovely carnival characters? You seem to me to be excellent fellows, very fine, but a bit pessimistic.
240 Great chief, I shall take you to Europe.

Montezuma. No, thank you, dear barbarian. You shall go back alone. I want to die beneath the debris of my empire. My race is finished—and my dynasty. Make way for the archaeologists!

Columbus. I want to share your plumes and your dancing death.

Montezuma. A hopeless desire! Death is a vocation. Whisky!

The Indians. Whisky! Whisky! *(The sailors, laden with bottles, which they distribute, come up from the hold.)*

Columbus. Since it is too late, I drink to America, to the last of the Aztecs, to your plumes. . . .

Montezuma. Wipe us out—you may do that; but make speeches, oh no! 250

Columbus. You are right, great chief. The Jesuits will come and preach to you. My feathered and fated friends, I drink to the sphere.

Montezuma. Drink to this America, which opens its arms to you—in a way. . . . *(He laughs heartily. Columbus hugs him. The crew and the Indians dance to the accordion in an access of irresistible fraternity. Curtain.)*

Scene III

(A building occupies the back of the stage. It has three doors. That on the right is red, with the inscription SHAME. *That on the left is black, with the inscription* SILENCE. *That in the center is gilt, with the inscription* GLORY. *Thus, one has, for the requirements of this scene, a triumphal arch in the center, a jail on the right, and a tomb on the left. At the top of the building is the base for a statue, on which one can read "In honor of . . ." The Crowd Man brandishes newspapers and dances about.)*

The Crowd Man. Hurrah! Day of triumph! Superman! What boldness! See him! Touch him! Crown him! Flowers! National Subscription! 10 Banquet! Down with the cops! Long live Lord Roberts![°]

(The gilt door lights up. It opens to allow Christopher Columbus to come through. He carries his case, and has a raincoat over his period costume.)

Columbus. It's me.

The Crowd Man. (Turning his back on the new arrival) Here he is! It's him! The conqueror! The conquistador! The toreador! Ah, magnificent fellow!

Columbus. Thank you, ladies and gentlemen. Your acclamation . . .

The Crowd Man. Is he going to crash, or isn't he? 20

Columbus. Who?

The Crowd Man. (Indicating the sky) The man who has discovered Europe! Long live Lindbergh! *(He takes stock of Columbus.)* Are you a globe-trotter?

Columbus. Exactly that. I am Christopher Columbus returning from America.

The Crowd Man. Have you made a fortune?

11. Lord Roberts. Field Marshall Earl Roberts who served Britain in major colonial wars and conquests from the Indian Mutiny (1856) to the Boer War (1899-1901) is the prototype of the colonial conqueror.

Columbus. No, but I am famous.

The Crowd Man. In that case, long live Christopher Columbus! 30 *(He dances.)* Long live the Grand Turk! Down with the Jews! *Vive la France! (He has gone. Silence. Columbus looks sadly at the triumphal arch, goes and puts out its light, then comes back and sits on his case.)*

Columbus. The fickleness of people! It serves me right. If I hadn't come back, they might have sung an oratorio in my honor. My mistake was in being homesick on the strength of a fantasy, whereas my homeland is the ocean. If only I had stayed with the pipe-smoking Indians, among the carved gods and the angry little monkeys! I end up without beauty, without gold, and, for all one knows, without reputation. A little adventurer! I dreamed of the sphere, whereas it was a matter 40 of something quite different. Showing that the earth was round wasn't a very sharp thing to do: the business of standing an egg on its end would have been more profitable to me. *(He sighs.)* I am old and I have not lived, because I have conceded too much to dreams. I have been far and I find myself nowhere. I have seen much and I have learned nothing. I have done a great deal and I have accomplished nothing. I only know that the world is small and illusion is great. I am neither conceited nor grasping nor lucky. I have neither the virtues of fools nor those of heroes. The scholarly books will say that I was an intrepid voyager, but the young will remember the business about the egg. 50 After death, that won't matter. But now? Times are hard for anyone whose sole possession is merely the formula for the volume of a sphere. *(He gets up.)* My dear savages with your pretty plumes, forgive me for not having followed your advice at all. I shall think of you, but I shan't write about your last dance nor your nostalgic death, for it's not a good thing to reveal everything when you are begging for a pension and when the Jesuits wish you well. *(He walks up and down.)* Let these disappointments strengthen me. Let me find in myself that philosophy of the humble which suggests an acceptable explanation for calamitous happenings. What does this gratitude, this indifference, matter to me 60 if I think myself famous, if I alone understand the meaning of my destiny? Why shouldn't I celebrate myself? *(He leaps up and throws his hat in the air.)* Long live Christopher Columbus! Glory and honor! Long live the famous navigator! *(He puts his hat on again.)* There! Knowing glory, it only remains for me to enjoy it in some quiet place where, unknown to anyone, I shall finish my days. *(He is going, dragging his feet.)* Oh glory! so like that America one has come back from. . . . *(But someone is at his heels.)*

The Minister. Hey! Columbus?

Columbus. He has just gone.

70 *The Minister.* It's you. I recognize you! *(He takes three steps backward, then, ceremoniously.)* Christopher Columbus, in my voice, the

State offers you its most spontaneous felicitations. It is aware of your worth, and hazards a guess at the consequences of your discoveries. The America which you give it is an excellent land for development, and consequently you contribute to the elevation of national prestige. Also, the State rewards you by decorating you with this coveted order, which is only bestowed on men of letters, on lifesavers, and on agronomists. Let your bosom swell with legitimate pride! On this occasion, the State has set the man of letters, the lifesaver, and the agronomist on the same footing, for you are eminently all of these. As a man of 80 letters, you have sent a report to the Geographical Society, who find it properly drawn up. As a lifesaver, you have shown proof of civic courage in setting sail, when it was known you can't swim, and in saving the kingdom's finances by the contribution of these magnificent colonies, which we have mortgaged without delay. As for agronomy, it owes you recognition for your samples of rare seeds and your observations on the Colorado beetle, the enemy of agriculture. No decoration has been more deserved, and your modesty can exhibit it without blushing. Let me embrace you, my dear Columbus. . . . *(Embrace and bestowing of decoration)* 90

Columbus. This will be a constant source of pleasure. Besides, you are very nice.

The Minister. Excuse me. I have to be. But, tell me, this America, where is it? There are animals there, aren't there? What do you think, now you are back?

Columbus. That one is never better off than when in the bosom of one's own family.

The Minister. (Shaking his hand) I am touched by those words.

(A bugle sounds the "Attention." The Minister goes off.)

Columbus. Wait! *(He picks up his case and is going, but The King,* 100 *on crutches and furnished with a bunch of keys, has arrived.)* He has seen me. Is he going to ask for his ship?

The King. Not long ago, an individual called Columbus set out across the sea. I envied him. This man has come back. I pity him. To have found Eden, and to have come back to my kingdom . . .

Columbus. Sire, I am the man. How are you getting along?

The King. On crutches, my friend. And the kingdom is getting along badly, too. It is in trouble through your fault. Here I am in conflict with all the powers, as though the internal quarreling weren't enough. What need have we of colonial Edens? And I who dreamed of hanging gardens 110 to promenade my infirmities! Anyway, everything considered, you have deserved well of the Nation. *(Familiarly)* You must be tired, Columbus.

Columbus. My bones, not my spirit.

The King. My council has decided that you should rest yourself.

The Nation is going to house and feed you. Since this decision could be misinterpreted, I myself wanted to lead you to your retreat. Come, Columbus. *(He goes toward the red door, which lights up.)* The King asks you to come to prison.

120 *Columbus.* Don't be distressed, Sire. I was just on the lookout for a hermitage. Providence wills that Your Majesty should offer it to me. *(He goes into the prison.)* And . . . the reason, Sire?

The King. Here is a profound one. It is human to belittle you and crush you in order to be able to glorify you all the better afterward. Then people will say there is justice after all.

Columbus. But . . . the reason, Sire?

The King. Since you persist. . . . It's to please the Jesuits. Don't go and think that they don't wish you well and that your freedom has been taken from you. Nothing of the sort!

130 *Columbus. (Thoughtfully)* My dear savages . . .

The King. This freedom . . .

Columbus. As a sailor, I have heard of it.

The King. (Pulling down a grille in front of Columbus) What are you going to do from now on?

Columbus. Travel.

The King. Good-by, Columbus. Your chains weigh the same as my crown. *(He goes off on his crutches. Columbus sits in his jail.)*

Columbus. The beginning of wisdom. And I am going to make the loveliest of voyages. It will be enough merely to close my eyes.

140 *(He becomes still. Pause. The Poet, wearing high heels, enters.)*

The Poet. Columbus, whom the world forgets, the poet remembers you!

Columbus. Forget me.

The Poet. You are suffering. I can sense it.

Columbus. Not at all.

The Poet. So! You are not suffering?

Columbus. No—and you?

The Poet. I? . . . Ah, you have been decorated?

Columbus. That is my least offense. You will be, one day, if you

150 suffer suitably.

The Poet. Nonsense! But tell me, what remarkable things did you see yonder in the new world?

Columbus. Poets.

The Poet. God! What school? What kind?

Columbus. Poets who are neither civil servants nor pimps. They have infinite culture and tact. They know the most ancient fables on earth. The stars are their concern and are the burden of their songs. These poets live in solitude and have no names. They make the beasts obey them. They are chaste. They write nothing, and they never reveal the secret of their ecstasies to the common folk. *(During this monologue, The Poet has gone out on tiptoe. Columbus, lost in his memories, goes on with his speech, and music, tender and sad, begins. Montezuma and three Indian dancers, resplendent in jewels, come in and dance to its rhythm. Under the burden of their plumes, they mime what seem to be the agonies of hieratic birds.)* From them I learned amazement—at the symphony of the seashores, the choir of the forests, the marriage of the constellations, the harps of the priests, the courage of the bee, the laments of women, the scent of spices, the lightning from God, the hills and plains of slumber, the dialogue of the serpent and the beetle, the tears and jewels of the betrothed, Life, Death, Metamorphosis, Numbers, Trance, the cure for all ills, the everlasting dance on the tombs. . . . *(He stands up in his prison.)* It is time to go. It is the auspicious time. It is the carnival of blood and plumes. The magnificent shadows act the farewell, the eternal departure. Like them, I have acquired the smiling indifference of ghosts. Only dead friends are kind. A new world isn't a long way off any more. Oh, disquieting navigation! Let us forget civilization and geography. I see signals. *(The dancers have disappeared. A bell rings. The prison grille rises. A ship's siren moans. Columbus comes forward on the stage. Death, an ageless naval officer, enters. Hands in pockets, he dances springily to the music whose rhythm has quickened.)* Great Admiral, Captain Columbus salutes you.

Admiral Death. Come aboard, Captain. Leave your human baggage at the harbor. Smash your compass. God is the pole. Fleming, Breton, or Spaniard, the infinite is a slack water with neither joy nor pain. Come aboard, soul of a captain. *(He dances off. The music has stopped. The prison light goes out. It is almost night.)*

Columbus. I have loved adventure too much not to love dying. It is with a light foot that I leave you, ancient Earth, and your obsolete sphere where everything is ashes, puerile and perverse. This time I am going to travel without returning, among the luminous bubbles which God blew on the first day that ever was. . . .

(He enters, through the black door, into the tomb. He has hardly gone from sight when a raging march in the manner of Sousa rings out. Everything lights up brutally. A human form covered by a sheet slowly climbs up the building. It stations itself on the base and remains motionless. Then come: The American, wearing a dress coat made from his national flag, and an opera hat of the 1840 style; Buffalo Bill [the most authentic cowboy of all, promoted colonel by the grace of children] with his goatee and revolvers, shooting in evidence of joy; a pretty girl of a dancer in a tutu; a Bombardon player; a big-drum beater. The procession halts facing the building. The musicians stop playing. The American takes out a paper, and Buffalo Bill tears down the sheet covering the

statue. It is Christopher Columbus. He looks petrified and abstract. He holds one hand on his breast, the other he stretches out to see if it is raining. The American yaps:)

The American. Ladies and gentlemen. In the name of America, I come to salute you, Columbus—but not the great man, only the statue. Stop. America does you great honor in saluting you, because you are 210 not an American, which is regrettable. In America there are not many great men. Americans are neither great nor small, but middling and of sound constitution. Stop. This tribute has its reservation. You discovered America four centuries too soon. You ought to be coming there now, yes sir! Still, it's all right as it is. It only remains for me to wish you good luck in this age in which it is possible that it will be shown that you did not exist, and in which statues go out of fashion remarkably quickly. Full stop. *(At a signal from the speaker, the musicians attack Luther's chorale,* Ein' feste Burg. *The American, The Ballerina, and Buffalo Bill—the last of these punctuating the song with revolver* 220 *shots—howl the following quatrain to the rudimentary music:*

Columbus, we extol thy name,
Nor ask we therefor pardon.
We sing to thy immortal fame
With voice and with bombardon.

The procession goes off cacophonically. Silence. The lights go out and the stage is drowned in shadow. On the base, Christopher Columbus moves. He takes out a handkerchief and begins to weep.)

Columbus. It's no good seeing things from up above. It does something to you . . . when you are sensitive like me. There's nothing you 230 can do about anything. You have to be a statue to understand. . . . *(Curtain.)*

Comments and Questions

The opening of the play, with Columbus blowing soap bubbles, immediately introduces several of the major strands of the web of symbols which Ghelderode spins to make his points, and which he uses to transform history into cosmic meaning. The immediate issue is of course that of roundness, the spherical shape of the world. But there is more to it: a soap bubble is a perfect sphere, more perfectly spherical than the planet earth, but also more ephemeral. The chasing of ephemera or the idea of ephemeralism therefore begins in the first speech.

Many ideas underlie the symbols of the play, ideas that are quite rightly generated by the character and trials of Columbus. Columbus says near the middle of Scene II: "Sailing for a hundred years and a hundred years more, I shall find the Eden that is at the center of myself, perfect silence, perfect solitude." What do you think he means? Does he succeed in achieving this condition of inaction and "not-being"? Why does he seem to want to? Consider other remarks of his, both before (especially in the opening speech) and after, that point to his motives for sailing to America and later for attempting to turn back at the point of sighting land, and, near the end, for his accepting the retreat of prison and then death.

Ghelderode has said that he felt "Columbus became a synthesis of all the travelers, all the wanderers, all the 'erratics' of his age and all ages. To my mind, Columbus was the man who escapes," for life offers "few joys in exchange for a great deal of pain, effort, and anxiety. . . ." In what way does Columbus appear to be both searching and escaping?

Do others, both in Columbus' time and ours, view his motives and accomplishments in the same way he does? As one might expect in a dream, characters have symbolic meanings, and, often, like the soap bubbles, in several ways. The Crowd Man is like one of the generalized characters in a medieval morality play, such as Everyman. *What other general symbolic characters can you find? Are there any characters that are more fully realized as individuals, like some of the type characters in* The Alchemist *or* Scapin? *The Reporter and the references to Lindbergh and Edgar Allan Poe are of course anachronisms; what do they signify? What other anachronisms can you find? Why is the angel Azuret introduced? Is there any significance in the fact that a supernatural guardian has a poor memory?*

What comment does Ghelderode appear to be making about the new in conflict with the old; about what man believes himself to be and what he really is? Is man's assurance that he is more civilized than the savages questioned or qualified? What happens in the course of reading the play to our faith in the validity of the accounts of past events and heroes as reported in history books? Finally, why do you think Ghelderode subtitles the play "A Dramatic Fairy Tale in Three Scenes"? Does the play have any characteristics in common with fairy tales you know? You might consider "The Emperor's New Clothes" for one.

Christopher Columbus *is part comedy, part serious play, and part morality play. In what ways does it resemble* The Visit, *with which it has these three characteristics in common?*

Thornton Wilder

SOME THOUGHTS ON PLAYWRITING

Thornton Wilder, whose play The Matchmaker *is included in this volume, is a contemporary American playwright and novelist.*

Four fundamental conditions of the drama separate it from the other arts. Each of these conditions has its advantages and disadvantages, each requires a particular aptitude from the dramatist, and from each there are a number of instructive consequences to be derived. These conditions are:

1. The theatre is an art which reposes upon the work of many collaborators;
2. It is addressed to the group-mind;
3. It is based upon a pretense and its very nature calls out a mul-
10 tiplication of pretenses;
4. Its action takes place in a perpetual present time.

I. The Theatre Is an Art Which Reposes upon the Work of Many Collaborators

We have been accustomed to think that a work of art is by definition the product of one governing selecting will.

A landscape by Cézanne consists of thousands of brushstrokes each commanded by one mind. *Paradise Lost* and *Pride and Prejudice*, even in cheap frayed copies, bear the immediate and exclusive message of one intelligence.

20 It is true that in musical performance we meet with intervening executants, but the element of intervention is slight compared to that which takes place in drama. Illustrations:

1. One of the finest productions of *The Merchant of Venice* in our time showed Sir Henry Irving° as Shylock, a noble, wronged, and indignant being, of such stature that the Merchants of Venice dwindled before him into irresponsible schoolboys. He was confronted in court by a gracious, even queenly, Portia, Miss Ellen Terry. At the Odéon in Paris, however, Gémier played Shylock as a vengeful and hysterical buffoon, confronted in court by a Portia who was a *gamine* from the
30 Paris streets with a lawyer's quill three feet long over her ear; at the close of the trial scene Shylock was driven screaming about the auditorium, behind the spectators' back and onto the stage again, in a wild

24. ***Sir Henry Irving*** (1838-1905), perhaps the most important Shakespearean actor of his time, was the chief artistic competitor of Sir Herbert Beerbohm Tree whose performance as Falstaff is reviewed by Bernard Shaw, p. 689.

Elizabethan revel. Yet for all their divergences both were admirable productions of the play.

2. If there were ever a play in which fidelity to the author's requirements were essential in the representation of the principal role, it would seem to be Ibsen's *Hedda Gabler*, for the play is primarily an exposition of her character. Ibsen's directions read: "Enter from the left Hedda Gabler. She is a woman of twenty-nine. Her face and figure show great refinement and distinction. Her complexion is pale and 40 opaque. Her steel-gray eyes express an unruffled calm. Her hair is of an attractive medium brown, but is not particularly abundant; and she is dressed in a flowing loose-fitting morning gown." I once saw Eleonora Duse° in this role. She was a woman of sixty and made no effort to conceal it. Her complexion was pale and transparent. Her hair was white, and she was dressed in a gown that suggested some medieval empress in mourning. And the performance was very fine.

One may well ask: why write for the theatre at all? Why not work in the novel where such deviations from one's intentions cannot take place? 50

There are two answers:

1. The theatre presents certain vitalities of its own so inviting and stimulating that the writer is willing to receive them in compensation for this inevitable variation from an exact image.

2. The dramatist through working in the theatre gradually learns not merely to take account of the presence of the collaborators, but to derive advantage from them; and he learns, above all, to organize the play in such a way that its strength lies not in appearances beyond his control, but in the succession of events and in the unfolding of an idea, in narration. 60

The gathered audience sits in a darkened room, one end of which is lighted. The nature of the transaction at which it is gazing is a succession of events illustrating a general idea—the stirring of the idea; the gradual feeding out of information; the shock and countershock of circumstances; the flow of action; the interruption of action; the moments of allusion to earlier events; the preparation of surprise, dread, or delight—all that is the author's and his alone.

For reasons to be discussed later—the expectancy of the group-mind, the problem of time on the stage, the absence of the narrator, the element of pretense—the theatre carries the art of narration to a 70 higher power than the novel or the epic poem. The theatre is unfolding action and in the disposition of events the authors may exercise a governance so complete that the distortions effected by the physical

43-44. Eleonora Duse (1859-1924) was one of the most internationally famous actresses of the early twentieth century.

appearance of actors, by the fancies of scene painters and the misunderstandings of directors, fall into relative insignificance. It is just because the theatre is an art of many collaborators, with the constant danger of grave misinterpretation, that the dramatist learns to turn his attention to the laws of narration, its logic and its deep necessity of presenting a unifying idea stronger than its mere collection of happenings. The dramatist must be by instinct a storyteller.

There is something mysterious about the endowment of the storyteller. Some very great writers possessed very little of it, and some others, lightly esteemed, possessed it in so large a measure that their books survive down the ages, to the confusion of severer critics. Alexandre Dumas had it to an extraordinary degree; while Melville, for all his splendid quality, had it barely sufficiently to raise his work from the realm of non-fiction. It springs, not, as some have said, from an aversion to general ideas, but from an instinctive coupling of idea and illustration; the idea, for a born storyteller, can only be expressed imbedded in its circumstantial illustration. The myth, the parable, the fable are the fountainhead of all fiction and in them is seen most clearly the didactic, moralizing employment of a story. Modern taste shrinks from emphasizing the central idea that hides behind the fiction, but it exists there nevertheless, supplying the unity to fantasizing, and offering a justification to what otherwise we would repudiate as mere arbitrary contrivance, pretentious lying, or individualistic emotional association spinning. For all their magnificent intellectual endowment, George Meredith and George Eliot were not born storytellers; they chose fiction as the vehicle for their reflections, and the passing of time is revealing their error in that choice. Jane Austen was pure storyteller and her works are outlasting those of apparently more formidable rivals. The theatre is more exacting than the novel in regard to this faculty, and its presence constitutes a force which compensates the dramatist for the deviations which are introduced into his work by the presence of his collaborators.

The chief of these collaborators are the actors.

The actor's gift is a combination of three separate faculties or endowments. Their presence to a high degree in any one person is extremely rare, although the ambition to possess them is common. Those who rise to the height of the profession represent a selection and a struggle for survival in one of the most difficult and cruel of the artistic activities. The three endowments that compose the gift are observation, imagination, and physical co-ordination.

1. An observant and analyzing eye for all modes of behavior about us, for dress and manner, and for the signs of thought and emotion in one's self and in others.

2. The strength of imagination and memory whereby the actor may, at the indication in the author's text, explore his store of observations

and represent the details of appearance and the intensity of the emotions —joy, fear, surprise, grief, love, and hatred, and through imagination 120 extend them to intenser degrees and to differing characterizations.

3. A physical co-ordination whereby the force of these inner realizations may be communicated to voice, face, and body.

An actor must *know* the appearances and the mental states; he must *apply* his knowledge to the role; and he must physically *express* his knowledge. Moreover, his concentration must be so great that he can effect this representation under conditions of peculiar difficulty —in abrupt transition from the non-imaginative conditions behind the stage; and in the presence of fellow-actors who may be momentarily destroying the reality of the action. 130

A dramatist prepares the characterization of his personages in such a way that it will take advantage of the actor's gift.

Characterization in a novel is presented by the author's dogmatic assertion that the personage was such, and by an analysis of the personage with generally an account of his or her past. Since, in the drama, this is replaced by the actual presence of the personage before us and since there is no occasion for the intervening all-knowing author to instruct us as to his or her inner nature, a far greater share is given in a play to (1) highly characteristic utterances and (2) concrete occasions in which the character defines itself under action and (3) 140 a conscious preparation of the text whereby the actor may build upon the suggestions in the role according to his own abilities.

Characterization in a play is like a blank check which the dramatist accords to the actor for him to fill in—not entirely blank, for a number of indications of individuality are already there, but to a far less definite and absolute degree than in the novel.

The dramatist's principal interest being the movement of the story, he is willing to resign the more detailed aspects of characterization to the actor and is often rewarded beyond his expectation.

The sleepwalking scene from *Macbeth* is a highly compressed 150 selection of words whereby despair and remorse rise to the surface of indirect confession. It is to be assumed that had Shakespeare lived to see what the genius of Sarah Siddons° could pour into the scene from that combination of observation, self-knowledge, imagination, and representational skill, even he might have exclaimed, "I never knew I wrote so well!"

II. The Theatre Is an Art Addressed to a Group-Mind

Painting, sculpture, and the literature of the book are certainly solitary experiences; and it is likely that most people would agree that the audience seated shoulder to shoulder in a concert hall is not an 160 essential element in musical enjoyment.

153. Sarah Siddons, (1755-1831), the most famous Shakespearean actress of her day.

But a play presupposes a crowd. The reasons for this go deeper than (1) the economic necessity for the support of the play and (2) the fact that the temperament of actors is proverbially dependent on group attention.

It rests on the fact that (1) the pretense, the fiction, on the stage would fall to pieces and absurdity without the support accorded to it by a crowd, and (2) the excitement induced by pretending a fragment of life is such that it partakes of ritual and festival, and requires a throng.
170 Similarly the fiction that royal personages are of a mysteriously different nature from other people requires audiences, levees, and processions for its maintenance. Since the beginnings of society, satirists have occupied themselves with the descriptions of kings and queens in their intimacy and delighted in showing how the prerogatives of royalty become absurd when the crowd is not present to extend to them the enhancement of an imaginative awe.

The theatre partakes of the nature of festival. Life imitated is life raised to a higher power. In the case of comedy, the vitality of these pretended surprises, deceptions, and *contretemps* becomes so lively
180 that before a spectator, solitary or regarding himself as solitary, the structure of so much event would inevitably expose the artificiality of the attempt and ring hollow and unjustified; and in the case of tragedy, the accumulation of woe and apprehension would soon fall short of conviction. All actors know the disturbing sensation of playing before a handful of spectators at a dress rehearsal or performance where only their interest in pure craftsmanship can barely sustain them. During the last rehearsals the phrase is often heard: "This play is hungry for an audience."

Since the theatre is directed to a group-mind, a number of con-
190 sequences follow:

1. A group-mind presupposes, if not a lowering of standards, a broadening of the fields of interest. The other arts may presuppose an audience of connoisseurs trained in leisure and capable of being interested in certain rarefied aspects of life. The dramatist may be prevented from exhibiting, for example, detailed representations of certain moments in history that require specialized knowledge in the audience, or psychological states in the personages which are of insufficient general interest to evoke self-identification in the majority. In the Second Part of Goethe's *Faust* there are long passages dealing
200 with the theory of paper money. The exposition of the nature of misanthropy (so much more drastic than Molière's°) in Shakespeare's *Timon of Athens* has never been a success. The dramatist accepts this limitation in subject matter and realizes that the group-mind

201. Molière's, in his play *The Misanthrope* (1666).

imposes upon him the necessity of treating material understandable by the larger number.

2. It is the presence of the group-mind that brings another requirement to the theatre—forward movement.

Maeterlinck° said that there was more drama in the spectacle of an old man seated by a table than in the majority of plays offered to the public. He was juggling with the various meanings in the word "drama." In the sense whereby drama means the intensified concentration of life's diversity and significance he may well have been right; if he meant drama as a theatrical representation before an audience he was wrong. Drama on the stage is inseparable from forward movement, from action. 210

Many attempts have been made to present Plato's dialogues, Gobineau's° fine series of dialogues, *La Renaissance*, and the *Imaginary Conversations of Landor;*° but without success. Through some ingredient in the group-mind, and through the sheer weight of anticipation involved in the dressing up and the assumption of fictional roles, an action is required, and an action that is more than a mere progress in argumentation and debate. 220

III. The Theatre Is a World of Pretense

It lives by conventions: a convention is an agreed-upon falsehood, a permitted lie.

Illustrations: Consider at the first performance of the *Medea,*° the passage where Medea meditates the murder of her children. An anecdote from antiquity tells us that the audience was so moved by this passage that considerable disturbance took place.

The following conventions were involved: 230

1. Medea was played by a man.

2. He wore a large mask on his face. In the lip of the mask was an acoustical device for projecting the voice. On his feet he wore shoes with soles and heels half a foot high.

3. His costume was so designed that it conveyed to the audience, by convention: woman of royal birth and Oriental origin.

4. The passage was in metric speech. All poetry is an "agreed-upon falsehood" in regard to speech.

5. The lines were sung in a kind of recitative. All opera involves this "permitted lie" in regard to speech. 240

Modern taste would say that the passage would convey much greater pathos if a woman "like Medea" had delivered it—with an uncovered face that exhibited all the emotions she was undergoing. For the Greeks,

208. Maeterlinck, Maurice Maeterlinck (1862-1949), Belgian-French dramatist. ***217. Gobineau,*** Joseph Arthur Court Gobineau, (1816-1882), French writer and diplomat. ***218. Landor,*** Walter Savage Landor, (1775-1864), English poet and essayist. ***226. Medea,*** by Euripides, presumably first performed in 431 B.C.

however, there was no pretense that Medea was on the stage. The mask, the costume, the mode of declamation, were a series of signs which the spectator interpreted and reassembled in his own mind. Medea was being re-created within the imagination of each of the spectators.

The history of the theatre shows us that in its greatest ages the stage employed the greatest number of conventions. The stage is funda-
250 mental pretense and it thrives on the acceptance of that fact and in the multiplication of additional pretenses. When it tries to assert that the personages in the action "really are," really inhabit such and such rooms, really suffer such and such emotions, it loses rather than gains credibility. The modern world is inclined to laugh condescendingly at the fact that in the plays of Racine and Corneille the gods and heroes of antiquity were dressed like the courtiers under Louis XIV; that in the Elizabethan age scenery was replaced by placards notifying the audience of the location; and that a whip in the hand and a jogging motion of the body indicated that a man was on horseback in the
260 Chinese theatre; these devices did not spring from naïveté, however, but from the vitality of the public imagination in those days and from an instinctive feeling as to where the essential and where the inessential lay in drama.

The convention has two functions:

1. It provokes the collaborative activity of the spectator's imagination; and

2. It raises the action from the specific to the general.

This second aspect is of even greater importance than the first.

If Juliet is represented as a girl "very like Juliet"—it was not merely
270 a deference to contemporary prejudices that assigned this role to a boy in the Elizabethan age—moving about in a "real" house with marble staircases, rugs, lamps, and furniture, the impression is irresistibly conveyed that these events happened to this one girl, in one place, at one moment in time. When the play is staged as Shakespeare intended it, the bareness of the stage releases the events from the particular and the experience of Juliet partakes of that of all girls in love, in every time, place and language.

The stage continually strains to tell this generalized truth and it is the element of pretense that reinforces it. Out of the lie, the pre-
280 tense, of the theatre proceeds a truth more compelling than the novel can attain, for the novel by its own laws is constrained to tell of an action that "once happened"—"once upon a time."

IV. The Action on the Stage Takes Place in a Perpetual Present Time

Novels are written in the past tense. The characters in them, it is true, are represented as living moment by moment their present time, but the constant running commentary of the novelist ("Tess slowly descended into the valley"; "Anna Karenina laughed") inevitably conveys to the reader the fact that these events are long since past and over.

The novel is a past reported in the present. On the stage it is always now. This confers upon the action an increased vitality which the novelist longs in vain to incorporate into his work. 290

This condition in the theatre brings with it another important element:

In the theatre we are not aware of the intervening storyteller. The speeches arise from the characters in an apparently pure spontaneity.

A play is what takes place.

A novel is what one person tells us took place.

A play visibly represents pure existing. A novel is what one mind, claiming to omniscience, asserts to have existed.

Many dramatists have regretted this absence of the narrator from the stage, with his point of view, his powers of analyzing the behavior of the characters, his ability to interfere and supply further facts about the past, about simultaneous actions not visible on the stage, and above *all* his function of pointing the moral and emphasizing the significance of the action. In some periods of the theatre he has been present as chorus, or prologue and epilogue or as *raisonneur*. But surely this absence constitutes an additional force to the form, as well as an additional tax upon the writer's skill. It is the task of the dramatist so to co-ordinate his play, through the selection of episodes and speeches, that, though he is himself not visible, his point of view and his governing intention will impose themselves on the spectator's attention, not as dogmatic assertion or motto, but as self-evident truth and inevitable deduction. 300 310

Imaginative narration—the invention of souls and destinies—is to a philosopher an all but indefensible activity.

Its justification lies in the fact that the communication of ideas from one mind to another inevitably reaches the point where exposition passes into illustration, into parable, metaphor, allegory, and myth.

It is no accident that when Plato arrived at the height of his argument and attempted to convey a theory of knowledge and a theory of the structure of man's nature he passed over into story telling, into the myths of the Cave and the Charioteer; and that the great religious teachers have constantly had recourse to the parable as a means of imparting their deepest intuitions. 320

The theatre offers to imaginative narration its highest possibilities. It has many pitfalls and its very vitality betrays it into service as mere diversion and the enhancement of insignificant matter; but it is well to remember that it was the theatre that rose to the highest place during those epochs that aftertime has chosen to call "great ages" and that the Athens of Pericles and the reigns of Elizabeth, Philip II, and Louis XIV were also the ages that gave to the world the greatest dramas it has known. 330

Raymond Williams

SOPHOCLES' *ANTIGONE*: A RECONSTRUCTION OF ITS PERFORMANCE

Raymond Williams, a lecturer at Cambridge University in England, published his essay on Antigone *as part of his book* Drama in Performance *in 1954.*

The Conditions of Performance

The occasion of the performance is the festival of the City Dionysia, in Athens, in the last days of March. On the first day of the festival, the image of Dionysus Eleuthereus° was carried in a brilliant procession to a shrine outside the city, where a bull was sacrificed to it; after dark on that day, the image was carried back in a torchlight procession and placed in the theatre.

4. *Dionysus Eleuthereus,* originally one of the Greek gods of fertility or vegetation, later worshipped as the god of wine; he was also the patron of the drama in whose honor festivals—the Dionysia—were held.

Plan of the Theatre of Dionysus at Athens, and of its immediate environs.

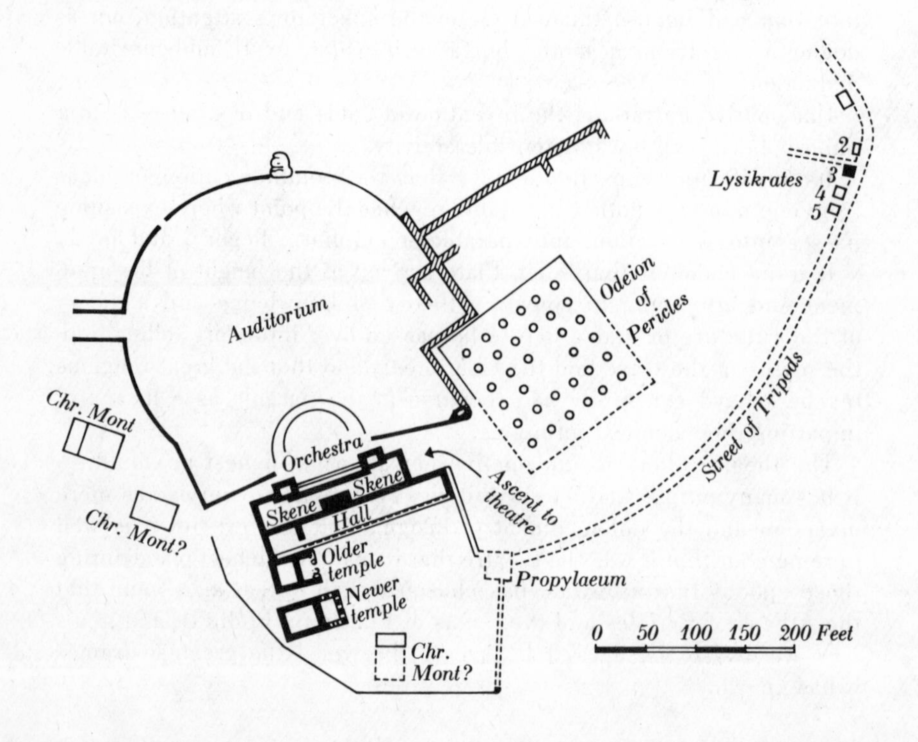

The whole dramatic festival is a ceremony of worship to Dionysus. Organised by the city, it will last for five days, during which three poets will each exhibit three tragedies and a satyric play, and there will also be performed five comedies and the singing, by boys' and men's choruses, of the dithyrambic hymns. The work of the three poets, like the dithyrambic singing, is competitive; as is also the playing of the chief actor, or protagonist. The ceremonies of each day begin at dawn in the theatre, with a purifying sacrifice, and the offering of libations. In the centre of the front row of the auditorium is the priest of Dionysus Eleuthereus, and sitting beside him the priests of Zeus and Athena. Behind them are a huge audience, as many as seventeen thousand men, women and children. All business in the city is suspended while the festival lasts.

The theatre of Dionysus, in which this audience is now assembled, lies on the south-eastern slope below the rock of the Acropolis. To the west, the audience can see the city and the harbour; to the east, the open country. Below the auditorium, in which the audience sit on wooden seats up the terraced slope, the dominant feature is the circular *orchestra*, the dancing-place *(orchesis*=dancing*)*. It is about sixty feet across, with a floor of beaten earth, and surrounded by a stone kerb. In the centre of the orchestra is an altar *(thymele)*, with

Detail of playing-area, Theatre of Dionysus at Athens. The skene *and* paraskenia *are indicated by the dotted line; the space between the* paraskenia, *into which the circle of the* orchestra *projects, is the* logeion.

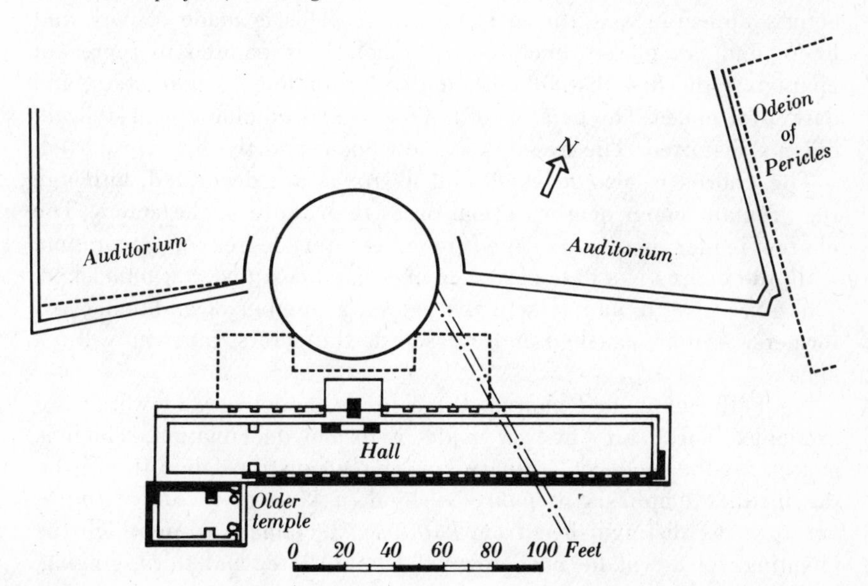

a step beside it. At the far side of the orchestra from the auditorium rises a wooden rectangular building, of one storey, about a hundred feet long. At each end of this building, wings *(paraskenia)* project towards the auditorium. Between these wings and the auditorium are two entrances to the orchestra *(parodoi)*. The wooden building is known as the *skene*, and a wide central door opens from it on to the space between the projecting wings; doors also open on to this space from the wings themselves. The space is the *logeion*, the speaking-place for the actors, as opposed to the *orchestra*, the dancing-place for the chorus. The *logeion* is not a stage in the modern sense; it is raised about a foot above the level of the *orchestra*, in a broad step running back to the front of the *skene*. On this front is a painted scene, representing a palace. Behind the *skene* building is the temple and precinct of Dionysus, in which the image that is now in the theatre is normally kept.

The performance of each play is heralded by a trumpet, and in the *Antigone* the central door is opened, and the first actors enter the *logeion*. The play will be acted by three actors, who will share between them the individual speaking parts, and a chorus of fifteen, of whom the leader *(coryphœus)* will also speak individually. Actors and chorus are all male. The actors wear a long robe, with a shorter over-mantle; these are richly coloured and decorated, but do not normally indicate character (except that a garment of open network may be worn to indicate a seer). On their feet the actors wear decorated shoes, with a thin sole (the shoes with soles of a thickness up to eight inches belong to a later period). The most significant feature of the actor's appearance is the mask he wears. This is made of cork and linen, and completely encloses his head. It is painted to represent character; the first distinction being white for female characters, and darker for males. The painting of the features is emphatic, and stylized, but not distorted. The eye-slits are left open, and the lips are parted.

The chorus is also masked, and its robes are decorated, although they remain much nearer normal dress than those of the actors. The chorus leader is distinguished by a greater degree of decoration. With the chorus is a flute-player, in decorated costume, but unmasked. There are also, to supplement the actors, a number of additional performers, who are masked and dressed as the actors, but who will not speak.

For both actors and chorus, three kinds of delivery of words are available. These are, first, a mode of formal declamation, which is nearest to the mode of ordinary speech, but distinguished from it by the distinct emphasis of metre; second, a kind of recitative *(parakataloge*, as distinguished from *kataloge*, declamation), in which the chanting voice will be accompanied by the flute; and third, singing, again accompanied by the flute, either in the form of a solo *(monodia)*, a duet or trio, singing between an actor and the chorus *(kommos)*, or the ode of the whole chorus. The particular form of delivery employed at any point in the play is determined by the nature of the metre in which the lines to be delivered are written.

Gesture, accompanying the delivery of the words, is so far as possible indicated in the composition of the lines to be delivered. It is formal in character, and controlled from moment to moment by the 80 words being delivered, "as if the words and the parts of the body were connected by strings which the former pulled." Dancing *(orchesis)*, in its general sense, includes the use of the whole body, and especially the hands, as well as movements of the leg. The purpose of any movement is mimetic—that is to say, the physical realization of what is being verbally expressed, either by the person speaking or singing, or in response to what is being spoken or sung by another. There are three classes of movement: indications (the pointing of an object or person); motions (the expression of a feeling); and postures, *schemata* (the positions which may be held, and fixed, when a motion is complete). 90 All these, as appropriate, will be employed by the actors, in the *logeion*. They will be employed also, in unison, by the chorus, in the *orchestra*. The chorus, which normally first enters the *orchestra* from the west, is formed into three files, each of five members of the chorus *(choreutæ)*. The leader of the chorus is in the center of the file which, when entering from the west, would be nearest to the audience; that is, in the centre of the front row. The flute player, who precedes the chorus in its entrance into the *orchestra*, then takes up his place on the step of the *thymele* in the centre. The chorus dance in that part of the *orchestra* nearest to the *logeion*. 100

These are the known conditions of performance. The trumpet has been sounded, and the performance of the *Antigone*, before this huge audience, gathered in the great open-air theatre for its most important religious festival, is about to begin. But before we look at parts of this performance, we need to look at Sophocles' text of the *Antigone*, which existed before the performance began, which controlled it during its realisation, and which has survived both performance and theatre.

Oscar G. Brockett

THE ELIZABETHAN THEATRE

Oscar G. Brockett, a professor at Indiana University, is the author of The Theatre: An Introduction *(1964) which includes the selection printed here. Professor Brockett discusses the open-air theatres, the so-called "public" playhouses, which were situated around London during the reign of Elizabeth I (1558-1603) and James I (1603-1625). In addition to these playhouses, indoor theatres were also in existence, particularly during the later period. Called "private" playhouses, they were smaller and more expensive and attracted a more select, or at least more affluent, audience. Most of Shakespeare's plays,* Henry IV *among them, were written for performance in the public playhouses.*

A number of public theatres were built before 1615. The first, erected in 1576, was called simply The Theatre. Others were: The Curtain (1577), Newington Butts (c. 1580), The Rose (1587), The Swan (1596), The Globe (1599, rebuilt in 1614), The Fortune (1600), and The Hope (1614). It is not certain that they were alike in their basic appearance; it is logical to assume that they differed considerably in details just as theatres in any period do.

The theatres varied in size, but the most elaborate seated from two to three thousand spectators. They were of differing shapes: round, 10 square, five-sided, eight-sided. Typically, they were laid out in this manner: A large central unroofed space, called the "pit" or "yard," was enclosed by three tiers of roofed galleries which formed the outside of the building. At the door to the theatre each person paid the same admission price. This entitled him to stand in the yard; if he wished to sit, he paid an additional fee and was admitted to the galleries.

A raised stage (from four to six feet high) extended to the center of the yard. This large platform, sometimes called the forestage or main stage, was the principal acting area. Spectators could stand around 20 three sides, and the galleries also commanded a view from at least three sides.

The greatest disagreement about the Elizabethan theatre concerns the "discovery" space (variously called the "inner below," the "study," and the "pavilion") at the rear of the forestage. In many plays of the period characters, objects, or places must be revealed or concealed. It is generally agreed, therefore, that there was an area at the rear of the main stage for this purpose. Its size and precise location, however, are disputed. The two major answers have been: (1) that this area was recessed into the back wall with a curtain across the front; and (2) that this area jutted onto the forestage like a pavilion and thus had curtains around three sides. Neither view can be established, though the weight of opinion is shifting toward the second. For our purposes it is sufficient to know that the large acting area jutting into the middle of the yard had two doors at the rear for entrances and exits, plus a space between these which could be used for revelations and concealments. It may have been large enough for scenes to be played inside it, or it may have been similar to the Medieval mansion (that is, only large enough to indicate a locale, while the forestage served as the *platea).*

Conclusions about the upper stage grow out of those about the discovery space. Those scholars who believe that there was an "inner below" state that there was a similar recessed space on the second level called the "inner above," while those who prefer the "pavilion" argue that there was an acting area on top of this forward projection. In either case, however, it is clear that there was an area on the second level which could be used by the actors. In addition, there were one or two windows on the second level out of which characters could lean or into which they might climb. The logical place for these would be above the two doors on the main stage. A third level was occasionally used by actors in scenes supposed to occur in very high places, but ordinarily this space was reserved for musicians.

The basic outlines of the stage, then, are simple: (1) a large platform (at the Fortune Theatre, approximately forty-three feet wide by twenty-seven-and-a-half feet deep) jutting to the middle of the theatre structure; (2) a door on each side at the rear of this stage; (3) a discovery space between these doors; (4) an upper acting area over the discovery space; (5) windows on each side of the upper stage; (6) a third level which might be used by actors, but which was usually reserved for musicians.

This stage seems to have been designed for a continuous flow of dramatic action. As the actors left the forestage by one door at the end of a scene, another group might enter at the other door and begin the next scene; or the discovery space might be opened and the stage would become a new place; or a scene on the forestage might be followed by one on the upper level; or more than one level might be used at the same time. One scene flowed into the next without pause. (The plays were not divided into acts; such divisions were made by later editors.)

It is usual today to assume that no scenery was used in the Elizabethan theatre, but the records kept by Philip Henslowe (a businessman associated with the Admiral's Men) list such items as rocks, trees, beds, a hell-mouth, and a cloth representing the "city of Rome." It is possible that there were a number of set pieces, or that mansions may have been put up occasionally as on the Medieval stage. It is also possible that mansions were used in the beginning and gradually were discarded. It seems unlikely that very much scenery requiring shifting was used, however, as it would have seriously interrupted the flow of scenes. The distinct possibility exists, nevertheless, that scenic elements were used at times.

(Right) A reconstruction of the Fortune Theatre built in London in 1600. The contract, which still exists, for this building is another principal source of information about the features of the Elizabethan theatre. (Bottom) The inner stage conceived of as a pavilion.

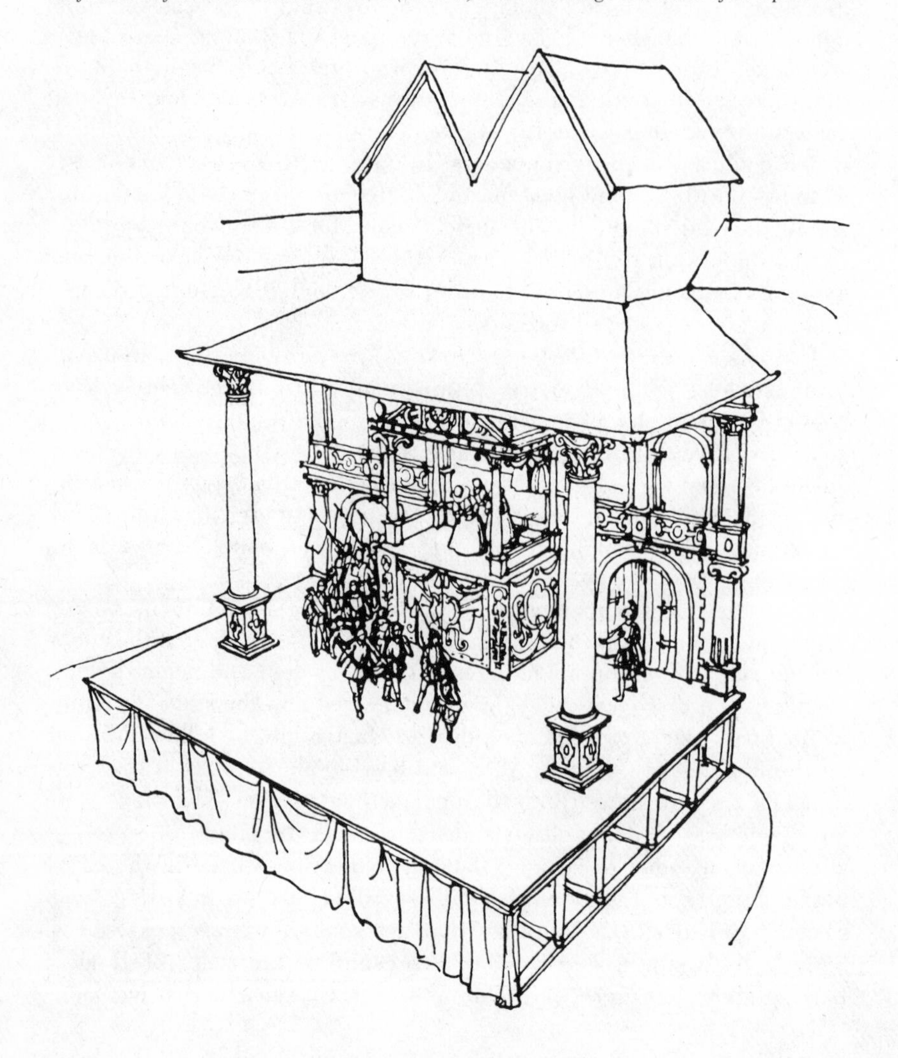

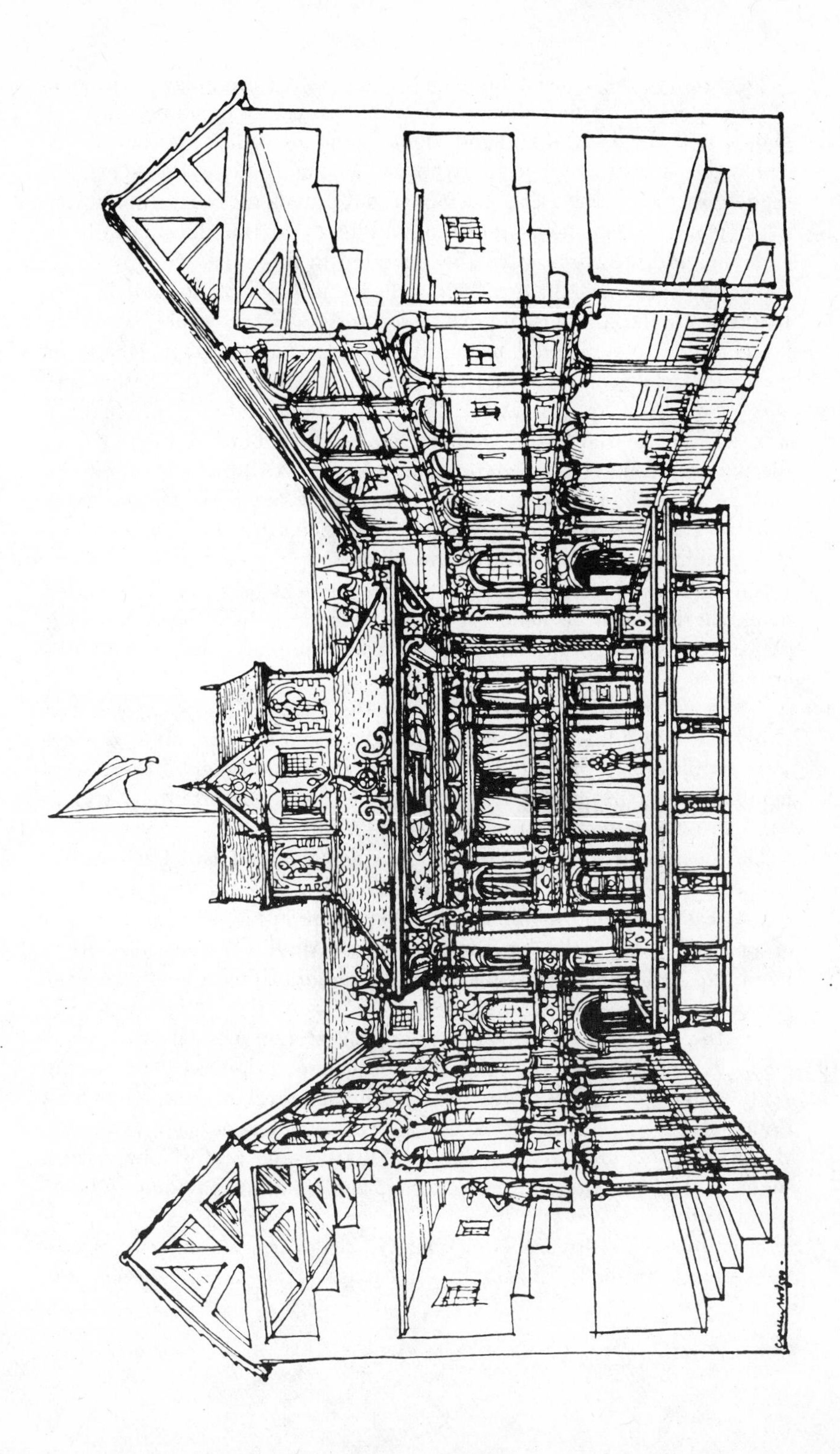

Machinery was housed both below and above the stage. A number of trap doors in the floor allowed for grave scenes, for the appearances of ghosts and devils, for fire and smoke, and for other special effects. Typically, a roof (supported by posts at the front of the stage) extended over the stage. Cranes, ropes, and pullies for raising and lowering objects were housed there. Sound effects for thunder, alarm bells, cannons, and fireworks were also operated in this area.

The Elizabethan theatre, with all its originality, included many features similar to those of past structures. For example, the Elizabethan theatre depended primarily on a permanent stage facade for its scenic background as had the Roman theatre, and the acting area was surrounded by spectators as in the Greek theatre. Some features were clearly related to the Medieval stage: the generalized acting area, the practice of having spectators stand in the yard, the special effects, and the possible use of mansions°—all of these recall Medieval theatre. But, the Elizabethan theatre combined these features in a unique structure which was both derivative and original.

Since theatres were roofless and performances occurred in the afternoon, there was little need for artificial illumination. Night scenes in plays were usually indicated by the presence of candles, lanterns, or torches.

While not much scenery was used, the Elizabethan stage was certainly not devoid of color and pageantry. Banners and other devices were employed to distinguish between armies and knights; there were many battles, processions, and dances. Most important, costumes were an ever-present source of visual pleasure.

The costumes for the Elizabethan stage were of two basic kinds, contemporary clothing and conventional dress. By far the majority of roles were costumed in Elizabethan garments appropriate to the rank or profession of each character. Like the Medieval, the Elizabethan mind had little sense of history, and characters from almost any place or time could be dressed alike.

On the other hand, however, certain stereotypes of the period made it necessary to set off some roles. The principal uses of conventionalized costumes were for: (1) special foreign groups, such as Romans, Turks, or Spaniards, (2) supernatural beings, such as fairies, classical gods, ghosts, and witches, (3) certain professional types, such as clerics, senators, and clowns, and (4) animals, such as lions, boars, and bears.

In spite of this apparent complexity, however, the majority of costumes were basically Elizabethan garments, and most of the conven-

93. mansions, a system of staging in which the scene was set with a series of "houses" (mansions) from which the actors emerged for their scenes.

tionalized costumes were created by superimposing a few simple elements on contemporary dress. For example, Roman characters were identified by the addition of a drapery to Elizabethan clothing. 120

Nevertheless, a large wardrobe was necessary, since each company changed its program almost daily and had a large number of plays in its repertory. An actor might wear his own clothing in some roles, but the company assumed primary responsibility for all other costumes.

Acting companies included from ten to twenty members, of which approximately ten were shareholders, the others were hired men. A company divided its receipts so that each shareholder was entitled to a specified percentage of the profits. The hired men (the "extras," 130 doorkeepers, musicians, and stage hands) were paid a set wage (in this period their pay was comparable to that received by skilled laborers in other trades). Shareholders obviously had an interest in the financial success of the company, and the largest shares were usually allotted to the most important members of the acting company. Typically, when a troupe was formed the shareholders agreed to stay together for a stated period of time, and the conditions under which a member might leave or under which new shareholders might be taken in were specified. The hired men were usually engaged for a period of two years. 140

If a company did not have enough money to build a theatre, and to buy costumes and other necessary equipment, it might enter into an agreement with another person or group to furnish the necessary items. In return, these "householders" were given half of the gallery receipts, while the company retained the other half, in addition to all of the general admission fees.

Besides the regular members of the troupes, there were also apprentices. Each company needed from three to five boys to perform the female roles. A boy began his apprenticeship when he was between ten and fourteen and continued in it until he reached the age of twenty- 150 one. At the end of his training, he might be taken into the troupe as a regular member, or might join another company. Each boy was apprenticed to an individual actor rather than to the company as a whole. He lived with his master, who gave him room and board and trained him. Payment for the boy's services was made to the master by the company.

Each of the regular actors probably specialized in certain types of roles. The playwright, as a rule, wrote for a specific company and he knew who would play each character in his play. Thus he often wrote for the special capabilities of specific actors. This may have placed 160 certain restrictions on the dramatist, but it also was an advantage since he knew what he could expect from each actor. Richard Burbage (c. 1567-1619) played most of Shakespeare's leading roles, and the range of these parts suggests that he was one of the great actors of the English stage.

The acting company performed a large repertory of plays, changing the bill almost daily. A play was repeated several times during a season if there was sufficient demand, and when it was no longer popular it was dropped from the repertory and a new work was added. Each actor
170 had to be prepared to perform a great number of roles each season and was kept busy rehearsing and performing both new and old plays.

Some companies had dramatists under contract to furnish a set number of plays in a given period and paid them a weekly salary. Other companies bought plays outright. The playwright was expected to supervise the original production of his own works, although subsequent rehearsals were conducted by the bookholder, who combined the functions of prompter and stage manager. Since the actor was supposed to know his trade, the playwright probably confined himself chiefly to explaining his intentions, though he no doubt suggested specific
180 pieces of business or line readings when he was not satisfied with an actor's inventions.

Before a play could be performed, it had to be approved by the Master of Revels. Each actor's part (complete with cues) was then copied and given to him. An over-all summary of exits, entrances, and the play's story line was posted backstage so that actors might consult it. The bookholder kept the master, or prompt, copy of the play in which were indicated exits and entrances, properties required for specific scenes, cues for stage hands and musicians. The bookholder probably stood behind one of the doors at the back of the stage and
190 followed the performance through a grating.

On days when plays were to be presented, a flag was raised above the theatre. Performances were given regularly except during a siege of the plague, during certain religious seasons, or upon the death or severe illness of a ruler or important public official. The audience was composed of all sorts of persons: noblemen, merchants, workmen, men, and women. No doubt the level of appreciation varied considerably among audience members. Some playwrights wrote disparagingly of them, especially the "groundlings" who stood in the yard, while others praised their perceptivity. Each performance ended with singing,
200 dancing, or a comic afterpiece designed to send the audience home in a jolly mood.

Maxwell Anderson

THE ESSENCE OF TRAGEDY

Maxwell Anderson (1888-1959) began his long career as an American playwright in the 1930's with several poetic dramas on historical events.

Anybody who dares to discuss the making of tragedy lays himself open to critical assault and general barrage, for the theorists have been hunting for the essence of tragedy since Aristotle without entire success. There is no doubt that playwrights have occasionally written tragedy successfully, from Aeschylus on, and there is no doubt that Aristotle came very close to a definition of what tragedy is in his famous passage on catharsis. But why the performance of tragedy should have a cleansing effect on the audience, why an audience is willing to listen to tragedy, why tragedy has a place in the education of men, has never, to my knowledge, been convincingly stated. I must begin by saying that I have not solved the Sphinx's riddle which fifty generations of skillful brains have left in shadow. But I have one suggestion which I think might lead to a solution if it were put to laboratory tests by those who know something about philosophical analysis and dialectic. 10

There seems no way to get at this suggestion except through a reference to my own adventures in playwriting, so I ask your tolerance while I use myself as an instance. A man who has written successful plays is usually supposed to know something about the theory of playwriting, and perhaps he usually does. In my own case, however, I must confess that I came into the theater unexpectedly, without preparation, and stayed in it because I had a certain amount of rather accidental success. It was not until after I had fumbled my way through a good many successes and an appalling number of failures that I began to doubt the sufficiency of dramatic instinct and to wonder whether or not there were general laws governing dramatic structure which so poor a head for theory as my own might grasp and use. I had read the *Poetics* long before I tried playwriting, and I had looked doubtfully into a few well-known handbooks on dramatic structure, but the maxims and theories propounded always drifted by me in a luminous haze—brilliant, true, profound in context, yet quite without meaning for me when I considered the plan for a play or tried to clarify an emotion in dialogue. So far as I could make out every play was a new problem, and the old rules were inapplicable. There were so many rules, so many landmarks, so many pitfalls, so many essential reckonings, that it seemed impossible to find your way through the jungle except by plunging ahead, trusting to your sense of direction and keeping your wits about you as you went. 20 30

But as the seasons went by and my failures fell as regularly as the leaves in autumn I began to search again among the theorists of the past for a word of wisdom that might take some of the gamble out of playwriting. What I needed most of all, I felt, was a working definition of what a play is, or perhaps a formula which would include all the elements necessary to a play structure. A play is almost always, probably, an attempt to recapture a vision for the stage. But when you are working in the theater it's most unsatisfactory to follow the gleam without a compass, quite risky to trust "the light that never was on sea or land"° without making sure beforehand that you are not being led straight into a slough of despond.° In other words you must make a choice among visions, and you must check your chosen vision carefully before assuming that it will make a play. But by what rules, what maps, what fields of reference can you check so intangible a substance as a revelation, a dream, an inspiration, or any similar nudge from the subconscious mind?

I shan't trouble you with the details of my search for a criterion, partly because I can't remember it in detail. But I reread Aristotle's *Poetics* in the light of some bitter experience, and one of his observations led me to a comparison of ancient and modern playwriting methods. In discussing construction he made a point of the recognition scene as essential to tragedy. The recognition scene, as Aristotle isolated it in the tragedies of the Greeks, was generally an artificial device, a central scene in which the leading character saw through a disguise, recognized as a friend or as an enemy, perhaps as a lover or a member of his own family, some person whose identity had been hidden. Iphigeneia,° for example, acting as priestess in an alien country, receives a victim for sacrifice and then recognizes her own brother in this victim. There is an instant and profound emotional reaction, instantly her direction in the play is altered. But occasionally, in the greatest of the plays, the recognition turned on a situation far more convincing, though no less contrived. Oedipus, hunting savagely for the criminal who has brought the plague upon Thebes, discovers that he is himself that criminal—and since this is a discovery that affects not only the physical well-being and happiness of the hero, but the whole structure of his life, the effect on him and on the direction of the story is incalculably greater than could result from the more superficial revelation made to Iphigeneia.

Now scenes of exactly this sort are rare in the modern drama except in detective stories adapted for the stage. But when I probed a little

46. From "Elegiac Stanzas Suggested by a Picture of Peele Castle" by William Wordsworth. ***48. slough of despond,*** part of the territory traversed by Christian in John Bunyan's *Pilgrim's Progress,* an allegorical description of the pitfalls on the road to salvation. ***64. Iphigeneia,*** in Tauris by Euripides.

more deeply into the memorable pieces of Shakespeare's theater and our own I began to see that though modern recognition scenes are subtler and harder to find, they are none the less present in the plays 80 we choose to remember. They seldom have to do with anything so naïve as disguise or the unveiling of a personal identity. But the element of discovery is just as important as ever. For the mainspring in the mechanism of a modern play is almost invariably a discovery by the hero of some element in his environment or in his own soul of which he has not been aware—or which he has not taken sufficiently into account. Moreover, nearly every teacher of playwriting has had some inkling of this, though it was not until after I had worked out my own theory that what they said on this point took on accurate meaning for me. I still think that the rule which I formulated for my own guidance is 90 more concise than any other, and so I give it here: A play should lead up to and away from a central crisis, and this crisis should consist in a discovery by the leading character which has an indelible effect on his thought and emotion and completely alters his course of action. The leading character, let me say again, must make the discovery; it must affect him emotionally; and it must alter his direction in the play.

Try that formula on any play you think worthy of study, and you will find that, with few exceptions, it follows this pattern or some variation of this pattern. The turning point of *The Green Pastures*,° for example, 100 is the discovery by God, who is the leading character, that a God who is to endure must conform to the laws of change. The turning point of *Hamlet* is Hamlet's discovery, in the play scene, that his uncle was unquestionably the murderer of his father. In *Abe Lincoln in Illinois*° Lincoln's discovery is that he has been a coward, that he has stayed out of the fight for the Union because he was afraid. In each case, you will note, the discovery has a profound emotional effect on the hero, and gives an entirely new direction to his action in the play.

I'm not writing a disquisition on playwriting and wouldn't be competent to write one, but I do want to make a point of the superlative use- 110 fulness of this one touchstone for play structure. When a man sets out to write a play his first problem is his subject and the possibilities of that subject as a story to be projected from the stage. His choice of subject matter is his personal problem, and one that takes its answer from his personal relation to his times. But if he wants to know a possible play subject when he finds it, if he wants to know how to mold the subject into play form after he has found it, I doubt that he'll ever discover another standard as satisfactory as the modern version of Aristotle which I have suggested. If the plot he has in mind does not

100. The Green Pastures, by Marc Connelly. ***104. Abe Lincoln in Illinois,*** by Robert Sherwood.

120 contain a playable episode in which the hero or heroine makes an emotional discovery, a discovery that practically dictates the end of the story, then such an episode must be inserted—and if no place can be found for it the subject is almost certainly a poor one for the theater. If this emotional discovery is contained in the story, but is not central, then it must be made central, and the whole action must revolve around it. In a three-act play it should fall near the end of the second act, though it may be delayed till the last; in a five-act play it will usually be found near the end of the third, though here also it can be delayed. Everything else in the play should be subordinated to this one episode—
130 should lead up to or away from it.

Now this prime rule has a corollary which is just as important as the rule itself. The hero who is to make the central discovery in a play must not be a perfect man. He must have some variation of what Aristotle calls a tragic fault; and the reason he must have it is that when he makes his discovery he must change both in himself and in his action—and he must change for the better. The fault can be a very simple one—a mere unawareness, for example—but if he has no fault he cannot change for the better, but only for the worse, and for a reason which I shall discuss later, it is necessary that he must become more admirable, and
140 not less so, at the end of the play. In other words, a hero must pass through an experience which opens his eyes to an error of his own. He must learn through suffering. In a tragedy he suffers death itself as a consequence of his fault or his attempt to correct it, but before he dies he has become a nobler person because of his recognition of his fault and the consequent alteration of his course of action. In a serious play which does not end in death he suffers a lesser punishment, but the pattern remains the same. In both forms he has a fault to begin with, he discovers that fault during the course of the action, and he does what he can to rectify it at the end. In *The Green Pastures* God's fault
150 was that he believed himself perfect. He discovered that he was not perfect, that he had been in error and must make amends. Hamlet's fault was that he could not make up his mind to act. He offers many excuses for his indecision until he discovers that there is no real reason for hesitation and that he has delayed out of cowardice. Lincoln, in *Abe Lincoln in Illinois*, has exactly the same difficulty. In the climactic scene it is revealed to him that he had hesitated to take sides through fear of the consequences to himself, and he then chooses to go ahead without regard for what may be in store for him. From the point of view of the playwright, then, the essence of a tragedy, or even of a serious
160 play, is the spiritual awakening, or regeneration, of his hero.

When a playwright attempts to reverse the formula, when his hero makes a discovery which has an evil effect, or one which the audience interprets as evil, on his character, the play is inevitably a failure on the stage. In *Troilus and Cressida* Troilus discovers that Cressida is a light woman. He draws from her defection the inference that all women are faithless—that faith in woman is the possession of fools. As a consequence he turns away from life and seeks death in a cause as empty as the love he has given up, the cause of the strumpet Helen. All the glory of Shakespeare's verse cannot rescue the play for an audience, and save in *Macbeth* Shakespeare nowhere wrote so richly, so wisely, or 170 with such a flow of brilliant metaphor.

For the audience will always insist that the alteration in the hero be for the better—or for what it believes to be the better. As audiences change the standards of good and evil change, though slowly and unpredictably, and the meanings of plays change with the centuries. One thing only is certain: that an audience watching a play will go along with it only when the leading character responds in the end to what it considers a higher moral impulse than moved him at the beginning of the story, though the audience will of course define morality as it pleases and in the terms of its own day. It may be that there is no absolute up or 180 down in this world, but the race believes that there is, and will not hear of any denial.

And now at last I come to the point toward which I've been struggling so laboriously. Why does the audience come to the theater to look on while an imaginary hero is put to an imaginary trial and comes out of it with credit to the race and to himself? It was this question that prompted my essay, and unless I've been led astray by my own predilections there is a very possible answer in the rules for playwriting which I have just cited. The theater originated in two complementary religious ceremonies, one celebrating the animal in man and one celebrating 190 the god. Old Greek Comedy was dedicated to the spirits of lust and riot and earth, spirits which are certainly necessary to the health and continuance of the race. Greek tragedy was dedicated to man's aspiration, to his kinship with the gods, to his unending, blind attempt to lift himself above his lusts and his pure animalism into a world where there are other values than pleasure and survival. However unaware of it we may be, our theater has followed the Greek patterns with no change in essence, from Aristophanes and Euripides to our own day. Our more ribald musical comedies are simply our approximation of the Bacchic rites of Old Comedy. In the rest of our theater we sometimes 200 follow Sophocles, whose tragedy is always an exaltation of the human spirit, sometimes Euripides, whose tragicomedy follows the same pattern of an excellence achieved through suffering. The forms of both tragedy and comedy have changed a good deal in nonessentials, but in essentials—and especially in the core of meaning which they must have for audiences—they are in the main the same religious rites which grew up around the altars of Attica long ago.

It is for this reason that when you write for the theater you must choose between your version of a phallic revel and your vision of what 210 mankind may or should become. Your vision may be faulty, or shallow, or sentimental, but it must conform to some aspiration in the audience, or the audience will reject it. Old Comedy, the celebration of the animal in us, still has a place in our theater, as it had in Athens, but here, as there, that part of the theater which celebrated man's virtue and his regeneration in hours of crisis is accepted as having the more important function. Our comedy is largely the Greek New Comedy, which grew out of Euripides' tragicomedy, and is separated from tragedy only in that it presents a happier scene and puts its protagonist through an ordeal which is less than lethal.

220 And since our plays, aside from those which are basically Old Comedy, are exaltations of the human spirit, since that is what an audience expects when it comes to the theater, the playwright gradually discovers, as he puts plays before audiences, that he must follow the ancient Aristotelian rule: he must build his plot around a scene wherein his hero discovers some mortal frailty or stupidity in himself and faces life armed with a new wisdom. He must so arrange his story that it will prove to the audience that men pass through suffering purified, that, animal though we are, despicable though we are in many ways, there is in us all some divine, incalculable fire that urges us to be better 230 than we are.

It could be argued that what the audience demands of a hero is only conformity to race morality, to the code which seems to the spectators most likely to make for race survival. In many cases, especially in comedy, and obviously in the comedy of Molière, this is true. But in the majority of ancient and modern plays it seems to me that what the audience wants to believe is that men have a desire to break the molds of earth which encase them and claim a kinship with a higher morality than that which hems them in. The rebellion of Antigone, who breaks the laws of men through adherence to a higher law of affection, the 240 rebellion of Prometheus, who breaks the law of the gods to bring fire to men, the rebellion of God in *The Green Pastures* against the rigid doctrine of the Old Testament, the rebellion of Tony in *They Knew What They Wanted*° against the convention that called on him to repudiate his cuckold child, the rebellion of Liliom° against the heavenly law which asked him to betray his own integrity and make a hypocrisy of his affection, even the repudiation of the old forms and the affirmation of new by the heroes of Ibsen and Shaw, these are all instances to me of the groping of men toward an excellence dimly apprehended, seldom pos-

242-243. They Knew What They Wanted, by Sidney Howard. ***244. Liliom,*** in Ferenc Molnár's play of that name.

sible of definition. They are evidence to me that the theater at its best is a religious affirmation, an age-old rite restating and reassuring man's be- 250 lief in his own destiny and his ultimate hope. The theater is much older than the doctrine of evolution, but its one faith, asseverated again and again for every age and every year, is a faith in evolution, in the reaching and the climb of men toward distant goals, glimpsed but never seen, perhaps never achieved, or achieved only to be passed impatiently on the way to a more distant horizon.

Arthur Miller

ON SOCIAL PLAYS

The contemporary American playwright, Arthur Miller, wrote this essay as his introduction to the published version of his play A View from the Bridge *(1955).*

A Greek living in the classical period would be bewildered by the dichotomy implied in the very term "social play." Especially for the Greek, a drama created for public performance had to be "social." A play to him was by definition a dramatic consideration of the way men ought to live. But in this day of extreme individualism even that phrase must be further defined. When we say "how men ought to live," we are likely to be thinking of psychological therapy, of ridding ourselves individually of neurotic compulsions and destructive inner tendencies, of "learning how to love" and thereby gaining "happiness."

10 It need hardly be said that the Greek dramatist had more than a passing interest in psychology and character on the stage. But for him these were means to a larger end, and the end was what we isolate today as social. That is, the relations of man as a social animal, rather than his definition as a separated entity, was the dramatic goal. Why this should have come to be is a large historical question which others are more competent to explain, as several already have. For our purposes it will be sufficient to indicate one element in the life of classical Greece that differs so radically from anything existing in the modern world as to throw a bright light on certain of our attitudes which we take for
20 granted and toward which we therefore are without a proper perspective.

The Greek citizen of that time thought of himself as belonging not to a "nation" or a "state" but to a *polis.* The polis were small units, apparently deriving from an earlier tribal social organization, whose members probably knew one another personally because they were relatively few in number and occupied a small territory. In war or peace the whole people made the vital decisions, there being no profession of politics as we know it; any man could be elected magistrate, judge, even a general in the armed forces. It was an amateur world compared to our stratified and specialized one, a world in which everyone knew
30 enough about almost any profession to practice it, because most things were simple to know. The thing of importance for us is that these people were *engaged,* they could not imagine the good life excepting as it brought each person into close contact with civic matters. They were avid argufiers. Achilles was blessed by the gods with the power to fight well and make good speeches. The people had a special sense

of pride in the polis and thought that it in itself distinguished them from the barbarians outside who lived under tyrannies.

The preoccupation of the Greek drama with ultimate law, with the Grand Design, so to speak, was therefore an expression of a basic assumption of the people, who could not yet conceive, luckily, that any man could long prosper unless his polis prospered. The individual was at one with his society; his conflicts with it were, in our terms, like family conflicts the opposing sides of which nevertheless shared a mutuality of feeling and responsibility. Thus the drama written for them, while for us it appears wholly religious, was religious for them in a more than mystical way. Religion is the only way we have any more of expressing our genuinely social feelings and concerns, for in our bones we as a people do not otherwise believe in our oneness with a larger group. But the religiousness of the Greek drama of the classical time was more worldly; it expressed a social concern, to be sure, but it did so on the part of a people already unified on earth rather than the drive of a single individual toward personal salvation. The great gap we feel between religious or "high" emotion and the emotions of daily life was not present in their mass affairs. The religious expression was not many degrees higher for them than many other social expressions, of which their drama is the most complete example.

It is necessary to add that as the polis withered under the impact of war and historical change, as commerce grew and a differentiation of interest separated man from man, the Greek drama found it more and more difficult to stand as a kind of universal mass statement or prayer. It turned its eye inward, created more elaborated characterizations, and slowly gave up some of its former loftiness. Men, as H. D. F. Kitto has said in *The Greeks*, replaced Man in the plays. Nevertheless, to the end the Greek drama clearly conceived its right function as something far wider than a purely private examination of individuality for the sake of the examination or for art's sake. In every dramatic hero there is the idea of the Greek people, their fate, their will, and their destiny.

In today's America the term "social play" brings up images which are historically conditioned, very recent, and, I believe, only incidentally pertinent to a fruitful conception of the drama. The term indicates to us an attack, an arraignment of society's evils such as Ibsen allegedly invented and was later taken up by left-wing playwrights whose primary interest was the exposure of capitalism for the implied benefit of socialism or communism. The concept is tired and narrow, but its worst effect has been to confuse a whole generation of playwrights, audiences, and theater workers.

If one can look at the idea of "social drama" from the Greek viewpoint for one moment, it will be clear that there can be only either a

80 genuinely social drama or, if it abdicates altogether, its true opposite, the antisocial and ultimately antidramatic drama.

To put it simply, even oversimply, a drama rises in stature and intensity in proportion to the weight of its application to all manner of men. It gains its weight as it deals with more and more of the whole man, not either his subjective or his social life alone, and the Greek was unable to conceive of man or anything else except as a whole. The modern playwright, at least in America, on the one hand is importuned by his most demanding audience to write importantly, while on the other he is asked not to bring onto the stage images of social function, 90 lest he seem like a special pleader and therefore inartistic. I am not attempting a defense of the social dramas of the thirties, most of which were in fact special pleadings and further from a consideration of the whole man than much of the antisocial drama is. I am trying only to project a right conception of what social drama was and what it ought to be. It is, I think, the widest concept of drama available to us thus far.

When, however, a contemporary dramatist is drawn for but a moment toward a concept of form even remotely Greek, certain lacks become evident—a certain abyss even begins to appear around him. When 100 you are writing in the name of a people unified in a self-conscious and rather small band, when you yourself as a writer are not an individual entrepreneur offering wares to a hostile market place but a member of a group who is in other ways no different from the rest—when, in short, the dramatic form itself is regarded as inevitably a social expression of the deepest concerns of all your fellow men—your work is bound to be liberated, freed of even the hypothesis of partisanship, if only because partisanship cannot thrive where the idea of wholeness is accepted. Thus in such a situation what we call social matters become inseparable from subjective psychological matters, and the drama is 110 once again whole and capable of the highest reach.

If one considers our own drama of the past forty years in comparison with that of classical Greece one elemental difference—the difference which seems to me to be our crippling hobble—will emerge. The single theme to which our most ambitious plays can be reduced is frustration. In all of them, from O'Neill's through the best of Anderson, Sidney Howard, and the rest, the underlying log jam, so to speak, the unresolvable paradox, is that, try as he will, the individual is doomed to frustration when once he gains a consciousness of his own identity. The image is that of the individual scratching away at a wall beyond 120 which stands society, his fellow men. Sometimes he pounds at the wall, sometimes he tries to scale it or even blow it up, but at the end the wall is always there, and the man himself is dead or doomed to defeat in his attempt to live a human life.

The tragic victory is always denied us because, I believe, the plays cannot project with any conviction what the society, in the playwrights' views at any rate, has failed to prove. In Greece the tragic victory consisted in demonstrating that the polis—the whole people—had discovered some aspect of the Grand Design which also was the right way to live *together*. If the American playwrights of serious intent are in any way the subconscience of the country, our claims to have found 130 that way are less than proved. For when the Greek thought of the right way to live it was a whole concept; it meant a way to live that would create citizens who were brave in war, had a sense of responsibility to the polis in peace, and were also developed as individual personalities.

It has often seemed to me that the Soviet Russians have studied classical Greece and have tried to bridge with phraseology profound differences between their social organization and that of Greece, while demanding of their writers what in effect is a Greek social drama. The word "cosmopolitan," as Kitto points out, was invented in Greece when the small polis were disintegrating, and when the drama itself was 140 beginning to turn inward, away from the largest questions of social fate to the fate of individuals alone. It was invented to describe a new kind of man, a man whose allegiance was not primarily to his society, his polis, but to others of like mind anywhere in the world. With it goes an intimation—or more—of skepticism, of self-removal, that presages the radical separation of man from society which the American drama expresses ultimately through themes of frustration. To supplant the polis and allegiance to it, the Soviets have a thousand kinds of social organizations, and, for all one knows, the individual Russian might well feel a sense of connection with civic affairs which the West does not 150 afford its citizens. The crucial difference, however, is that only the most theoretical Russian can trace the effects, if any, of his personality upon the policies of his country, while the Greek could literally see what he had done when he made his speech and swayed or failed to sway his fellow men.

Thus the Russian drama after the Revolution, much as ours, is a drama of frustration, the inability of industrialized men to see themselves spiritually completed through the social organization. But in the Soviet case the frustration is not admitted; it is talked away in large phrases having to do with a victory of the people through tragic 160 sacrifice. The fact remains, however, that nowhere in the world where industrialized economy rules—where specialization in work, politics, and social life is the norm—nowhere has man discovered a means of connecting himself to society except in the form of a truce with it. The best we have been able to do is to speak of a "duty" to society, and this implies sacrifice or self-deprivation. To think of an individual fulfilling his subjective needs through social action, to think of him as living most completely when he lives most socially, to think of him as doing this, not as a social worker acting out of conscientious motives, 170 but naturally, without guilt or sense of oddness—this is difficult for us to imagine, and when we can, we know at the same time that only a few, perhaps a blessed few, are so constructed as to manage it.

As with Greece, so with us—each great war has turned men further and further away from preoccupation with Man and drawn them back into the family, the home, the private life and the preoccupation with sexuality. It has happened, however, that at the same time our theater has exhausted the one form that was made to express the private life—prose realism. We are bored with it; we demand something more, something "higher," on the stage, while at the same time we refuse, or do 180 not know how, to live our private lives excepting as ego-centers. I believe it is this paradox that underlies the kind of struggle taking place in the drama today—a struggle at one and the same time to write of private persons privately and yet lift up their means of expression to a poetic—that is, a social—level. You cannot speak in verse of picayune matters—at least not on the stage—without sounding overblown and ridiculous, and so it should be. Verse reaches always toward the general statement, the wide image, the universal moment, and it must be based upon wide concepts—it must speak not merely of men but of Man. The language of dramatic verse is the language of a people profoundly at 190 one with itself; it is the most public of public speech. The language of prose is the language of the private life, the kind of private life men retreat to when they are at odds with the world they have made or been heirs to.

The social drama, then—at least as I have always conceived it—is the drama of the whole man. It seeks to deal with his differences from others not *per se*, but toward the end that, if only through drama, we may know how much the same we are, for if we lose that knowledge we shall have nothing left at all. The social drama to me is only incidentally an arraignment of society. *A Streetcar Named Desire* is a social drama; 200 so is *The Hairy Ape*, and so are practically all O'Neill's other plays. For they ultimately make moot, either weakly or with full power, the ancient question, how are we to live? And that question is in its Greek sense, its best and most humane sense, not merely a private query.

The social drama, as I see it, is the main stream and the antisocial drama a bypass. I can no longer take with ultimate seriousness a drama of individual psychology written for its own sake, however full it may be of insight and precise observation. Time is moving; there is a world to make, a civilization to create that will move toward the only goal the humanistic, democratic mind can ever accept with honor. It is a world 210 in which the human being can live as a naturally political, naturally private, naturally engaged person, a world in which once again a true tragic victory may be scored.

But that victory is not really possible unless the individual is more than theoretically capable of being recognized by the powers that lead society. Specifically, when men live, as they do under any industrialized system, as integers who have no weight, no *person*, excepting as either customers, draftees, machine tenders, ideologists, or whatever, it is unlikely (and in my opinion impossible) that a dramatic picture of them can really overcome the public knowledge of their nature in real life. In such a society, be it communistic or capitalistic, man is not tragic, he is pathetic. The tragic figure must have certain innate powers which he uses to pass over the boundaries of the known social law—the accepted mores of his people—in order to test and discover necessity. Such a quest implies that the individual who has moved onto that course must be somehow recognized by the law, by the mores, by the powers that design—be they anthropomorphic gods or economic and political laws—as having the worth, the innate value, of a whole people asking a basic question and demanding its answer. We are so atomized socially that no character in a play can conceivably stand as our vanguard, as our heroic questioner. Our society—and I am speaking of every industrialized society in the world—is so complex, each person being so specialized an integer, that the moment any individual is dramatically characterized and set forth as a hero, our common sense reduces him to the size of a complainer, a misfit. For deep down we no longer believe in the rules of the tragic contest; we no longer believe that some ultimate sense can in fact be made of social causation, or in the possibility that any individual can, by a heroic effort, make sense of it. Thus the man that is driven to question the moral chaos in which we live ends up in our estimate as a possibly commendable but definitely odd fellow, and probably as a compulsively driven neurotic. In place of a social aim which called an all-around excellence—physical, intellectual, and moral—the ultimate good, we have set up a goal which can best be characterized as "happiness"—namely, staying out of trouble. This concept is the end result of the truce which all of us have made with society. And a truce implies two enemies. When the truce is broken it means either that the individual has broken out of his ordained place as an integer, or that the society has broken the law by harming him unjustly—that is, it has not left him alone to be a peaceful integer. In the heroic and tragic time the act of questioning the-way-things-are implied that a quest was being carried on to discover an ultimate law or way of life which would yield excellence; in the present time the quest is that of a man made unhappy by rootlessness and, in every important modern play, by a man who is essentially a victim. We have abstracted from the Greek drama its air of doom, its physical destruction of the hero, but its victory escapes us. Thus it has even become difficult to separate in our minds the ideas of the pathetic and of the tragic. And behind this melting of the two lies the overwhelming power of the modern industrial state, the ignorance of each person in it of anything but his own technique as an economic integer, and the elevation of that 260 state to a holy, quite religious sphere.

What, after all, are our basic social aims as applied to the individual? Americans are often accused of worshiping financial success, but this is, first of all, not an American monopoly, and, second, it does not as a concept make clear what is causing so much uneasiness and moral pain. My own belief, at any rate, is that America has merely arrived first at the condition that awaits every country that takes her economic road without enforcing upon every development of industrial technique certain quite arbitrary standards of value.

The deep moral uneasiness among us, the vast sense of being 270 only tenuously joined to the rest of our fellows, is caused, in my view, by the fact that the person has value as he fits into the pattern of efficiency, and for that alone. The reason *Death of a Salesman*, for instance, left such a strong impression was that it set forth unremittingly the picture of a man who was not even especially "good" but whose situation made clear that at bottom we are alone, valueless, without even the elements of a human person, when once we fail to fit the patterns of efficiency. Under the black shadow of that gigantic necessity, even the drift of some psychoanalytic practice is toward the fitting-in, the training of the individual whose soul has revolted, so that he may 280 once again "take his place" in society—that is, do his "work," "function," in other words, accommodate himself to a scheme of things that is not at all ancient but very new in the world. In short, the absolute value of the individual human being is believed in only as a secondary value; it stands well below the needs of efficient production. We have finally come to serve the machine. The machine must not be stopped, marred, left dirty, or outmoded. Only men can be left marred, stopped, dirty, and alone. Our pity for the victim is mixed, I think. It is mixed with an air of self-preserving superiority—we, thank God, know how to fit in, therefore this victim, however pitiful, has himself to thank 290 for his fate. We believe, in other words, that to fit into the patterns of efficiency is the ultimate good, and at the same time we know in our bones that a crueler concept is not easy to arrive at.

Nor may the exponents of socialism take heart from this. There is no such thing as a capitalist assembly line or drygoods counter. The disciplines required by machines are the same everywhere and will not be truly mitigated by old-age pensions and social-security payments. So long as modern man conceives of himself as valuable only because he fits into some niche in the machine-tending pattern, he will never know anything more than a pathetic doom.

300 The implications of this fact spread throughout our culture, indeed, throughout the culture of the industrialized parts of the world. Be it

in music, literature, drama, or whatever, the value of a work is, willy nilly, equated with its mass "acceptance," i.e., its efficiency. All the engines of economic law are, like the mills of the gods, working toward that same end. The novel of excellence which could once be published without financial loss if it sold two or three thousand copies can no longer be published, because the costs of production require that every book sell at least ten, twelve, or fifteen thousand copies. The play that might have been produced at a decent profit if it could fill half a house for a few months can no longer be produced, for the costs of 310 production require a play to draw packed houses from the first night.

When one has the temerity to suggest that the Greek theater was subsidized, that so much of the world's great music, art, and literature was stubbornly patronized by people who found honor in helping to bring beauty onto the earth, one is not quite suspect, to be sure, but the suggestion nevertheless has an unreal air, an air of being essentially at odds and possibly in dangerous conflict with some unspoken sense of values. For we do believe that a "good" thing, be it art or toothpaste, proves its goodness by its public acceptance. And at the same time we know, too, that something dark and dreadful lies within this concept. 320

The problem, then, of the social drama in this generation is not the same as it was for Ibsen, Chekhov, or Shaw. They, and the left-wing playwrights of the thirties who amplified their findings and repeated their forms, were oriented either toward an arraignment of some of the symptoms of efficiency men or toward the ultimate cure by socialism. With the proliferation of machine techniques in the world, and the relative perfection of distributing techniques, in America first and the rest of the world soon, the time will shortly be upon us when the truth will dawn. We shall come to see, I think, that Production for Profit and Production for Use (whatever their relative advantages—and each 330 has its own) leave untouched the problem which the Greek drama put so powerfully before mankind. How are we to live? From what fiat, from what ultimate source are we to derive a standard of values that will create in man a respect for himself, a real voice in the fate of his society, and, above all, an aim for his life which is neither a private aim for a private life nor one which sets him below the machine that was made to serve him?

The social drama in this generation must do more than analyze and arraign the social network of relationships. It must delve into the nature of man as he exists to discover what his needs are, so that those needs 340 may be amplified and exteriorized in terms of social concepts. Thus, the new social dramatist, if he is to do his work, must be an even deeper psychologist than those of the past, and he must be conscious at least of the futility of isolating the psychological life of man lest he fall always short of tragedy, and return, again and again and again, to the pathetic swampland where the waters are old tears and not the generative seas from which new kinds of life arise.

It is a good time to be writing because the audience is sick of the old formulations. It is no longer believed—and we may be thankful for it—
350 that the poor are necessarily virtuous or the rich necessarily decayed. Nor is it believed that, as some writers would put it, the rich are necessarily not decayed and the poor necessarily the carriers of vulgarity. We have developed so democratic a culture that in America neither the speech of a man nor his way of dressing nor even his ambitions for himself inevitably mark his social class. On the stage social rank tells next to nothing about the man any more. The decks are cleared. There is a kind of perverse unity forming among us, born, I think, of the discontent of all classes of people with the endless frustration of life. It is possible now to speak of a search for values, not solely from the
360 position of bitterness, but with a warm embrace of mankind, with a sense that at bottom every one of us is a victim of this misplacement of aims.

The debilitation of the tragic drama, I believe, is commensurate with the fracturing and the aborting of the need of man to maintain a fruitful kind of union with his society. Everything we learn, everything we know or deem valuable for a man to know, has been thrown into the creation of a machine technology. The nuclear bomb, as a way of waging war, is questioned only now—because we have it, because we have invented it: not before both sides knew how to make
370 it. Both sides have the bomb and both sides have the machine. Some day the whole world will have both and the only force that will keep them from destructive use will be a force strange to machine psychology, a force born of will—the will of man to survive and to reach his ultimate, most conscious, most knowing, most fulfilled condition, his fated excellence.

History has given the social drama its new chance. Ibsen and Shaw had to work through three acts to prove in the fourth that, even if we are not completely formed by society, there is little left that society does not affect. The tremendous growth in our consciousness of social
380 causation has won for these writers their victory in this sense: it has given to us a wider consciousness of the causes that form character. What the middle of the twentieth century has taught us is that theirs was not the whole answer. It is not enough any more to know that one is at the mercy of social pressures; it is necessary to understand that such a sealed fate cannot be accepted. Nor is courage alone required now to question this complex, although without courage nothing is possible, including real dramatic writing. It is necessary to know that the values of commerce, values which were despised as necessary but less than noble in the long past, are now not merely perversely

dominant everywhere but claimed as positive moral goodness itself. 390
The question must begin to be asked; not whether a new thing will work or pay, not whether it is more efficient than its predecessor, more popular, and more easily accepted; but what it will do to human beings. The first invention of man to create that response in all nations was the atomic bomb. It is the first "improvement" to have dramatized for even the numbest mind the question of value. Over the past decade this nation and this world have been gripped by an inner debate on many levels, a debate raised to consciousness by this all-destroying "improvement." Alongside it is the "improvement" called automation, which will soon displace workers who mass-produce in industry. The 400
conquest of poverty and hunger is the order of the day; the refusal of the dark peoples to live in subjection to the white is already a fact. The world, I think, is moving toward a unity, a unity won not alone by the necessities of the physical developments themselves, but by the painful and confused re-assertion of man's inherited will to survive. When the peace is made, and it will be made, the question Greece asked will once again be a question not reserved for philosophers and dramatists; it will be asked by the man who can live out his life without fear of hunger, joblessness, disease, the man working a few hours a day with a life-span probability of eighty, ninety, or perhaps a hundred 410
years. Hard as it is for most people, the sheer struggle to exist and to prosper affords a haven from thought. Complain as they may that they have no time to think, to cultivate themselves, to ask the big questions, most men are terrified at the thought of not having to spend most of their days fighting for existence. In every sphere, and for a hundred hard reasons, the ultimate questions are once again becoming moot, some because without the right answers we will destroy the earth, others because the peace we win may leave us without the fruits of civilized life. The new social drama will be Greek in that it will face man as a social animal and yet without the petty partisanship of so much 420
of past drama. It will be Greek in that the "men" dealt with in its scenes —the psychology and characterizations—will be more than ends in themselves and once again parts of a whole, a whole that is social, a whole that is Man. The world, in a word, is moving into the same boat. For a time, their greatest time, the Greek people were in the same boat—their polis. Our drama, like theirs, will, as it must, ask the same questions, the largest ones. Where are we going now that we are together? For, like every act man commits, the drama is a struggle against his mortality, and meaning is the ultimate reward for having lived.

Louis Kronenberger

SOME PREFATORY WORDS ON COMEDY

Louis Kronenberger, drama critic, writer, and editor, published The Thread of Laughter *(1952), from which the selection below is taken.*

Comedy is not just a happy as opposed to an unhappy ending, but a way of surveying life so that happy endings must prevail. But it is not to be confused, on that account, with optimism, any more than a happy ending is to be confused with happiness. Comedy is much more reasonably associated with pessimism—with at any rate a belief in the smallness that survives as against the greatness that is scarred or destroyed. In mortal affairs it is tragedy, like forgiveness, that seems divine; and comedy, like error, that is human.

One might perhaps begin by talking about comedy in its philosophic
10 sense, as an attitude toward life, rather than as a mere technical aspect of the theater. One might begin, in other words, by speaking of the comedy that unites such writers and writings as Lucian and Aristophanes, the *Decameron* and *Candide*, Congreve and Peacock and Sterne, *Pride and Prejudice* and *Le Bourgeois Gentilhomme*,° rather than of the comedy that is the official label for such diverse plays as *Measure for Measure* and *The Man of Mode*, or *All's Well That Ends Well* and *The Importance of Being Earnest*, or *The Misanthrope* and *Private Lives.*° For obviously—despite immense differences—the same spirit animates an Aristophanes and a Jane Austen; whereas a vastly
20 different spirit separates *Measure for Measure* from *The Importance of Being Earnest*. *Measure for Measure*, we feel, is not really comedy; and *The Misanthrope*, again, is something more than comedy. But coarse as Aristophanes can be and genteel as Jane Austen, broadly as Aristophanes can clown and exquisitely as Jane Austen can annihilate, the two have much the same vision of life, much the same eye for its absurdities. They have in full measure the comic point of view, as other writers have the tragic point of view. In the theater, comedy and tragedy are forms that can be used with some purity. Much Restoration comedy was indeed written with some purity. Today, when the

12-14. Lucian, a sophist philosopher in ancient Greece; Aristophanes, also a Greek, was the first great writer of comedies whose work has come down to our time; Boccaccio, author of the *Decameron*, a collection of stories, lived in fourteenth century Florence; Voltaire's satire *Candide* was published in 1759; Congreve wrote comedies in Restoration England, in the late seventeenth century; Thomas Love Peacock was a nineteenth century English satirist; *Pride and Prejudice*, Jane Austen's novel, was published in 1813; Molière's comedy *Le Bourgeois Gentilhomme* was first performed in 1670. ***16-18.*** The plays mentioned are, in order, by Shakespeare, Etherege, Shakespeare, Wilde, Molière and Noel Coward.

theater is debased by the naturalistic drama, when the drama itself is three parts play to seven parts production, when the only comedy that most playwrights try for is standing-room comedy—today very little in the theater really expresses the comic sense of life. Far from probing, it seldom even honestly paints the surface. And the real trouble is not that the contemporary stage aims at artifice, but that it professes to aim at naturalness. It was one of the real virtues of the Restoration stage that it never sought—and never managed—to be "natural." It lied its head off about a good many of the appurtenances of life, but it managed to capture a surprising amount of the thing itself; and even its lies squared with the partial truth that life is a masquerade.

Comedy appeals to the laughter, which is in part at least the malice, in us; for comedy is concerned with human imperfection, with people's failure to measure up either to the world's or to their own conception of excellence. All tragedy is idealistic and says in effect, "The pity of it"—that owing to this fault of circumstance or that flaw of character, a man who is essentially good does evil, a man who is essentially great is toppled from the heights. But all comedy tends to be skeptical and says in effect, "The absurdity of it"—that in spite of his fine talk or noble resolutions, a man is the mere creature of pettiness and vanity and folly. Tragedy is always lamenting the Achilles tendon, the destructive flaw in man; but comedy, in a sense, is always looking for it. Not cheaply, out of malevolence or cynicism; but rather because even at his greatest, man offers some touch of the fatuous and small, just as a murderer, even at his cleverest, usually makes some fatal slip. In tragedy men aspire to more than they can achieve; in comedy, they pretend to more.

The difference, again, between the two is the very question of difference. A great tragic hero—an Oedipus or Lear—strikes us as tremendously far removed from common humanity. But comedy, stripping off the war-paint and the feathers, the college degrees or the military medals, shows how very like at bottom the hero is to everybody else. Tragedy cannot flourish without giving its characters a kind of aura of poetry, or idealism, or doom; comedy scarcely functions till the aura has been dispelled. And as it thrives on a revelation of the true rather than the trumped-up motive, as it is in one way sustained by imposture, so in another it is sustained by incongruity. Here is the celebrated philosopher cursing the universe because he has mislaid a book. Here are all those who, like King Canute, would bid the clock go backward or the waves stand still. Here is not only the cheat, but the victim who but for his own dishonest desires could never be cheated.

Comedy, in brief, is criticism. If through laughing at others we purge ourselves of certain spiteful and ungenerous instincts—as through tragedy we achieve a higher and more publicized catharsis—that is

not quite the whole of it. Comedy need not be hostile to idealism; it need only show how far human beings fall short of the ideal. The higher comedy mounts, the airier and more brilliant its forms, the more are we aware of man's capacity for being foolish or self-deluded or complacent; in the very highest comedy, such as the finale of Mozart's *Marriage of Figaro*, we are in a very paradise of self-deceptions and misunder-
80 standings and cross-purposes. At the heart of high comedy there is always a strain of melancholy, as round the edges there is all gaiety and ebullience and glitter; and Schiller was perhaps right in regarding high comedy as the greatest of all literary forms.

Comedy is criticism, then, because it exposes human beings for what they are in contrast to what they profess to be. How much idealism, it asks, shall we find entirely free from self-love? How much beneficence is born of guilt, how much affection is produced by flattery? At its most severe, doubtless, comedy is not just skeptical but cynical; and asks many of the same questions, returning many of the same answers,
90 as that prince—or at any rate duke—of cynics, La Rochefoucauld. "Pride," La Rochefoucauld remarked, "does not wish to owe, and vanity does not wish to pay." Or again: "To establish oneself in the world, one does all one can to seem established there." Of these and many similar maxims, a play or story might easily be written; from each much cold and worldly comedy, or harsh and worldly farce, might be contrived. But comedy need not be so harsh, and seldom is: though it can be harsher still, can be—as in Ben Jonson—gloating and sardonic. But always it is the enemy, not of virtue or idealism, but of hypocrisy and pretense; and what it does in literature is very much, I suppose,
100 what experience does for most of us in life: it knocks the bloom off the peach, the gilt off the gingerbread.

But though the comic spirit is, in Meredith's phrase, "humanely malign," it is also kindly and even companionable, in the sense that it brings men together as fellow-fools and sinners, and is not only criticism but understanding. Comedy is always jarring us with the evidence that we are no better than other people, and always comforting us with the knowledge that most other people are no better than we are. It makes us more critical but it leaves us more tolerant; and to that extent it performs a very notable social function. Its whole character, indeed
110 —quite aside from that point—is rather social than individual.

The social basis rests in the very subject-matter of comedy—in all that has to do with one's life as part of a group; with one's wish to charm or persuade or deceive or dazzle others. Thus no exhibitionist can exist in solitude, no hypocrite or poseur can work without an audience. There are indeed so many social situations that engender comedy that many of them are notably hackneyed. There are all kinds of classic family jokes—the mother-in-law joke preëminently; but equally the rich-uncle theme, or the country cousin, or the visiting relative who forgets to leave, or the one that proffers advice, or the one that prophesies disaster. Right in the home there is the precocious brat or the moping adolescent; there are countless varieties of comic servants; and there is finally the question, though it perhaps belongs in a different category, of who heads the family—the husband or the wife.

The idea of husband and wife more likely belongs with the social aspects of sex, with the War Between the Sexes as it is fought out in the drawing room. As a purely sexual conflict, this war would not be social; but by the same token it would not be comedy. The question whether man really makes the decisions—including the decision to marry—or is merely permitted to think he does, is, whatever the answer, thoroughly social in nature. Or there is the business of how men and women perform in society for one another's benefit: being the fearless protector or the clinging vine, the woman who always understands or the man who is never understood. We have social comedy again when we pit one nationality as well as one sex against another, when the American puritan is ensnared by a continental siren, or when the suitor is German and humorless, and the besought one is French and amused. There is still another social aspect when we add a third person to the situation, a mistress as well as a wife, or a lover as well as a husband; or—for the situation need not be illicit, it need only be triangular—when the wife's old beau or the husband's old flame reappears on the scene. Or there is the man who does not know which of two sisters, or two heiresses, or two widows to marry; or the girl which of a half dozen suitors.

Comedy, indeed, must gain admittance into any part of the world—including prisons and sickrooms and funerals—where people are thrown together. Any institution involving hierarchies and rivalries—for example, a university—is a perfect hotbed of it. There will be everybody's relation to the President or the President's wife; or the President's relation to the President's wife; or to his trustees; all the struggles for precedence and the problems of protocol; the progressives on the faculty and the die-hards; the wives who can't help looking dowdy, the wives who suppose they look chic. For obviously any institution, whether a college or a department store, an artist colony or a country club, provides a cross-section of social types and traits, and brings us face to face with a hundred things out of which comedy is distilled: ambition and pride, arrogance and obsequiousness; a too-slavish following or a too-emphatic flouting of convention; all the stratagems men use in order to outwit or get their way.

And of course comedy becomes purely social in that best known and perhaps best liked of all its higher forms—the comedy of manners.

Here we have hardly less than a picture of society itself; here the men and women are but parts of a general whole, and what survives—if we have it from the past—is likely to be known as the Restoration Scene, or Regency London, or Victorian Family Life. Here the drawing room is not merely the setting of the play or novel, but the subject and even the hero; here enter all the prejudices, the traditions, the taboos, the aspirations, the absurdities, the snobberies, of a group. The group, to constitute itself one, must partake of a common background and accept a similar view of life: though there will usually exist some outsider, some rebel, some nonconformist who, as the case may be, is ringing the doorbell or shattering the window panes; trying desperately to get in or desperately to get out; bending the knee or thumbing his nose. Or the comedy of manners will contrast one social milieu with another—the urban and the rustic, the capital and the provinces, Philistia and Bohemia, America and Europe. And in the comedy of manners, ignorance of good form has much the same value that, in straight drama, ignorance of some vital fact has.

And with ignorance of one kind or another we begin coming close to the very mainspring of comedy, or at any rate of comedy in action. For most comedy is born of ignorance or false knowledge; is based on misunderstanding. (Obviously not knowing the truth—though here one might add "until it is too late"—applies to much tragedy also.) At the level of ordinary farce or romantic comedy, the lovers are estranged until a quarter of eleven because the young man misunderstood why the young lady was walking with Sir Robert in the garden. At a higher level, it will not be mere circumstance or coincidence, but qualities of character that block the way. Envy proves an obstruction, or arrogance; or a too-great tendency to be suspicious or to take offense. In *Pride and Prejudice* the very title makes this clear. In Jane Austen's finest novel, *Emma*, there is every variety of misunderstanding, but the greatest misunderstanding of all, and the one that leads to so many of the others, is Emma's concerning her own nature. Emma—so high-handed and so wrongheaded, so often reasonable and so seldom right—is herself a wonderfully modulated comic character. And what matters is not so much the realistic consequences of her mistakes as the assured and benevolent air with which she commits them. And now moving higher still, to Meredith's *The Egoist*, we see self-deluded character constituting, really, the whole book. Sir Willoughby Patterne is the supreme example of self-centeredness in literature—the man who, in his absorption with the creature he is and the role he plays and the impression he makes, can care about nobody else. He tramples on the emotions and even the liberties of all who come his way, only cherishing such people so far as they cherish or pay homage to him. He is stunned by what seems to him *their* selfishness when, appalled by his, they walk out or turn away. And as we watch Meredith's great demonstration of human egoism, as we see with what comic flourishes and farcical leaps and wild extravagant motions it proceeds—as we smile and even laugh—we become increasingly uncomfortable. The more monstrous Sir Willoughby seems, the more we realize that in some 210 sense this man is ourselves. If no one ever misunderstood his own nature worse, no one has ever pointed a moral better. Comedy at its greatest is criticism indeed; is nothing less, in fact, than a form of moral enlightenment.

The Egoist is sometimes declared to be comedy in name only, to be at bottom tragic. I would myself disagree—Meredith carries his theme to so extreme a length as to transform his hero from a man into a sort of sublime caricature, and gives him a purely comic intensity, an intensity quite disproportionate to what it is intense about. If just this is the "tragedy" of most human beings, it must yet serve to expose 220 rather than exalt them; otherwise what shall we call genuine tragedy when we encounter it? Malvolio in *Twelfth Night*, who has also been looked upon as tragic, comes somewhat closer to being so. For pretension with him does partake a little of aspiration; his vanity, moreover, is stung because he is a servant, and stimulated by the mischievousness of others. But Malvolio, like Sir Willoughby, is really too trivial for tragedy, as he is also too priggish. What happens to him seems painful rather than tragic; it is not quite our modern idea of fun.

And this brings up the point that though Comedy has its permanent subject-matter and even its body of laws, it is liable, like everything 230 else, to changes in fashion and taste, to differences of sensibility. One generation's pleasure is the next generation's embarrassment: much that the Victorians shuddered at merely makes us laugh, much that they laughed at might well make us shudder. One always reacts—and quite fortunately—from the vantage-point of one's own age; and it is probably a mistake, and certainly a waste of breath, to be arrogant or snobbish or moral about what amuses or does not amuse one: we may fancy we are less callous than our grandfathers and only be less callous about different things. The cuckold was clearly, in Restoration comedy, a figure to hoot at. Simply for being cuckolded we do not today 240 find a man so comic, or even comic at all: though the moment we add an extra element to his role, such as his elation over cuckolding others, he becomes a comic figure for us. To what extent sex itself is a comic theme must naturally vary with the morality of a particular age: there are times when it seems shocking for a man ever to have a mistress; there are times when it seems even more shocking for a man never to have one. Right in the same age, what is considered virtue by the parson may be termed repression by the psychiatrist; and in such an age, which is usually one of moral transition, we may well find conflicting comedy

250 values. The pendulum-swing of taste always makes it hard for people to know what they really like: if they are in revolt against gentility, they are likely to confuse what is funny with what is merely bold or obscene; if they are converts to gentility, they will be too much outraged by the indecent to inquire whether it is funny. There is nothing at which the Comic Spirit must smile more than our fickle and inconstant notions as to what constitutes comedy. We need not always look back to Shakespeare's drearier clowns as an instance of how tastes change: sometimes we need only attend a revival of what convulsed us ten years before.

Max Beerbohm

ARMS AND THE MAN (Review)

Sir Max Beerbohm (1872-1956), writer and caricaturist, was Bernard Shaw's successor as drama critic for the London Saturday Review. *(See Shaw's review of Shakespeare's* Henry IV, *page 689.)* *Here, on January 4, 1908, Beerbohm reviews a revival of Shaw's play* Arms and the Man.

I do wish I had been in the Avenue Theatre on that night, fourteen years ago, when "Arms and the Man" was first produced. It would be amusing, as a gauge of the changes that time has wrought on me and on things in general, to compare my sensations on that night with my sensations at the Savoy Theatre last Monday. It is on young men, for the most part, that the revolutionary pins his faith. And that is the reason why so few revolutions succeed. The very people who are counted on as co-operators are the very last to co-operate. It is well known that schoolboys are always strictly conservative; but it is not so well known that their conservatism lingers in them for some time after they have left school. Quite young men do not think for themselves: they are dependent on what they have been told. They kneel ever at such altars as are already well illuminated. All the ardour of their youth goes to the worship of well-established gods. For unsanctified new forms, methods, ideas, they have no use. They regard that sort of thing as an impertinence, and are as down on it as the quite old men are. It is only in the interval between eld and youth, before the crabbedness of youth has had time to rest and pull itself together for its reappearance as the crabbedness of eld, that we are really capable of welcoming and understanding new things. I am quite sure that if I had been in the Avenue Theatre on that historic first night I should have been very indignant against the whole affair. In a sense, of course, I should have enjoyed it. I should have admitted that Mr. Shaw was very clever. But his gifts would have been the measure of my indignation: to think that such talent should be turned to such evil uses! I should have heartily agreed, next morning, with the elderly men who at that time monopolised dramatic criticism on the daily papers, that it was a very cheap joke to represent a soldier as shivering and whining after he had been for three days under fire, and as being in the habit of carrying chocolates into battle. I should have been revolted by Mr. Shaw's cynicism in making a young woman stoop to the telling of fibs—and she no villain-ess! Sergius Saranoff would have seemed to me "a hound," and I should have been ashamed of having been compelled to laugh at him instead of hissing him. The whole play would have seemed to me a disagreeable fantasy. If one must invent, I should have said, the invention must be of a beautiful kind; and I should have had some very severe things to say about jesting on such themes as war and love.

Since that time, and since the time when "Plays Pleasant and Unpleasant" were published, I have come to see that much of this seeming 40 fantasy and flippancy was a mere striving after sober reality, and that the reason why it appeared fantastic was that it did not conform with certain conventions of the theatre which the majority of playgoers took as a necessary part of truth to life. Far be it from me to suggest that Mr. Shaw in "Arms and the Man" gives a wholly truthful picture of life in the Balkan States. There is a rich fantastic streak in Mr. Shaw, and it runs through all his work. What I mean is that he has given us more of the truth than we could have got from the average playwright who has no fantasy whatsoever. A platitude? It would have been a daring paradox fourteen years ago, and is worth enunciating as a measure- 50 ment of the distance we have meanwhile covered. Mr. Shaw himself has covered some distance. Fourteen years ago he was not so far ahead in form, as he was in matter, of the average playwright. In form, indeed, he was merely abreast of the time. I should have had nothing to say, fourteen years ago, against the form of "Arms and the Man." How strange and rickety that form seems now! One studies with something of an antiquarian interest the elaborate intrigue that centres around the adventures of Major Petkoff's old coat. How ingenious, but to us how jejune nowadays, that intrigue is! And to think that this sort of thing was what all the dramatists used to labor at and to pride them- 60 selves on! Towards the end of the play, when Louka the servant becomes the affianced bride of Sergius Saranoff, we cudgel our wits to find some meaning in the strange conjunction. Does Mr. Shaw mean that the idealist must necessarily—? Peace, peace! There *is* no meaning. Saranoff has been thrown over by Raina, who is going to marry Bluntschli; and in the drama of the early 'nineties it would have been untidy, an offence against symmetry, not to mate Saranoff with somebody before the fall of the curtain. Louka is the only unmarried girl besides Raina, and so it is she who is requisitioned. There would have been "no questions asked" fourteen years ago. Certainly we have prog- 70 ressed. Nor has Mr. Shaw progressed merely in finding the proper form for expression of his peculiar qualities in drama. Those qualities themselves have much developed since he wrote "Arms and the Man." It is a brilliant thing, this play; but shrill in tone, and narrow in outlook, and shallow, as compared with the work of Mr. Shaw in his maturity.

Bernard Shaw

HENRY IV, PART I

Bernard Shaw (1856-1950) was the drama critic of the London Saturday Review *when, on May 16, 1896, he reviewed a revival of Shakespeare's* Henry IV, *Part I, produced by the famous actor-manager Herbert Beerbohm Tree (1853-1917) at the Haymarket Theater. Beerbohm Tree, incidentally, was the brother of Max Beerbohm, whose review of Shaw's* Arms and the Man *appears on page 687.*

This is a miserably incompetent world. The average doctor is a walking compound of natural ignorance and acquired witchcraft, who kills your favorite child, wrecks your wife's health, and orders you into habits of nervous dram-drinking before you have the courage to send him about his business, and take your chance like a gentleman. The average lawyer is a nincompoop, who contradicts your perfectly sound impressions on notorious points of law, involves you in litigation when your case is hopeless, compromises when your success is certain, and cannot even make your will without securing the utter defeat of your intentions if anyone takes the trouble to dispute them. And so on, down to the bootmaker whose boots you have to make your tortured feet fit, and the tailor who clothes you as if you were a cast-iron hot-water apparatus. You imagine that these people have professions; and you find that what they have is only, in the correct old word, their "mystery" —a humbug, like all mysteries. And yet, how we help to keep up the humbug! I know men of quite exceptional intelligence—men so sceptical that they have freed their minds from all philosophic and religious dogma, who nevertheless read the Lancet° and the British Medical Journal from end to end every week as devoutly as any superstitious washerwoman ever read Zadkiel or Old Moore,° and not only believe it all, but long tremblingly for the next symptom that will give them an excuse for calling in the medicine man to mistake typhoid fever for influenza or paint their tonsils with caustic when their kidneys are out of order. Every week they have some joyful tidings for me. Another disease has been traced to its germ; an infallible destroyer of that germ has been discovered; the disease has been annihilated. What wonderful triumphs has not science enjoyed in my time! Smallpox has been made totally impossible; hydrophobia has vanished; epilepsy has yielded to the simplest of operations; the pangs of angina pectoris have

18. *Lancet*, a British medical journal. **20. *Zadkiel or Old Moore*,** examples of astrological literature, used to imply superstition.

30 been relieved as if by magic; consumption is a dream of the past; and now there is to be no more diphtheria. Instead of vainly seeking, as of old, for a universal remedy, we are the proud discoverers of a dozen, and can change with the fashion from one to another. Mercury, salicylic acid, iodide and bromide of potassium, hashed thyroid, antipyrine, with lymphs innumerable: there they are, making us all safe and happy until we are unfortunate enough to fall down in a fit, or get bitten by a mad dog, or fall sick with an ugly rash and a bad pain in our backs, when we promptly place ourselves in the hands of the very gentleman who wrote to The Times to pledge his honor and reputation, founded 40 on a pyramid of vivisected rabbits, that such things could never happen again. Depend upon it, if Macbeth had killed Macduff, he would have gone back to the Witches next day to ask their advice as to the best way of dealing with Malcolm.

It is the same with all the professions. I have other friends who are law-mad—who believe that lawyers are wise, judges high-minded and impartial, juries infallible, and codes on the brink of perfection. The military-mad and the clergy-mad stalk at large throughout the kingdom. Men believe in the professions as they believe in ghosts, because they want to believe in them. Fact-blindness—the most common sort of 50 blindness—and the resolute lying of respectable men, keep up the illusion. No mortal, however hard-headed, can feel very safe in his attempts to sift the gold of fact and efficiency out of the huge rubbish heap of professionalism.

My own weakness is neither medicine, nor law, nor tailoring, nor any of the respectable departments of bogusdom. It is the theatre. The mystery-man who takes me in is not the doctor nor the lawyer, but the actor. In this column I have prated again and again of the mission of the theatre, the art of the actor, of his labor, his skill, his knowledge, his importance as a civilizing agent, his function as a spiritual doctor. 60 Surely I have been in this the most ridiculous of all dupes. But before you lay me down in derision, never to read my articles again, hear my excuse. There is one sort of human accomplishment that cannot be dismissed as a figment of the spectator's imagination. The skill with which a man does that which he has done every day for twenty years is no illusion. When the operative at his mule in the cotton-mill pieces the broken yarn, when Paderewski° at his Erard grand plays a sonata, he is not hypnotizing you, or inviting you to make-believe. He is actually doing things that would be miracles if done by an untrained man. Or take him who, with no eye to cotton cloth or the interpretation of 70 Beethoven, does difficult things for the sake of their difficulty, simply as marvels: for instance, the acrobat. You cannot deny the reality of

66. Paderewski, Ignace Paderewski (1860-1941), Polish pianist and composer.

his feats. His complete physical self-possession, his ambidextrous grace, his power of making several deliberate movements in the space of a pang of terror—as when, for example, he will coolly alter the disposition of his body at a given moment, whilst he is falling headlong through the air: all these accomplishments of his really exist, and are by no means the product of the imagination of an innocent clergyman sitting in the auditorium with his nose buried in a volume of Shakespear, and ready to take the word of the newspapers next day for what is happening on the stage. Now, am I to be greatly blamed for having 80 supposed that the actor was a genuinely skilled artist like the acrobat, only adding to the skilled mastery of his powers of movement a mastery of his powers of speech, with an ear for verse, a sense of character, a cultivated faculty of observation and mimicry, and such higher qualities as Nature might throw into the bargain? There were great examples to mislead me: Kean° was a harlequin as well as a Hamlet; Duse's Camille° is positively enthralling as an exhibition of the gymnastics of perfect suppleness and grace; and I have seen Salvini° come out before the curtain to accept a trophy from an admirer in a stage box with more art and more fascination—the whole thing being 90 carried out in strict accordance with certain rules of his art—than an ordinary skirt dancer could get into the clumsy imposture she calls dancing after two years' hard practice. Further, it has been a matter of common observation in my generation that the burlesque of the Byron-Farnie-Reece-Burnand period° did not, as it turned out, prove a bad training for the people who played in it. Nobody will contend, I imagine, that the training was intellectual: the secret lay in the music, the dancing, the marching, the fantastic walks round, the boundless scope for physical agility, the premium which the very barrenness and vulgarity of the entertainment placed on personal feats and on mimicry. 100 Even that terrible stage calamity the stock actor of the old régime learnt something more from the Christmas pantomime than he would have known without it.

I plead, then, that acting is potentially an artistic profession, and that by training and practice a person can qualify himself or herself to come to a manager or author and say, "Within the limits imposed by my age and sex, I can do all the ordinary work of the stage with perfect certainty. I know my vowels and consonants as a phonetic expert, and can speak so as to arrest the attention of the audience whenever I open my mouth, forcibly, delicately, roughly, smoothly, prettily, harshly, 110

86. Kean, Edmund Kean, an English actor in the early nineteenth century. ***87. Camille,*** one of the great roles of the Italian actress Eleonora Duse (1859-1924), as of many other major actresses in the nineteenth century, was the title role in *Camille (La Dame aux Camélias,* 1852), by Alexandre Dumas the younger. ***88. Salvini,*** Tommaso Salvini (1829-1916), an internationally famous Italian actor. ***95. Byron-Farnie-Reece-Burnand period,*** in the mid-nineteenth century.

authoritatively, submissively, but always artistically, just as you want it. I can sit, stand, fall, get up, walk, dance, and otherwise use my body with the complete command of it that marks the physical artist." An actor might know all this, and yet, for want of the power to interpret an author's test and invent the appropriate physical expression for it, never, without coaching, get beyond Rosencrantz or Seyton.° It is, therefore, only the minimum qualification of a skilled stage hand; and if an actor is not that, then he is merely a stagestruck unskilled laborer or handy man, and his "conceptions" of Ibsen or Shakespear are mere
120 impertinences. I naturally concluded that the minimum was in force, and acting a real profession. Alas! that only proves that my desire and hope got the better of my observation—my imagination of my experience.

However, I am cured now. It is all a delusion: there is no profession, no art, no skill about the business at all. We have no actors: we have only authors, and not many of them. When Mendelssohn composed Son and Stranger for an amateur performance, he found that the bass could only sing one note. So he wrote the bass part all on that one note; and when it came to the fateful night, the bass failed even at that. Our
130 authors do as Mendelssohn did. They find that the actors have only one note, or perhaps, if they are very clever, half a dozen. So their parts are confined to these notes, often with the same result as in Mendelssohn's case. If you doubt me, go and see Henry IV at the Haymarket. It is as good work as our stage can do; but the man who says that it is skilled work has neither eyes nor ears; the man who mistakes it for intelligent work has no brains; the man who finds it even good fun may be capable of Christy Minstrelsy but not of Shakespear. Everything that charm of style, rich humor, and vivid natural characterization can do for a play are badly wanted by Henry IV, which
140 has neither the romantic beauty of Shakespear's earlier plays nor the tragic greatness of the later ones. One can hardly forgive Shakespear quite for the worldly phase in which he tried to thrust such a Jingo hero as his Harry V down our throats. The combination of conventional propriety and brute masterfulness in his public capacity with a low-lived blackguardism in his private tastes is not a pleasant one. No doubt he is true to nature as a picture of what is by no means uncommon in English society, an able young Philistine inheriting high position and authority, which he holds on to and goes through with by keeping a tight grip on his conventional and legal advantages, but who would
150 have been quite in his place if he had been born a gamekeeper or a farmer. We do not in the first part of Henry IV see Harry sending Mrs Quickly and Doll Tearsheet to the whipping-post, or handing over

116. Rosencrantz or Seyton, minor characters in *Hamlet* and *Macbeth.*

Falstaff to the Lord Chief Justice with a sanctimonious lecture; but he repeatedly makes it clear that he will turn on them later on, and that his self-indulgent good-fellowship with them is consciously and deliberately treacherous. His popularity, therefore, is like that of a prizefighter: nobody feels for him as for Romeo or Hamlet. Hotspur, too, though he is stimulating as ginger cordial is stimulating, is hardly better than his horse; and King Bolingbroke, preoccupied with his crown exactly as a miser is preoccupied with his money, is equally 160 useless as a refuge for our affections, which are thus thrown back undivided on Falstaff, the most human person in the play, but none the less a besotted and disgusting old wretch. And there is neither any subtlety nor (for Shakespear) much poetry in the presentation of all these characters. They are labelled and described and insisted upon with the roughest directness; and their reality and their humor can alone save them from the unpopularity of their unlovableness and the tedium of their obviousness. Fortunately, they offer capital opportunities for interesting acting. Bolingbroke's long discourse to his son on the means by which he struck the imagination and enlisted the 170 snobbery of the English people gives the actor a chance comparable to the crafty early scenes in Richelieu.° Prince Hal's humor is seasoned with sportsmanlike cruelty and the insolence of conscious mastery and contempt to the point of occasionally making one shudder. Hotspur is full of energy; and Falstaff is, of course, an unrivalled part for the right sort of comedian. Well acted, then, the play is a good one in spite of there not being a single tear in it. Ill acted—O heavens!

Of the four leading parts, the easiest—Hotspur—becomes preeminent at the Haymarket, not so much by Mr Lewis Waller's superiority to the rest as by their inferiority to him. Some of the things he 180 did were astonishing in an actor of his rank. At the end of each of his first vehement speeches, he strode right down the stage and across to the prompt side of the proscenium on the frankest barnstorming principles, repeating this absurd "cross"—a well-known convention of the booth for catching applause—three times, step for step, without a pretence of any dramatic motive. In the camp scene before the battle of Shrewsbury, he did just what I blamed Miss Violet Vanbrugh for trying to do in Monsieur de Paris:° that is, to carry through a long crescendo of excitement by main force after beginning fortissimo. Would it be too far-fetched to recommend Mr Waller to study how 190 Mozart, in rushing an operatic movement to a spirited conclusion, knew how to make it, when apparently already at its utmost, seem to bound forward by a sudden pianissimo and lightsome change of step,

172. Richelieu, a play by Edward Bulwer-Lytton (1839). ***188. Monsieur de Paris,*** a play by Alicia Ramsay, then playing in London.

the speed and force of the execution being actually reduced instead of intensified by the change? Such skilled, resourceful husbandry is the secret of all effects of this kind; and it is in the entire absence of such husbandry that Mr Waller shewed how our miserable theatre has left him still a novice for the purposes of a part which he is fully equipped by nature to play with most brilliant success, and which he
200 did play very strikingly considering he was not in the least sure how to set about it, and hardly dared to stop blazing away at full pitch for an instant lest the part should drop flat on the boards. Mr Mollison presented us with an assortment of effects, and tones, and poses which had no reference, as far as I could discover, to the part of Bolingbroke at any single point. I did not catch a glimpse of the character from one end of his performance to the other, and so must conclude that Shakespear has failed to convey his intention to him. Mr Gillmore's way of playing Hal was as bad as the traditional way of playing Sheridan. He rattled and swaggered and roystered, and followed every sentence with
210 a forced explosion of mirthless laughter, evidently believing that, as Prince Hal was reputed to be a humorous character, it was his business to laugh at him. Like most of his colleagues, he became more tolerable in the plain sailing of the battle scene, where the parts lose their individuality in the general warlike excitement, and an energetic display of the commonest sort of emotion suffices. Mr Tree only wants one thing to make him an excellent Falstaff, and that is to get born over again as unlike himself as possible. No doubt, in the course of a month or two, when he begins to pick up a few of the lines of the part, he will improve on his first effort; but he will never be even a moderately good
220 Falstaff. The basket-work figure, as expressionless as that of a Jack in the Green; the face, with the pathetic wandering eye of Captain Swift belying such suggestion of character as the lifeless mask of paint and hair can give; the voice, coarsened, vulgarized, and falsified without being enriched or colored; the hopeless efforts of the romantic imaginative actor, touching only in unhappy parts, to play the comedian by dint of mechanical horseplay: all that is hopeless, irremediable. Mr Tree might as well try to play Juliet; and if he were wise he would hand over his part and his breadbasket to Mr Lionel Brough, whose Bardolph has the true comic force which Mr Tree never attains for a moment.
230 Two ideas have been borrowed from the last London revival of Henry V by Mr Coleman at the Queen's Theatre in Long Acre. One is the motionless battle tableau, which is only Mr Coleman's Agincourt over again, and which might just as well be cut out of cardboard. The other is the casting of Miss Kate Phillips for Mrs Quickly. As Mrs Quickly is plainly a slovenly, greasy, Gampish old creature, and Miss Phillips is unalterably trim, smart, and bright, a worse choice could not have been made. One would like to have seen Miss Mansfield in the part.

Mrs Tree, as Lady Percy, did what I have never seen her do before: that is, played her part stupidly. The laws of nature seem to be suspended when Shakespeare is in question. A Lady Percy who is senti- 240 mentally affectionate, who recites her remonstrance with Percy in the vein of Clarence's dream in Richard III, and who comes on the stage to share the applause elicited by the combats in the battle of Shrewsbury, only makes me rub my eyes and wonder whether I am dreaming.

Besides Mr Lionel Brough and Mr Lewis Waller, there were three performers who came off with credit. Mr Holman Clark played Glendower like a reasonable man who could read a Shakespearean play and understand it—a most exceptional achievement in his profession, as it appears. Mr D. J. Williams, who played William in *As You Like It* the other day at the Métropole, and played him well, was a Smike- 250 like and effective Francis; and Miss Marion Evans was a most musical Lady Mortimer, both in her Welsh song and Welsh speech.

The chief merit of the production is that the play has been accepted from Shakespear mainly as he wrote it. There are cuts, of course, the worst of them being the sacrifice of the nocturnal innyard scene, a mutilation which takes the reality and country midnight freshness from the Gadshill robbery, and reduces it to a vapid interlude of horseplay. But the object of these cuts is to save time: there is no alteration or hotch-potch, and consequently no suspicion of any attempt to demonstrate the superiority of the manager's taste and judgment to 260 Shakespear's, in the Daly° fashion. This ought to pass as a matter of course; but as things are at present it must be acknowledged as highly honorable to Mr Tree. However, it is not my cue just now to pay Mr Tree compliments. His *tours de force* in the art of make-up do not impose on me: any man can get into a wicker barrel and pretend to be Falstaff, or put on a false nose and call himself Svengali. Such tricks may very well be left to the music-halls: they are altogether unworthy of an artist of Mr Tree's pretensions. When he returns to the serious pursuit of his art by playing a part into which he can sincerely enter without disguise or mechanical denaturalization, may I be there to 270 see! Until then let him guard the Haymarket doors against me; for I like him best when he is most himself.

261. Daly, Augustin Daly (1838-1899), theatrical producer.

John Masefield

KING HENRY IV, PART I

John Masefield, the Poet Laureate of England since 1930, has written poetry and poetic dramas since the turn of the century.

Written. (?) *Published.* 1598. *Source of the Plot.* Most of the comic scenes are the fruit of Shakespeare's invention. A very popular play, *The Famous Victories of Henry V*, by an unknown hand, gave him the suggestions for an effective comic scene. In the historical scenes he follows closely the *Chronicles* of Holinshed.

The Fable. The play treats of the rising of Henry Hotspur, Lord Percy, against Henry IV of England, and of the turning of the mind of Henry, Prince of Wales, from low things to things more worthy his birth. It ends with the killing of Hotspur, by the Prince of Wales, on the battlefield at Shrewsbury. Hotspur is an uncommon man, whose uncommonness is unsupported by his father at a critical moment. Henry, Prince of Wales, is a common man, whose commonness props his father, and helps him to conquer. The play is about a son too brilliant to be understood, and a son too common to understand.

The play treats of a period some four years after the killing of King Richard II. It opens at a time when the oaths of Henry Bolingbroke, to do justice, have been broken on all sides, lest the injustice of his assumption of kingship should be recognised and punished by those over whom he usurps power. The King is no longer the just, rather kind, man of affairs who takes power in the earlier, much finer play. He is a swollen, soured, bullying man, with all the ingratitude of a king and all the baseness of one who knows his cause to be wrong. Opposed to him is a passionate, quick-tempered man, ready to speak his mind, on the instant, to any whom he believes to be unjust or false.

This quick-tempered man, Lord Percy, has done the King a signal service. Instead of asking for reward he tries to persuade the King to be just to a man who has suffered wounds and defeat for him. The King calls him a liar for his pains.

Percy, stung to the quick, rebels. Others rebel with him, among them some who are too wise to be profitable on a council of war. War does not call for wisdom, but for swiftness in striking. Percy, who is famed for swiftness in striking, loses half of his slender chance because his friends are too wise to advise desperate measures. Nevertheless, his troops shake the King's troops. The desperate battle of Shrewsbury is very nearly a triumph for him. Then the Prince meets him and kills him. He learns too late that a passionate longing to right the wrong goes down before the rough and stupid something that makes up the bulk of the world. He learns that

"Thought's the slave of life, and life, time's fool;
And time, that takes survey of all the world, 40
Must have a stop"—

and dies. The man who kills him says a few trite lines over his body, and leaves the stage talking of Falstaff's bowels.

Prince Henry, afterwards Henry V, has been famous for many years as "Shakespeare's only hero." Shakespeare was too wise to count any man a hero. The ways of fate moved him to vision, not heroism. If we can be sure of anything in that great, simple, gentle, elusive brain, we can be sure that it was quickened by the thought of the sun shining on the just and on the unjust, and shining none the less golden though the soul like clay triumph over the soul like flame. Prince Henry is not 50 a hero, he is not a thinker, he is not even a friend; he is a common man whose incapacity for feeling enables him to change his habits whenever interest bids him. Throughout the first acts he is careless and callous though he is breaking his father's heart and endangering his father's throne. He chooses to live in society as common as himself. He talks continually of guts as though a belly were a kind of wit. Even in the society of his choice his attitude is remote and cold-blooded. There is no good-fellowship in him, no sincerity, no whole-heartedness. He makes a mock of the drawer who gives him his whole little pennyworth of sugar. His jokes upon Falstaff are so little good-natured that he stands 60 upon his princehood whenever the old man would retort upon him. He impresses one as quite common, quite selfish, quite without feeling. When he learns that his behaviour may have lost him his prospective crown he passes a sponge over his past, and fights like a wild cat for the right of not having to work for a living.

There is little great poetry in the play. The magnificent image—

"Baited like eagles having lately bathed"—

the speech of Worcester (in Act V, sc. i) when he comes with a trumpet to speak with the King, and the call of Hotspur to set on battle—

"Sound all the lofty instruments of war, 70
And by that music let us all embrace"—

are all noble.

To many, the play is remarkable because it introduces Sir John Falstaff, the most notable figure in English comedy. Falstaff is that deeply interesting thing, a man who is base because he is wise. Our justest, wisest brain dwelt upon Falstaff longer than upon any other character because he is the world and the flesh, able to endure while Hotspur flames to his death, and the enemies of the devil are betrayed that the devil may have power to betray others.

Robert C. Elliott

SHAW'S CAPTAIN BLUNTSCHLI: A LATTER-DAY FALSTAFF

Robert C. Elliott is Professor of English at the University of California at San Diego.

In the first act of *Arms and the Man*, Bluntschli, the professional soldier, explains matter-of-factly to Raina that on the battlefield he never carries cartridges for his pistol; he carries chocolate instead. One inevitably thinks of another equally unconventional soldier: "Ay, Hal; 'tis hot, 'tis hot; there's that will sack a city," cries Falstaff as he pulls a bottle of sack instead of a pistol from his holster. The parallel unorthodoxies point up a relationship between the plays that goes deeper than the chuckles we get at the deplorably unmilitary conduct of the two characters.

Cleanth Brooks and Robert Heilman have made abundantly clear, in their fine analysis of *Henry IV*, *Part One* (an analysis on which I rely heavily), the importance of the problem of honor to the structure of the play.[13] Hotspur and Falstaff are foils to one another in respect to this theme: Hotspur with his romantic, hot-blooded conception of honor:

> By heaven, methinks it were an easy leap,
> To pluck bright honour from the pale-faced moon . . . ;

Falstaff with his characteristic realism: "Can honour set to a leg? no: or an arm? no: or take away the grief of a wound? no" (I, iii, ll. 201-202; V, i, ll. 130-131). *Arms and the Man* has a similar theme, made explicit most succinctly in Sergius's final comment on Bluntschli, the last line of the play: "What a man! Is he a man?" It is a crucial question. Manhood for Sergius, at least in his "public" character, is the kind of manhood exemplified by Hotspur. Sergius is disillusioned with soldiering, which he has found to be "the coward's art of attacking mercilessly when you are strong, and keeping out of harm's way when you are weak" (p. 54). (Hotspur, we remember, insisted on attacking at Shrewsbury when his forces were weak.) "Oh," Sergius cries fervently to Louka, "give me the man who will defy to the death any power on earth or in heaven that sets itself up against his own will and conscience: he alone is the brave man" (p. 74). His fiancée, Raina

13. ***Understanding Drama*** (New York, 1945, 1948), pp. 376-387. Quotations from *Henry IV*, *Part One* and *Arms and the Man* correspond to those in this text.

(again, in her public character), shares these ideals; she goes into raptures at the news that Sergius (contrary to orders) has led a wild cavalry charge against the enemy. Her romantic ideals have been justified, and Sergius is worthy of "the higher love." "Oh, to think that it was all true! that Sergius is just as splendid and noble as he looks! that the world is really a glorious world for women who can see its glory and men who can act its romance! What happiness! what unspeakable fulfilment!" she cries to her mother (p. 35).

But hard on the heels of this cry comes Bluntschli, the anti-hero, 40 through the bedroom window. Just as Falstaff, with his realism and humor, tests the world of Hotspur ("... there's honour for you," says Falstaff, looking at the dead body of Sir Walter Blunt. "God keep lead out of me! I need no more weight than mine own bowels" [V, iii, ll. 33-34]), so Bluntschli, with his realism and practicality, tests the world to which Sergius and Raina profess such devotion. We quickly learn how flimsy that world is. Sergius's "heroic" cavalry charge against machine guns, Bluntschli makes clear, was comical folly, successful only by accident. Against the "professional point of view," all that Sergius and Raina publicly stand for shows as childish nonsense—a fact 50 that Sergius explicitly recognizes. Speaking of his meeting with Bluntschli after the battle, Sergius says to Major Petkoff: "We were two children in the hands of that consummate soldier, Major: simply two innocent little children" (p. 54). (Compared to Falstaff, Hotspur sometimes seems a child—though a genuinely heroic one—in his naïveté.) But Sergius's praise is heavily qualified; for him, the modern soldier, perfectly exemplified in Bluntschli, is nothing but a tradesman, a "commercial traveller in uniform." Sergius withdraws his challenge to Bluntschli because "it takes two men—real men—men of heart, blood and honor—to make a genuine combat . . . youre not a man: 60 youre a machine." "Quite true, quite true," says Bluntschli (p. 78).

Sergius's final comment ("What a man! Is he a man?") clearly has its ambiguities. If Bluntschli is not a man, then who is? Sergius himself? The problem is one of history. In *Henry IV*, the bravery, the wild romanticism of Hotspur are enormously attractive; and if those qualities, even in the world of *Henry IV*, are not adequate as a way of life for a "full" man, still they are qualities to which a man could commit himself wholly and unselfconsciously. But for Sergius the case is different. Sergius knows that if he attempted "To pluck bright honour from the pale-faced moon" he would stub his toe. His Byronic self- 70 doubt, his ironic self-questioning measure the inadequacy of the Hotspurian values in the world of the late nineteenth century. The major test of those values comes from the common-sense probings of Bluntschli. But devastating as the probings are, the test lacks conviction; for Bluntschli is but a pale imitation of Falstaff. He has not Falstaff's "wholeness" (realist that he is, he confesses to "an incurably romantic disposition" [p. 83]), nor anything like Falstaff's stature (in any of a dozen senses). Raina's furious accusation, "You have a low shopkeeping mind" (p. 71), turns out to be good characterization. The only man in 80 Bulgaria Bluntschli really admires is Nicola, the butler, who pimps for his fiancée Louka so that he can get her custom when he sets up his own shop. "This is either the finest heroism or the most crawling baseness," says Sergius of Nicola's renunciation of Louka. "Never mind whether it's heroism or baseness," answers Bluntschli; and then he adds admiringly, "Nicola's the ablest man I've met in Bulgaria" (p. 82), thus placing himself on a moral level with the butler, who in truth has "the soul of a servant" (p. 58).

In *Henry IV* the world of the court, the world of the tavern, and the world of chivalry (Hotspur's world) are in conflict, as it were, for the 90 soul of Prince Hal. Each world has its valid claims, and each throws light on the others. When the time for action comes, Hal is forced to choose among them; and he chooses well. But in *Arms and the Man* no choice between the conflicting worlds is possible, for neither has the power to command serious allegiance. (Surely this is Shaw's ironic comment—a comment implicit in the mock-heroic title of the play—on his own time.) The "chivalric" ideals of Sergius and Raina are so anachronistic and so artificial that not even they can really believe in them. And the "practicality" of Bluntschli is so practical and so low that one cannot take it seriously. The only character in *Arms and the* 100 *Man* who in any sense transcends these worlds (as Hal transcends his), and is thus the real "man" of the play, is Louka, the servant girl with a soul above her station. Louka is eminently practical, certainly, but she despises Nicola's "cold-blooded wisdom" (p. 73); and, finally, she has the spirit and the pride to bring the swaggering Sergius to heel.

Barnard Hewitt

THORNTON WILDER SAYS "YES"

Barnard Hewitt, a professor at the University of Illinois, is the author of books and essays on the theater.

The prefatory note to the volume, *Three Plays by Thornton Wilder*, states that he is regarded by many as America's greatest living playwright. We may discount this considerably as a publisher's exaggeration, but there is no question that his name will appear on almost anyone's list of major contemporary American playwrights—and probably nearer the top than the bottom.

This is a little surprising when one stops to think that his reputation rests almost entirely on three plays, one of them an adaptation. True, he has written a number of one-act plays, one or two of which have become classics of the amateur theatre. He has translated 10 André Obey's *Lucrèce* for Katharine Cornell and he has adapted *A Doll's House* for Ruth Gordon. His trilogy on the Alcestis story, *A Life in the Sun*, was seen at the Edinburgh Festival in 1957. But his name and fame as a playwright depend on *Our Town*, first produced in 1938, *The Skin of Our Teeth* in 1942, and *The Matchmaker* in 1954. A small output in twenty years.

Moreover, these three plays have not been universally hailed as masterpieces, or even as original contributions to American drama and theatre. On the contrary, both *The Skin of Our Teeth* and *Our Town* have been attacked as derivative. Joseph Campbell and Henry 20 Morton Robinson, authors of the *Skeleton Key to Finnegan's Wake* were shocked to discover that *The Skin of Our Teeth* drew a good deal from James Joyce's puzzling work and ended their inventory of the borrowings by suggesting that if the play shows genius it is the genius not of Wilder but of Joyce.

Julian Sawyer concurred about *The Skin of Our Teeth* and pointed out that *Our Town* owes a considerable debt to Gertrude Stein's *The Making of Americans.* He pronounced this stern judgment: "the superficial and escapist treatment that Thornton Wilder bestowed upon his all too derivative material makes him anything but a purloiner 30 of the great thought, beauty, and feeling which constituted those works of art resulting from the genius of Gertrude Stein and James Joyce."

Francis Fergusson, writing in the *Sewanee Review* in 1956, although he expressed admiration for Wilder's theatrical virtuosity, pronounced him fundamentally sentimental and pretentious.

Wilder has been attacked too as a shallow optimist, out of touch with the dark realities of American life today. His plays have been extremely popular in Germany, as indeed elsewhere in Europe, since 40 World War II, and when Wilder visited Germany a few years ago he received an enthusiastic welcome. Paul Fussell, Jr. in *The Nation*, noting this phenomenon with a cynical eye, observed that of living American writers Wilder is the least touched by the social, intellectual and psychological currents of America as it is. Europeans, seeking a soothing picture of the country, upon which their own future appears so largely to depend, have seized not upon Williams or Faulkner with their deep wells of envy, anger, hatred, and terror but upon the mild Wilder. To quote Mr. Fussell: "Here, gratifying the European image of what he should be, was the American Writer, with all his folksy inno- 50 cence of evil, with all his touching devotion to Love, and with all his inspiring and efficient optimism." According to Mr. Fussell, Thornton Wilder is hoodwinking Europeans—who of course are asking to be hoodwinked. He offers them in *The Skin of Our Teeth* a vitalistic, cosmic optimism out of tune with our time, and in *Our Town* an image of America that is "pastoral, complacent, coy, charming, and entirely unreal."

None of Thornton Wilder's critics mentions *The Matchmaker*, perhaps because it is offered as an adaptation not as an original work, but more likely because it is labeled a "farce" and serious critics of 60 the drama have almost always ignored farce as mere diversion for the unthinking. Moreover, farce has been pretty much out of favor in the theatre for nearly thirty years. However, there are signs that it may be returning to fashion: witness the success not only of *The Matchmaker* but of *Hotel Paradiso.*° Moreover, Eric Bentley has rediscovered farce as a subject for analysis by the critic and theorist of drama. His essay "The Psychology of Farce," which introduces the volume of French farces recently published in the Mermaid Dramabook series, gives every appearance of being only a beginning. We may expect more on the subject from Bentley, and other critics may well follow his lead.

70 If *The Matchmaker* is subjected to analysis, it is likely to draw adverse criticism of the same kinds that have been leveled against *Our Town* and *The Skin of Our Teeth*. Since *The Matchmaker* is acknowledged to be an adaptation of an Austrian play by Johann Nestroy, which was based upon an English play by John Oxenford, perhaps no one will look for further borrowings. But if they do, they will find that the scene in Act I in which Dolly Levi describes to Horace Vandergelder Ernestine Simple's wonderful qualifications to be his wife,

64. Hotel Paradiso, by Georges Feydeau (1862-1921), a prolific French writer of intricately plotted farces. *Hotel Paradiso* (1894) as adapted by Maurice Desvallieres appeared successfully on Broadway in 1957.

in which she flatters Horace and extracts money from him, is right out of Molière's *The Miser*. Before any critic cites this as further evidence that Thornton Wilder is lacking in original creative power, let us hope 80 he will recall that Molière's *The Miser* drew very heavily upon Plautus' *Aulularia*.

What do we discover, if we examine *The Matchmaker* according to Eric Bentley's view of farce? Bentley finds the function of farce in Freud's *Civilization and Its Discontents* and describes that function as follows: "...when we buy civilization, as we do, at the price of frustration, the frustrated impulses become a potential source of trouble. The pressures are enormous and perpetual. We ought to welcome any relief from them, however slight or trivial, provided it is harmless. Dreams are the commonest relief but are usually unpleasant. 90 The most pleasurable relief is to be found in the arts." One of these arts is farce. The farce, like the dream, pictures the disguised fulfillment of repressed wishes. Many repressed wishes are gross and all are in revolt against our culture. Since the family is at the center of our culture, gross wishes are mainly directed against the family. "Outrage to family piety and propriety," says Bentley, "is certainly at the heart of farce." Hence, the farcical ubiquity of the bed. The energy which is one of the earmarks of farce derives from the repression of primitive instinct. The violence, which is another of its earmarks, is aggression against established forms, against established values. 100 The physical exertions of the characters in farce provide release and relief for conflicts which for the most part lie buried beneath the conscious life of civilized man. To quote Mr. Bentley once more: "Man, says farce, may or may not be one of the more intelligent animals; he is certainly an animal, and not one of the least violent; and one of the chief uses to which he puts his intelligence, such as it is, is to think aggression when he is not committing it."

From Bentley's point of view, farce is a moral and highly useful form of drama. It provides in enjoyable and harmless fantasy a substitute for aggressive thoughts and destructive actions—wife-beating, 110 adultery, rape, incest, patricide—to which we are all impelled by the beast within us. Farce is an efficacious tranquilizer. An evening at *Hotel Paradiso* is as good as an hour on the psychiatrist's couch.

Thornton Wilder's *The Matchmaker* is full of energy, but the energy is not destructive. The wildly absurd action of the play is precipitated and complicated by the determination of its principal characters to lead freer, fuller lives than circumstances have imposed upon them. Cornelius Hackl one day rebels against the narrow limits of his life in Yonkers as Horace Vandergelder's chief clerk, and, with his youthful assistant, Barnaby Tucker, sets out for a day of adventure in New 120 York, determined before he returns to have a good meal, get almost

arrested, spend all his money, and kiss a girl. Ambrose Kemper is determined to marry Horace's niece Ermengard in spite of her uncle's opposition. Irene Malloy, weary of the restrictions which widowhood, her millinery business, and standards of decorum placed upon her, kicks over the traces. She goes to dinner at the Harmonia Gardens with what she thinks are two gay blades. Dolly Levi is determined to marry Horace Vandergelder in order to put his money into circulation and thus make the world a pleasanter place for her and lots of other people.
130 Horace Vandergelder stands for the cautious, careful, safe existence—everything the others are rebelling against. Horace prides himself on his good sense. In comparison with him, nearly everyone is foolish. To be young is foolish. To fall in love is foolish. To marry is foolish. To be poor is foolish. In order to be rich one must work hard and spend money only for necessities. To be sensible, therefore, is to be old and rich like Horace Vandergelder.

And yet the revolt against Horace and the cautious, careful life he stands for is without malice, without vindictiveness. It is entirely light-hearted. The two clerks encourage some cans of tomatoes in
140 Horace's store to explode, thus providing an excuse for their holiday, but the cans of tomatoes were spoiled to begin with. Otherwise Horace does not suffer from their revolt. Horace is not forced or tricked into allowing Ermengard to marry Ambrose; he does so of his own free will. Dolly Levi succeeds in marrying Horace, but she does not deceive him. He knows she is going to help him spend his painfully accumulated money, but he wants to marry her anyhow.

This is not hard to believe, for we know that Horace, in spite of all his talk about what is sensible and what is foolish, in spite of his treatment of Ambrose and Cornelius and Ermengard, is not really
150 so different from the rest of them. In the first act, immediately after his stuffy sermon on folly and good sense, he declares that he is contemplating getting married again, not only in order to have his house run with order, comfort, and economy (a *sensible* reason) but also because he hankers after "a little risk and adventure after many years of caution and hard work," (a very *foolish* reason). Having taken one cautious step out of his safe, sensible, and lonely world into the adventurous, foolish, and convivial world, he inevitably takes another step, and another, until he is running with the majority of mankind. To use Dolly Levi's words, he has "joined the world," he has "re-
160 joined the human race."

Thus, Horace only *seems* to be a symbol for the sensible, humdrum side of life, against which everyone else is rebelling. Underneath his crusty exterior he longs as much as anybody to shake off the shackles of security and good sense. Once the crusty exterior is cracked, it rapidly disintegrates.

Cornelius, Ambrose, Dolly Levi, and Irene Malloy do not represent repressed wishes in revolt against our culture. Their revolt is not aggression against the established forms, the established values of our civilization. They are not really rebelling against anything outside themselves. They are in conflict with the drive toward self- 170 preservation, security, and peace, which exists in most human beings side by side with its opposite, the drive toward change, adventure, and excitement.

Aggression in *The Matchmaker* is not directed against the family. Indeed, the opposite is true. Aggression, if it can be called that in this play, is directed against ideas and attitudes which discourage marriage. The immediate result of the rebellions it presents is three marriages, all of which have every prospect of being happy marriages, thus strengthening the family and the culture of which it is the center.

In *The Matchmaker*, Wilder has used the form and method of farce 180 to celebrate—in very simple, almost childlike terms—the radical, the pioneering, the exploring, the creative spirit in man. Even if one ignores the playwright's statement of his theme as he puts it into the mouths of some of his characters or overlooks these explanations in the hurly-burly of the action, this meaning, as Harold Clurman has noted "is in the doing of it, the sheer physical exhilaration of its theatrical pattern." *The Matchmaker* is gay; it is exhilarating. It is not a tranquilizer but a tonic.

If *The Matchmaker* is a lively song in praise of adventure, *Our Town* might be called a hymn to the humdrum. As Wilder has said, 190 "*Our Town* is not offered as a picture of life in a New Hampshire village; or speculation about the conditions of life after death. . . . It is an attempt to find a value above all price for the smallest events of daily life." *The Matchmaker* is a play of extraordinary action, lighthearted rebellion, and high spirits. *Our Town* is a play of everyday activity, poignant feeling, and the peace which comes with acceptance.

In spite of its success with audiences, or perhaps because of that success, *Our Town* has been attacked by some critics as sentimental, untrue. It presents a false picture, they say, because it contains none of the ugliness of small-town life in America as it exists and as it has 200 been represented in the drama by William Inge and in other literary media by Sherwood Anderson, Carl Sandburg, and Edwin Arlington Robinson. Eric Bentley has criticized the use of the Stage Manager as condescending to the audience and as productive of repetition and platitude. The disuse of scenery and properties has been termed quaint, coy, and distracting.

The ugly side of American small-town life is not entirely missing from *Our Town*. Simon Stimson, the drunken, disappointed organist is there. In a play by Tennessee Williams or William Inge, he would

210 be stage center. Wilder keeps Simon close to the wings. His purpose is not to present a complete picture of small-town life but rather through its little cycle of daily activity and its big cycle of birth, marriage, and death to discover for us the value of the ordinary in human life any time, anywhere, every time, everywhere. *Our Town,* though it contains little ugliness, does not evade the pain of life. It is full not only of the pleasure and joy of ordinary living but of the little troubles of growing up, the terror of youth before the mystery of marriage, and the anguish of the bereaved before the terminal fact of death. To have given more prominence to Simon Stimson and his like would only have 220 distracted from Wilder's purpose.

The frame supplied by the Stage Manager is essential to that purpose. The Stage Manager is not merely an easy means to exposition, to setting the scene in Grover's Corners. He is the principal means to the double vision, the intermeshing of past and present, which permeates the whole play, as Winfield Townley Scott has noted in "Our Town and the Golden Veil" in the *Virginia Quarterly Review.* Although the Stage Manager knows Grover's Corners well, he exists in our time. He can call in Professor Willard to place Grover's Corners and its inhabitants for us in the scale of geologic and historic time. He can him- 230 self remind us that Babylon once had two million people in it, and though all we know about them is the names of the kings and some copies of wheat contracts, every night all those families sat down to supper, and the father came home from work, and the smoke went up the chimney, same as in Grover's Corners, same as here. And he can glance into the future of Grover's Corners and tell us what is to change and what is to remain.

The double vision the Stage Manager permits is responsible for the play's two-fold effect. *Our Town* appears somehow to have to do simultaneously with very ordinary people and with the shining 240 galaxies of stars, with the smallest of small towns and with the universe, with time and with eternity. Oddly enough, Grover's Corners and the Webbs and the Gibbs do not appear insignificant against the backdrop of eternity; they are not lost in the vastness of the universe. The daily routine and the individual life cycle of birth, marriage, and death are revealed as part of the eternal rhythm of the universe.

The absence of scenery and of realistic properties in *Our Town* may strike the sophisticated playgoer as coy or the less sophisticated playgoer as quaint, and therefore prove distracting to both, but I believe not for long. If the play is reasonably well acted, one quickly 250 accepts the convention and forgets that the real stove, the real dishes, the real newspaper are not there. And this convention is no affectation. It is integral to Wilder's concept. Although the action of the play takes place in a small town in New Hampshire at a specific time and it is concerned with individuals, yet it aims to illustrate a truth that holds for men and women everywhere, in the big city as well as the small town, and in every time, in 1938 or 1959 as well as in 1901. Scenery and realistic properties would have tied *Our Town* too firmly to the particular time and place, would have made it the nostalgic, sentimental play of life in the vanished American small town, for which it is sometimes mistaken. Thornton Wilder has said exactly this in another way: 260

> Emily's joys and griefs, her algebra lessons, her birthday presents—what are they when we consider all the billions of girls who have lived, who are living, and who will live? Each individual's assertion to an absolute reality can only be inner. . . . And here the method of staging finds its justification. . . . Our claim, our hope, our despair are in the mind—not in things, not in 'scenery.' The climax of this play needs only five square feet of boarding and the passion to know what life means to us.

It is hard to imagine how the climax of *Our Town* could be achieved at all under the conditions imposed by the presence of scenery. Without scenery, the transitions in scene can be as swift as the imagination, not only in time and place but back and forth from life to death. Emily has died in childbirth and she comes to take her place among the dead in the Grover's Corners cemetery. She learns that it is possible to return, to relive the past among the living, and she goes back, in spite of warnings from the dead and from the Stage Manager who says: "You not only live it but you watch yourself living it. And as you watch . . . you know what's going to happen afterwards." Emily has chosen to relive her twelfth birthday. From its beginning, every moment of that day is transfigured by her double awareness. Each moment is almost unbearably beautiful, and each moment goes so fast! Finally the dead Emily of fourteen years later cries: "Mama, just for a moment we're happy. Let's look at one another!" But the living have no time to look and they cannot hear the voice out of the future. Emily, unable to bear the happiness and the pain, flees back to the disinterested dead. And she cries out to the Stage Manager, "Do human beings ever realize life while they live it? every, every minute?" "No," he answers, "The saints and poets maybe—they do some." 270 280

Thus, *Our Town* asserts the value of human life, no matter how apparently trivial, no matter how apparently insignificant. It does so, not by ignoring or belittling change and death, but by reminding us that change is necessary to the recognition of beauty and that death in a very fundamental way gives meaning to life. *Optimism,* even unmodified by the derogatory adjective *shallow,* does not seem to me quite the word to describe this view of the world. I should call it *affirmation.* 290

In *The Matchmaker*, and in a playful mood, Thornton Wilder affirms the value of change, of the new. In *Our Town* and in a reverent mood, he affirms the value of the unchanging, of the habitual and the familiar. In *The Skin of Our Teeth* he extends his dramatic image to include both the ordinary and the extraordinary, the domestic and the political, the personal and the public, the petty and the world-shaking. Again Wilder makes use of the double vision. The Antrobus family is living both in prehistoric times among dinosaurs and in Excelsior, New Jersey, today. As in *Our Town*, the events of ordinary daily life are presented against the vast dimensions of time and space; but the present is not seen *against* the panorama of the past; it is inextricably mixed with the whole history of human life on this planet. Mrs. Antrobus, wife, mother, and preserver of the home is Mrs. Gibbs or Mrs. Webb swept out of the backwater of Grover's Corners into the main stream of life where she is buffeted by glaciers and floods and wars. And Mr. Antrobus is Cornelius Hackl, lifted out of Horace Vandergelder's store into the arena of great events where danger is real and omnipresent, and where he is transformed into the inventor, the discoverer, the fighter for human progress and liberty. We see the Antrobus family—that is to say the human race—survive the perils of the ice age, of the flood, of world war, each time by the skin of its teeth. And we see too that both Mr. Antrobus and Mrs. Antrobus—both the radical and the conservative, the adventurer and the stay-at-home, the explorer of new frontiers and the protector of the hearth—contribute to its survival.

The Skin of Our Teeth includes the ugly as well as the beautiful, the destructive as well as the creative. Sabina is not only the Antrobus' maid; she is also Lily Fairweather, hostess in an Atlantic City bingo parlor and beauty contest winner, threat to the Antrobus marriage, camp follower in the war, the universal pleasure girl and temptress, Lilith. Henry Antrobus is not only the unruly son; he is the juvenile delinquent, the murderer, the fascist, the leader of the Enemy. Clearly the forces which threaten to destroy the human race are not all forces from without. Sabina's origins, like Lilith's, are lost in the fog of prehistory but Mr. Antrobus raped her home from the Sabine hills, and she has been a member of the Antrobus household ever since. There is no doubt about Henry's parentage. He is an Antrobus, strange, embarrassing, and frightening offspring of George and Maggie, those two high-principled, well-intentioned parents. The point is clear: the destructive forces of hate and lust are as much a part of man as the constructive forces of charity and love. The history of man is one of continual struggle for survival through mastery not only of the world without but also of the world within.

Like *Our Town, The Skin of Our Teeth* has been criticized for its 340 theatricality, for its flouting of the conventions of realistic playmaking. Some of this theatricality may seem, as Wilder has said, to be merely making fun of old-fashioned drama and not so old-fashioned production, but it is indispensable to the double vision he is providing. Only in an atmosphere of obvious, though completely earnest make-believe, is it possible to present the Antrobus family at once in the ice age and in Excelsior, New Jersey in 1942, at once in the time of the flood and in modern Atlantic City, and thus by inference as the human family in every age, past, present, and future.

Moreover, once the atmosphere of make-believe is established, 350 Wilder is able to express his theme in another dimension by pretending to return to reality. He is probably aware of the tendency we have as spectators at a play to regard what we see on the stage as diverting or moving perhaps but no direct concern of ours. However, when Sabina suddenly becomes the actress Miss Somerset and refuses to play the seduction of Mr. Antrobus because it will be unbearably painful to a friend in the audience we are jolted into a new awareness. And when Sabina stops the fight between Henry and Mr. Antrobus because she is afraid the actor of Henry will really strangle the actor of Mr. Antrobus, and for a few minutes we have the 360 actors discovering in themselves destructive feelings which parallel those of the characters they are playing, the universality of blood guilt is really driven home to each of us.

In *The Skin of Our Teeth*, Thornton Wilder affirms his belief in man, in human life, in all of human life, ordinary and extraordinary, petty and heroic, ugly and beautiful, evil and good.

If Thornton Wilder is an optimist, his is no shallow optimism. He recognizes that pain, cruelty, failure, and death are a part of living but he feels strongly that they can never completely define life. Gerald Weales has observed that Wilder, like the heroine of his novel *The* 370 *Woman of Andros*, seems to say, "I have known the worst that the world can do . . . nevertheless, I praise the world and all living." He says "yes" to life.

Thornton Wilder says "yes" to the theatre also. He recognizes and accepts the fact that theatre is a collaborative art, that director and actors necessarily intervene their bodies, minds, and imaginations between the playwright and his vision of his play. In his essay "Some Thoughts on Playwriting," he says he seeks "to organize the play in such a way that its strength lies not in appearances beyond his control, but in the succession of events and in the unfolding of an idea, in 380 narration." The details of the physical realization of his play he is happy to leave to actors and director. He recognizes too that a play is addressed not to individuals but to a group, and he accepts the fact that the "group-mind imposes upon him the necessity of treating materials understandable by the larger number."

Above all, Thornton Wilder believes in the theatricality of the theatre. The theatre, he says, is a world not of illusion but of pretense, of make-believe. It lives by conventions, that is, by agreed upon falsehoods, by permitted lies. "When it tries to assert that the 390 personages in the action 'really are,' really inhabit such and such rooms, really suffer from such and such emotions, it loses rather than gains credibility." Convention, he maintains, provokes the spectator to collaborate in the dramatic creation, and it raises the action from the specific to the general. The element of pretense reinforces the continual effort of the stage to present generalized truth.

Of course, the theatre of "illusion," as Wilder uses the term, is also a theatre of pretense. No one mistakes its personages for real people. And like the theatre of "make-believe," it depends upon conventions—agreed upon falsehoods, permitted lies. But its con- 400 ventions are different conventions. They tend to make the audience a spectator rather than a collaborator; they tend to make the drama particular rather than general.

The theatre of "illusion"—as opposed to the theatre of "make-believe"—is, in a way, theatre that denies itself. Not only the realistic theatre of Belasco and Stanislavsky but the symbolistic theatre of Gordon Craig and Adolphe Appia° seeks to create by means of text, actors, scenery, and light a world separate from the audience—not the world of the theatre, but the world of Peter Grimm or Madame Ranevsky° or Hamlet or Tristan and Isolde. The proscenium arch is not only the 410 symbol of that separation but the principal means whereby the illusion is created.

Thornton Wilder's plays in one way or another break down the barrier of the proscenium arch. They involve the spectator directly by frankly making him once more a participant in a theatrical experience. These plays have been and continue to be highly successful. They point the way the living theatre should go, for if it is to survive as anything but a luxury for the few, it must discard the conventions of "illusion" and revive the older conventions of "make-believe." It should leave the creation of "illusion" to the moving picture and 420 to television, both of which are infinitely better equipped for it. The

405-406. Belasco and Stanislavsky . . . Gordon Craig and Adolphe Appia. David Belasco (1854-1931), American playwright, actor, and producer; Stanislavsky, stage name for Constantine Alexeev (1863-1938), Russian actor and producer, called the father of the modern Russian theater; Edward Gordon Craig (1872-), British stage designer and writer on the theater; Adolphe Appia (1862-1928), Swiss stage designer. ***408. Peter Grimm or Madame Ranevsky.*** Peter Grimm is the main character in *The Return of Peter Grimm* (1911) by David Belasco; Madame Ranevsky is the heroine of Chekhov's *The Cherry Orchard* (1904).

theatre should reaffirm itself as an art of "pretense" not of "illusion," of living actors not real people, and of an active not a passive audience.

Thornton Wilder is important in today's American theatre because he is a believer, a yea-sayer. He says "yes" to the life of the theatre, still struggling to escape the strangling embrace of realism and illusion. And through the theatre he says "yes" to human life. In what sometimes seems an unbroken chorus of aggression and rejection by contemporary American playwrights, his is one strong, affirmative voice.

Robert E. Knoll

HOW TO READ *THE ALCHEMIST*

Robert Knoll, professor of English at the University of Nebraska, published Ben Jonson's Plays: An Introduction *in 1964.*

The plot of *The Alchemist*—which Coleridge linked with *Oedipus Tyrannus* and *Tom Jones* as one of the three most perfect in literature—is generally regarded as tremendously involved. Una Ellis-Fermor (*The Jacobean Drama;* 1936, 1953; p. 115) calls it "one of the most complex groups of plots in English comedy." My students often lose their way in its seeming convolutions and come to class not knowing what they have read. They are confused by so many persons rushing on and off stage engaged in so much constant activity. The truth is, the action is nowhere nearly so involved as it appears to be, and in some respects it is quite simple. The incidents are arranged according to a simple pattern.

In the following paragraphs I want to indicate some of the ways *The Alchemist* might profitably be read. The play has its own peculiar rewards, different from those offered by *Twelfth Night* and *The Taming of the Shrew.* The central questions I seek to answer here are these: What kind of dramatic satire is *The Alchemist* and what are its peculiar virtues? Why is *The Alchemist* as it is and not different (and more like Shakespeare)? To answer I must give an account of the dramaturgical organization of the play and then of its theme.

The play begins with a long first scene in which we see that Face and Subtle, aided by Dol Common, have set themselves up as confidence men. One should note two elements in this first scene: first, the game is played in the house of Face's master while he is away in the country; and, second, the alliance between the scoundrels is very precarious. We know from the beginning that they will turn on each other at the first opportunity, and we are reminded from time to time during the course of the action of this precarious yoking. With this necessary exposition out of the way—and note how it is given dramatic tension by the quarrels among the principals—the play moves immediately to a merry-go-round of activity. We are introduced in successive scenes (1) to Dapper—I, ii—who aspires to be a gambler, (2) to Drugger—I, iii—who wants to be shown how to turn a fast buck, (3) to Sir Epicure Mammon accompanied by Surly—I, iv; II, i, ii, iii—who wants to be richer than God, and (4) to Ananias—II, iv, v—the Anabaptist who wants the property of his church turned to gold. Only one other set of characters is introduced to us after this parade of gulls:

(5) Kastril—III, iv—who wants to be taught to be a Roaring Boy; he is accompanied by his sister, the rich widow Dame Pliant. Each of these persons comes to Subtle and Face as a client, for each wants to make money more quickly than can be managed legitimately. 40 They have common aspirations.

Already Jonson's central dramatic technique is obvious. It is duplication. As in fairy stories and nursery tales, a central dramatic conflict is reiterated with variable characters in a number of situations. In the story of the Three Pigs, for example, three times the wolf has occasion to cry, "I'll huff and I'll puff and I'll blow your house in." In "Billy Goats Gruff," the Troll says repeatedly, "Who is that trip-trip-tripping on my bridge?" and in The Three Bears, somebody is always asking, "Who has been sitting in my chair, or eating my porridge, or sleeping in my bed?" Similarly here, Face and Subtle are approached 50 five times with five similar requests. In *The Alchemist*, our interest is with the scoundrels rather than with the victims as (generally) in the nursery stories, but the pattern of action is the same. In both Jonson and the folk tale, a conflict between an attacker and different sets of defendants is repeated several times. Each repetition is riskier than the previous conflicts and increases narrative tension. Each new goat in "Billy Goats Gruff," each new house in "The Three Pigs," each new character in *The Alchemist* is bigger and stronger than his predecessors. Altogether the plotting of *The Alchemist* is hardly "complex" as the critics say; it consists simply of a number of duplications 60 of a single nursery situation. The plotting is really quite straightforward. Compared to this, *A Midsummer Night's Dream*, with all its cross allegiances and complicated identities, is a labyrinthine confusion.

The duplicating stories in this play differ from one another more in intensity than in complexity. As each new situation is introduced, we see not only that its protagonist is more corrupt than those previously introduced, but that he introduces a more profound moral problem. If Dapper, the first applicant for Face's illicit assistance, wants to win at gambling, no worthy man is hurt thereby. If Drugger, client number two, 70 wants to attract customers by trickery (one thinks of Madison Avenue), gullible but relatively innocent customers are the losers. Sir Epicure Mammon, client number three, by aspiring to unlimited power promises to corrupt the world and all its people. He deserves a low circle in hell. Ananias and Tribulation Wholesome, in bringing the property of the orphans to be metamorphosed to gold, are already corrupted; they are hypocrites and sophists. They find a place even lower in the ever-burning pit of sulphur. The various gulls are introduced one at a time, in a descending order of moral depravity. We have met them all, successively, by II, v. 80

In their later, as in their initial, appearances each of these five groups of characters is kept artfully and marvelously separated from all the others; if these situations were historical rather than dramatic, Ananias, Sir Epicure, Drugger, and Dapper could not be kept from meeting. More important the dramatic experience of each group duplicates the dramatic experience of every other. Dapper, who wants to gamble, after I, ii appears again in III, v; then he is bound and gagged and "laid aside" for the rest of the play. Even in III, v he is only momentarily our exclusive concern. Our experience with Drugger, the tobacconist, is similar. After his introduction, he reappears alone only in II, vi, promising to bring Kastril and Dame Pliant to the gullers; thereafter he never holds the center of the stage. He is, in effect, dropped. Sir Epicure, after his spectacular entrance (II, i, ii, iii) repeats his Godlike aspirations only once, in IV, i; and then in IV, v he is gulled and dismissed. The fifth group of characters also appears only a couple of times. After a lengthy introduction of the Puritans (II, iv, v) we see them again in III, i, ii (only one scene separates these two appearances) and then we are through with them until their brief appearance at the end of the fourth act. Kastril, the only remaining character, after his delayed introduction (III, iv), appears only twice in IV; Dame Pliant is completely passive and is more a piece of furniture than an actor. The situations dealing with Dapper, Drugger, Sir Epicure Mammon, and Ananias are each handled separately and briefly and reach their climaxes independent of one another. Our interest alternates among them. Jonson uses a single dramaturgical technique for all of them: First an introduction, then an interval of neglect, finally the gulling. This duplication of action is a triumph of artifice; but it is not complicated. A simple situation is repeated five times. One must not mistake quantity for complexity.

There are two plot elements which I have passed over until now because they seem rather unlike the five situations which I have been discussing. One deals with Surly and the other with Lovewit. Surly alone sees through the rogues' pretensions. Whatever crossplotting the play contains comes through him. He ties the disparate elements together. And yet even when he tries to expose Subtle and Face to the others (in IV, vii), the five plot lines are separated. As a result right down to the end of the fourth act Jonson juggles his five plots, never allowing their actions to become tangled, scarcely allowing them to intersect one another. Lovewit appears exclusively in the last act. When it begins, the confidence men have been successful. Now the central dramatic conflict shifts. During the first four acts, the principal conflict has been Face versus the gullible. But Face at last is in conflict with Lovewit, and he is on the defensive. Suddenly all the gulls appear on stage simultaneously, for the only time in the play in which they appear together. Even now, it should be noted, they are a collection, not a group. In a brilliant maneuver Face recovers from their attacks and, thanks to Lovewit, comes off scot-free. But though the avaricious fools are thus finally lost, Face for the first time does not win. For the first and only time, the biter is bitten. We leave the play unconvinced that Face will suffer much or for long; Lovewit had best 130 watch his step or he too will be outsmarted. Given a chance, Face will surely play Mosca to Lovewit's Volpone.

For all the multitude of detail, the pattern of plotting in the play is clear. The action alternates among five different intrigues, all of which duplicate one another in outline—introduction, interval, gulling. It is imperative to note that there is no development in the play; each character and each action remains at the end substantially what it was at the beginning. Jonson merely tells the same story over five times with five different sets of trappings. The five groups appear as a quintet only in the last scene. By this time Face is engaged in intrigue number 140 six, with Lovewit. The action of the play is not complicated; it is only multiplied. Compared to Shakespeare, this is the simplest kind of plot; Shakespeare is never so redundant. If the action does not develop, it constantly accelerates; and this increasing speed of action is the cause of its very real charm. The pace of acceleration is uniform. (Miss Ellis-Fermor makes this point in her book, pp. 45-46.) Each new incident moves a bit faster, requires a bit faster thinking on the part of the cony catchers, comes on the heels of its predecessors a bit sooner, than the one ahead of it. But it is not basically different from its predecessors. 150

The formal arrangement of *The Alchemist* is repetitive. The single didactic theme is equally repetitive and equally lacking in development. It has been said that this play is a gigantic attack on avarice, that underlying all the actions of all the characters is an inordinate desire for gain. "Be rich," Sir Epicure cries. The theme of this play, however, should not be so oversimplified. The "meaning" of the play is a good deal more complex than this even if its characterizations and plotting are not. *The Alchemist* is essentially a Christian play. Jonson is here concerned with showing how false gods may usurp the very name and ritual of the true God. His play deals with religious per- 160 versions. Ananias and Tribulation Wholesome obviously hide irreligious acts under religious cloaks. The scenes in which they speak in the accents of Old Testament prophets accentuate their distance from the prophets and show their meanness. To overlook the Biblical echoes in their speeches (who can?) is to miss half the fun of the satire, and its point. The climactic scene with Dapper also has its Christian significance; but it is not, I think, so obvious. It depends for its ultimate success on reference to Christian ethics and rituals. In III, v, Face,

Subtle and Dol persuade Dapper that to earn the favor of "her Grace,"
170 the Queen of Faery—that is, to persuade her to respond to his prayerful petitions—he must "throw away all worldly pelf" and "keep nothing that is transitory" about him (III, v, 17, 30). The means to "grace," they tell Dapper, are the traditionally Christian humility, poverty, and obedience; Dapper puts these virtues to service of the wrong god and they cease to be virtues and become ridiculous. The scene reads like a Tudor interlude, for here as in the morality plays the protagonist is bedevilled by demons attempting to force him into a decision. The joke is that the decision is "moral" only by a wild stretch of the imagination and the "demons," far from being supernatural, are Dol, Face,
180 and Subtle. The scene is a burlesque, almost a parody, of the old ritual drama.

The Ananias-Tribulation Wholesome scenes are clearly an attack on sophistical religion; the scenes with Dapper are a burlesque of traditional beliefs turned to false purpose. The scenes with Sir Epicure Mammon also have their religious significance. Sir Epicure wants to correct that nature which is a manifestation of the Almighty; he wants to improve on God. When he cries to Surly, "Be rich," he echoes God's commandment that there be light. Subtle says of him:

He will make
190 Nature ashamed of her long sleep: when art,
Who's but a step-dame, shall do more than she,
In her best love to mankind, ever could.
If his dream last, he'll turn the age to gold. (I, iv, 25-29)

Like Faustus he is drunk with the idea of power, and like Faustus the power to which he aspires is directed to no service but his appetite. Sir Epicure is more than avaricious. In attempting to outGod God, he is sacrilegious. His is a mortal not a venial sin.

Subtle, the alchemist, also aspires to the Godhead. He even conceives of himself as a kind of God already. Though his philosopher's
200 stone is only a ruse, he thinks himself something of a manmaker. When he addresses Face, for instance, his words remind us of the Voice out of the Whirlwind, the incomprehensible Creator:

Slave, thou hadst had no name—[without me] . . .
Never been known, past *equi clibanum*,
The heat of horse-dung, under ground, in cellars,
Or an ale-house, darker than deaf John's; been lost
To all mankind, but laundresses, and tapsters,
Had not I been. (I, i, 81, 83-87)

Subtle, Sir Epicure, all the persons of the play, suffer from this sin
210 of pride. They want to turn the world to their purposes, whereas they

ought, in the Christian view, to seek the place themselves humbly in the service of this world's God.

So far I have simply pointed out religious overtones in some parts of *The Alchemist.* As a matter of fact, the whole play is a reworking of the Parable of the Talents. There was a certain man who, going into the country, called his servant to him and delivered to him his house and his property which he was to keep against the master's return. With industry the servant made the property pay him great dividends; and when the master returned, he called him to an accounting. The servant in fear turned his profit over to the master, for the master reaps where he does not sow and gathers where he does not reap; and he received back his own with interest. The servant's unprofitable assistants were cast out of the house, and the profitable servant was received into the master's bosom. This parable can be used and no doubt was used by persons like Tribulation Wholesome to defend all kinds of eccentric business practices. In the Parable, the Master does not inquire how the servant had increased the wealth; he does not even ask the rate of interest; he does not seem to notice the "interest" which was forbidden by traditional Christian (medieval) strictures against usury. In fact the Parable can be made to indicate that the Master would have us all make money; in this view material prosperity is both a responsibility laid upon us all and a means to Divine favor. The view that prosperity is *evidence* of Divine favor is not dead even now. In this play Jonson gives a Puritan reading of the Bible to show up its shabbiness. Its relevance to modern times needs no development.

The Alchemist deals with avarice obviously, but it deals with avarice in the context of a full system of religious morality. What Jonson objects to essentially is not that one man can and does cheat another, or that one group takes advantage of another. He treats the rascals and the fools with equal dispassion. This satire is not primarily concerned with what man has made or can make of man. Jonson objects to excessive ambition because it is an offense against God's ordering of things. When a man aspires to be more than he was born to be, he is in effect assuming that he knows better than God the place to which he should have been called. Seen in this light, *The Alchemist* is a religious not a social tract, directed against the impious not against the anti-social. It is not, in final analysis, a social satire tied to the changing conditions of a single society. This central religious meaning is discoverable in every character, in every scene, of the play. Jonson drives his point home by repetition. It is this principle of repetition which organizes the plot and determines the characters. Jonson presents impiety in a number of aspects, in a number of similar situations. But like the plot, the central idea is not developed. The essential brilliance of the play can be seen when one observes the simplicity of the central dramaturgical principle. If Shakespeare is rich, Jonson is elegant. He takes the simplest character and situation and repeats it with a virtuosity that hides its redundancy. And when one becomes aware of this redundancy, one can get to the moral heart of the play.

Leonard Cabell Pronko

JEAN ANOUILH'S *ANTIGONE*

Leonard Cabell Pronko of Pomona College, Claremont, California, is the author of books on the French avant-garde *theatre and on Jean Anouilh.*

The story of Antigone is the story of the individual against the state, the eternal opposed to the temporal, the hero to the mass, purity to compromise, and absolute values to the merely expedient. Anouilh's Antigone represents many of these things for us, and in her we can see preserved much of the polyvalence of the original myth. The beginning of the play makes clear at once that we are neither in ancient Greece, nor in some modern country like that depicted in *Eurydice*. Instead we find ourselves before "a neutral setting," peopled by characters dressed in simple evening clothes—the most neutral costumes possible. If the cut of the costumes seems too modern and the card-playing of the guards has a note of contemporaneity, Prologue, who advances to the footlights, immediately reminds us that we are within a certain tradition, and that these characters are about to play the story of Antigone. His simple explanation of the characters and of the story they are going to enact establishes the conventional nature of the play. Chorus will enter several times to comment upon the action, and to converse with certain of the characters. His role is similar to that of the Greek Chorus, although his function is purely dramatic, never lyric. "Not the least of the achievements of this method," comments Raymond Williams, "is that it restores to the dramatist major control of the form of his play."° There is no suspense in the modern sense, for we know how the play will end; we have no doubt but that Antigone will die. Even if we did not know the myth, the Chorus is there to tell it to us and to remind us that tragedy is restful because there is nothing we can do but accept it. The interest of the play arises, as in the Greek theater, from something much more profound than the plot: the moral struggle between two wills, both of which are right, and the intensity of the heroine, which is reflected in every aspect of the play of which it is the dominant note.

Anouilh has made a liberal use of anachronism in his play. This serves several purposes: it furnishes a humor to contrast with the tension of the greater part of the play, and it reminds us that we are not in Greece, but in a timeless ground where antiquity and modernity

21. Raymond Williams, *Drama from Ibsen to Eliot* (London: Chatto and Windus, 1952), p. 198.

can touch fingertips without becoming ridiculous. It is another indication of the neutrality of setting and the universality of application and appeal which the author attempts in his play.

Anouilh's *Antigone* is not a translation or an adaptation of Sophocles' play—it is a re-creation.[38] The general outline of the story is the same, but, as we found in *Eurydice*, there is considerable alteration and omis-
40 sion of details. The seven parts of Sophocles' tragedy are as follows: I Antigone invites Ismene to share with her the "risk and toil" of burying Polynices. Ismene decides to take the way of moderation, to follow Creon's decree. II Creon explains his decree; the guard comes to tell Creon that someone has cast the sacrificial burial dust upon the body of Polynices. III The guard, having caught Antigone as she sprinkled the dust and performed the libations a second time, brings her to Creon. She admits her guilt, and Creon, his pride hurt and his authority challenged, condemns her to be buried alive. IV Haemon tells his father that the citizens admire Antigone, and begs him to reconsider. He
50 refuses, and Haemon leaves, his "mind distressed." V Antigone is led to burial. VI Tiresias warns Creon that the gods are angry at his pollution of Polynices' body, and Creon consents, much against his will, to bury the body and to release Antigone. VII The Messenger tells how Creon, after burying the dead, arrived too late at the cavern in which Antigone was immured. Tearing down the stones, he discovered she had hanged herself. Haemon, by her side, looked loathingly at his father and attempted to strike him, then stabbed himself. The Queen, Eurydice, hearing the Messenger's report, retires to her palace, where, as a second Messenger relates to Creon, she kills herself. Creon is left
60 in hopeless despair, realizing that he is the cause of his own suffering, and the Chorus sings a brief song in praise of wisdom and censuring "unholy pride."

Several of these scenes are repeated in Anouilh's play—not word for word, but in their basic outlines, although Anouilh tends to add to those scenes that are most important in relation to the Antigone-Créon struggle which is the central agon of his play, and to subtract from those that have no direct bearing on their conflict. Both plays begin at sunrise with a conversation between Antigone and her sister. (The Antigone-Nurse scene in Anouilh's play is a preparation for the Antigone-Ismène
70 scene which is to follow.) It is in this first scene that we learn of Antig-

38. Sophocles' play is used as the basis of comparison here because it is the first and best-known treatment of the story of Antigone. In the plays of Aeschylus, Euripides, and Seneca, Antigone is not one of the major characters in the struggle, nor is she depicted as the same proud and fearless woman we see in the plays of Sophocles and Anouilh. Anouilh has clearly followed Sophocles' development of the plot and has even borrowed certain speeches from him. . . . This chapter is concerned with Anouilh's treatment of myth, and the question of influences is not taken into consideration. What we hope to see is what Anouilh offers us through the medium of myth as compared to what is offered by the primitive myth itself, or its earliest literary representation. [Pronko's note.]

one's choice. Both authors depict her as a free being who chooses her way, but whereas in Sophocles' play she describes her choice and what she is about to do, in Anouilh's, she describes what she has already done, for she has just returned from burying Polynices. Ismène, in both plays, shrinks from any extravagant action, and chooses the way of obedience to Creon's decree. Later Antigone tells her: "Thou mad'st thy choice to live and I to die"; and in Anouilh: "Tu as choisi la vie et moi la mort."[°]

Anouilh has inserted here a scene between Antigone and Hémon. It not only serves to reveal the love between the couple and the heroism of Antigone in renouncing this love, but it heightens the pathos of her death, and prepares us for what is to happen later.

The story then continues along the same lines as in the Greek play, as the Guard brings Créon news of the burial of Polynices, leaves frightened by the King's threats, and returns later with Antigone who has been apprehended. Then ensues the central scene of Anouilh's play, in which Antigone and Créon come to grips over their problem. In the Greek original the scene is rather brief, and we learn from it that Antigone's reason for burying her brother was that divine immutable law demanded it. She represents the "unwritten laws of God which know not change." Creon, on the other hand, represents what is best for the state. His first duty is to the kingdom he rules. He conceives of himself as the symbol of the kingdom, and brooks no interference in his rule. In showing his concern that his pride has suffered and his authority been challenged to the point of humiliation, he becomes less sympathetic than Anouilh's Créon, but also more absolute. The French Créon is more humane: he would save Antigone if he could, for her sake and for Hémon's. He is also a more clearsighted monarch: he knows that what he is doing is in the best interests of state, but at the same time he realizes it is a compromise, and that Antigone is right to a certain extent. Actually, both protagonists are right, and Sophocles felt this as much as Anouilh, but the latter gives emphasis to the fact by making his Créon more humane and keenly intelligent, and his Antigone more desperately strong in her resistance to what Créon represents. We cannot say that Anouilh's Antigone has a stronger will than Sophocles', but she appears to, because she is heroic will personified. Her action rises not from a desire to satisfy the religious law, for she feels it is meaningless. Rather, it is an inner compulsion, a desire to be true to herself, that motivates her actions, and the only way she can be true to herself is by refusing the compromise of life represented by the policy of Créon. Her action is a symbol of her liberty. Créon with all his logic cannot batter down her defenses, and if she insists

77-78. Tu as choisi la vie et moi la mort, "You have chosen life, I death."

upon death even in the face of the absurdity of her reasoning, it is because she has the courage to be her truest self.

This conception of Antigone's struggle is an interpretation, and in that respect a reduction of the original myth to specific terms that reason can understand. If Anouilh found this perspective, it is because it lay inherent in Sophocles' play, suggested below the rational level —implicit there, but explicit here in the French version. Anouilh has
120 helped us to see certain facets of Sophocles' play of which we might otherwise have been unaware because we lack the proper background for accepting any play we see as a treatment of man's ultimate problems —a celebration of the mystery of human life. The solitude of these heroic individuals, the compromise of life, the freedom of choice, problems of state, the meaning of happiness—all these lie behind or beneath Sophocles' drama. Anouilh has only brought them to the fore as any modern dramatist must do if today's audience is to be made aware of at least the partial meaning of myth. As Fergusson points out, the modern dramatist is almost compelled to preach, invent, and argue
130 to accomplish what Sophocles or Shakespeare, writing for audiences with a certain awareness, could accomplish by "appealing in both cases to ancient and publicly accepted values and modes of understanding."°

The scene between Créon and Hæmon which follows in Anouilh's play is brief and to the point. There is none of the expression of filial obedience and admiration we find in Sophocles. There is only the desperate cry of disappointment of the youth who has suddenly seen what growing up means, and sees his father as he really is. He can only refuse to accept the compromise, and follow Antigone.

140 The greater development of the scene between Haemon and Creon found in Sophocles is another example of the multiple aspects of reality to be found in the myth. If the scene were merely an additional one, unrelated to the central conflict, it would indeed be superfluous, but a feeling of unity is retained because the Creon-Haemon relationship—the admiration of son for father, the sense of obedience conflicting with the despair over loss of Antigone—is a reflection on another plane, in a different area, of the central conflict.

Anouilh remembers Sophocles, and his heroine, for a moment assuming the lyric tone of the Greek theater, cries out, "O tombeau! O lit
150 nuptial! O ma demeure souterraine . . ."° But this is said in the midst of the ironic scene in which the Guard prates on about ranks, advancement, and salaries. As the heroine in the Greek play is led to her death,

132-133. Francis Fergusson, *The Idea of a Theater* (Garden City, N. Y.: Doubleday Anchor Books, 1953), p. 130. ***149-150. O tombeau! O lit nuptial! O ma demeure souterraine,*** "O tomb! O bridal bed! Alone!"

she greets the cavern, "O tomb, my bridal chamber, vaulted home . . ." and she dies in the hope that she will join her loved one in Hades.

Anouilh's omission of the Tiresias section of the Greek play might be praised on the grounds that it avoids diversity in the play, which is not concerned with any conflict between Créon and the gods, or even between Créon and Tiresias as a representative of the people's opinion. The Créon-Antigone agon is the central experience of Anouilh's play, and since this is the partial perspective he wishes to emphasize, his 160 tightening of the plot by this omission is to be commended. Such is not the case with the Greek *Antigone* where the Tiresias episode is another aspect of the complex reality whose multiple perspectives are suggested to us by Sophocles, or would be had we the requisite background to grasp the full significance of each character and each act.

At the end, Anouilh's Chorus comes again to remind us that tragedy is restful because the outcome is inevitable. Now all is over: "all who were to die are dead. . . . A great and sad calm falls over Thebes and over the empty palace where Créon must begin to wait for death."

Into the mold of the *Antigone* of Sophocles, unified by certain omis- 170 sions, Anouilh has poured a drama whose breadth of appeal is enhanced by a variety of themes and by neutrality of setting and characters—two characteristics shared by the ancient and the modern theaters. Although lacking the multiplicity of perspectives that Sophocles' play had for the people of his day, Anouilh's *Antigone* is still broad in its appeal and a richly suggestive treatment of myth for audiences of our age.

The absence of a ritual theater has not prevented Anouilh from presenting more than one aspect of the myth, for this modern *Antigone* contains much of the suggestiveness of myth, and at the same time says something to men today. The legend is pure and comprehensible, un- 180 obscured by surrealistic magic or by the complex overwrought language that makes of Giraudoux's beautiful Electra° an enigma until it is studied thoroughly. The story and characters are treated with dignity; the audience is made to feel itself a part of the play insofar as it is directly addressed by Prologue and Chorus. A classic austerity reigns in the tightness of the plot, the tension achieved, and the simplicity of means. The tortured irony of the scenes with the guards brings us into closer relationship with the characters in the play, as we are jarred to laughter by the contrast between the guards and Antigone, and immediately are filled with shame, realizing that we too are like the 190 guards and incapable of making the sacrifice of an Antigone.

If Anouilh's *Antigone* comes closer to the universality of the Greeks than do most other modern re-creations of myths, it is not only because

182. Giraudoux's . . . Electra. Jean Giraudoux (1882-1944), French dramatist. *Electra* was written in 1937.

of the inherent expressiveness of the myth and the author's ability to see below the rationalized surface of the story. In addition to these important factors, we should remember that *Antigone* was written and produced during the Occupation. Even if we do not believe Anouilh intended it as a thrust at the occupiers and at Vichy, we must still recognize that he could rely on a heightened sensitivity in his audience, 200 and a feeling of a collective religious kind of experience before a spectacle depicting the struggle for individual liberty and showing the physically vanquished as essentially free.

Nathaniel Hawthorne

MY KINSMAN, MAJOR MOLINEUX

After the kings of Great Britain had assumed the right of appointing the colonial governors, the measures of the latter seldom met with the ready and general approbation which had been paid to those of their predecessors, under the original charters. The people looked with most jealous scrutiny to the exercise of power which did not emanate from themselves, and they usually rewarded their rulers with slender gratitude for the compliances by which, in softening their instructions from beyond the sea, they had incurred the reprehension of those who gave them. The annals of Massachusetts Bay will inform us, that of six governors in the space of about forty years from the surrender of the old charter, under James II., two were imprisoned by a popular insurrection; a third, as Hutchinson inclines to believe, was driven from the province by the whizzing of a musket-ball; a fourth, in the opinion of the same historian, was hastened to his grave by continual bickerings with the House of Representatives; and the remaining two, as well as their successors, till the Revolution, were favored with few and brief intervals of peaceful sway. The inferior members of the court party, in times of high political excitement, led scarcely a more desirable life. These remarks may serve as a preface to the following adventures, which chanced upon a summer night, not far from a hundred years ago. The reader, in order to avoid a long and dry detail of colonial affairs, is requested to dispense with an account of the train of circumstances that had caused much temporary inflammation of the popular mind.

It was near nine o'clock of a moonlight evening, when a boat crossed the ferry with a single passenger, who had obtained his conveyance at that unusual hour by the promise of an extra fare. While he stood on the landing-place, searching in either pocket for the means of fulfilling his agreement, the ferryman lifted a lantern, by the aid of which, and the newly risen moon, he took a very accurate survey of the stranger's figure. He was a youth of barely eighteen years, evidently country-bred, and now, as it should seem, upon his first visit to town. He was clad in a coarse gray coat, well worn, but in excellent repair; his under garments were durably constructed of leather, and fitted tight to a pair of serviceable and well-shaped limbs; his stockings of blue yarn were the incontrovertible work of a mother or a sister; and on his head was a three-cornered hat, which in its better days had perhaps sheltered the graver brow of the lad's father. Under his left arm was a heavy cudgel formed of an oak sapling, and retaining a part of the hardened root; and his equipment was completed by a wallet, not so abundantly stocked as to incommode the vigorous shoulders on which it hung. Brown, curly hair, well-shaped features, and bright, cheerful eyes were nature's gifts, and worth all that art could have done for his adornment.

The youth, one of whose names was Robin, finally drew from his pocket the half of a little province bill of five shillings, which, in the depreciation in that sort of currency, did but satisfy the ferryman's demand, with the surplus of a sexangular piece of parchment, valued at three pence. He then walked forward into the town, with as light a step as if his day's journey had not already exceeded thirty miles, and 50 with as eager an eye as if he were entering London city, instead of the little metropolis of a New England colony. Before Robin had proceeded far, however, it occurred to him that he knew not whither to direct his steps; so he paused, and looked up and down the narrow street, scrutinizing the small and mean wooden buildings that were scattered on either side.

"This low hovel cannot be my kinsman's dwelling," thought he, "nor yonder old house, where the moonlight enters at the broken casement; and truly I see none hereabouts that might be worthy of him. It would have been wise to inquire my way of the ferryman, and doubtless he 60 would have gone with me, and earned a shilling from the Major for his pains. But the next man I meet will do as well."

He resumed his walk, and was glad to perceive that the street now became wider, and the houses more respectable in their appearance. He soon discerned a figure moving on moderately in advance, and hastened his steps to overtake it. As Robin drew nigh, he saw that the passenger was a man in years, with a full periwig of gray hair, a wide-skirted coat of dark cloth, and silk stockings rolled above his knees. He carried a long and polished cane, which he struck down perpendicularly before him at every step; and at regular intervals he uttered 70 two successive hems, of a peculiarly solemn and sepulchral intonation. Having made these observations, Robin laid hold of the skirt of the old man's coat, just when the light from the open door and windows of a barber's shop fell upon both their figures.

"Good evening to you, honored sir," said he, making a low bow, and still retaining his hold of the skirt. "I pray you tell me whereabouts is the dwelling of my kinsman, Major Molineux."

The youth's question was uttered very loudly; and one of the barbers, whose razor was descending on a well-soaped chin, and another who was dressing a Ramillies wig, left their occupations, and came to the 80 door. The citizen, in the mean time, turned a long-favored countenance upon Robin, and answered him in a tone of excessive anger and annoyance. His two sepulchral hems, however, broke into the very centre of his rebuke, with most singular effect, like a thought of the cold grave obtruding among wrathful passions.

"Let go my garment, fellow! I tell you, I know not the man you speak of. What! I have authority, I have—hem, hem—authority; and if this be the respect you show for your betters, your feet shall be brought acquainted with the stocks by daylight, tomorrow morning!"

Robin released the old man's skirt, and hastened away, pursued by an ill-mannered roar of laughter from the barber's shop. He was at first considerably surprised by the result of his question, but, being a shrewd youth, soon thought himself able to account for the mystery. 90

"This is some country representative," was his conclusion, "who has never seen the inside of my kinsman's door, and lacks the breeding to answer a stranger civilly. The man is old, or verily—I might be tempted to turn back and smite him on the nose. Ah, Robin, Robin! even the barber's boys laugh at you for choosing such a guide! You will be wiser in time, friend Robin."

He now became entangled in a succession of crooked and narrow streets, which crossed each other, and meandered at no great distance from the water-side. The smell of tar was obvious to his nostrils, the masts of vessels pierced the moonlight above the tops of the buildings, and the numerous signs, which Robin paused to read, informed him that he was near the centre of business. But the streets were empty, the shops were closed, and lights were visible only in the second stories of a few dwelling-houses. At length, on the corner of a narrow lane, through which he was passing, he beheld the broad countenance of a British hero swinging before the door of an inn, whence proceeded the voices of many guests. The casement of one of the lower windows was thrown back, and a very thin curtain permitted Robin to distinguish a party at supper, round a well-furnished table. The fragrance of the good cheer steamed forth into the outer air, and the youth could not fail to recollect that the last remnant of his travelling stock of provision had yielded to his morning appetite, and that noon had found and left him dinnerless. 100 110

"Oh, that a parchment three-penny might give me a right to sit down at yonder table!" said Robin, with a sigh. "But the Major will make me welcome to the best of his victuals; so I will even step boldly in, and inquire my way to his dwelling."

He entered the tavern, and was guided by the murmur of voices and the fumes of tobacco to the public-room. It was a long and low apartment, with oaken walls, grown dark in the continual smoke, and a floor which was thickly sanded, but of no immaculate purity. A number of persons—the larger part of whom appeared to be mariners, or in some way connected with the sea—occupied the wooden benches, or leather-bottomed chairs, conversing on various matters, and occasionally lending their attention to some topic of general interest. Three or four little groups were draining as many bowls of punch, 120 which the West India trade had long since made a familiar drink in the colony. Others, who had the appearance of men who lived by regular and laborious handicraft, preferred the insulated bliss of an unshared potation, and became more taciturn under its influence. Nearly all, in short, evinced a predilection for the Good Creature in some of its various shapes, for this is a vice to which, as Fast Day sermons of a hundred years ago will testify, we have a long hereditary claim. The only guests to whom Robin's sympathies inclined him were two or three sheepish countrymen, who were using the inn somewhat after the fashion of a Turkish caravansary; they had gotten themselves into the darkest corner of the room, and heedless of the Nicotian atmosphere, were supping on the bread of their own ovens, and the bacon cured in their own chimney-smoke. But though Robin felt a sort of brotherhood with these strangers, his eyes were attracted from them to a person who stood near the door, holding whispered conversation with a group of ill-dressed associates. His features were separately striking almost to grotesqueness, and the whole face left a deep impression on the memory. The forehead bulged out into a double prominence, with a vale between; the nose came boldly forth in an irregular curve, and its bridge was of more than a finger's breadth; the eyebrows were deep and shaggy, and the eyes glowed beneath them like fire in a cave.

While Robin deliberated of whom to inquire respecting his kinsman's dwelling, he was accosted by the innkeeper, a little man in a stained white apron, who had come to pay his professional welcome to the stranger. Being in the second generation from a French Protestant, he seemed to have inherited the courtesy of his parent nation; but no variety of circumstances was ever known to change his voice from the one shrill note in which he now addressed Robin.

"From the country, I presume, sir?" said he, with a profound bow. "Beg leave to congratulate you on your arrival, and trust you intend a long stay with us. Fine town here, sir, beautiful buildings, and much that may interest a stranger. May I hope for the honor of your commands in respect to supper?"

"The man sees a family likeness! the rogue has guessed that I am related to the Major!" thought Robin, who had hitherto experienced little superfluous civility.

All eyes were now turned on the country lad, standing at the door, in his worn three-cornered hat, gray coat, leather breeches, and blue yarn stockings, leaning on an oaken cudgel, and bearing a wallet on his back.

Robin replied to the courteous innkeeper, with such an assumption of confidence as befitted the Major's relative. "My honest friend," he said, "I shall make it a point to patronize your house on some occasion, when"—here he could not help lowering his voice—"when I may have more than a parchment three-pence in my pocket. My present business," continued he, speaking with lofty confidence, "is merely to inquire my way to the dwelling of my kinsman, Major Molineux."

There was a sudden and general movement in the room, which Robin interpreted as expressing the eagerness of each individual to become his guide. But the innkeeper turned his eyes to a written paper on the wall, which he read, or seemed to read, with occasional re- 180 currences to the young man's figure.

"What have we here?" said he, breaking his speech into little dry fragments. "'Left the house of the subscriber, bounden servant. Hezekiah Mudge,—had on, when he went away, gray coat, leather breeches, master's third-best hat. One pound currency reward to whosoever shall lodge him in any jail of the province.' Better trudge, boy; better trudge!"

Robin had begun to draw his hand towards the lighter end of the oak cudgel, but a strange hostility in every countenance induced him to relinquish his purpose of breaking the courteous innkeeper's head. 190 As he turned to leave the room, he encountered a sneering glance from the bold-featured personage whom he had before noticed; and no sooner was he beyond the door, than he heard a general laugh, in which the innkeeper's voice might be distinguished, like the dropping of small stones into a kettle.

"Now, is it not strange," thought Robin, with his usual shrewdness,— "is it not strange that the confession of an empty pocket should outweight the name of my kinsman, Major Molineux? Oh, if I had one of those grinning rascals in the woods, where I and my oak sapling grew up together, I would teach him that my arm is heavy though my 200 purse be light!"

On turning the corner of the narrow lane, Robin found himself in a spacious street, with an unbroken line of lofty houses on each side, and a steepled building at the upper end, whence the ringing of a bell announced the hour of nine. The light of the moon, and the lamps from the numerous shop-windows, discovered people promenading on the pavement, and amongst them Robin hoped to recognize his hitherto inscrutable relative. The result of his former inquiries made him unwilling to hazard another, in a scene of such publicity, and he determined to walk slowly and silently up the street, thrusting his 210 face close to that of every elderly gentleman, in search of the Major's lineaments. In his progress, Robin encountered many gay and gallant figures. Embroidered garments of showy colors, enormous periwigs, goldlaced hats, and silver-hilted swords glided past him and dazzled his optics. Travelled youths, imitators of the European fine gentlemen of the period, trod jauntily along, half dancing to the fashionable tunes which they hummed, and making poor Robin ashamed of his quiet and natural gait. At length, after many pauses to examine the gorgeous display of goods in the shopwindows, and after suffering some rebukes 220 for the impertinence of his scrutiny into people's faces, the Major's kinsman found himself near the steepled building, still unsuccessful in his search. As yet, however, he had seen only one side of the thronged street; so Robin crossed, and continued the same sort of inquisition down the opposite pavement, with stronger hopes than the philosopher seeking an honest man, but with no better fortune. He had arrived about midway towards the lower end, from which his course began, when he overheard the approach of some one who struck down a cane on the flag-stones at every step, uttering, at regular intervals, two sepulchral hems.

230 "Mercy on us!" quoth Robin, recognizing the sound.

Turning a corner, which chanced to be close at his right hand, he hastened to pursue his researches in some other part of the town. His patience now was wearing low, and he seemed to feel more fatigue from his rambles since he crossed the ferry, than from his journey of several days on the other side. Hunger also pleaded loudly within him, and Robin began to balance the propriety of demanding, violently, and with lifted cudgel, the necessary guidance from the first solitary passenger whom he should meet. While a resolution of this effect was gaining strength, he entered a street of mean appearance, on 240 either side of which a row of ill-built houses was straggling towards the harbor. The moonlight fell upon no passenger along the whole extent, but in the third domicile which Robin passed there was a half-opened door, and his keen glance detected a woman's garment within.

"My luck may be better here," said he to himself.

Accordingly, he approached the door, and beheld it shut closer as he did so; yet an open space remained, sufficing for the fair occupant to observe the stranger, without a corresponding display on her part. All that Robin could discern was a strip of scarlet petticoat, and the occasional sparkle of an eye, as if the moonbeams were trembling on 250 some bright thing.

"Pretty mistress," for I may call her so with a good conscience, thought the shrewd youth, since I know nothing to the contrary,—"my sweet pretty mistress, will you be kind enough to tell me whereabouts I must seek the dwelling of my kinsman, Major Molineux?"

Robin's voice was plaintive and winning, and the female, seeing nothing to be shunned in the handsome country youth, thrust open the door, and came forth into the moonlight. She was a dainty little figure, with a white neck, round arms, and a slender waist, at the extremity of which her scarlet petticoat jutted out over a hoop, as if she were standing 260 in a balloon. Moreover, her face was oval and pretty, her hair dark beneath the little cap, and her bright eyes possessed a sly freedom, which triumphed over those of Robin.

"Major Molineux dwells here," said this fair woman.

Now, her voice was the sweetest Robin had heard that night, the airy counterpart of a stream of melted silver; yet he could not help doubting whether that sweet voice spoke Gospel truth. He looked up and down the mean street, and then surveyed the house before which they stood. It was a small, dark edifice of two stories, the second of which projected over the lower floor, and the front apartment had the aspect of a shop for petty commodities. 270

"Now, truly, I am in luck," replied Robin, cunningly, "and so indeed is my kinsman, the Major, in having so pretty a housekeeper. But I prithee trouble him to step to the door; I will deliver him a message from his friends in the country, and then go back to my lodgings at the inn."

"Nay, the Major has been abed this hour or more," said the lady of the scarlet petticoat; "and it would be to little purpose to disturb him to-night, seeing his evening draught was of the strongest. But he is a kind-hearted man, and it would be as much as my life's worth to let a kinsman of his turn away from the door. You are the good old 280 gentleman's very picture, and I could swear that was his rainy-weather hat. Also he has garments very much resembling those leather small clothes. But come in, I pray, for I bid you hearty welcome in his name."

So saying, the fair and hospitable dame took our hero by the hand; and the touch was light, and the force was gentleness, and though Robin read in her eyes what he did not hear in her words, yet the slender-waisted woman in the scarlet petticoat proved stronger than the athletic country youth. She had drawn his half-willing footsteps nearly to the threshold, when the opening of a door in the neighborhood 290 startled the Major's housekeeper, and, leaving the Major's kinsman, she vanished speedily into her own domicile. A heavy yawn preceded the appearance of a man, who, like the Moonshine of Pyramus and Thisbe, carried a lantern, needlessly aiding his sister luminary in the heavens. As he walked sleepily up the street, he turned his broad, dull face on Robin, and displayed a long staff, spiked at the end.

"Home, vagabond, home!" said the watchman, in accents that seemed to fall asleep as soon as they were uttered. "Home, or we'll set you in the stocks by peep of day!"

"This is the second hint of the kind," thought Robin. "I wish they 300 would end my difficulties, by setting me there tonight."

Nevertheless, the youth felt an instinctive antipathy towards the guardian of midnight order, which at first prevented him from asking his usual question. But just when the man was about to vanish behind the corner, Robin resolved not to lose the opportunity, and shouted lustily after him,—

"I say, friend! will you guide me to the house of my kinsman, Major Molineux?"

The watchman made no reply, but turned the corner and was gone; 310 yet Robin seemed to hear the sound of drowsy laughter stealing along the solitary street. At that moment, also, a pleasant titter saluted him from the open window above his head; he looked up, and caught the sparkle of a saucy eye; a round arm beckoned to him, and next he heard light footsteps descending the staircase within. But Robin, being of the household of a New England clergyman, was a good youth, as well as a shrewd one; so he resisted temptation, and fled away.

He now roamed desperately, and at random, through the town, almost ready to believe that a spell was on him, like that by which a wizard of his country had once kept three pursuers wandering a whole 320 winter night, within twenty paces of the cottage which they sought. The streets lay before him, strange and desolate, and the lights were extinguished in almost every house. Twice, however, little parties of men, among whom Robin distinguished individuals in outlandish attire, came hurrying along; but, though on both occasions they paused to address him, such intercourse did not at all enlighten his perplexity. They did but utter a few words in some language of which Robin knew nothing, and perceiving his inability to answer, bestowed a curse upon him in plain English and hastened away. Finally, the lad determined to knock at the door of every mansion that might appear worthy to be 330 occupied by his kinsman, trusting that perseverance would overcome the fatality that had hitherto thwarted him. Firm in this resolve, he was passing beneath the walls of a church, which formed the corner of two streets, when, as he turned into the shade of its steeple, he encountered a bulky stranger, muffled in a cloak. The man was proceeding with the speed of earnest business, but Robin planted himself full before him, holding the oak cudgel with both hands across his body as a bar to further passage.

"Halt, honest man, and answer me a question," said he, very resolutely. "Tell me, this instant, whereabouts is the dwelling of my kins- 340 man, Major Molineux!"

"Keep your tongue between your teeth, fool, and let me pass!" said a deep, gruff voice, which Robin partly remembered. "Let me pass, I say, or I'll strike you to the earth!"

"No, no, neighbor!" cried Robin, flourishing his cudgel, and then thrusting its larger end close to the man's muffled face. "No, no, I'm not the fool you take me for, nor do you pass till I have an answer to my question. Whereabouts is the dwelling of my kinsman, Major Molineux?"

The stranger, instead of attempting to force his passage, stepped back into the moonlight, unmuffled his face, and stared full into that of Robin. 350

"Watch here an hour, and Major Molineux will pass by," said he.

Robin gazed with dismay and astonishment on the unprecedented physiognomy of the speaker. The forehead with its double prominence, the broad hooked nose, the shaggy eyebrows, and fiery eyes were those which he had noticed at the inn, but the man's complexion had undergone a singular, or, more properly, a twofold change. One side of the face blazed an intense red, while the other was black as midnight, the division line being in the broad bridge of the nose; and a mouth which seemed to extend from ear to ear was black or red, in contrast 360 to the color of the cheek. The effect was as if two individual devils, a fiend of fire and a fiend of darkness, had united themselves to form this infernal visage. The stranger grinned in Robin's face, muffled his party-colored features, and was out of sight in a moment.

"Strange things we travellers see!" ejaculated Robin.

He seated himself, however, upon the steps of the church-door, resolving to wait the appointed time for his kinsman. A few moments were consumed in philosophical speculations upon the species of man who had just left him; but having settled this point shrewdly, rationally, and satisfactorily, he was compelled to look elsewhere for his amuse- 370 ment. And first he threw his eyes along the street. It was of more respectable appearance than most of those into which he had wandered; and the moon, creating, like the imaginative power, a beautiful strangeness in familiar objects, gave something of romance to a scene that might not have possessed it in the light of day. The irregular and often quaint architecture of the houses, some of whose roofs were broken into numerous little peaks, while others ascended, steep and narrow, into a single point, and others again were square; the pure snow-white of some of their complexions, the aged darkness of others, and the thousand sparklings, reflected from bright substances in the walls 380 of many; these matters engaged Robin's attention for a while, and then began to grow wearisome. Next he endeavored to define the forms of distant objects, starting away, with almost ghostly indistinctness, just as his eye appeared to grasp them; and finally he took a minute survey of an edifice which stood on the opposite side of the street, directly in front of the church-door, where he was stationed. It was a large, square mansion, distinguished from its neighbors by a balcony, which rested on tall pillars, and by an elaborate Gothic window, communicating therewith.

"Perhaps this is the very house I have been seeking," thought Robin. 390

Then he strove to speed away the time, by listening to a murmur which swept continually along the street, yet was scarcely audible, except to an unaccustomed ear like his; it was a low, dull, dreamy sound, compounded of many noises, each of which was at too great a distance to be separately heard. Robin marvelled at this snore of a sleeping town, and marvelled more whenever its continuity was broken by now and then a distant shout, apparently loud where it originated. But altogether it was a sleep-inspiring sound, and, to shake off its drowsy influence, Robin arose, and climbed a window-frame, that he might 400 view the interior of the church. There the moonbeams came trembling in, and fell down upon the deserted pews, and extended along the quiet aisles. A fainter yet more awful radiance was hovering around the pulpit, and one solitary ray had dared to rest upon the open page of the great Bible. Had nature, in that deep hour, become a worshipper in the house which man had builded? Or was that heavenly light the visible sanctity of the place,—visible because no earthly and impure feet were within the walls? The scene made Robin's heart shiver with a sensation of loneliness stronger than he had ever felt in the remotest depths of his native woods; so he turned away and sat down again be- 410 fore the door. There were graves around the church, and now an uneasy thought obtruded into Robin's breast. What if the object of his search, which had been so often and so strangely thwarted, were all the time mouldering in his shroud? What if his kinsman should glide through yonder gate, and nod and smile to him in dimly passing by?

"Oh that any breathing thing were here with me!" said Robin.

Recalling his thoughts from this uncomfortable track, he sent them over forest, hill, and stream, and attempted to imagine how that evening of ambiguity and weariness had been spent by his father's household. He pictured them assembled at the door, beneath the tree, the great 420 old tree, which had been spared for its huge twisted trunk and venerable shade, when a thousand leafy brethren fell. There, at the going down of the summer sun, it was his father's custom to perform domestic worship, that the neighbors might come and join with him like brothers of the family, and that the wayfaring man might pause to drink at that fountain, and keep his heart pure by freshening the memory of home. Robin distinguished the seat of every individual of the little audience: he saw the good man in the midst, holding the Scriptures in the golden light that fell from the western clouds; he beheld him close the book and all rise up to pray. He heard the old thankgivings for daily mercies, 430 the old supplications for their continuance, to which he had so often listened in weariness, but which were now among his dear remembrances. He perceived the slight inequality of his father's voice when he came to speak of the absent one; he noted how his mother turned her face to the broad and knotted trunk; how his elder brother scorned, because the beard was rough upon his upper lip, to permit his features to be moved; how the younger sister drew down a low hanging branch

before her eyes; and how the little one of all, whose sports had hitherto broken the decorum of the scene, understood the prayer for her playmate, and burst into clamorous grief. Then he saw them go in at the door; and when Robin would have entered also, the latch tinkled 440
into its place, and he was excluded from his home.

"Am I here, or there?" cried Robin, starting; for all at once, when his thoughts had become visible and audible in a dream, the long, wide, solitary street shone out before him.

He aroused himself, and endeavored to fix his attention steadily upon the large edifice which he had surveyed before. But still his mind kept vibrating between fancy and reality; by turns, the pillars of the balcony lengthened into the tall, bare stems of pines, dwindled down to human figures, settled again into their true shape and size, and then commenced a new succession of changes. For a single moment, 450
when he deemed himself awake, he could have sworn that a visage—one which he seemed to remember, yet could not absolutely name as his kinsman's—was looking towards him from the Gothic window. A deeper sleep wrestled with and nearly overcame him, but fled at the sound of footsteps along the opposite pavement. Robin rubbed his eyes, discerned a man passing at the foot of the balcony, and addressed him in a loud, peevish, and lamentable cry.

"Hallo, friend! must I wait here all night for my kinsman, Major Molineux?"

The sleeping echoes awoke, and answered the voice; and the pas- 460
senger, barely able to discern a figure sitting in the oblique shade of the steeple, traversed the street to obtain a nearer view. He was himself a gentleman in his prime, of open, intelligent, cheerful, and altogether prepossessing countenance. Perceiving a country youth, apparently homeless and without friends, he accosted him in a tone of real kindness, which had become strange to Robin's ears.

"Well, my good lad, why are you sitting here?" inquired he. "Can I be of service to you in any way?"

"I am afraid not, sir," replied Robin, despondingly; "yet I shall take it kindly, if you'll answer me a single question. I've been search- 470
ing, half the night, for one Major Molineux; now, sir, is there really such a person in these parts, or am I dreaming?"

"Major Molineux! The name is not altogether strange to me," said the gentleman, smiling. "Have you any objection to telling me the nature of your business with him?"

Then Robin briefly related that his father was a clergyman, settled on a small salary, at a long distance back in the country, and that he and Major Molineux were brothers' children. The Major, having inherited riches, and acquired civil and military rank, had visited his cousin, in great pomp, a year or two before; had manifested much 480 interest in Robin and an elder brother, and, being childless himself, had thrown out hints respecting the future establishment of one of them in life. The elder brother was destined to succeed to the farm which his father cultivated in the interval of sacred duties; it was therefore determined that Robin should profit by his kinsman's generous intentions, especially as he seemed to be rather the favorite, and was thought to possess other necessary endowments.

"For I have the name of being a shrewd youth," observed Robin, in this part of his story.

490 "I doubt not you deserve it," replied his new friend, good-naturedly; "but pray proceed."

"Well, sir, being nearly eighteen years old, and well grown, as you see," continued Robin, drawing himself up to his full height, "I thought it high time to begin in the world. So my mother and sister put me in handsome trim, and my father gave me half the remnant of his last year's salary, and five days ago I started for this place, to pay the Major a visit. But, would you believe it, sir! I crossed the ferry a little after dark, and have yet found nobody that would show me the way to his dwelling; only, an hour or two since, I was told to wait here, and Major 500 Molineux would pass by."

"Can you describe the man who told you this?" inquired the gentleman.

"Oh, he was a very ill-favored fellow, sir," replied Robin, "with two great bumps on his forehead, a hook nose, fiery eyes; and, what struck me as the strangest, his face was of two different colors. Do you happen to know such a man, sir?"

"Not intimately," answered the stranger, "but I chanced to meet him a little time previous to your stopping me. I believe you may trust his word, and that the Major will very shortly pass through this street. 510 In the mean time, as I have a singular curiosity to witness your meeting, I will sit down here upon the steps and bear you company."

He seated himself accordingly, and soon engaged his companion in animated discourse. It was but of brief continuance, however, for a noise of shouting, which had long been remotely audible, drew so much nearer that Robin inquired its cause.

"What may be the meaning of this uproar?" asked he. "Truly, if your town be always as noisy, I shall find little sleep while I am an inhabitant."

"Why, indeed, friend Robin, there do appear to be three or four 520 riotous fellows abroad to-night," replied the gentleman. "You must not expect all the stillness of your native woods here in our streets. But the watch will shortly be at the heels of these lads and"—

"Ay, and set them in the stocks by peep of day," interrupted Robin, recollecting his own encounter with the drowsy lantern-bearer. "But, dear sir, if I may trust my ears, an army of watchmen would never make head against such a multitude of rioters. There were at least a thousand voices went up to make that one shout."

"May not a man have several voices, Robin, as well as two complexions?" said his friend.

"Perhaps a man may; but Heaven forbid that a woman should!" 530 responded the shrewd youth, thinking of the seductive tones of the Major's housekeeper.

The sounds of a trumpet in some neighboring street now became so evident and continual, that Robin's curiosity was strongly excited. In addition to the shouts, he heard frequent bursts from many instruments of discord, and a wild and confused laughter filled up the intervals. Robin rose from the steps, and looked wistfully towards a point whither people seemed to be hastening.

"Surely some prodigious merry-making is going on," exclaimed he. "I have laughed very little since I left home, sir, and should be sorry to 540 lose an opportunity. Shall we step round the corner by that darkish house, and take our share of the fun?"

"Sit down again, sit down, good Robin," replied the gentleman, laying his hand on the skirt of the gray coat. "You forget that we must wait here for your kinsman; and there is reason to believe that he will pass by, in the course of a very few moments."

The near approach of the uproar had now disturbed the neighborhood; windows flew open on all sides; and many heads in the attire of the pillow, and confused by sleep suddenly broken, were protruded to the gaze of whoever had leisure to observe them. Eager voices hailed 550 each other from house to house, all demanding the explanation, which not a soul could give. Half-dressed men hurried towards the unknown commotion, stumbling as they went over the stone steps that thrust themselves into the narrow foot-walk. The shouts, the laughter, and the tuneless bray, the antipodes of music, came onwards with increasing din, till scattered individuals, and then denser bodies, began to appear round a corner at the distance of a hundred yards.

"Will you recognize your kinsman, if he passes in this crowd?" inquired the gentleman.

"Indeed, I can't warrant it, sir; but I'll take my stand here, and 560 keep a bright lookout," answered Robin, descending to the outer edge of the pavement.

A mighty stream of people now emptied into the street, and came rolling slowly towards the church. A single horseman wheeled the corner in the midst of them, and close behind him came a band of fearful wind-instruments, sending forth a fresher discord now that no intervening buildings kept it from the ear. Then a redder light disturbed the moonbeams, and a dense multitude of torches shone along the street, concealing, by their glare, whatever object they illuminated. 570 The single horseman, clad in a military dress, and bearing a drawn sword, rode onward as the leader, and, by his fierce and variegated countenance, appeared like war personified; the red of one cheek was an emblem of fire and sword; the blackness of the other betokened the mourning that attends them. In his train were wild figures in the Indian dress, and many fantastic shapes without a model, giving the whole march a visionary air, as if a dream had broken forth from some feverish brain, and were sweeping visibly through the midnight streets. A mass of people, inactive, except as applauding spectators, hemmed the procession in; and several women ran along the sidewalk, piercing 580 the confusion of heavier sounds with their shrill voices of mirth or terror.

"The double-faced fellow has his eye upon me," muttered Robin, with an indefinite but an uncomfortable idea that he was himself to bear a part in the pageantry.

The leader turned himself in the saddle, and fixed his glance full upon the country youth, as the steed went slowly by. When Robin had freed his eyes from those fiery ones, the musicians were passing before him, and the torches were close at hand; but the unsteady brightness of the latter formed a veil which he could not penetrate. The 590 rattling of wheels over the stones sometimes found its way to his ear, and confused traces of a human form appeared at intervals, and then melted into the vivid light. A moment more, and the leader thundered a command to halt: the trumpets vomited a horrid breath, and then held their peace; the shouts and laughter of the people died away, and there remained only a universal hum, allied to silence. Right before Robin's eyes was an uncovered cart. There the torches blazed the brightest, there the moon shone out like day, and there, in tar-and-feathery dignity, sat his kinsman, Major Molineux!

He was an elderly man, of large and majestic person, and strong, 600 square features, betokening a steady soul; but steady as it was, his enemies had found means to shake it. His face was pale as death, and far more ghastly; the broad forehead was contracted in his agony, so that his eyebrows formed one grizzled line; his eyes were red and wild, and the foam hung white upon his quivering lip. His whole frame was agitated by a quick and continual tremor, which his pride strove to quell, even in those circumstances of overwhelming humiliation. But perhaps the bitterest pang of all was when his eyes met those of Robin; for he evidently knew him on the instant, as the youth stood witnessing the foul disgrace of a head grown gray in honor. They stared at each 610 other in silence, and Robin's knees shook, and his hair bristled, with a mixture of pity and terror. Soon, however, a bewildering excitement began to seize upon his mind; the preceding adventures of the night, the unexpected appearance of the crowd, the torches, the confused din and the hush that followed, the spectre of his kinsman reviled by that great multitude,—all this, and, more than all, a perception of tremendous ridicule in the whole scene, affected him with a sort of mental inebriety. At that moment a voice of sluggish merriment saluted Robin's ears; he turned instinctively, and just behind the corner of the church stood the lantern-bearer, rubbing his eyes, and drowsily enjoying the lad's amazement. Then he heard a peal of laughter like 620 the ringing of silvery bells; a woman twitched his arm, a saucy eye met his, and he saw the lady of the scarlet petticoat. A sharp, dry cachinnation appealed to his memory, and, standing on tiptoe in the crowd, with his white apron over his head, he beheld the courteous little innkeeper. And lastly, there sailed over the heads of the multitude a great, broad laugh, broken in the midst by two sepulchral hems; thus, "Haw, haw, haw,—hem, hem,—haw, haw, haw, haw!"

The sound proceeded from the balcony of the opposite edifice, and thither Robin turned his eyes. In front of the Gothic window stood the old citizen, wrapped in a wide gown, his gray periwig exchanged for 630 a nightcap, which was thrust back from his forehead, and his silk stockings hanging about his legs. He supported himself on his polished cane in a fit of convulsive merriment, which manifested itself on his solemn old features like a funny inscription on a tombstone. Then Robin seemed to hear the voices of the barbers, of the guests of the inn, and of all who had made sport of him that night. The contagion was spreading among the multitude, when all at once, it seized upon Robin, and he sent forth a shout of laughter that echoed through the street,—every man shook his sides, every man emptied his lungs, but Robin's shout was the loudest there. The cloud-spirits peeped from 640 their silvery islands, as the congregated mirth went roaring up the sky! The Man in the Moon heard the far bellow. "Oho," quoth he, "the old earth is frolicsome to-night!"

When there was a momentary calm in that tempestuous sea of sound, the leader gave the sign, the procession resumed its march. On they went, like fiends that throng in mockery around some dead potentate, mighty no more, but majestic still in his agony. On they went, in counterfeited pomp, in senseless uproar, in frenzied merriment, trampling all on an old man's heart. On swept the tumult, and left a silent street behind. 650

. . . . .

"Well, Robin, are you dreaming?" inquired the gentleman, laying his hand on the youth's shoulder.

Robin started, and withdrew his arm from the stone post to which he had instinctively clung, as the living stream rolled by him. His cheek was somewhat pale, and his eye not quite as lively as in the earlier part of the evening.

"Will you be kind enough to show me the way to the ferry?" said he, after a moment's pause.

"You have, then, adopted a new subject of inquiry?" observed his 660 companion, with a smile.

"Why, yes, sir," replied Robin, rather dryly. "Thanks to you, and to my other friends, I have at last met my kinsman, and he will scarce desire to see my face again. I begin to grow weary of a town life, sir. Will you show me the way to the ferry?"

"No, my good friend Robin,—not tonight, at least," said the gentleman. "Some few days hence, if you wish it, I will speed you on your journey. Or, if you prefer to remain with us, perhaps, as you are a shrewd youth, you may rise in the world without the help of your kinsman, Major Molineux."

Bibliography

The lists which follow do not, of course, pretend to be definitive with respect to any of the topics below. They were compiled with some general considerations in mind:

Whenever possible works are included which the editors expect to be useful to students whose previous experience with plays is limited.

Recent works which contain good bibliographies are noted accordingly. In many cases earlier works on similar subjects are then not listed.

Special attention is paid to reasonably inexpensive paperbacks; these are marked with an asterisk (*).

I. The Theater

Listed here are some works, mostly recent, which give an introduction to the physical aspects of theater, and to its development.

Bieber, Margarete. *The History of the Greek and Roman Theatre.* Princeton: Princeton University Press, 1938.

Bowman, Walter Parker. *Theater Language; a Dictionary of Terms of the Drama and Stage from Medieval to Modern Times.* New York: Theatre Arts Books, 1961.

Brockett, Oscar G. *The Theatre: An Introduction.* New York: Holt, Rinehart and Winston, 1964.

Cheyney, Sheldon. *The Theatre: Three Thousand Years of Drama, Acting, and Stagecraft.* New York: Tudor, 1929.

Flickinger, R. S. *The Greek Theater and Its Drama.* Chicago: University of Chicago Press, 1926.

Freedley, George and J. A. Reeves. *A History of the Theatre.* Revised ed. New York: Crown, 1955.

*Gassner, John and Ralph G. Allen. *Theatre and Drama in the Making.* 2 vols. Boston: Houghton, Mifflin, 1964. An annotated anthology emphasizing methods and materials of research in theatre history and dramatic criticism.

Gorelik, Mordecai. *New Theatres for Old.* New York: Samuel French, 1940.

Hartnoll, Phyllis. *The Oxford Companion to the Theatre.* New York: Oxford University Press, 1951.

Hewitt, Barnard W. *Theatre U.S.A. 1668-1957.* New York: McGraw-Hill, 1959. Not a history but a book containing excerpts from primary source materials.

Hunt, Hugh. *The Live Theatre: An Introduction to the History and Practice of the Stage.* New York: Oxford University Press, 1962.

Macgowan, Kenneth and William Melnitz. *The Living Stage: A History of the World Theatre.* Englewood Cliffs: Prentice-Hall, 1955.

*Matthews, Brander, (ed.) *Papers on Acting.* New York: Dramabooks—Hill and Wang, 1958.

Nagler, Alois. *Sources of Theatrical History.* New York: Dover, 1952. (*As *Source Book of Theatrical History.* Dover, 1959)

Roberts, Vera Mowry. *On Stage: A History of the Theatre.* New York: Harper and Row, 1962.

*Simonson, Lee. *The Stage Is Set.* New York: Theatre Arts Books, 1964.

Whiting, Frank H. *An Introduction to the Theatre.* New York: Harper, 1961.

Wright, Edward A. *A Primer for Playgoers.* Englewood Cliffs: Prentice-Hall, 1958.

II. The Drama in General

Listed here are histories of the drama, histories of a few major national dramatic literatures, with emphasis on the modern, and some critical studies of the drama.

*Abel, Lionel. *Metatheatre: A New View of Dramatic Form.* New York: Dramabooks—Hill and Wang, 1963.

*Barnet, Sylvan, Morton Berman and William Burto. *Aspects of the Drama; a Handbook.* Boston: Little, Brown & Co., 1962. Includes a dictionary of dramatic terms.

Bentley, Eric. *The Life of the Drama.* New York: Atheneum, 1964.

*Bentley, Eric. *The Playwright As Thinker.* 2nd ed. revised. New York: Meridian, 1955.

Brustein, Robert. *The Theatre of Revolt: An Approach to the Modern Drama.* Boston: Little, Brown, 1962. See especially for chapters on Ibsen, Shaw, and O'Neill.

Chiari, Joseph. *The Contemporary French Theatre: The Flight from Naturalism.* New York: Macmillan, 1959.

Clark, Barrett H. *European Theories of the Drama.* Revised by Henry Popkin. New York: Crown, 1965.

Clark, Barrett H. and George Freedley, (eds.) *A History of Modern Drama.* New York and London: Appleton-Century, 1947.

*Cole, Toby. *Playwrights on Playwriting: The Meaning and Making of Modern Drama from Ibsen to Ionesco.* New York: Hill and Wang, 1960.

*Downer, Alan S., (ed.) *American Drama and Its Critics.* Chicago: University of Chicago Press, 1965.

Downer, Alan S. *British Drama.* New York: Appleton-Century-Crofts, 1950.

Downer, Alan S. *Fifty Years of American Drama.* Chicago: Henry Regnery, 1951.

Fergusson, Francis. *The Idea of a Theater.* Princeton: Princeton University Press, 1949. (*Anchor Books, 1953.)

*Fowlie, Wallace. *Dionysus in Paris: A Guide to Contemporary French Theatre.* New York: Meridian, 1960.

Garten, H. F. *Modern German Drama.* London: Methuen, 1959. (*Evergreen, 1962.) In addition to bibliography, has a list of English translations of German plays.

Gassner, John. *Direction in Modern Theatre and Drama.* New York: Holt, Rinehart and Winston, 1965.

Gassner, John. *Masters of the Drama.* 3rd ed. New York: Dover, 1954.

Gassner, John. *Theatre at the Crossroads: Plays and Playwrights of the Mid-Century American Stage.* New York: Holt, Rinehart and Winston, 1960.

Gassner, John, (ed.) *Ideas in the Drama.* New York: Columbia University Press, 1964.

Grossvogel. *Four Playwrights and a Postscript.* Ithaca: Cornell University Press, 1962. (*as *The Blasphemers*, Cornell Paperbacks, 1965)

Guicharnaud, Jacques. *Modern French Theatre from Giraudoux to Beckett.* New Haven: Yale University Press, 1961. (*Yale Paperbound, 1961.)

Krutch, Joseph Wood. *American Drama Since 1918.* Amplified ed. New York: George Braziller, 1957.

Krutch, Joseph Wood. "*Modernism*" *in Modern Drama.* Ithaca: Cornell University Press, 1953.

Lewis, Allan. *The Contemporary Theatre.* New York: Crown, 1962.

Lumley, Frederick. *Trends in Twentieth Century Drama: A Survey Since Ibsen and Shaw.* 2nd revised ed. (Essential Books) New York: Oxford University Press, 1960.

*Matthews, Brander, (ed.) *Papers on Playmaking.* New York: Dramabooks—Hill and Wang, 1957.

Nicoll, Allardyce. *British Drama.* 5th ed. London: G. G. Harrap, 1962. Has a comprehensive bibliography by dramatic periods.

Nicoll, Allardyce. *The Theatre and Dramatic Theory.* London: G. G. Harrap, 1962.

Nicoll, Allardyce. *World Drama.* New York: Harcourt, Brace, 1950.

Parrott, T. M. and R. H. Ball. *A Short View of Elizabethan Drama.* New York: Scribner, 1943. (*Scribner Library, 1960.)

Peacock, Ronald. *The Art of Drama.* London: Routledge and Kegan Paul, 1957.

Quinn, Arthur Hobson. *A History of the American Drama from the Civil War to the Present Day.* Revised ed. New York: Crofts, 1936.

Weales, Gerald. *American Drama Since World War II.* New York: Harcourt, Brace, 1962.

Williams, Raymond. *Drama from Ibsen to Eliot.* New York: Oxford University Press, 1953.

III. Types of Plays

Listed here are books which deal with the major dramatic types, such as comedy or tragedy.

Aristotle. *Poetics.* See *Aristotle on the Art of Poetry.* Revised ed. by Leon Cooper. Ithaca: Cornell University Press, 1947. Numerous translations of the *Poetics* are available.

Aylen, Leo. *Greek Tragedy and the Modern World.* London: Methuen, 1964.

Bentley, Eric. *The Life of the Drama.* New York: Atheneum, 1964. See Part II on types of plays: melodrama, farce, tragedy, comedy, and tragi-comedy, pp. 195-353.

Blistein, Elmer M. *Comedy in Action.* Durham, N. C.: Duke University Press, 1964.

Boulton, Marjorie. *The Anatomy of Drama.* London: Routledge and Kegan Paul, 1960.

Bowra, C. M. *Sophoclean Tragedy.* London: Oxford University Press, 1945. (*Oxford Paperbacks, 1964)

Bradley, A. C. *Shakespearean Tragedy.* London: Oxford University Press, 1946. (*New York: St. Martin's Press, 1963.)

Esslin, Martin. *The Theatre of the Absurd.* Garden City: Doubleday, 1961. (*Anchor Books, 1961)

Feibleman, James K. *In Praise of Comedy: A Study in Its Theory and Practice.* New York: Macmillan, 1939.

Kitto, H. D. F. *Greek Tragedy.* Garden City: Doubleday, 1954. (*Anchor Books, 1958)

Kronenberger, Louis. *The Thread of Laughter: Chapters on English Stage Comedy from Jonson to Maugham.* New York: Knopf, 1952.

*Levin, Richard, (ed.) *Tragedy: Plays, Theory, and Criticism.* New York: Harcourt, Brace, 1960.

Mandel, Oscar. *A Definition of Tragedy.* New York: New York University Press, 1961.

*Michel, Laurence and Richard B. Sewall, (eds.) *Tragedy: Modern Essays in Criticism.* Englewood Cliffs: Prentice-Hall, 1963.

Meredith, George. *An Essay on Comedy and the Uses of the Comic Spirit.* Ed. by Lane Cooper. Ithaca: Cornell University Press, 1956. (Also reprinted in **Comedy.* Anchor Books, 1956)

Monro, D. H. *Argument of Laughter.* London: Cambridge University Press, 1951.

Muller, Herbert J. *The Spirit of Tragedy.* New York: Knopf, 1956. (*Washington Square Press, 1960)

Olson, Elder. *Tragedy and the Theory of Drama.* Detroit: Wayne University Press, 1961.

Potts, L. J. *Comedy.* London: Hutchinson, 1949.

Ribner, Irving. *The English History Play in the Age of Shakespeare.* Princeton: Princeton University Press, 1957.

Sewall, Richard B. *The Vision of Tragedy.* New Haven: Yale University Press, 1959.

Steiner, George. *The Death of Tragedy.* New York: Knopf, 1961. (*Drama Books, 1963)

Tillyard, E. M. W. *Shakespeare's History Plays.* New York: Macmillan, 1944. (*Colliers, 1962)

IV. Collection of Plays

Listed here are a few, mostly recent, collections of plays, for those who want to gain a wider view of the development of the drama.

*Bald, R. C., (ed.) *Six Elizabethan Plays.* Boston: Houghton-Mifflin, Riverside Edition, 1963.

*Bentley, Eric, (ed.) *The Classic Theatre.* Vol. 1: Six Italian Plays; Vol. 2: Five German Plays; Vol. 3: Six Spanish Plays; Vol. 4: Six French Plays. Garden City: Doubleday Anchor Books, 1961.

*Bentley, Eric, (ed.) *The Modern Theatre,* 6 vols. Garden City: Doubleday, 1955-1960.

Block, Haskell, and Robert Shedd, (eds.) *Masters of the Modern Drama.* New York: Random House, 1961.

*Clark, Barrett H., (ed.) *World Drama.* 2 vols. New York: Dover, 1960.

*Corrigan, Robert W., (ed.) *Laurel British Drama: The Twentieth Century.* New York: Dell, 1965.

Corrigan, Robert W., (ed.) *The Modern Theatre.* New York: Macmillan, 1964.

*Clurman, Harold, (ed.) *Famous American Plays of the 1930's.* New York: Dell, 1959.

Gassner, John. *Treasury of the Theatre.* 2 vols. New York: Simon and Schuster, 1950.

Grene, David, and Richard Lattimore, (eds.) *The Complete Greek Tragedies.* 4 vols. Chicago: University of Chicago Press, 1959.

*Hewes, Henry, (ed.) *Famous American Plays of the 1940's.* New York: Dell, 1960.

*MacAndrew, Andrew, (transl.) *Nineteenth Century Russian Drama.* New York: Bantam, 1963.

*MacAndrew, Andrew, (transl.) *Twentieth Century Russian Drama.* New York: Bantam, 1963.

*MacGowan, Kenneth, (ed.) *Famous American Plays of the 1920's.* New York: Dell, 1959.

*Parone, Edward, (ed.) *New Theatre in America.* New York: Dell, 1965. Plays of the 1960's.

*Strasberg, Lee, (ed.) *Famous American Plays of the 1950's.* New York: Dell, 1960.

*Warnock, Robert, (ed.) *Representative Modern Plays.* Vol. 1, British; Vol. 2, American; Vol. 3, Ibsen to Tennessee Williams. Glenview: Scott, Foresman, 1952-1964.

V. Individual Playwrights

Listed here are critical and biographical studies of the works of the playwrights represented in this volume. Editions of collected works are given when available. Inexpensive paperback editions of other plays by these playwrights can be found in *Paperbound Books in Print*, New York: R. R. Bowker Co., a cumulative index published monthly.

JEAN ANOUILH

Harvey, John. *Anouilh: A Study in Theatrics.* New Haven: Yale University Press, 1964.

Pronko, Leonard Cabell. *The World of Jean Anouilh.* Berkeley: University of California Press, 1961.

FRIEDRICH DÜRRENMATT

Askew, Melvin W. "Dürrenmatt's *The Visit of the Old Lady,*" *Tulane Drama Review,* V (June 1961), 89-105.

Dürrenmatt, Friedrich. "Problems of the Theatre," *Tulane Drama Review,* III (October 1958), 3-26.

Klarman, Adolf. "Friedrich Dürrenmatt and the Tragic Sense of Comedy," *Tulane Drama Review,* IV (May 1960), 77-104. Reprinted in **Modern Drama: Essays in Criticism.* Ed. by Travis Bogard and William I. Oliver. New York: Oxford University Press, 1965.

Rogoff, Gordon. "Mr. Dürrenmatt Buys New Shoes," *Tulane Drama Review,* III (October 1958), 27-34. This essay and those by Askew and Dürrenmatt are reprinted in **The Context and Craft of Drama.* Ed. by Robert W. Corrigan and James L. Rosenberg. San Francisco: Chandler, 1964.

MICHEL DE GHELDERODE

See special issue on Ghelderode, *Tulane Drama Review,* VIII (October 1963), 11-71.

Herz, M. "Tragedy, Poetry, and the Burlesque in Ghelderode's Theatre," *Yale French Studies,* No. 29, 1962, pp. 92-101.

HENRIK IBSEN

Bentley, Eric. "Ibsen, Pro and Con, " **In Search of Theatre*. New York: Knopf, 1953.

Bradbrook, Muriel. *Ibsen, The Norwegian*. New York: Macmillan, 1948.

Brustein, Robert. "Ibsen and Revolt," *Tulane Drama Review*, VII (Fall 1962), 113-154.

Firkins, Ina Ten Eyck. *Henrik Ibsen: a Bibliography of Criticism and Biography with an Index to Characters*. New York: H. W. Wilson, 1921.

Fjelde, Rolf, (ed.) *Ibsen: a Collection of Critical Essays*. Englewood Cliffs: Prentice-Hall, 1965.

Ibsen, Henrik. *Collected Works*. Ed. by William Archer. New York: Scribners, 1906-1912.

Northam, John. *Ibsen's Dramatic Method*. London: Faber & Faber, 1953.

Shaw, George Bernard. *The Quintessence of Ibsenism*. New York: Brentano's, 1913. (*Dramabooks—Hill and Wang, 1960)

Tennant, P. F. D. *Ibsen's Dramatic Technique*. Cambridge: Cambridge University Press, 1948. New York: Humanities Press, 1966.

BEN JONSON

Barish, Jonas A. *Ben Jonson and the Language of Prose Comedy*. Cambridge: Harvard University Press, 1960.

Chute, Marchette. *Ben Jonson of Westminister*. New York: Dutton, 1953. (*Dutton Paperbacks, 1958)

Jonson, Ben. *Works*. 11 vols. Ed. by C. H. Herford and Percy Simpson. Oxford: The Clarendon Press, 1925-1952.

Knoll, Robert E. *Ben Jonson's Plays: An Introduction*. Lincoln: University of Nebraska Press, 1964.

Partridge, Edward Bellamy. *The Broken Compass: A Study of the Major Comedies of Ben Jonson*. New York: Columbia University Press, 1958.

ROBERT LOWELL

Brustein, Robert. "We Are Two Cultural Nations," *New Republic*, CLI (November 21, 1964), 25-29. A review of *The Old Glory*.

Lowell, Robert. *The Old Glory*. New York: Farrar, Straus, 1965. Includes *My Kinsman, Major Molineux*.

Ricks, Christopher. "The Three Lives of Robert Lowell," *New Statesman* LXIX (March 26, 1965), 7.

Stables, Hugh B. *Robert Lowell: The First Twenty Years.* New York: Farrar, Straus, 1962.

MOLIÈRE

Fernández, Ramón. *Molière the Man Seen Through the Plays.* New York: Hill and Wang, 1958.

Lewis, Wyndham. *Molière, The Comic Mask.* London: Eyre and Spottiswode, 1959.

*Moore, Will Grayburn. *Molière, a New Criticism.* Garden City: Anchor Books, 1962.

EUGENE O'NEILL

Bryer, Jackson R. "Forty Years of O'Neill Criticism: A Selected Bibliography," *Modern Drama*, IV (September 1961), 196-216.

*Cargill, Oscar, N. Bryllion Fagin, and William J. Fisher, (eds.) *O'Neill and His Plays: Four Decades of Criticism.* New York: New York University Press, 1961. Selected critical essays and an extensive bibliography.

*Gassner, John, (ed.) *O'Neill: A Collection of Critical Essays.* Englewood Cliffs: Prentice-Hall, 1964.

Gelb, Barbara and Arthur. *O'Neill.* New York: Harper and Row, 1962. The most complete and authoritative biography, with bibliography, play list, and dates of first performances. (*Delta Books, 1964)

Miller, Jordan Y. *Playwright's Progress: O'Neill and the Critics.* Glenview: Scott, Foresman, 1965. Selected criticisms.

O'Neill, Eugene. *The Plays.* 3 vols. New York: Random House, 1951.

SHAKESPEARE

*Berman, Donald. *A Reader's Guide to Shakespeare's Plays: A Discursive Bibliography.* Glenview: Scott, Foresman, 1965.

Chute, Marchette. *Shakespeare of London.* New York: Dutton, 1949. (*Dutton Paperbacks, 1953) A pleasant introductory biography.

*Harrison, G. B. *Introducing Shakespeare.* New York: Penguin, 1961.

Nagler, Alois M. *Shakespeare's Stage.* New Haven: Yale University Press, 1964. (*Yale Paperback, 1966)

*Sanderson, James L., (ed.) *William Shakespeare's Henry the Fourth, Part I.* (Norton Critical Edition.) New York: Norton, 1962. An annotated text with essays in criticism, extracts from the major sources, and bibliography.

BERNARD SHAW

*Bentley, Eric. *Bernard Shaw, 1856-1950.* Norfolk, Conn: New Directions, 1957.

Broad, C. Lewis. *Dictionary to the Plays and Novels of Bernard Shaw, with Bibliography of His Works.* New York: Macmillan, 1929.

Chesterton, G. K. *George Bernard Shaw.* New York: Lane, 1909. (*Dramabooks, 1958)

Ervine, St. John. *Bernard Shaw: His Life, Works, and Friends.* New York: Morrow, 1956.

Farley, Earl, and Marvin Carlson. "George Bernard Shaw: A Selected Bibliography" (1945-1955), *Modern Drama,* II (1959), 188-202, 295-325.

Henderson, Archibald. *George Bernard Shaw: Man of the Century.* New York: Appleton-Century-Crofts, 1956.

Kronenberger, Louis, (ed.) *George Bernard Shaw: A Critical Survey.* Cleveland and New York: World, 1953.

Pearson, Hesketh. *G.B.S: A Full Length Portrait.* New York and London: Harper, 1942.

Shaw, Bernard. *Complete Plays* (with prefaces). 6 vols. New York: Dodd, Mead, 1962.

Shaw, Bernard. *Dramatic Opinions and Essays.* New York: Brentano's, 1907.

Shaw, Bernard. *Sixteen Self-Sketches.* London: Constable, 1949.

Williamson, Audrey. *Bernard Shaw: Man and Writer.* New York: Crowell-Collier, 1963.

SOPHOCLES

Hamilton, Edith. *The Greek Way to Western Civilization.* New York: Norton, 1942. (*Mentor Books, 1948) A valuable introduction to classical Greece; see especially chapter 11, "The Idea of Tragedy" and chapter 13 on Sophocles.

Kitto, H. D. F. *Sophocles: Dramatist and Philosopher.* London: Oxford University Press, 1958.

(Sophocles). *Sophocles.* Vols. 1 and 2 of *The Complete Greek Tragedies*, ed. by David Grene and Richmond Lattimore. Chicago: The University of Chicago Press, 1959.

Waldock, A. J. A. *Sophocles the Dramatist.* Cambridge: Cambridge University Press, 1951.

Webster, T. B. L. *An Introduction to Sophocles.* Oxford: The Clarendon Press, 1936.

Whitman, C. H. *Sophocles: A Study of Heroic Humanism.* Cambridge: Harvard University Press, 1951.

THORNTON WILDER

Bogard, Travis. "The Comedy of Thornton Wilder," Intro. to *Three Plays by Thornton Wilder.* New York: Harper and Row, 1962. Reprinted in *Modern Drama: Essays in Criticism.* Ed. by Travis Bogard and William I. Oliver. New York: Oxford University Press, 1965, pp. 355-373. Of special interest for Bogard's distinction between farce and comedy.

Burbank, Rex. *Thornton Wilder.* New York: Twayne, 1961.

Edelstein, J. M. *A Bibliographic Checklist of the Writings of Thornton Wilder.* New Haven: Yale University Press, 1959.

*Goldstein, Malcolm. *The Art of Thornton Wilder.* Lincoln: University of Nebraska Press, 1965.